The Book of Strzyzow and Vicinity Poland

Translation of
Sefer Strzyzow ve-ha-seviva

Original Book Edited by: Itzhok Berglass and Shlomo Yahalomi-Diamond

Originally published in Tel Aviv, 1969

A Publication of JewishGen, INC
Edmond J. Safra Plaza, 36 Battery Place, New York, NY 10280
646.494.5972 | info@JewishGen.org | www.jewishgen.org

©JewishGen, Inc. 2022. All Rights Reserved
An affiliate of New York's Museum of Jewish Heritage – A Living Memorial to the Holocaust

The Book of Strzyzow and Vicinity, Poland

Translation of *Sefer Strzyzow ve-ha-seviva*

Copyright © 2022 by JewishGen, INC All rights reserved.
First Printing: May 2022, Iyar 5782

Editors of Original Yizkor Book: Itzhok Berglass and Shlomo Yahalomi-Diamond
Project Coordinator: Phyllis Kramer z"l
Layout and Name Indexing: Jonathan Wind
Reproduction of Photographs: Stefanie Holtzman
Cover Design: Rachel Kolokoff Hopper

This book may not be reproduced, in whole or in part, including illustrations in any form (beyond that copying permitted by Sections 107 and 108 of the U.S. Copyright Law and except by reviewers for public press), without written permission from the publisher.

JewishGen INC. is not responsible for inaccuracies or omissions in the original work and makes no representations regarding the accuracy of this translation. Digital images of the original book's contents can be seen online at the New York Public Library website or the Yiddish Book Center website.

Printed in the United States of America by Lightning Source, Inc.

Library of Congress Control Number (LCCN): 2022931815

ISBN: 978-1-954176-24-9 (hard cover: 530 pages, alk. paper)

About JewishGen.org

JewishGen, an affiliate of the Museum of Jewish Heritage - A Living Memorial to the Holocaust, serves as the global home for Jewish genealogy.

Featuring unparalleled access to 30+ million records, it offers unique search tools, along with opportunities for researchers to connect with others who share similar interests. Award winning resources such as the Family Finder, Discussion Groups, and ViewMate, are relied upon by thousands each day.

In addition, JewishGen's extensive informational, educational and historical offerings, such as the Jewish Communities Database, Yizkor Book translations, InfoFiles, Family Tree of the Jewish People, and KehilaLinks, provide critical insights, first-hand accounts, and context about Jewish communal and familial life throughout the world.

Offered as a free resource, JewishGen.org has facilitated thousands of family connections and success stories, and is currently engaged in an intensive expansion effort that will bring many more records, tools, and resources to its collections.

Please visit https://www.jewishgen.org/ to learn more.

Executive Director: Avraham Groll

About the JewishGen Yizkor Book Project

Yizkor Books (Memorial Books) were traditionally written to memorialize the names of departed family and martyrs during holiday services in the synagogue (a practice that still exists in many synagogues today).

Over the centuries, as a result of countless persecutions and horrific atrocities committed against the Jews, Yizkor Books (Sefer Zikaron in Hebrew) were expanded to include more historical information, such as biographical sketches of famous personalities and descriptions of daily town life.

Following the Holocaust, the idea of remembrance and learning took on an urgent and crucial importance. Survivors of the Holocaust sought out other surviving residents of their former towns to memorialize and document the names and way of life of those who were ruthlessly murdered by the Nazis. These remembrances were documented in Yizkor Books, hundreds of which were published in the first decades after the Holocaust.

Most of these books were published privately, or through landsmanshaftn (social organizations comprised of members originating from the same European town or region) that still existed, and were often distributed free of charge. Sadly, the languages used to document these crucial histories and links to our past, Yiddish and Hebrew, are no longer commonly understood by a significant percentage of Jews today. As a result, JewishGen has undertaken the sacred responsibility of translating these books into English so that the culture and way of life of these communities will be preserved and transmitted to future generations.

In 1986, a group of farsighted JewishGenners started a project to pool their efforts together in groups based upon their ancestors from each town and donate money to get the Yizkor books of their ancestral towns translated into English. As the translated material became available, it was made accessible for free at www.JewishGen.org/Yizkor. Hardcover copies can be purchased by visiting https://www.jewishgen.org/Yizkor/ybip.html (see below).

It is our hope that the translation of these books into English (and other languages) will assist the countless Jewish family researchers who are so desperately seeking to forge a connection with their heritage.

Director of JewishGen Yizkor Book Project: Lance Ackerfeld

About the JewishGen Press

JewishGen Press (formerly the Yizkor Books-in-Print Project) is the publishing division of JewishGen.org, and provides a venue for the publication of non-fiction books pertaining to Jewish genealogy, history, culture, and heritage.

In addition to the Yizkor Book category, publications in the Other Non-Fiction category include Shoah memoirs and research, genealogical research, collections of genealogical and historical materials, biographies, diaries and letters, studies of Jewish experience and cultural life in the past, academic theses, and other books of interest to the Jewish community.

Please visit https://www.jewishgen.org/Yizkor/ybip.html to learn more.

Director of JewishGen Press: Joel Alpert
Managing Editor - Jessica Feinstein
Publications Manager - Susan Rosin

Notes to the Reader

The images in the original book were reproduced from photographs from the time of the first edition. These reproductions were already of poor quality, being pre-war and at least 30 or more years old. As a result the images in the book are not very good and the best achievable.

A reader can view the original scans of the book on the websites listed below.

The original book can be seen online at the Yiddish Book Center website:

https://www.yiddishbookcenter.org/collections/yizkor-books/yzk-nybc314023/berglas-yitshak-yahalomi-sefer-strizov-veha-sevivah

and

https://www.yiddishbookcenter.org/collections/yizkor-books/yzk-nybc314230/berglas-yitshak-yahalomi-the-book-of-stryzow-and-vicinity

or at the New York Public Library Digital Collections website:

https://digitalcollections.nypl.org/items/504dea30-3541-0133-a9fe-00505686a51c

and

https://digitalcollections.nypl.org/items/c2e1c6d0-3543-0133-3c47-00505686a51c

To obtain a list of Shoah victims from Strzyzow the reader should access the Yad Vashem web site listed below; one can also search for specific family names using family name option. These lists are continually updated by Yad Vashem, so it is worthwhile to periodically search these lists.

There is more valuable information (including the Pages of Testimony, etc.) available on this website: https://yvng.yadvashem.org/

A list of all books available from JewishGen Press along with prices is available at: https://www.jewishgen.org/Yizkor/ybip.html

Credits for Book Cover

Front cover photograph:
The Leviathan painting on the vaulted ceiling above the Bimah, page 376 [Page 473]

Front and back cover texture, color, and background photograph: Rachel Kolokoff Hopper

Back cover poem:
From a poem by Uri Tzvi Greenberg Page 8 [Page 4]

Back cover photographs:
Top left: *Rachel, the daughter of Fishel Goldberg,* page 418 [Page 501]
Top right: *The Schefler family. Sitting: Shimon and Reisl Schefler. Standing: Joshua, Sarah, David, Shoshana, Tzvi and Moshe,* page 445 [Page 525]
Bottom left: *Joseph Chaim Diamand, his wife Dvoray with her mother, Chana Katz and children Shlomo and Heschel,* page 420 [Page 503]
Bottom right: *Moshe and Freda Guzik with their child,* page 416 [Page 499]

GeoPolitical Information

Strzyżów, Poland is located at 49°52' N 21°48' E and 168 miles SSE of Warszawa

	Town	District	Province	Country
Before WWI (c. 1900):	Strzyżów	Strzyżów	Galicia	Austrian Empire
Between the wars (c. 1930):	Strzyżów	Strzyżów	Lwów	Poland
After WWII (c. 1950):	Strzyżów			Poland
Today (c. 2000):	Strzyżów			Poland

Alternate Names for the Town:

Strzyżów [Pol], Strizev [Yid], Strezow [Ger], Strizhev, Schizuv, Strisev, Strishuv, Strizhuv, Strizov

Nearby Jewish Communities:

Niebylec 4 miles E
Czudec 6 miles NNE
Frysztak 8 miles WSW
Domaradz 9 miles SE
Wielopole Skrzyńskie 10 miles NW
Korczyna 10 miles S
Jasienica Rosielna 10 miles SE
Zgłobień 11 miles NNE
Jedlicze 12 miles SSW
Tyczyn 12 miles NE
Krosno 13 miles S
Błażowa 13 miles E
Sędziszów Małopolski 15 miles NNW
Brzozów 15 miles SE
Ropczyce 15 miles NNW
Rzeszów 15 miles NE
Kołaczyce 17 miles WSW
Jasło 17 miles WSW
Brzostek 17 miles W
Zabratówka 19 miles ENE
Dynów 20 miles E
Rymanów 20 miles S
Głogów Małopolski 21 miles NNE
Nowy Żmigród 21 miles SW

Dębica 21 miles NW
Dukla 21 miles SSW
Osiek Jasielski 21 miles SW
Jawornik Polski 22 miles E
Zarszyn 22 miles SSE
Jodłowa 22 miles W
Pilzno 23 miles WNW
Widełka 23 miles N
Łańcut 24 miles NE
Ulucz 25 miles ESE
Markowa 25 miles ENE
Siedleczka 26 miles ENE
Biecz 26 miles WSW
Dubiecko 26 miles E
Kolbuszowa 27 miles N
Sanok 27 miles SE
Przecław 27 miles NNW
Kańczuga 29 miles ENE
Jaśliska 29 miles S
Raniżów 29 miles NNE
Sokołów Małopolski 29 miles NNE
Bukowsko 29 miles SSE
Ryglice 30 miles W
Rzochów 30 miles NNW

Jewish Population: 859 (in 1880), 1,104 (in 1921)

Map of Poland with **Strzyżów** indicated

The Book of Strzyzow and Vicinity

TABLE OF CONTENTS

Article	Author	Page
Welcome to Strzyzow (Coordinator's introduction)		3
Dedication		7
Acknowledgment		7
Commemoration of Martyrs		7
Quotation from poems of Reb Yehuda Halevi, and Uri Tzvi Greenberg		8
Strzyzow my little town	Shlomo Yahalomi	5
The book of remembrance	Itzhok Berglass	10
Do Not Forget	Shlomo Yahalomi	11

ABOUT THE RABBIS IN STRZYZOW — Shlomo Yahalomi

Article	Page
The spiritual Strzyzow	14
Rabbis who served in Strzyzow and became famous	14
Rabbi Aryeh Leib Halevi	14
The godly kabalist, Rabbi Eliezer Fishel	15
The Tzadik from Ropczyce, Rabbi Naphtali Horowitz	15
Rabbi Tzvi Elimelech Shapiro	15
The holy Rabbi Elazar from Lancut and Strzyzow	16
Rabbi Israel Dov Gelernter	16
Rabbi Shlomo Shapiro	17
The Tzadik Rabbi Alter Zev Horowitz	20
The Assistant Rabbis in Strzyzow	20

STRZYZOW AND ITS INHABITANTS — Itzhok Berglass

Article	Page
Strzyzow my birthplace	23
The population in Strzyzow	24
How did the Jews make a living	25
The Rabbis in Strzyzow	25
Stryzow and its inhabitants	26
The Rabbi from Sassov	27
The community leadership. "The Kehillah"	28
The spiritual and social life of the Jews	29
Sabbath and holidays in Strzyzow	30
Family life in Strzyzow	33
Emigration	34
The synagogues in Strzyzow	34

The public bathhouse		36
The cemeteries in Strzyzow		36
Charity institutions and their activities		37
Jewish traditional education in Strzyzow		39
Secular education		42
Political parties in Strzyzow		44
The Zionist Movement in Strzyzow		45
Professionals and intelligentsia in Strzyzow		49
Negative types		49
Converts		49
The relationship between Jews and Poles		49
The Ritter story		50
The pogrom in 1898		50
Memories from the 1898 pogrom	Tzvi Sternberg	51
The pogrom in Strzyzow in 1918		53
The blood libel in Strzyzow		53
Strzyzow and its inhabitants		56
These I Will remember	Shlomo Yahalomi	58
People who studied the Torah	Shlomo Yahalomi	59
The Yeshiva Eitz Chaim In Strzyzow	Shlomo Yahalomi	60
The cheders and the melamdim	Shlomo Yahalomi	60
Reb Mordechai Rosenbaum	Shlomo Yahalomi	61
Reb Yechezkiel Gorgel - adam's apple	Shlomo Yahalomi	61
Reb Yosl from Brzozow	Shlomo Yahalomi	61
Reb Israel Leib Karp	Shlomo Yahalomi	62
The Agudat Israel	Shlomo Yahalomi	62
The relationship between Agudat Israel and Zionists	Shlomo Yahalomi	63
One among thousand	Moshe Mussler	64
When did the Jews settle in Strzyzow	Moshe Mussler	65
First rays of progress in Shtetl	Moshe Mussler	66
The forbearers Of the Holocaust	Moshe Mussler	67
To you, Kaddish I say my dear shtetl	Pinchos Klotz Aloni	68
Strzyzow	Yechezkiel–Harry Langsam	71
The Bais Yacov School in Strzyzow	Golda Miller–Langsam	72
Hassidim in Strzyzow	Mordechai Schiff	73
My Shtetl	Eliezer Gruber	74
How Mordechai Goldberg saved the town	Tzvi Elazar Sternberg	75
My Shtetl Strzyzow	Leah Loos	76

PERSONALITIES AND EVENTS

About the old Strzyzow	Itzhok Berglass	81
A royal visit at Reb Aaron Kanner	Shlomo Yahalomi	82

Reb Joel Margalit, of blessed memory	Shlomo Yahalomi	82
Reb Itzikl Diller makes a choice between Sandz and Sadigora	Shlomo Yahalomi	82
How Rabbi Chaim from Sandz gave a thrashing to Reb Shlomo from Zyznow	Shlomo Yahalomi	83
Rabbi Alter Zev Horowitz	Shlomo Yahalomi	83
Rabbi Nechemiah Shapiro	Shlomo Yahalomi	85
The Assistant Rabbi Yacov Shpalter	Shlomo Yahalomi	87
Memories from Strzyzow	Itzhok Deutch	88
A Miracle	Itzhok Deutch	88
A Jewish Heart	Itzhok Deutch	90
Hanukkah in Shtetl	Harry Langsam	90
Piquant stories from Strzyzow	Heschel Diamand	91
An awful story about "Rev'EE"	Heschel Diamand	92
How Reb Yosl, the sexton, had suddenly gone deaf	Heschel Diamand	92
Reb Baruch Berglass	Shlomo Yahalomi	93
Reb Avrehmal'E Goldman	Shlomo Yahalomi	94
Reb Hershel Gelander who Chanted the Mussaf Prayers	Shlomo Yahalomi	94
My father, my teacher, Reb Joseph Diamand	Shlomo Yahalomi	95
Reb Elazar Wurtzel. The Man of hints and gestures	Shlomo Yahalomi	97
Reb David Wiener	Shlomo Yahalomi	98
Reb Feitel Last and his son Shlomo	Shlomo Yahalomi	98
Reb Chaim Mandel	Shlomo Yahalomi	100
Reb Yeshayahu Mandel Hacohen	Shlomo Yahalomi	101
Reb Chaim Yacov Nuremberg	Shlomo Yahalomi	102
"A prayer of the afflicted when he is overwhelmed"	Shlomo Yahalomi	103
Reb Yacov Schiff	Shlomo Yahalomi	107
Half of the rewards in the hereafter	Shlomo Yahalomi	108
"When the world shall be perfected under the reign of the Almighty"	Shlomo Yahalomi	110
The righteous and the beloved, Reb Eisik Holles	Moshe Mussler	113
Reb Eisik the Sexton	Moshe Mussler	114
The Teachings of Moshe Mendelsohn	Moshe Mussler	115
A Tree Was Cut Down Prematurely	Moshe Mussler	116
The Faultless	Moshe Mussler	117
Meir Hertzkes	Moshe Mussler	118
The clever and the not so clever. Shlomo Bier	Moshe Mussler	119
Meir Ber who was intimate with the authorities	Moshe Mussler	120
The eccentric Heschel Holoshitz. "Heschel the peasant"	Moshe Mussler	121
The needy	Moshe Mussler	123
The unfortunate families	Itzhok Berglass	124
The first Zionist in Strzyzow	Itzhok Berglass	126
Rizhi, the righteous woman	Itzhok Berglass	127
There were four of us	Itzhok Berglass	128
Reb Simcha Feingold, of blessed memory	Ben Ami Feingold	130
The large, well-rooted families in Strzyzow	Shlomo Yahalomi	130

The Adest family, The Berglass family, The Diamond Family	Shlomo Yahalomi	131
The Holles family, The Kanner family, The Mandel family	Shlomo Yahalomi	133
The Mintz family	Shlomo Yahalomi	134
Reb Hershel Resler and his sons–in–law	Shlomo Yahalomi	134
The Rosen brothers, The Schefler Family, The Sturm Family	Shlomo Yahalomi	134
The Tenzer family	Shlomo Yahalomi	136

ABOUT DAILY LIFE AND TRIVIAL EVENTS IN STRZYZOW. ODD STORIES

Gentiles Reciting the Prayer "Shema Israel"	Itzhok Berglass	138
The District Commissioner's Party	Itzhok Berglass	138
The Thousands That Were Burned	Itzhok Berglass	139
The Prescription	Itzhok Berglass	139
A Conscientious Ignoramus	Itzhok Berglass	140
The "Resolution" by the Rabbis to Observe the Sabbath Twice a Week	Itzhok Berglass	140
The Relations Between the Jews and Gentiles	Itzhok Berglass	141
The Jews Extinguished the Fire in a Gentile House	Itzhok Berglass	141
How the Jews Saved Gentile Property during the Flood	Itzhok Berglass	141
The Zionist Movement and my Road to Zionism	Leah Loos	141
Repentance	Leah Loos	142
The Deal with the Ukrainians	Itzhok Berglass	143
The Elections to the City Government	Itzhok Berglass	143
The Unsuccessful Intervention	Itzhok Berglass	145
Jewish Contact with the Authorities	Itzhok Berglass	146
How the Word "Choshiver" was Changed to "Hashomer"	Itzhok Berglass	146
The Election to the Polish Parliament	Itzhok Berglass	147
The Kindergarten Inspection	Itzhok Berglass	148
This Also Happened in Our Town	Moshe Mussler	149
Long Live the Kaiser	Moshe Mussler	151
Books Burned on the Auto–Da–Fe	Moshe Mussler	151
Inference	Moshe Mussler	152

FROM THE DISTANT AND NOT SO DISTANT PAST OF STRZYZOW

The Man Who Was No Coward	Shlomo Yahalomi	154
A Proper Answer	Shlomo Yahalomi	154
A Clever Jew	Shlomo Yahalomi	154
The Merchandise is Already Packed	Shlomo Yahalomi	155
A Powerful Word	Shlomo Yahalomi	155
Everything Has To Be Her Way?	Shlomo Yahalomi	155
What was Reb Hersh Ber the Sexton Doing?	Shlomo Yahalomi	156
The Rabbi's Insinuation	Shlomo Yahalomi	156
The Righteous Who Never Sinned	Shlomo Yahalomi	156

Good Morning	Shlomo Yahalomi	156
The Story About the Treasurers Who Were Forced to Resign	Shlomo Yahalomi	156
Reb Baruch Diller Explained That the Willingness is the Essence	Shlomo Yahalomi	157
The "Dreadful Story" about Mother's Earrings	Shlomo Yahalomi	157
With or Without a Permit	Shlomo Yahalomi	157
What is a Mitzva and How Did Joshua's Spies Cross the River Jordan	Shlomo Yahalomi	158
He Used Hands Without Having Said the Proper Blessing	Shlomo Yahalomi	158
The special "Sabbatical Inspiration"	Shlomo Yahalomi	158
The Father and Son's Card Game	Shlomo Yahalomi	158
The Son Sued the Father	Shlomo Yahalomi	159
Reb Hershal'e Schiffs Eye Glasses	Shlomo Yahalomi	159
Reb Israel Gertner Opposed Buying on Credit	Shlomo Yahalomi	159
Such a "Repentant Sinner"	Shlomo Yahalomi	159
Yacov or Yacov Chaim	Shlomo Yahalomi	160
Every Rabbi Specializes in a Different Sickness	Shlomo Yahalomi	160
Which Fast Was the Best?	Shlomo Yahalomi	160
And What is Called a "Ruined Holiday"	Shlomo Yahalomi	160
"We Implore Thee, O Lord, Prosper Us"	Shlomo Yahalomi	160

MEMORIES FROM STRZYZOW

In The Days Past -	Professor Dr. Ch. Lehrman	163
Contrasting Worlds	Professor Dr. Ch. Lehrman	170

THE HOLOCAUST AND THE AFTERMATH

The Second World War and the Holocaust	Itzhok Berglass	180
Children in captivity	Itzhok Berglass	192
After the war and the Holocaust	Itzhok Berglass	194
1967	Itzhok Berglass	196

WORDS OF CONTEMPLATION AND THOUGHTS

Judaism and Nationalism	Rabbi Israel Frenkel	199
A Partial Answer, Regret and Guilt	Rabbi Israel Frenkel	201
Our Strength Against a Hostile World	Rabbi Israel Frenkel	203
Martyrdom and the Sanctity of Life	Rabbi Isaac Glikman	204
I Shall See the Holocaust Before My Eyes Forever	Shlomo Yahalomi	205
Remembrance and Forgetfulness	Rabbi Samuel Nachum Frenkel	208

WRITTEN BY SURVIVORS

In Memory of My Family – Obliterated in the Holocaust	Itzhok Berglass	211

My Family	Shoshana Ginsberg (Scheffler)	212
My mother	Pinchos Klotz–Aloni	212
Father Said: Do Not Remain Here	Shulamit Grinwald–Hasenkopg	213
The Bitter Account	Shlomo Yahalomi	214
My Father Reb Chaim Itzhok Kalb	Ben Zion Kalb	217
The People of Israel Shall Live!	Leah Loos	218
In Memory of My Parents Who Perished Somewhere in Poland	Dr. Chanan Lehrman	219
Memories from My Father's House	Seryl Fishler–Mandel	220
My Holy Father the Martyr, Reb Abraham Kalb the Shochet, of Blessed Memory	Ben Zion Kalb	221
In Memory of My Father and My Town	Menachem the son of Moshe Kandel–Nuremberg	222
In Memory of My Family	Ruth Kremerman–Russ	222
In Memory of My Father, Sister with Her Family	Harry Langsam	223
Days and Years in Strzyzow	Chana Schiff–Shmulewicz	224
Eta Hacker, (From the Landesman–Diamand Family)	Shlomo Yahalomi	226
How I Found Out About the Town of My Origin, Strzyzow	Shlomo Neumann	226

FROM THE LEGACY OF THE MARTYRS

Naphtali the Son of Reb Chaim Mandel...May G–d Avenge His Blood		229
Why Did G–d Punish Me So Severely?	Eta Federbush–Diamand	229
Excerpt From a Letter Written to Leah Loos in Eretz Israel	Liba Greenblatt and Sarah Alta Mandel	230
Letter From the Nazi–Occupied Territory	Eta Falk–Dembitzer	230
A Letter to Itzhok Berglass in Pimia, Siberia	Chaya Feirush–Berglass	231
A Letter to Itzhok Berglass in Pimia, Siberia	Nechama Bernstein–Berglass	231
A Plea for Support to the Secretary of the Strzyzow Society in the United States		231
Letter of Recommendation from Itzhok Berglass		234
Letter of Recommendation from Abraham Tenzer		235
Letter from the Free Loan Society in Strzyzow To the Strzyzow Relief Committee in New York		236

THE VICINITY

The Little Towns	Itzhok Berglass	238
The Villages	Itzhok Berglass	238
The Village Lutcza	Itzhok Berglass	239
The Jewish Villagers were the Pillars of Benefaction	Shlomo Yahalomi	240
Reb Eliyahu Bilut from Lutcza	Shlomo Yahalomi	240
Reb Yechezkiel Wallach from Lutcza	Shlomo Yahalomi	241
The Large Diamand Family	Shlomo Yahalomi	241

MEMORIES FROM THE DAYS OF THE HOLOCAUST

The cup of sorrow from which I drank during the Holocaust years	Moshe Mussler	243
At the edge of the Sheol	Shlomo Yahalomi	248
On the third anniversary of my exile	Shlomo Yahalomi	248
Seven Rosh Hashanahs	Shlomo Yahalomi	249
Purim in jail	Shlomo Yahalomi	249
Passover. The festival of freedom in prison	Shlomo Yahalomi	251
Rosh Hashana 1940 in the Odessa prison	Shlomo Yahalomi	252
Shavuoth night, 1941	Shlomo Yahalomi	252
Rosh Hashanah, 1941. In the collective farm "Mocry Maidan" near Saratov	Shlomo Yahalomi	253
Go ahead. Pray! Rosh Hashanah 1942	Shlomo Yahalomi	254
"In the land of the free". Rosh Hashanah 1943. "Peat Enterprises"	Shlomo Yahalomi	254
United with my brother once again. Rosh Hashanah, 1944.	Shlomo Yahalomi	255
Rosh Hashanah 1945. The last Rosh Hashanah in Soviet Russia	Shlomo Yahalomi	256
Memories from the land of Exile	Itzhok Berglass	256
The location of our exile	Itzhok Berglass	257
The protest	Itzhok Berglass	258
"Give thanks to the Lord for He is good"	Itzhok Berglass	259
The holidays in Siberia	Itzhok Berglass	259
Memories of the first days of Poland's occupation by the Nazi	Simcha Langsam	261
The situation in Strzyzow	Simcha Langsam	262
Memories	Simcha Langsam	263
Zitomir	Simcha Langsam	265
Ben Zion Kalb saved many Jewish lives during the Holocaust	Shlomo Yahalomi	268
Letter from the Jewish Agency		269
Letter from Rabbi Weismandel to Ben Zion Kalb		272
A postcard from the valley of death		277
Letters to Ben Zion Kalb from Taivia Lubetkin and "Antek" Itzhok Zukerman, leaders in the Warsaw ghetto		277
My last Simchat Torah in Strzyzow	Harry (Yechezkiel) Langsam	281
Memories from the days of horror. Jumping off the death–train	Itzhok Leib Rosen	282
The struggle with the Jewish "Kapos"	Itzhok Leib Rosen	283
"Yiddishkeit" in the German concentration camps	Itzhok Leib Rosen	284
The horrible years. 1942–1945	Hilda Mandel-Feit	285
Surviving in the Lion's den	Pearl Strengerwoski–Rosen	286
"Kol Nidrei" in Auschwitz	Joseph Weinberg	287
My road of suffering	Reuven Greenbaum	288

FOR THE HOMELAND

The Fighters	Itzhok Berglass	291
Yacov Feingold, of blessed memory	Itzhok Berglass	291

To the Laterbaum Sisters	Itzhok Berglass	291
The Casualties	Itzhok Berglass	293
Joseph Asher, of blessed memory	Leah Laos	293
My brother Michael Kalb, of blessed memory	Aryeh Kalb	295
Moshe Lehrman, of blessed memory	Aryeh Kalb	296
Parting, Eulogy by Rabbi M. Shapiro	Aryeh Kalb	297
My comrade Moshe	Shlomo Levi	297
Tzvi Navon, of blessed memory	Shlomo Levi	298
Tzvi Navon, of blessed memory, on the shloshim of his death	Zalman	299
To my brother	Chaya Levin	300
Aaron, the son of Yacov Kanner, of blessed memory	Chaya Levin	301
Aaron Kanner	Chaya Levin	301
Chanan Abraham Kalb, of blessed memory	Chaya Levin	302

THE DESTRUCTION OF FRYSZTAK

How the Nazis annihilated a Hassidic shtetl	Menashe Unger	304
The Rabbi of Koloszyce in Frysztak	Menashe Unger	305
The holy headscarf	Chaim Lieberman	306

LIST OF THE MARTYRS OF STRZYZOW AND VICINITY

Of thee I cry, my eye is shedding a tear	Simcha Langsam	311
The list of martyrs		312
The martyrs of Frysztak and Czudec		339
The departed in the Holy Land		341

IN MEMORY OF OUR BROTHERS, THE JEWS OF STRZYZOW

The Monument	343
The Torah Scroll	343
The text of the inscription on the plaque	346

REMNANTS OF THE COMMUNITY

Natives of Strzyzow throughout the world	Itzhok Berglass	348
Israel		350
United States of America		352
Canada, Latin America, Brazil		354

REMNANTS OF THE COMMUNITY IN EUROPE

Poland, Germany, England, Belgium, France, Switzerland, Italy, Austria	358

To the conclusion of this book	Shlomo Yahalomi	361
Update on Strzyzow		363
A memorial to Chudnov, in the district of Zitomir, U.S.S.R.	Harry Langsam	364
Pictures from Stryzow		367
Memorial Pages		414
Glossary		455
Name index (Original Book)		463
List of Photographs from Strzyzow		496

NAME INDEX 500

The Book of Strzyzow and Vicinity (Poland)

49°52' / 21°48'

Translation of
Sefer Strzyzow ve-ha-seviva

Edited by: Itzhok Berglass and Shlomo Yahalomi-Diamond

Published in Tel Aviv, 1969

Acknowledgments

Project Coordinator:

Phyllis Kramer z"l

Our sincere appreciation to Genia Hollander & Helen Rosenstein Wolf for typing up the English text to facilitate its addition to this project.

The Hebrew-Yiddish text was printed in Israel and translated by Harry Langsam in Los Angeles, USA

Our sincere appreciation to Harry Langsam for permission to put this material on the JewishGen web site.

This is a translation from: *Strzyzow, Poland: Sefer Strizhuv ve-ha-seviva*
(Memorial Book of Strzyzow and vicinity), Editors: J. Berglas, Sh. Yahalomi (Diamant),
Tel Aviv, Former Residents of Strzyzow in Israel and Diaspora, 1969 (H, Y 480 pages).

Note: The original books can be seen online at the NY Public Library site: Strzyzow (1969) and Strzyzow (1990)

This material is made available by JewishGen, Inc. and the Yizkor Book Project for the purpose of fulfilling our mission of disseminating information about the Holocaust and destroyed Jewish communities. This material may not be copied, sold or bartered without JewishGen, Inc.'s permission. Rights may be reserved by the copyright holder.

JewishGen, Inc. makes no representations regarding the accuracy of the translation. The reader may wish to refer to the original material for verification.

JewishGen is not responsible for inaccuracies or omissions in the original work and cannot rewrite or edit the text to correct inaccuracies and/or omissions.

Our mission is to produce a translation of the original work and we cannot verify the accuracy of statements or alter facts cited.

Welcome to Strzyzow

Strzyzow (also known as Strizev in Yiddish and Strezow in German) is today a major town in southern Poland (it was in Galicia, an Imperial Province of Austria Hungary, from 1776 to 1919). The earliest known Jewish community appeared in the 16th century, but it was not until the 18th century that the synagogue was built. Strzyzow is located in the **Rzeszow** region at **latitude 49 52', longitude 21 48'**, 40 km south of Rzeszow, 75 km west of Przemysl. Today there are no Jews in Strzyzow.

My great grandmother **Frieda Necha KANDEL** was born in Strzyzow in 1860 (the photo is from 1913). Frieda married **Josef SCHEINER**, a Schochet from the nearby town of Dubetsk. They emigrated to the United States in the late 1890s.

In loving memory of those who lived and died there, and of those who ventured out, I have created two web pages, one devoted to the town (on JewishGen's Shtetlinks), and this one, devoted to the Yizkor Book.

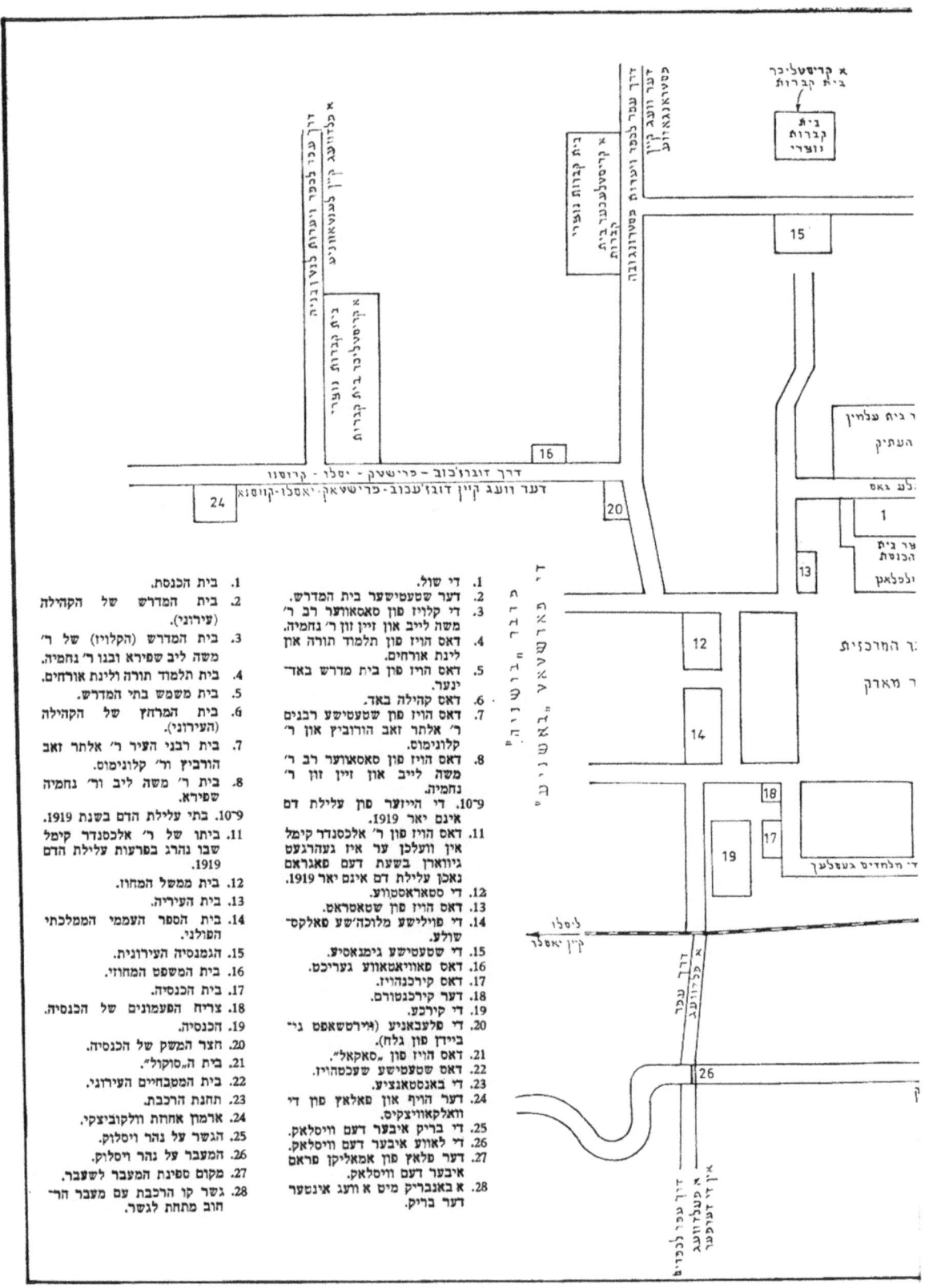

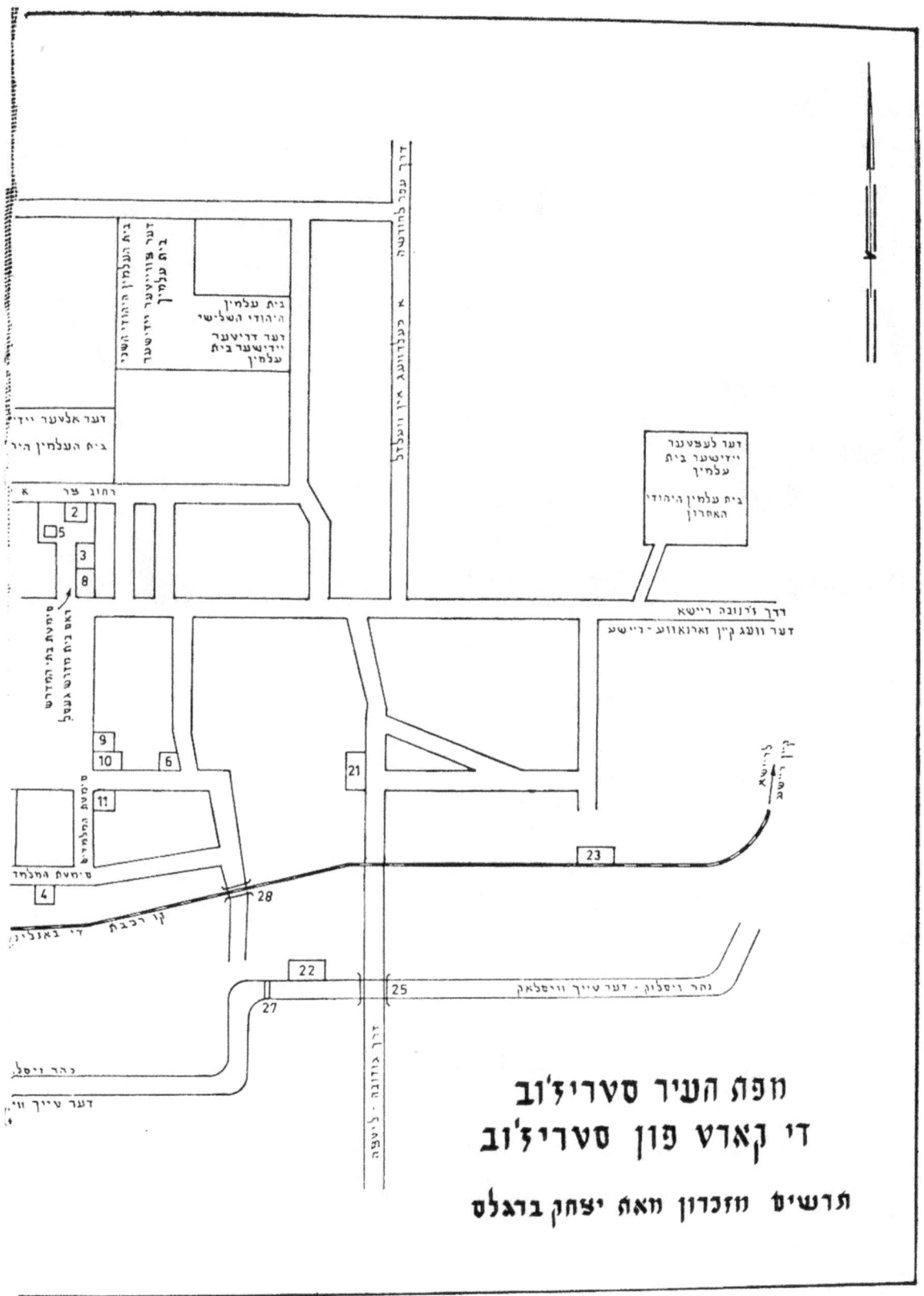

Sefer Strizhuv, the Yizkor Book

The Yizkor Book, Sefer Strizhuv, was published in 1969 in Tel Aviv. It has 480 pages; mostly Hebrew and Yiddish. In 1990, Harry Langsam translated it into English, and published it in Los Angeles, entitling it "The Book of Strzyzow and Vicinity". Harry Langsam has given JewishGen permission to reproduce the contents on this web page. To date, I have entered the table of contents, the list of names, the index and a few of the most poignant stories. With time, I will add other stories to this page.

I hope you will find this interesting and helpful. Please contact me if you have questions or comments. As with any genealogical research, this is an evolving project.

Phyllis Kramer z"l

* * * *

The Book of Strzyzow and Vicinity
published by the "Natives of Strzyzow Societies" in Israel and the Diaspora;

edited by Itzhok Berglass, and Shlomo Yahalomi-Diamand;

supervised by the publishing committee:

Itzhok Berglass, Shlomo Yahalomi, Pinchos Aloni, Simcha Langsam,
Leah Loos, Moshe Mussler

[Page 1]

> In memory of my father, sister, her husband and their children and all our relatives. I am translating this memorial book of the martyrs of Strzyzow to the language spoken by my children and my grandchildren so they will know what happened to the Jewish people who lived amidst the civilized nations of Europe during World War II, between the years 1939-1945.
>
> **Harry Langsam**

[Page 2]

Acknowledgment

> I would like to express my gratitude to my daughter, Rema Nadel and to my son-in-law, Michael Friedberg for the time spent with me helping in the translation of this memorial book. Without them it would have been difficult for me to achieve my goal.
>
> **The translator**

[Page 3]

Commemoration of Martyrs

May the merciful Father who dwells on high, in his infinite mercy, remember those saintly, upright and blameless souls, the holy communities who offered their lives for the sanctification of the Divine Name. They were lovely and amiable in their life and were not parted in their death. They were swifter than eagles and stronger than lions to do the will of their Master and the desire of their stronghold. May our G-d remember them favourably among the other righteous of the world; may he avenge the blood of his servants which has been shed as it is written in the Torah of Moses, the man of G-d: "O nations make his people joyful! He avenges the blood of His servants, renders retribution to His foes and provides atonement for His land and people". And by Thy servants, the Prophets, it is written: "I will avenge their blood which I have not yet avenged; the Lord dwells in Zion". And in the holy writing, it is said: "Why should the nations say 'where then is their G-d? Let the vengeance for Thy servants' blood that is shed be made known among the nations in our sight". And it is said: "The avenger of bloodshed remembers them. He does not forget the cry of the humble". And it is further said: "He will execute judgment upon the nations and fill (the battle-field) with corpses: He will shatter the (enemies) head over all the wide earth. From the brook by the wayside he will drink, and then he will lift up his head triumphantly".

[Page 4]

>On such sadness,
>tears should be endless.
>Each person should be concerned
>and each heart distressed.
>
>**(Reb Yehuda Halevi)**

Because between us and the Western World,
the bodies of the untainted martyrs are lying.
From my murdered people, young and old,
killed in the season of bloom and season of snow....
The dust that supposedly had them covered did not cover.
Their exalted faces...They radiate in their exposure.
And we the heirs:
For all the goodness and honour that they paid for
with their blood, here we shall be burdened
to carry for ever the eternal light.

From a poem by Uri Tzvi Greenberg

[Page 5]

Strzyzow my little town

By Shlomo Yahalomi

Here is a story, a very sad story
About a town which vanished with all its glory.
Horrible is the story, behold!
In this book the story will unfold.

There was once a town
A very small town
Surrounded with hills, and valley galore,
It belonged to me, you and more.

Although its territory was small,
A few hundred families in all,
Two thousand people or maybe less –
Her importance everyone impressed.

There were rabbis a score,
Great scholars blessed by G-d they were.
Sons and grandsons, descendants
Of holy men, and in Torah studies valiant.

From Ropczyce Rabbi Naphtali the men
Who, with wisdom, the Hassidic world ran.
Rabbi Mendele of the book **Sova Smachot** the author,
From which people our traditions learned to adore.

The author of **Drishat Ari**, the book
Turned our town into his study nook,
To study with diligence he was keen,
With his cousin the Yismach Moshe he was always seen.

To enchant the hearts and revive the souls,
Was the author of **Bnuyot Ramah's** goal.
And with his penetrating preaching
He brought for the souls a healing.

The one from Dynov, the extreme,
Fighting G-d's war was his dream.
Rabbi Tzvi Elimelech the holy,
In our town wonders performed, truly.

The Tzadik Rabbi Elazar from Lanzut
Was popular and looked good,
His father name him as his heir
And he proudly filled the rabbinical chair.

[Page 6]

Rabbi Shlomo, the lion of the group,
Was our Rabbi and leader of troop,
His ways were benevolence and might,
He was our guiding light.

Rabbi Shlomo with his roaring voice,
His chanting split heavens and we rejoiced.
Aroused the pious and those non-devout,
Never tolerated a weakening of belief in G-d.

town was once upon a time
A home, when they were in their prime
Two Baal Shem Tov lads
Who always lived in a world above their heads.

Rabbi Elazar Fishel, the kabbala man
Thought that to speed the redemption he can.
He authored several books and also studied mysticism,
Always a dreamer far removed from realism.

We had many more personalities
Who nowadays are considered rarities.
For their good deeds they were well-known
Because here in town they were born.

Simple people and scholars abundant
Who studied Torah daily and kept the covenant.
With crystal clear hearts beyond fault
Never did they dare G-d to insult.

Hassidim truly and stirring
From exaltation like fire burning
Always joyful and happy
Never became tired, always snappy.

Light they spread like a candle
With G-d fearing spirit, everyone's heart they kindled.
For sacrifice – always ready,
Generous to the poor, never greedy.

Young men with brains acute
Spent their days in Gemara's sophistry.
Their energy and power they spent
To find in the commentaries for their questions answers at hand.

Our merchants and tradesmen
Were hospitable to strangers and kinsmen.
Our town also was blessed
To have good leaders among the best.

[Page 7]

There were also women righteous and modest,
With hearts of gold and with mercy possessed.
And Psalms – reciting Jews who did their best
During the prayers for redemption G-d addressed.

Whatever there was, whatever there has been
This town disappeared entirely from the scene.
Woe! Woe! What a tragedy! What an end.
They all perished. It is hard to comprehend.

Once upon a time there was a town
What left is a piece of stone
Which is Strzyzow's monument
Mounted on a wall in the martyr's basement.

The Book of Remembrance
Dedicated to the Holy Community of Strzyzow and Vicinity;

For the generations who remained buried in foreign lands, and for those whose burial place nobody know, because the cemeteries have been turned into public parks and their gravestones used for sidewalks; only a few gravestones were saved after the intervention of the survivors from Strzyzow; they were removed from the sidewalks and returned to the site of the last Jewish cemetery before the war.

For the last generation who worked for the beginning of the redemption but had not lived to see it, they sanctified the name of heaven with their martyrized deaths during the European Holocaust and have not had even a Jewish burial.

To the natives of Strzyzow and vicinity who are spread throughout the four corners of the world, may this book be a bond with their perished brothers and sisters, and to their offspring, a way of getting acquainted with their origin.

Itzhok, the son of Baruch Berglass

[Page 8]

Do Not Forget!

In the very ancient times, the people of Israel in Egypt, in the land of Goshen, resided among the Egyptians but did not mingle with them. They were quiet and humble. They were faithful to the Kind and obeyed the laws. As it is written: "And the children of Israel were fruitful and increased abundantly, and multiplied and vaxed exceedingly might. And the land was filled with them".

"Behold! The people of the children of Israel are too many and too mighty for us". They became rich from exploiting us. The King got smart and published the "White papers" which in reality were black. The proclamation said: "All first-born Jewish males should be killed".

On appearance, the Egyptians were very civilized and did not question this ordinance. On the contrary, they faithfully obeyed this order without hesitation and for a time, it seemed that there would be no Jewish male child survivor, Heaven forbid.

But one Jewish mother by the name of Yochebed, succeeded in hiding her first-born son in a wooden box and putting it in the Nile River. When Batyah, the daughter of Pharaoh came to the river to bathe, she heard a baby crying. Immediately she understood that this baby is probably one of the last Jewish children and she could not be so merciless not to spare this child's life.

But here is what happened in our century – a tragic and terrible Holocaust – nothing like that ever happened to the Jews in the Diaspora. The corpses are still before our eyes. The orphans, the very few who survived, small children and adults, they were standing before our eyes. It happened almost yesterday but they already seemed far away, almost forgotten. Few remember that once upon a time there were a Jewish people great in numbers and quality amongst the Europeans, to so-called "civilized" nations. The Jewry of Poland, Lithuania, Galicia, Hungary, Czechoslovakia, Romania and Russia. All categories, Hassidim, Mitnagdim, plain Jews, Jewish tradesmen, Jewish farmers, Rabbis, heads of Yeshivot – millions of them – also scientists, poets, writers, politicians and philosophers. A Jewish life full of energy and creativity. And suddenly, a poisonous snake – Hitler – came to power and ordered the final solution, to annihilate all Jews – which no one should survive.

These cultured, intelligent German people of composers, poets and philosophers, turned loose their animal instincts to kill mercilessly and in a most cruel way. Old and young indiscriminately, of all ages. They killed, murdered, burn and even buried alive, six million! Six million! Can they be forgotten? And yet, in a miraculous way, a few survived.

[Page 9]

One from a shtetl, two from a family, remnants of the European Jewry. And they are the ones who have sworn not to forget.

Those who heard about the Holocaust from far away might be inclined to forget, but not the people who witnessed this tragedy. Those individual survivors who lost their wives, husbands, parents, children – they keep reminding us and are warning us ever minutes, every hours of the day and in every place: DO NOT FORGET!

And from the general destruction to the destruction of our beloved home, our beloved shtetl Strzyzow. Although it was small, to us it was a great place.

Once there was a place in Poland, at the foothills of the Carpathian Mountains, the name of this place was Strzyzow. Small, but important enough to write about. About the Torah scholars, the Hassidim and about how the sound of Torah never ceased to be heard from the inside of the Beit Hamidrash, the kloyz. About the beginning of Hassidim which goes back to the time of the Baal Shem Tov, the founder of the Hassidic movement.

We will write about all the stories and legends that were told in this town. The lights and shadows which existed and had their influence on the town. This place has a historical value to tell about her past. All the tales I have heard from the elders and what I have read here and there. It is worthwhile to collect all this in a book, particularly when this is our town where we were born and raised until the destruction by the cursed Nazi.

This book will serve as a perpetuation of the town, for our sake and for the sake of the martyrs who went up in flames to heaven and died for sanctification of the Divine Name. It is the duty of all those who survived to do everything possible, that this place should not be forgotten. Not by us, nor by future generations. With G-d's help, I have told here the stories which I collected from my notebook which were written not with ink, but with blood and tears.

May G-d help us to succeed in our task.

Shlomo Yahalomi (Diamand)
The son of Joseph Chaim.
A remnant rescued from fire.

[Page 10]

About the Rabbis in Strzyzow
Shlomo Yahalomi

The Spiritual Strzyzow
By Shlomo Yahalomi

When I started to write about Strzyzow in general, and about the Rabbis in particular, I started with a prayer: "Dear G-d, help me not to exaggerate where I do not intend to and not to belittle anybody who deserves to be praised. Therefore, I apologize to everyone, the victims and the survivors, if I over looked anything or anybody".

If an average book is holy, this book about the Holocaust victims is holier than holy. And if someone would ask me: "Who are you to undertake such a task?" my reply would be: "Sorry! Not too many of us survived, somebody had to do it in order that Strzyzow would not be forgotten". I felt that we are obliged to memorialize the martyrs of Strzyzow.

Nobody really knows when the Jews settled in Strzyzow. The old people used to say that Strzyzow was founded about four centuries ago. There was one gravestone in the oldest cemetery which was located in the centre of the town. The inscription read as follows: "here rests the holy man Eliyahu and his wife who died in the year 1740".

There was a story going around that this holy man wrote in his will that in time of trouble or sickness, people should come and pray at his grave. And the people carried out the man's request. Also, two pupils of the Baal Shem Tov lived in Strzyzow of which the town was very proud. To the writer of these memories, it was told by one old man that in his father's writings he found a story about these two pupils. One was well known in town and was supported by the community. However, the other man did not divulge his identity, and was very poor, making a living as a water carrier. His wife knowing what a Tzadik he was, demanded that he should stop being so humble, so the people of the town would help him out. But he refused her demands with all kinds of excuses. Subsequently, their situation reached the point of desperation and he surrendered to his wife's request. He announced that the coming Sabbath he would preach in shul G-d's words. On the Sabbath, the shul attracted more people than usual. People attended out of curiosity, wondering what a water carrier could possibly tell them. But lo and behold, they heard a sermon from this man that everybody was astounded. His words penetrated in their souls. People were crying. Everyone said that a sermon like this, they had never heard in their lives.

Strzyzow was once visited by Rabbi Levi Itzhok from Berditchev. He stayed in town over the Sabbath as well as Rabbi Mendele from Rymanov who often visited the town. Both Rabbis were considered the pillars of Hassidism and Strzyzow was very proud to host such visitors.

Rabbis who served in Strzyzow and later became famous

Even though the Jews settled in Strzyzow four hundred years ago, I did not succeed to trace the names of the Rabbis who had served during the first two hundred years. The reason is that apparently none of them authored any books or commentary by which we could have identified them. Indeed, there were no gravestones of any Rabbis in the cemeteries except for one – the gravestone of Rabbi Alter Zev Horowitz. The elders in town and Rabbi Tzvi Elimelech Shapiro who served as Rabbi of Strzyzow, confirmed that fact by saying that no Rabbi who served the community of Strzyzow ever died in Strzyzow because they always moved to a better place which meant a bigger community.

[Page 11]

Rabbi Aryeh Leib Halevi

Rabbi Aryeh Leib Halevi was the first Rabbi of whom we know. He was the uncle of Rabbi Moshe Teitelbaum, the author of the book "Yismach Moshe". Rabbi Aryeh Leib Halevi was the Rabbi of Strzyzow for twenty five years, from 1740-1765. He was the author of several books on various subjects, strictures and rules, on circumcision and phylacteries and also about Sabbath and holidays. The book "Even Hapina" was left unfinished because he was suddenly summoned before the Creator.

The Godly Kabbalist and Rabbi Eliezer Fishel

Rabbi Eliezer Fishel was the author of two Kabbalistic books: Olam Hagado and Midrash Lepirushim. He signed the book as a native of Strzyzow. He was the grandson of the famous Rabbi Itzhok from Krakow who was called, in Yiddish: "Der groiser Rebbe fun Krakow". Rabbi Eliezer Fishel was also, at one time, the preacher in Brody. Although the historian Dr. Gelber, wrote that Rabbi Eliezer was born in Czeszanov, however, this is incorrect. Apparently, Dr. Gelber never referred to the above-mentioned two books where Rabbi Eliezer Fishel clearly indicated that he was born in Strzyzow. While speaking of Rabbi Eliezer Fishel, let us mention his son, Rabbi Moshe Yechiel who served as Rabbi in Biala, Lithuania. The son was one of the staunchest admirers of Rabbi Mendele from Kock. Rabbi Moshe Yechiel was a wealthy man having received a hefty dowry in the sum of a hundred thousand rubbles from his rich father-in-law.

The Tzadik from Ropczyce, Rabbi Naphtali Horowitz

Rabbi Naphtali served as Rabbi in Strzyzow a short time only. He was born on the day when the Baal Shem Tov, the founder of Hassidism died. Rabbi Chaim, the Rabbi from Sandz said that there was a sunset and a sunrise at the same time. Rabbi Naphtali studied Torah at his uncle's house, the famous Rabbi Meshulam who lived in Tiszmienice and he was also a pupil of the Rabbi Elimelech from Lezajsk. Rabbi Naphtali was famous for his jokes, however, some Hassidim disapproved, especially his father-in-aw. His father-in-law complained to Rabbi Naphtali's father about his joking and light-headedness and asked him to intervene. Rabbi Menachem Mendel, Rabbi Naphtali's father, went to Dukla where Rabbi Naphtali lived to attend a wedding where his son was supposed to be the jester and amuse the guests. When he heard his son's jesting, he said to his son's father-in-law: "You call this jesting? Behold! He recites whole chapters from Rabbi Chaim Vital's book – The Tree of Life".

After Rabbi Naphtali from Ropczyce left Strzyzow, a very famous scholar from Tarnov became Rabbi of Strzyzow. His name was Menachem Mendel, the author of the book: Sova Smachot – a commentary of the Talmudic tractate Kidushin. This is the tractate that sets the rules and laws of marriage and the relationship between husband and wife.

[Page 12]

Strzyzow was very proud to have him as its religious leader. He died in 1871. After his departure, Rabbi Tzvi Elimelech Shapiro was invited to Strzyzow to be its Rabbi.

Rabbi Tzvi Elimelech Shapiro

Rabbi Tzvi Elimelech was loved by everyone. He served as Rabbi in five communities: Rybotycze, Strzyzow, Oleszczyce, Dynov and Munkatch. In each city, he served a few years only. Ultimately, he returned to Dynov where he spent the rest of his life. He was once asked why he changed places so often and he replied: "If a man has several barrels and keeps rearranging them, does someone ask him why? The boss above does it; he knows where to put his barrels".

He was the author of many books: Agra D'Pirka, Agra D'Kala, Beni Yesoschor, Regel Yesharim, Derech P'Kudecha, Magid Taalumot, Vehayah Beachs and Reach Dodaim. Very interesting commentaries on Torah, Zohar and Talmud.

Rabbi Tzvi Elimelech was a fighter. He fought against the spreading of the Berlin Haskala Movement and its founder Mendelsohn. He saws them as the destroyers of Judaism. He was apprehensive that the Haskala movement would cause mass conversion.

Rabbi Tzvi Elimelech was born in Javornik. His father was Reb Pesach Langsam and his mother was the sister of Rabbi Elimelech from Lezajsk. A whole volume could have been written about this Rabbi and his sons, Rabbi Elazar from Lancut and Rabbi David from Dynov, about whom the father said that his soul was drawn from aristocratic stock. But we were limited in space and could not possibly write everything about them, but without intention of demeaning their reverence. The elders in town were proud of their Rabbi and his offspring who added glory to the Jewish world for generations.

The Holy Rabbi Elazar from Lancut and Strzyzow

Rabbi Elazar Shapiro was the son of Tzvi Elimelech from Dynov. Rabbi Elazar was name Rabbi of Strzyzow in the year 1838. Rabbi Tzvi Hersh from Ziditchov said about him that he never saw such elegant looks as this young man possessed. Rabbi Elazar was always the first to come into the Beit HaMidrash on Friday afternoon alone to welcome the Sabbath. Once he came very early and his son, Shlomo was with him. In the Beit HaMidrash there was only one man sitting at the oven, dressed in simple Sabbath clothes like the poor people wore and recited psalms. When the man saw Rabbi Elazar coming in, he stood up, merrily greeted the Rabbi and returned to his seat. Said Rabbi Elazar to his son Shlomo: "You know what my father Rabbi Tzvi Elimelech said about this man? He said that this man is the pillar of a third of the world".

Once, Rabbi Elazar and his son Rabbi Shlomo accompanied by the holy Rabbi Shalom from Kaminka, travelled together to visit the famous Rabbi from Ryzyn. On their way back, their funds ran out. This was near the city of Stanislawow where they stopped at an inn to rest. While discussing among themselves about their situation, a blind wanderer came in and approached Rabbi Elazar who, at that time, served as Rabbi of Strzyzow, and told him about a woman relative who lived in Wysoka, a village near Strzyzow, if he would be so kind to take some money for her. The Rabbis agreed happily to deliver the money. In the meantime, they obtained some money on their own. When they reached Strzyzow and inquired about the woman, they found out that there never was a woman by that name in that village. They were sure that the money was sent to them from heaven.

[Page 13]

An interesting story happened before Rabbi Elazar's wedding. During the engagement, the father of the bride, Reb Joshua Heshel Holles, a very wealthy man, promised a dowry in the sum of four hundred golden guldens to be paid before the wedding ceremony. The father of the groom, Rabbi Tzvi Helimelech insisted on the full amount to be paid as promised, before the ceremony. The father of the bride became angry and made up his mind to break off the engagement. And so he did. On the way home the father noticed the sadness and the painful expression on his daughter's face. He returned to Rybotycze and paid the dowry and the wedding took place after all. But, it was G-d's will that the money should be lost.

When Rabbi Elazar lived with his father, Rabbi Helimelech, who by then was the Rabbi of Munkatch, his mother Tova Chava gave the money to a wealthy man for which she was to be earning interest. However, when the people in town found out that Rabbi Elazar had deposited a large sum with the wealthy man, they kept coming to ask for loans. Rabbi Elazar, being a goodhearted man, kept giving notes to the holder of his money until it was all gone.

In 1857, Rabbi Elazar was elected as Rabbi of Lancut and there he lived until the end of his days. He passed away in Vienna in 1865. By the intervention of Baron Rothchild and the pleas of his son, Rabbi Shlomo, with the approval of Rabbi Chaim from Sandz, his remains were brought to rest in Lancut.

Rabbi Israel Dov Gelernter, of Blessed memory, from Jasienice

After Rabbi Elazar left Strzyzow, Rabbi Israel Dov took his place. He was the author of the book <u>Ravid Zahav</u>. He absorbed Torah from many great scholars in Galicia, especially from Rabbi Naphtali from Ropczyce, with whom he studied for fifteen years. He venerated very much his Rabbi and always talked about his wisdom and skills. Here is an episode that Rabbi Israel Dov Gelernter told about his Rabbi. Rabbi Israel Dov had a very good friend, Reb Joseph, the son of the Rabbi from Plantch. They always sat together at the Rabbi's table. It was customary that Rabbi Naphtali gave small challahs to his admirers who were sitting around his table, and to these two friends, he always gave a large challah. Once, something happened to their friendship and when the Rabbi gave everyone the challah on Friday night, he gave to these two men two separate challahs. After the meal, when they went home, they began to do some thinking about what the Rabbi did. Suddenly they realized that the Rabbi noticed their broken friendship. They apologized to each other, drank "l'Chaim" and made up. The next day at the Sabbath noontime meal, the Rabbi gave them again a double challah.

[Page 14]

Rabbi Shlomo Shapiro of Strzyzow-Munktach

As it was told in the previous chapter, when Rabbi Elazar was elected Rabbi of Lancut, Rabbi Israel Dov Gelernter became Rabbi of Strzyzow. However, when he found out that Rabbi Elazar was not pleased with his replacement, he left Strzyzow in the middle of the night. Later, Rabbi Shlomo Shapiro, son of Rabbi Elazar, became Rabbi of Strzyzow.

Rabbi Shlomo was born in 1832 in Rybotycze, a small town in Galicia. He married Chaya from Ryvka, the granddaughter of Rabbi Moshe Leib from Sassov.

Rabbi Shlomo Shapiro had a good voice to sing and chant with, for which he was famous all over Galicia and Hungary. As a child, he was a prodigy. He authored the book 'Beit Shlomo', a commentary on the Five Books of Moses. Before he became Bar Mitzvah, he travelled to Rabbi Israel from Ryzin to ask for his blessing. When the Rabbi asked him what was his wish, he replied: "My wish is to achieve purity in serving G-d and the people". Rabbi Shlomo later said that whenever he was praying he felt Rabbi Israel's spirit within him. Rabbi Shlomo was the third generation to serve as Rabbi in Strzyzow. The time he served as Rabbi was marked by scandals and controversy. He handed in his resignation several times but he always came back after the community leaders pleaded with him and apologized for the trouble they caused.

Rabbi Shlomo Shapiro was an ardent admirer of Rabbi Chaim Halberstam from Sandz and stood by him during the controversy which broke out between him and Rabbi Israel of Ryzin. The controversy was about a different approach to Hassidism. The majority of Strzyzow sided with the Rabbi from Ryzin and this caused a lot of friction in the community. Then, another controversy was added on top of this.

In 1882, the Kehillah in Strzyzow wanted to hire a cantor, a retired Austrian officer, about whom rumours were circulating that he did not observe the Sabbath even when he was able to. Reb Shlomo fiercely opposed the hiring of the cantor. This opposition escalated dissention even further and reached a point where a Kehillah member insulted Rabbi Shlomo. Ultimately, Rabbi Shlomo accepted an invitation to serve as Rabbi of Munkatch, a much bigger and more respectable community in Hungary.

Being apprehensive that his admirers might try to persuade him to remain in Strzyzow, he left the town during the night and stayed at my grandfather's farm. This time, he also took his family with him, unlike the previous times. Rabbi Shlomo Shapiro left Strzyzow in 1882 after he served as its Rabbi for twenty four years. His two sons, Rabbi Tzvi Hersh and Rabbi Moshe Leib were also with him, including his little grandson, the child prodigy, Reb Chaim Elazare, who later became the famous Rabbi of Munkatch. After Rabbi Shlomo left Strzyzow, his followers and his opponents realized what a great loss Strzyzow suffered. They sent him a letter with an apology and asked him to return, but he refused. Later, the Kehillah leaders turned to his son, Rabbi Moshe Leib, and asked him to take his father's place. Not only did he refuse but he sent back a nasty letter to the Kehillah leaders. Finally, the town gave up on the Shapiros and turned to somebody from the Ropczyce Dynasty.

[Page 15]

Rabbi Chaim Elazar Shapiro - The Rabbi of Stryzow-Munkatch

[Page 16]

Rabbi Alter Zev Horowitz - The Rabbi of Strzyzow

[Page 17]

Reb Wolf Deutch, one of the most active and Efficient Kehila leaders in Strzyzow

[Page 18]

Heschel Diamand
The last presiding Kehila leader in Strzyzow

[Page 19]

The Tzadik Rabbi Alter Zev Horowitz

A letter of invitation was sent to Rabbi Alter Zev Horowitz, the great-grandson of the famous Rabbi Naphtali from Ropczyce. He accepted the invitation and peace returned to the community. However, it did not last long.

Suddenly, Rabbi Moshe Leib Shapiro returned to Strzyzow. At his arrival, he was asked by the community leaders for the reason of his return and what his future plans were: "I came back just to live here" he replied. Soon the people who still remembered the greatness of his father and also knew Rabbi Moshe Leib's qualifications, began to urge him to claim back his rabbinical post. And another dispute began brewing between his followers and the followers of Rabbi Alter Zev Horowitz who, meanwhile, had established himself in town and was respected by everyone. Ultimately, it was decided to bring the dispute before a rabbinical court.

Three well-known Rabbis were chosen as judges: The Rabbi from Tarnov, the Rabbi from Rawa-Ruska and the Rabbi from Bergsaz, Hungary. However, their decision was inconclusive – two were in favour of Rabbi Alter Zev and one against. And the dispute lasted for generations.

Rabbi Moshe Leib Shapiro was Rabbi in Sassov before his return to Strzyzow. Even though he never got back his rabbinical post, his devoted admirers supported him materially. When World War I began, Rabbi Moshe Leib moved to Vienna where he passed away during the war.

Rabbi Alter Zev Horowitz passed away in 1930 and his grandson Reb Kalonymus Horowitz inherited the rabbinical post, including the unresolved dispute. Hitler put an end to all the arguments.

Rabbi Nechemiah Shapiro, the son of Rabbi Moshe Leib, remained in Vienna after his father's death until the rise of anti-Semitism forced him to return home. He returned to Strzyzow in 1930.

The Assistant Rabbis in Strzyzow

Although there were Assistant Rabbis in Strzyzow as in other towns in Galicia in the early years, to us, are known, only a few highly revered Assistant Rabbis during the second half of the nineteenth century and the beginning of the twentieth century up until World War II.

Rabbi Joseph Mordechai Wiener served during Rabbi Shlomo Shapiro. He was a popular scholar, distinguished and a faultlessly righteous man. Reb Joseph Mordechai was admired by the Rabbi of Sandz, Rabbi Chaim Halberstam. He continued to serve after Rabbi Shlomo left and Rabbi Alter Zev Horowitz took over the rabbinical chair. His son, Reb David Wiener was one of the jewels of the town. We will tell more about him in another section in this book. A second son of Reb Joseph Mordechai was Reb Isachar Dov, a great scholar, pious and G-d fearing about who it was said that he was holy since conception. He lived in Brzozov. His daughter was the wife of Reb Leib Friedman, the Shochet in Strzyzow. The second daughter, Bracha, was married to Reb Yacov Schiff who was also a pious and humble man and we will also tell more about him in another section of this book. The offspring of Reb Joseph Mordechai perished in the Holocaust, except one son of Reb David Wiener who survived in France.

[Page 20]

Later, Rabbi Alter Ezra Seidman was elected as Assistant Rabbi. He served side-by-side with Rabbi Alter Zev. He was acute and clever. He chanted during the High Holidays. His children were Reb Moshe Meir, one of the smartest people in town; daughter Sarah who was the wife of Reb Elazar Weiss and Luba who lived in Limanov. One daughter moved to Rzeszov where she established a large family and Taubha resided in Pilzno.

After Reb Alter Esra passed away, the town remained without an Assistant Rabbi for a long time. It was hard to find a replacement. The more qualified Rabbis refused to settle in Strzyzow and the less qualified we refused by Strzyzow after having a tradition of such good and highly qualified Assistant Rabbis. Finally, Reb Yacov Shpalter from Illitch was named Assistant Rabbi. He was a learned man, well versed in Talmud and Halacha but more relaxed in structures which caused tension between him and Rabbi Nechemiah Shapiro. Reb Yacov Shpalter and his entire family were wiped out in the Holocaust except for one grandson, Ephraim, who lives with us in Israel.

Recently, the book Toldot Noah which was first published in Przemysl in 1929 and re-issued in Jerusalem in 1966, came into my hands. In this book it is written that the author, Rabbi Naphtali Nutman, of blessed memory, served as Assistant Rabbi in Strzyzow. His grandson, Reb Israel Nutman from Strzyzow tells in his foreword to the above book, that the father of Rabbi Naphtali Chaim Nutman was a wealthy man but his son left the house to study Torah with the author Maleh Haroyim. He studied day and night and became a great Torah scholar. He was well versed in religious rules and strictures, especially in authoritative laws. A second grandson of the author, Reb Abraham Pinchos Weisman, told at the end of the book, that before his grandfather's departure (this was on a Friday), Reb Naphtali Chaim asked what time it was and when he was told that it was already afternoon, he said: "Master of Universe, please let me live in this world until after the Sabbath". Soon he began to feel better. He prayed the afternoon prayer with great exaltation not appearing to be sick at all. On a Saturday night in May 1840, he passed away at the age of forty-two. During the Hassidic controversy between Sandz and Ryzin, he remained neutral.

[Page 21]

Strzyzow and its Inhabitants

Itzhok Berglass

Strzyzow my birthplace

In my survey about the shtetl Strzyzow and its Jews during the last fifty years, I tried to paint a clear and truthful picture about life in the shtetl without any prejudice or glorification. I did not exaggerate the negative because the dead cannot defend themselves. However, certain facts I could not hide in order to be truthful.

In my writing, I relied strictly on my memory during more than forty years of my life in my birthplace. My parents and grandparents were also born in Strzyzow. I heard the Ritter story from my father and also from Reb Shlomo Yahalomi. An important source of information for me was Reb Levi Itzhok Schiff who immigrated with his family to Eretz Israel before the Holocaust. The blood libel of 1919 and the pogrom that followed, I witnessed myself. As to what happened during the Holocaust, I mostly relied on what Reb Itzhok Leib Rosen told me. He lived through the tragedy and survived and also from another survivor, Reb Shimon Mandel who just happened to be in Strzyzow when the war broke out. He was visiting his grandfather and was forced to remain in Strzyzow. I was unable to obtain any information about the Jews who lived in the villages around Strzyzow, about their lives and sufferings during the Holocaust years. I wrote in general about common life in various cities throughout Galicia of which Strzyzow was no exception.

In describing life in Strzyzow and about the Zionist movement, I had to mention also the part I played in it as a leader for eighteen years. By mentioning my part in the movement I did not intent to boast about it but I could not avoid it either. If I left somebody out or told something incorrectly, my apology. It was not intentional.

Strzyzow

Strzyzow was located in central Galicia in the southern part of Poland, midway between Rzeszow and Yaslo. The Wisloka River flows through the city. To strangers, the name Strzyzow does not mean much. It was known only to Jews living in the nearby cities in the foothills of the Carpathian Mountains, bordering Slovakia and Hungary. It was also known to the admirers of Rabbi Shlomo Shapiro and his son who left Strzyzow and moved to Munkatch. To researchers who wrote history about Galician Jews and their Rabbis, Strzyzow was well-known because very famous Rabbis resided in Strzyzow. At one time or another, these Rabbis became religious leaders all over Galicia.

Cities like Strzyzow one could find in the thousands in that part of the Austro-Hungarian Empire. Strzyzow had interrelations with man cities of the Empire, commercial and by marriage, until the end of World War I when Galicia was included in the re-established independent Poland. To those who were born in Strzyzow and spent most or part of their life there, particularly their childhood, Strzyzow never ceased to exist and they can never forget it because of the memories, whether they were happy or sad ones.

[Page 22]

I will begin my story about the last period before the Holocaust, from about the end of the nineteenth century until the destruction, since I have very little information of life in Strzyzow before that period.

Spiritually, it was a very rich life, a life of work, study and spiritual fulfilment. Youths lived a life of dreams about a better future that never materialized. We like to commemorate those people who were always busy doing something for other people, helping the poor and the sick, lending money interest-free to the less fortunate; our parents, brothers and sisters, relatives and friends who perished by the Satan of Europe. Such a tragedy should never be forgotten.

In 1895, a big fire destroyed the attic and roof of the shul and the entire structure of the Beit HaMidrash. The attic of the shul was used as a storage place for the pinkasim. These pinkasim were an irreplaceable source of information for the community. The period of which I am writing is about its ups and downs in the social life of the community and also about its economic life, especially after World War I. The Zionist movement contributed to the progress and modernization of life in Strzyzow.

Nobody knows exactly when the Jews settled in Strzyzow. In Polish history books, Jews were mentioned since the beginning of the sixteenth century. In the first and oldest cemetery was an old gravestone dated 1703. There were other gravestones but the dates were worn off. The tree trunks in the cemetery showed signs of very old age. The shul was built four hundred years ago. According to the Polish history books, Strzyzow was founded in the tenth century and most inhabitants were shepherds who specialized in sheep-shearing. Strzyzow in Polish means shearing, that is how the name Strzyzow originated. In 1241, Strzyzow was still mentioned as a village but at the end of the thirteenth century, Strzyzow was proclaimed a city.

Since Strzyzow served as an overnight stop-over for travellers on their way from Poland to Hungary, they were permitted to sell wine and spirits and that contributed to the economy of the city.

In the sixteen century, the Arians (a Christian sect) settled in Strzyzow and its vicinity. These settlers contributed to the improvement of life in the city, culturally and economically. The entire area was ruled by feudalism for centuries. They owned the land, flour mills, brick yards and breweries, which by the way was the main industry of Strzyzow and its vicinity until World War II.

The ownership of these enterprises changed hands. It was passed on from generation to generation. Names like Jan and Mikolay Olva, Stanislaw Wielkopolski and Strazowski were still remembered by some old people. One of the last feudal lords was the head of the Wolkowitzki family whom the Jews used to call "the old man" to distinguish between him and his son who lived in our time.

The old Wolkowitzki took part in the Polish uprising against the Russian Tzar and escaped to Galicia where he married a daughter of one of these wealthy families in town and settled in Strzyzow.

[Page 23]

At the beginning of the century, feudalism was abolished by the Austrian government. Old man Wolkowitzki gained his Austrian citizenship with the title of "Count". He was awarded the monopoly to sell wine and spirits and other taxable merchandize and later leased these rights to Jews. These Jewish lessees had a bad reputation in the community as being mistrustful for their association with the local non-Jewish people. However, they mustered respect out of fear and therefore were always elected to the community leadership. I still remember three such personalities who served as heads of the community. I will write about them later on in this book.

Until the end of the nineteenth century, most of the buildings in Strzyzow were wooden structures except for a few houses that were built from stone. All the wooden houses were destroyed during the big fire which I mentioned before and were replaced with brick buildings. The big fire started in the house of Reb Yacov Sturm – the hat maker. The oven which he used to dry the hats caught fire and within minutes the whole town was engulfed in flames. The wooden houses with their straw roofs burnt down to the ground and from the stone houses, all that remained was the walls and chimneys. The City Hall, the roof of the shul, the entire structure of the Beit HaMidrash, everything went up in smoke. The local fire fighters with their primitive equipment were unable to help, especially when most of the equipment was used to save the local church. This fire was remembered for generations. It served as a milestone during conversations. People used to ask when did it happen – before or after the big fire? The townspeople of which the majority were Jewish, suffered heavy losses and it took many years to rebuild the town because fire insurance was unheard of. Therefore, Strzyzow looked like a new little town just built. The town was remarkably clean and the air was clean and fresh because of the green meadows and fields that surrounded the town – a perfect natural landscape with the Wisloka River flowing through the city. Strzyzow was located in the foothills of the Carpathian Mountains, 800 ft. above sea level, surrounded by pine woods. After the railroad was built at the end of the nineteenth century, Strzyzow was connected with the rest of the country and this was an important factor in the development of the city.

The Population in Strzyzow

The population in Strzyzow was about six thousand people, evenly divided between gentiles and Jews. When Poland became independent after World War I, in 1918, a redistricting took place in which a few nearby villages were annexed to the city in order to create a non-Jewish majority. Although the people were not happy with the annexation because of higher taxation, no protestation helped because the order came from the central government in Warsaw. Since then, the population remained one third Jewish to two thirds gentiles.

Most of the Poles were farmers, even those who lived within the city boundaries. Some were employed by the government and a few were professionals: teachers, doctors, judges, etc. The farmers sold their products to the Jews and in return, they bought from the Jews supplies and items.

[Page 24]

How did the Jews make a living?

Most of the Jews had little stores in the marketplace. On Market day, which used to be on Tuesday, the farmers brought to town all their agricultural products, poultry and cattle for sale. The local Jews and the Jews from nearby towns who came to Strzyzow on Market day displayed their wares on tables and sold it to the farmers. Of course, there were as many sellers as buyers and everyone struggled to eke out a living. Every city had a different Market day. During the rest of the week, the people from Strzyzow travelled to markets in nearby cities. There were many Jews who went to the villages and bought directly from the farmers. Since they did not have any means of transportation and had to walk to the villages, whatever they bought they had to carry home on their backs. There were no factories in town except a lumber mill owned by two Jewish partners. The workers in the mill were all gentiles. There were a few tradesmen, tailors, dressmakers, shoemakers, barbers and a few sheet-metal craftsmen in town. Jews in the free professions such as doctors, lawyers and dentists were very few. They all came from other places. After they obtained their diploma they settled in Strzyzow.

Livelihood was very hard. The people struggled all their lives to make a living. From time to time, a salesman from out of town or an agent would show up in Strzyzow to conduct some business. Preachers, scribes and watchmakers often visited Strzyzow and offered their services. They stayed a few days and left.

On Market days, an acrobat or a magician would come and perform in the market place and, until the end of the day, nobody would even know if they were Jewish or not until they appeared in the shul for the evening services.

There was a group of Jews about whom nobody knew exactly what their occupation was and how they made a living. These people were intelligent self-educated and used their knowledge to buy all kinds of freight bills or some kind of discount papers, and since the average Jewish merchant did not know how to read or write, they had to rely on these people as middlemen. Book sellers often came to display their wares in the Beit HaMidrash, sold religious and story books in Yiddish. Occasionally they would secretly sell to young people books from the New Hebrew literature. Out-of-town beggars frequented the town and went from door-to-door begging alms. Of course, nobody ever refused them a donation.

The Rabbis in Strzyzow

The most famous of the Rabbis who served in Strzyzow was Rabbi Tzvi Elimelech Shapiro from Dynow, the founder of the Dynow Rabbinic Dynasty. After he left Strzyzow, his son, Rabbi Elazar was elected to replace his father. After serving a few years in Strzyzow, Reb Elazar left and his son, Rabbi Shlomo became Rabbi of Strzyzow.

Reb Shlomo served the community in the second half of the nineteenth century. The older people in Strzyzow remembered him well. They called him the Munkatcher Rabbi because he left Strzyzow for the rabbinical post in Munkatch, the capital of the Carpathian-Ruthenia district.

[Page 25]

Stryzow and its inhabitants

Rabbi Shlomo was beloved and admired in Strzyzow. He left Stryzow because Munkatch was a much larger community and his father and grandfather served as Rabbis of Munkatch. The people in Stryzow were unhappy about his leaving. Therefore, he left Stryzow during the night. Rabbi Shlomo's mistake was that he did not secure a replacement. While living in Munkatch, he groomed his older son, Rabbi Tzvi Hersh to take his place and returned to Stryzow with the intent to put his younger son Reb Moshe Leib in the rabbinical chair. However, it was too late. The post was filled by a young Rabbi, Alter Zev Horowitz from the Ropczyce Dynasty. This young Rabbi had just married and was looking for a place to settle and it was then that the everlasting rabbinical dispute began.

The young rabbi was a bright young man and the community took a liking to him especially the members of the Kehillah Committee and other influential people in the community. Rabbi Alter Zev bought an old house which he demolished and replaced with a three-story building, the first such building in Strzyzow's history. He served the community close to fifty years. He was a very strict and demanding leader, a scholar and spent most of his time studying Torah. He was a pious man, strictly and meticulously observing all religious laws and chanted the prayers with special melodies of his own compositions. Before the High holidays, he trained a choir to assist him in chanting the High Holiday prayers and a few of his choir boys grew up to be good cantors.

Rabbi Alter Zev Horowitz had many opponents in the community and there were always scandals and arguments, especially when Rabbi Alter Zev ignored some of the Kehillah members who sided with the Shapiros in the rabbinical dispute, which never ceased up to the Holocaust. Rabbi Alter Zev always came out a winner having the support of the central and local non-Jewish authorities. In order to understand why, I would describe the relationship between the Poles, the Jews and Austrians.

At that time, in the last twenty years of the Austro-Hungarian Empire, when western and eastern Galicia were one entity and the city of Lwow was the capital, the Governor of the district was always a Polish aristocrat, a devoted sympathizer of the Hapsburg Dynasty. There was an existing animosity between the Poles and the central government in Vienna and, as always, the Jews were the victims. Austria granted to the Poles complete autonomy. The German language was used in the army and railroad administration only. The Poles also ruled the Ukrainian minority who lived mostly in rural areas. The majority of the rich landowners were Poles and very few Jews. The Poles, in order to strengthen their influence with the Austrian government, claimed that the Jews were considered Poles of Hebrew persuasion. The majority of the cities in Galicia were Jews. One of the paradoxes was that in the 1910 census, the majority of the Orthodox Jews and the assimilated Jews declared that their mother tongue was Polish, just to bootlick the Poles. Many of these Orthodox Jews did not even know how to speak Polish. In contrast, the Zionist intelligentsia who frequently used Polish, declared Yiddish to be their mother tongue.

The Hassidic movement made an alliance with the assimilated Jews to help Polish candidates win their seats in the Austrian Parliament just to hurt the Zionist candidates. Many Rabbis, leaders of the Hassidic movement, especially the Rabbi from Belz and the Rabbi from Munkatch, and many smaller Rabbis urged their followers not to vote for the Zionists.

[Page 26]

This disunity in the Jewish camp caused the Poles to consider the Jews as pawns in their political machinations. Therefore, all these Rabbis from Strzyzow and other places, by supporting the Polish rulers, have secured their rabbinical posts.

Whenever Rabbi Alter Zev felt threatened in Strzyzow, he always had the support of the Polish authorities. His position with the authorities improved even more after his son Reb Chaim Yehuda grew up and became an active politician because he was not qualified to be a Rabbi. Reb Chaim Yehuda Horowitz was famous all over Galicia and was known in the government for his influence among the Jews.

Rabbi Alter Zev was an anti-Zionist in general but he never fought the local Zionists claiming that the Zionists in Strzyzow just happen to be good religious people. There was plenty of antagonism between his son the politician and the Zionist movement in Poland on the political area.

The fighting between Rabbi Alter Zev and Rabbi Moshe Leib Shapiro slackened during World War I when both Rabbis lived in Vienna as refugees during the Russian occupation of Strzyzow. In Vienna, these two Rabbis met each other often like old friends. It seemed that they had declared a cease-fire. During the war, Rabbi Moshe Leib passed away and his son, Rabbi Nechemiah Shapiro remained in Vienna for a few more years after the war.

When Rabbi Alter Zev went on in years, he and his family began to worry about securing the rabbinical seat for his grandson, Kalonymus since his son; Reb Chaim Yehuda had no intention and was not qualified to take his place. Rabbi Alter Zev decided to hand over his rabbinical post to his grandson while he was still alive. Rabbi Alter Zev passed away the first day of Passover 1930. He was the first Rabbi in the Jewish history of Strzyzow to die and be buried in Strzyzow. Around his gravesite, a mausoleum was erected. In 1946, when the survivors of the Jewish community visited Strzyzow, they only found a pile of rubbles at the site of the mausoleum. Rabbi Kalonymus Horowitz was a very pious, G-d fearing man, humble and well-liked by the community just like his grandfather. In the last few years before the Holocaust, he was active in the community, aiding the German-Jewish refugees and cooperating with the Zionists. When World War II began, he escaped to the eastern part of Galicia which was occupied by the Soviet army. When the Soviets arrested all refugees and exiled them to Siberia, for some unknown reason, he was spared and was given a Russian passport. He lived in Rohatyn and from there he sent food packages to Siberia where the people of Strzyzow were exiled. After the Germans occupied Rohatyn, he was killed with the rest of the Jews. His father, Reb Chaim Yehuda Horowitz lived in the ghetto of Rzeszow and died of starvation together with his family while hiding from the Nazis in an underground bunker.

[Page 27]

The Rabbi from Sassov

Rabbi Moshe Leib Shapiro was called the Rabbi from Sassov. He was the son of Rabbi Shlomo who left Strzyzow and went to Munkatch. When he was a young man, he served as Rabbi in Biecz and later became Rabbi in Sassov. Therefore, they were both called the Rabbi of Sassov. As it was mentioned before, he did not succeed to regain the rabbinical chair.

Nevertheless, he remained in Strzyzow and was supported by his ardent followers who never recognized Rabbi Alter Zev as a legitimate Rabbi. Before every holiday, people used to send him donations. From time to time, the Kehillah also gave him cash allowances. He often left Strzyzow and travelled throughout Czechoslovakia and Hungary where his father was well known, to ask for financial support.

Rabbi Moshe Leib was a very capable man and after the big fire in Strzyzow, he built himself a beautiful house with a chapel which he used as a study and to pray. He later converted the chapel into a big prayer house which was called "The Kloiz". The kloyz contributed to his income and also added to his influence in the community.

Rabbi Moshe Leib had a very pleasant voice and chanted the prayers on every holiday. He was an excellent Torah reader, outspoken and refused to compromise when it concerned religious laws or traditions. He concerned himself particularly with the religious upbringing of the younger generation. If he did not like how certain parents brought up their children, he would refuse to let them come to the pulpit to lead the prayers. He himself kept an eye on the youngsters and as soon as he noticed some reading a newspaper, he would grab the paper and tear it into shreds. (In those days, reading a newspaper was a cardinal sin in Hassidic circles).

Rabbi Moshe Leib passed away during World War I in Vienna and his son, Rabbi Nechemiah remained there until 1930. Rabbi Nechemiah was an official mohel and performed most of the circumcisions in the hospitals. When he returned to Strzyzow, he also was supported by his father's admirers.

Rabbi Nechemiah was very handsome with a well-groomed beard, very educated in the holy books and knowledgeable in secular subjects as well. But, he opposed Zionism like all other rabbis. He visited the United States twice, and when he met emigrants from Strzyzow, he urged them to be faithful to their upbringing especially in observing the Sabbath and keeping kosher. Rabbi Nechemiah had a very high moral standard. While in the United States, he refused to accept a thousand dollar donation from a "rabbi" who, it was rumoured, that he earned the money unethically.

After Rabbi Nechemiah returned from Vienna, the dispute over the rabbinical seat flared up again, in a stronger form than before, especially after Rabbi Alter Zev passed away. It should be added to the credit of the Shapiros that during all the years of dispute, they avoided involving the non-Jewish authorities.

When the Nazi came, Rabbi Nechemiah did not leave Strzyzow. At the beginning he went into hiding but later, during the occupation, he moved back to his house.

[Page 28]

One of the Nazi officers who was an Austrian took a liking to him for his knowledge of the German language and the Rabbi another son of Rabbi Nechemiah, who lived in Dukla, Reb Yeshayahu Napthali Hertz with his family and a daughter Fruma Ryvka with her husband and children also perished. May their memory be blessed.

(The translator of this book, before escaping the Nazi, went to see Rabbi Nechemiah to ask for his advice and for his blessing. Despair was the expression on his face and he said with a sigh: "In a time when the whole world is in turmoil and nothing makes sense anymore, what possible advice can I give you? May G-d watch over you).

The rest of the clerical functionaries in Strzyzow, like the sextons, the ritual slaughterers, the assistant rabbis, had little impact on the community. Their function was to obey the rabbis and the community leaders.

Besides the two official assistant rabbis, Reb Joseph Mordechai and Reb Alter Ezra Seidman who served the town, one before World War I and the other immediately after the war, there was one outstanding personality who lived in Strzyzow and I would like to tell something about him. He was a descendant of the Shapiro Rabbinical Dynasty but his father was a simple merchant. His name was Reb Eisik Holles.

Reb Eisik Holles' occupation was to study day and night, literally, and to serve G-d. He had no official function in the community but people, instead of going to the rabbi with their problems, preferred to ask Reb Eisik. When the holiday came around, they never forgot to send him a donation.

The last rabbinical assistant was Reb Yacov Shpalter. The last two ritual slaughterers were: Reb Chaim Friedman, the grandson of the assistant rabbi Joseph Mordechai and Reb Mendel Rosen. They were both natives of Strzyzow. Reb Mendel Rosen had a good voice and served sometimes as an unofficial cantor. They all perished in the Holocaust.

The community leadership. "The Kehillah"

The function of the Kehillah members was to supervise Strzyzow's few public institutions: The prayer houses, the bath house including the mikva and the cemeteries. They also provided flour for matzoth and emergency charity needs. The Kehillah paid the salaries of the rabbi and the ritual slaughterers. The funds came from three sources: The fee for slaughtering poultry and cattle, burial fee (only from those who could pay) and a special annual tax was collected from all the community members, which was assessed by the Kehillah with the approval of the authorities. The taxes were very progressive, not too burdensome and based on income. The upkeep of the prayer houses and the provision of firewood were funded by the Kehillah but small daily expenses were donated by the worshippers. The income from the sale of kosher flour for Passover was distributed among the poor. To purchase land for cemeteries and their upkeep, an inheritance tax was collected, similar to the tax which is collected nowadays. This tax was also very progressive and poor people did not pay. The amount of the inheritance tax depended on the wealth of the deceased and his generosity when he donated to charity.

[Page 29]

The Kehillah members were not paid for their services. On the contrary, it was an honour to be elected to the Kehillah. In the second half of the nineteenth century and at the beginning of the twentieth century, the head of the Kehillah was always nominated by the gentile landowners of the surrounding land, villages and the town. Such a nominated head of the Kehillah was Reb Zalman Mohrer who was a very simple man. He was followed by Reb Yacov Kanner, a member of a very rich family who lived in Strzyzow for many generations. Reb Yacov Kanner was one of the last community leaders nominated by the non-Jewish authorities.

After the abolishment of feudalism at the beginning of the twentieth century, the system changed and the Kehillah leaders were elected by the Jewish community. Reb Tzvi Brav who was a newcomer to Strzyzow was the first head of the community elected by Jews. Names of other Kehillah leaders are: My father, Reb Baruch Berglass, Reb Wolf Deutch, Reb Moshe Diamand, Reb Alter Nechemiah and Reb David Dembitzer, just to name a few. These community leaders had their advisers who ran the show behind the scenes.

One time, the rabbinical dispute and the arguments over who should serve as rabbi went so far that the Kehillah leader that sided with the Shapiros fired outright Rabbi Alter Zev. But, as mentioned before, because the authorities were on his side, they opposed his firing and there was nothing the Kehillah could do about it.

Before World War I, Strzyzow had two outstanding community leaders: Reb Tzvi Brav and Abraham Keh. Later, the leadership went to Reb Wolf Deutch. They all passed away during the war. At the time of the transition from the Austrian rule to the Polish rule in 1918, the head of the Kehillah was Reb Abraham Tenzer. It was very hard times for the Jews. Pogroms occurred almost daily all over Galicia and in the rest of Poland. After Reb Abraham Tenzer, the leadership passed on to Reb Yacov Greenblatt, followed by Michael Schitz. They also had plenty of trouble because this was the time when the rabbinical dispute was at its peak. Reb Yacov Greenblatt sided with Rabbi Nechemiah Shapiro and Reb Michael Schitz was rabbi Alter Zev's man.

The last Kehillah leader that was elected in a free election was Reb Heschel Diamand. He was young, energetic, and sympathetic to the Zionist cause and was neutral in the rabbinical dispute. Before the Nazi occupation, he escaped to eastern Poland and spent the Holocaust years in a Soviet labour camp. After the war, Heschel Diamand immigrated to the United States.

During the Nazi occupation, the Nazi nominated as head of the Jewish community the so-called "Juden Rat", Abraham Brav and his assistants were Yacov Rosen and Aaron Deutch. The Nazi selected these three men because they were the sons of former Kehillah leaders. These three men did all they could to help the Jews in Strzyzow. They never betrayed anybody in order to improve their own lot and, of course, they perished with the rest of the people from Strzyzow.

[Page 30]

The spiritual and social life of the Jews in Strzyzow

Life in Strzyzow was based on an orthodox-Hassidic foundation but not too extreme. The relationship between the Hassidim and the progressive segment of the population was very good. The rabbinical dispute which lasted for generations never affected the relationship between the people. Besides siding with the rabbi or the other, in other aspects of day-to-day life, there was always peaceful cooperation.

The controversy between the admirers of the rabbi from Ryzin (later Sadigora) and the rabbi from Sandz occasionally reached violent outbursts and once went too far when the Hassidim of Sadigora caused the arrest of Rabbi Shlomo Shapiro by the local non-Jewish authorities.

The Hassidim of the rabbi from Sadigora were a well-organized group. They used to organize Saturday night get-togethers and helped each other in time of need. Their political representative was Reb Levi Itzhok Schiff and the spiritual leaders were Reb Baruch Diller and his son-in-law Reb Hershel Gelander.

Reb Hershel Gelander was a fine religious man, a Torah scholar with a good voice who for years chanted the prayers on the High Holidays. In later years, the animosity between the Hassidim subsided and the two opposing groups became more tolerant of each other.

Until the end of the nineteenth century, one could hardly see anyone in town not wearing the typical black coat on weekdays and a silk coat with a fur hat, called a "shtreimel" on Saturday. Women shaved their heads after marriage and wore wigs. Women did not use cosmetics. Jewellery, which was handed down from generation to generation, was worn. All the people in town observed all the commandments and stringent religious rules both at home and outside. Trimming beards, reading books and newspapers was forbidden.

At the beginning of the twentieth century, many changes occurred in Strzyzow. People began to wear modern clothes, wearing stylish haircuts, trimmed their beards and many even shaved them off altogether. People began to subscribe to newspapers and read secular books. But still and until the Holocaust, one could not find anyone in Strzyzow who would not observe the Sabbath or eat non-kosher food. Traditions were strictly observed and everybody spoke Yiddish.

The day usually started by going to the Beit HaMidrash for the morning services. Many people used to get up earlier to study the Talmud and other holy books. During the day, everybody went about their business or occupation. At the end of the day, the synagogue filled up with worshippers again who came to the evening services. After the services, people remained in the synagogue, some to study and some just to chat. There were organized study groups. The long winter nights in particular were used for studying. During summertime, people loved to spend more time outdoors enjoying the freshness of the summer air.

Women generally stayed indoors doing household chores and raising children. They rarely visited their women neighbours for a chat. Many women helped their husbands in the stores especially on market days. In later years, younger couples allowed themselves to take a stroll on a Sabbath afternoon, sometimes even a few couples together. Boys and young men spent their time studying Torah and praying. On summer afternoons the young people also allowed themselves to go outdoors for a breath of fresh air or even to take a swim in the Wisloka River. But of course, girls were excluded from such activities.

[Page 31]

In the late twenties and early thirties, the Zionists organized the youth and taught them how to enjoy life by singing songs together, playing an instrument or organizing a play. They read books in Yiddish or Polish. In front of the shul was a big lawn with lust green grass where the children felt free to run around and play games. However, many times the sexton who wanted to save the grass for his goats would close the gates for the children. Sports were unknown in Strzyzow except summertime swimming in the river and wintertime riding down the hill on a sled.

Sabbath and holidays in Strzyzow

The preparations for the Sabbath began on Thursday when the women did their shopping. Friday at noon, the bath house keeper appeared in the centre of the market place and blew his horn announcing that the bath house was ready to receive visitors. Taking a bath for the Sabbath was a joyous occasion. Even the gentiles frequented the bath house. Later in the day, women carried pots of cholent to the bakeries to put them in the oven to keep warm until the next day for the midday Sabbath meal.

At candle lighting time, late customers would rush into the store for last minute shopping and the sexton, Reb Eisik, circled around the market place and called to close the stores, announced that the Sabbath had arrived and time had come to go to the shul to welcome the Sabbath queen. After Reb Eisik passed away, this tradition was discontinued.

Dressed in their best for the Sabbath, the men went to G-d's house for the Friday evening services. On Sabbath day, the services lasted until noon. After a scrumptious meal, the older people took their afternoon naps and the young people went for a stroll in the fields or nearby woods. Taking a nap on a Sabbath afternoon was one of the luxuries reserved for the Sabbath only. On weekdays, nobody had time for such a luxury. Later, after the nap, everyone went back to the shul for the evening services and if it was too early for the end of the Sabbath, they would stroll up and down the market place which was also the main street in town.

When the holidays were approaching, the town was bustling with preparations and excitement especially the Passover holiday. Actually, soon after one Passover was over, people began to get ready for the next Passover. Sumer time, when fruit season started, the women busied themselves preparing all kinds of preserves for Passover. Then, when the grain harvest came along, the Jewish farmers from the villages around Strzyzow took extra care while harvesting wheat in order to keep it dry and kosher for matzo flour.

At the beginning of the winter and around Hanukkah time, the geese were at their best. Goose fat and chicken fat were staple food in every Jewish home. This was the only fat used on Passover and, therefore, it had to be prepared during the winter. On Passover, nobody, even the closes friends, ever share food or for that matter, any dishes with anybody else out of fear that they were not careful enough in observing the laws concerning kashrut and chometz.

[Page 32]

At the beginning of this century, the wheat for matzo flour was stone ground. Later, the rabbis permitted under their supervision the preparation of flour in water mills. Flour for matzo was sold exclusively by the Kehillah and the profits went to the poor.

A month before Passover, the bakers began to prepare their bakeries and made them kosher for baking matzo. Every household prepared a barrel of borsch for Passover. Normally the fermentation of the beets for the borsch took about a month. And of course, everybody made his own wine from raisins for the required four cups on the Seder nights. Those who could afford it, allowed themselves to order from the big city a bottle of Carmel wine from Eretz Israel.

Everybody participated in baking their own matzo. The fresh baked matzo were carefully put into a white sheet and carried home on a pole on the shoulders of two people. At home, the matzo was hung up from the ceiling on a special hook put there for that purpose. On the eve before Passover, the Passover dishes were brought down from the attic where they were stored during the year. The everyday dishes were taken away and hidden out of sight. All these preparations were made with inner spiritual happiness in anticipation of the spring and freedom festival.

In the synagogues, the big chandeliers were glistening from the polish they just received. All the children wore new clothes. This was their happiest moments of the year. Later into the night, the sound of Passover songs were heard from all the homes in town. Between the first two days and the last two days of Passover, which is called "Chol-Ha-Moed", guests from out of town came to visit their relatives and prearranged meetings by matchmakers of marriage candidates took place. Only on the last day of Passover was the strict observance of Passover kashrut relaxed and people visited each other to taste the delicacies which each housewife had prepared and was anxious to show off.

A distinctive feature of Passover was the escorting by Jewish family members of the gentile water carriers to and from the city water pumps. The Jews feared that the water carriers might tamper with the water and would not be kosher for Passover. (Until the destruction, Strzyzow did not have running water or electricity).

Between Passover and Shavuot, a light mourning period was observed. No weddings, haircuts or swimming in the river was permitted. (The water in the river was cold anyway). On Lag-B'Omer, the morning stopped for a day and it was a children's holiday. The melamdim and their helpers took the children out into the fields – every child was armed with a bow and arrow and they played soldiers. The arrows sometimes caused light injuries.

On the Shavuot holiday, the homes were decorated with greenery which symbolized spring. This was the peak season for dairy products and the menu was: cheese cakes, cheese kreplach, sour crème and sour milk – everything homemade.

On Tisha B'Av, the day when the Holy Temples were destroyed by the Romans and the Greeks, the tables and benches in the synagogues were turned upside down as a sign of mourning. No kerosene lamps were used, only candles, everybody fasted that day and leather shoes were forbidden. After Tisha B'Av, when the days became shorter and the evenings longer, people remained in the synagogues after the service to study the holy books. These studies continued all winter until Passover.

[Page 33]

As the High Holidays were approaching, the sound of the shofar was heard daily from the interiors of the synagogues as it is customary to blow the shofar daily. Some people blew the shofar during the day for training purposes for the upcoming High Holidays. Many people were traveling to other cities to visit their parents' or relatives' graves as it is customary before the High Holidays. Many strangers were also seen in Strzyzow who came to visit the graves of their relatives.

Traditional "Slichot" were conducted in the early morning hours of the last Sunday before Rosh Hashanah. The Hassidim of Sadigora conducted their services at midnight. In the pre-dawn hours, the sexton went from door to door, knocked with a wooden mallet and called: "Children of Israel, arise and come to worship the Almighty". The services on Rosh Hashanah and Yom Kippur were solemn. On the second day of Rosh Hashanah, the entire community turned out at the river to say "Tashlich". There was a tradition that after finishing the prayer, people emptied their pockets into the river symbolizing the throwing of their sins away. The children used to fill their pockets with challah crumbs and empty these into the river and the fish happily devoured these crumbs. It seemed that the fish were waiting for such a treat which only came once a year.

Early in the morning on Erev Yom Kippur, the Shohet went from house to house to slaughter the "Kaparot". This is an old tradition that every Jew is required to get a chicken for each female and a rooster for each male in the family – hold it over the head and recite a prayer. After this ceremony, the chickens were either given away to the poor or slaughtered and a donation given instead. Yom Kippur started early afternoon with afternoon prayers in the synagogues. At the completion of the services, everybody passed a table with collection plates for different charities and donated generously. There was another tradition on Erev Yom Kippur after the afternoon services and a very peculiar one as well! A small rug was spread out on the floor and all adult men lay down while the sexton with a whip in his hand flogged them symbolically as atonement for their sins. And of course, the sexton was given gratuity for his service.

At home, a lavish meal with kreplach stuffed with meat was waiting for the whole family. After the meal was finished, the head of the family, with teary eyes, bestowed a blessing upon the children's heads and wished everyone a Happy New Year. Of course the women also joined in the shedding of tears while wishing each other a Happy New Year, asking each other for forgiveness for any misbehaviour during the year. Then, the entire family went to the synagogue. On the way to the synagogue they stopped at the neighbours' homes and extended best wishes and asking their forgiveness for any transgressions that they may have committed during the past year. The Jewish farmers from the vicinity around Strzyzow used to leave their homes and their households in the hands of their non-Jewish friends, and came to town for the High Holidays. In later years, they established their own places of worship where they conducted the services lead by people they had hired from the city.

[Page 34]

Soon after Yom Kippur, the peasants from the villages knew already that it was time to bring to town pine branches and sell them to the Jews for the Sukkoth holidays. The branches were used to cover the Sukkoth. In every backyard, a Sukkah was erected for the holiday. The decorations for the sukkah were the children's responsibility, especially the girls. A lot of effort was invested by the youngsters to show their artistic talents by decorating the Sukkah and preparing flags for Simchat Torah. There were no ready-made flags in those days, therefore, all the children had homemade flags. Men spent time in the Sukkah not just to eat meals but also to sing songs and entertain their neighbours. In fact, in those days, the Sukkoth holiday was exclusively a man's holiday. The women were busy preparing and delivering food to the Sukkah and the men enjoyed themselves. Since Sukkoth is always in the fall, and in Eastern Europe fall is sometimes very cold, often the rain disturbed the sitting in the Sukkah and forced the people to escape into the house. Then, the town joker used to say that when it rains, he enjoyed best the holiday by eating in the house. When the weather was cold, everybody had to bundle up to keep warm but nevertheless, it was fun.

On Simchat Torah night, the rabbi was escorted to the synagogue with dance and songs. After an afternoon of drinking and celebrating, the spirits were high. The shul, the Beit HaMidrash and the kloyz were lighted brightly, filled with people with shining faces and children were parading with their multi-coloured flags topped with apples. Stuck in the apple was a burning candle, and not one flag went up in flames, to the children's sorrow. A remarkable thing in all the holidays was that on the second night of any holiday, during the intermission between Mincha and Maariv services, the prayer houses were packed to capacity with people studying the holy books and it was hard to find a seat or the desired book. People were rested and did not have to be up early the next morning so they studied in a most relaxed way.

Hanukkah was not much of a holiday. However, it was a happy time for the children. When the sexton lit the Hanukkah candles in the Beit HaMidrash or kloyz and while he recited the blessing, the children were allowed to make all kinds of disturbances – screaming and throwing snowballs at the poor sexton. This was a tradition of unknown origin. During Hanukah, people used to gather at the Rabbi's house to watch him light the Hanukkah candles and sing Hanukkah songs together. During the ceremony the rabbi wore his Sabbath shtreimel and his silk coat. As the people started to leave, everyone handed the rabbi Hanukkah gelt. No presents were exchanged in those days. The Zionists had fund raising parties for the Jewish National Fund. The next holiday was Tuv B'Shvat which was celebrated only by eating fruit from the Holy Land – Eretz Israel.

When the Purim holidays was approaching, signs were put up in the prayer houses with pictures of two fish, a glass of wine and clasping hands. In Jewish tradition, the symbol of the month Adar is fish because fish is considered good luck. Therefore, the month of Adar in which the Purim holiday is celebrated, is considered to be a lucky month for Jews.

The clasping hands wishing l'chaim symbolized merrymaking.

On Purim, the streets were crowded with masked people, who went from house to house, performing a Purim spiel, or singing songs, for which they received a donation. Also messengers were hurrying with plates covered with embroidered handkerchiefs and filled with delicacies as it is customary on Purim to send Mishloach Manot.

Purim was a holiday of giving charity. The head of the family sat at the head of the table loaded with cakes, cookies, hammantashen, candies, fruit, wine and liquor. When people soliciting donations, or poor people who were asking alms came into the house, they were invited to sit down, have a drink and taste the delicacies. Then everybody received a generous donation. On every holiday, including Hanukkah and Purim, the clerical functionaries used to get gifts from the well-to-do, and also from the average people. An exception were the ritual slaughterers. They had a regular salary, and wintertime, one leg from each goose or chicken belonged to them. They also had free meat from the butchers.

Family life in Strzyzow

Family life in Strzyzow was generally good, even though romance as we know it nowadays did not exist. Matchmaking was made by professional matchmakers or by friends. Therefore, whenever a matchmaker proposed a match for a son or a daughter, the concerned parents begun to gather information about the family background of the marriage candidate, his or her parents, and their financial situation. The information gathering was done with the help of friends and relatives who lived in the city of the proposed match. If what the matchmaker told about the candidate turned out to be true, a meeting was arranged, and both parties worked out an agreement about the dowry, wedding, and any other problems concerning the welfare of the young couple. And at last, love came for the young couple.

If the parents of the bride did not fulfill all the promises, then a dispute broke out before the wedding. However, the parents always found a way to smooth things out. These arguments never affected the newlyweds.

In later years when the Zionist organization sprang up all over Galicia, and young people of both sexes began to meet more freely, as a result of such fraternization, some marriage came about without matchmakers.

Jewish life was very conservative. Even the people who were rich and better off than others, led a thrifty life, always saving money for dowries, for their daughters, and in some cases, also for their sons. Family celebrations such as wedding or the birth of a child were celebrated only within the family or very close friends. When a baby was born, especially when the baby was a boy, men were invited Friday night to a welcome male party, during which beer and garbanzo beans were served. This was a tradition for generations. Lavish parties were unknown. However, wedding celebrations were celebrated on a larger scale. Even the not so well-to-do people used to borrow money and make a rich looking wedding. The parents of the bride had to provide the dowry and to furnish the place where the young couple intended to live. Therefore, poor people with daughters found themselves in a helpless situation. The only solution for the girl from a poor home was to learn a trade and to earn her own dowry, or leave town and emigrate. A seamstress was the most popular trade.

[Page 36]

Emigration

The emigration from Strzyzow was mainly to two countries – Germany and the United States. After World War I, many young people moved to Upper Silesia, the industrial centre of Poland. Most of the emigrants were young people who could not find employment in Strzyzow and their parents' little stores could not absorb them. Therefore, they left Strzyzow in search of a better life elsewhere for themselves and to be able to support their parents at home. In some cases, the head of the family was forced to emigrate and later to bring his family over. All those who left Strzyzow never forgot their relatives and friends. They never lost contact with the shtetl. In all the strange places of emigration, the people from Strzyzow always met and were in close contact.

After World War I, emigration rose to even higher proportions. Many families who left Strzyzow during the war never returned. They remained in Western Europe. Many young men were forced to emigrate to escape the military service in the Polish army which was known for its hatred of the Jews. Rabbi Alter Zev Horowitz and Rabbi Nechemiah Shapiro used to receive financial support from these émigrés, particularly from people who had immigrated to the United States. In the later years, a Strzyzow Society was founded in the United States with the purpose of helping the poor in Strzyzow.

The Synagogues in Strzyzow

Strzyzow had three synagogues. A shul, the Beit Hamidrash and the kloyz which Rabbi Moshe Leib Shapiro built. Rabbi Alter Zev Horowitz had a small sanctuary in his house. In the thirties, the religious Zionists established their own place of worship.

The shul, with its enormously thick walls, was four hundred years old. It was located in the centre of the town with a big lawn in front of the building. Surprisingly, the Catholic Church was on a side-street. This was a paradox because in most Galician cities, the Catholic Church was always located in a central place.

The entrance to the shul was though a narrow low gate and to the left of the entrance was a small window with a heavy iron grill. At the end of the nineteenth century, this window was converted to a second entrance. The entrance hall had a giant column in the centre, supporting the vaulted ceiling. On the right side of the entrance to the sanctuary, there was a niche in the wall with a big copper collection box. Upon entering the sanctuary, worshipper dropped coins for charity. When entering the sanctuary, a person had to bend down because it was very low and you had to descend a few steps to reach the floor. The ceiling in the sanctuary was also vaulted. The windows were located high, just below the ceiling as a protection against rock throwing by the mob in time of pogroms. In the centre was the bimah surrounded by four heavy columns supporting the ceiling. The ark was simple as were the benches, because all the wooden parts of the shul including the ark, an artistic woodcraft, burnt down in the big fire of 1895.

[Page 37]

Paintings which adorned the ceiling were also ruined in the fire. Only one big fish, the Leviathan, which was painted on the ceiling right in the centre above the bimha, survived. A few chapters from Psalms were carved in the wall that also remained intact. These carvings and the paintings on the ceiling were painted hundreds of years ago. During the fire, a few courageous young men jumped into the shul and saved the Torah scrolls. The huge chandelier made of brass was carried out by a young and very strong man and whose name was Elimelech Korn. He worked in the bakery of Reb Aaron Kanner.

After the fire, the walls were whitewashed and remained that way until 1930 when they were repainted by a painter from Przemysl by the name of Samuel Garfunkel and his son Aaron. Aaron was married to the daughter of the shul treasurer, Reb Leib Sternberg. Father and son teamed up and painted the shul in beautiful colours and Bible pictures. In one corner of the shul, an eternal light burned over which the sexton watched and refuelled with oil whenever it was necessary. There were two small rooms adjacent to the big sanctuary which was used for meetings of the community leaders, and sometimes, a room was rented out for a cheder.

To the left of the main entrance, on the west side of the building, were stairs leading to the attic. The attic was filled with torn prayer and study books and maybe writings and Kehillah ledgers that were hundreds of years old but that no one had ever checked them for historical purposes.

There was a little window in the attic which was used for displaying the national flag on national holidays because it was facing the market place. Before World War I, the Austro-Hungarian flag was flying and later, the Polish flag.

After the big fire, a new roof was constructed to replace the one that had burned down. This time, the roof was covered with metal sheets. All the repairs were made at the time that Reb Tzvi Brav was head of the Kehillah.

On weekdays, the shul was closed in the evenings. As the shul was near the cemetery, people were afraid to pass by at night especially the children. There was a superstitious belief that the deceased from the cemetery would gather in the shul every night to worship and to read the Torah, and if a by-passer was called by his name to the Torah, he would shortly die. Daily and Sabbath services were only conducted in the summer.

Wintertime, the only services held were on the Sabbath because it was very cold in the shul as it was not permitted to have an oven in the shul. The people who attended services in shul were mostly simple people, peddlers, tradesmen – people who hardly knew how to pray or chant Psalms. Hassidim and Torah educated people worshipped in the Beit Hamidrash or at the kloyz.

In the last twenty or thirty years, when the Zionist idea started to make in-roads in Galicia, the shul served as a place where Zionists congregated to worship. On High Holidays, Rabbi Shlomo Shapiro and later, Rabbi Alter Zev Horowitz used to conduct the services.

[Page 38]

Under the Austro-Hungarian rule, whenever there was a national holiday or the Emperor's birthday, special services were conducted in shul under the auspices of the Rabbi and the presence of government officials. In the last twenty five years, the shul was also used for political meetings organized by the local Zionist activists.

All wedding ceremonies in town were performed in front of the shul. The young couple were led from their houses escorted by all the guests while the klezmorim were playing joyous tunes to and from the chuppa.

For many years, the cantor in shul and also the Torah reader was Reb Leib Sternberg who conducted these services free of charge. He was very well liked by all the worshippers. The only reward he received for his services was that on Simchat Torah, the entire congregation came to his house to escort him with song and dance all the way to the shul. The treasurers of the shul were always fine people doing their best to manage the shul's needs. It would not be fare not to mention a few of them. Abraham Minc was treasurer at the end of the previous century. In this century, the treasurers were: Reb Feivel Diamand, Reb Moshe Henig and Reb Yehuda Gruber. During Yehuda Gruber's treasurer ship, all the above-mentioned remodelling and re-paintings took place.

The Beit HaMidrash was built during Rabbi Shlomo Shapiro's service as Rabbi at the end of the nineteenth century. The Beit HaMidrash was located in an alley which was called the Beit HaMidrash Alley.

The building was a simple structure from the outside and simple furniture inside. The ark where the Torah scrolls were kept was a beautiful piece of artwork made of oak and adorned with beautiful wood carvings. Along the western wall were huge bookshelves filled with holy books, Bibles and Talmud tractates. This library belonged to the congregation and nobody was allowed to remove any books. In the centre of the sanctuary, a big kerosene lamp hung from the ceiling surrounded by half a dozen chandeliers. Looking out through the windows on the north side, the oldest cemetery in town could be seen. The Rabbis in Strzyzow worshipped in the Beit HaMidrash all year round except on the High Holidays when they led the prayers in shul.

After Rabbi Shlomo Shapiro built his own prayer house which was called kloyz, he did not worship in the Beit HaMidrash any longer. The Beit HaMidrash had no steady cantor. On Saturdays and holidays, the prayers were led by lay-men but there was a steady Torah reader. On the High Holidays, Reb Hershel Gelander led and chanted the prayers all his life. On weekdays, services began early in the morning and continued until noon. In the evening, the Beit HaMidrash was filled with worshippers especially in the winter months when the shul was closed on weekdays. Torah studying was a tradition that never ceased. People, old and young, were studying Torah and other holy books.

Although the shul was a very nice and representative building and was loved by everyone in Strzyzow, still, the Beit HaMidrash was the place where people came to meet and share their time in prayers and learning Torah. In time of trouble or sickness, candles were lit, prayers were recited in Beit HaMidrash, and everyone joined in reciting Psalms and pleading G-d for help.

[Page 39]

The upkeep of the Beit HaMidrash came from donations. People gave when they were called to the Torah or on happy family occasions. Treasurers were always elected by the worshippers. However, since the Beit HaMidrash was Rabbi Alter Zev's domain, and because he worshipped there all year round, the treasurer was always on of his followers.

The kloyz was a big solid building with a gallery for women. Actually, it served the same purpose as the Beit HaMidrash. The only difference was that it was private property belonging to the Shapiros.

The house where the Shapiros resided was adjacent to the kloyz. The kloyz had simple furniture except for the ark which was adorned with wooden carvings of lions and other Biblical animals. When Rabbi Moshe Leib built his house, he added an extra room for a permanent Sukkah, with a movable ceiling and roof. The Sukkah was used during the year as a study. This was one of the most modern Sukkahs in the entire area. The architect always sought Rabbi Moshe Leib's advice in every step of the building. Like the Beit HaMidrash, the kloyz also had a huge collection of books; some of them were very rare. The people, especially the young men, had the responsibility to watch over the books, to re-shelves them and if there was need for repair, it was their job to take them to Reb Zalman Brauner, the only book-binder in town. Funds for the upkeep and the purchase of new books were collected from the worshippers. Every Friday, a youth went around from house to house and asked for a donation.

Seats in shul and in the Beit HaMidrash were private property. Everybody in town owned a seat and whoever was able to pay more, owned a better seat at the western wall. The seats were passed on from father to son as an inheritance and so were the women's seats. In the kloyz, seats were only on a yearly rental basis.

As mentioned above, in the last two years before the Holocaust, the religious Zionists had their own place to congregate and worship. The majority of the Zionists continued to worship where their fathers and grandfathers had done so before them.

The Public Bathhouse

The bathhouse, including the mikva, was built hundreds of years ago – soon after the first Jews settled in Strzyzow. The bathhouse was the property of the Kehillah and was leased to a bathhouse keeper. At the time when Hersh Brav was the head of the Kehilla, he modernized and remodelled the bathhouse so that Strzyzow's bathhouse was up to par with many bathhouses in bigger cities.

The Cemeteries in Strzyzow

Strzyzow had four cemeteries. The oldest cemetery bordered with the shul, and the next oldest, bordered with the Beit HaMidrash. The first, the second and the third cemetery were all connected with a path leading to each other.

[Page 40]

The last cemetery which existed up to the Holocaust was located out of town on a hill on the way to the village of Zarnowo. In addition, there was one cemetery which was shared by the Jews and gentiles. In 1880 a cholera epidemic swept through the town and hundreds of people died and were buried in this cemetery. This cemetery was called the "Cholera Cemetery". The cemeteries were divided into separate sections for men, women and children. Many times when someone passed away, arguments occurred about the gravesite selections. A section near the fence was reserved for people who committed suicide. In the old cemetery, the inscriptions on the gravestones were unreadable but in all other cemeteries, the gravestones were easily identifiable. Almost everybody in town had some relatives buried in one of the three cemeteries. In the beginning of this century, a stone and cement wall was erected around all cemeteries.

Charity Institutions and their activities

As in many cities, Strzyzow had many charitable institutions – some to help the local poor and some for the people who came from out of town. The well-known local poor used to receive support regularly but those unfortunate who were embarrassed to ask for help, for them, there was always a friend who knew about their predicament and through these friends, help was extended whether a one-time help was needed or more, especially before holidays when help was always there.

Since the majority of people in Strzyzow could not afford the luxury of a hospital, when somebody became seriously ill, hurriedly, one or two people went around town to make a collection. The patient was sent on the next train to the nearest hospital which was in Krakow, a distance of seventy miles. Collections like this sometimes had to be made during the night to enable the sick person to leave with the morning train because there were only two trains a day.

Strzyzow had some tight-fisted people from whom it was very hard to extract a donation befitting their ability. But nobody could shirk the responsibility entirely and everybody participated in giving to charity. There were those volunteers who were always collecting charity, ignoring the fact that they themselves hardly made a living.

There were some well-to-do merchants about whom rumours were not so kind when charity was concerned. But these rumours were not always accurate because they just gave in their own way without fanfare and publicity. As an example, I like to mention two names about which people were talking that they did not do their fair share. They were my father Reb Baruch Berglass and Reb Israel Gertner. But the fact was that Reb Israel Gertner had his own private free-loan bank. The village peddlers and small store owners always turned to him for a loan whenever they needed cash to buy merchandize for the upcoming Market Day. On the other hand, he was very particular in setting a due date for the loan and strictly adhered to collection on time.

My father, Reb Baruch Berglass never refused to anybody when asked for charity but he always tried to haggle and give less than asked, but he never let anybody out the door without giving. On the other hand, feeding the poor was his life's goal. His house was always open whether on a weekday, Saturday and holiday. There were always one or two strangers sitting at his table together with his family. He simply did not enjoy the Sabbath meal without having a poor man at his table.

[Page 41]

Reb Joseph Schacher, before his impoverishment, used to send checks to the needy by mail, anonymously, and nobody knew from where the checks came. Women like Rizha Rosenblith and Hena Rachel Unger specialized in collecting challah and fish for the poor. Whenever a poor Jewish wanderer was arrested, these two women always stood by to help with kosher food and bail when it was needed.

And Reb Joseph Klotz, who hardly made a living for himself, used to bring hot coffee or tea every Saturday for the poor who slept in the Beit HaMidrash. Reb Yeshayahu Mandel, a poor little man himself, always collected charity for some cause. The Shohet Reb Leib Friedman had a bed reserved in his house in case someone needed lodging. Of course, he had a guest every night.

Strzyzow was a little town with many permanent charity institutions. Some existed continuously and some ceased to exist for lack of funds and later reorganized. Food for Passover Appeal was activated every year to provide the poor with food for the holiday. In the last few years before the war, funds for this purpose were received from the Strzyzow Society in the United States for distribution among the poor.

There were people who were embarrassed to accept charity at home but from the Strzyzow Society they gladly accepted. It would not be fair not to mention Reb Samuel Mussler and Hersh Unger in New York who were active all their lives to collecting and sending money for their fellow countrymen in Strzyzow.

One of the most important institutions in Strzyzow was the Talmud Torah. Their goal was that no poor Jewish child should remain without Torah education. Every Jewish child was required to study Torah and if the parents were unable to pay, the town's responsibility was to provide such education. A special committee was elected to collect donations regularly on a weekly basis to pay for teaching the poor children. There was a tradition in Strzyzow that at every happy occasion, plates were put on the tables for different charities and Talmud Torah was one of them.

Every year in the fall, a one-time appeal was made to help the poor prepare for the winter with potatoes, firewood and warm clothes. Strzyzow also had a Free Loan Society which provided loans without interest to small storekeepers and tradesmen. Dr. Chaim Frenkel, a lawyer, was in charge of the distribution of these loans.

After Hitler's rise to power, funds were raised to help the Jewish refugees who were expelled from Nazi Germany and all their possessions confiscated. Most refugees were concentrated in a refugee camp on the Polish-German border in Zbonszin, a place in no-man's land, because the Polish government refused to let them in.

When the wave of oppression started and refugees began to arrive into Poland, a mass protest meeting was called in Strzyzow, as in all other cities in Poland, under the leadership of all organized groups in town. Everybody in Strzyzow came to the meeting. The speakers were: Avigdor Diamand, the head of the Zionists, Dr. Chaim Frenkel, on behalf of the intelligentsia and Reb Shlomo Diamand, representing the orthodoxy(Yahalomi) who was a very bright young man. Reb Shlomo Diamand resides now in Israel. A collection was made at the meeting and everybody signed up a pledge which had to be paid monthly to the refugee fund.

[Page 42]

A few families who immigrated from Strzyzow to Germany were expelled and came back to settle in Strzyzow. These families were helped locally and funds collected monthly were sent to a central committee in Warsaw.

The Bikur Cholim Society in Strzyzow was an organization whose members' main duty was to stay with the sick at night to enable the family members of the sick to rest. And, in many cases, they also paid for the prescriptions.

Of course a city cannot exist without a Hevra Kadisha to take care of everything, from removing the body from the house to preparing the funeral and digging of the grave. An initiation fee was required from each member and yearly membership dues were collected from all members.

When a member passed away, a fee for the gravesite had to be paid separately. They money was used for the upkeep of the cemeteries and if extra funds were available, it went to charity. Of course, all these assessments were made according to the financial situation of the concerned. Everybody in Strzyzow belonged to the Hevra Kadisha because, sooner or later, everybody needed them.

There were two Mishnayot Learning Societies that studied a few chapters of Mishnayot in memory of the deceased society members. The first year, when a member passed away, ten members studied a few chapters daily and, thereafter, on each yahrzeit, Mishnayot was studied again by ten members, a minyan. There was an elected committee with a record keeper who kept the records with the dates of the yahrzeits. To be a member in the Mishnayot Learning Society, a one-time fee was assessed according to the financial ability of the candidate. From members who did not know how to study, a higher fee was collected.

There was once a man in Strzyzow by the name of Reb Moshe Diamand, a very rich man. He owned land and forests for timber. He left a bequest in his will that the firewood for the oven in the Beit HaMidrash should be supplied from his estate forever. After many years, when the heirs wanted to sell the inheritance free of debts, they could not do so until they satisfied the Kehillah. The agreement called for the heirs to build a two story building which would serve as a Talmud Torah School where children would study Torah. The upper floor was to be used for classes and the ground floor as a shelter for poor people where they could spend the night. The furniture was later donated by Reb Abraham Tenzer in memory of his two sons who died in their youth.

The writer of these memories, Itzhok Berglass and his two sisters, Nechama and Chaya donated the equipment for the Talmud Torah but, to our sorrow, the building never served the purpose because it was finished just when the war started.

[Page 43]

Jewish Traditional Education in Strzyzow

Until the second half of the past century, the Jewish children in Strzyzow received religious education only. A boy, when reached the age of three, was required to begin his education. At that time, his hair was shorn and only side-locks remained. A ritual four-cornered garment was put on him with tzitziot and, wrapped in a tallit; he was carried off by his father to the melamed in cheder. At first, he was taught the Hebrew alphabet and then the vowelization.

At the age of four or five, depending on the capability of the child, he began to learn the Pentateuch. A small party was given in honour of the boy who started to study Chumash. Relatives were invited on a Saturday afternoon – the boy made a traditional speech which was taught for generations. The speech was actually a question and answer dialogue with the help of another boy. The guests were treated with apple cider and cake.

Every melamed had a helper whose job was to bring the children to cheder and to return them home. The helper's job was also to provide the children with a flag for Simchat Torah and a bow and arrow for Lag B'Omer. Lag B'Omer is a holiday in springtime, halfway between Passover and Shavuot. On that day, the children were free from studies and the helpers took the children for a day out into the woods where they played soldiers. There was also a tradition in Strzyzow that whenever a boy was born, the helper took the children to welcome the new born. The children recited a prayer and were given treats.

At the age of six, the child passed on to a melamed who taught the older children Talmud. And so the children kept passing from one melamed to another according to their progress in learning until they reached the age of Bar Mitzvah. After Bar Mitzvah, they were capable and prepared to dwell in the Beit HaMidrash to study Torah and other holy books alone or in groups but always under the supervision of the older scholars who were studying Torah as a permanent occupation.

The melamdim who were teaching the children were not professional pedagogues and did not have a manual from which they could prepare their lessons. Each had a system of his own by which he taught and the results were generally satisfactory. There were melamdim who specialized in teaching the alphabet, and then others took over and taught Chumash, Talmud and son on. Some melamdim taught only the Prophets and the Talmud. The melamdim were also required to teach how to write in Yiddish.

The melamed prepared the boy for his Bar Mitzvah. He taught him how to put on the Tefilin. Reading the Torah or chanting the Haftorah was not necessary because in Galicia this tradition was unknown.

As I mentioned above, every melamed had his system in teaching. It all depended on the disposition of the teacher. If he was an angry man, he was very strict with the children and if he was soft-hearted, he took it easy with the youngsters.

Reb Mordechai Rosenbaum who specialized in teaching little tots was nicknamed "murderer" because he was very strict. But parents preferred him over Reb Eliyahu who was very soft-spoken. With Reb Mordechai, the parents were sure that the child would know how to read. Reb Yaacov Dym, who had a cheder for many years, taught the 7-10 age groups. He was well-liked by both the parents and the children.

[Page 44]

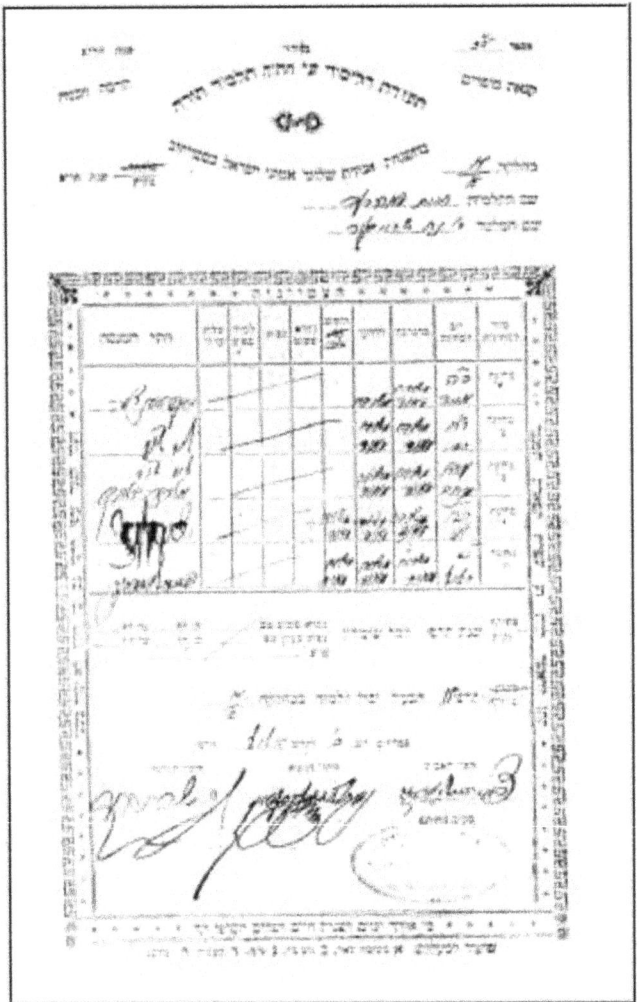

Photocopy of a report card issued by the Talmud Torah in Strzyzow

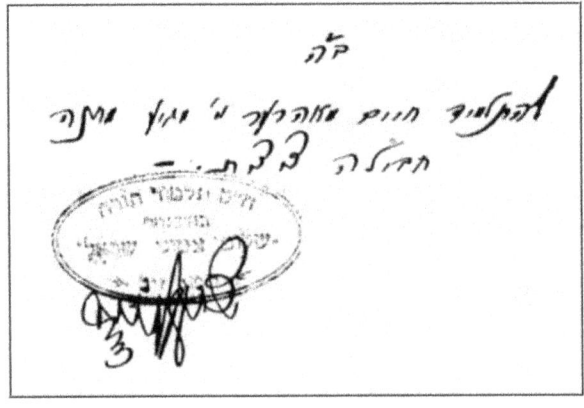

Certificate of award given to an outstanding student. The award: A bundle of Tzitzioth

[Page 45]

Rules and Regulations for students attending the Talmud Torah

Every student is required:

1. Not to be tardy and not to miss any school day.
2. To obey and respect the teacher, the parents and adult people.
3. To behave properly in the street, not to get involved in a fight, not to insult anyone, not to run in the street, not to associate with such persons who do not study the Torah and do not observe Jewish law and rituals.
4. Always wear the ritual garment with tzitzioth, wear a yarmulke even while asleep, to wash the hands first thing in the morning, to wear clean clothes, to say the blessing before and after consuming any food or drink, to pray from the prayer book and not from memory, not to converse during prayers and always respond 'amen' when the cantor is chanting.

[Page 46]

Chaim Yacov Nuremberg taught Talmud exclusively to the 10-13 groups. His specialty was to break up the boredom of studying the Gemara with interesting stories and legends. By contrast, Reb Moshe Samuel Friedman did not want to waste time with story-telling. Pupils who graduated from Moshe Samuel came out with a perfect knowledge of the Talmud and also knew how to write a perfect Yiddish and Hebrew. Of course, it was the old-fashioned Hebrew which was called Lashon Hakodesh. Reb Moshe Samuel did not use a pen; he wrote with a quill.

Every generation which grew up in Strzyzow had a certain type of a melamed. The melamdim had not special training. On the contrary, in the old days, nobody wanted to grow up and be a melamed. Being a melamed was a shameful profession. When somebody was unsuccessful in life, being a melamed was the only way to earn a living. Usually, they began with one or two children and if they were successful, then they started a cheder.

There was no special location for the cheders in town. Every melamed used his living quarters as a classroom, sometimes with the permission from the authorities and sometimes without. Even if the melamed obtained a licence, it was always for a smaller number of children than he taught. In case of an inspection by the authorities, the extra children always disappeared.

The melamed's wife served as a nurse. When somebody hurt himself or cut his finger, she treated it with a piece of bread and butter that she put on the finger and wrapped it around with cobweb, and it always helped.

In the thirties, at the initiative of the Kehillah and the generosity of a few well-to-do people, a Talmud Torah school was built. As I already mentioned before, the children in Strzyzow did not live to study there. it was finished just when the war started. Presently, the Polish government is using it for a school.

The Agudat Israel, who had a strong following in Strzyzow, began to work toward modernization of educational systems for the children. They demanded better qualified teachers, instituted report cards with grades and rewards for outstanding students. One particular teacher whom I would like to mention was Reb Noah Schreiber who had a very progressive way of teaching children. As a matter of fact, he was recruited by another city to teach in a regular Talmud Torah School because of his qualifications. The payment to the teachers was seasonal, from Passover to Rosh Hashanah and from the High Holidays to Passover. Wintertime, every student had to pay extra for kerosene used to light the cheder.

Studying Torah was sacred among the Jews in the shtetl, whether you could afford it or not. Parents who were able to pay, paid themselves, and the community paid for the poor. But not child was deprived of education, heaven forbid!

One of the painful problems was how to teach the girls to read the prayers and how to write. In the second half of the nineteenth century, the majority of women were illiterate. In the synagogue, there were always one or two women who knew how to read the prayers and the rest were sitting and repeating after them. On this account, many jokes were born about how women twisted the words of the prayers. Rarely could anyone in Strzyzow afford to hire a private tutor to teach his daughters. In the beginning of the twentieth century, people started to send the girls to cheder once or twice a week after the boys had left. But, the melamdim had no training whatsoever to teach neither boys nor girls. Eventually, a couple of young men came up with the idea to start a private class for girls for a nominal fee and later, a few of those girls started to teach the younger ones.

[Page 47]

In the thirties, the Agudat Israel solved the problem of educating girls by opening a Bais Yacov School for girls. They brought a teacher, Ms. Diller from another town. She was not happy in Strzyzow and left after one year. Her replacement, Miss Wasserman, was a very qualified and devoted teacher. The parents and the students were very happy with her. Unfortunately, within five years, the school folded for lack of funds.

Soon after, the Zionist organization started a kindergarten for girls and taught Hebrew to older girls. This school lasted until the beginning of World War II.

Secular Education

During the nineteenth century, no Jewish boy and only a few Jewish girls attended a secular school. Those who knew Polish or German were self-educated. Rarely would anybody engage a private tutor.

Men who were about to get married and planned to join their father's business tried to obtain some education by private means. There were a few self-educated people in Strzyzow who passed on their knowledge to others for a fee. I would like to mention Reb Zalman Zagner who authored a textbook for mathematics and accounting in Yiddish. He was very popular in Galicia. Mr. Zagner moved to another city where he became a regular teacher in a school.

Another well-educated man who never received formal education was Reb Tzvi Mohreer. He was the official registrar who registered the Jewish new born and the deceased. He had this concession from the government and collected a fee whenever his service was needed. He received no regular salary. Mr. Mohrer was also a teacher who taught young people to read and write. Reb Tzvi Mohrer worked for the post office under the Austrian government on a temporary basis so they would not force him to work on the Sabbath or Jewish holidays. There was one very intelligent person who had an unofficial law office. His name was Alter Nechemiah. He knew the law as thoroughly as a lawyer though he never attended any school. The Greenblatt family were all self-educated and were always willing to share their knowledge with others.

In the last twenty years before the war, all the children were required to attend elementary school, whether boys or girls. It was hard for a Jewish boy to attend a secular school because of the way they were dressed with side-locks and a yarmulke. The gentile boys were very hostile to the Jewish students. It was also hard for Jewish boys because they had to attend the secular school as well as cheder. They could not neglect the studying of the Torah.

[Page 48]

The Hebrew Kindergarten and Nursery in Strzyzow

1. Schiff. 2. Deutch. 3. Lustgarten. 4. Goldman-Last. 5. Meisels. 6. Thim. 7. Schlisselberg. 8. Berglass. 9. Gertner. 10. Taub-Gertner. 11. Lichtman. 12. Hina Feit, daughter of Samuel and Rachel who volunteered their time and helped with the children. 13. Salzman. 14. Karp. 15. Schacher-Hagel. 16. Rosenblith. 17. Berglass. 19. Rosenthal. 20. Assistant teacher. 21. Teacher Elka Shulman

[Page 49]   A class in the Polish elementary school in Strzyzow

The majority of students were Jewish, but no Jewish teachers

[Page 50]

In the last ten years before the war, the number of young people who continued studying Torah and dwelled in the Beit HaMidrash, dwindled to a few only. Strzyzow had also a secular high school in which Jewish students from out-of-town attended but not the local children because of forced attendance on the Sabbath and holidays.

Political parties in Strzyzow

Strzyzow had two political parties only. The Central Zionist Organization which was an umbrella organization for different groups and the Agudat Israel which opposed Zionism as such. The Zionist Organization was very strong in the last thirty years before the war. They influenced the youth and inspired them to work for the Zionist cause, namely, a Jewish homeland in Erets Israel which was under the British rule. About the Zionist activities, I will write in broader form in a later chapter.

The Agudat Israel was founded by Reb Naphtali Chaim Halbersten, a grandson of the famous Rabbi Chaim from Sandz. He came to Strzyzow after he married the daughter of Rabbi Alter Zev Horowitz. My brother-in-law, Reb Itzhok Bernstein, Reb Joel Glickman and a very capable young man – Shlomo Diamand (Yahalomi), helped him to establish the party. The most active member who ran the organization was the secretary, Moshe Schwartzman. The main task of the Agudat Israel was in the field of orthodox education, especially among the girls. The girls group was called Baos Agudat Israel. With all due respect, the organization had very little success. From time to time they awakened and renewed their activity but it soon cooled off again. Something was amiss and nobody could figure out why. Maybe it was lack of a goal or idealism, or because the opposed Zionism?

The majority of the people in Strzyzow were religious anyway and did not need an organization for that purpose. Even the Zionists were all religious people and there was no need for religious propaganda.

The Zionists and the Agudat Israel had a very peaceful coexistence. The relationship became strained only once in 1921 when the Zionists began a fundraising campaign for the just-established Jewish National Fund in which they tried to include the entire population of the town. The Agudat Israel did not succeed in their opposition and the campaign was very successful.

In most elections to the Polish Parliament, the Zionists were in coalition with the Agudat Israel. But in local politics, and in the rabbinical disputes, there were people from both parties aligned on both sides. Normally, in time of elections to the city government, the Jews always split their support between the opposing non-Jewish candidates.

Once, at the beginning of this century, all the Jews united to fight the Priest Jablecinski who was an outspoken anti-Semite. At that time, the Jews were still fifty percent of the population and with a little support from some non-Jews, they succeeded in their opposition and a more liberal mayor was elected. Every time when a candidate for mayor wanted to be elected, he had to make a promise not to discriminate against the Jews.

[Page 51]

For many years, a fight for the mayoral chair was going on between two aristocratic Polish families – the Konieczkowskis and the Patryns. Konieczkowski was patronized by the church which was very anti-Jewish. Of course, the Jews gave their support to Dr. Patryn and he ruled the town for many years.

Dr Joseph Patryn, the son of a big family, was an interesting figure. The origin of the Patryn family was Swedish. Their ancestor was a Swedish soldier who remained in Strzyzow after the Swedish-Polish War at the time when King Casimir ruled Poland. The Patryn family were very rich, well-rooted in the area and Dr. Patryn was in our time the patriarch of the family. He was a good doctor and a shrewd politician which is why he had so many opponents in Strzyzow. He was devoted to his allies whether Jews or gentiles and was helpful whenever necessary.

When Dr. Patryn died, Reb Joseph Diamand eulogized him with these words: "Since I am older than he, I wish I would have died instead". This was said with true sincerity. Although Dr. Patryn himself attended church very rarely, the Patryn family were good Catholics. They even built a little chapel on a hill overlooking the city. This man had no bigotry in him and when he disliked somebody it was purely politics.

As mayor, Dr. Patryn did many favours. He had four brothers and each had big families. They owned almost all the land around Strzyzow. They had many Jewish business associates and helped the Jewish needy with farm produce. Many times they set an example to other Polish families. All the Jews in Strzyzow attended his funeral and the stores were closed for the day. Even after his death, Jews continued to support his friends in local politics.

The Zionist movement in Strzyzow

The Zionist ideal and its movement which had spread worldwide finally reached Strzyzow also. There were a few lovers of Zion before but they were not organized. The first Zionists in Strzyzow when Dr. Herzl, the founder of political Zionism was still alive, was Reb Moshe Meir Seidman. He spread the Zionist ideal in Strzyzow but did not organize anything. Following Seidman was a young man by the name of Shalom Flaumenhaft. He dwelt in Beit HaMidrash studying Torah but nevertheless, was active in spreading the Zionist ideal without much success.

A man by the name of Simcha Feingold who came to Strzyzow as a representative of a lumber company and remained in Strzyzow for a long time, was a real lover of Zion. His grandson, Ben Ami Feingold, wrote an article in this book about his activities in Strzyzow.

Before the Feingold family immigrated from Strzyzow, their oldest son, Moshe met with a group of young men, the most intelligent young men in Strzyzow, and explained to them the importance of political Zionism. Their names were: Mordechai Brav; Joel Greenblatt; Aryah Diamand; Tzvi Elazar Sternberg and Itzhok Tenzer. During this meeting, he asked to serve on the first Zionist committee and the first Zionist organization was established. The Feingolds left Strzyzow in 1907.

As presiding officer, they elected Mordechai Brav who was elected for two reasons: because he was the community leader's son and most importantly, he was the only young man with a secular education. The rest of the committee were pious young men who dwelt in Beit HaMidrash studying Torah and secretly reading secular books. The treasurer in the committee was Itzhok Tenzer who held this office until the outbreak of World War I. During the war, everything fell apart.

[Page 52]

After the war, a new generation of young people grew up. A group of self-educated boys and girls took upon themselves to restore the organization. They named as leader the prestigious Reb Tzvi Pfeffer who came to Strzyzow after the war and opened the only printing shop in the entire area. He was very intelligent and a capable leader.

In general, the people in Strzyzow did not oppose the establishment of a Zionist organization as long as it did not interfere with the religious upbringing of the younger generation and they continued to observe the religious code. Only once during the first Jewish National Fund campaign in 1921 did the Zionist meet a strong opposition from the extreme Hassidim. The Zionists tried to recruit donors on a permanent basis but afterwards, the opposition weakened and the Zionists continued to be active in the community life and in local politics. There were no extremists in Strzyzow from either side.

One of the first important acts by the Zionists was the establishment of a library. After contacting the Zionist headquarters in Lwow, the organization received the first shipment of books. They rented a small room and a Jewish library came into existence. The library was used as a home for the Zionists. The Zionist committee frequently held their meetings in the library. Now having a home of their own, they organized campaigns for the Jewish National Fund by distributing the blue and white collection boxes and the sale of shkalim, which was equivalent to buying a membership card.

On Simchat Torah, the Zionists borrowed a Torah scroll from the shul and all the members worshipped in the library and donations went partly to the library and partly to the Jewish National Fund. This tradition lasted until the outbreak of the war in 1939.

At the beginning, the Zionist movement was an entity unlike today. There were no different groups aiming at different social directions. There was only one general Zionist Party. The library gained popularity among the boys and girls, the young and old, because everybody was anxious to read books, to get acquainted with Bialik, Sholem Alsichem, Peretz and others and many began to learn Hebrew. For the boys it was not hard to learn Hebrew but for the girls it was more complicated because they did not attend the cheder.

In 1910, the committee in Strzyzow was asked to help the Zionists from the nearby shtetl of Frysztak to establish a library. But their library did not last for very long. This little shtetl was ultra-Hassidic with many extremists who opposed such progress like a library. One night, they broke into the place where the borrowed books from our library in Strzyzow were kept and made a bonfire destroying all the books. After this shameful act, the Zionists from Strzyzow wanted to press charges and take them to court for destroying their property. However, when the storm calmed down, they realized that it would not be dignified for Jews to fight in a non-Jewish court. Therefore, the Zionists dropped the whole matter.

[Page 53]

Under the Austro-Hungarian rule, the Zionists in Strzyzow always supported Zionist candidates to Parliament. In 1911, the Zionists had as their candidate, Dr. Tzvi Syrup from Sandz who ran against a Pole, Dr. Leopold Jaworski. Because of Dr. Syrup's Zionism, the Orthodox Jewry decided to support Dr. Jaworski. When Reb Moshe Deutchar from Krakow, a representative of the Orthodox Jewry came to campaign for Jaworski, he received such a reception from the Zionists that he had to leave town under police protection. However, our candidate was not elected because the majority of rabbis and the Orthodox Jewry in Galicia were against Zionist candidates.

During the war, between 1914-1918, the Zionist activity stopped completely because many young people were in the war fighting and many were evacuated from the town. Strzyzow was twice occupied by the Russians. After the war when life returned to normality, the former Zionist committee, with the help of a few younger members, reactivated the Zionist committee with renewed energy. The first task was to restore the library because during the war, all the books had been destroyed. There were many teenagers who during the war grew up to be conscientious young men, eager to participate in all Zionist activities. Tzvi Elazar Sternberg taught Hebrew to the boys and the girls organized a girls' club named "Ruth". The programme included studying Jewish history, Hebrew and current events relating to Jewish life in the Diaspora.

When the Central Committee of the Zionists relocated to Krakow, Dr. Itzhok Schwarzbarc was elected leader. He visited several times Strzyzow and his visits were very inspirational.

In the 1919 elections to the new Polish Parliament, the Zionists worked very hard, campaigning for their candidates. This time, the hard work paid off because the majority of the Jews in Galicia supported them and every Zionist candidate won.

The success of the elections caused rivalry among the Zionist leadership. The younger generation was growing up and they demanded to share the leadership. In Strzyzow this dispute had settled by itself after most of the adult Zionists immigrated and the few who remained got saddled with families and withdrew from activism. The younger leaders were very intelligent, self-educated and devoted to the Zionist cause.

Avigdor Diamand was elected as leader of the Zionist organization. He took over the leadership from his older brother Aryeh. Abraham Brav took over the treasury from his older brother Mordechai and also the responsibility of the library. There was an outstanding group of girls including Hana Nechemiah, Feiga Greenblatt, Feiga Weinberg, Eta Dembitzar, Sarah Zilber and Vita Loos. All these girls played a very important role in the Zionist activities in Strzyzow. Later, I, the writer of these memoirs, took over the leadership and served as the secretary of the Zionists in Strzyzow.

In 1921, the World Zionist Organization proclaimed a fund-raising campaign for the Jewish National Fund with a goal to raising twenty-five million pounds sterling. The money was needed to help the first pioneers who began to redeem the land and settle in Eretz Israel. We the Zionists in Strzyzow began this campaign with the slogan: "Every Jew in Strzyzow helps build a Jewish Homeland".

[Page 54]

We influenced and inspired the majority of the people in Strzyzow by organizing a mass meeting in shul. However, at the last minute, the Polish authorities withdrew their permit, under the pretext that this shul was designated only for worshipping. By the withdrawal of the permit, the Polish authorities helped us in the success of the campaign. The meeting was held in a small room adjacent to the main sanctuary of the shul. Everyone in Strzyzow, even non-Zionists contributed to this campaign. There were people who pledged their jewellery. Even though these pieces of jewellery had no big monetary value, the act itself had a tremendous moral uplift.

After this huge campaign, the Zionists realized that funds would be continuously needed so we organized a monthly membership contribution to the Jewish National Fund. These contributions continued until September, 1939. Of course, faces in the organization's leadership and the membership kept changing. The most active in collecting funds in the thirties were: Yacov keh, Vita Loos, Sarah Rabhun, Naphtali Roth and Peretz Pinsel from the Mizrachi, a very active Zionist.

At the beginning of each year, the Zionist activists asked for pledges and during the year, these pledges were paid off.

I was the leader until 1938. Not only were we active in fund raising for the Zionist causes but we took an active role in the community life and the Kehillah. In time of elections to local and central government, we always made sure that the right candidate got the deserved Jewish support. We also helped chalutzim who were leaving for Eretz Israel, most of whom had no means to pay for their passage. We even helped the well-known anti-Zionist, Reb Shalom Schwartzman who went to the Holy Land and joined the Netursi Xarta. We saw to it that he got a certificate from the British authorities permitting his emigration. The Zionists used to organize all kinds of festivities for fund raising purposes. The first time we organized such an affair in 1919, when we used an egg packing plant belonging to one of our friend's father. The news about the party reached the worshippers in the Beit HaMidrash. A group of older people came to pay us a visit to see with their own eyes what the Zionists were up to. But to their consternation, their attitude changed when they did not see anything extraordinary. From then on, these parties were well accepted. In the later years, the Zionists celebrated every Tub B'Shvat with a big party in the Polish club hall. Tzvi Shapiro, a local resident who spent some years in Eretz Israel, was the spiritual leader of these affairs.

The relationship along the different Zionist group and between the rest of the population was very good.

In 1925, a group of young men organized the first religious youth group under the sponsorship of the Mizrachi. They began to spread the idea of "Aliya" to Eretz Israel, and this idea never ceased to inspire the young generation in Strzyzow. In a village not far from Strzyzow lived a Jewish landowner, Reb Yechezkiel Wallach with his son-in-law, Reb Israel Wilner. They were ardent Zionists and enabled the young people of Strzyzow to establish a "Hachshara" where the chalutzim could obtain agricultural training by working in the fields. Many young people from Galicia came there to be trained before leaving for Eretz Israel.

[Page 55]

Generally, it was hard to find a place for the Zionist groups to obtain agricultural training before fulfilling their dream to make Aliyah. Eretz Israel had just begun to develop as a Jewish Homeland. Aktiva Diamand, a farmer's son, was the first chalutz to emigrate to Eretz Israel and after him, many followed. Many young people had to emigrate illegally because it was almost impossible to obtain a certificate from the British rulers.

After the Nazi came to power in 1933, many who immigrated from Strzyzow to Germany were forced to leave so they immigrated to Eretz Israel. People, who escaped the Nazi in 1939 and spent their war-years in Russia, when they returned, most of them also settled in Israel. This is the reason why we have such a big concentration of people from Strzyzow in Israel.

In the late thirties, the Zionists in Strzyzow were active in illegal Aliyah. After the death of Reb Hersch Mohrer, who was the official registrar of the Jewish population in Strzyzow, his son – Chaim – a member of the Zionist-Revisionist Party and his friend, Nahtali Diamand, took a stack of blank birth certificates and gave them to the Central Zionist Office which used them as they were needed.

Joseph Diamand, a young man from Krakow who came to work as a clerk in Strzyzow, organized the Revisionist group – "Menorah" and the affiliate youth group "Beiter". This group, under the leadership of Eliezer Gruber, Feivel Schacher, Baruch Nuremberg and Joseph Deutch, attracted many youngsters to the organization. The leader of the youth group was Tzvi Schefler and the coordinators were: Chaim and Eta Mohrer, Pesha Roth, Chava Gruber and Leah Kracher. They did tremendous propaganda work for the Zionist cause and especially by inspiring the young people to make Aliyah, whether legally or illegally. Joseph Diamand later went to Krakow ad became the economical editor for the Zionist Polish newspaper.

The desertion of the Revisionists from the mainstream of the Zionist organization caused shock to the local Zionists which were soon overcome, after recruiting more members into the Zionist organization. They organized two youth organizations: "Akiba" and "Hanoar Hazioni". These young people worked feverishly to spread the Zionist idea and urged their members to leave Poland before it was too late. Their leaders were Joseph Schiff, Naphtali Diamand and Naphtali Roth.

More and more youth groups were organized under the auspices of the Zionist organization. The boys' group was called Bar Kochba and the girls' group – Shoshana. These groups were very energetic in their work, helping young people to leave Poland and immigrate to Eretz Israel. They had Hebrew classes and many other cultural activities. On the library was closed by the authorities for no reason at all except that it was a Jewish library. After an appeal to the higher authorities, the library which was named "Hatikva" reopened with a special section for younger readers.

The Mizrachi organized a religious group under the leadership of Elimelech Waldman, Reuven Zelig Mandel, Moshe Dym and Yacov Adest. Waldman was a graduate from a Hebrew teachers' seminary. He taught Hebrew in a nearby city but lived in Strzyzow and helped with teaching Hebrew locally. Moshe Dym was later recruited to work for the head office of the Mizrachi in Krakow where he helped many from Strzyzow to obtain certificates for Aliyah.

[Page 56]

In general, the dominant atmosphere in Strzyzow was Zionism. All the young people in Strzyzow found their way to Zionist youth groups except the extreme Orthodox and those who joined the Agudat Israel.

There were no leftists in town. People who came from places where the leftists and influence, changed their attitudes and became active in the Zionist movement.

There was a lumber mill in Strzyzow which belonged to Jewish owners – Reb Moshe Johannes and Reb Tzvi Kracher. They had a foreman, Reb Yacov Eisner who was very intelligent and a devoted Zionist although he was strictly orthodox. Eisner had a very good voice and always chanted in the Beit HaMidrash. He organized a Hachshara in the lumber mill for chalutzim who were getting ready to immigrate to Ertez Israel. There they gained experience and were introduced to manual labour in order to be ready for the hardship in the Jewish Homeland. In those times, very few young people learned a so-called non-Jewish trade like cabinet making, mechanical work, etc.

In 1936, the Zionists in Strzyzow did the most daring thing considering the financial situation in town. They added a few classes to the existing kindergarten and turned it into a regular Hebrew school for which they hired a qualified Hebrew teacher – a graduate from the religious teacher's seminary – Yavneh.

A committee of devoted mothers was elected to provide all the assistance the school needed. Women like Nechama Gertner, my wife, Sarah Berglass, Rachel Feit and Sarah Shapiro, who, with the help of the entire Zionist movement, overcame all the hardships and thanks to their commitment and devotion, the school lasted until the outbreak of war in September, 1939.

In 1938, I resigned from the leadership of the Zionist organization and my successor was Dr. Acht, a young lawyer who just settled in Strzyzow. He was a very active Zionist and he continued to be the leader until the outbreak of the war. The last summer before the war started, a big campaign was proclaimed by the World Zionist Movement for the redemption of the Galil. A general meeting was called in the shul where Dr. Poretzky, a special emissary from Eretz Israel spoke. In his speech he warned the people to wake up from apathy and immigrate to Eretz Israel legally, if possible or illegally because Europe was not safe anymore. Who could have imagined at that time that the disaster was so close and the end of European Jewry so imminent? On September 1, 1939 war broke out and on 10th September, the Germans occupied Strzyzow. And the destruction of the Jewish community of Strzyzow, Poland and the rest of Europe began.

[Page 57]

Professionals and the Intelligentsia in Strzyzow

All the professionals who resided in Strzyzow in the last fifty years were all out-of-towners who settled in Strzyzow to practice their profession. There were doctors, lawyers, dentists and a few clerks. The majority of them did not socialize with the gentiles and neither were they too close with the Jews. They were isolated in their own circle. A few supported the Zionist movement but they were not active members. They also participated in local charities. During the High Holidays they worshipped in shul. They were the only Jews in town who dared to violate the Jewish tradition by not wearing hats and not observing the Sabbath and their behaviour was reluctantly accepted. When the Hebrew school was established, only a few agreed to send their children to study Hebrew.

Negative Types

There were a few bad characters among the Jews in Strzyzow. However, types like professional informers who would report to the authorities about violations of certain government rules when they contradicted the Jewish traditions were unknown. The widow of one custom official, whose record was not without blemish, lived a long life and suffered for her husband's misdeeds. There were no Jewish thieves or swindlers and when business or inheritance disputes occurred, it was always settled by the rabbi or by arbitration through a third party. Jews did not like to bring their problems before the non-Jewish court. There were one or two men who continuously had litigations in court but they were considered disreputable although, in no other way, were they different from the rest of the Jews. When it came to support charitable causes, they supported it wholeheartedly. Generally, the Jewish people in Strzyzow lived like one big family.

Converts

Strzyzow had its converts too, though very few. A story circulated that a few generations earlier, a rabbi with a few of his followers from Grzybow, a city sixty miles from Strzyzow, were brought by the church to Strzyzow for the baptism ceremony at a well on the outskirts of the town. Later, a statue was erected in their honour. We all remember the statue because it was located in a pine grove where we used to stroll on a Sabbath afternoon. Nobody was sure about the authenticity of the story.

Once, two girls who were cousins fell in love with two gentile boys and converted to get married. Their relatives lived in town but no one carried a grudge against them knowing that they could not prevent it.

After World War I, when Poland won her independence, a railroad station manager, for the sake of preserving his job converted to Catholicism as well as his family. The conversion ceremony took place in the church with a big fanfare. His oldest son who studied in Rzeszow refused at first because of his association with a Zionist group but later relented. This Jewish official apparently had a traditional Jewish upbringing.

[Page 58]

He knew a lot about Jewish traditions and rituals. After his conversion, he kept his job and continued his friendly relationship with the Jewish people in Strzyzow. Apologetically, he used to remark to his Jewish friends that Moses did not lose anything and that Jesus did not gain much by his conversion, meaning that he had not been a good Jew and was not a good Catholic either. But still, after the conversion, he never missed the Sunday mass. However, before the conversion, he rarely attended services in shul. His conversion helped him and his family to survive the Holocaust. Long before the war, he was transferred to another place where no one knew his origins. The latest convert was a lawyer's daughter whom no one paid attention to because her father was much assimilated and had nothing to do with the Jews and nor did the girl.

The relationship between the Jews, the Poles and the Pogroms

Regarding the inter-relationship between the Poles and the Jews, or rather, the behaviour of the Poles towards the Jews in the past, I do not know. They probably were the same as those towards the rest of the Jews who lived all over Poland. In the last generations, the Jews resided in Strzyzow and nearby villages among Poles and conducted their business relations as good neighbours and off-times, even very friendly. But there was no danger of being assimilated except in a few rare cases. The Jews knew everything about the Polish history because they had studied it in the secular school. As for the Poles, the Jews were like a closed book. Neither one of the two nationalities ever socialized with each other. There were Jewish representatives in the city hall who worked with the Poles but that is all. No Jew ever attended a Polish wedding or another family affair and neither did the Poles attend Jewish affairs.

But even in the good times, the Jews knew and felt who the ruler of the country was. In the restless times when anti-Semitic propaganda strengthened its influence among the Poles, the hatred appeared openly. In the pogroms of the years 1898-1918 and 1919, the most active participants were the peasants and the illiterates but the city people just stood by, not reacting one way or another.

Before the turn of the century, one Jew was killed in a mysterious way near a crossing and nobody ever found out who killed him.

The Ritter Story

The Ritter story which shook the Jews in Strzyzow and vicinity happened at the end of the nineteenth century.

It happened in spring just before Passover when a body was found at the time when Reb Itzhok Ritter's manure was spread on the fields. Ritter was a farmer who lived in a nearby village. The body was identified as the daughter of a Ukrainian farmer from a nearby village who was a servant in the house of a local priest. A few months before, she disappeared and no one knew her whereabouts. Ritter was a simple, religious, seventy year-old-man. Soon after the discovery of the body, he was arrested, tried and sentenced to death even though there was no evidence that he had anything to do with this murder, and the body was found in a pile of manure in an open field.

[Page 59]

After appealing the sentence, his death sentence was commuted and he was sentenced to life imprisonment. However, his family, being sure of his innocence, did not rest. With the help of influential Jewish leaders in Galicia, including Rabbi Leib Broide from Lwow, Rabbi Gedalyahu Shmelkis from Przemysl, they succeeded in getting an audience with Kaiser Franz Joseph, Emperor of the Austro-Hungarian Empire. At the audience, Ritter's daughter, two lawyers, the above-mentioned rabbis and Reb Mordechai Wilner, a family friend who stood by during their ordeal, were present. At the short audience with the Emperor, he told them not to worry. Soon after, Ritter was pardoned and freed. The Kaiser was well-informed about the case.

A short time later, a relative of the village priest confessed on his death-bed that he had killed the girl as a favour to the priest after the priest had made her pregnant. He was also the person who hid her in the pile of manure.

The Pogrom in 1898

A few years after the Ritter affair, pogroms broke out all over Galicia. Under the influence of the anti-Semitic priest Stoilowski, Jews were beaten, store windows broken and Jewish goods looted. The Austrian governor was forced to call in a military unit to restore order. The soldiers acted very reluctantly and, of course, nobody was arrested. On the contrary, two Jews in Strzyzow were arrested. Reb Yacov Hagel was arrested for refusing to let the military use the shul for a stable. He not only refused but even dared to ask the officer why there were not using their Catholic church. The other Jew was arrested because he dared to call the mob 'robbers'.

Luckily, Strzyzow was spared the bloodshed during the pogrom. On Sunday after mass, a big crowd gathered near the church waiting for a signal to begin the assault and start looting again even though the military unit was still in town. The officer ordered the soldiers to load their rifles and get ready to fire. Still, the mob refused to retreat. It was a matter of seconds before the officer was ready to give the order to fire when the old priest Jablocinski appeared in front of the church and spoke to the mob. He told them that this was the wrong way to get rid of the Jews. The proper way, he said, would be to stop dealing with them, not to buy anything from them and that would make the Jews leave the country. Subsequently, the mob dispersed.

In Frysztak, a nearby town, the mob was not that lucky. The soldiers were forced to open fire and a few Poles were killed.

Right after the pogrom, the preaching of the priest Jablocinski began to materialize. He urged a few Poles to open a cooperative which would compete with the Jews.

They made a big opening ceremony with the priest consecrating the store and held anti-Jewish speeches. In his opening speech, the priest urged all Christians to boycott the Jews and only buy in the Christian stores.

[Page 60]

The priest made a remark to the peasants that those who intended to steal should continue their visits in the Jewish stores. He knew well his flock. However, Jews being forced to be merchants for generations knew much better the trade than the Christians. They knew how to be flexible and reduce prices by lowering profit margins. Therefore, the Christian cooperatives which mushroomed all over Galicia, did not succeed in pushing out the Jews from businesses. The simple village people upon whom the Polish aristocrats always looked down on preferred to buy in Jewish stores. Therefore, no matter how much the priest kept preaching each Sunday to support the Christian cooperatives, they did not succeed in doing much damage. In Strzyzow, after the Christians opened two stores, one for groceries and hardware and the other for agricultural supplies, they were soon forced to close the agricultural supply store. The grocery department existed only because the government granted them a licence to sell monopolized items which nobody else was allowed to sell, neither wholesale or retail. The government controlled items were: salt, sugar, tobacco and matches.

After the 1898 pogroms, the situation improved somewhat. Liberal winds were blowing from higher up and inter-relationship between the two nationalities – Jews and Poles – were cordial. Both respected each other. They fully cooperated in the city government. A Jewish section in the slaughter house was provided for kosher slaughtering and whenever a Jewish holiday fell on a Tuesday – the weekly market day – it was postponed to another day. The attitude toward the Jewish students changed drastically for the better. Whenever Polish students tried to harass the Jews, they were protected by the teachers. Nevertheless, the Jews had to occupy the seats in the last rows. No Jewish child dared to leave the perimeter of the town. If he did, he was always attacked by the Polish youngsters.

During World War I, anti-Semitism rose to an all-time high, notwithstanding the fact that many Jews served in the army on the front lines and many gave their lives for the country. Many more were wounded and remained invalids for life. The hatred went so far that a member of the Austrian Parliament dared to question the government about why Jews did not fulfil their obligations when it concerned the army. This Parliament member happened to be elected from our district, representing the farmers' party and they pretended to be liberal-minded.

In the last year of the war, more and more anti-Semitic incidents occurred. In Krakow, one Jewish father on his way to a hospital to visit his injured son, a soldier, was thrown out of the train and killed. In 1918 at a protest meeting in Strzyzow against the just-concluded peace treaty between Germany and the Soviet Union, the Poles did not blame Germany for the treaty but the Jews. After the meeting, they went on a rampage and began looting Jewish stores and homes.

[Page 61]

Memories from the 1898 Pogrom
By Tzvi Elazar Sternberg

In the second half of 1898, the skies over the children of Israel became gloomy with dark clouds. Wicked winds began to blow and a pogrom atmosphere was felt in Strzyzow. The enemies of the Jews raised their heads and spread all kinds of lies and falsehoods using it to their advantage. The clergy from their church pulpits preached that the Jews were to be blamed for all their tribulations. Father Stoilowski, known for his obloquy, travelled from village-to-village and incited to riot against the Jews. No wonder then that the peasants attacked, murdered, robbed and looted our brothers. In addition to the anti-Jewish campaign, this was also a year of drought and the Austrian government did not extend any help to the farmers. Consequently, the time was ripe for the anti-Semites to blame their misfortune on the Jews – the eternal scapegoats.

After the first pogrom in the vicinity, the band-leaders declared that Sunday, August 18th would be the day of pilferage and murder in our town. Bad news about robberies and beatings had already reached Strzyzow from nearby towns such as Frysztak, Niebylec, Czudec and the surrounding villages. The Jews in Strzyzow trembled with fear, worrying about what was going to happen to them. Delegation after delegation ran to the mayor of the town asking him to take preventive actions. The mayor promised that with his intercession, everything would pass peacefully. The old man Wyzikowski, a venerable citizen and the head of the fire brigade, had put on his uniform which was decorated with medals from the 1866 war as well as his fancy hat and his rusty sword that dangled from his belt. He came out into the street assuring the Jews that he would see to it that no harm would come to them. Whoever saw him in his outfit and did not know him could have believed that this man was a powerful personality and could do anything he wanted to do.

My father, of blessed memory, made shutters for windows from such thin boards that the lightest breeze could have blown them down in a second. Friday morning, units of infantry and cavalry which consisted of Hungarians, Germans and Ukrainians, arrived in town. They came from Easter Galicia. There were also a few Jews among them. The Jewish people of Strzyzow breathed a sigh of relief. Everybody invited the Jewish soldiers for the Sabbath to their homes for two reasons: to fulfil the commandment of hospitality and to feel more secure in their homes.

The cavalry stationed their horses in the front yard of the shul. Reb Yacov Hagel, the shul treasurer, refused to allow the horses to station near the shul. He went to the commanding officer and after a heated discussion; he was arrested for insulting the Christian religion and was kept in prison until the trial. At the trial he was sentenced to a year and a half imprisonment. Handcuffed, he was led away to Rzeszow to spend his jail term. During the trial, we found out what constituted an insult to the Christian religion: he had asked the officer why he did not put the horses in front of the Catholic Church!

My father invited two soldiers for the Sabbath. They happened to be from Sieniawa, his birthplace, and he knew the soldier's parents.

[Page 62]

They told us not to be frightened, that with the presence of the soldiers in the house, nobody would dare harm us. Nevertheless, my mother cried bitterly during the Sabbath candle lighting. We, my dad, the soldiers and I, went to the services in the Beit HaMidrash where many worshippers were missing and Jewish soldiers took their places. It just so happened that a son was born to my uncle Reb Joseph Hersh, his third son, Joel, but out of fear, nobody showed up to the traditional "welcome to the male party" which usually took place on a Friday night. Whatever food Reb Joseph Hersh had prepared was given away to the soldiers. We ate together and sang Sabbath songs when a sudden knock at the door was heard. We were startled and afraid to open the door until a soldier grabbed his bayonet and in a ready-to-fight position, slowly opened the door. Then, Reb Menashe from Lutcza, a nearby village, burst in breathlessly. After my father poured him a drink, he pulled himself together and began to tell his story.

He told us that his neighbours attacked him and looted his house. They robbed him of everything. He hid behind the door with a board in his hands. After they departed with the loot, he attacked the last few who were still in the house. He beat them until they were bleeding and then ran away to Strzyzow.

We knew Menashe. He used to sell us eggs from time to time. He was a pious peasant Jew who spoke Yiddish like a gentile.

On Sunday, August 18th, the day the anti-Semites had designated to pogrom the town; peasants came from the surrounding villages, some with carts and some on foot with sacks ready for looting. The market place was swarming with peasants. Again, Wyzikowski came out all spruced up in his uniform. He went around in the crowd and scolded loudly the peasants, urging them to disperse. But no one paid any attention to him. Then the infantry and the cavalry soldiers arrived. They attacked the mob that started to run toward the churchyard with the soldiers chasing after them. Then, the old priest Jablocinski came out and pleaded with the soldiers, promising them that he would see to it that the crow would leave peacefully. The crowd dispersed and the Jews sighed a breath of relief.

The 1918 Pogrom in Strzyzow

In November, 1918, after the Austro-Hungarian Empire fell apart and Poland became independent, the demobilized Jewish soldiers who had just returned from the battle fields organized a self-defence group because the Jews felt insecure and needed protection. They were armed by the temporary Polish authorities. When the Polish authorities found out that the Polish mob was planning to attack the Jews, they called in all the guns and the Jews remained defenceless. The pogrom began during an anti-Jewish meeting which was called by Jew haters and agitators. While the meeting was in progress in the local clubhouse, another group of hooligans did not even bother to attend the meeting. They began looting and destroying Jewish stores and homes.

[Page 63]

They started looting the grocery store of the partners Feit and Tenzer and continued to rob all the stores on the south side and west side of the market place, stopping at our store.

When the leaders of the meeting heard about the looting, they interrupted the meeting and asked the people to disperse, claiming that this was not the way to get rid of the Jews. The same spiel that we had heard twenty years earlier from the priest Jablocinski. Now another priest, Bulok, was his name. He was the leader and the main speaker for the anti-Semites. He also claimed that by looting Jewish property, they were doing a disservice to the Polish government which had just won her independence and were defaming Poland's reputation as a democracy. The pilfering stopped. However, on the side street, out of sight of the authorities, looting continued. The material damage to the Jews was tremendous, particularly the wine merchant Reb Israel Kanner. He was ruined forever. He lost his wife and a son just before the pogrom and after the pilferers became drunk, they broke the wine barrels in the wine cellar. One Pole died on the spot from drunkenness.

Winter of 1918-19 was very depressing for the Jews in Poland in general and for the people in Strzyzow in particular. The Polish soldiers, under the command of General Haller and on their way from the western front to the Easter front, went berserk. Beating and pilfering the Jews was the order of the day. Jews were thrown out of trains and in Strzyzow, a man by the name of Margolis, was beaten and kicked off the train. In the city of Lwow, after the Poles won back the city from the Ukrainian rebels, they organized a pogrom in which many Jews were killed. Demobilized army personnel instead of going home and returning to civilian life, were roaming around in villages and cities, destroying and looting Jewish property. The Polish authorities were weak and also not anxious to stop these excesses whenever it affected the Jewish population.

These pogroms caused many young Jewish men to leave Poland in search of a better future in Western Europe or in the U.S. But for the remaining Jews, there was uncertainty in their future.

The blood libel in Strzyzow

It happened in the spring of 1919 on a Monday, the seventh day of Passover. It was the second day of the Easter holiday. (In Europe, the Christians celebrate Easter for two days). Before noon during the morning services, two Polish women – one in her middle age and the other a young woman, burst into the Beit HaMidrash which was filled with worshippers. The women demanded vociferously the return of the older woman's fourteen-year old daughter. They searched everywhere, under tables, benches and when they had finished searching, they left. Some people ignored it but some took it very seriously knowing that such incidents could cause a tragedy for the entire community.

The same afternoon, the Chief of the Police appeared in the house of Reb Levi Itzhok Schiff accompanied by the older woman who earlier had searched the Beit HaMidrash, and a little girl of about fourteen years of age.

The Police asked the little girl if she recognized the Jew who had locked her up in the basement of this house, from which she claimed to have managed to escape through a small window.

[Page 64]

The Places where the alleged blood libel took place

This is the northeast side of the market place in Strzyzow

1. The small opening where the girl allegedly was held.
2. The stoop where Golda Horowitz was sitting and waiting for her father to wake up.
3. The window where Reb Levi Itzhok Schiff lived.
4. The community bathhouse.

The building belonged to Eliezer Glatt

[Page 65]

The Chief of Police ordered the Schiff family to line up and asked the girl to identify the man who had dragged her into the basement. When the girl hesitated to identify anybody, the Chief of Police tried to persuade her to point at Reb Levi Itzhok Schiff. Luckily, the police could not convince the girl and they left. On their way out they saw the woman, Golda Horowitz, sitting on the stoop of her father's house. Suddenly the girl pointed at the redhead woman that she recognized as the person who had dragged her into the basement. This woman suffered a lot during the war. She was struggling to bring up two small children on her own because her husband was in the U.S. and could not help her being on the opposite side of the warring countries. On this holiday, she had come to visit her father, Reb Joshua Selligman. Her father was asleep and she had decided to wait until he woke up. Next door lived the milkman, Reb Israel Aaron Berger. When he heard the commotion outside, he came out to see what was going on. He too was read-headed and the girl pointed at him as well claiming that Berger and Gold Horowitz were the two people, both red-headed, that had abducted her and dragged her into the basement. According to the girl, she was called into the Horowiz family house to remove the candlesticks from the table. The plotters of the blood libel did not know that there was a difference between a regular Sabbath and a holiday which fell on a weekday. On a Sabbath, Jews are forbidden to handle candlesticks but not so on a holiday. After she did what she was asked to do, she said the woman fed her with milk and matzo and afterwards she was dragged by the red-headed woman with the help of the red-headed man into the basement. When she screamed, they gagged her.

Both Golda Horowitz and Israel Berger were arrested. Soon the police produced an eyewitness, a semi-retarded man, who used to sleep in the Jewish bath-house. The witness claimed that he just happened to be sitting nearby and saw the entire episode.

Within hours, a mob gathered in the market place and began to terrorize Jewish homes, attacking the Jews who were on their way to the evening services. Most of those who suffered were those in the Beit HaMidrash because they were an easy target. The mob just burst into the sanctuary and began to hit everyone indiscriminately. But the young Jews did not surrender meekly. They fought back and repulsed the attackers. They pushed them out of the Beit HaMidrash. Meanwhile, the news of the libel spread to villages around Strzyzow and the peasants joined the city hooligans who quietly surrounded the Beit HaMidrash, blocked the exits and some went up to the women's gallery. Simultaneously, they started a rock throwing attack at the people inside. The beating and looting went on until midnight when the mob got tired and went home.

Early the next morning, my sister Chaya Berglass and Aryi Diamand secretly slipped out of town and went to Rzeszow, a large city nearby, to appeal for help. Their appearance caused fear and frightened the local Jews so they decided that a delegation of Jewish representatives with Rabbi Nathan Levin would turn to the Polish authorities and ask for help.

[Page 66]

Strzyzow and its inhabitants

But soon the Jews realized that no help would be forthcoming. The delegation immediately departed by train to Krakow to intervene with the regional authorities with the help of Dr. Schwarzbart, the Chief Secretary of the Zionist Central Committee.

While the search for help was going on, in Strzyzow the pogrom continued into the second and third day. On the third day, a military unit arrived in town and order was restored.

During these three days, two hundred people, men, women and children were wounded and one man killed. Reb Alexander Kimmel, of blessed memory, was killed. A Polish neighbour had a grudge against him over a fence dispute so he took advantage of the situation and killed him.

The blood libel was planned in advance, preparing the alleged victim as a live witness and a second witness who claimed he saw the crime was committed. Who the plotters were was never found out. A short time later, the stepfather of the girl was killed and rumours were that he knew too much and had been opposed to putting his girl through such an ordeal. The facts were that the Police Chief and the local priest with the local politicians were involved.

It was evident from the first moment by the way the Chief behaved in the house of the Schiff family when he tried to coax the girl to pointing at Reb Levi Itzhok as the man who took her to the basement. The police never bothered to investigate who the plotters were and the Jews were troubled with the upcoming trial. The local non-Jewish population was inclined to believe in the whole story fanatically that the Jews were using Christian blood to prepare matzos for Passover. It was remarkable how far this belief penetrated their minds. Even a person like the mayor, Dr. Patryn, when approached to do something about the pogrom, responded: "Why did you need the whole problem?" meaning that he believed the story and he was considered to be a liberal and an intelligent man.

After the pogrom was suppressed, the city was calm but tense. The Jews were afraid that the smallest disturbance would bring back another pogrom. Another delegation went to Krakow, representatives of the Kehillah, Reb Abraham Tenzer, and Reb Chaim Yehuda Horowitz on behalf of his father, Reb Alter Zev and my sister Chaya Berglass, who spoke Polish very well. In Krakow, they recruited Dr. Itzhok Schwarzbart, the Zionist leader, to intervene with the authorities about the plot and expressed their fear of another bloodbath. And the delegation's anxiety was justified as you will read later on.

A few weeks after the pogrom, a Jewish self-defence group which was active in Krakow and its vicinity, came to Strzyzow to support and protect the Jews. At the same time, a Polish military unit arrived in town. Their arrival had no connection with the Jewish group. Apparently, the Polish authorities knew that something was brewing. The local Polish authorities did not allow the Jewish defence group to act, claiming that they would cause anger among the Polish people seeing armed Jews.

On Tuesday, the market day in Strzyzow, an unusually large crowd arrived from near and far. Since this was springtime, the Visloka River was over flowing and the passage into the town was limited to only two narrow bridges from the east and south. The roads from the north and the west were impassable.

[Page 67]

Therefore, the Polish officer ordered his soldiers to block the bridges and prevent the crowd from coming to town. When the mob tried to push their way into town, the officer warned them that he had orders to shoot and begged them to avoid bloodshed. That is how the town was fortunate enough to have escaped another pogrom.

Other cities in the area did suffer. In Kolbuszow, a nearby town, ten Jewish people were killed and hundreds wounded.

Mrs. Golda Horowitz and Reb Aaron Berger were put on trial for attempted murder but the religious aspect of the story was not mentioned by the prosecution. It would have looked ridiculous to mention that the Jews were using Christian blood for matzos. The Jews were represented by the most famous criminal lawyer in Poland, Dr. Leib Landau from Przemysl. Although the two witnesses for the prosecution testified against the accused, the two were freed for lack of evidence. The two Poles who were tried for murdering Reb Alexander Kimmel during the pogrom were also freed. The Pole who killed Kimmel died in a mental hospital and the witness who testified in the blood libel was around for many years. He kept coming into Jewish homes begging for food, and as usual, people soon forgot what he had done to the Jews. The pogroms and the blood libel left an impression on the town for many years to come. After a Jewish delegate to the Polish Parliament protested about this incident, a commission was nominated to investigate the pogroms and the blood libel. The commission came to Strzyzow and questioned some witnesses but nothing was resolved.

Reb Alexander Kimmel's widow, who was left with small children and without any means of support, immigrated to the U.S. Golda Horowitz also immigrated to the U.S. and Reb Israel Aaron Berger moved with his family to another town.

Soon people in Strzyzow forgot the Austrian government and began to adjust to life under Polish rule. In the first years of the Polish independence, Jews had their own elected delegates to the Polish Parliament. In the local government, Jews always supported someone who pretended to be friendly with them. Culturally, Jews did not mix with the Poles.

The situation of the Jews in Poland between the two World Wars was not too bad. Politically, the Zionists strengthened their influence among the Polish Jewry. Economically, the Jews may have been better off than under the Austrian rule until the beginning of the thirties. Then, anti-Semitism swept through Poland, an anti-Jewish campaign started again in which the Poles were urged to boycott the Jewish businesses. The Polish government tolerated it and did nothing to stop the campaign. In Strzyzow, a few Christian stores were opened as a result of that campaign.

The Jewish farmers in the villages were forced out and many of them moved to the cities, economically ruined. The mood among the Poles was anti-Jewish and wherever they could, they demonstrated their feelings. In Strzyzow, the people liked to spend their Sabbath afternoons in the woods which belonged to Count Wolkowitzki. Suddenly, a sign appeared: "Entrance to Jews forbidden!" After my intervention, the sign was removed. The market day used to be postponed whenever it fell on a Jewish holiday but suddenly an ordinance was issued by the city that it would not be postponed anymore. After a few market days with the Jews, they relented to the postponement again because the farmers did not come to town. Some Poles threatened the Jews by saying: "Wait –Hitler is coming soon and that will be the end of you". In school, the Jewish students felt the hatred and were defenseless.

[Page 68]

The majority of the Poles continued the formal relationship until the outbreak of World War II.

These I will remember
by Shlomo Yahalomi

In memory of the young students and teachers who dwelt in the Beit HaMidrash and studied the Torah.

The synagogues in the cities of Poland, Galicia and the Lithuanian Yeshivot were the creators of the Jewish soul. Between the walls of these institutions you could find people of all ages and walks of life – the poor and the rich. Everybody studied Torah, the holy books of the Bible with all its commentaries, day and night without interruption. There were some young men who considered studying the Torah as a permanent occupation and they were supported by their families. The less fortunate could study only in the morning and evening hours because during the day they had to struggle for their daily bread. Some students studied individually and some in groups. The younger boys never hesitated to bother their elders with questions and asking for help. In Strzyzow, as in all other cities in Galicia, the Beit HaMidrash was always full of people learning on their own or teaching others. The long rectangular tables were always cluttered with open books and around these books; people were discussing various religious problems and response. There were young men who studied all night. The majority came at four in the morning to take up their holy studies. They studied everything that was written from the early sages to the latest rabbinical geniuses. The young men who studied in the Beit HaMidrash or kloyz were obligated to take care of the books and also to obtain funds for new books. Every Friday, all the books were shelved by category.

It is impossible to list all the names of the students and scholars who spent time in the Beit HaMidrash or kloyz in Strzyzow, from the early rabbis, generations ago, to the latest generation who perished in the Holocaust. The geniuses and religious people, who dwelt in the synagogues and later graduated to become famous rabbis, would make a very long list. I will only mention a few starting with rabbi Moshe Teitelbaum – the author of the book "Yismach Moshe"; rabbi Aryeh Leib – the author of "Otot Hahamayim"; rabbi Tzvi Elimelech Shapiro whose most important book was the "Beni Yisoschor and several other books. Rabbi Tzvi Hersh Shapiro – author of "Darkei Tshuva"; Reb Naphtali Nutman, author of "Toldot Noah" and many more famous rabbis from the early centuries. There were scholars who studied just to fulfil their own thirst for knowledge without the desire to win fame such as: Reb Moshe Krym; Reb Mendel Mannis Friedman, the son of Reb Moshe Samuel, the teacher who taught pupils for many years.

[Page 69]

He was a righteous man, gentle, with a wonderful disposition and patience to explain the most complicated passages in the Talmud to his students. Reb Mendel Mannis Friedman's son survived and is now a member in kibbutz Tirat Tzvi, one of the biggest religious kibbutzim in Israel. Another son of Reb Moshe Samuel was Reb Pinchos Friedman who married the daughter of the Assistant Rabbi from Frysztak. He authored the book "Meah Kshita". In an introduction to this book, Rabbi Shlomo Shapiro wrote that the author is a young man who knows the Torah by heart. Reb Pinchos authored a second book by the name of "Divrei Yehonathan" – a commentary on the Five Books of Moses. I would also like to mention Reb Moshe Nuremberg who left Strzyzow to be assistant rabbi in Keln, a city with the biggest Jewish community in Germany.

A few of the young men in the class before us who spent time and studied G-d's teachings in the synagogues of Strzyzow were: Reb Mendel Groskopf, a scholar, a G-d fearing man, and humble, who gave charity discretely without fanfare. After his marriage, he moved to a nearby town, Brzostek. When the Nazi occupied his town, they selected him to be the Jewish community leader. Soon the Nazi Chief ordered him to prepare a list of all Jews who were physically able to work. He made a list with only one name – his own and was executed on the spot. (The translator of this memorial book visited Reb Mendel Groskopf in his home during the Nazi occupation when he was on his way to Strzyzow to take farewell from his father, of blessed memory, before his escape to Russia. It was Hoshana Raba, the seventh day of Sukkoth, 1939. He arrived early in the morning before the services which were held illegally in his house with barely a minyan. The tears of the worshippers were so heart-breaking that the scene will never be forgotten and will follow him all his life. They needed an Etrog and a Lulav to recite the Hoshanot but there was none. There was only a dry Lulav from the previous year which reminded them of better times). I wish also to commemorate Reb Mendel Sturm, the son of Yacov. A humble and righteous man, a Talmudist and knowledgeable in all religious strictures. After he married a girl from another town, he moved there where he shared the fate of all his brethren.

The brothers Yacov and Mendel Rosen who never became angry at anyone and were always in good spirits, always hoped for better times to come. They were sincere G-d fearing people. Further on in this book, more will be said about them.

Reb Wolf Mandel, one of the finest young men, knowledgeable in the depths of Torah and all the commentaries, always shared his knowledge with others. He was friendly and smiling to everybody. He loved singing Hassidic melodies, especially the happy ones.

Reb Moshe Yacov Schwartzman, the leader of the Agudat Israel, was a devoted Jew who gave much of his spare time for the organization. He was an intelligent young man, always willing to give a helping hand when Torah education was concerned, especially for the girls' education. He helped to open the Bais Yacov School for girls.

Reb Chaim Friedman, one of my closest friends, was the grandson of Reb Joseph Mordechai – the Assistant Rabbi in Strzyzow for many years. Reb Chaim made his grandfather proud of having a grandson like him.

[Page 70]

He learned to be a shochet and later became a shochet after his father, Reb Leib Friedman, retired. Pinchos, his brother, was also a G-d fearing, sharp-minded individual.

Wolf Zilberman who dwelt in the Beit HaMidrash day and night always discussed the Talmud and defended his position fiercely.

Aaron Samuel Beitler was a fledgling Hebrew poet with a gentle soul. The brothers Itzhok, Mendel, Tzvi Elimelech and Yacov Goldman, the sons of Avrehmale Goldman were all dear and likeable. Itzhok was a mathematician who could put together a Jewish calendar for hundreds of years ahead. He once met the poet Chaim Nachman Bialik and after a conversation with Itzhok, Bialik was overwhelmed about Itzhok's knowledge and intelligence in many subjects, besides the teachings of the holy books. All of the Goldman brothers secretly read Yiddish and world literature.

Yacov Landesman who, although he lost his father as a child, grew up to be one of the best young men. His home environment was not of the best because of his mother's second marriage. Still, he was able to overcome all of the hardships and turned out to be a Talmudic genius.

Elazar Loos, a very humble but smart, soft-speaking and straight-forward young man, survived the Holocaust physically but was mentally impaired. A few months after liberation from the concentration camps, he put an end to his life. His sister in Eretz Israel never had a chance to stretch out her helping arm to him.

Meir Schiff, Samuel Schreiber, Pinchos Kracher, Israel Hauben, Motel Weitman, Paltiel Kneller and his brothers Itzhok and Eisik, Mordechai and Hersh Tenzer, Shimon Hochdorf, David Bernstein, Joseph Mordechai and David Hersh Schiff and Meir Mordechai Schwartzman were young men, the best that Strzyzow had. A promising young generation which was capable and ready to follow their elders to continue the Jewish community life were all so untimely cut-down in the prime of their lives and in the cruelest way. May G-d avenge their untainted blood.

The people who always studied the Torah
by Shlomo Yahalomi

Almost all the adults in Strzyzow, no matter how busy they were making a living, found time to study Torah. Whoever did not know how to study at least recited a few chapters of King David's psalms daily. About twenty or thirty people regularly took part in learning Mishanyoth every evening. Reb Shalom Schwartzman, the teacher, possessed a unique talent to teach and explain the most complicated subjects in a way that simple people would understand. Every Sabbath afternoon, Reb Chaim Yacov Nuremberg taught Midrash, the chapter of the week with its commentaries and books of ethics. He was a master teacher. He used to tell all kinds of interesting stories related to his teachings and the simple folk loved him for it. On Friday nights, people used to gather in groups and study Torah and Chassidic books. The teacher of this study-group was the writer of these lines. Afterwards, tales about Hassidic rabbis followed to which the participants listened with great enthusiasm.

All this took place in the Beit HaMidrash. The best people in town, whether rich or poor, took part in these studies. People like Reb David Wiener, Reb Chaim Mandel, Reb Ephraim Kneller, the brothers Yacov and Mendel Rosen and even a man like Reb Baruch Berglass, who was one of the wealthiest people in town, spent every day until noon studying the Scriptures. These were the inhabitants of the town.

[Page 71]

Of course, the list is not complete. We can go on and on. We did not mention Reb Abraham Tenzer who studied religious philosophy, Reb Shalom Schwartzman who studied the Zohar every day and last but not least, the town's most famous intellectual, Reb Alter Nechemiah who studied and knew the Prophets and the commentaries on them.

The Yeshiva Etz Chaim in Strzyzow
by Shlomo Yahalomi

In 1930, by the initiative of a few young men, a small Yeshiva was established in Strzyzow. Even though the Yeshiva was under the auspices of the Agudat Israel, it succeeded in enrolling students from Hassidic families, followers of rabbis from Bobow, Belz and Munkatch, and also from the religious group – Mizrachi. They taught Talmud with daily commentaries and on Friday nights or Sabbath afternoons, the Pentateuch was taught. The Assistant Rabbi, Yacov Shpalter, Reb Chaim Mandel, Reb Mendel Rosen and the writer of these memoirs, were the teachers. Every Thursday, the students were examined in the presence of the fathers and supporters. The Yeshiva did not last long because the enthusiasm of the students and the teachers which at the beginning was strong soon faded. Only a few students survived the Holocaust.

Besides the Yeshiva, there was a Talmud Torah Society which provided religious education for the children of the poor. Funds for this purpose had to be raised continuously year-round. Collections were made at weddings and other family celebrations. The Talmud Torah Society members kept a watchful eye on the quality of the teachings and examined the students from time-to-time. The outstanding students were awarded small symbolic prizes such as a prayer book or a four-cornered ritual garment with tzitziyot. The Society also urged the melamdim to hand out report cards. Boys who were supported by the Talmud Torah Society had to obey to certain rules and ways of behaviour. These rules were mentioned earlier in this book in the chapter on education in Strzyzow.

The Cheders and the Melamdim
by Shlomo Yahalomi

Many used to criticize the cheders of the earlier generations. Even now, there are plenty of critics. The complaints were that the teachers had no pedagogic experience and the cheders were not sufficiently clean. However, even though part of the criticism was justified, it has to be pointed out that, although the teachers had not studied in teacher's seminaries or universities, they did have a wonderful way of interpretation and exceeded the professionals of today with their skills. There were also cheders which were immaculate. It is a fact that no one can deny that the alumni of cheders turned out to be scholars and educated men. Therefore, the teachers deserve a monument for their achievements. A few of them have already been mentioned and I will tell about a few more teachers that taught me or were close to me personally.

[Page 72]

Reb Mordechai Rosenbaum
by Shlomo Yahalomi

They called him Reb Mordechai melamed. His silver beard and the look in his eyes gave the impression of a very strict teacher, and he was. He did not spare the whip. In his cheder the children learned to read in a prayer book and as soon as a child knew how to read, he was immediately transferred to another teacher. His wife Basha helped him with the children in a very energetic way. From his entire family, only one daughter with her family survived because they had immigrated before the Holocaust.

Reb Yechezkiel Gorgil (Adam's Apple)
by Shlomo Yahalomi

He taught the Five Books of Moses with Rashi's commentary and the beginning of Talmud. Gorgil was his nickname and very few in Strzyzow knew his last name. He was also called "Yechezkiel Godower" because he came to Strzyzow from the village Godowa. He was a teacher par excellence. His method of explanation was remarkable especially when he taught the children about how the Israelites on their way from Egypt built the Tabernacle and about the breast-plate which the High Priests wore. He drew a blueprint and explained it to the children in such detail that it undoubtedly remained in the children's minds even after they grew up. I still remember a little speech he used to make before he began to teach the Talmud.

"Dear Children. Have no fear for the studying that we are about to begin. Nobody knows before he learns and he never regrets it afterwards". Illiterate people, he used to say, are like dry wood ready for burning. Of course, he did not spare the whip either. When somebody did something unbecoming to a Jewish boy, he would call him over with a melodic voice and tell him the following:

"If you voluntarily remove your pants and lay down like a nice little boy, you will get only two lashes but if I will have to use force, you will get five lashes over your behind…"

On one occasion, I too almost got to be a victim of such a lashing. It happened when we decided to play a game of imitating a gentile funeral. We picked on student who would pretend that he was dead. We dug a shallow grave and buried him. Next, we covered him with boards exactly according to the rules. After a few seconds, the deceased panicked and began to scream. Neighbours hearing his screaming came out to the rescue. And because I was the ring-leader of this action, the teacher was going to give me a lashing ceremony, but my friend the "deceased" begged Reb Yechezkiel not to punish me because he forgave me. And that is how I escaped the punishing ordeal.

Reb Yechezkiel was a Hassid of the rabbi from Sadigora and he had the support of the Hassidim of that rabbi. All of his offspring perished in the Holocaust but he died years before. After he passed away, his son-in-law took over the cheder.

[Page 73]

Reb Yosl from Brzozow
by Shlomo Yahalomi

Reb Yosl the teacher from Brzozow was one of the best Strzyzow ever had. He taught Talmud only to the best students in town. Reb Yosl was well respected not only because he was an out-of-town teacher but also because he taught the students the principles of mathematics and other secular subjects. He also had a wonderful singing voice. He knew all the liturgical music and songs from famous cantors around the world. Reb Yosl knew how to read music which he taught his students. Whenever he was invited to a wedding, he was always asked to entertain with his sweet voice and the chorus of his students.

Reb Yosl was a pious Jew and a good teacher. One of his many daughters survived the Holocaust and lives in Israel.

Reb Israel Leib Karp
by Shlomo Yahalomi

Reb Israel was a teacher without any outstanding qualifications. He himself did not know too much but just enough to teach the eight to ten year-olds. But he did teach the children all the ritual rules and customs which other teachers ignored. He was poor but a Hassid of the rabbi from Sadigora so the Hassidim of that rabbi made him a melamed. Reb Israel Leib was a soft-spoken man, never raising his voice to a child. Therefore, the discipline in cheder was weak. However, in the rare occasion when he did get angry, he slapped on the face with such a force that the child never forgot. Reb Israel Leib was a G-d fearing man and tried very hard to teach the children and to satisfy the parents. There were a few other teachers who taught in Strzyzow but they did not leave any strong impression on those whom they taught.

The Agudat Israel
by Shlomo Yahalomi

The Agudat Israel was founded in Strzyzow in 1922. It was not easy for the organizers to overcome all the obstacles and hardships in establishing the party in town. There was opposition from every direction. To begin with, the majority in Strzyzow were followers of the rabbi from Munkatch who opposed any party or organization whether Zionist or Orthodox. The plain religious people claimed that they had no need for a religious party because everyone was religious anyway.

The Orthodox activists realized that the Zionist idea kept making inroads rapidly among the youth and they did not want to lose their chance to influence the religious youth.

The Agudat Israel did succeed in influencing the strictly orthodox Hassidic youth, contrary to the opinion of the writer of this article who thought it was wrong to engage the Beit HaMidrash boys in party politics. In the late thirties, I realized that I was wrong when I found out that many of these Beit HaMidrash dwellers belonged already to the Zionist religious organization.

At the helm of the party was Reb Yacov Itzhok Bernstein, a Hassid of the famous rabbi Tzvi Elimelech from Blazow, a very religious man and the devoted leaders were: Reb Naphtali Chaim Halberstam, the son-in-law

[Page 74]

The Bais Yacov School for girls in Strzyzow
The girl with the X over her head is Gitl Feldmaus, the translator's cousin

[Page 75]

of Rabbi Later Zev Horowitz, a very pleasant man who acted quietly but decisively; Reb Moshe Schwartzman – the secretary and a capable, talented young man who was the moving spirit of the party and Reb Joel Glickman, a scholar and a G-d fearing man who was a noted leader of the party. He and Reb Yacov Itzhok Bernstein acted with devotion. Their goal was to keep the Jewish youths strictly religious.

The Agudat Israel in Strzyzow helped to obtain qualified teachers for the Bais Yacov, a girls' school. They also kept a watchful eye on the melamdim and tried to modernize the teaching system in Strzyzow.

The relationship between the Agudat Israel and the Zionists
by Shlomo Yahalomi

The two opposing parties in Strzyzow had a correct relationship without animosity. They opposed each other ideologically but in a peaceful way, unlike in other cities in Galicia. Both the Zionists and the Agudat Israel were strictly observant Orthodox Jews. The only difference between them was that the Zionists strove §to build and to settle immediately in the Jewish Homeland in Eretz Israel and the Agudat Israel wanted to wait for the Messiah to come. The only issue that really split the community into two camps was the rabbinical dispute.

There were families where fathers supported Rabbi Alter Zev and the sons Rabbi Nechemiah Shapiro, or vice-versa. Women had no influence in the rabbinical dispute. This was strictly a man's world in those days. Many times during the elections to the Kehillah, a father who supported one rabbi would run against his son who supported the other rabbi.

[Page 76]

One among thousands
by Moshe Mussler

It is hard for me to imagine how our shtetl looks now without the Jews. It seems to me that if the Jews have gone then there is no justification for Strzyzow's existence. Our roots were there for generations. We built it. We developed it. The non-Jewish inhabitants looked like outsiders when they were in the centre of town. The air in the streets and in the alleys was breathing with Yiddishkeit.

Friday at sunset when the shutters of the stores came down and the Jewish stores were closed, you could feel the holiness of the Sabbath had arrived. It came down from heaven. In all my wanderings in this world, I never had such feelings similar to those I felt on the Sabbath day in Strzyzow.

Reb Eisik, the old sexton, started his stroll from door-to-door equipped with a wooden mallet in his hand knocking on every door and announcing that the holy Sabbath had arrived. He called out loudly. "Let's go to G-d's house to welcome the Sabbath Queen". Everyone hurried not to be late, Heaven forbid, and not to desecrate the Sabbath.

The peasants from the villages who parked their carts in the market place were also rushing home not wanting to disturb the holiness of the Jewish Sabbath. The polish government clerks who, at the end of the day were returning home from their offices were also rushing through the Jewish centre. Even though they were the rulers of the land, nevertheless, at this time of the day, they felt out of place among the Jews.

Those who were late finishing their attendance in the bath-house were rushing home while others were already on their way to the synagogues all spruced up in their best clothes. Many wore silk frocks and the traditional shtreimel worn by almost everyone on the Sabbath in Galicia. The simple people, tailors, cobblers and village peddlers all worshipped in shul where Reb Mordechai, the tailor, led the services and Reb Leib Sternberg pleasantly sang the L'cha Dodi welcoming the Sabbath Queen. The services in shul did not take very long because the worshippers were tired from the labour they had done all week and they were more than happy to hurry home to a festive meal with a little schnapps which their wives had prepared.

In Beit HaMidrash, the pace was slower. Everybody recited the Songs-of-Songs. The words came out from their depths of heart with a sigh and happiness simultaneously. The congregation waited for the Rabbi's arrival. But he was not in a hurry either. When the rabbi finally arrived, everybody rose from his seat and the entire congregation began to chant the evening prayers.

From the open windows of the kloyz the sweet voice of Reb Samuel Moshe was heard singing the Sabbath song "L'cha Dodi". The sound of his voice penetrated deeply into everyone's soul. These are the unforgettable memories which I remember from my childhood about a Sabbath in my shtetl.

And what happened to this town? To my shtetl?

The shul turned into a warehouse, the Beid HaMidrash where our parents spilled their tears begging and praying before the Almighty was levelled to the ground. From the gravestones, sidewalks were built. The streets and alleys were orphaned – no more Jewish children playing in these places. Teachers are not teaching anymore. Strzyzow share the fate of many thousands of other cities in Galicia.

[Page 77]

May their memory never be forgotten by her sons.

When did the Jews settle in Strzyzow
by Moshe Mussler

When we were young, none of us cared about the historical past of Strzyzow as a Jewish town. To my best knowledge, the Kehillah never had a "Pinkas" which is a sort of diary and nothing was ever recorded. The only information we could gather at the time when we planned to write these memoirs came from different books authored by different Rabbis in Galicia who, in their correspondence and response, mentioned Strzyzow on different occasions. From several remarks in these books, we learned more or less when the Jews settled in Strzyzow. We assume that much valuable data was destroyed during the big fire in 1895, in which more than half of the town burnt down including the Kehillah house and the Beit HaMidrash. Not too many of us ever bothered to record anything important about Strzyzow, a fact which we now regret. However, we will try our best.

There were not many Jews who were interested in historical research to supply us with data about when and how Jewish life began in Strzyzow. In a Hebrew quarterly magazine "Zion" we found a map of Jewish communities in Galicia in which Strzyzow was included. This magazine was printed at the end of the seventeenth century. My father, who liked to study the past, found a gravestone dated 1650. The most convincing proof about the time of the establishment of the Jewish community in Strzyzow is the shul which is still intact. If, to judge by the style, the shul was built in the year 1600, in those years every public building was built like a fortress to protect the inhabitants from outside invaders such as the Tatars and the Swedes. The thickness of the walls is about two metres and is all built in solid rock.

There were repairs made at the end of the nineteenth century after the big fire in which the roof, tables, benches and the Holy Ark were burnt. Except for the walls, only the big menorah which weighed over two hundred kilos and a few smaller candelabras which were hanging from the vaulted ceiling, survived.

At the right side entrance door into the shul, an iron ring extended from the wall at the level of a man's height. Apparently, the ring was used to tie up the violators of the Jewish customs and all who passed them had to spit on them.

When entering, you had to descend a few steps to fulfil a quotation from the Psalms: "Out of the depths I call to thee O Lord". The bimah was at the centre of the shul to which you had to ascend seven steps. The acoustics were excellent even though the ceiling was very high. During the High Holidays when the shul was packed with worshippers and they raised their voices to pray, the prayers were heard outside like the roar of the sea.

The first and second cemetery was close to each other but the third cemetery was about two hundred metres away. They were all ancient cemeteries from earlier centuries and were not used in our time.

[Page 78]

In my youth, I would have been able to read the inscriptions and dates on the gravestones but there was a superstitious belief that reading from the gravestones would cause forgetfulness.

In the month before the High Holidays, it is customary to visit the graves of relatives so I used to go out with a collection box to collect charity from people who were visiting their relatives' graves. But I never say anybody visiting these three cemeteries. Only once was I approached by someone from another city to help locate her mother's grave. This woman was only ten years old when her mother died years ago which meant the first half of the nineteenth century.

All the houses surrounding the market place were almost new, rebuilt after the big fire in the nineteenth century. In contrast, the houses in the alley where most of the melamdim lived were old shacks. The oldest one was Reb Yehuda Nosen's house which, to this day, I cannot understand how this house did not collapse. Apparently, there were miracles in those days. The cheder of Reb Eli Dovid was very old and I think it was built at the time when Queen Maria Theresa was sitting on her throne.

The conclusion to all of this is: It is very hard for me to establish the exact date of the establishment of the Jewish community in Strzyzow.

It breaks my heart that we do not know exactly when the Jews settled in Strzyzow but the sorrow is even greater in that Strzyzow ceased to exist in our time and shared the fate of the rest of the Jewish communities in Europe. The earth is saturated with the blood of our parents, brothers and sisters.

"Earth! Do not conceal their blood to prevent from hearing their voice of lamentations".

First rays of progress in shtetl
by Moshe Mussler

It is hard to pinpoint exactly when enlightenment and progress reached our town. Even a researcher in history would not have been able to establish the exact date. In any case, it did not happen before the end of the nineteenth century. When the twentieth century began, a wave of enlightenment spread all over Galicia including our shtetl Strzyzow. This wave caused a cultural revolution in Strzyzow's quiet life.

Like many other cities in Galicia, Strzyzow was very conservative, religious and family-oriented. People never travelled and had little knowledge of the wide-world which existed outside of the town. Echoes from the outside world did begin to filer in at the beginning of the twentieth century.

The dwellers of the Beit HaMidrash began to neglect their studying of the Torah. These studies did not satisfy their thirst for secular knowledge which was not available on the bookshelves of the Beit HaMidrash. As a result, they began to read stealthily Yiddish and modern Hebrew books.

The knowledge of Polish and German was also very important for those who decided to obtain secular education.

In a very short time, without the help of any teachers, we began our secular education. Most of the young people in town participated in this so-called "Haskalah" movement. Only a few sons of very Hassidic families remained outside the wave of enlightenment for fear of their parents.

[Page 79]

One of the first steps by a few bold young men was to establish a library. The library contained Hebrew, Yiddish, Polish and German books. Polish books were introduced to pacify the local authorities and German books were there to assure the licence from the Central Austrian Government, knowing that they would not dare to hinder the opening of a library in the official language.

I have to confess that the anxiety of the Hassidic segment demonstrated by their opposition to the opening of a library as well as the Zionist movement was justified. Many of us, after learning certain things in the secular books, started to ignore a few traditions. Of course, we did not turn atheists right away.

There were a few among us who progressed in their secular knowledge so much so that the books available in our library were not enough to satisfy our hunger for more education. Therefore, they left town. But even so, I do not know of anyone who reached any fame in the literary or educational field.

When the Zionist movement first began in Strzyzow and the first lecturers from out of town were invited, we could never find a place for them to speak. Once we had to force our way into a locked Beit HaMidrash when Dr. Frenkel came to Strzyzow from the Central Zionist Committee. Dr. Frenkel was later a teacher in a Tel Aviv High School. When the speaker began to speak, little by little, people gathered out of curiosity and what they heard was surprisingly satisfactory. This was the first time in Strzyzow that progress won over extremism and from there on, things went easier. The ice was broken.

The thirst for secular education and knowledge about the world of literature was so strong that a peculiar incident which happened to me comes to mind. My friend, Itzhok Berglass was the only person who could afford to buy his own books. For this reason, everybody treasured books so much that nobody would even think of loaning a book to another person. Itzhok Berglass had in his possession a book of Chaim Nachman Bialik's poems. I wanted to read it so much that when I found out that he gave this book to the bookbinder for repair, I stealthily went into the workshop and spent the better part of the night reading the whole book. I was so happy and enjoyed so much Bialik's poems that I could not fall asleep until morning. How can we forget those long winter nights sitting around the hot stove, or the summer Friday nights when a group of young men enjoyed having what is now called an Oneg Shabbath?

We used to sing all the songs we knew about Zion and Jerusalem and we then discussed the latest editorials in the Hebrew papers to which one of us had subscribed to in secret. Who could imagine that some of us would live to see an established Jewish Homeland called Israel? If one of the readers of these lines is interested in knowing in greater detail about how renaissance of Hebrew and the Zionist movement began, let him read the book of Shalom Yacov Agnon "Young and Old".

[Page 80]

There were rumours in town that a few young men had some modern ideas and progressive thinking but would not dare to share these with others such as Reb Alter Nechemiah and Hersh Pfeffer. Also, the son of the assistant rabbi, Reb Alter Ezra Seidman, because of his progressiveness, was forced to leave Strzyzow when his father found out that he was skipping prayer services and somebody saw him reading a forbidden book. Still, progress made its inroads in Strzyzow. The writer of the memoirs was also swept away with the waves and left Strzyzow. I never saw my shtetl gain but it always remained in my memories.

The forbearers of the Holocaust
by Moshe Mussler

Although more than sixty years have passed since that time, still, jitters go through my body when I recall one spring evening when I was sitting on my father's lap in our store when suddenly a rock flew in through the display window. My father hurriedly dropped the shutters and went into the backroom for safety.

The sound of smashed windows and the screaming of the mob were accompanied by looting and beating of Jews until midnight.

The only policeman who served the town disappeared somewhere in a tavern. And no authority was in sight as though the earth had suddenly swallowed them.

That night, nobody slept in his bed. Clothed, we sat in apprehension that at any moment, the mob would attack us.

Such waiting was unnerving and one does not forget it for the rest of one's life.

The next day was market day in a nearby shtetl called Frysztak. All the local Jews whose livelihood depended on these market days could not afford to stay at home and not travel to the market.

After a few hours, they returned with bandaged heads and other wounds. The pogrom had reached them there too. Peasants who usually came to the market to do their shopping at this time did not shop but looted the Jewish stalls and beat the Jews. The Jews were defenceless.

Days of fear and anxiety went through our shtetl until a military unit came and restored order.

Although I was a little boy at the time, right there and then I made up my mind that I would not live in Strzyzow anymore, or for that matter, in Galicia. I realized then that there was no future in Poland for the Jews.

When World War I ended, I was a war prisoner in Italy. Returning home after Poland won her independence, I could not recognize my little town. Everybody was depressed. Sad faces walked around and very few of my contemporaries were present. I could not take it anymore, such sadness and helplessness so one dark night, I turned around and left Strzyzow – my birthplace – never to return. I never missed it because it was not my motherland – to me it was my step-motherland.

[Page 81]

To you, Kaddish I say my dear shtetl
by Pinchos Klotz Aloni

When I decided to write a bundle of memories about my childhood which I spent in Strzyzow, I faced a difficult dilemma. How to describe the years of my childhood? Should the impressions be written the way I saw them as a child or the way I see them in the present? I left Strzyzow thirty–two years ago. I might not have become wiser but I became more experienced than before. Therefore, my memories might seem childish and naïve.

I believe that writing about what I have gone through might, in a certain way, reflect the lives of others from the same town because life in a little shtetl was monotonous, eventless whether small or large. Whatever happened, it happened more or less the same to everyone with minor variations.

Today, for instance, if I reminisce about how we spent our Friday nights, it seems a bit old–fashioned. But then, we all were deeply impressed and could not forget those nights so soon.

I recall when we used to gather on wintery Friday nights in the warm Beit HaMidrash by the weak light of two or three flickering candles which were on the verge of expiring. Or, on the summer nights, on the lawn in front of the shul, telling stories about the righteous, the rabbis and miracle performers, or stories about ghosts and spirits which the childish souls absorbed with jitters, believing every word. We visualized all kinds of imaginations and scary things. We looked out of the corner of our eyes toward the old cemetery and it seemed we saw or heard something. Even though we were sure that it was only a night bird, still we were afraid that it might be the soul of a sinner in the image of a bird which was complaining that she could not get emendation. Fright was imposed upon us by the stories of children who fell asleep during the evening services and later woke up when the deceased came to their night services.

I still remember the dusk hours of Saturday evening before the candles were lit and the old Beit HaMidrash was full of mysterious shadows while the sounds of songs were heard from the people who gathered for the Sabbath's third meal.

I also recall the early mornings of the Slichot days when, looking through the windows, I noticed the night becoming paler and the stars expiring and disappearing one after another and the day began. Such a scene I did not see during the year, only during the Slichot services.

Today, when I think about all these things, they seem childish to me. But then they possessed so much charm and I was strongly affected by them.

Since there was no entertainment in a small shtetl, we had to invent our own. One of the entertainments was to go to the railroad station to meet the trains, especially on Chol Hamoed. Even though we did not see anybody off and did not meet anyone, it was still worthwhile to walk three kilometres to see who was coming and who was leaving.

An important event in the shtetl was a wedding. Everyone took part in it and we, the children, were the happiest. We mingled with the musicians and I was proud when they hung a big drum on my neck. I marched in the streets and the musician banged with his sticks. From time to time, he laughingly would bang on my head. My back hurt for several days after that, but it still made me happy.

[Page 82]

Another important occurrence was the rabbinical dispute and when something happened in connection with it. Also, when the famous rabbis came to visit, for instance, the rabbi from Munkatch – Rabbi Chaim Elazar Shapiro who came every year for a visit, Jews and non–Jews all went to see him and the whole town was in an uproar.

When a fire broke out this was a holiday for us children. Even a fight among drunks on a Sunday or on market day was a happy occasion for us.

The town came to life when it was visited by a cantor, with or without a choir, preachers and homilists who preached in the Beit HaMidrash, a weeding jester or a Zionist speaker.

A major adventure was the required appearance of the boys before the military draft board. All the recruits changed their normal lives and these quiet, tranquil Beit HaMidrash dwellers almost went berserk. The pious young men from the Beit HaMidrash neglected their studies, the serious idealistic Zionists, their books, the apprentices of all trades left their work benches and the helpers in the stores did not come to work. They all spent the nights in the Beit HaMidrash reciting Psalms, singing songs and melodies, telling stories and sometimes also played cards. In addition, they busied themselves with all kinds of mischiefs. They burnt the oven with the wood that they had brought from Jewish yards, ate everything they found in the pantries and also did all kinds of despicable deeds. In the morning, many of the merchants found their signs on somebody else's store and some had to go and look for them altogether. Door knobs were smeared with tar and the owners stood and polished them clean. Many fences also disappeared. I and other youngsters who were not even of military age dragged along and participated in these activities.

On the day when the recruits had to report to the draft board, many peasant boys from the villages came to town drunkenly singing even though they were still sober! It was dangerous for a Jew to encounter these groups. In contrast, the Jewish recruits who had gone wild days before became serious, realizing that the decision of the draft board would decide their destiny for several years or sometimes for their entire lives.

It seems funny now but then, for twelve, thirteen year–old boys, it was especially and primitively charming.

The years that I spent in cheder belong to another period. For me, they were difficult years. I happened to be a very good student but my grandfather, Reb Moshe Samuel Friedman, was my teacher. I always sat at his right and another grandson from Dynov at his left. We both were beaten for others. My grandfather was seventy years old and it was hard for him to get up and walk over to the other students. So he yelled at them and hit us!

Therefore, I took advantage of every free moment and ran to the river for a swim. It was a beautiful river with beautiful surroundings – forests, mountains, refreshing air and wells about which were believed to cure eye and skin diseases. On the way to one well, there was a portrait of a Catholic Saint about whom a legend circulated that he was the rabbi from Grzybow who came to Strzyzow for conversion. I am not sure about the truthfulness of this story. Nobody thought about doing any research. The grown–ups had plenty of other worries and the children thought only about playing and having fun.

[Page 83]

People who were dong folklore research would have found a very rich field for their research. They would have even found the source of the wonderful language which the children used during their play and was passed on from generation to generation. "En ten tina, sovoroka bena" and others. The researchers could also have found the source of everyone's nickname which traditionally everyone possessed besides his given name and last name. Until this day, people are more remembered for their nicknames than their last names. But, alas, the childhood years were gone and then the real hardship began. For me too, my fight with my parents had begun. It is the eternal dispute between the parents and their offspring and it was particularly sharp in the later years in the little towns of Galicia. The children strove to go forward into the big world and towards broader horizons. Those who became influenced by the Zionist ideal strove to make Aliyah to Eretz Israel, but the parents wanted to keep their children within crowded space, fearing that, Heaven forbid, they might forfeit Judaism. The tragedy was that both sides were right.

I also belonged among those who began to dream of Eretz Israel. The first step was to learn a trade and join the Zionist organization. It was then that my parents demonstrated the strongest opposition. If you learn a trade you automatically stop learning Torah and, if you join the organization, you will read books and you will also congregate with the opposite sex.

However, parents were not able to stop life's progress. The stream was too strong. The Jewish youth saw that Poland held no future for them. Anti–Semitism was growing, Jews were pushed out of their livelihood and there were no jobs. Ultimately, the parents realized that they could not stop the children.

Only then was I permitted to learn cabinet–making in Strzyzow. For lack of a Jewish cabinet–maker, I learned the trade from a gentile. Later, I moved to Rzeszow and to a training camp where I made Aliyah to Eretz Israel. There I went through a lot but I do not want to write about that.

Now, our shtetl, like a thousand other cities and towns in Poland and generally in Europe, does not exist anymore. Our shtetl was not better than other shtetls. However, to us, this shtetl was dear because it was ours. We were born, brought up and lived through sad and happy occasions here. That is where our parents lived, our sisters and brothers and now they are all gone. They are no longer alive. My dear father and mother struggled all their lives, like all the other Jews and, in the end, the murderers exterminated a third of these tortured people and put an end to my dear shtetl.

May these few pages serve as an eternal Kaddish for my shtetl, for my parents who were truly "Mentchen" and toiled hard to make ends meet.

We shall not dare to forget our martyrs. It is everybody's duty to remember and not to forget. "Remember what the Amalekites did to you".

[Page 84]

S omewhere there was a shtetl, charming, beyond dispute;
T hough it was little and minute
R ooted in my heart, forever engrained;
Z ionists, devoted to a Homeland to restore;
Y ear in year out, tranquil it always remained;
Z estful Hassidim, lively people. I sadly remember,
O ffspring with parents killed by the world's worst murderer;
W hile all of them, literally all, perished.
W e will not forget you dear shtetl, we will not.

Strzyzow
by Yechezkiel–Harry Langsam

In the foothills of the Carpathian Mountains, surrounded by groves, in a valley of lush greenery, at the banks of the Visloka River, there was a charming little Jewish shtetl – Strzyzow.

This shtetl has never gained worldwide fame for its personalities but all its inhabitants were one big personality. The people from Strzyzow participated in every national or religious activity of the Polish Jewry. The Jewish youths in Strzyzow were a group of highly intelligent, national conscious boys and girls. They were members in all national and religious parties from Agudat Israel to the leftist, Hashomer Hatzair. (In the last elections to the Zionist Congress, for the first time in Strzyzow, there were five votes for the leftists).

The centre of the town was the market place. A big square, surrounded by houses most of which belonged to Jews. On the south–western corner of the market a little bit into an alley, the Catholic Church stood – the tallest building in town. The building resembled a guard who was guarding the city from approaching enemies.

Regrettably, it was the source of hatred toward the Jews. The south–east corner of the market place served as an exit gate which led to the Jewish bath–house and further on, to the railroad bridge, to the cattle market and slaughterhouse. The same road also led to the Visloka River.

It quietly flowed the Visloka River with weeping willow trees on both sides of its banks whose twigs were used for hoshanot on Hoshana Raba. Not only happiness and childish laughter did the river absorb but also a lot of pain and sorrow when somebody drowned.

It was a paradise on earth to take a stroll on a Sabbath afternoon on the narrow road on the other side of the river to which we had to cross upstream behind the church on a narrow, single plank. Crossing the river on that plank was an ordeal. We had to hold on to a cable, and our young hearts trembled with fear and mixed with joy.

[Page 85]

Wintertime, the hills that led to the bathhouse was used for sledding and it was one of the greatest pleasures. This road also witnessed another pleasant event: On Friday afternoons, men trudging downhill after the bathhouse keeper blew his pipe that simulated a bugle and repeatedly yelled: "To the bathhouse!"

To the north–east corner of the market place simulated an entrance gate into town. Coming from Rzeszow, you arrived there by descending from the Zarnowo Hill. Right there at the entrance there was a mud puddle which never dried out. Two or three houses into the market place, there was the alley that led to the Beit HaMidrash and the kloyz of the rabbi from Sassov. Further on, on the same side, was the shul with a lush green lawn in front of it. It was the second biggest building in town.

Strzyzow was surrounded with charming mountains, forests and meadows. The scenery and natural beauty around Strzyzow was eye–catching and the clear air was overwhelming.

The older generation included every segment of Hassidim – from Belz to Munkatch, from the Sadigora Dynasty to the small rabbis from the nearby small towns. As tiny as this shtetl was, it had a larger number of institutions whose main goal was the education of the younger generation. There was a Hebrew kindergarten, a Bais Yacov school for girls, a Yeshiva for boys and in addition, everyone studied at home too. Among the charity institutions there were the Free Loan Society, the Talmud Torah Society to support the education of poor children and two societies taking care of the repair and obtaining books for the Beit HaMidrash and the kloyz. Also, there was a welfare society for the poor wanderers to save them from being forced to traverse the town and going from door–to–door asking for alms.

A major part of the youth joined the Zionist pioneer movement and left their homes for the hard life in Eretz Israel.

Of the young people who immigrated to other countries and those who escaped to Russia, these are now the remnants of Strzyzow.

With the devastation of European Jewry in general and particularly the Polish Jewry, our shtetl of many hundreds of years was destroyed together with her customs and traditions, the poor and the wealthy, the scholars and the simple Jews. Hassidim, Zionists, the prayer houses and the cemeteries are all gone now. It does not exist anymore. Not a trace remains of all the things that were so dear to us.

Cursed and forsaken shall be those who caused such destruction, such a disaster. G–d shall avenge the innocent and untainted blood.

The Bais Yacov School in Strzyzow
by Golda Miller–Langsam

It pains the heart when you stop for a moment and reminisce about the past. The nice and good things are unforgettable. It was once upon a time…. What is left for us? Only memories!!! A few single people, spread and strew all over the world remained. But the shtetl does not exist anymore. Everyone's heart smoulders from the memories. They cannot be forgotten.

[Page 86]

Please remember the martyrs and the untainted!

With a few simple words, I would like to commemorate the children of our shtetl. The pure, holy souls who are hovering above us. They were young and beautiful, full of life, filled with devotion to G–d, Torah and the people of Israel. They wanted to be the builders of the Jewish nation, of the Jewish future, but they did not live to reach their goal. They were torn away from their fathers and mothers, from their people and were thrown into one grave.

Such dear and beloved children of our shtetl!

Earth! Please do not cover their innocent blood!

Children from all segments of the town, boys from the cheder, youths from Agudat Israel, girls from the Bais Yacov School, the Zionists youth movement – they all contributed so much for the children of the town. They aroused feelings, love and responsibility for our nation in the children, reverence for everything that was theirs, respect for the Jewish culture, for Jewish Sabbaths and holidays, for Jewish songs and dance and for our own society.

The Bais Yacov School added to this entire programme a Judaic consciousness and a Jewish culture according to the Torah.

The devoted teacher of the Bais Yacov School in Strzyzow was my good friend Breindl Wasserman, of blessed memory. She was a role model of devotion, attachment to the children and sacrifice for Jewish religious education. Let me remember the young man Moshe Schwartzman, the active public servant, the founder of the school. He worked wholeheartedly and devotedly for the existence of the school. Especially outstanding was the student Seryl Friedman who later became a teacher in the nearby city of Wielopole where she herself established a Bais Yacov School under the supervision of the teacher Wasserman from Strzyzow. Actually, I was only a guest in town but when I used to come home for the holidays, I frequented the streets and observed a fresh, growing young generation. I prided myself and saw them as a promising future for our suffering people.

I still see before my eyes the big dancing circles, hand–in–hand, poor and rich, small and large, their sparkling eyes against the setting sun hiding behind the surrounding hills. Those heart–warming words still ring in my ears.

> We are like the birds, free
> We are like the flowers in the field;
> Our friendship is our shield,
> We, the children from the tents of Yacov's tribe.

Yes, children, you really were the flowers in the field. You blossomed, you were affectionate, and you were the hope for the nation's future.

To our sorrow, you were plucked during the most beautiful blossoming together with the rest of the nation, you perished by the defiled murderous hands.

G–d! Avenge their untainted blood.

[Page 87]

Hassidim in Strzyzow
by Mordechai Schiff

When my thoughts take me back to the days before the big and bitter destruction, I remember my place of birth, Strzyzow, with its dear people.

Our town stood out with her colourful population. There were simple people, hearty Jews, scholars, intellectuals and the majority were Hassidim of different rabbis: Fiery Hassidim of the rabbi from Belz like Reb Shalom Schwartzman, Reb Yacov Schiff, Reb Leib Friedman, the shochet and also devoted Hassidim of the rabbi from Munkatch: Reb Yeshayahu and Reb Chaim Mandel, Reb Chaim Yacov Nuremberg, Reb Samuel Moshe Groskopf and many more simple Jews. These people still remembered Rabbi Shlomo Shapiro the rabbi from Strzyzow. There were also Hassidim of the rabbi from Blazow, the Tenzer family, the Feit family and others with their leader Reb Itzhok Berstein, and many more Hassidim of the rabbi from Sadigora.

About the latter, to which my whole family belonged and among whom I grew up, I would like to write in a broader form because of their extraordinary character.

Among the Sadigora Hassidim were several groups: The Boyan, Chortkow and the Husiatin group. They all emerged from the Ryzin dynasty. In Strzyzow there were about thirty or forty people who belonged to the so–called "People of the clan". They had a special, brotherly relationship, like one big family. On every occasion they got together with a bottle of vodka on the table. They drank L'chaim, spoke about rabbis and Hassidism, became enthusiastic and began to dance, even on a simple week–day. They always found a reason for a get–together, a Yahrzeit, or a small unimportant holiday. They celebrated the anniversaries of the departures of all the rabbis of the dynasty, starting with rabbi Reb Israel from Ryzin. On every holiday, they sat around a table, drank beer, told about rabbinical miracles and, if they received a new commentary spoken by their rabbi on a verse in the Bible, this would really call for a celebration. They mediated and thought about every word or meaning that they had just heard from their rabbi's mouth and they derived great pleasure from it. These new expressions and commentaries were sent to my grandfather, Reb Hersh, of blessed memory, who was called endearingly: "Reb Hershale B'li Neder" because to every sentence he pronounced, he added the words "B'li Neder" which meant, not to consider it a vow (just a precaution in case it could not be fulfilled, it might not become a broke promise).

I still remember the hearty late Saturday night Melaveh Malka meals, especially on the long winter nights in my father's Reb Levi Itzhok Schiff's house, which my mother, the graceful Ryvka, nee Horowitz, of blessed memory, prepared for the Hassidim. There was a hot borsht, potatoes and leftovers from the Sabbath kugel. The Hassidim sat together until after midnight, chatting about the rabbis and their greatness, or repeating the rabbi's teachings.

[Page 88]

My mother was very hospitable and we were familiar with her expression whenever a wayfarer showed up. "Reb Yid, go wash your hands", which meant to come to the table and eat. She also provided lodging. It was for her a privilege to cater to and serve Hassidim and scholars.

I remember when we were young, we always listened to the Hassidic tales breathlessly and stared at the flushed faces of the older Hassidim like Reb Baruch Diller, Reb Hersh Gelander, Reb Jonah Freiwirth, Reb Yechezkiel Gorgel, Reb Zalman Brauner and my grandfather. Some of these Hassidic veterans had visited the old rabbi from Ryzin and they repeated what they had personally heard from the rabbi's holy mouth. What a joy it was when preparing for a trip to visit the rabbi on a holiday. It was a preparation for a holy deed. The Hassidim who did not go, sent messages to give to the rabbi and asked those who went to bring back the rabbi's blessings. When the Hassidim returned home, their faces shone with a spiritual glow. They came back with an inner solemnity and peacefulness as though they had achieved the most important achievement, to have merited have sitting at the rabbi's table and listening to the teachings from the rabbi's holy mouth. Their enthusiasm and belief in the rabbi had inspired them in their daily struggle for existence.

Of thee I cry, and bitterly my heart is saddened, of all those dear, faultless, innocent martyrs who so brutally perished at the hands of the Nazi murderers whose names shall be erased forever.

My Shtetl
by Eliezer Gruber

When I wrote these few memories about the town of my birth, I remembered the beautiful nature that surrounded her, the mountains, forests, water–falls and the lovely river, which in some places flowed tranquil and in some with strong rapids. There we strolled, enjoyed the fresh air and grew up into maturity. I also remember the comrades from the older generation who implanted into the young hearts the ideal of Eretz Israel, Jewish culture, the Hebrew language which was then called: "Lashon Hakodesh" and pioneering. At the head of these comrades was Itzhok Berglass with his co–worker Avigdor Diamand, Abraham Brav, Sarah Zilber, Feiga Greenblatt, Eta Dembitzer, Vita Loos, Hena Nechemiah and others. Also, Zeinvel Greenblatt who taught us Hebrew. They all met that horrible fate together with our six million brothers.

Thanks to the influence of the above–mentioned leadership, the youth in Strzyzow were different from the youth of the nearby town of Frysztak. The youth of Strzyzow were Jewish, progressive and Zionists.

We, the younger ones, cooperated with the older comrades in all Zionist activities. We learned Hebrew and prepared for Aliyah to Eretz Israel. Later, we taught the younger boys and girls and continued to teach them the same ideals. We now enjoy the fruits, here in our land of the State of Israel.

In 1925, we the youngsters under the leadership of Chaim Weinberg and Pinchos Zilber organized a spiritual centre in which the entire Zionist groups were included. With the help of Baruch Nuremberg, Feivel Schacher, Joseph Deutch, Joseph Weinberg, Joshua Sturm, Mordechai Schiff and the girls: Beila Auerhun (who later became my wife), Mishkit Mandel,

[Page 89]

Rachel Leah Deutch (the wife of Mordechai Schiff), Ronie (Ruth Russ, Bat–Sheva Russ, Chana and Sarah Fleisher and others. We divided the youngsters into groups, taught them Hebrew, Jewish history, etc. The centre was the first to organize the practical pioneer movement and later became the foundation of the Revisionist organization: "Menorah".

The Revisionist Organization was organized by the young man, Joseph Diamand from Krakow who later became the chief of the economic department of the Zionist newspaper in the Polish language "Nowy Dziennink". He befriended me and, through me, became acquainted with a wider circle of young men. He contributed strongly to the youth of Strzyzow, both culturally and organizationally and he also influenced the youth not to wait for legal certificates but to make Aliyah to Eretz Israel illegally.

From the "Menorah", the Beitar branched out which Yacov Presser helped to organize. Yacov Presser came from Rzeszow to study in the gymnasium of Strzyzow. The commander of the Beitar was Tzvi Schefler and the activists were: Chaim and Eta Mohrer, my sister Eva Gruber, Leah Kracher, Pesl Roth, Chana Auerhun, Feiga Springer, Hagel and others. They were active until the outbreak of the war.

Besides the Zionist youth, I would also like to mention a few people from our town who stood out with their good deeds.

Everyone knew Joseph Schacher. However, few knew that before each holiday, he secretly mailed checks to the needy that were happy to receive money unexpectedly in order to be able to prepare food for the holiday. Rizhi Rosenbluth was well known in Strzyzow for her good deeds. I remember as a boy I once collected money for charity together with Abraham Mintz and when she saw us, she was so overwhelmed that we were active in charity, that she gave us more than anybody else and wished us to continue doing good deeds.

I would like to mention Joseph Klotz, the city sexton who in winter, on Sabbath mornings, collected all the strangers and the poor from the Beit HaMidrash and took them home for a hot coffee or tea. Chana Rachel, the wife of Reb Zalman Diamand from Wysoka, never allowed a poor man to pass her house without giving him a meal and a few coins. When the poor wayfarers came to town on horse and buggy, they always had a place in Reb Fishel Goldberg and his wife, Feiga's barn.

Feigale'h, as she was called with endearment, treated the wayfarers properly and charitably. During the last war, the Goldberg resided in Lwow. Even though they were themselves refugees, all the lone refugees from Strzyzow who were without their families, found a home in their house. They ate there, washed their laundry and felt as though they were at home. She was helped by her daughter–in–law Leah, the daughter of Reb Feivel Diamand. Later, the Goldberg sent packages to those people who were exiled to Siberia.

All these people were before my eyes when I wrote these lines. Let this be my small contribution to their memory in this book.

[Page 90]

How Mordechai Goldberg saved the town
by Tzvi Elazar Sternberg

I would like to tell a story which, when it happened, was known in the entire region and made a tremendous impression. It is worthwhile that the younger generation should know about it and see how the Jews of the past, simple, uneducated Jews, were willing to sacrifice for others. It happened in the year 1860. The cholera had spread its black wings over the town and had torn away many inhabitants, men, women and children. The deceased were given a Jewish burial in a mass grave on the field that belonged to Mr. Kociela and it called, until this day, the Cholera Hill.

At that time the town rabbi as Rabbi Shlomo Shapiro who, in 1882, became rabbi of Munkatch. The rabbi was sitting at his table and was deeply enmeshed in studying the Talmud. From time to time he heaved a heavy sigh for the misfortune that befell his shtetl. Suddenly, his personal assistant, Reb Berish Weinberg (father–in–law of Reb Chaim Nuremberg) came running and bitterly sobbing turned to the rabbi and said: "Rabbi, have mercy! We already did everything possible. We measured the cemetery, we married off Zerach the crazy in the cemetery** and there is no let up from the cholera epidemic! Reb Pinchos Kanner, Reb Hersh Yacov and others have fallen ill. The sadness is horrendous and it is a great danger. Save us Rabbi". Rabbi Shlomo lifted his large eyebrows and with his swollen eyes from crying, looked mercifully at Reb Berish and said: "Go quickly to Mordechai Goldberg and tell him in my name to help the Jews from Strzyzow…." Reb Berish did not believe his ears. But there was nothing he could do. The rabbi's request had to be obeyed.

Mordechai Goldberg, Mordechai the horse trader as he used to be called, lived in an old broken–down shack behind Yechiel Rosen's house which consisted of two little chambers. In one chamber he lived with his wife Sarah and the second chamber was occupied by Reb Nachum Teitelbaum where he also had a study and taught little children. On the left side of that house was a barn with straw which served as a lodging place for the poor. On the right side was a stable with a few old sick horses – Mordechai's merchandize. Every day, Mordechai carried a pot with barley and a loaf of bread which his wife Sarah had prepared for the poor. Reb Berish arrived with the message from the rabbi and approached Mordechai thinking: "from this simpleton is expected help? Maybe he is one of the thirty–six righteous in this world…?" He almost addressed him as Holy Rabbi but restrained himself from doing it. He just said: "The rabbi has sent me to you and said that you ought to help the shtetl". Mordechai burst out in laughter. "You are mistaken. It is not me the rabbi meant. I am a simple Jew. I was orphaned when I was a child and was raised by my sister Chaya, Reb Samuel Rosen's wife. As soon as I grew up, I was inducted into the military and served the Kaiser. I cannot help. Go tell this to the rabbi".

There was a belief that marrying off retarded people in the cemetery or measuring the cemetery would end the epidemic

[Page 91]

After Reb Berish returned to the rabbi with his response, the rabbi explained that what he meant was that Mordechai should cheer up the people and help them to get rid of their depression and sadness because sadness is one of the main causes that increase the cholera. After Reb Berish went and explained to Mordechai Goldberg what the rabbi wanted from him, Mordechai promised to fulfil the rabbi's request. The next morning, Mordechai walked in the street on wooden stilts, his face blackened and the klezmorim played the instruments, sang Polish songs accompanied by the singing of the children of the town and he made the town merry. Everybody came out into the streets to see Mordechai play and dance on his stilts. He changed the words of the Polish songs to words from the Sabbath prayers. Mordechai continued his stunts for quite a while until the cholera disappeared. Rabbi Shlomo later said that a reward awaited Mordechai in the hereafter. However, first he promised him and his children a long life in this world and that his children would become heroes and would impose fear in the hearts of the gentiles. The blessing materialized. Reb Mordechai with his sons, Fishl and David as well as his grandchildren, have always defended Jews from gentile hands. The gentiles were afraid of them. In 1898 when Father Stoylowski and his party incited the peasants to make pogroms in our part of Galicia and also in Strzyzow, Mordechai's sons saved many Jews from being beaten and from having their properties looted. In 1918, when Poland became independent and the blood libel in Strzyzow occurred, the Goldbergs heroically fought off the mob.

My Shtetl Strzyzow
by Leah Loos

I confess! I never liked you, my shtetl! I did not like the place where I was born and grew up. Where my family lived for centuries. I left you many many years ago and went to Eretz Israel. Why didn't I like you? I stopped loving you the day I started to feel how restricted I was, how limited my freedom was and how everybody interfered in my personal life.

I never appreciated your beauty, never felt the positive in you but only the negative. Like a healthy person never appreciates health until he becomes sick, so am I. Now, after the horrible catastrophe when all my dear ones are gone and murdered, I now begin to feel the loss and all my complaints against you have ceased to exist. My heart is filled with love toward you my shtetl and to your Jews. I feel now like a little girl who suddenly realizes how big a family she has lost. I regret that I am not blessed with the talent of a singer and cannot sing an ode of praise which I feel inside me. If only I were a sculptor and could present the most interesting individuals of my Jewish shtetl the way I see them in the eyes of my soul. If only I were an historian and could write the history of my mother's family. Only by the many heirlooms which were locked up in the bottom drawer of our antique chest could I describe each personality. Each item contained a story about spiritual personalities, geniuses and leaders of many communities going back hundreds of years.

[Page 92]

I am sorry that I am not blessed with any artistic talents in order to express what I visualize. Therefore, I will try to retrieve some memories about the daily life in the shtetl as remembered by one of her orphaned daughters. And this should be a monument to my dear ones.

I feel like the peasant boy in the story of J.L. Peretz who came to shul on Yom Kippur. When he saw how the Jews prayed with reverence but not knowing how to pray, he was unable to participate. He too wanted to express his feelings before the Almighty so he did it with a whistle.

Now everyone in Strzyzow is dear to me, not only my immediate family. My heart is bleeding for them. Even the hot–headed, red–bearded man who threatened that if I continued to attend secular high school he would spill a pail of filthy dishwater over my head. I hated him then but I miss him now because he was the one who guarded us and kept a watchful eye on the children of Israel not to deviate from our customs and traditions. He was alarmed that our involvement with other cultures would be detrimental to our existence.

I did not bear a grudge against him now, on the contrary, I am begging forgiveness from his soul.

With deep love and admiration, I remember our distant relative, the Rebetzin with her matriarchal face. She always carried safety pins in her pocket and when she noticed a little over–exposure in a girl's dress, she would ask her to close it with a pin.

And my teacher, Reb Eli Dovid who, when he found out that I considered enrolling in a secular high school, chased me out from his cheder even though teaching was his profession and his livelihood depended on teaching. I still remember that he lived on bread and potatoes which I always saw him eat. Notwithstanding his poverty, he refused to teach me. I still visualize the rectangular shape of the dark room as well as his wife Nechama with her high–pitched voice. She was his second wife and they married not for love but for convenience. After Reb Eli Dovid lost his first wife, he needed a housekeeper and she was a widow who needed a breadwinner. She was always complaining that he did not provide her with all her needs for the household.

My memories are still fresh on how Reb Eli Dovid, dressed in his Sabbath cloak, used to appear in our house on the Sabbath afternoons to examine my brother Elazar. He wanted to show off to my father how well his son was doing in his studies. A treat for the teacher always followed which, for us children, was an enjoyable experience.

The Sabbath in our shtetl. The preparations for the Sabbath began on Thursday evening. The first thing that everybody had to do was buy a ticket for the slaughtering of a chicken. Without a ticket the shochet would not slaughter chicken. The slaughtering itself was for us children an unforgettable experience.

Next came the scrubbing of the wooden floors in the house which had to be done every Sabbath. Baking the challahs, a smooth one for Friday night and a twisted one for the Sabbath day was done at the bakery of Malka Rosa, and this was an ordeal. She was always angry and hollering but she had a heart of gold. Any hungry person who came into her house was fed, Jew or non–Jew. Yasha Kopitchuk, the town idiot who was the star witness for the prosecution at the blood libel trial, even he found shelter in her house.

[Page 93]

Friday afternoon: The men were hurrying to the bath–house and the women were carrying pots of cholent to the bakeries where they were kept warm in the ovens for the Sabbath midday meal. The stores were closed. In each house, tables were covered with white tablecloths, freshly polished antique candlesticks with candles burning, one for each member of the family. The challahs on the table, the wine cups and the wine next to the challahs. All the men were on their way to the synagogues. And while the men were at the synagogues, weather permitting, women sat on the stoops in front of the houses dressed in their best, waiting for their husbands and sons to return home, always accompanied by a poor stranger who would be a guest for the Sabbath meal.

Of course, not every table in Strzyzow had the same delicious food. In general, Strzyzow was not rich but nobody missed having a challah, fish and a chicken for the Sabbath meal. There were many righteous women who knew who needed help and provided it. And if it happened that a Jew was jailed, he too was not forgotten.

Strzyzow, like many other cities in Galicia, consisted of a square market place surrounded with one–story houses. Only a few were two–stories high. All the houses belonged to the Jews. One main street led to the railroad station. The rest of the alleys and narrow streets were mud puddles most of the year. The houses were built from bricks not because of wealth but because of the fire which had destroyed wooden structures years ago. Tuesday was the market day when the farmers came to town. They brought their products for sale and bought necessities for their households.

The Jews in town waited anxiously for market day because their livelihood depended on it. Sunday was a day of rest that was forced upon the Jews by law. On this day, the only policeman in town showed up in the market place to see that all the stores were closed. Notwithstanding the fact that Sunday was Sabbath for the Christians, they all tried to shop after Sunday mass. They used to sneak in through the back doors of the Jewish stores and the owners played cat–and–mouse with the policeman. When the policeman showed up at the back door, he collected his bribe and left.

Strzyzow was a quiet town. The only time it was noisy was when the Count, who lived in a nearby estate, showed up in in 1927 Model T Ford. Everyone came out to see this devilish wagon which drove without horses and roared like a lion as though a devil or a ghost was pushing it.

On the eastern side of the market place, in front of the nicer homes in town, women and fruit peddlers were sitting and displaying their produce. They sold fruit of the season which they had bought from the farmers on market day. Their business was not very good but the location was in such a strategic point that they saw and heard everything that went on in the shtetl.

These women had plenty of time to gossip. Whenever a marriage candidate arrived for a pre–arranged meeting with a bride, they had the first look and also gave their approval or disapproval. They also had a talent for nicknaming everybody in town.

[Page 94]

The railroad station was located about a mile from the centre of the town, and we had two coach drivers who drove the passengers back and forth from the station. They also transported freight which arrived by train. One of the coach drivers was killed during the pogrom in 1919 and another man took his place.

Rzeszow was a bigger city about twenty miles from Strzyzow. This was a commercial centre for the entire area. Regrettably, there are no Jews left in this town either. In the late twenties, a bus line connected Strzyzow with Rzeszow which hurt the coach drivers. They were the victims of progress. They hardly made a living before but the bus line reduced their livelihood even further. The coach drivers in Strzyzow were a happy bunch and liked to play tricks on the people in town, especially on the Sabbath before Passover, which is called Shabbat Hagadol. I remember once on such a Sabbath afternoon after a restful nap which followed the cholent, when my mother proudly approached the borsht barrel, removed the white cloth wrapping and removed the wooden cover. Then, she took a wooden spoon and stirred the borsht and after tasting a little, she had a satisfied expression on her face. She also gave us some to taste and to our father, of blessed memory. After my father expressed enthusiastically that the borsht tasted like the finest wine, my mother put the covers back and told us to leave. We suddenly heard a commotion outside. What happened?

The gentile boy who worked for one of the coach drivers brought his coach to a very respectable bald–headed citizen and delivered to him an invitation for a free trip to Egypt. There was a superstitious belief that somehow baldness was connected with the sixth plague in Egypt. "The Boils'. Every year for as long as I remember, this joke was played on the bald–headed people in town. We, the children, used to gather around and even made up a special song for this occasion: "Shabbat Hagadol is a hot day so all the bald ones go by train". Of course, it rhymes better in Yiddish. Some bald men took this joke lightly and laughed with the crowd but some became very angry.

The preparations for the Passover holiday actually took place all year. As soon as the first fruit of the season appeared, the women began preparing all kinds of preserves and fruit wine for Passover.

At Hanukkah time, my mother prepared chicken and goose fat for Passover. She stored the fat in earthenware pots and the cracklings which remained after cooking (grivenenss) belonged to the children.

We always baked our own matzoth on a Sunday when the store was closed. Our whole family participated in this endeavour and everybody had an assignment. We, the girls, had to put on cotton dresses which could be washed and cleaned before Passover to be sure that none of the dough stuck to our dresses. When I was a little girl, my job was to pour water for the mixing of the dough. When I got older, I was given a roller to roll out the matzoth. Every Pesach, men only baked shmura matzoth made out of flour especially preserved and watched over since the day of harvesting. We, the children, enjoyed these matzoth very much because they had a special flavour. There was always a mystery surrounding these matzoth and we considered them a delicacy although they were very hard to chew.

[Page 95]

I never saw a queen on her throne. But a real queen was my mother on the Seder night. Tired from the back–breaking work preparing for the holiday, weariness showing on her face but still her wig was perfectly combed. She wore the most expensive earrings, a golden chain around her neck and her fingers were adorned with diamond rings. She wore her black silk dress in which she resembled a real queen after coronation. Those experiences were renewed every year on the Seder nights.

Of course, the reading of the Haggadah was a little boring because we did not understand what we were reading except when my father translated some passages from time to time. When time came to fill Elijah's cup, I watched the cup and convinced that he took a few sips from the cup.

Even Tisha B'Av, which is a day of mourning, was sort of a happy day for us children. We could not wait to be twelve years old and to be able to fast. Fasting was an adventure for us. Even though we went into the woods frolicking and all around us the underbrush was full of all kinds of berries, none of us dared to pick a single one.

When Rosh Hashanah came along, we could not wait to go to the shul to hear the shofar. When the sound of the shofar reached us, we got goose bumps from fear and we were sure that the whole word was trembling. The women's balcony was packed like sardines. I remember once I fainted from lack of air. There was a woman who said that the reason I fainted was that I spoke a sentence in Polish to another girl which, in her opinion, was blasphemy. And I foolishly agreed.

On Yom Kippur, before I was old enough to fast, I used to enjoy this holiday tremendously by eating a lot when others were forbidden to eat. I just could not understand why the neighbours had to ask each other's forgiveness even though they were friendly to each other all year round. We went to shul to hear Kol Nidrei with fear in our young hearts and tears in our eyes. We joined the older people in their cries without knowing the reason therefor. My mother always prepared treats for the children to eat during the day so that kept us busy running home every now and then. It seems to me that we ate more on this day than on a regular day. My mother was suffering from migraine headaches after fasting and this destroyed my fun from the day's eating.

Soon after Yom Kippur, we helped the adults in building the Sukkah. But running back and forth from the house with the food was no fun. We were rewarded when Simchat Torah came along as, with flags in our hands, we were dragged in by the grown–ups to dance with them and everybody gave us candy.

These are the memories from my shtetl which probably all Jewish daughters from other cities share. Such a rich life came suddenly to a stop and in such a cruel way.

[Page 96]

Personalities and Events

by Shlomo Yahalomi

In this section of "Personalities and Events" we will write about known personalities in Strzyzow and the occurrence of events which, in our opinion, should be perpetuated in this book. I will write about interesting characters, some from the previous generations and some from the last generation. About people who were G–d fearing, Talmudic scholars and some plain, good Jews, humble in their behaviour, doing day after day good deeds without fanfare and also about a few exceptional people.

I will write about small and big happenings that I heard from the mouths of the elderly in our shtetl or that I personally witnessed.

I will begin from the earlier times and later about the Holocaust generation. The stories which I selected were chosen objectively without any prejudice to other stories about which I did not write. I will write about the ones which are most familiar to me and please forgive me for those I have omitted. It was not intended to discriminate.

About the old Strzyzow
A Royal visit at Reb Aaron Kanner the First
by Itzhok Berglass

I heard this story from Elazar Wurtzel and he heard it from Rabbi Moshe Leib Shapiro, the rabbi of Sassov–Strzyzow who heard it told by the famous rabbi from Sandz, Rabbi Chaim Halberstam.

Rabbi Naphtali from Mielec was the son–in–law of the rabbi from Sandz. When his wife died, somebody suggested he marry the daughter of Avishal Kanner who lived in Strzyzow. But, Rabbi Naphtali hesitated because he was afraid that such a marriage may offend his former father–in–law as the suggested bride was not from a rabbinical family. So he decided to ask his former father–in–law, Reb Chaim, if he objected. When the rabbi from Sandz heard the name of Avishal Kanner, he agreed right away saying: "I am very happy that we are going to be related with the Kanner family".

And the rabbi from Sandz told a story that happened between him and Reb Aaron Kanner, the father of Avishal.

The grandson of the famous rabbi from Lezajsk was very poor and also shy and no matter how much his friends urged him to ask for help from his grandfather's admirers, he refused. When things got worse and his family was starving, he finally agreed to visit a few cities to ask for support under the condition that the rabbi from Sandz and the rabbi from Kaminka would travel with him for moral support. On the way, the rabbis told rabbi Naphtali that they would pretend to be his attendants and that he should act as a rabbi. They visited a few cities with little success. Then, one Friday, finding themselves near Strzyzow, they decided to spend the Sabbath in Strzyzow. On the way and walking in the direction of Strzyzow, they met Reb Aaron Kanner, the father of Avishal who was speeding in a carriage with a pair of fine horses. When Reb Aaron Kanner noticed the three men, he had the impression that they might be famous rabbis.

[Page 97]

Reb Aaron Kanner stopped for a while to greet them with a loud "Shalom Aleichem" and then went to his carriage to continue his voyage. He drove a short distance when his carriage broke down. Reb Aaron immediately realized that this mishap had something to do with the recently–met rabbis whom he did not offer a ride. He approached them, turned to Rabbi Naphtali, the grandson of the rabbi from Lezajsk and apologized, explaining that he was in a hurry to reach a sick Count in a nearby village who owed him money and he was afraid that the Count might die before he reached him. Rabbi Naphtali responded by pointing his finger toward the rabbi from Sandz and the rabbi from Kaminka saying: "I am innocent; it is they who did it to punish you for being rude and not offering us a ride". The rabbis accepted the apology and told Reb Aaron to continue to his destination and collect the money. Reb Aaron Kanner then told them that upon their arrival in Strzyzow, they were to go directly to his house because he wanted them to be his guests for the Sabbath. They accepted the invitation and spent a very pleasant Sabbath. The whole town was very happy to have such important rabbis among them.

Saturday night, Reb Aaron Kanner asked the rabbis what was the reason for their travel? They explained the situation and the predicament rabbi Naphtali found himself in. That he was the grandson of the famous rabbi from Lezajsk.

The rabbi from Sandz also informed Reb Aaron Kanner that they were already a week in to their journey with little success and, if the second week would not improve, Reb Naphtali would return home empty–handed. Then Reb Aaron Kanner asked them how much they expected to collect. They told him that they hoped to collect five hundred guldens (at that time it was a sizeable sum). After Reb Aaron heard of their ambition, he suggested that he would give them the money on condition that they stay with him another week. Of course they happily agreed and every day was a holiday for the people in Strzyzow. At the end of the second week, Reb Aaron paid his pledge and the rabbis went home. That is how rabbi Chaim from Sandz told the story and added: "Of course, I would not dare to oppose such a match". Years later, the grandchildren of the rabbi from Sandz married the grandchildren of Avishal Kanner. One of these great–grandchildren is Rabbi Avishal Kanner of Haifa, Israel.

I would also like to mention that the house where these rabbis stayed was where my parents, Reb Joseph and Dvora Diamand, of blessed memory, lived until their departure to the other world. This visit was called by the people in town, a Royal visit.

[Page 98]

Reb Joel Margalit, of blessed memory
by Shlomo Yahalomi

Reb Joel Margalit was a wealthy man, an admirer of the Tzadik from Ropczyce. Once, he went to the rabbi for a Sabbath and, after the Sabbath was over, he went into the Beit Hamidrash to take farewell from the Hassidim who dwelt there and to give each Hassid a donation. When he ran into Reb Hersh, a fiery Hassid, he refused to take the donation and demanded from Reb Joel fifty guldens saying: "I have a one and only daughter and the time has arrived for her to get married but I do not have a dowry for her". Reb Joel was very agitated and angrily took back the donation he had wanted to give in the first place. When Reb Joel went in to see the rabbi from Ropczyce, he complained of the "hutzpa" of Reb Hersh who sometimes served as the attendant of the rabbi. The rabbi listened to the complaint and said, wondering: "Is that so? He demanded the sum of fifty guldens?" That is what he had asked, responded Reb Joel. Then Rabbi Naphtali from Ropczyce said: "If that is the case, who knows, maybe you should have bargained with him. Perhaps he would have agreed to take less. Go back and, if you do not succeed, you may be forced to pay him the amount he asked from you". If Rabbi Naphtali asks, who would challenge the rabbi's wish? Reb Joel went back to Reb Hersh and bargained with him, pleading and threatening him but to no avail. The man did not budge. Reb Joel went back to the rabbi and told him that he failed to persuade the Hassid Reb Hersh to take less than the fifty guldens. "Well", the rabbi sighed, "Go back and pay him". Reb Joel had no choice. He would not leave without bidding farewell to Rabbi Naphtali of Ropczyce, so he paid Reb Hersh the money.

Later, Reb Hersh, the servant, turned out to become one of the most righteous rabbis in Galicia. This was Rabbi Hersh from Rymanow. He blessed Reb Joel and his blessing came true and Reb Joel became even wealthier than before.

Reb Itzikl Diller makes a choice between Sandz and Sadigora
by Shlomo Yahalomi

There was one exceptional person in Strzyzow during the time when Rabbi Shlomo Shapiro served in Strzyzow and this was Reb Itzikl Diller. He was a pupil of Rabbi Tzvi Elimelech Shapiro, the author of the book "Beni Yisochor" and the grandfather of Rabbi Shlomo Shapiro. Reb Itzikl was not just an ordinary Jew; he was a man of many attributes, a scholar, skilled in the mystical teachings and an enthusiastic Hassid. Notwithstanding the fact that he was Rabbi Tzvi Elimelech's pupil, and Rabbi Shlomo was his grandson, he opposed Rabbi Shlomo fiercely. There were many reasons for Itzikl's opposition which cannot be divulged. However, one of the main reasons was that Rabbi Shlomo was an admirer of the rabbi from Sandz who fought the rabbi from Sadigora and his Hassidim.

Reb Baruch Diller, Reb Itzikl's son, told me that his father used to travel intermittently – once to the rabbi from Sandz and once to the rabbi from Sadigora and when the dispute between the two rabbis broke out, Reb Itzikl decided to make his mind up once and for all, either to follow the rabbi from Sandz or the rabbi from Sadigora. As soon as he

[Page 99]

Went for a Sabbath to Sandz, he returned enthusiastically. He liked the rabbi's way of Hassidism. But, the following week when he went to see the rabbi from Sadigora, he saw a different world. There, everything was done quietly, without noise and without outwardly expression. He thought to himself: "In Sandz they serve G–d out of fear; in Sadigora they service him with love, and our sages prefer to serve G–d with love rather than out of fear". And so he decided to follow the Rabbi from Sadigora.

Reb Itzikl's decision hurt Rabbi Shlomo very much and this was reflected in their relationship. Rabbi Shlomo could not forgive him because he knew that Reb Itzikl was his grandfather's pupil.

This is not the only story that I heard from Reb itzikl's son. Every time we talked about old times he used to say: "What do you know about those Hassidim and their ways?"

How Rabbi Chaim from Sandz gave a thrashing to Reb Shlomo from Zyznow
by Shlomo Yahalomi

My grandfather, Reb Shlomo from Zyznow was a very rich man. He owned a lot of farmland and timberland. In his youth, he worked very hard and struggled to make ends meet. His life changed after he visited the famous Rabbi from Sandz. Here is the story as my father, may he rest in peace, told it to me.

Reb Eli Bilut who leased farmland from a big landowner in a nearby village called Lutcha, was on his way to Sandz to see the Rabbi. When he passed the village where my grandfather lived, he stopped and suggested to my grandfather to join him on his journey to Sandz. My grandfather happily accepted the proposition and they went together. When they arrived in Sandz they went to the Beit HaMidrash. Everybody was happy to see Reb Eli Bilut because he was known for his generosity. He always gave a big donation for the Beit HaMidrash dwellers and treated them with a bottle of vodka to drink L'chaim. Soon Reb Eli ordered a bottle to drink L'chaim for his safe arrival and it was not long before everyone was in high spirits. In fact, Reb Eli was a little bit drunk and my grandfather realized that he was in no condition to appear before the Rabbi for the traditional greeting.

Reb Eli ordered his driver to take him to the river for a dip in the cold water to sober up and to cool off because it was a hot summer day. As soon as they went into the water, and attendant of the Rabbi came running with a message from the Rabbi. The Rabbi wanted to see Reb Eli immediately because he wanted to go for a drive in Eli's coach.

Reb Eli was a husky man and it was not easy for him to scramble out of the water. My grandfather, who was much younger and faster, jumped out at once, grabbed the horse and carriage and left Reb Eli Bilut behind. The Rabbi did not ask about Reb Eli. He just climbed into the coach and went for the ride.

When the Rabbi returned home and went into the house, my grandfather followed him in without asking permission which was against the rules. Immediately, he asked the Rabbi of Sandz for a blessing, spilling out before him his bitter situation and how hard he was struggling to make a

[Page 100]

living. Rabbi Chaim from Sandz who walked with a limp and used a cane for support, grabbed his cane and began to hit my grandfather, yelling at him; "have you seen a hutzpa this young man has? It is not enough that he stole Rebi Eli's privilege to take me for a drive', but he also demands a reward, a blessing!" He kept hitting him and calling him names and in the end gave him his blessing.

You can imagine how happy my grandfather felt because it was a well–known fact that whoever was thrashed by the rabbi could rest assured that the rabbi's blessing would be upon him. Hassidim used to try very hard to make the rabbi angry. Of course, all his life, Reb Eli regretted inviting my grandfather to join him on this trip.

And from then on, my grandfather succeeded in all his endeavours and turned out to be a very rich man.

Rabbi Alter Zev Horowitz
by Shlomo Yahalomi

In the days when Rabbi Alter Zev Horowitz occupied the rabbinical chair in Strzyzow, people were not too generous to bestow unearned titles. When someone was called Rabbi, genius or righteous man, it had to be well–deserved. Therefore, I would like to tell something about our rabbi, Reb Alter Zev who was a man of G–d, righteous, honest and holy during his entire life.

Reb Shalom Schwartzman told me that once, when Rabbi Alter Zev was in Belz to visit the famous rabbi, the rabbi from Belz saw him passing by his window and he called his son asking him: "Would you like to see a truly G–d fearing man? If you do, look out the window". Rabbi Alter Zev was only nineteen years old then and Reb Shalom added: "Now you know who our rabbi is!"

The rabbi from Sieniawa once said that Rabbi Alter Zev could have been one of the biggest rabbis in Galicia, and could have had a big Hassidic following. However, his humbleness prevented it.

In his childhood, he perplexed many with his behaviour and the following story will tell you how devoted he was in observing every rule and custom, be it large or small. Rabbi Alter Zev's father once became very upset when his son Alter Zev was only thirteen years old. It was on Purim when his father read the Megillah and Reb Alter Zev was not sure that he had absorbed every word as is required. So he asked his friend Hersh Ber to stay with him the Beit HaMidrash to read the Megillah again. Being afraid that somebody would disturb them, they barricaded the door with tables.

When Rabbi Alter Zev's father saw that his youngest son had not yet returned home after a day of fasting (the day before Purim is the fast of Esther), he went to look for him. The first place he went was the Beit HaMidrash. When he found the door locked he began to knock. Not knowing who was knocking, Her Ber told Alter Zev's father: "Go and knock your head against the wall". The father became angry and demanded the door be opened immediately. Soon, Hersh Ber realized that this was the voice of Rabbi Alter Zev's father and removed the tables from the door then hurriedly jumped out of the window. Reb Alter Zev did not pay attention to what was happening around him. He continued the reading of the Megillah. The father angrily slapped his son's face, an act he regretted in later years.

[Page 101]

The following year, Reb Alter Zev got smarter. He went home first to participate in the Purim meal and later secluded himself and read the Megillah a second time to make sure that he did not miss a word. When Rabbi Alter Zev became Bar Mitzva, he made a vow never to laugh in his life thus fulfilling the command of our sages that people should always be sombre. He never laughed thereafter!

When Rabbi Alter Zev was elected as the rabbi of Strzyzow, he was not even twenty years old. He was a good–looking man, especially when he matured and his beard turned the colour of salt and pepper. He had an angelic face. Even the gentiles admired this aristocratic figure. He had a very sweet voice and rumours were that in his youth, he composed a melody to the lyrics of a Sabbath song. It was well–known that all members of the Ropczyce Rabbinical Dynasty were blessed with musical talents.

Rabbi Alter Zev sang and led the prayers and was upset when his helpers sang off–tune. His prayers were always prolonged but people did not mind. It was a pleasure to listen to his chanting. He was truly G–d's servant and he studied the Torah day and night. His daily prayers lasted until later afternoon. He was very charitable and sometimes gave away his last penny. The Rebitzin knew better than anybody else what a righteous man he was and, therefore, she watched him closely since he was the apple of her eyes. She always put money in his pocket so he would not be embarrassed if somebody asked him for alms.

On more than one occasion and on a Friday, after his wife lit the candles, he declared that he was not going to shul because he pledged his Shtreime for charity. Since he was short in change to put in the charity boxes, he placed his shtreimel near the boxes as a pledge. In those days there were many charity boxes in every Jewish home and every Friday, before candle–lighting, people donated small change into the boxes. Rabbi Alter Zev's wife had to go to her neighbours to borrow money to put in the boxes so that the Rabbi would be able to go to shul. Meanwhile, the congregation were waiting for him, and grumbling that the Rabbi was burdening them unnecessarily.

And if all year–round he was so absorbed in serving G–d, imagine how he was on holidays. Let us begin first with Passover: They used to tell about the rabbi from Ropczyce that his soul was obsessed with the mitzva of Sukkoth because, all year round, he either talked about the Sukkah or did something for the Sukkah. His grandson, Rabbi Alter Zev was obsessed with Passover, especially with the importance of having kosher matzos.

Rabbi Alter Zev went to the field in person to oversee the harvesting of wheat. He then stored the wheat in an especially dry place to prevent any moisture from getting on to the wheat. He stood by when the wheat was ground with grinding stones and the matzos that he ate were the ones he baked on Erev Pesach, the day before the Seder night. To the baking of the matzos, the rabbi invited almost the entire town. Everyone was anxious to help in such a holy endeavour.

[Page 102]

During the baking of the matzos, the people sang and recited Psalms with the traditional melodies from Ropczyce. When the baking ended, everybody was rewarded with three matzos for the first Seder night. People carried these matzos home with pride. Rabbi Alter Zev also invited the young men who had participated in baking the matzos to be his guests for the second Seder night and many accepted his invitation.

Who could forget a Seder with Reb Alter Zev? There was no electricity in Strzyzow but when the rabbi sat at the head of the table surrounded by his family and guests, a brightness of light shone upon us all. It seemed like the angels from heaven provided a special heavenly light. His white gown had a special whiteness and the rabbi himself, with his majestic face, expressed only holiness. When he began reciting the Haggadah, silence fell upon the room. No one wanted to miss a word while he chanted the Haggadah. They used to say that if people knew how the rabbi conducted a Seder, everyone would leave his house and would come to the rabbi's Seder. The rabbi always added some interesting anecdotes about how his ancestors and other famous rabbis celebrated their Seder nights. Even in the way he ate was worth watching. He ate with a certain devotion and reverence, not just to fill his stomach. The rabbi used to tell jokes that had been told by his grandfather, the famous Rabbi Naphtali from Ropczyce who was known as an amusing man.

And how was Rabbi Alter Zev on the High Holidays? I don't know if anybody is able to describe Rabbi Alter Zev during the Silent Prayer on Rosh Hashanah when tears, the size of pearls, rolled down his face or, for that matter, his dancing on Simchat Torah during the Hakafot. I will never forget the Rabbi's last Rosh Hashanah when he was unable to walk and was carried to shul on a chair. Still he led the Mussaf prayers and when he reached the prayer: "Unesanei Tokef", the verse where it says who shall live and who shall die, we realized that he knew that his end was near.

Like all other Jews, his family had its share in the Holocaust. His sons and daughters and their families all perished. Only a few of his family survived and they continue to serve G–d. Some live in the United States and some in Israel.

[Page 103]

Rabbi Nechemiah Shapiro
by Shlomo Yahalomi

"Out of the depths I called to Thee"
(Psalms, Ch.130, ver.1)

Attributes which are listed by the sages in the Talmud such as: good looks, cleverness, stature and wisdom were all possessed by Rabbi Nechemiah. Even now I still see him standing right in front of me, upright and with a lively expression on his face. He had sparkling eyes through which you could see his purity and good–heartedness. All the Shapiros, going back to the founder of the Shapiro Dynasty – Rabbi Tzvi Elimelech Shapiro, were blessed with all the above–mentioned merits. Rabbi Nechemiah was a very humble man. Although he was well–known as a Torah scholar, he never seemed to be arrogant about it or boastful. On the contrary, many times during conversations with me, he told me that he wished that he had been born into a poor family and was a simple Jew rather than to be from a Rabbinical Dynasty. He explained it by saying that G–d does not ask much from simple and uneducated Jews as long as they serve G–d the way they know. But, from Rabbi Nechemiah, G–d expected more and more all the time. He used to recall how the rabbi from Ropzyzce always asked: "What is the difference between a simple uneducated Jew and a rabbi of his stature?" And he answered that a simple man gets up in the morning, says his prayers, does a few good deeds and thinks that he did G–d's will the best he could. I, a rabbi of the stature of Rabbi Naphtali from Ropczyce, no matter how much I try to fulfil G–d's will and study Torah day and night, still feel that it is not enough. Nevertheless, Rabbi Nechemiah did overcome his "tragedy" and was not an embarrassment to his forefathers. Rabbi Nechemiah inherited from his grandfather, the Rabbi from Sassov, the love for his fellow man and Jew. He loved everybody, friend or foe. He literally embraced them, patted their backs, gave encouragement and strengthened their belief that G–d the Almighty had not forsaken them. Was it any wonder that the simple folk, tradesmen, hard–working people loved him so much? These people were ready to sacrifice their lives for their rabbi if, Heaven forbid, somebody would show any disrespect to the rabbi. He called them G–d's people. Come and see the remnants of these simple Jews who are in Israel now, some of whom, to my sorrow, left their parent's ways. Come and see how their souls simply go out at the mention of the revered name "Rabbi Nechemiale" as he was called in endearment.

From this maternal grandfather, the rabbi from Sandz, he inherited devotion to G–d and obedience of the laws of Moses down to the smallest command. He did not inherit the rabbi's extremism. Notwithstanding all the above attributions, Rabbi Nechemiah was unlucky his entire life. He was never rich and whatever he had, he gave away. In spite of the Sandz–Sadigora dispute, he preserved the friendship of Sadigora offspring. When he lived in Vienna, he had friendly relationship with the rabbi's, grandchildren who also lived in Vienna.

[Page 104]

He did not follow their way of Hassidism – it did not go that far. He followed his own ancestor's traditions especially that of Rabbi Tzvi Elimelech. The reason for this adherence was not only because he was the fifth generation of the Shapiro Dynasty but out of his conviction that this was the right way to serve G–d. Rabbi Nechemiah was the son–in–law of Rabbi Yeshayahu Hertz from Dynow who was a grandson of Rabbi Tzvi Elimelech.

Rabbi Nechemiah's father established his own Hassidic customs and did not follow his father's footsteps and neither did Rabbi Nechemiah follow his father's customs. When Rabbi Nechemiah was asked why not? He responded that he was doing exactly as his father did. His mother was not pleased but she could not change his mind.

Rabbi Nechemiah had his staunchest admirers in Strzyzow. They were the Hassidim of the Rabbi from Munkatch: Reb Elazar Wurtzel, Reb Chaim Yacov Nuremberg and Reb Chaim Mandel. They supported him out of allegiance to the rabbi of Munkatch who was his cousin and they had a very close relationship.

Not only did these fiery Hassidim stand by Rabbi Nechemiah but also simple folks supported him, especially in his dispute over the rabbinic seat.

Rabbi Nechemiah! Where are you now? I wish you could see us now, remnants of your congregation. Now we would like to hear you chanting the Sabbath afternoon prayer – the "Vaani Tefilati" with your strong voice. How sweet it sounded. I remember one Sabbath afternoon before the Shavuot holiday. You, Rabbi, had not felt so well. The people asked you to relax and not to lead the prayers but you refused. Later, you began to recite the "Vaani Tefilati" (which means: "I pray before you, O G–d"). It is time to help your folk in Israel and you also added in Yiddish your own words: "Derbarimdiger G–d, derbarim zich shoin" (which means: "O merciful G–d, have mercy and respond to our prayers"). Suddenly, a shriek was heard in the kloyz. This was the retarded epileptic, Eliezer Mussler. He fell to the floor and fainted. People whispered that you tried to help this unfortunate boy with your prayers.

When the High Holidays approached, especially at the first day of Slichot which begins one week before Rosh Hashanah, Rabbi Nechemiah in his prayers demanded mercy for his flock. He always chanted and led the prayers himself with a sweet melodic voice. The kloyz was packed and Rabbi Nechemiah began the prayers mixing in Yiddish words such as "Oy tate, heiliker tate". ("Father, holy Father, please listen to your flock's prayers and respond positively". There was such a silence in the kloyz that a fly could be heard. Rabbi Nechemiah, perspiring and his face pale, prayed with such an ecstasy that his body and soul were in it. The Rabbi always blew the shofar. He was a very skilled man in many fields; mohel, architect and writer. Nowhere can you hear, nowadays, chanting like those that Rabbi Nechemiah chanted on the High Holidays. The young generation does not comprehend how Jews prayed before the Holocaust.

When the war began, Rabbi Nechemiah wondered aloud and asked by the Almighty could not leave the Jews alone. Rabbi Nechemiah did not lament only on the trouble which had befallen the Jews but also spoke about all of mankind.

[Page 105]

At the beginning of the war, he tried to cheer up the people as much as he could. He, the sickly man who in normal times endured several diseases, suddenly gained strength to help his flock in these troubled times. He tried to strengthen the broken–hearted of his community. He mobilized his entire energy to convince people that Hitler's downfall was imminent. He told them stories about similar situations in the past when somehow the Jews survived and help had come unexpectedly.

However, Rabbi Nechemiah himself was not very optimistic. He confided to a few close friends that he foresaw tragedy of large dimensions to the people of Israel. He tried to prevent panic. Apparently, it was decided in heaven to help him ease the suffering of his community a little bit.

One day during the Nazi occupation of Strzyzow, a few Nazi came into his house. They began to terrorize the rabbi but the rabbi did not demonstrate any fear. In a loud voice and in perfect German which he knew because he had resided in Vienna, he asked them if they were able to converse in a civilized way. Surely, if such a question would have been put to the Germans by a simple man, the response would have been a bullet in his body! However, Rabbi Nechemiah was tall, husky and handsome. His attitude startled the Nazi and caught them off–balance. They did not harm him. They just left the house silently. After they had left, the Rabbi thanked G–d that he had escaped a tragedy. But this was not the end of the story. When the commanding officer of the Nazi heard about the Rabbi's knowledge of the German language, he ordered the rabbi to report to his office. It is not hard to imagine how the rabbi must have felt hearing of such an invitation. He decided that he would not deny what he had said to the soldiers in his house. He would say exactly what had happened and that all he had asked was for a civilized behaviour.

When the rabbi came to the office, he noticed that the commanding officer was a middle–aged man with a gentle expression on his face. Indeed, the thought that there were good and bad Nazi was far from his mind, but the looks of the officer encouraged him. "Are you Herr Rabiner Shapiro?" When the rabbi responded positively, they developed a conversation in a Viennese accent. The officer told the rabbi that he was also from Vienna. They ended the conversation in an almost friendly atmosphere. The officer never mentioned the incident with his soldiers. When the rabbi left, the officer told him to let him know if he had any problems. Everybody wondered what had caused the officer to behave in the way that he had. Many thought that maybe he knew the rabbi from Vienna.

The rabbi spent sleepless nights thinking on whether he should develop a friendship with the officer and use him to extort favours for the Jews. He was not sure if it was proper for a Jew, especially a rabbi, to have anything to do with a Nazi. He also wondered what the non–Jewish neighbours would say. HE feared that they would call him a traitor. But his love for his flock convinced him to do everything possible to make life a little easier for the Jews in Strzyzow.

[Page 106]

For a whole year and as long as the commandant was stationed in Strzyzow, Rabbi Nechemiah succeeded in calling off a few decrees which the local Polish Jew–haters tried to instigate against the Jews.

When I was on my way to escaping the Nazi, I stopped in Strzyzow (by that time I was living in another shtetl) and I went to see the rabbi. He was sitting in his room surrounded by a few of his friends and admirers. All of them had sad expressions on their faces, knowing that heavy clouds were hanging over the Jews. Someone asked the rabbi a question: "Is it true that this was the last stage of suffering for the Jews before the Messiah's coming?" The rabbi asked the man: "Why do you think so?" And the man responded innocently: "If it is not for the Messiah, why is G–d tormenting us? Is it perhaps for the sins that we have sinned?" Rabbi Nechemiah got up from his chair and started pacing across the room, back and forth. His face turned pale and he suddenly raised his voice in anger and stated emphatically: "No! No! No such talk in my presence. You do not mean to tell me that we are supposed to justify the Almighty's treatment of his children". He sat down and after a while he started to tell the following story: Once a woman came to Rabbi Moshe Leib from Sassov and complained bitterly that her children kept dying one after the other. In her complaint, she said that G–d was not fair to her. The Rabbi's wife, overhearing the woman, scolded her and told her that G–d knows what he is doing and that she should not behave this way. Rabbi Moshe Leib turned to the woman and said: "Dear woman, you are right and your complaints are justified. I will pray for you and I promise you that the next child you will bear, G–d will help you and you will live to see him or her under the wedding canopy". When the rabbi finished the story, everybody understood that the moral of the story was that there may be a time when the children of Israel felt that G–d's treatment was not too merciful.

When I left the rabbi, he told me: "My child, you know the prayer and the meaning of the words – "out of the depths I called to thee". And the rabbi began to cry. He then said: "Nobody is able to help us now, only G–d Almighty. The Jewish people are now in deep trouble but let us hope that G–d will eventually have mercy on us".

The Assistant Rabbi Yacov Shpalter
by Shlomo Yahalomi

Rabbi Yacov Shpalter was born in Illitch, a very small town in Galicia. He came to Strzyzow after the previous assistant rabbi, Reb Alter Ezra Seidman passed away.

Rabbi Yacov Shpalter was an interesting personality. He was very sharp and well–educated in all response books concerning Jewish religious code and strictures. He was also well–versed in many other holy books. Several times he had harsh disputes with Rabbi Nechemiah Shapiro and other rabbinical authorities. But, Rabbi Yacov Shpalter never gave up in his discussions. He was very persistent and loved to discuss. Most of the time, he found a source or precedent in the books to prove that he was right to rule the way he did.

[Page 107]

When the Kehillah refurbished the mikva in Strzyzow, under the supervision of the assistant rabbi, everything was done the way Rabbi Yacov Shpalter wanted and he ruled that the mikva was kosher. However, when Rabbi Nechemiah came to inspect it, he ruled that the mikva was not kosher.

According to Jewish law, if a rabbi rules or makes a certain decision, a party concerned is not permitted to turn to another rabbi for a second opinion and another rabbi is not permitted to rule otherwise. Once Rabbi Nechemiah forbade something and notwithstanding this decision, Rabbi Yacov Shpalter ruled differently. Rabbi Nechemiah was very angry and upset and he turned to a few famous rabbis and Torah scholars for support in his criticism of Rabbi Yacov Shpalter. However, Rabbi Yacov also recruited a few scholars whom he convinced with his arguments that his viewpoint was also correct.

This dispute was never solved because many rabbis disliked such disputes and hated to be dragged into such arguments. Rabbi Yacov never felt insulted by his opponents. On the contrary, he used to joke about it and laughed about them.

He knew all the tricks and manoeuvres in the business world and when he was asked to arbitrate a dispute between two businessmen, he was well qualified to make the right decision. Rabbi Yacov lived in our house and many times had asked me to be present during litigation or to look up a precedent in a similar case in order to make the right judgment.

It was a well–known fact, in those days, that Jews avoided bringing their problems to a gentile court and, therefore, they always brought their disputes before a rabbinical judge. It is impossible for me to re–tell all the stories or jokes that I had a chance to hear from Rabbi Yacov Shpalter. To our sorrow, he and his family including his grandchildren all perished in the Holocaust. Only one grandson, Reb Ephraim Shpalter, survived and now lives in Israel.

Memories from Strzyzow
by Itzhok Deutch

This story was told to me by Reb Shalom Schwartzman when I went to see him in Jerusalem after my arrival in Israel. He told me that he saw this story recorded in the chronicle of the Kehillah before the great fire of 1895 destroyed the chronicle and other old documents.

It happened when Rabbi Mendele from Rymanow was very old. When he was ill, Rabbi Naphtali from Ropczyce went to see him. There was no train in those day so the rabbi travelled by horse and buggy. The road led through Strzyzow where Rabbi Naphtali arrived at dawn. He prayed in shul and rested for a few hours.

At noon, Rabbi Naphtali resumed his journey and was escorted out of town by many Hassidim. When they reached the village of Dobrzechow, the horses refused to continue and they remained standing in the middle of the road. Everyone was astonished and looked at the Rabbi.

Rabbi Naphtali became immersed in his thoughts and it seemed as if he was trying to remember something. He then said to the crowd: "I am supposed to convey greetings here to a great Tzadik. Please lead me to him".

The Hassidim were astounded and began to tremble because they all knew that there were no Jews in Dobrzechow.

[Page 108]

The Hassidim did not know what to tell the rabbi and where to lead him.

Finally, somebody remembered that on a side-road that led to the village of Wysoka, there was a little house where a poor and simple Jew lived. This Jew was called the "Psalm Jew" and they took the rabbi there.

When Rabbi Naphtali stepped in through the door, the Psalm Jew rose and said loudly: "Welcome Rabbi Tarphon"

Later, Rabbi Naphtali continued on his journey to Rymanow. However, in Strzyzow, this incident made a deep impression. The fact that there lived a hidden righteous among them and that nobody knew it could not be ignored. The shtetl was in uproar. The sick ran to Dobrzechow to seek healing. People came from near and far, handing him notes about all kinds of problems. But the Psalm Jew refused to see anybody or to accept notes (Quitlach) insisting that he was a simple man and not a rabbi. The people did not relent. They demanded to know what the meaning of the greeting was: "Welcome Rabbi Tarphone". So he declared to them that in the previous incarnation, many generations ago, Rabbi Naphtali was the Tanai Rabbi Tarphon.

In his old age the Psalm Jew moved into the city. He did not become a rabbi but he did lead Torah discourses. That is how he spent the last days of his life and he was considered holy by the people of the town.

A Miracle
by Itzhok Deutch

It was known in Strzyzow that many members of the local rich family, the Patryns, were friends of the rabbi from Sassov. One of them, Jan Patryn who was called "the ox driver" because he ploughed his field with oxen, was an admirer of the Shapiros. Not once did I see him unloading produce from his fields at Rabbi Nechemiah Shapiro's house.

Curious about the beginning of this friendship, I once asked Jan Patryn about it.

"Yes", said Mr. Patryn. "I owe the Shapiros a lot. I owe them my life. Their holy grandmother saved me from a sure death".

"How was it possible?" I asked, wondering. "Their grandmother was already dead for many years". "Listen to this wonderful story and you will wonder no more". And Mr. Patryn began to tell his story.

It was in 1914. The Russians had just occupied Strzyzow. There were rumours circulating that the Russians were committing cruelties to the civilian population and everyone sat in their locked homes and were afraid to walk in the streets. We already heard that they had stabbed a leather merchant by the name of Mandel in the nearby town of Czudec. The stores in town had been robbed of all merchandize and we thought that now they would start to rob the houses.

About a week after the occupation began when I and my family were sitting in the house depressed, we heard a knock on the door. We all remained silent and, at first, we did not open the door. However, the knocking became stronger and we were forced to open the door.

Two Russian soldiers appeared at the door and immediately began to look around for something to take. Apparently, they did not like my poor belongings but they soon noticed the boots which I was wearing.

[Page 109]

"Give me your boots and we will not take anything else", they said.

The boots were made from good black leather and I had no desire to part with them. I knew I could not afford to buy another pair. There was already a shortage in everything especially footwear for the winter. Afraid of being robbed, I had stashed away some money but not enough to replace such a pair of boots.

I decided I was not giving up my boots. "Take whatever you want", I said "but not my boots. The winter is approaching and they are the only ones I have. I cannot walk around barefoot in the winter".

One of the soldiers withdrew his sword from its sheath, raised it over me and said: "Take off the boots or I will kill you".

Both soldiers grabbed and tried to pull the boots off my feet. I fought them with all my power and, during the struggle, I grabbed the sword and broke it in two.

The two soldiers became confused and I took advantage of the situation and ran out of the house. However, I did not know where to run to in order to escape the attackers. I felt that they were chasing after me and were getting closer. I was sure that if they caught me, it would be my end.

My inner instincts told me to run into the Jewish cemetery which was not far from my house. I ran between the gravestones and noticed a big double gravestone which consisted of three parts: one large flat stone which lay on the ground and a steel bar which connected the head stone with the stone at the foot. An inner voice told me: "here is the place to hide". It seemed to me that I heard a voice from the grave: "Yashek, stay here".

When I stood at this grave I saw the two Russians coming after me. I swiftly threw myself on the ground along the stone and laid there drenched with sweat. I saw the Russians and heard their steps. Nonetheless, even though they were so near to me, they did not see me. After they had searched the entire cemetery and failed to find me, they left. Only then did I breathe with relief. I rose and thoughtfully looked at the grave. I understood that there probably was a holy person buried here and who had saved my life and I was overpowered with a feeling of reverence. I solemnly bowed my head to the grave. But who was this holy person who had performed a miracle? I did not rest but quickly went to town to find a Jew who could tell me whom this grave belonged to. The first man I encountered was Reb Zalman Brauner, the bookbinder.

"Come with me!" I said to him. "Read to me the inscription on that gravestone in the Jewish cemetery. You will render me a big favour".

"What happened?" he said. "Why do you want to know and why are you so excited?"

"I will tell you all about it later. But first, let's go to the cemetery". I went with Reb Zalman, pointed to that gravestone and asked him whose gravestone it was? "Oh, here lies the holy Rebetzin, of blessed memory, from Lancut, the Shapiros' grandmother".

I remained a friend of the Shapiros forever. I also assembled me.

[Page 110]

Entire family to tell them this miraculous story and asked them to support the rabbinical family of the Shapiros because they were holy people.

I also told this story to my relative, Dr. Joseph Patryn and he was so impressed with it that he decided to withdraw his resignation from the mayoralty (from which he had earlier resigned) in order to be able to help the Jews during the hard and difficult times of the occupation.

A Jewish Heart
(The luck of the poor man)
by Itzhok Deutch

It is common knowledge that a rich person is lucky. But sometimes it also happens that a poor man gets lucky not to lose the last thing he owns.

Reb Leibush Hochdorf, Reb Reuven's Shapiro's son–in–law, owned a small store with yard goods located in the house of his father–in–law adjacent to the shul in Strzyzow. From this store, he barely made a living. Once, on a Wednesday morning after the Tuesday market day, Reb Leibush took all the money that came in yesterday, borrowed some more money from his neighbours and went to Rzeszow to buy new merchandize for his store. He hoped that buying for cash would have him pay a lower price and, therefore, would be able to sell easily.

After his arrival in Rzeszow, he immediately went to the wholesaler, Reb Shimon Fleisher, and announced to the salespeople that he had cash and wanted to buy cheap. He selected the merchandize for the entire sum that he had and was happy about the prices.

When the time came to pay, he became pale and horrified because he could not find the money that he had brought with him. He searched in every pocket of his clothes but alas, he had no money. It was gone! The salesman advised him to retrace his steps back to the railroad station where he might possibly have lost his money.

Leibush went back and searched the streets in vain. He could not find his money. He remained standing in the middle of the station in desperation and, out of great sorrow; tears came out of his eyes.

Accidentally, Reb Yacov Nathan Kanner, an important man in Rzeszow who knew Reb Leibush and his status, happened to be at the railroad station. "What happened? Why are you crying?" asked Reb Yacov. "Some kind of misfortune?" Leibush burst out sobbing and told him about the money he had lost. Not only his money but money that did not belong to him. And now, how could he buy merchandize in order to be able to repay the money he had borrowed?

"Do not despair, the Almighty will help and you will find your money", said Reb Yacov. Thinking for a while, he continued. "How much money was there? Do you remember the denominations? Where did you keep it? And how was it wrapped?" Reb Leibush told him: "Four hundred zlotys in ten zloty bills wrapped in a newspaper and tied with a string".

"Calm down. I will go into the street and inquire of the local Jews. Maybe someone has found it?" Reb Yacov Kanner, the noble and charitable Jew, speedily went among his rich acquaintances and collected four hundred zlotys in ten zloty bills, wrapped it in a newspaper, tied it with a string and, with a radiant face, quickly brought the money to Reb Leibush Hochdorf who sat with a trembling heart in the waiting room of the station.

[Page 111]

Leibush, bewildered with joy, thanked Reb Yacov several times and wished him success and long life. With great joy he ran back to the wholesale place of the Fleisher firm, showed the just–found package of money and told about the miracle that Reb Yacov Kanner had brought the found money. The face of the salesman who had waited on Hochdorf before and had heard the story, became white as chalk because he knew very well that nobody had found the money. He himself had stolen it when Hochdorf absent–mindedly had put the money on the table. The salesman realized what the noble Reb Yacov Kanner had done. He was very touched and a feeling of remorse arose in his heart. He could stand it no longer. He pulled the money out of his pocket and returned it to Reb Leibush.

Hanukkah in Shtetl
by Harry Langsam

Can someone imagine the joy of us children when Hanukkah was approaching? The joy was overwhelming for many reasons. First of all, we were free from studying in the evening because soon after services, the lighting of the candles was required. Afterwards, we were supposed to gaze at the burning candles and sing songs for at least half an hour. Therefore, there was not much time left to return to the cheder.

The air was frosty outdoors and tiny, crisp snowflakes were falling from heaven. It was only the beginning of the brutal winter. The ovens in kloyz and in the Beit HaMidrash were warm and cosy and the regular occupants of the benches nearby sat there before the services and talked politics or reminisced about World War I, stories that had been told many times. It seemed that every winter, these same stories were re–told. How they evacuated to Bohemia and Hungary and how some escaped from prisoner–of–war camps in Italy.

Of course, the rich had not need to sit around the ovens in the Beit HaMidrash because their homes were warm enough and, at Hanukkah time, they already enjoyed the taste of Passover food. Hanukkah was the time when housewives prepared schmaltz for Passover and the goose cracklings were devoured immediately.

When Hanukkah eve arrived and the Almighty was good to us children and sent us down the first pure white snow, it was for us the greatest happiness and exhilaration. Snowballs were thrown at the sextons while they were reciting the blessings during the candle lighting ceremony.

I have no idea how such a tradition of throwing snowballs at the sexton started. Maybe tens or hundreds of years ago. One thing we were sure of was that the sexton would have felt deprived if, Heaven forbid, nobody threw snowballs at them! No sexton would have relinquished the privilege of being hit with a snowball on his head. And, when snow was not available, a wet towel or a bucket of cold water, which someone dared to spill over them from the women's gallery, was also acceptable. In addition, the sexton was forced to stay under such an avalanche and still try to light the wet Hanukkah candles.

[Page 112]

In later years, the Rebetzin, of blessed memory, made sure that the gallery was closed thinking that what the sexton received downstairs in the sanctuary was enough without the additional bucket of water.

The festivities began an hour or so before the services while Reb Itzikl, the sexton, was busy preparing the big metal Hanukkah lamp, and putting in the candles. We, the youngsters, began to carry ammunition into the kloyz and storing them under the benches. Until this day, I cannot understand how these snowballs did not melt. When the services were over and the mourners finished saying Kaddish, Itzikl Dayches, the sexton, (Dayches was his wife's name by which he was called), was standing with a candle in his hand like a conductor with his stick ready to begin. He began with a drawn–out and festive voice: "Baaruch A–a–ta". Son the children began yelling and screaming and the show began.

Hanukkah possessed many more pleasurable activities. For instance, attending the official City Rabbi's candle lighting ceremony or, as my father and I did, attending the ceremony at the home of Rabbi Nechemiah from Sassov. To be present when the rabbi lit the candles was a spiritual uplifting. Every night a few quorums gathered in the rabbi's house to hear him recite the blessings and light the candles in the beautiful silver menorah. Until the ceremony began, the Hassidim sat around and told Hassidic tales. The room was warm and cosy and a festive mood reigned everywhere.

Meanwhile, we, the children, were playing with the dreidel and many of us lost our "Hanukkah gelt".

Soon, the rabbi was slowly putting on his Sabbath fur hat and his wide silk belt on his long silk coat. He poured oil into the bright and shining silver Hanukkah menorah while the Hassidim rose and began to sway back and forth, like a wave. The rabbi then recited the blessings with devotion and sang "Al Hanisim".

The soul felt so good during the ceremony. It seemed to me that these little wicks that were burning in oil brought a ray of hope and told the people who gathered here in the rabbi's house that somewhere far away, there was a land which, a long time ago, belonged to us. Then the gentiles tried to expel us but a miracle occurred and we overcame them. Afterwards, a small vial of oil was found, surely not bigger than the vial that the rabbi used and that miraculously found vial of oil keeps bringing light for the Jews until this day.

The rabbi sang "Maoz Tzur" and asked Reb Moshe Yacov Mandel to sing "Mizmor Shir". Reb Samuel Moshe Grosskopf sang "Or Haganuz". Next, Reb Elazar Wurtzel began a Torah discourse with the participation of Reb David Wiener and the rest of the congregation.

On Hanukkah, it was also permitted to play cards. It was not a sin. On this account, gambling was taking place in several candy stores and it lasted longer than Hanukkah. The Hassidic young men played in private homes but only on Hanukkah and on Christmas Eve. The days of Hanukkah were over and were followed by harsh winter days but the pleasant experience of Hanukkah remained in our memory forever.

[Page 113]

Piquant stories from Strzyzow
by Heschel Diamand

Our shtetl was loved and dear to us all and we all deserve to be proud of the good deeds by the town in general and by many individuals in particular especially of our glorious past, including the great rabbis who served our community. The rabbis contributed to the glory and brightness of Strzyzow and they also made us well–known around the world. Nonetheless, there were some events that also brought shame and loss of respect. For instance, the rabbinical dispute caused many small disputes among the inhabitants. These disputes seem frivolous nowadays but at the time, they occasionally aggravated the whole town and not only resulted in hatred but also caused us to be laughed at by others. Now I would like to tell a few tragi–comical episodes from the last years before the horrible devastation.

An awful story about "Rev'EE"
by Heschel Diamand

Who amongst us does not know that there exist nice, medium and ugly aliyot (ascending to the bimah and Torah)? The third, sixth and maftir are the choice aliyot. One who is called before maftir is medium. The fifth person who was called to the Torah was neither the best nor down and out. In contrast, if you were the fourth calling, may G–d help you. If a revered citizen (and who did not consider himself revered?) was called to the Torah, "Rev'ee", the fourth, it was considered an insult. The frivolous gang had a ball with such a person and they endlessly kidded him. "They could not find anybody else whom to give Rev'ee?" They kept pestering him and that caused strong resentment and arguments between the unfortunate victims and the trustee in shul, in kloyz and in Beit HaMidrash.

Well, one day, it happened during the time when the Rosen brothers, Yacov and Mendel, were trustees in the Beit HaMidrash. They decided to put an end to this ridiculous predicament. I was the leader of the Kehillah and they came to me to seek my support for their suggestion that from this Saturday onwards, "Rev'ee" would be given to the most prosperous and revered worshippers and that should put an end to the discriminatory feelings. The trustees proposed that I, the head of the Kehillah, should be the first to jump into the fire. Of course, I agreed and I was called the fourth person to the Torah reading. The town came to life and caused a tremendous uproar. And from then on, it became standard procedure. No more special privileges for the more affluent worshippers when called to the Torah. Logically, order should have returned. But not so! Yacov and Mendel Rosen, the trustees, declared that the rabbi too should get Rev'ee. At first I was reluctant to agree to their proposition. I later told them; "If the rabbi agrees, it would be fine with me". The rabbi was traditionally called the sixth: "Shishi", once a month. The rabbi was asked and he philosophically responded "I will keep getting my "Shishi" once a month and also Rev'ee whenever they will call me".

[Page 114]

Understandably, such an event was historical for the town. However, the idyllic situation did not last long. A short time later, someone (out of reverence to the martyr of which I cannot reveal his name) complained to the Ministry of Religion in Warsaw that the rabbi was given an aliyah which was usually reserved for simpletons and such an act was demeaning and an outrage. It brought shame to the entire community. The district commissioner summoned the leader of the Kehillah to report to him for an explanation and he also called the rabbi for an inquiry. (The rabbi was innocent because it was done without his knowledge). The community leader took with him Reb Chaim Mandel – a Torah scholar who intended to prove to the commissioner that according to the rules of the Torah reading, Rev'ee is even better than Shishi. Before we went into the office of the commissioner, the rabbi begged me to do everything possible to avoid blasphemy. I suggested to the rabbi that he declare that Rev'ee is as good as the other aliyoth. The rabbi did as I told him and the explanation was forwarded to the Ministry in Warsaw…

How Reb Yosl, the sexton, had suddenly gone deaf
by Heschel Diamand

The trustees were not always capable of running the business. There were trustees who distributed aliyot to members of their clique. Once it happened that the trustees belonged to one party and the head of the community to another. Somebody decided to teach the trustees a lesson and arranged a deal with the sexton, Rob Yosl – a clever man who knew from where the wind blew – and saw that the majority was on the opposite side of the trustees. On a holiday eve, he agreed to accept a list of names of those that he should call to the Torah reading from the trustees' opponents and here is what happened: When the trustee told the sexton whom to call, he called someone else from the list. The trustees looked at each other and asked the sexton: "What happened?" But Reb Yosl played dumb and claimed he had not heard them correctly. At the next calling, the same thing happened. The trustee said: "Shlomo" and the sexton called: "Yacov". Finally, the trustees understood what was going on and they capitulated.

Reb Baruch Berglass
by Shlomo Yahalomi

Medium height, his back bent forward, a long beard, deep penetrating eyes, slow and carless walk, this is the description of Reb Baruch Berglass. One of the most beloved men in town. In certain ways, he was one of a kind, a rare breed. The town elders used to say that in his youth, he was as sharp as a needle, brilliant, intelligent and knowledgeable in both Talmud and many holy books. At seventeen, he was a diligent student, studying from three in the morning to eleven o'clock at night. He was fascinated with figures and counted each line, letter and punctuation mark that he had studied.

[Page 115]

He also had a knack for finding any subject in the Talmud. When he matured and got married, he studied less but did not stop.

His friend, colleague and avid opponent was Reb Shalom Schwartzman who was also one of the beloved men in town, and about whom we will tell later in this book. They never agreed on anything. Sometimes their discussions were so overpowering that they almost insulted each other but remained friends and respected one another. Both were G–d fearing men, realizing that their arguments were only to enhance their devotion to G–d and abiding his commands.

Reb Baruch Berglass was a rich man and prosperous in his business. He had customers not only on market days but every day of the week. Although he knew that he was needed in the store and his family would have liked him to shorten his morning prayers, he took his time and disregarded their wishes. His prayers lasted more than an hour and were followed by one hour studying. He did not just speedily whisper his prayers. No! He enunciated each word separately with devotion and reverence, understanding the meaning of each word. Certain words he would repeat several times especially the "Shema Israel" concentrating on each syllable. If some strange thought came to his mind that interrupted his concentration, he would start all over again. Reb Shalom Schwartzman loved to poke fun at him for his repetitiousness. But Reb Baruch did not surrender. Angrily he told him: "Mind your own business! I did not ask for your advice". Or he would laughingly say: "are you chastising me? Very well, you fulfilled your duty, thank you". And that is how he disarmed him.

Reb Baruch Berglass was a kind and charitable man but people whispered behind his back that he was miserly. People who knew him well knew that although he did not throw his money around, he always gave with a smile and friendliness. Of course, being known as a wealthy man, more was demanded from him and he enjoyed negotiating over the amount. Whenever he asked for a donation, he never let anyone leave empty–handed. And, concerning hospitality, he was the first to offer it. He always fed the poor Jewish wanderers who passed through Strzyzow. Whenever a poor man appeared hungry in shul in in Beit HaMidrash, he was immediately directed to Reb Baruch Berglass' house. For breakfast or lunch, he could be sent without advance notice but for dinner, the household had to be notified in advance.

Reb Baruch served for many years as a member of the Kehillah, always alert to community needs and generous with money and advice. He was highly respected and he always avoided political arguments. He was a truthful man and hated hypocrisy.

His son, Itzhok Berglass survived the Holocaust by escaping to Soviet Russia and later went to Israel to realize his life–long dream of living in an independent Jewish homeland. Also, many of Reb Baruch's grandchildren live in Israel and in the Diaspora.

[Page 116]

Reb Avrehmal'E Goldman
by Shlomo Yahalomi

It is doubtful whether anybody in town was as popular as Avrehmal'e Goldman. Not because of his merits but because of his wife's merits. Her name was Dvoirah Sarah. The whole family had long names. His name was Abraham and his father–in–law's name was Zelig. That is why he was called Reb Avrehmal'e Zelig's. His wife's name was Dvoirah Sarah so they called her: Dvoirah Sarah, Avrehmal'e Zelig's. Their son, Itzhok, was called Itzhok, Dvoirah Sarah's Avrehmal'e Zelig's and so they called all the sons and daughters. Reb Avrehmal'e was as poor as can be. He himself used to joke about his poverty. He used to say that he was poor by a miracle: "If someone is poor because of bad luck, lacking a trade or business – that is natural, but I, a jack–of–all–trades, a wholesale businessman, having dealt with everything: building material, plasterboards, cement, roofing materials and this is only the physical merchandize. Besides the above, I have also dealt with spiritual merchandize, like being a melamed, a cantor and I still remain poverty–stricken. This can only happen by a miracle".

Reb Avrehmal'e was very educated in Talmud and Halacha. He was a teacher for many years, a highly qualified teacher who taught only teenagers, students capable of studying Talmud and the various commentaries on the Talmud. Reb Avrehmal'e had a fine chanting voice of which his wife was very proud. She used to boast to the peasants in the market about her husband's cantorial endeavours. Reb Avrehmal'e once had a lawsuit in court against his competitor and the case did not look so good. Suddenly, Dvoirah Sarah stood up in front of the judge and declared, proudly, pointing in the direction of his opponent: "You have the nerve to challenge my husband? When my husband begins to chant the Sabbath prayer –"Shochen Ad" all the worshippers are chanting with him". Reb Avrehmal'e himself was always ready to sing and display his talent. He never complained about having a sore throat or being hoarse. He was always happy, telling jokes and making fun of others and he never got insulted if people laughed at him. Even his own sons use to tell jokes about him and right to his face. About his talented sons, we will tell more later in this book. G–d shall avenge his and his family's blood. No one of his family survived.

Reb Hershel Gelander who chanted the Mussaf Prayers
by Shlomo Yahalomi

As if they were alive today, I see before me standing the wonderful townspeople and each one deserves to be written about and perpetuated in this book so that the future generations will know who the victims of the Holocaust were – the victims who did not leave behind their equals. These dear Jews were entirely wiped out; and some offspring who did survive, do not follow in their parent's traditions. Some distant relatives who did survive rarely remember the martyrs' names. However, a few did inherit nice sayings and expressions of scholars which were used by these townspeople in their daily conversations. But Reb Hershel Gelander, in addition to a son and daughter, left behind him a special form of chanting.

[Page 117]

You saw before you a man of middle height, long side–curls that looked if as though somebody had ironed them and a charcoal black beard. When he was standing behind the oven humming in a sweet melodic voice – the "Zohar" – you stood perplexed: whose are those big burning eyes expressing softness and strength at once, submerged in the book as an inseparable entity, desiring only to unite and merge the holy letters from this wonderful book? And, what is the source of the aristocratic smile hovering on his lips?

Reb Hershel Gelander grew up and was educated in the courtyards of the Sadigora Rabbinic Dynasty. There he spent his day and nights in Torah, Hassidism and songs. He was a choirboy and helper of cantors Reb J. Shorr and Samuel from Ustrzyki and others. From them, he learned how to chant. He used to say that it was very important to know how to chant properly and not only to intone loudly. The principal rule was: a cantor must not be an actor. As blowing the shofar is a science and not a trade, so is chanting. The science of chanting is to remember that we are praying before the King of the Universe. He who realizes that he is praying to the King of the Universe will not fail and will be assured that his prayers will be accepted in heaven and on earth.

Reb Hershel was a clever man, vigorous, a scholar, pious and an enthusiastic Hassid of the rabbi from Sadigora. He did not ponder about it. He just believed firmly in Hassidism. Not because he was unable to ponder but, he said: "A person should be straight. As the sages would say, 'One who is straight cannot be crooked'. Generally speaking, who needs to rake and research? There is no benefit in climbing a mountain and trying to understand things which are above our perception. We will never comprehend the ways of the holy ones (meaning the rabbis of Sadigora). But what? Whoever has open eyes and good sense understands that the important thing is not the knowledge but the belief. Is it not what the rabbis of Sadigora preached?" This prefaced each of Reb Hershel's discussion about his rabbis and, he added: "I do not intend to recruit believers in my rabbis". But still, he could not resist demonstrating his beliefs. He learned from his rabbi to love his fellow Jew, every Jew. He opposed Zionism fiercely but never insulted a Zionist personally. When he once overheard someone cursing the Zionists, he became very upset. He was very conservative and he always remained in the background. Few people knew that he got up every day of the year at four o'clock and headed straight for the mikva – summer or winter. After the immersion in the mikva, he studied the holy books at home until nine o'clock. He then went to shul for morning services. He prayed quietly with devotion. He used to tell the rabbi, Reb Israel from Ryzin: "It is better to move one little finger for G–d than to make a big noise dishonestly".

All year–round, he made a living as a small merchant but in the anticipation of the High Holidays, he stopped his secular trade and began his preparations for the holidays, rehearsing the holiday chanting. He prepared himself not only physically but spiritually as well. His chanting penetrated into each Jewish soul. On those days, he never laughed or joked, spending his time in the Beit HaMidrash where he led the prayers every year.

[Page 118]

His voice was not loud. It was a sweet mellow voice. People followed him in the prayer book word–by–word. People from other prayer houses used to come in to listen to his chanting. In the High Holidays, he was assisted by a group of young people whom he trained before the holidays. The writer of these memoirs was one of these youngsters. I was so well acquainted with his chanting that it made Reb Hershel proud to think that someday I would take his place.

When I was getting ready to escape to Russia, I went to see Reb Hershel to say goodbye. We embraced and kissed each other. Then Reb Hershel said: "It is G–d's will that the Jewish people should suffer so much. Only G–d knows how long this will last, but if….". And at this point he broke down and began to cry. Later, he composed himself and finished his sentence by saying: "You are younger and healthier than I. Please do not forget me and my prayers". May G–d avenge his innocent blood. He perished and shared the fate of his six million brothers and sisters. However, I carried with me his form of chanting throughout Siberia and after the war, to Germany and finally, to Israel. Since then, whenever I, his pupil, chant, I always see his face before me.

My father, my teacher, Reb Joseph Diamand
by Shlomo Yahalomi

My father was a highly esteemed and outstanding citizen in town. His spiritual features were: Strong faith in G–d and perpetual belief in eternity of Israel. He had a fatherly approach to every individual as well as to the community. He was a social activist, always occupied with the need of the community and with no expectation of reward. He was also blessed with positive merits: always being content, always happy, and always full of hope that everything will turn out alright, and he shared his happiness with everyone who came in touch with him. These merits in addition to his cleverness and wisdom put in in the centre of community activism. Although there was no lack of disputes in town, whether spiritual or not (in which he was sometimes involved), but people knew that even when he was angry, his anger was only pretended. More than once during a heated exchange, he would throw in a funny remark or tell a joke and soon the tempers were cooled off and the loud–mouths lost their tongues. He knew how to raise himself from his individuality and judge each problem from the perspective of what is good for the community. Whenever an urgent need arose to mediate between real or imagined adversaries or to extricate someone from mire, they turned to Reb Joseph and he, with his cleverness and patience, settled everything in a way that left both parties feeling victorious. It was all done with a smile on his face. They said about him – according to Rabbi Alter Zev: "What he could achieve with a funny and sharp remark in the right place and at the right time, ten wise men could not accomplish". Generally speaking, he was never agitated or angry and if, on occasion he became agitated, it was very easy to appease him. He used to say: "My theory is if somebody tells me 'Shalom Aleichem', my answer is 'Aleichem Hashalom'.

He had a warm Jewish heart and helped whoever turned to him, no matter what kind of help was needed, advice on how to extricate oneself from entanglement or for help to obtain a favour from a gentile master.

[Page 119]

He was active in a very sensitive and delicate field: freeing Jewish sons from military service. As it was known in Galicia, every year and in each shtetl, a military commission visited and gave physical examinations to those who were eligible for military service. Our Jewish brothers were not too happy to serve in the gentile military. On the contrary, everybody tried to avoid this "privilege" to suffer and sometimes to get killed for a fatherland which was not his. And it is an old story that you could always find a good Jew who acted to free our Jewish brothers from the claws of the gentile military. In our shtetl, there was also one who was active in this field and this was my father Reb Joseph Diamand. He did this holy work without any expectation of being rewarded. He always tried to contact the members of the commission and to come to an "agreement" in this sensitive matter. The middle–man between the military doctor and the Jews most often was Dr. Patryn, the mayor of the town who was a medical doctor by profession. The fact that he was a doctor gave him a change to express his professional opinion that the Jewish recruits' physical condition might not be suitable for military service. Sometimes he influenced the military doctor without a bribe and sometimes there was a need to pay a sizeable sum. On very rare occasions, somebody from the shtetl was recruited but, if such an incident did occur, the townspeople did not leave a stone unturned – they always found a way to cancel the first commission's decision and to bring the recruit before a second commission and be freed.

At this point, I would like to tell a terrible incident that happened once in town. On the initiation of my father, Dr. Patryn offered a sizeable sum of money to a military doctor on the condition that he free all the Jewish recruits who would appear before him.

However, the military doctor refused to accept the bribe but he fulfilled the request anyway. But, this episode had unfortunate results. This is what happened: The military doctor told about the proposition to his colleague, the presiding officer of the commission – a major. Subsequently, when the major quarrelled with the doctor, he reported the affair to the military prosecutor. The mayor, Dr. Patryn was summoned to a trial as a defendant accused in an attempt to bribe the military doctor for which he could have received a severe punishment. If the court would have found him guilty he might have been sentenced not only with imprisonment but they would have also revoked his right to practice medicine and not be permitted to continue to serve as mayor of the city. It is easy to imagine the uproar that this trial stirred in the whole region and especially in the town. Most of all, this affair touched the heart of the Jews. If the mayor would have been convicted, it could have caused distress and resulted in dire consequences for the Jews.

This incident hurt my father directly because he was the cause of it. In his defence, the mayor claimed to have said: "If they, the military, will not discriminate against the Jews, the Jews will make a sizeable donation to the Red Cross". Since the military doctor did not understand Polish very well, he misunderstood what was said. But the military doctor said resolutely that there was no misunderstanding: "Ihrtum–ausgeschlossen". (Misunderstanding – impossible).

[Page 120]

After many intercessions and tremendous effort, the defence was able to get a change of venue from Vienna to Rzeszow, a central city in Western Galicia and to arrange a second investigation of the parties and witnesses. My father was also summoned to the second trial as a witness for the defence, besides the defendant and the army doctor. My father was supposed to have testified that Dr. Patryn told him that the Jews would make a donation to the Red Cross as the defendant had claimed. Torah authorities requested that everything possible should be done to save the defendant who had endangered himself in favour of the Jews. Their biggest worry was how to save the Jewish reputation since a harsh sentence might provoke vengeful feelings among the gentiles towards the Jews.

The night before the trial was dreadful to all participants. The military doctor was probably angry because he was dragged from Vienna to Rzeszow and was probably anxious to testify and name the accused in order to teach the gentile mayor of Strzyzow a lesson. He himself was Jewish. Although the mayor was a friend of the Jews, he could not ignore the fact that it was because of them that he found himself in such a predicament. My father, Reb Joseph, thought and searched for a tactic that would relieve them from the bad situation unscathed. That is to say – how to save the mayor and the shtetl? As much as he tried, he came up with only one bit of advice: the quotation of our sages: "The only one to lean on is our Father who rules the Universe". He hoped that at the last moment, he would somehow find an exit from this entanglement. Oh yes, one more person – someone very special – was awake that night before the trial: The Town's rabbi, Reb Alter Zev, blessed be his memory. He did not let out of his hands the book of Psalms and other mystical books. He summoned all his righteous ancestors, calling out to them by their names: The Holy Shlah, Reb Itzhok Horowitz, the Baal Shem Tov and especially his grandfather, Rabbi Naphtali from Ropczyce. He called them all out and demanded help for the shtetl in distress. At dawn when my father went to him to ask for his blessing before his trip to the trial, the rabbi said to him: "By the authority of my righteous ancestors, I hereby bless you that you shall succeed in your mission". He thought for a while and added: "The month of Nissan is the month of many great miracles and the holiday of freedom. May it be the will that G–d should make a miracle and show us wonders".

When Reb Joseph disembarked the train in Rzeszow he unexpectedly saw the military doctor leaving the train which had just arrived from Vienna. At this moment, he felt as though somebody had pushed him forcibly towards the doctor and they suddenly were face–to–face. Both turned pale as chalk. The doctor tried to look the other way but as he later told, it seemed to him than an elderly man with a dignified face insistently pushed him to Reb Joseph's side…. And Reb Joseph? Girded with strength and with a clear and decisive voice, as if he were giving an order, thundered at the doctor: "Would you listen, my master, revered doctor? Today they are going to prosecute a gentile who wanted to help Jews. The only accuser is you, a Jew. Have you thought about how many more Jew–haters you will create after the gentile is found guilty? Jew–haters who will probably in time strike you too, my revered master!"

[Page 121]

These energetic words were said dangerously but from a warm Jewish heart and they did the job. When he appeared before the judges, the doctor said: "Ihrtum ncht ausgeschlossen" (there is a possible mistake). And there was light and relief for the Jews in the shtetl.

Reb Joseph passed away in 1929. Of his offspring a son survived, Abraham Joshua Hesel who was the last president of the Kehillah in Strzyzow, presently in New York and a second son, Shlomo Yahalomi, the writer of this story. Blessed be G–d from above for the privilege to build anew our house and beget sons and daughters – may they live a long life.

Reb Elazar Wurtzel. The Man of hints and gestures
by Shlomo Yahalomi

If he would have said that Reb Elazar did not talk too much, that would have been an understatement. He spoke less than people who do not talk much. His problem was that he spoke in cues and hints, half sentences but, if you were lucky and guessed what he wanted to say, you enjoyed it.

He was a distinguished scholar in the scriptures, Talmud and all Talmudic commentaries. He did not study fast like one doing piece work. No! He studied slowly and in depth, spending unlimited time penetrating the depth and the mysteries of the subject. He always asked: "What is there to rush?" And apropos, he told a story that once Rabbi Itzhok Shmelkis from Lwow visited Rzeszow where his son–in–law served as rabbi. Traditionally, when a famous scholar came to town the local students and the Beit HaMidrash dwellers gathered for a discourse with the visiting scholar on different Torah subjects and to hear from him some new interpretations. One student, who was a prodigy, brought before the Rabbi a very complicated problem being certain that the rabbi would explain it to him. The student spoke very fast. The rabbi stopped him and said to him: "Slow down, let me hear you word–by–word on this problem of yours". After the student slowed down and told about his problem, he suddenly realized that there was no problem at all. That is what Reb Elazar wanted to point out; studying slowly and thoroughly would make it easier to understand. He studied day and night. If something was not clear to him, he was never tired to study it again and again until he understood it. When this happened, a sparkle lit up his eyes and a smile appeared on his face. His studying was not in quantity but in quality.

If one of the younger students asked him to explain something he would spend unlimited time with him until the student understood the subject. Not many dared to bother him because of his peculiar way of explaining, that is, with hints and gestures. He used to advise the student to look up in this or that book, or maybe in a third source and then come back to him if it was still unclear to him.

Reb Elazar was a very humble and soft–spoken man and he never raised his voice even when his opponent, during a discussion, got excited and angry, not realizing that he was wrong. It did not bother Reb Elazar at all.

[Page 122]

Reb Elazar showed no interest in local politics especially in the Rabbinical dispute which never ceased. Neither did he participate in the dispute between the Zionists and their opponents. Although he was related to one of the rabbis with whom he sympathized, he never openly expressed his opinion. I remember once, when somebody said something derogatory about Doctor Herzl, the founder of the Zionist Movement, he objected right away with a hint and gesture like: "Nu' Oh'" and that is all that he said, meaning that it was wrong.

Few knew that he was well–informed in current events. At least once a day he spent a short while scanning the headlines in the daily newspaper. Some people in town frowned upon it and there were even rumours that he carried around progressive ideas in his head, although whenever expressed them. But, he had everybody's admiration. There were certain times when Reb Elazar was talkative. This was only when he spoke about the rabbis he admired most, such as the rabbi from Sandz, Reb Chaim Halberstam and his son, Rabbi Yechezkiel from Siniawa. He became a master storyteller when he began to tell about their greatness, holiness and about all the miracles they had performed.

He was also talkative at the Passover Seders when everybody was required to tell and re–tell the story of the redemption of the Jews from Egypt and the miracles that happened at the Red Sea. Many of the Beit HaMidrash dwellers used to pay him a visit on Passover night to hear him tell the Passover story.

Reb Elazar was a widower and lived with his daughters. The son–in–laws were not big Torah scholars. They were simple people but they respected their father–in–law and put up with all his whims. If I would have had the foresight of the annihilation of European Jewry, I would have taken notes of all my conversations with Reb Elazar, whether on Torah subjects or secular subjects. What I do remember, I hope I will someday put it in print for future generations. Unfortunately, no one from his family survived the Holocaust.

Reb David Wiener
by Shlomo Yahalomi

Reb David Wiener was a special asset to the community, a wonderful type, a great scholar and a G–d fearing man. On one hand he was a shrewd and clever businessman and on the other, a schlemiel in his personal life. He studied Torah with devotion. He never did both at the same time and he always knew what to do and when to do it. When he studied Talmud he always hummed a melody. It was a pleasure to listen to him because it seemed as though you were listening to a wonderful composition. Reb David liked the Beit HaMidrash dwellers who studied Torah daily. He preached to them the ethics of Jewish behaviour, not in a strict way but in a fatherly way. Reb David spoke softly, like a father to his sons, never uttering a bad word and, when he wanted to needle somebody, he did it jokingly.

On occasion, when he detected that a young man shaved his face which was strictly forbidden according to the Jewish custom, he touched the fellow's face with his hands. When the culprit smiled blushingly as if he were caught in a misdeed, Reb David remarked to him: "You are Laughing and I am hurting" because the stubble always irritates when you caress it, both literally and figuratively.

[Page 123]

The young people in Beit HaMidrash used to complain that although he was such a wise man, he would not accept a little progress. He insisted that once you ignore a small infraction, you never know when to stop. He used to say: "my father was a g–d fearing man and I am a G–d fearing man and so should everyone be". He father was the assistant rabbi in Strzyzow. His name was Reb Joseph Mordechai Wiener.

When the Nazi came to town, he said: "Now the time is ripe to get ready for sanctification of the Divine Name". He did not pay attention to what was happening around him but he continued to lead the same life style as though nothing had changed. He studied even more and when the Nazi came to his house to take him away, they found him bent over the Talmudic tractate and studying with a sweet melodic voice. He did not pay any attention to the representatives of the master race. The Nazi were enraged with such behaviour. When they asked him why he did not respond, he said: "I have nothing to say to you. All I want is time to study the scriptures and not be interrupted". He was killed immediately and that is how he gave his life for the sanctification of the Divine Name while humming a song.

Reb Feitel Last and his son Shlomo
by Shlomo Yahalomi

You saw before you a Jew of medium height, lean and gaunt with a long silvery beard which covered almost a third of his height. His head was a little tilted and it looked like it was coming off of his very thin neck. His back was also bent a little forward and only his face was attractive and gentle. Sometimes radiant and sometimes expressing some anger.

Reb Feitel was not a great scholar but he absorbed in his youth the fragrance of Torah and most of all, the belief in the Righteous Ones especially in the offspring of the Dynow Dynasty and its founder, Rabbi Tzvi Elimelech Shapiro. If someone dared to criticize his rabbi in his presence, he would attack him, ready to tear him apart like a fish. On a good day, if he was in a good mood, happy, content and relaxed, he would react with only a scolding and name–calling.

Reb Feitel was a model of cleanliness. You could never find a spot on his ancient clothes. The jokers in town use to say that he inherited those clothes from his great–grandfathers. In every spare moment he would moisten his finger with his tongue and pick the tiniest piece of lint from his coat, pants or shoes which, according to the testimony of the town elders, he bought on his wedding day, approximately forty years hence. They were always polished and looked like new as if they had just left the shoemaker's hands yesterday. It was no wonder that he walked so slowly, counting each step so as not to soil the soles. When he saw people walking fast and carelessly, he would stop them and shout a fatherly reproach: "Nu, you are ruining your shoes, you are violating the commandment 'You shall not waste'".

Reb Feitel was a happy Jew jesting at the weddings of his good friends. He was an unpaid jester. He knew many folk songs and Hassidic melodies.

[Page 124]

On Saturday nights after the Sabbath was over he strolled back and forth in the kloyz of the rabbi of Sassov and sang the traditional song: "Hamavdil" in a melody and lyrics which he himself had composed. The lyrics were about how said it was that the holy Sabbath Queen was leaving us and the drab week began. His admirers formed a chorus around him and they sang with him. Woe to those who sang a false tune.

On the yahrzeit of his parents', he led the prayers and tried to show off his cantorial talent which, unfortunately, he did not possess. At one such performance and on a Friday night, Reb Feitel began to chant the Kabalat Shabbath prayer which begins with: "L'cha n'rannah" and repeated the word L'cha several times which means: "let's go". Rabbi Moshe Leib became irritated and told him: "Go, go and come back tomorrow night to sing the Hamavdil".

And now let us return to the Saturday nights. When Reb Feitel concluded his singing, he sat down at the table and began to tell tales. He had a few stories that he repeated hundreds of times. His favourite two stories were about a pupil of the Baal Shem Tov who wanted to convert to Christianity but the Jewish legendary preacher from Mezritch saved him with his powerful preaching. And the second story was about Rabbi Meir from Premishlan who, in his childhood, used to tell his neighbour the butcher, which cattle would be kosher and which would not. IF one of the Beit HaMidrash dwellers wanted to have fun with Reb Feitel, he would interrupt him and tell him that the story was not exactly the way it happened. Reb Feitel would raise his head with his angular chin and long bear, put his hand under his chin and say: "Nu, by all means, let us hear it!" And the young man would intentionally twist the story around. Soon Reb Feitel would stop him and with mockery, he would declare that the teller did not know what he was talking about and silenced him. Then Reb Feitel would continue the story with a victorious look on his face.

He used to say, with a sigh: "What do you know? There was once…. What do you know children? Where can you get today a holy Reb Shlomo? He was a Tzadik". He was referring to Rabbi Shlomo Shapiro who served as rabbi in Strzyzow and ran away to Munkatch, as it was told earlier in this book.

Reb Feitel's biggest opponent was his son Shlomo. The son was his "adversary" and, in general, a big philosopher. The father called him: "my son the philosopher". And there was a lot of truth in it.

Shlomo was really an enlightened young man who studied many research books and books on ethics. He could not tolerate his father's tales about the miracles of the rabbis and on this subject; there were eternal discussions and arguments between father and son. "Your destructors and demolishers will come from among your own", a quotation from the Prophet Jeremiah which his father used to quote with sadness and complaint. And if they did so all year round, on the Sabbath and holidays, they argued even more. His father practiced all kinds of customs on the Sabbath and holidays, imitating the rabbis from Dynow, of which his son, the intellectual, did not approve. And so they always fought. Whatever the father did, the son refused to do and sometimes the son even joked about it.

[Page 125]

Just as much as Shlomo was more educated and enlightened that his father, so was he sharper than his father.

For understandable reasons, this is not the forum to tell about all the fights between father and son. We will tell only about a fearful true story which could have ended in a bitter tragedy. Only through a miracle was the outcome good. It appeared that Reb Feitel was a good provider for his household. They were never deprived of anything. Even though he was a little stingy on weekdays, he spared nothing for the Sabbath and the holidays. It happened on the first Seder night of Passover. As in every Jewish home, they prepared in his house "maror" (bitter herbs). And as it might seem strange and amazing, these bitter herbs were, year–after–year, the source of a heated exchange between the naïve father and the enlightened son. The father prepared an oversized portion of bitter herbs that would be sufficient for each member of the family to consume as much as it was required by the commandment, and he intended to force everybody to eat the entire portion. The son not only disagreed with his father's intention, but tried to prove to his father that he was wrong about the size of the portion. Shlomo called his father a "bitter herbs glutton"… This bitter fight over bitter herbs brought bitterness and more than once, the father had called his son "Goy" but the son also reacted with sharp words. This argument took place not only before the Seder but during the Seder as well. There were a few people who stood in the back of Reb Feitel's house on the Seder night and listened to the bitter arguments and poked fun at them.

Once a dreadful incident happened during the eating of the bitter herbs. Reb Feitel, while eating the oversized portion and being angry and shouting at his son, a piece of horseradish stuck in Reb Feitel's throat and almost choked him. At first the family did not realize the seriousness of the matter and the son continued screaming: "maror, maror". Suddenly, he saw his father had lost consciousness and a tragedy was imminent. The family began to scream: "Please help! Mercy!" One of the neighbours ran to bring the doctor to help save Reb Feitel. After he regained consciousness, Reb Feitel's first word to his son was: "Goy".

When he recovered his disposition, Reb Feitel said: "Do you know who saved me? Nu, by all means, tell me who?" The son who had also recovered from the ordeal was almost ready to start the fight again. But he restrained himself as his father continued: "You know who saved my life? None but Rabbi Tzvi Elimelech himself. His spirit should protect us and all of Israel. I swear by my life". He continued to speak with emotion and enthusiasm. "When I thought that my end was near, I saw him, the Rabbi Tzvi Elimelech, may he be remembered with blessings. He simply approached me, stuck his finger in my throat and pushed the 'maror' down my throat. When I wanted to kiss his hand and thank him for the favour that he did to me, he disappeared and ascended into heaven...."

It is superfluous to remark that the educated son did not believe the story, but this time he did not react.

Reb Feitel was more fortunate than others. He died of natural causes but his son Shlomo and the rest of his large family perished in the Holocaust.

[Page 126]

Reb Chaim Mandel
by Shlomo Yahalomi

You saw before you a short, shrunken, thin man, with veins visible from under his facial skin; an oblong head, a wide forehead and a few strands of hair instead of a beard; big clever eyes illuminated and happy and also expressing a lot of energy and fiery sparks. He was always on the move. He did not walk – he flew. A renowned Talmudic scholar, skilled, sharp, acute, quick–oriented and capable of resolving complicated Talmudic problems. This was Reb Chaim Mandel. He dealt with leather but in reality, he was everything except a merchant. His mind was in the Talmud, Hassidic tales, and local politics and in his continuous fight against Zionism. He was also active in the rabbinical dispute, a teacher to many students and finally, he conducted a little business. His supposed livelihood was from the leather business but his main source of support was his mother–in–law, the woman of valour, the capable Esther Hinda who owned a big grocery store which was like a present–day supermarket. From all these resources the income was not enough to feed the family but he never complained and you never saw him worried. On the contrary, he was always content, always had a happy face and was not one to sigh. By nature, he was an optimist. He always put his fate in the Almighty and most of the time, a smile hovered on his lips with a little irony hidden behind his eyebrows.

Reb Chaim Mandel was considered a little more sophisticated and different from his fellow townspeople who never left town. He did some traveling in his youth and spent some time in Hungary and in Germany. In Hungary, he studied with the famous Rabbi Saul Brach where he befriended many rabbis and Torah authorities. No one in town knew as much about the customs of the Hungarian Jews as did Reb Chaim Mandel. Their customs were different from the Galician customs and he made fun of many of these customs.

Reb Chaim was an amazing man. There was no one like him in town. A man who was nicknamed: "the burner" because when he prayed or entered into a discussion, he always became so ecstatic that his face turned red as if a fire burned inside of him. On the other hand, he was also beloved and amiable and liked to listen to a good joke.

He opposed Zionism fiercely. When his daughter Seryl announced that she was leaving for Eretz Israel, he let out a bitter cry saying that not only had she converted and left the Jewish fate, but she would cause the conversion of his entire family.

"Those hands will not build Eretz Israel". He used to say sarcastically, pointing to the hands of a few who, according to him, unloaded their religious yoke for their convenience and joined the Zionists. Nevertheless, many at a time during an angry tirade on the Zionists and loud screamed about those "Goyim", he would let out a sharp–witted jesting remark and a smile appeared on his lips at once lowering the heat by ninety degrees.

In his opposition to Zionism, he was influenced by Rabbi Chaim Elazar Shapiro, the rabbi from Munkatch. Reb Chaim Mandel was an enthusiastic Hassid of his rabbi who was born in Strzyzow.

[Page 127]

When the Rabbi's grandfather, Rabbi Shlomo, left Strzyzow, the grandson, rabbi Chaim Elazar was eight years old. Most people in Strzyzow admired the rabbi from Munkatch because his ancestors, Rabbi Tzvi Elimelech and his father, rabbi Shlomo both served as rabbis in Strzyzow. Reb Chaim Mandel was a confidante of this rabbi. He was the teacher of the rabbi's future son–in–law, Reb Baruch Rabinowitz who, at present, lives in Cholon, Israel. (He later moved to Petach Tiqua). Reb Chaim Mandel taught him Torah when Reb Baruch spent some time in Strzyzow with his grandmother, the righteous Rebetzin Chana Shapiro. She was the grand–daughter of the rabbi from Sandz. Even after Rabbi Baruch's engagement (at is Bar Mitzvah) the rabbi from Munktach invited Reb Chaim Mandel to continue to teach his future son–in–law. Therefore, Reb Chaim's opposition to Zionism was natural. Still, nobody believed that someone like Reb Chaim Mandel was capable of hatred. He was beloved by the people and he respected them. But, he said: "Because I love them – I must warn them to stay away from the Zionist agitators".

During prayers and when he studied, his whole body swayed to and fro. All the parts of his body participated in the action. He was always well prepared before giving a lesson to his students. He had a very good memory and knew how to locate the source of his interpretation. He used to get fired up when he failed to convince someone that he was right. Once, he had trouble with me, the writer of these memoirs. He became so angry that he slapped my face for daring to challenge him. This was on a Thursday night when we used to be up all night studying. Early next morning, Reb Chaim walked into the Beit HaMidrash with a book under his arm. He slowly approached me and asked for my forgiveness. It appeared that he too was up all night and searched for the disputed subject after the previous night's discussion and found out that I was right.

Both his sons were scholars too. Reb Wolf the older son was a very fine and pious man who was not such a sworn opponent of Zionism. The younger son Naphtali, although he dwelled in the Beit HaMidrash and studied Torah, secretly belonged to the Religious Zionists and studied philosophy. The father, Reb Chaim, was no fool. He knew about this but hid his frustrations.

His wife Kreindl Bracha was a righteous woman. She adored her husband and put up with him lovingly. They had six daughters, all good looking and self–educated. Two of them left Strzyzow and went to Eretz Israel and, at present, live there with their families. But the rest of the family perished in the flames of the Holocaust.

Reb Yeshayahu Mandel Hacohen
by Shlomo Yahalomi

A G–d fearing man with unlimited merits. Reb Yeshayahu was an enthusiastic Hassid and an ardent admirer of the rabbi from Munkatch but he was not just a blind follower in agreeing to whatever the rabbi said or did no say. He did not like to hear anyone slander people, even Zionists. His principal belief was that all Jews are good Jews.

During the absence of Rabbi Nechemiah Shapiro from Strzyzow, Reb Yeshayahu conducted the prayers in the kloyz on the High Holidays.

[Page 128]

After Rabbi Nechemiah returned to Strzyzow, Reb Yeshayahu chanted only part of the prayers. He was a charitable man and was always busy doing something useful for others. A week did not go by that he would not collect money for some worthy cause. Reb Yeshayahu was always in debt because he borrowed money for charitable needs and later raised money to pay it back. That was the custom in Galicia. If someone came to town, whether a charity case himself or raising funds for others, he either collected right away or Reb Yeshayahu borrowed from someone and gave it to him and, on a later date, Reb Yeshayahu collected from the townspeople to repay the person from whom he had originally borrowed the money. He himself had no money. Reb Yeshayahu was the one who took care of these charity cases. He did it with such simplicity and without fuss so naturally as though that was the way it should be done. His motto was: If he would not worry about others, who would?

Being used to constantly borrow money from the rich people in town and later pay them back, people used to tease him that he was collecting money for the rich.

He was a dear soul, a rarity in the days before the Holocaust. Imagine if he were alive today?

From his entire family, only one son survived a Torah scholar and G–d fearing like his father, of blessed memory. He passed away in Israel. Also, a grandson lives in Israel and also a concentration camp survivor. One son of Reb Yeshayahu who immigrated long ago and right after World War I lives in Switzerland.

Reb Chaim Yacov Nuremberg
by Shlomo Yahalomi

Reb Chaim Yacov was one of a kind. There is a Hassidic tale that Rabbi Baruch from Mezibush once said to Rabbi Hersh Leib Malik: "Haven't you heard – people consider me to be one of a kind?" Then Rabbi Baruch asked him: "How is it possible to have tow of a kind?" Reb Hersh told him: "Why not? The Passover Haggadah song: 'Chad Gadia' is about one lamb and we repeat 'Chad Gadia' twice!" Reb Baruch thought for a while and replied: "Yes, indeed. It is possible to have even four of a kind. I am one of a kind – a Torah scholar; you are one of a kind in wisdom. Reb Mordechai is one of a kind, a G–d fearing man and Reb Shalom from Prohobeshitz is one of a kind, a staunch believer in the Kingdom above".

This dialogue explains in a simple way the expression: "One of a kind". It does not mean one in the whole world. It means that there can be a few one of a kind of different kinds. There were in our town a few dear personalities who were one of a kind, each one being something special. Reb Chaim Yacov Nuremberg was one who possessed many merits and virtues. He was a scholar, a lover of Jews and a complete believer in G–d and his teachings. His chanting was like a burning fire. When he chanted the prayer: "and for our sins we were exiled from our land", the thresholds trembled. If Reb Chaim Mandel was called "The Burner" while he chanted, then Reb Chaim Yacov exceed him in pouring out his soul and tears. Our sages stated: "The gates of tears never closed".

[Page 129]

This saying refers to people who prayed like Reb Chaim Yacov. Many people were swept away by his tears, especially the simple folk who were influenced by his style of chanting.

The majority of the simple folk in town were Reb Chaim Yacov's followers. He was a successful teacher of Torah and his teaching of the Midrash was especially interesting.

Reb Chaim Yacov was a master storyteller of Hassidic tales. His tales were a thoughtful work of art. He knew how to describe in detail the geographical surroundings and the appearance of the houses of the heroes in his stories even the smallest detail of the clothes they wore. He imitated the voices of the long–departed rabbis of his stories. Everything was filled with mystery. Whoever heard Reb Chaim Yacov tell a story seemed to see those righteous people vividly and not as in a dream. Once he told a terrible story about trouble in a shtetl and how the people came to the rabbi to ask for help. Reb Chaim Yacov was so carried away with the story, imitating how the people were yelling: "Help! Help!" that outside, passers–by ran into the Beit HaMidrash frightened, thinking G–d knows what had happened and wondering what all the screaming was about. Soon they realized that Reb Chaim Yacov was only telling a story. No wonder that Reb Chaim Yacov attracted the young who were always ready to listen to his stories even for the hundredth time. His stories always sounded new because of his talented storytelling and the extra flavour he added which only an artist could portray.

Meritoriously, part of Reb Chaim Yacov's family survived and live in Israel and the Diaspora.

"A prayer of the afflicted when he is overwhelmed"
(Psalms, chapter 102, v.1)
by Shlomo Yahalomi

In memory of Reb Shalom Schwartzman

Morning services on the Sabbath and holidays consist of three parts: P'sukei D'Zimra, Shacharit and Mussaf. The P'sukei D'zimra contains chapters from psalms which express praise to the Almighty for his wonderful creation of man and nature. The Shacharit portion is a service which contains the Amidah and Kriat Shema in which the Jew expresses his devotion to G–d, Torah and Israel. These two parts are recited daily and on holidays but the third part, the Mussaf, is recited only on the Sabbath and holidays. It is a prayer in which we reminisce about the way these holidays are celebrated at the time of the Holy Temple before the destruction, and in which we express the sadness of losing the Holy Temple and our land.

After we memorialized the personalities who chanted the prayers on the High Holidays, Reb Hershel Gelander who chanted the Mussaf prayers and Reb Yacov Schiff who chanted the Shacharit, it would be proper to mention the ones who chanted the P'sukei D'zimra. Indeed, they did not have to sing or chant them at all. Only a nice recital was sufficient… but they did split heavens with their fiery enthusiasm. Their prayers ascended to the heavens to appear before the Almighty. After their P'sukei D'zimra, the road was paved, easy and smooth for the chanters of Shacharit and Mussaf that followed. The Satan had already received a stinging slap in the face, his power was weakened and it was easy to subdue him. It is worthwhile to mention the chanters of P'sukei D'zimra, whether from the aspect of their personalities or their chanting. They were men who stood tall spiritually in the days before the Holocaust, and if they were alive today, they would have been prominent in their righteousness and exalting merits. Let us describe the first one, Reb Shalom Schwartzman.

[Page 129]

You saw before you a man who stood out in a crowd, tall, upright and strong; a marvellous and distinguished man with a full, long beard, hair on his big head and the very long side–locks, straight like sticks that had prematurely turned white from much grief and sorrow. His big eyes penetrated your inner chambers, expressing indescribable energy and fiery sparks that added outward splendour and majesty to his inner being. Reb Shalom's life was a long chain of trouble, pain and tragedy on one side and a high spiritual strength, withstanding many difficult trials and sanctifying the Heavenly Name on the other side. He was a G–d–fearing enthusiastic Hassid who fought G–d's battles; a proselytizer, a preacher of morality and reverence to G–d. He watched over the young people in the Beit HaMidrash so that they would not become corrupt, Heaven forbid! He led the fight against atheism. Since his youth, he taught and educated young and old in the Torah and the reverence of G–d. He particularly emphasized reverence. His net was spread over the Beit HaMidrash. He was the spiritual father and guide of the innocent lambs, the Torah students. He preached ethics, Hassidism, told Hassidic tales and guarded the watch–post so that the youth would not deviate and reach out toward secular cultures and read secular books such as Bialik's poems. Corrupt was considered he who bought a Zionist "Shekel" and, of course, a real Zionist! Reb Shalom was an extremist who stubbornly fought Zionism. He was even against the Mizrachi. Once, when a Zionist speaker came to town and wanted to speak in the Beit HaMidrash, Reb Shalom organized his young people, the Beit HaMidrash dwellers, and his mature students to whom he taught Mishnayoth, to study aloud so that nobody would be able to hear the speaker. However, truth has to be told. His fight was not against the Zionists but against Zionism. He loved every Jew and he had a good relationship with the Zionist activists in the shtetl.

The Zionists on the other hand never insulted him. They revered and respected him knowing that all his deeds were for heavenly purpose. They were not angry at him even when Reb Shalom rebuked those who spoke during prayers: "Sha Goyim…." He was adored by every soul in town because of his honesty, righteousness and his rare spiritual strength.

Reb Shalom's suffering was very heavy as in the Biblical story of Job. In spite of his suffering, he remained righteous from the beginning to the end. His young wife suffered an untimely death. His only son, the dear Moshe Joshua, was perfect and pious; a scholar with many merits; humble and his spirits were exceeded only by his youth. His daughters, the righteous and educated Risha and Yetta, who were married to wise and G–d–fearing men, and all the grandchildren, passed away.

[Page 131]

He himself suffered a lot of pain besides these many troubles. Nevertheless, Job – Reb Shalom – did not sin and never questioned why. Habitually, he quoted the saying of older Hassidim: "The believer has no questions, the non–believer has no answers". He remained righteous – he remained Reb Shalom. On every happy occasion and especially on Simchat Torah, he sang and danced as though he was the happiest man in the world.

Reb Shalom's material situation was not any better. He always made a meagre living and sometimes even lived in poverty. There were times when he worked for others and his providers treated him with reverence and respect. My father, Reb Joseph Diamand, told me that when Reb Shalom worked as a trustee in his father's business, Reb Joseph was in charge over him. At the same time he was also Reb Shalom's Torah student. On weekdays, my father was the boss, directing the work of his employee – Reb Shalom – and on the Sabbath, Reb Shalom was the teacher, directing and giving orders to his student, Reb Joseph. The relationship between boss and employee and teacher and his pupil were friendly and most intimate. Sometimes they teased each other. On weekdays when Reb Shalom felt like "aggravating" my father, his provider, he kiddingly would say to him: "wait, wait, soon the Sabbath will be here and the situation will reverse. I will be ordering you around". On the Sabbath when Reb Shalom disciplined my father during the third Sabbath meal, my father used to threaten him: "Soon the Sabbath will be over" – meaning that he would be the boss. Such was the relationship between the boss and his employee. After a time, Reb Shalom went out on his own and began selling alcohol and wine but he hardly earned a living. Reb Shalom divided his day half for Torah and worship and the other half for his livelihood. His nights were also divided: half for midnight prayers and the other half for sleep and rest.

He was number one in the Mishnayoth Society. An hour and a half before evening services in the summer and after the services in the winter, he sat and daily taught Mishnayoth to many residents, among whom were the rich and distinguished. He was an excellent lecturer and did not spare his labour and exertion until all the pupils understood that Mishna completely. It was a pleasure to watch Reb Shalom and his students when he explained to them the mathematics of the tractate "Kilaim" (Diverse Kind). Like a born mathematician, he spread before them the mathematical principles of the Rambam and Bartenura and the people drank his words with thirst.

Reb Shalom was also an excellent letter writer – most significant in those days. When he was very young and dwelled at the Beit HaMidrash, a book with exemplary letter–writings was published containing a few of his letters. His style and penmanship were wonderful. He formed buds and flowers with a double purpose – for the beauty of the handwriting and the beauty of the rhetoric according to the best compositions of our holy language. The young men in the Beit HaMidrash, who were engaged to be married and did not know how to write a nice letter to their bride's parents, turned to Reb Shalom for assistance. And of course, he also wrote to the bride with holy purity.

[Page 132]

When a young man went to visit the bride's home (although Reb Shalom was not comfortable with it) Reb Shalom instructed him on his behaviour; what to do and how to find grace in the eyes of G–d and man and, of course, in the eyes of the bride as well. Everything was for the sake of heavens.

How innocent Reb Shalom was.. This writer, who had strong, intimate bonds with him and revealed his heart to him, knows many many things to tell. The innocence and naivetÃ© which were derived only because of his righteousness. He was convinced that no secular writer was capable of writing a letter to a bride that she would like as well as one written by a believer. He and only he, knew, with the help from above, how to find the key to the heart of a bride because G–d helped him and all his expressions such as:" to the beautiful, the gracious, as the sun and the moon, whose wisdom reaches the highest height and the deepest depth". He used to include verses from the love songs of Reb Yehuda Halevi, not forgetting to point out the source. It is easy to understand how proud a groom was, seeing how wonderful and splendid his letter was and thinking that when it would reach the bride, it would surely make a strong impression.

And, because it is written: "You shall be active in many ways", Reb Shalom was active in the community needs, and sometimes in things that seemed small and insignificant "There is no vacuum in this world. Everything is Torah, everything is reverence for G–d!" He expressed his opinion on every problem be it small or large. He sometimes clashed with his most intimate friends, like Reb Baruch Berglass, the rich man who prayed mystically and dared to pronounce fully the mystical "Names". In spite of their friendship and closeness, they always disagreed. Not only did Reb Shalom warn Reb Baruch that is was forbidden to pronounce those "Names" but in other subjects, they also had sharp disagreements. What one built, the other tore down and vice–versa. This writer also had many disagreements with Reb Shalom but, whether we agreed or disagreed, Reb Shalom had all our respect!!!

Add to Reb Shalom's merits swiftness and you find him to be perfect. He was very swift in performing a mitzvah, a deed of merit, quick with everything. Everything he did was done with the maximum speed. Whether it was for lack of time or whether such was his nature, young men could not compete with him when it concerned quickness. He was that way in his childhood and when his hair turned white. He was that way in days of ease and days of trouble. "The day is short and there is a lot to accomplish" was his motto.

We already described enough about his personality in general but we missed the most important attribute: Reb Shalom's praying.

As one of the great righteous used to say: "There are three kinds of chanters and three kinds of chants. Chanters like Moses and his chant, King David and his chant and the poor man's chant". Moses and his chant means one who chants but has no voice and does not know how to intone a melody or to sing. He may also stutter a little but he is considered in the category of Moses who stuttered but was our teacher. Such chanting is satisfactory and acceptable. Kind David and his chanting means a cantor who chants pleasantly, has a sweet voice and is fluent in the prayers like King David who was the singer of Israel. Such chanting ascends and goes through to the heavens.

[Page 133]

Besides these two, there is the chanting of a poor man, a man who is necessarily the most righteous man of his generation and is not in the category of the singer of Israel, but he is a man distressed, in pain and poverty, whose heart is broken. Of such a man it was said: "G–d is close to the broken–hearted and the spiritually distressed, he helps". And such chanting is received in the heavens as the chants of Moses and David bound together. In addition, sometimes such chanting ascends to the highest heavens. And the preacher of Mezrich already said: "There are different keys to locks but there are thieves who can open any lock without a key. They just break the lock. G–d the Almighty likes such a thief who can break such a lock and spill his heart before him".

That is how Reb Shalom Schwartzman was. Although he was qualified to chant as Moses because he was very G–d fearing, and as King David, although he did not know how to sing, his voice was strong and heart–rendering; most of all, he was qualified because there was no one like him in the shtetl to chant as a poor, inhumanly pain–suffering person. Who else could express in his prayers all the sadness and hurt, sorrow and bitterness accumulated in his heart and move the will of the Lord? Even in the weekdays, his prayers were flaming and inspirational. Imagine how he prayed in the High Holidays. It was enough to see him going to the mikva and immersing himself in the cold water before his prayers to recognize that a tempest was nearing. He was all terror and fear even before he reached the pulpit. And the chanting itself – only he who had seen and heard him knew what chanting was. He began with the blessings and his bones trembled. He said them with a loud and strong voice, word–by–word, especially emphasizing words which expressed the thankfulness of man for the mercy of G–d. These words were said with much feelings and mighty weeping. His voice kept going stronger from minute–to–minute and suddenly, he was hoarse and began choking with tears.

He chanted: "Weeping may lodge with us at evening but in the morning, there are shouts of joy" (Psalms). At this point his heart almost stopped. Drops of sweat fell on his white beard as though he was entirely drowning in sweat. All eyes turned on Reb Shalom. Will he come through? Will he return to roar in his strong voice? Soon came the answer: "To you G–d, I call and of You G–d, I plead". This outcry sounded as though a bombshell had fallen from heaven. At this point, the congregation felt that he had broken the lock! That is how Reb Shalom chanted, alternating, first begging for mercy and compassion and next, issuing a demand to be helped like a son who sinned before his Father in heaven and then, with a bit of chutzpa, demanding forgiveness. First slowly but then with the speed of lightning that made the thresholds tremble.

When he uttered: "Until now you helped me compassionately", he was unable to continue. A long silence ensued – everyone felt that he had reached the drowning point and, in the women's section, they realized that Reb Shalom was in danger of collapsing, Heaven forbid! A gruesome wailing was heard from there. Everyone cried as though the world had come to an end. They all lost their places in the prayer book.

[Page 134]

Then, the voice of Reb Baruch Diller was heard. He was an ardent Hassid of the Rabbi from Sadigora who never became excited or aroused from wailing "Nu! Oh". He protested. According to the tradition of the Sadigora Hassidim, you are not supposed to wail. You just pray with heart. Some worshippers were ready to lynch Reb Baruch for such a rude interruption and some said: "on the contrary. Reb Shalom needs to be encouraged". In the meantime, the storm passed. Reb Shalom woke up and with more enthusiasm, ended his chanting in the tradition of the rabbi from Dynow. When he finished, he returned to his seat perspiring and his clothes looked as if they were just laundered. Thank G–d he survived and was well.

To encourage Reb Shalom after such chanting, the people used to ask him to speak on the subject of prayers. Reb Shalom willingly and with great satisfaction told them the Hassidic stories, Hassidic quotations and teachings from the Torah and Ethics. When someone asked Reb Shalom why he perspires so much during his chanting, his response was: "It is sufficient for a person to merely realize before whom he is praying and his entire body turns into water. Whoever is praying and does not perspire from fear of his Creator is only reciting prayers and is not really praying". He would add: "Do we know how to pray? The Rabbi from Blazow, he knew how to pray! However, he who heard the rabbi from Blazow chant, at least know how much a person needs to pray to G–d, to be worthy of praying properly."

Still, the story of Reb Shalom Schwartzman's life is not finished. His livelihood kept collapsing from day–to–day. To put it simply, he went broke without a penny left in his pocket. From all his labour, he was left with only one grandson and with a second wife. They were both sickly people and needed medical attention but the house was empty. Reb Shalom decided to do everything possible and immigrate to Eretz Israel. He forgot about his previous opposition to Zionism and turned to the Agudat Israel and to the Zionists for help. He also turned to the famous Rabbi Cook and some other famous rabbis with a plea: "Please help me emigrate from Poland!" After much intervention, his own and that of his friends (in which I too had my share in this mitzvah), he emigrated with this wife and grandson, Meir Mordechai. His life in Eretz Israel was not pleasant either. Maybe someday we will describe it in more detail what happened to him there. As of now, we will only mention the bitter epilogue, as was written in the newspaper "Hatzofeh" dated August, 1938.

"The hands of the murderers attacked again from their hideout in Jerusalem and tore the thread of life from a Yeshiva–dweller, the young Meir Mordechai Hacohen Gutwirth who was nineteen years old.

Yesterday at 11:15 p.m. an Arab truck traveling on the road between Sanhedriyah and Ramah, about one kilometre from Sanhedriyah, found the body of Meir Mordechai alongside the road. The driver immediately notified the neighbours who called the police and the Red Cross. His head had holes from knife stabbing and from stoning… This martyr immigrated three years ago from Strzyzow near Rzeszow in Western Galicia with his grandfather, Reb Shalom Schwartzman who settled in Meah Shearim. This was the only grandchild left to the grandfather. A sizeable crowd participated in the funeral, mostly young men from the Yeshivat.

[Page 135]

He was eulogized by Henoch Sienkewicz, the Dean of the Yeshiva 'Sfat Emet'. At the request of the grandfather, he was buried in the brotherly cemetery of Galicia".

That is how the martyr Meir Mordechai Hacohen died. The last of Reb Shalom's family. Meir Mordechai was my pupil.

A few years ago, Reb Shalom Schwartzman passed away in Jerusalem. He was ninety and some years old. He performed many good deeds in his lifetime. Because of his merits and the merits of his chanting, the chanting of the poor, the remnants of Strzyzow survived, to remember his every day of the years, especially on the High Holidays and moreover, what chanting the prayers is all about.

Reb Yacov Schiff
by Shlomo Yahalomi

Reb Yacov Schiff was a holy man, literally. Reb Yacov was the son–in–law of the assistant Rabbi, Joseph Mordechai Wiener. It was enough to take one look at this short man with blue childlike eyes and lean face, to realize that before you stood a man of holiness and glory. Even the gentiles called him: "the godly man". And what was the greatness of this adorable man? He was not one of the great scholars in town. He was considered an average learned man who never discussed the Talmud with others. He was a shy man who kept to himself. Even though he did study in the Beit HaMidrash day and night, nobody ever bothered to draw him into a discussion. Therefore, it was hard to judge the extent of his knowledge. Reb Yacov was an ardent admirer of the Rabbi from Belz and was very much respected by the rabbi. He had many students whom he taught Talmud but he was modest about it. Everyone in town knew that he was second–to–none in his piety and faultless in his devotion. To Reb Yacov, every day of the year was like Yom Kippur. His reverence of his Creator was constant. He was humble, quiet as the flow of water in a quiet river and low as meadow grass. That is how the rabbi from Belz described Reb Yacov Schiff's personality.

Reb Yacov Schiff never stood out. He never argued with anyone, never chastised anyone and never preached morality. But when he taught his students, he was very strict and demanding. He taught older students only, those in the ages between seventeen and twenty. He watched over them not only when they were his students but also when they studied on their own. He always wanted to know how they progressed. Sometimes he surprised them by peeking in through the windows of the Beit HaMidrash, standing on his toes because he was a short man. He stood there without uttering a word. His silence had inspired the young men more than the yelling of others. The students feared him when they were caught off–guard away from their books, embarrassment covered their faces.

Reb Yacov used to chant Shacharit on the High Holidays. If you think that he was a good cantor – absolutely not! But what? What was his power? The townspeople declared: "we have not found a better defender before G–d than Reb Yacov Schiff". Not with a strong voice but rather a low–key voice with a broken heard and reverence. And such a man cannot be ignored by G–d.

[Page 136]

Reb Yacov ate very little and many days he fasted altogether, especially during the month of Elul, before the High Holidays. Reb Yacov Schiff did not sleep much either. Only as much as was necessary to sustain his health. His wife used to beg him: "have mercy on yourself", but to no avail. He claimed that he could not indulge himself on such fearful days, days when fish in the sea would tremble with fear of the Day of Judgment. And this was only before Rosh Hashanah. Can anybody imagine when Rosh Hashanah came along? He slept even less. Twice a day, he went to the mikva to cleanse himself. Reb Yacov Schiff claimed that he was the congregation's messenger to the Almighty.

When he began his chanting, the entire women's section started to cry and the whole congregation followed. No wonder! Who could compete with words emanating from the heart? And a heart like Reb Yacov's at that! His chanting was not stylish. He chanted and sang simple traditional melodies thus not copying any rabbis. His words were heard loud and clear but with reverence. When Reb Yacov chanted, no one dared to speak. Everybody remained quiet and still and felt assured that all the gates to heaven were open for Reb Yacov's prayers. When he finished, he was in perspiration and his clothes were soaked in sweat. Everyone in the congregation went over to compliment him and shake his hands. Not only because they wanted to thank him but to receive his response: "Blessed be thou". An opponent of Hassidism once remarked: "If Reb Yacov would like to become a rabbi, I would be one of his first followers".

In later years, Reb Yacov was mortally ill and could not continue to chant or even to study. His wife had to be the breadwinner. She had a little grocery store from which they barely eked out a living but they stubbornly refused to accept help. People used to send them checks by mail anonymously. When the writer of these memoirs once made a remark to Reb Yacov that he was wrong not to accept help, he responded by saying: "He who gives life will also sustain and support".

Because of his righteousness, he was more fortunate than others in Strzyzow. He died of natural causes. His family perished in the Holocaust and nobody; absolutely nobody survived from his family.

Half of the rewards in the hereafter
by Shlomo Yahalomi
Part I

Whoever saw this man for the first time could not avoid being impressed by his aristocratic looks and his beautiful and majestic expression. Upright and tall, with a gentle face that expressed joy and happiness and his childlike eyes that expressed honesty and innocence. His oversized white beard and his hearty laugh subdued many hearts and attracted the attention of strangers. He was not very intelligent but he sometimes said certain things that even wiser people than he would have wished that they had said it. He was one of a few or maybe the only one in town who finished all the Talmudical tractates year–after–year. People used to say that he studied the Talmud wholesale. He kept advancing without stopping at complicated portions or twisted segments in the Talmud.

He used the simplest commentaries and if by chance a student from among the Beit HaMidrash dwellers would ask him to explain something, he would explain it the way he though was right. When the student later found out that he was wrong, he would go over to him and challenge him. As soon as he was told that he was wrong, he would become angry and call his opponent names claiming that they were ignorant.

His name was Reb Levi Joseph Wind. There was only one student whom, upon receiving a wrong answer from Reb Levi Joseph, would quietly tell him that he had made a mistake. To him, Reb Levi Joseph would reply: "You devil! You have such a sharp mind. How come I did not think of it?" And that student was I, the writer of these memoirs. Reb Levi Joseph was a Hassid of the rabbi from Sieniawa and visited his rabbi often. Later, when the rabbi from Sieniawa passed away, he travelled to his grandson, the rabbi from Koloszyce. He always told of the miracles his rabbi had performed. If someone expressed doubts about his stories he felt very insulted. I used to listen to his tales patiently and pretend that I believed in these stories.

Reb Levi Joseph was not a poor man. People may have considered him to be richer than he really was. Nobody knew the truth.

His only trouble was that he had no sons, only daughters who were very particular in selecting their mates. When they finally got married, they all remained childless. He pleaded with the rabbi to pray for them and he sent his daughters to famous specialists. But nothing helped. Finally, he received a promise from his rabbi that he would have a grandchild and his older daughter gave birth to a baby girl. The joy of the grandfather was tremendous and the whole town shared in his happiness. Then Reb Levi Joseph gleefully challenged everyone saying: "Nu, you see? You did not believe that my rabbi could perform miracles". His granddaughter grew up to be a beautiful girl and made her grandfather proud.

Part II

In 1946, I arrived in the Displaced Persons Camp in West Berlin, Germany. Soon after my arrival, I was asked to see the camp Rabbi immediately about an urgent matter. When I arrived, the Rabbi welcomed me with the following words: "I waited for you like the Jews are waiting for the Messiah". And he soon revealed to me the following story:

There is an unfortunate Jewish woman with a husband who is not Jewish. They have two boys. She visits daily and spills out her bitterness before me. The man with whom she lives risked his own life during the Holocaust to save her from the Nazi. At the beginning, he did it without an ulterior motive, but later, she could not ward off his demands and bore him two sons. He promised her that after the war would be over he would convert to Judaism. Now, he wants to fulfil his promise and is willing to go through the circumcision ritual together with the two boys. The boys are Jewish anyway... According to the laws of Moses, children born to a Jewish mother are considered Jewish. The camp's Rabbi's opinion was that the man should be permitted to convert without delay. But there is another rabbi, a Lubavitcher Hassid who opposes the conversion.

[Page 138]

His reason is lack of trust in the whole–heartedness of the man. Therefore, I was asked to help the camp rabbi to convince the other rabbi that he was wrong.

When I heard this story I was astounded. I could not believe it. How could anybody, especially a rabbi and a Lubavitcher Hassid, stand in the way of such a conversion? Even from a humanitarian point of view, it was wrong to deny this Jewish woman her happiness.

In the books of Ethics, our sages warned us to be careful in solving problems in general and in particular, marital problems. Therefore, I decided first of all to pay a visit to the couple and speak to them. When I entered the people's home, my head began to spin and I had the shock of my life. Before me stood the granddaughter of Reb Levi Joseph Wind from Strzyzow.

From this day on, I was restless. Not only was the fate of this woman touching my heart but the memory of her grandfather shadowed me wherever I went. I dreamt at night that he was standing behind my back and demanding justice for his granddaughter. And I was thinking to myself: "Is it possible? Hitler destroyed his entire family and she is the only survivor and we dare to deny her a chance to build a Jewish family? No! Never! Whatever happens, this family belongs among us. I cannot do this to her".

A few days later when I went to the office of the camp rabbi, the Hassid – the other rabbi was there and they were discussing the matter. The Hassidic rabbi still refused to give in. I told him a story about Rabbi Dov Ber from Mezritch how he once heard a voice from heaven telling him that he should not expect any reward in the hereafter because of some trespass or sin. At the beginning the rabbi was sad but later he announced that he was very happy because from then on, his devotion to G-d would not depend on the expectation of a reward. I paused a second and then I said to them that after all the tragedies that had befallen the Jewish people, every Jew should be prepared to help his fellow Jew without expecting a reward in the hereafter. Continuing the argument, I said: "Let's consider for a moment that I am wrong and, by prodding you to permit this man's conversion I am committing a sin for which might lose my reward. Even so, I am ready and prepared to bear the consequences".

I looked straight in the eyes of the Hassidic Rabbi and noticed that my statement had impressed him. I continued: "On second–thought, since you are a rabbi and a Hassid, why should I lose my reward in the hereafter? Let us both lose. I should lose half and you should lose half. At least something will remain for me and you".

The Hassid of the rabbi from Lubavitch began to laugh and said: "you convinced me. Let's be partners".

I left Berlin and in a few weeks, the camp celebrated the Brit Milah of the man and his two sons.

A few years later while walking in the streets of Tel–Aviv, the writer of these memoirs saw this Hassidic rabbi and we recognized each other. After a few polite exchanges I asked him what he was doing. To my surprise, he told me that he had joined a kibbutz where his son was a member.

[Page 139]

What kibbutz did he join? A kibbutz which is affiliated with the non–religious kibbutzim. Suddenly it dawned on me to ask him: "And what about the other half of the reward? Maybe you don't need it anymore?" He departed without a response. Apparently he was afraid I might ask him some more questions.

"When the world shall be perfected under the reign of the Almighty"
(quotation from the prayer "Aleynu")
by Shlomo Yahalomi

In memory of the faultless and simple Jews

This time I would like to tell about the plain Jews of Strzyzow. In essence, when you looked at one of them you would think that there was nothing much to tell about him. But this writer thought otherwise. Namely, these types of people were the real human kinds who were often misjudged by others. In heaven, they do know about these people. They know who was big and who was small.

Since all the stories which are told here have only one purpose and that is to light a memorial candle in the memory of the martyrs who perished in the Holocaust, so is the intention of this story to perpetuate the simple people of Strzyzow. In reality, these simple people, when they were alive, were almost unnoticed in the community. But they do deserve to be remembered at least as much as the upper–class in town, if not more. Although to us they were simple in comparison to the present Jews, they were holy and righteous in their daily lives.

And so let us remember one of these simple and uneducated men, Reb. X and his family.

You saw before you a man of middle height, wide shoulders, a stout body, an enormously big head and with a face mostly covered by his beard. On his face you could notice the signs of beauty and charm. His forehead was described by the town jokers as the forehead of the Rambam, the rabbinical philosophical personality of the tenth century. It meant, in simple words, that he had a forehead of a genius. His eyes expressed softness and warmth, love, mercy and good–heartedness, notwithstanding the myth that redheads are angry and explosive people.

His only vulnerability was, a derogatory remark aimed against the apple of his eye, Reb Chaim Elazar Shapiro from Munkatch (which he pronounced "Umkatch") and for which he was prepared to explode into violence.

Indeed, his material situation could never disturb his patient nature and contentment. All these attributes stemmed from one basic merit with which he was blessed; namely: humility. He recognized how little education he had and how little he knew about proper behaviour. Therefore, he never dared to be ill–tempered. If you ask: What did you expect of him? Wasn't he lacking education, wisdom and in addition was he an oppressed poor man? The answer to this question would be that there are plenty of poor and uneducated people who are not humble at all.

With all the above–mentioned merits, his manners befitted in many way an uncultured and ignorant man because he lacked the education and the elementary rules of behaviour in his parents' house. Therefore, he Was routinely seen doing things that boggled the mind.

[Page 140]

He walked around in the market with a pocketful of bread, pinching off pieces and stuffing them in his mouth. This was almost a daily ritual for him after which he would go over to the water pump, bend down and drink a third of a pail of water. He also loved horses. He would go over to the horses, embrace and caress them as people caress their only child. Fortunately, or unfortunately, he had two very enlightened sons. Especially the younger son who possessed a sensitive heart with a poetic and gentle soul. His father's behaviour hurt him and caused him a lot of pain. The son spent a lot of energy lecturing his father and asking him to cease the deeds that degraded him and the rest of the family. All the begging was in vain. This is how his father responded: "before you preach morality to your father about his outwardly faults, you had better go and teach ethics to those 'nice' Jews and tell them about their hidden faults, about their hypocrisy, haughtiness, self–elevation, etc". Indeed, one might ask from where did Reb X get such nice and wise words. Where did such meaningful words reach him? It was a legitimate question. The answer to this question is that it is doubtful whether he realized the meaning of such piercing words. Indeed, he often heard such words from the mouth of Rabbi Nechemiah Shapiro, of blessed memory, who habitually inserted such words in his sermons on the ethics of our forefathers at his Sabbath third meal table. The hero of this story was a faithful admirer of Rabbi Nechemiah and he heard these words from him and repeated them. Although Reb X did not fully comprehend the meaning of such words, the son who was thoughtful and diligent in morality and philosophical books, knew very well how right his father was.

Here the writer wishes to tell something about the son. The son in his father's house was like a rose among thorns because his mother was no more distinguished in education and merits than his father. Therefore, he suffered a lot. He felt inferior and unhappy. He confided in me, his best friend, many times. Even though I was the son of a rich family, he chose me as a friend because we had the same level of education and knowledge. "How I envy you. You have it so easy to fulfil the commandment: 'Honour thy father and they mother'. You honour them not only because G–d ordered you to do so but because they are truly worthy of your respect. But I…." I tried to console him. Respecting his parents was even a greater mitzvah. But he did not seem to accept my consolation.

Now let us return to Reb X. In his behaviour he was not outstanding because there were a few more like him, in one field, a very important field; he was the only one in town. Namely, in reciting Psalms. At present, in Israel, when people are suffering from too much leisure time, they are searching for ways to kill time with nothingness. However, the shtetl, such a problem was non–existent. Either they studied Torah or they just came into the Beit HaMidrash to see, hear and enjoy the echoes of the sound of Torah coming from the Beit HaMidrash dwellers. Others just sat there with Psalters in their hands and recited psalms. The hero of this story had a great deal of spare time on his hands because he did not own a store and he did not have a permanent livelihood. How did he make a a living?

[Page 141]

He used to go around in the nearby villages and buy "bargains" from the peasants and in return, sold them something they needed. On his way to the villages he would recite Psalms which he knew by heard having recited those hundreds of times. Wherever he went or travelled, Psalms always escorted him. He did not understand what these words meant but he knew their importance. He had heard from the rabbi from Munkatch, or in his pronunciation, the rabbi from Umkatch, if you recited Psalms with tears in your eyes, G–od would help. Therefore, you could always see him wandering the villages whispering with tears flowing from his eyes. He often complained that the travel in the villages was getting harder for him not because he had to walk a lot but because he could not refrain himself from crying. This all happened when he was away. However, in his house and more so in the Beit HaMidrash or kloyz, he cried freely. His voice thundered like thunders in heaven and surely his crying was heard there. He simply attacked the Psalms although he did not understand them and the words did not come out perfectly. According to what he heard from rabbi Nechemiah, the most important thing in reciting Psalms is the good intentions. And what did he intend with the Psalms? To beg for a livelihood? Heaven forbid! He would not dare to think of such foolishness while reciting Psalms. Only when you would pray were you permitted to ask for something. That was his theory. But what was the recital of Psalms for? Only for the coming of the Messiah. The subject of the Messiah was for him of utmost importance. And this is how he explained it. "When the Messiah will come there will be a resurrection. And when all the dead will be resurrected, that means…. (and here a smile appeared on his face), people will no longer die which means no more dead". Apropos, a wise man once said: "What an uneducated man can invent out of his simplicity and innocence, ten wise men cannot invent".

If during the year Reb X was busy reciting Psalms, imagine how busy he was when the days of mercy and repentance arrived! He gained an additional past–time, the recital of Slichot. There is no need to point out again that here, in the Slichot, was altogether lost, turning the words around with an off–tune melody. The language of Slichot was for him a double puzzle. He did not understand the words and because of their mystery, they brought out in him a deep admiration for these prayers. When he was reciting the Psalms he needed to recite a few chapters to warm up and begin to cry. With the Slichot, all he needed was to open the book and soon the pages were wet. Reb Mendel, a fiery Hassid and scholar, remarked to those who would tease Reb X: "Believe it or not, Satan is more afraid of his tears than the reverence of R.H." (Out of respect to the deceased, I will not mention who R.H. was).

This was all in normal times.

When the terrible years of the Nazi came, a double suffering began – both physical and spiritual which affected everyone, the poor and the rich. The rich were the first targets of the wicked who degraded and disrespected them publicly, requiring them to do all sorts of back–breaking labour. The poor were the first to starve from hunger, not having food even for a day. Reb X was dazed. He used to consider as natural the division of the town in particular and the world in general into two categories of people: people who had everything and respect belonged only to them with all the splendour that came with it and; people like him – the real poor who though that such is their fate to suffer silently.

[Page 142]

Suddenly before him – such an upset. Everyone was suffering. He tried very hard to digest the abnormal phenomenon without success. At first, he did console himself that the division between the rich and poor, notwithstanding their degradation, still existed. The rich still had food to eat but not the poor. Later, when hunger penetrated everywhere, he was lost. The world had come to an end, he stated: "I am telling you, gentlemen, it is the end of the world. There was a world since the Creation ruled by a permanent order. There were smart, foolish, poor, rich, the respected and the despicable. Now they have come and they want to make a new order. They are crazy! They will never succeed!"

A small consolation for Reb X was that the clothes of the rich were still in better shape than the clothes which the poor wore. That meant that the world was not in complete anarchy yet. He consoled himself in opposition to a statement made by an acquaintance of his who happily declared openly: "The equality of the poor and the rich has arrived". Reb X could not stand it. With his great humility and suffering, the spiritually depressed and true lover of Israel could not bear the shame and suffering of those whom he always considered to be superior and privileged. And surely, he would not think of finding satisfaction in his so–called "equality" and moreover, expressing happiness about it.

Indeed, worse times had arrived when, not only was he equal to the privileged but suddenly, he saw that everyone had to stand in line for selections, the same line for the rich and the poor. Not only being in the same line but such dear privileged were equally beaten. He, the simpleton, the eternal beggar was liked by "them". He never considered his strong body and muscles to be an asset. On the contrary, a Jew should look like a Jew and not look like a peasant and here he was preferred for his strength. When they began to send Jews to the place of no return, he and others like him were left behind, being needed for the war effort. It pained him to see all the abnormal things. He thought that he would gladly go in their place. He suffered a lot. He suffered for his family and for others and I could not decide which suffering hurt him most.

And so, on these High Holidays, these days of awe which held a double fear: fear as High Holidays and fear and danger of being caught by the Nazi praying together. Reb X was among the secret worshippers. I want to point out here that despite those hard times during the rule of the despicable, the Nazis, Reb X did not carry on so much with his recital of Psalms. He actually never stopped reciting whenever it was possible but quietly, almost in a whisper. You could hardly hear him and he did not cry. Surprised? How come? Was it because his situation had improved? In the days of murder and mass killing, logic dictates to the contrary. But here is what he said: "In a time when everyone is crying, the Rabbi, scholars, the rich and the educated, why should I mix my cheap tears with theirs? If G–d will not respond to their crying, would he listen to me?"

Nobody paid attention to the change in Reb X's behaviour. Who was he that he should interest anybody?

[Page 143]

But the holy Rabbi Nechemiah Shapiro did notice and did not rest. He was not calm. He pledged to do everything to open Reb X's well of tears. Rabbi Nechemiah said that in such troubled times; all the tears were needed from every Jew, especially the tears of the innocent. If in normal times G–d lusts for tears of the simple people, surely in times of fright and darkness he craves them even more.

Before the High Holidays, the rabbi gave Reb X a prayer book with a Yiddish translation so that he could read and understand what he was saying. Reb X began to read in Yiddish and his eyes lit up as a whole new world opened up to him. How sweet those prayers were. How unfortunate that for years he did not understand the words of the prayers and now....with the translation, the well of tears reappeared. Beginning in the days of Slichot, he started to cray and cry and when Rosh Hashanah came along, he let himself go. He knew when the congregation recited the prayer: "Unesanei Tokef", everyone was supposed to cry, especially at this time and in their situation. There was no limit to the tears that he spilled.

"As a shepherd seeks out his flock making the sheep pass under the rod, so doust thou make all the living souls pass before Thee". At this juncture, he exploded in a bitter spasm because he had reached the most sensitive point of the prayer to him personally. The words: "All the living souls" shocked his heart deeply. "All are equal, large and small – can the world exist this way? …. Master of the Universe, he began to sob, return the world to its former state that all shall know that there is a G–d and that all are equal".

His crying grew stronger until suddenly he became silent and fainted with the words: "Make the world a better world…."

The righteous and the beloved Reb Eisik Holles
by Moshe Mussler

There never lacked and there never would lack of pious, G–d fearing people as long as there is a Jewish people in this world who are anxious to fulfil the Creator's commandments, whether a light mitzvah or a harsh one. There were numerous such people and you could have found them mostly in the small towns throughout the Diaspora. Our shtetl was also considered to be a shtetl of Hassidim and the majority were men of deeds.

In fact, even among the pious, there were different categories – some who names themselves pious or were crowned by others without deserving such a title.

Among the few who reached the upper level of piety and reverence to the fullest, according to my humble opinion, was Reb Eisik Holles. He was endearingly called Reb Eisik'l by all the people of the town. Even though he was not officially nominated by the community leaders to judge and solve religious problems. To judge was forbidden and what was not, had many people knocking on his door to ask and always obeyed his decision.

[Page 144]

He served the public without expectation of reward and revered everyone especially children who were sent by their mothers with questions about kashrut.

Indeed, he lived in such meagreness that in this day and age, we can hardly comprehend. To me, it was a wonder how this man had the energy to study literally day and night. His face radiated from the light of the Torah and he had an expression of natural humility spread all over his face. I think that the painter who painted the portrait of the Genius from Wilno used Reb Eisik's face as a model. Whenever I remember him, even though many years have passed since then, I still feel the deep respect which my soul felt at that time.

My father, of blessed memory, who was not considered a Hassid and was well known as an opponent of Hassidism, was an ardent admirer of Reb Eisik'l. My father was a frequent visitor in his home and I accompanied too. I remember wintertime when we returned home after such a visit, we were frozen to death. The oven in his house never knew the taste of heat.

A testimony to his kind–heartedness will be the following episode which happened in his private life. After his wife did not bear children during the ten years of their marriage, his mother demanded from him that he divorce her. Reb Eisik'l refused, justifying his refusal by saying: "She married me when she was young and pretty and now, where would she find someone to marry her?"

When he was among people he never raised his voice and, of course, there was never a complaint on his lips. He suffered silently and the not–too–many years of his life were spent praying and studying.

Reb Eisik the Sexton
by Moshe Mussler

It is a well–known fact which no one in his right mind could deny that being head of the Kehillah was preferable to serving as a sexton in the community. The first has its rewards – respect and power but the second has only poverty and degradation.

However, in the case of Reb Eisik the sexton, the above well–known fact was null and void. People from our shtetl awarded Reb Eisik more respect than to the community leader. They related to him as to a person without whom the shtetl could not exist.

On Friday and holiday eves, as soon as the sun disappeared from the treetops, Reb Eisik appeared in the market equipped with a heavy wooden mallet which was passed on to him from past generations. Notwithstanding his advanced age, he ran hurriedly around the marketplace knocking on each gate once or twice and announcing in a loud voice: "In shul a–r–a–a–n". (come in shul).

His voice echoed all over the market and immediately the stores were closed. You could not find a person who would risk his soul and leave his store open after Reb Eisik's announcement.

One day, a new district commissioner arrived in town that did not like the tradition of door knocking and decided to abolish the community leader was summoned to appear before the commissioner and was warned to stop this tradition. it.

[Page 145]

Indeed, the community leader tried to claim that this tradition had been in the shtetl for many generations and it was part of the religious worship just as ringing the church bells was traditional for the Christians. However, the commissioner who was a well–known anti–Semite did not bend and the order remained intact.

When Reb Eisik found out about it, he went to the community leader, reported to him with a knock of the mallet on the table and said: "It never entered my mind nor will it in the future to obey the commissioner even if it means being arrested; I will not stop this tradition. Mitzva emissaries never get hurt. I was promised by the Rabbi from Sandz, the founder of the Sandz Dynasty, when his holy hands rested on my head, that as long as I live, nothing will ever happen to the shul where I serve as a sexton".

The end of the story was that in the same week that the Commissioner issued the order, he was ordered to leave the town and never return. Needless to say, the order was rescinded and the commissioner's replacement ignored the whole thing.

Reb Eisik was very much respected and adored by the children. He ruled not only over the living but also over the dead.

There was a myth believed by all inhabitants of the shtetl that the deceased gathered nightly in shul to pray. No one dared to enter the shul in night hours. If someone happened to pass nearby after sunset, particularly in the alley between the shul and the cemetery, he would cut it as short as he could as though his life were in danger.

Imagine how much more we, the children, were frightened and afraid of the dead. For nothing in this world could entice us to be found in the vicinity during evening hours. However, where Reb Eisik was concerned, fear for the dead did not exist. Maybe it id but we did not know it.

In the days of forgiveness and mercy, the High Holiday times, Reb Eisik walked into the shul in the early hours on his own. First, he knocked once or twice on the gate with his mallet to notify the deceased to clear the premises and return to their resting places. Later, he refuelled the eternal light which was located in a niche, lit the lights in G–d's house and then ran to knock on the doors of each house. While knocking he called out in a monotonous voice and in Hebrew and in Yiddish: "Arise to serve the Creator. In shul, a–r–a–a–n".

In addition to his service as a sexton, which brought very little income, he also dabbed in to baking. His cakes and bagels were not the most attractive but they were distinguished by their special Jewish taste. That is to say that they were peppered and salted in the winter and stuffed with blackberries and raspberries in the summer.

Notwithstanding his old age we, the children, were afraid of him. It was enough for him to lift his cane and we disappeared.

Only once a year he would let us turn the shul upside down. This was on Tisha B'Av. As soon as we were released from cheder and were free, we began the job of turning all the tables and benches in the shul upside down. Everything that was not tacked down to the floor was moved to make the destruction look like the destruction of the Holy Temple which we mourn on Tisha B'Av.

[Page 146]

Reb Eisik was a simple man but he merited to see two of his sons to become scholars who taught Torah in our shtetl. His third son immigrated to London and became a leader of the London Jewish community.

When he passed away, the glory of the shul went with him. The community felt orphaned by losing one of the best sextons the community so respected.

The Teachings of Moshe Mendelsohn
by Moshe Mussler

It is certain that we, the seniors of Strzyzow, whatever we achieved as youngsters in learning Torah and prayers, ought to be thankful to the cheder of Reb Eli Dovid and his two helpers. And we should not forget the whip which hung on the wall over his head and the pointer which he constantly held in his hand. Undoubtedly, these two tools went to heaven with Reb Eli Dovid where they received their reward.

The people in Strzyzow knew that Reb Eli Dovid was authorized by the Rabbi of Sandz, of blessed memory, to be a melamed. The people were also certain that their offspring would grow up to become Torah scholars and G–d fearing Jews.

Reb Eli Dovid was not the biggest scholar in town but in the elementary teachings of reading the Pentateuch, he was the best. What he had hammered into the child's head remained there forever.

If someone were to ask where Reb Eli Dovid obtained his knowledge and ability to teach and explain the chapter of the week, nobody knew. We, the little four–year–olds who repeated after him like parrots, still remember it now, never looked to the source of the matter.

Moreover, after I grew up and had studied many, many books, I was still puzzled and did not understand where our teacher, Reb Eli Dovid, learned all those German words which he used in his explanations since he had never left town and had no knowledge of any foreign language. This mysterious puzzle I solved many years later and here is how it happened:

During World War I, I had the "honour" of being a solder in the army of Kaiser Franz Joseph I and I wore his uniform. During my service, I once received a furlough for a few days to visit my parents.

After I had rested for a while, I noticed that my little brother was not in the house. I asked my mother, of blessed memory, where he was and she told me that little Avrom was in Reb Eli Dovid's cheder. So I decided to surprise him and pay him a visit.

When I entered the cheder wearing my uniform, Reb Eli Dovid jumped up from his chair startled and almost fainted. It was known that the Polish District Commissioner forbade the Jews to teach their children unless they had proper and approved accommodations similar to those which the Austrian authorities provided for the government schools. Otherwise, they did not issue a licence to teach children in a cheder. From time to time, gendarmes would come into the alley where most cheders were located to check if the teachers were abiding the law.

If they found a teacher who had no licence or had more children than he was licenced for, a report was issued and the children were dispersed and sent home. The teacher was also warned not to teach anymore. The fine was paid by the Kehillah because teachers were all poor, and hardly eked out a living. Surely they could not afford to pay fines.

[Page 147]

In fact, as soon as the trial of the melamed was over, he started to teach again. The commandment that it is forbidden to interrupt the teachings of the Torah to Jewish children was stronger than the order of the Commissioner. Although there is another commandment that Jews should not break the law of the land in which they live, the Jews were convinced that these laws were discriminatory and their purpose was to obstruct the religious teachings of the Jews. Therefore, the Jews ignored these rules.

No wonder then that Reb Eli Dovid thought I was a gendarme and that is why his face turned pale. He remained in his seat as if he were suddenly paralyzed.

I rushed up to him and asked him to relax as I greeted him with the traditional "Shalom Aleichem". It took him a while to relax and regain his composure as his breath returned to him. My eyes began to wander around the room as I tried to find my kid brother. To my surprise, nothing had changed since I had been a toddler. The whip, the pointer and the books from which I obtained my knowledge were in the same places. The whip was at his left side, the box with the snuffing tobacco at his right and his pointer was behind his ear. The pillow which he used to lean his elbows on had gained a few more spots and his beard had changed colour.

I suddenly found myself looking at a book from which he had taught me the first chapter from the book: "Vayikra" with all the outlandish words the teacher used to teach me….although many times, I did not totally comprehend their meaning, I still remembered them word–for–word.

Like a man finding a fortune, I grabbed the book and opened it. On the title page an acknowledgement was printed saying that this book was translated by the scholar of the German language, Moshe Mendelsohn. This was Mendelson the scholar and philosopher from Berlin who was excommunicated. (He started the Reform Movement in Germany). It was known that the Orthodox–Hassidic world had censured this book and had forbidden its use. Surely it was forbidden to teach children from this book. I then realized where my teacher had learned all these German words of explanation.

I suppose that G–d was patient with this simple, innocent man and did not punish him for his deviation because the progressive free thinking ideas of Mendelsohn were unknown to Reb Eli Dovid. The children's parents never found out about the book and with regard to the blessing that he claimed to have received from the Rabbi of Sandz, of blessed memory, to be a melamed, I am not responsible for its accuracy. I only repeated what I heard from the elders in town. His blessing partially came through because a few of us grew up to be G–d fearing Jews.

A Tree Was Cut Down Prematurely
by Moshe Mussler

Our city was not listed among the cities that produced men and writers that became famous in the Jewish world. I am referring to secular knowledge only. Indeed, with regard Torah literature and everything connected with it, I am not a qualified authority to judge.

To tell the truth, there were among us a few who were outstanding in their knowledge. But, there were such people among the Beit HaMidrash dwellers in every shtetl who, had they been given the opportunity to receive a standard education, would probably have reached the ranks of scholars in Judaism and, maybe also in secular professions.

[Page 148]

One of them undoubtedly was our comrade Chaim Gertner who specialized in bibliography. He possessed a remarkable memory. He remembered every article and the names of the authors as well as the place and date of publication. There were among us a few that, although they had never attended school, knew perfect German and were very knowledgeable in the German literature. The thirst for knowledge and enlightenment overcame many obstacles. We, the younger generation of half a century ago, were used to such intelligent types and they did not seem to us to be out of the ordinary. They were everywhere in Galicia, not only in Strzyzow.

What I am about to tell happened in the summer of 1938. On a Saturday night, a man suddenly appeared in my apartment in Antwerp, Belgium. He was young, about thirty–five or a little older and he introduced himself as Itzhok Goldman from Strzyzow, the son of Reb Abraham Goldman who was once my teacher. During our conversation, he told me that two years ago he and his family left Strzyzow and travelled to England to see if they would be able to settle there.

He lived there for a while but could not legalize his residence in London in spite of the intervention of well–known personalities. Therefore, he was forced to settle in Amsterdam where he was a teacher giving private Talmud lessons to Jewish students.

When he found out that there was an opening in the religious community school in Antwerp, he came to ask my advice on whether to accept the position and move to Antwerp as I was from Strzyzow and was his father's pupil.

I remembered him sitting on his father's lap when his father taught me the most complicated segment of the Talmudical tractate: "P'sachim".

Who would have thought that this child would, in time, reach the rank of a scholar, an expert in the Talmud and a phenomenal mathematician?

In my conversation with him I had a chance to recognize a little of his quality and character. Consequently, I found out that he was authoring a book on the principle of determining leap years, a commentary to Reb Moshe Maimonides (Rambam). (See the letters of Chaim Nachamn Bialik who read part of his essay and urged him to continue his important work). It would not be an exaggeration to say that whoever dared to get involved in such a complicated subject would be considered a prodigy.

It was past midnight when we parted. I never saw him again. After the war, I found out that he had died a sanctified death with the rest of the Dutch Jews in the ovens of Auschwitz. Neither he nor we attained to enjoy the fruit of his labour. If he would have survived, we would all have been proud of his achievement.

I searched everywhere and questioned many people, remnants of the Amsterdam Jewish community. I asked if they knew anything about him or his book which had remained in manuscript. To my sorrow, not many had heard of him. The unfortunate one was wise but humble and nobody had paid attention to him. What a pity that such a tree was cut down before its time.

[Page 149]

The Faultless
by Moshe Mussler

Even though sixty–five years have passed since then, I still visualize him as if he were alive. Short, his back bent, his fast walk and his cane in in his hand marching ahead of him.

He was a rich, poor man; that is to say, he owned a house which was named: "The ruins of Reb Yehuda Nosen". I doubt that whoever wrote it knew how to appraise the quality of this man. I am convinced that it was the stereotype text that was used for the average person who, let us say, prayed three times daily. It sounded like this: "Here rests an innocent, straight man, etc".

Such a description was not always true. Not everyone who was innocent was also straight, and vice–versa. Indeed, when it concerned Reb Yehuda Nosen, it was completely true. He was innocent and straight; without a speck of exaggeration. And this is not even a small part of the deserved praise. In my humble opinion, he deserved an epitaph on his gravestone consisting of a few words: "The most righteous of his generation". This is what he really was.

When he was younger, his livelihood was teaching. As he grew older, he sold vodka and bagels in the Beit HaMidrash. He kept his merchandize in a locked box under one of the benches.

The highest grade of humility was endured by him but nevertheless, no complaint ever reached his lips. Moreover, I am sure he never dwelled on the way the Creator handled things.

Once a native of Strzyzow came from the United States to visit his parents' gravesite and to observe the Yahrzeit of their departure. After the services, the guest invited everyone who was present in the Beit HaMidrash to have a drink. Reb Yehuda Nosen's hands got very busy. Such a sale did not happen every day…Guests from overseas were a rarity in Strzyzow, particularly people who still followed their parents' footsteps.

When the reception and the traditional well–wishing was over, the guest handed Reb Yehud Nosen a dollar banknote with the remark: "Keep the change". Reb Yehuda Nosen put his glasses on, examined the bill from both sides and returned it saying: "This is not acceptable currency, please give me sixty Austrian groshen".

All the explanations from bystanders that this piece of paper was worth twice as much as he was asking, did not help. He insisted on sixty groshen and that was it. At the end, the visitor took back the bill and paid him the sixty Austrian groshen. Only then did Reb Yehuda Nosen's face brighten up.

Since that day, Yehuda Nosen kept praying for visitors from overseas. But his prayers were never answered. There never was a repetition of such a miracle.

People said that in his entire life he never held a gold coin worth ten Austrian crowns. He probably doubted if such a coin existed. And what are people saying about the Jewish love for money? Is it not an eternal lie about the children of Abraham, Isaac and Jacob?

[Page 150]

Meir Hertzkes
by Moshe Mussler

There were only a few people in Strzyzow who were called by their names without adding the title "Reb". Meir Hertzkes was one of them. He was the simplest of the simple. But Meir had one characteristic of which few could boast about. He knew his value. He never made himself heard when he was among the distinguished.

But when he was among the village peddlers, it was a different story. Here he expressed his opinion loudly especially when the subject was death.

On Sabbath and holidays he came to the Beit HaMidrash and treated the better folks including the Rabbi with a sniff of tobacco. No one dared to refuse. "I inherited this tradition from my father, of blessed memory, to treat the townspeople with a sniff from my box and as a reward; I bury them when the time comes for their departure".

And hereby, let it be known that Meir was the grave–digger of the community. On days when somebody passed away, Meir did not go to the villages. He remained in town and prepared himself for the job.

Firstly, he tasted the bitter drop from the bottle which was always ready in his pocket. Then he went to the descendant's house, looked at the descendant's face and announced: "Dead! We will do what is proper for him!" and left.

After he finished digging the grave, Meir Hertzkes returned to town and participated in the purification of the deceased. Understandably, during the purification of the deceased, he used Hebrew words only as it was habitual among the members of the Burial Society. "Hold the hands. Catch the water", etc. (These expressions he knew by heart). At the funeral procession he was among the first who followed the casket. He walked and counted the virtues of the deceased. At the filling of the grave, Meir stood and gave directions on how to fill the dirt for the comfort of the deceased.

This simple Jewish man achieved what others did not. Namely, his only son Hertzke dwelled in the Beit HaMidrash and was counted with other young men as an intellect in the Talmud.

The poor man spared the food from his mouth to pay the teachers. I remember that every Thursday, on his way to the services, he stopped at the melamed's house to pay for the teaching.

After World War I when the gates of the United States opened, Meir and his son left town and settled in New York. There he found his eternal rest. May his soul be kept alive forever. Amen.

[Page 151]

The clever and the not so clever Shlomo Bier
by Moshe Mussler

Reb Shlomo was an average citizen. He was not counted among the more respected Jews. But, his conduct was like that of an important personality. You never could find a speck of dirt on his clothes. His strut was that of a Polish aristocrat. He had a sharp eye and an acute tongue but always careful to express his opinion about people whom, for some reason, he did not like. And such were numerous in town. From time–to–time he did let escape into the empty space a sharp, off–hand, double–meaning remark addressed to no one in particular.

Reb Shlomo was a clever man. Nevertheless, he did not succeed in establishing himself in town business–wise. Therefore, he went to Germany as did many others in town who did not want to, and perhaps were ashamed to emigrate overseas. He found his livelihood there by wandering through villages with a pack of merchandize on his back. He visited his family once a year at Passover time, took off the German clothes and changed into traditional clothes, namely: a black coat and a shtreimel on the Sabbath and like the rest of the Jews, returned his side–locks, which were hidden behind his ears to, the proper place – his beard was always well groomed and he looked like everyone else.

When his feet weakened from much walking and of age, he divorced himself from Germany and returned home. His two sons took over his route and supported him, fulfilling the fifth commandment: "Honour they father and mother".

When he advanced in age he spent his winter days sitting near the oven in the kloyz studying a book. In such hours, we gathered around him and begged him to tell us his adventures in the strange land. I can testify that he was a great artist in story–telling about all kinds of events which happened in the great world outside of our town. Mainly, we never tired of hearing the story of the suicide of Kaiser Franz Joseph who was "beloved" by us all. I am still puzzled to this day where Reb Shlomo obtained all the details. It is possible that during the years, he learned to read German newspapers and German books but all this is only a supposition. I never saw him reading a German newspaper although they were available in town. I tend to think that he obtained the information about this matter from others and his memory did not betray him.

What occurred between the prince and his beloved and the reason for his suicide – he breezed through with a few words. We were eleven and twelve years old and Heaven forbid that he should describe what happened between him and her…. Our share in grief of the Kaiser was real, from the bottom of our hearts because he was the shield and patron of the Jews. That we were mistaken, we only found out after the dissolution of the Hapsburg Dynasty.

[Page 152]

Another story which Reb Shlomo knew and told us in the smallest of details, was a story that inflamed our imaginations – a story about a Major Mikopnik. Reb Shlomo told the story with Prussian precision, repeating the orders from the Prussian captain in a pure German accent as though he himself was the captain in charge of the military unit. This was not a story; it was a theatrical performance in the smallest of details.

It is my opinion that this man was blessed with talent of a first–class declaimer. However, in our town, no one including Reb Shlomo himself recognized this talent.

In summer time after sunset when the peasants departed from the market place, Reb Shlomo took up a position on the corner of the Beit HaMidrash alley and immediately, a group of idlers and peddlers gathered around him. He began to tell about the daily events when all of a sudden he noticed that one of the court clerks, whom we nicknamed "the pauper king", was approaching. The pauper king was said in the traditional High Holiday sing–song. Why did this clerk merit such a nickname? I have no clear answer. Perhaps because of his gaudiness wearing his official hat while the rest of his clothes were tattered and worn out. In addition, he was also constantly drunk. When the pauper king came closer to Reb Shlomo and the surrounding group, Shlomo rushed out to the curb to be more visible and began shaking his hat as if to separate it from his yarmulke. The honourable pauper king thought that the hat was shaken to great him and he rushed to take his hat off in response to the greeting. Meanwhile, Reb Shlomo, with his hat in hand, pretended that he was only cleaning his hat with his sleeve.

On another occasion when a local gentile passed in a hurry in his carriage, Shlomo pointed his cane towards the wheels. When the man stopped and descended from the carriage to check if there was any problem with the wheels and seeing that nothing was wrong, asked Reb Shlomo what he meant. Reb Shlomo distanced himself from him and said: "Nothing. I was just noticing how the wheels are turning…" And he soon disappeared into the alley.

This man, with all his acuteness and cleverness, was submissive to his wife who was a woman of valour. No comment on that one.

Meir Ber who was intimate with the authorities
by Moshe Mussler

It is obvious that this story is not about the famous Jewish–German composer of the opera: "Huguenots" who was a convert, but it is about Meir Bert the barber of Strzyzow. He specialized in giving enemas, extracting teeth and was also a little bit of a musician.

It seems that the angel in charge of music forgot to include him among the world geniuses. Nonetheless, this fact did not diminish his popularity in town and particularly his closeness with the authorities.

This "genius" was not a native of our town. He came from Domaradz, a down–trodden little town less esteemed that ours, buried somewhere on the road to Dynow and without a railroad connection.

In those days, the profession of a barber was considered a respectable profession. It was related to the art of medicine….

Therefore, he behaved like an intellectual which separated him from the rest of the Jews.

[Page 153]

Already then, half a century ago, the Polish language ruled in his house. His spouse and three daughters were apprehensive of socializing with daughters of their own faith and socialized only with Christian girls fearing that their accent would be influenced. Meir used to boast before his gentile clients about the Polish upbringing of his daughters and their close association with their daughters.

He was the only one in town without a beard and side–locks. Indeed, he did not fail to come to shul for the Sabbath service dressed in silk with a small worn–out shtreimel which hardly covered his bald head. In the middle of the afternoon long before the evening prayers, he shed his Sabbath clothes, put on his derby hat and left the house pretending that he was going for a stroll. But, in reality, he headed toward the houses of the District Commissioner and other important officials to give them a shave and haircut for their Sunday day of rest. Meir was particularly proud that the Commissioner was his client. While he was busy with the Commissioner's beard, he chatted as it is habitual with barbers. Meir joked about his co–religionists' traditions and inadvertently disclosed some of the town's business for which discretion would have been preferable. On the other hand, he was also close to the Rabbi and once a month, paid his a visit to cut his hair. Here he presented himself to be a G–d fearing Jew boasting about his strictly kosher household and about his many interventions with the Commissioner in favour of his co–religionists. The truth was that the Rabbi and the rest of the community knew that he desecrated the Sabbath but for understandable reasons, they avoided admonishing him directly.

On market day he had his hands full; mainly extracting rotten teeth from peasants' mouths. These peasants, even though they suffered pain during the removal, did not dare to scream. To lessen the pain, they downed a half a dozen glasses of vodka which his neighbour, the Assistant Rabbi's wife had sole to them. So she also benefitted from their pain.

On Yom Kippur, the special day of the year, Meir turned very religious. He hardly left the shul the whole day. His head submerged in the prayer book saying quietly the portions of prayers that he thought to be important with reverence because he had difficulty in reading the "small print".

When the hour of the concluding prayers arrived, an expression of solemnity spread over his face. Isolated in a corner, he raised his voice in the prayer: "Avinu malkeinu". Meir told himself innocently that he had one request from the Ruler of the Universe: "To be inscribed favourably". At the end of the fast, Meir feared that perhaps G–d may not have forgiven him his many sins which were registered in heaven above…. But he did believe, after all, that the Merciful would relent and that he doubtlessly merited a good inscription.

After World War I, he disappeared from town with the many thousands of wanderers who were forced out of the newly established independent Poland because of their dislike of Jews. Meir too found his way to the free U.S.A. and, if he is still living, he probably lives a well–respected life as an intimate with the authorities.

[Page 154]

The eccentric Heschel Holoshitz
"Heschel the peasant"
by Moshe Mussler

There was not a town in the Jewish Diaspora which did not have its share of eccentrics and various types who, with their behaviour, distinguished themselves from the rest of the townspeople.

Our Hebrew and Yiddish literature is rich with these characters. These creatures were particularly outstanding and, therefore, they are lingering in my memory. It seems to me as if they are now alive and standing before my eyes.

One of them was the rich man, Heschel Holoshitz, who came to settle in town, as I heard from my grandfather, from Bonaruvka, a Ukrainian village near Strzyzow.

Heschel lived in a large, dark and damp room in the house of Shimon "The Horse trader" behind my grandfather's house. The room served as a kitchen, a bedroom and also as a store. His merchandize was extra–especial because of its smelly character. He sold naphtha, tar, low–quality soap, herring and cod liver oil which had a sharp stench and also matches. The smell of these articles caused dizziness.

His customers were Ruthenians from distant villages who gathered in his house with their wives and children to buy and also eat there. And, maybe, that is the reason why he was nicknamed: "The Peasant" because he dealt with them and behaved like them.

I doubt if Heschel knew how to write even one letter. His walls were marked with straight and diagonal lines. In addition to those lines, there were also some mysterious marks which were clear only to him.

Heschel Holoshitz was a miser without comparison. He bemoaned every penny which he avoided spending as much as he could even for food. He and his wife lived on stale bread dressed with onions or a bowl of sauerkraut. Even on the Sabbath and holidays, they satisfied themselves with a poor meal, just so that their fortune should not decrease.

No wonder then that the man accumulated during his lifetime a sack full of gold coins. It was said that his wealth reached several thousand guldens. This treasure he kept in a chest reinforced with forged steel bands and locked with an antique lock. The chest was hidden under the bed and covered with rags.

The poor people of the town, tradesmen and also small store–keepers who were in need and pressed for a little cash, were forced to set foot in his house to borrow a few guldens. Understandably, for a usurious fee.

This man loved his money more than himself; was careful not to lend it unless the borrower brought valuable collateral. The well–informed testified that his chest contained tens of wedding rings, strings of pearls, gold chains, earrings, bracelets and other silver and gold heirlooms which were inherited from parents or acquired during better times.

This wealth that Heschel kept in his chest had robbed him of his peace of mind, fearing robbers day and night. He was hated by all the townspeople. Nobody wished him well, particularly the debtors. A poor man never stepped across his threshold. He never opened the palm of his hands to give alms. He walked around like an outcast, angry and vexed with himself and others.

[Page 155]

His clothes were shabby and filthy and so were his wife's. She wore dresses whose origin could hardly be identified; remnants of fashions from the seventies of the past century or maybe even earlier.

When the spring of their lives was over and they became older, they suddenly remembered that there existed a hereafter. And, in their minds, they began to worry. The question arose as to how to secure a corner in paradise. Indeed, how could one achieve such a corner when there was no heir to say Kaddish after their departure, because they were childless. In spite of their wealth, the woman was not blessed to bear an offspring.

After all, only if someone says Kaddish and learns a chapter of Mishnayoth for the departed soul, is it possible to overcome the obstacles on the road leading to paradise.

In town there existed a society: "Good Remembrance" which was founded by Rabbi Moshe Leib Shapiro. The goal of this society was to study a chapter of Mishnayoth daily for the first year of a member's departure and, thereafter, on the anniversary day of the departure to also say Kaddish if the member had no heir.

Every year on Passover, a general meeting was called and held in the rabbi's house. The rabbi's family were busy preparing treats for all the members of the society. The effort was worthwhile because the rabbinical family derived much financial support from the society's funds.

Heschel Holoshitz and his spouse reluctantly decided to join the society. In those days, no Jewish person was ready to relinquish his share in paradise. The Holoshitzes knew that they would have to pay up a fortune, possibly a few hundred guldens. It was painful, very painful for them to separate themselves from the money which had been so hard to accumulate. But the fear that they might die before joining the society overpowered their lust for money. And they were forced to accept their verdict.

This Passover when the society members were discussing the acceptance of Heschel and his wife, I succeeded with other boys to sneak into the meeting room. Not only to witness the show but also to enjoy the treats of the Rabbi's wife.

The amount asked of them was large even for those times. The value of the Austrian coin was as good as gold and this almost caused Heschel to faint. He cried, begged, and swore by his health and by his wife's health that he never in his life saw such a huge sum. He claimed to be a poor and oppressed man and if they would insist on such a sum, he would not have money left for his next meal and would be forced to go out and ask alms from door–to–door.

Of course, all his swearing did not help. Everyone knew that his chest was full of gold coins, coins engraved with Kaiser Franz Joseph's likeness and it was a pity that they should lie there useless. Heschel was not enjoying them but the society would know how to use his money.

[Page 156]

The hours of negotiation lasted longer than usual. At the end, Heschel and his wife surrendered and, heavy–hearted, they rushed home and brought the money. It appeared that this was the first time and the last time in the society's history that such a big sum came into their treasury.

When I returned to town after World War I, Heschel and his wife were deceased and I was told that during the Russian occupation; they were attacked by robbers who robbed and killed them. Hopefully, their place in paradise was secured for them.

The needy
by Moshe Mussler

In the time when Galicia, including our town, was under the protection of the powerful Hapsburg Dynasty, there were only a few wealthy people in our town: their number could be counted on one hand. The concept of "wealth" meant that they need not worry about tomorrow. Even so, I have doubts that such men fully enjoyed their wealth and had peace of mind. Below those rich ones, townspeople who seemed to have enough bread to eat were always worrying about the next day. Making a living was as hard as dividing the Red Sea and everyone begrudged each other.

Many store keepers lived from day to day and their situation hung on a thread. Everybody pushed everybody, desperately fighting for a customer. They argued for every cent. The bread they ate was dipped in bitterness. Instead of rich people, our town was blessed with several kinds of poor people which our language has named as follows: Poor, poverty–stricken, beggars, wretched people, those who go from door–to–door and others who barely ate from one Sabbath to another. The highest poverty was reached by the brothers Shlomo and Mendel and their unfortunate mother. They were poor as poor can be.

The older brother Mendel worked in the store of Moshe Reicher. He loaded and unloaded sacks of flour, distributing them to different stores. Mendel himself looked like a sack of flour and a funny smell emanated from him. These two brothers were also the only Jewish water carriers in town, at a time when all the rest were gentiles.

Mendel was very easy going and never bitter at children who teased him. Even though there was no shortage of poor girls in town, nevertheless, a match for him was not found and he remained single all his life. On the Sabbath and holidays, he wore a torn and patched–up frock. He stood in the corner of the shul with a prayer book in his hand. It is doubtful that he knew how to pray or even to say the blessing over the Torah. Therefore, he was never called to the Torah.

If somebody asked Mendel why he did not take a wife, a broad smile appeared on his face and he meekly responded: "I too have the same question. Apparently my mate was not born yet".

Remembering him, I could see him representing all the innocence in town. He never hurt anyone, not even a fly and I mean it literally. He surely could not hurt his fellow man. He walked on the side of the road so as not to disturb anyone. Mendel spoke very little and he suffered his poverty in silence.

[Page 157]

If he were alive today, the psychiatrists would diagnose Mendel's brother Shlomo as retarded. His mind was that of a two–year old. Not only did he behave like a child but his mother treated him as such. She did not call him Shlomo but "Shloimele". Only on rare occasions did Shlomo help his brother Mendel in loading and unloading sacks of flour. He treasured the few cents he earned until he lost them or his mother emptied his pockets.

Girls shied away from him as if he were a ghost. He himself avoided facing them. Instead, he liked the company of older women and enjoyed sitting amongst them.

I remember when Shlomo reached military age, the mayor of the city presented him before the selection committee while his mother stood outside crying bitterly and praying to G–d to save him from gentile hands (of course, needlessly).

On the Sabbath and holidays, his mother dressed him up in a multi–coloured jacket, riding pants of a cavalry man with two big patches in the back and a vest of a page. Dressed in such splendour, she sent him off to shul to show him off to the worshippers.

Shlomo did whatever his mother told him to do. In wintertime, his favourite place in the Beit HaMidrash was behind the oven. Summertime, he walked proud as a peacock, back and forth with a smiling, dumb–founded expression on his face. Habitually, he would tickle a worshipper and disappear.

Outside on the law in front of the shul, little children waited for him. In their company he felt equal and spent the time playing until the end of the services.

How long these brothers lived and how their lives ended, I have no information. After World War I ended, I turned my back on the town and the memories of the inhabitants paled and were forgotten, except these written lines which I brought out from the depths of oblivion or forgetfulness.

The unfortunate families
by Itzhok Berglass

Strzyzow was a troubled town. Livelihood was hard to come by because the main customers, the Polish peasants whose farm products were very cheap, haggled over the price of everything and the competition among the merchants was tremendous. The Jews had all kinds of worrisome problems. Above all was the worry about their health. In spite of the clean air, many youngsters and adults died of tuberculosis and, in spite of the quiet conservative life, people also died of heart diseases and other illnesses that befall mankind.

There were two families in town that saw very little joy in their lives and drank from the cup of bitterness to the end.

The first such family was Reb Shalom Schwartzman who was called Reb Shalom the Trustee. He was the son of an assistant rabbi from Sokolow near Rzeszow. He came to our town to oversee and to be a trustee of Reb Yacov Kanner's business. That is how he got his nickname.

[Page 158]

Later on he became independent and opened a combined business, a tavern, restaurant and inn, all in his living quarters. His main customers were the Jews of the town who used to drink a glass of beer after the Sabbath meal and during weekdays, out–of–town agents who came to the town on business. His customers were also local gentiles who wanted to indulge in Jewish food. The attraction of Reb Shalom's customers was not only the food and drinks which he served but also Reb Shalom himself. He was a clever Jew, a scholar who pleased his guests with his wisdom and education. His first wife bore him two daughters and a son and it seemed that he had achieved success. The then the first tragedy struck. His wife died of tuberculosis in the bloom of her life. Reb Shalom bore his grief with self–restraint and, after a while, he married a second time. She did not give him offspring but she was a good wife and mother, devoted to his children like their real mother.

His children grew up and got married. His older daughter bore three sons to the delight of the parents and grandparents. Suddenly a tragedy again befell Reb Shalom. In one winter, his son Moshe, who lived in Rzeszow, became ill with pneumonia, a serious illness in those days in particular for those who had weak lungs. This was a defect apparently inherited from his mother. Moshe died. Next, his older sister, the mother of the three sons, became ill as a result of running around in the harsh winter during her brother's illness. She neglected her own weak health and passed away. After her death, the younger sister, who lived in Strzyzow with her father, also became ill and died shortly in spite of the energetic care from her parents and husband who was very devoted to her. Reb Shalom and his wife took the oldest grandson, Meir Mordechai into their house and the two other children were left with their father in Rzeszow. These two children then died after a short time of scarlet fever. The grandparents raised Meir Mordechai as a son, taught him Torah and piety.

In spite of these tragedies, Reb Shalom's spirit did not break. He did not rebel against the Creator. He continued to teach Torah and to lead the Mishnayoth studying group in the Beit HaMidrash as before. But with all the outward calmness, these many tragedies shook Reb Shalom and his livelihood was not as before because he was forced to neglect it. Then he decided to do something that was not popular to do in his circles. He decided to immigrate to Eretz Israel. Reb Shalom obtained a permit to emigrate as a rabbi, of course, not without the Zionists' help. Our comrade, Avigdor Diamand intervened in this matter at the Central Zionist office. Although Reb Shalom opposed Zionism, his opposition was good natured, without hypocrisy or personal hatred. We, the Zionists, understood that a man of Reb Shalom's stature could not do otherwise but be opposed to Zionism. He went to Eretz Israel and settled in the Meah Shearim section of Jerusalem, the Holy City. Here he continued his studies of Torah and prayer. He raised his grandson in the spirit of the community where he settled for a peaceful life in his old age.

But his misfortune followed him to Eretz Israel and robbed him of his last offspring.

[Page 159]

One evening during the excesses by the Arabs against the Jews in 1938, Meir Mordechai went for a stroll to breathe in the clean air of Jerusalem which he needed for his health. He accidently lost his way in the maze of Meah Shearim and walked into an Arab alley where he was attacked by Arabs. He was put in a sack and killed. This murder shook the whole Meah Shearim neighbourhood and outraged the Jews of Strzyzow. But the bereaved Reb Shalom bore the pain with courage and continued his life as before, studying Torah and praying.

Reb Shalom lived a long life and attained the satisfaction of welcoming Strzyzow's returnees from Russian refuge that arrived in Israel after the war. He died at a very old age and was buried in the Holy City of Jerusalem.

The second family struck by the hands of fate was the family of Reb Israel Kanner. He was a son of the aristocratic Kanner family whose roots in Strzyzow went back many generations. He was not as rich as his brother Reb Yacov. He was a quiet and humble man, toiling to provide for his family. He earned his livelihood from a tavern and a small inn. Reb Israel's speciality was dealing in wine. He was a great wine specialist. His customers included peasants, local gentiles and Jews who only bought wine for the Sabbath and holidays and, in particular, for Passover.

The tragedies began to befall him when he was still young, when his wife Freidel, a daughter of the famous Landau family, became ill. She was sick for a long time. She also bore him a retarded son. After a few years his wife recovered and they became accustomed to the retarded son. In 1910, Reb Israel lost the licence for the tavern which cut deeply into his livelihood.

He overcame the hardship because of his and his family's diligence. But when World War I began, the worse tragedies that can happen in a person's life – sickness and death – befell upon him.

During the war their retarded son disappeared without a trace. Within a year of the son's disappearance, their oldest daughter Chaya became ill and needed surgery. However, when the local doctor diagnosed the illness it was too late to operate and she died in the bloom of her life. Their younger son, Itzhok became ill with tuberculosis and passed away. The wife became sick from grief and shortly after, also passed away.

During the pogrom of 1918, Reb Israel suffered more than others. The rioters, after becoming drunk on his wine, broke all of the wine barrels in the cellar in which he had invested all of his savings.

All these blows were not discernible in the shrunken and silent Reb Israel. He did not shed one tear, not even during the mourning period. These blows, however, touched his inner soul and weakened his health. Reb Israel became sick and died of a serious and prolonged illness – an untimely death after much suffering.

The tragedies kept befalling the family even after the parents' death. The second daughter Yehudit and her new born twins died at childbirth. A son, Joseph——Bendet, an educated young man, had an unsuccessful marriage. At the outbreak of World War II, he lived in Lwow.

[Page 160]

The two other daughters of Reb Israel Kanner – Chana who was married and had a child and Bella, who was single, remained in Strzyzow in their parents' house. They all perished in the annihilation of the European and Polish Jewry by the Nazi who exterminated all the Jews both fortunate and unfortunate.

The first Zionist in Strzyzow
by Itzhok Berglass

The first Zionist, as I wrote before, was Moshe Meir Seidman – the only son of the assistant rabbi, Reb Alter Ezra.

In his youth, when he studied in the Beit HaMidrash and even after he was married until he left Strzyzow in 1908, his behaviour was no different than other young men in Strzyzow. He wore a bear with side–locks, wore the traditional silk frock on the Sabbath, and after his marriage, he wore a shtreimel. He prayed and studied Torah and did not do anything detrimental to the Jewish religion or tradition. Nevertheless, he had a bad reputation in town which lasted for years, until the people became used to Zionist creatures like him. He was the symbol of a man gone astray. His sin was that he peeked into secular books despite his father's opposition and openly propagated Zionism – a new idea which was not well accepted in the Hassidic circles.

Although he never succeeded in organizing the Zionist movement in Strzyzow, he demonstrated his devotion to Zionism on every occasion. He named his first–born son Benjamin Zev in memory of the Zionist leaded who had just passed away.

In 1908, Moshe Seidman moved to Drohobycz, the city of oil wells where he became one of the most energetic activists in local Zionist movement.

During World War I and due to his shrewd commercial tactics, he became rich and bought an estate near Lwow.

From then on, Moshe Meir Seidman's house was run as befits a wealthy man. But under his wife's influence, the house was empty of Jewish tradition and was run in an entirely secular way, devoid of the Jewish spirit. Moshe Meir, in whom the Jewish tradition was implanted since childhood at his parents' home, suffered greatly from his wife's behaviour to which he never agreed. His troubled soul caused him to do a desperate deed. Namely, he left his estate and went to the rabbi of Komarno who lived in Lwow where he spent a year with the Hassidim whom he supported generously.

Subsequently, he returned to his wife but he did not find his peace. In 1923 he left again. Wishing not to be recognized, he disguised himself. He grew a beard and side–locks like he had done in his youth and decided to be in exile and repent for his sins. He was a regular in the Beit HaMidrash of the rabbi from Komarno, without being recognized. Notwithstanding the disguise, the rabbi recognized him without letting him know. Then, one Saturday night, the rabbi told him that his father had passed away and he arrived for the funeral just on time.

From then on, he struggled with his wife about keeping the household in a traditional Jewish spirit until he partially succeeded. Strzyzow, his birthplace, was always close to his heart and he was always happy to meet people from Strzyzow and help them out.

[Page 161]

He was twice as happy when, in 1913, he met Moshe Mussler – his friend Eliyahu's son – who came to Lwow to enrol in a Hebrew Teacher's seminary. He saw in this student a realization of the Zionist ideal which he propagated in his youth.

At the beginning of World War II and during the triumphant march of the Nazi through Poland, his older son, Benjamin Zev, was killed trying to escape from Rzeszow. The loss of his son greatly depressed him.

After the Russians took over Eastern Galicia, Moshe Meir Seidman changed his name to Alterowich and lived alone in Lwow. Because of his wealth, he did not want to be recognized and avoid being exiled to Siberia. He continued his attendance in the Komarno rabbi's Beit HaMidrash.

To distance himself even further from his family which had caused him so much grief, le left Lwow and settled in Truskawiec – a resort town near Drohobycz. There he found his sanctified death together with his Jewish brothers. His family was filled on the estate where they had lived.

Rizhi, the righteous woman
by Itzhok Berglass

There was no lack of righteous women in Strzyzow. The majority of the town's women deserved such a noble title. Not only the women who attended the services each Sabbath but also those who came only once a month were all righteous. They were kind and unpretentious to their husbands. They worried about the children, took care of their household and also helped carry the burden of earning a living.

An important fact about these women was that each and every one was active in charitable deeds. Although normal charity work was done by the heads of the families, the men, the women were active in a different way. They discreetly helped women in need who accepted without their husband's knowledge, because had they known they would have been embarrassed and might have refused such charity.

One woman in town who was outstanding charity and maybe the most outstanding was Rizhi Rosenblith, whom everyone called Rizhi the Righteous.

Her husband, Reb Elazar Rosenblith, had a hard time making a living in spite of the fact that he was a high–pitched peddler. On market days while others displayed their wares on a simple table, he built a whole Sukkah which resembled a mobile store. Notwithstanding all this, his wife had to help him earn a living.

All his life Reb Elazar complained of pressures in his head. But nobody paid attention to him because he was a tall, husky man with ruddy cheeks. On account of his constant complaining, he was nicknamed: "The complainer". Whoever heard in those days of high blood pressure?

Reb Elazar did not need any help in the business. Besides, Rizhi was not a business woman. She was a very straight person who was not able to convince a buyer to buy anyway. She therefore opened a private bakery in her quarters and people who knew that she was trustworthy, gave her ingredients on Thursday to bake challahs from them for the Sabbath.

[Page 162]

She was good–hearted and patient. She never became angry at customers, not even at those who were always late bringing the cholent on Friday afternoon to keep warm in her oven.

Her second and most important job was charitable activity. Her heart and hands were always open for the needy. The poor were part of her household. They came to her in times of need and she always found time, whether day or night, to help out with her own means or from others. She provided the poor with all their needs.

Her happiness was seeing others active in charity especially the young people. She considered charity the greatest mitzvah.

There were four of us
by Itzhok Berglass

In memory of my three friends during my youthful years: Reb Samuel Zeinvel Greenblatt; Naphtali Herz Weber and Chaim Gertner and who are no longer among the living.

We were sixteen or seventeen years old then, the best period in our lives both in our dreams and ambitions. The time itself was a time of transition from conservatism of the old Beit HaMidrash to the new Zionist movement which marched in step with our yearning for enlightenment and renewal of the structure of our lives.

In general, we the Zionist youth and the Beit HaMidrash dwellers were still friends. But this was a time when we began to split up into small groups which met in our spare time, strolled in the streets and the beautiful surroundings where we discussed world problems. The four of us were a tight circle. The three that I have mentioned about and I who feel that it is my duty to perpetuate them in our memorial book.

Reb Yacov Greenblatt whose son was one of the four, was called Yank'l the writer. (Almost everyone in town had a nickname. Many people were known only by their nicknames and not by their last names. There were whole families who shared the same nickname and nicknames were inherited by the sons from their fathers). Reb Yacov Greenblatt had no schooling. He was a self–educated man who knew all the laws and as a lawyer he acted as legal adviser and wrote petitions. That is how he obtained the nickname: "the writer". During the years he advanced and became the secretary of the Kehillah. During World War I and the mayoralty of Dr. Patryn, he was also the Secretary of the city. Subsequently, he established his own bank and named himself as president. He was also elected as president of the Kehillah.

The most mature and the strongest intellectually was Samuel Zeinvel Greenblatt who was well educated in Hebrew and secular subjects. The three of us thirstily drank in his words of wisdom. We called him simply: "Zeinvel". His whole family was self–educated. Zeinvel's older brother, Joel, was a member of the first Zionist committee. Joel was sharp and knew Hebrew and German to perfection. The knowledge of German came to him from reading German books about Jewish wisdom and philosophy. The German language was the only language that had so many books on Jewish subjects.

[Page 163]

He too never attended any school, not even the Polish elementary school. Joel immigrated to Germany and enrolled in the Rabbinical Seminary of Dr. Brauer in Frankfurt. However, he soon left because he could not get accustomed to the extreme religious spirit which prevailed in the Seminary. He subsequently succeeded in business and when Hitler came to power, he left for England.

Reb Zeinvel Greenblatt did not attend school either. Their Orthodox mother wanted her sons to grow up Torah scholars and pious men. But Zeinvel turned into a bookworm. He knew Hebrew and German perfectly and he was an expert in literature. At the age of fifteen he was influenced by the book "Reishit Chochma" and became extremely pious. His extremism did not last long but he remained religious all of his life. In spite of his being religious, our parents did not favour our companionship with Zeinvel who, because of his Zionism, was considered to have gone astray religiously. He taught Hebrew privately and he was among those who laid the cornerstone of Hebrew education in Strzyzow.

In later years, he immigrated to Germany where he hoped to settle with his brother's Joel help. He returned disappointed and remained in Strzyzow for the rest of his life working for his father as a clerk in the bank. Zeinvel died a sanctified death. He was murdered by the Nazi during the massacre as it will be told later in this book. Zeinvel's two sisters were active Zionists and both died in the Holocaust.

My second friend was Naphtali Hertz Weber whose name was shortened to Hertzke. Hertzke's father, Reb Meir, was a poor village peddler who never missed a recital of Psalms on Saturday afternoons. He was known as an avid "Amen" sayer after everyone who made a blessing. Reb Meir strived ambitiously for his son to grow up a Torah scholar and he did not let the son help him earn a livelihood. Reb Meir spent as much as the wealthy people for his son's education. After Hertzke finished his studying in cheder and legally required elementary school, he continued studying in the Beit HaMidrash. But at home, he completed a secular education on his own and became a private tutor to help out his parents. He tutored boys and girls who fell behind in their elementary school studies. He taught girls to read and write Yiddish and taught both sexes Modern Hebrew. Hertzke also contributed a lot to Hebrew education in town. In 1920 Hertzke and his parents immigrated to the United States, joining his three sisters who had previously emigrated. At the beginning, Hertzke had a hard time finding a steady job in the United States. Although they were from Strzyzow, his employers had fast become accustomed to the American way of life, along with the other Jewish immigrants and they conducted their business on the Sabbath as usual. As soon as Hertzke failed to appear on the job on Saturday, they refused to let him work on Sunday or Monday. And this was supposed to be the progressive Zionist from Strzyzow. He finally became acclimatized in the United States, got married and lived there for the rest of his life.

My third friend, the youngest in the group, was Chaim Gertner. He was the son of Reb Israel Gertner, one of the wealthiest people in town. Chaim Gertner went through the stages of religious and secular education, as I and Hertzke did. Chaim helped his father in the business and so did I, the writer of these memoirs. We studied Torah together in the Beit HaMidrash and the secular studies at home. We were the youngest members in the Zionist organization, a movement which had just started in town. Chaim's father, who was apprehensive about his family's reputation, did not relate favourably to his son's Zionism.

[Page 164]

In his opinion it was the diminution of reputation for a son from such a respectable family. For that reason, Chaim's father had put all kinds of obstacles in the way of his Zionist activities. But the flexible Chaim knew how to overcome the hardship and did not deviate from his path. He left town together with his parents during World War I when Strzyzow was occupied by the Russians. Chaim never returned. After the war, he settled in Krakow.

Before World War I, when we were sixteen years old, we attended the funeral of Reb Leibush Shipper, of blessed memory*** On the way back from the funeral we, the four friends, promised ourselves with a hand shake that, at the appropriate time, we would immigrate to Eretz Israel, the land of our dreams. In the winter of 1931–1932, I suggested to Chaim Gertner that we should fulfil our promise and realize our dream. To my sorrow, Chaim not only refused but also failed to give me the necessary encouragement which I needed to overcome my family's opposition. Chaim lived comfortably in Krakow, a city heavily populated with Jews. It had many synagogues, rabbis and Torah scholars and also many Jewish intellectuals.

During World War II, I met Chaim Gertner as a refugee with his family in Lwow. Apparently, he somehow managed to receive a Soviet passport or maybe he was just lucky enough to have escaped exile to Siberia along with his brother Moshe. He remained in Lwow until the German occupation and he and his family perished together with millions of his brethren.

***Reb Leibush Shipper was one of a few interesting personalities in town. At the beginning of the 20th century, he came from another town to settle in Strzyzow. In his old age, he married a woman from Strzyzow. His children from a previous marriage supported him. So all he did was sit in the Beit HaMidrash and study the Talmud from early morning to late at night.

He used only one commentary. He studied with much speed as though he were reading a detective story. His wife Nechama brought him all the meals to the study table. Finishing the sixty two Talmudical tractates was, for Reb Leibush, a simple routine when for others it took years to accomplish.

Reb Simcha Feingold, of blessed memory
by Ben Ami Feingold

My grandfather, Reb Simcha, was born in Radomisl, Galicia in the middle of the past century (1863). He spent his youth in, the traditional way – in cheder and Yeshiva. After he married he settled in Strzyzow where he lived until just before World War I. He then immigrated with the big wave of immigrants to the United States. He made his livelihood in Strzyzow by working in the forests. He supervised timber cutting and marketing.

[Page 164]

Reb Simcha was not only a Torah scholar who studied continuously, but he was also a thinker. He concentrated his thoughts on the timing of the redemption of the Jewish people. He even secretly authored a composition on this subject. He wrote it, chapter by chapter, and only the later years of his life, when he came to Eretz Israel, did he complete his book as scholars have been doing throughout history.

His thinking about the redemption made him a Zionist in his youth. Therefore, his house in Strzyzow became a centre for Zionists with the help of his spouse, – my grandmother. When a Zionist speaker came to town he always stayed in Reb Simcha's house. The greatest day in his life was when his son, Yacov (my father), of blessed memory, went to Eretz Israel as a member of the American Jewish Legion. My father went with both his grandparents' blessings, interwoven with Reb Yehuda Halevi's poems, wishing success in his endeavour.

Grandfather was a believer but not a zealot. With love and understanding, he reached out to his grandchildren, the so–called "agnostics". With understanding, wisdom and patience, he implanted love for Israel.

My grandfather's Zionism brought him to Eretz Israel in 1934 and he settled near his son in Schunat Borochov. Here he continued his studies and research. He kept on writing and spent many hours in the libraries reading ancient books and manuscripts. However, Schunat Borochov was a secular settlement and he did not like the environment. Thus, he looked for a more traditional atmosphere and settled in B'nai Brak. Later, he moved to Schunat Montefiore where he remained until the last days of his life. He lived the life of a scholar, in piety and love of mankind.

Reb Simcha Feingold passed away on the eve of the establishment of Medinat Israel having achieved an abundance of years and good deeds. He did not live to see the realization of his dream of redemption for which he longed for all his life. My good grandmother soon followed him. They were buried on the Mount of Olives in a gravesite they had purchased for themselves. Nobody visits their graves which are over the border across from the Temple Mount. (This article was written before the Six Day War. The Mount of Olives is now under Israeli rule).

The large, well–rooted families in Strzyzow
by Shlomo Yahalomi

Strzyzow had many large, well–rooted families who, after many generations, branched out and, by inter–marriage, reached a point wherein the majority of the people in town were related. Before I list the names of these families, I would like to apologize for any omissions. I only mentioned those families which were well–known to me or were my relatives. I only wish that others could have filled in the names which I have omitted. I will list them in alphabetical order. Each family had their own interesting personalities, scholars and ordinary everyday Jews.

[Page 166]

The Adest family
by Shlomo Yahalomi

The Adest family was well respected in Strzyzow. The family began with Reb Yacov Adest. Yacov had three sons and a daughter: Feivel, Moshe, Zelig and Dvoire Sarah. The sons were sophisticated men who were all involved in town politics but never ran for office. They only pulled the strings behind the curtains. The youngest son, Moshe, was very clever and sharp. His jocularity and stinging remarks offended many people. Nevertheless, everybody enjoyed hearing them even those who were offended. Moshe had a son who was a great impersonator. He impersonated cantors, preachers and righteous women. He was a beloved and fine young man. Reb Zelig Adest's son–in–law, Avrehmal'e Goldman, was a scholar. He was sharp and acute and a man about whom we wrote a well–deserved separate chapter.

The Berglass family
by Shlomo Yahalomi

The Berglass family was an old, rich and well–established family in Strzyzow. They had a hardware store which they claimed was established in Napoleon's time. The family began with Reb Avrom Mendel from the village of Glinik near Strzyzow. From the trunk of the Berglass family tree came the branches of Reb Israel Gertner's family and Reb David Liberman's family. These families were rich and shrewd business people. There were two Berglass families in Strzyzow. Reb Baruch Berglass was a very man who inherited the above–mentioned hardware store. Reb Hersh Ber Berglass was known not for his material situation but for his spiritual richness. Hersh Ber never missed being the first one in the Beit HaMidrash, whether summer or winter. When people came at four o'clock in the morning, he was already there studying. He was a dear and pious Jew. His son and daughter lived in Strzyzow until the Holocaust.

The Diamand Family
by Shlomo Yahalomi

They were one of the largest, most branched–out families in Strzyzow and vicinity. The Diamand family, including the people who inter–married with them, consisted of a few hundred people. I will list only those who were known to me.

The first of this huge family that I remember are: Reb Aryeh Leibush Diamand from Dobrzechow and Reb Akiba Samuel Diamand. They were the founders of the Diamand family. Reb Aryeh Leibush was the grandfather of my grandmother Sarah. Reb Akiba Samuel was the father of my grandfather. Reb Aryeh Leibush was a Hassid and a very hospitable man. He travelled to the righteous rabbis of his time. He was particularly attached to Reb Shlomo Zalman Frenkel, the holy rabbi of Wielopole. According to family legend, they were related. I remember that the Rabbi and righteous Reb Joseph Frenkel from Sedziszow, when writing to my father, of blessed memory, addressed him as "my dear relative and friend". Reb Aryeh Leibush had four sons who settled in the surrounding villages following the advice of the rabbi from Wielopole.

Reb Yacov, his first son, had eight children and like his father, he was also a Hassid and his home was always open to wanderers. The majority of this ancient family perished in the Holocaust.

[Page 167]

Reb Arye Leibush's second son, Reb Moshe, also had eight children. He left part of his estate to the poor in Strzyzow. One of his daughters immigrated to the United States and had a large family in America.

Of the offspring of Reb Aryeh Leibush's third son, Avrohom, I only know of two sons and two daughters. One son had eleven children who lived throughout Galicia. The second son lived in Strzyzow. He was a very clever man who possessed many merits, chanted the prayers and only had one son, but many daughters and grandchildren. They all perished in the Holocaust.

Reb Avrohom's daughters married local young men and all had big families of their own. The fourth son of Reb Aryeh Leibush was Reb Akiba who also had a big family. From Akiba's family, one a great–granddaughter survived in a village near Strzyzow. When a relative found out about her, he had to pay ransom for her release. He gave a horse and wagon to the peasant for her release.

The second founder of the Diamand family, Reb Akiba Samuel Diamand, was my father's grandfather. He had four sons and one of his sons was my grandfather, Reb Shlomo, after whom I was named. He lived in Zyznow close to Strzyzow.

My grandfather, Reb Shlomo, owned a tavern and much property in the village where he permanently resided. Even though he lived in the village, he was one of the community leaders in Strzyzow. He was very influential in town and in the entire vicinity. He was well–known for his charity. He was clever and sharp, compassionate and forceful, merits which he applied where necessary, always at the right time and in the right place. My grandfather had twelve children; three from his first marriage and after his wife died and he married her sister, nine more children were born. The children lived in different places where they established families of their own. Ninety percent of these families perished in the Holocaust. It was G-d's will that we, the brothers Heschel and Shlomo, the sons of Reb Joseph and Dvoire Diamand, the grandchildren of Reb Shlomo from Zyznow, survived. There are also a few other grandchildren who survived, some live in Israel and a few others in the United States.

The other son of Reb Shlomo from Zyznow, Reb Hersh from Bonarowka, had a son–in–law who was self–educated and about whom we will write later in this book. Reb Shlomo's third son, Reb Aryeh Leib Diamand, had many children who also had large families of their own. One of his off–spring, Dr. Akiba Samuel Milgraum–Diamand, lived in Haifa, Israel. He was well–known for his generosity because in many instances, upon making house calls to the poor, he would also leave money to buy the prescription. He passed away in 1945. I could not have mentioned everyone in such a large family. Therefore, I beg forgiveness.

Reb Yacov Moshe Diamand, the grandson of Reb Shlomo from Zyznow, was one of the important citizens in town. He married Reizi Wiesenfeld from Pilzno who bore him two sons: Aryeh Leibush and Avigdor. Both were enthusiastic Zionists and important personalities in town. Reb Aryeh Leibush married a daughter from the Montag family in Jaroslaw. At the outbreak of World War II, when the Nazi entered Jaroslaw, they were expelled to Przemysl from where they later moved to Lwow. They perished together with their only daughter. May G-d avenge their blood.

[Page 168]

Reb Avigdor Diamand was married to the daughter of Reb Yechiel Hollender, the leader of the Kehillah in Gorlice. They were childless. A few days before the outbreak of the war, Avigdor arrived in Krakow sick and was admitted to the University Hospital. His wife stayed with a nephew, Aryeh Diamand, and they all perished in the Holocaust.

This is not a complete list of the Diamand offspring. There were many more victims. G-d shall forgive me for those that I have omitted.

The Holles Family
by Shlomo Yahalomi

The Holles family belonged to a big Rabbinical Dynasty, related to the Shapiro family and particularly to Reb Chaim Elazar Shapiro who was rabbi in Strzyzow and Munkatch, respectively. Rabbi Shlomo Holles was the assistant rabbi of Lwow at the time when the genius, Rabbi Yacov Orenstein served as rabbi. Rabbi Shlomo Holles' son, Joseph, lived in Strzyzow. His son, Reb Eisik'l, was known for his piety and righteousness and he was also one of a few interesting types in the town heretofore described. From this whole family, only a few offspring survived. They reside in Israel.

The Kanner Family
by Shlomo Yahalomi

One hundred and fifty years ago, Reb Aaron Halevi Kanner lived in Strzyzow. He was the father of the famous Kanner brothers: Reb Avishal; Reb Yehuda Leibush; Reb Itzhok and Reb Joseph. Reb Aaron was very wealthy and his fame as a hospitable, charitable and graceful man reached far and wide. Most of Reb Aaron's sons were also very rich. They were scholars, pious and charitable people. The most famous of them was Reb Avishal who moved to Sanok. His sons, Moshe and Aaron, were learned men and are mentioned by Reb Shmuel Engel in his responsae. Three famous rabbis: Rabbi Naphtali Horowitz; Rabbi Joseph Rubin and Rabbi Yehuda Eichenstein married daughters of the Kanner family. The grandchildren of Reb Avishal entered into matrimonial bonds with the grandchildren of Rabbi Chaim Halberstam from Sandz. As of today, there are two great–grandchildren who are rabbis in Israel: Rabbi Avishal Kanner, the Rabbi of Tczchow who lives in Haifa and Rabbi Moshe Halberstam of Jerusalem. The whole Kanner family assimilated into large rabbinical families.

Reb Aaron's second son, Reb Pinchos Kanner, lived in Strzyzow and was also very rich. He was a scholar with many merits and his offspring inter–married famous rabbinical families. Two of his sons, Reb Yacov and Reb Israel Kanner as well as his daughter, resided in Strzyzow. Reb Israel Kanner married a daughter of rabbinical ancestors; a relative of the author of the book "Noda Bayehuda". Reb Israel Kanner was a righteous man without luck in his personal life. His misfortunes followed him all of his life, as we wrote in the previous pages of this book.

[Page 169]

Reb Yacov Kanner, the second son of Reb Pinchos who was my great–grandfather, was a rich man with a capital R. He was intelligent and served the community for many years. Reb Yacov's first wife, Dvoire was from the Komarno Rabbinical Dynasty which goes back to the famous Rabbi from Lezajsk and the rabbi from Lublin called "The Seer".

My mother, Dvoire, was a great–great–granddaughter of Reb Yacov Kanner. Reb Yacov's second wife bore him many sons and daughters. Two sons lived in Strzyzow. The rest of the children spread throughout Galicia. To list all the names of the Kanner family is simply impossible. Here and there, some great–great–grandchildren of the Kanners survived the Holocaust but most of them were annihilated by the Nazi. Many families in Strzyzow were related to the Kanners.

One of Reb Pinchos Kanner's sons, Reb Aaron, moved to Germany where a large family branched out. They were expelled from Germany in 1936. One of Reb Aaron's sons was caught on the German–Swiss border where he suffered a heart attack and died in Switzerland.

The Mandel Family
by Shlomo Yahalomi

The founder of the Mandel family was Reb Moshe Yacov Mandel from Scuzcin. His son settled in Strzyzow. They were all Kohanim. All the Mandels, generation after generation, were ardent admirers of the Shapiro Rabbis. We already wrote about Yeshayahu and Chaim Mandel. One grandson, Shimon Mandel, survived and is now an officer in the Israel army.

The Mintz Family
by Shlomo Yahalomi

The head of the Mintz family was Reb Abraham Mintz, a well-respected man in Strzyzow. He was the treasurer of the shul and accepted by everyone. His son Michael was, like his father, a very nice person. One son immigrated to France where he soon passed away. Reb Shlomo, another son of Reb Abraham, immigrated to the United States at a very young age. There he raised a large family and lived very happy. One of Reb Abraham's daughters married Feivel Adest from Strzyzow. Fortunately, many of Reb Abraham's family spread throughout the world and survived.

Reb Hershel Resler and his sons-in-law
by Shlomo Yahalomi

Reb Hershel lived in Tilkowice, a village near Strzyzow. He was known for his sons-in-law: Reb Benjamin Baumel, Reb David Dembitzer and Reb Moshe Aaron Zilber. Reb Benjamin was a worthy, faultless Jew, a Hassid of the Rabbi from Sadigora who chanted nicely and had an easy-going personality. He raised his children to study Torah and to do good deeds. Of all his children, only a son and daughter survived. They reside in the United States.

Reb David Dembitzer was a clever and good-hearted man, beloved by everyone. His sons were active Zionists and Torah students. One son and two daughters reside in the United States.

[Page 170]

Reb Moshe Aaron Zilber was a pious, humble and straight man. His sons Joshua, Pinchos and his daughter Sarah were fervent activists in the Zionist movement. His son-in-law, Reb Tzvi Shapiro was a devoted Zionist who went to Eretz Israel and lives amongst us here in Israel.

The Rosen brothers
by Shlomo Yahalomi

The first of the Rosen family was Reb Shmuel Rosen who came from Wielopole. Rabbi Alter Zev extended a friendly welcome to him and respected him greatly. On Purim, the rabbi let him wear his shtreimel. Reb Shmuel Rosen had two sons: Reb David and Reb Yechiel. Reb David's son, Reb Joseph Hersh, lived in Strzyzow and was an ardent admirer of Rabbi Alter

Zev Horowitz. Reb Joseph Hersh, even though he was an irascible man, had a good heart, gave a lot to charity and was very hospitable. Reb Joseph Hersh had three sons: Yacov, Mendel and Joel. Reb Yacov was a Torah scholar. He was very clever, full of energy, blessed with capabilities and was very active helping the community during the Holocaust years. I, the writer of these memoirs, was his student. Yacov had a son, a child prodigy who died in his boyhood. The second son of Reb Joseph Hersh, Reb Mendel, was also a scholar. He had a good voice and often chanted in the Beit HaMidrash. He later became the ritual slaughterer in town. The third son, Reb Joel, did not live in Strzyzow. The Rosens were all killed by the Nazi.

Reb David Rosen had two sons–in–law. The first was Reb Leib Sternberg, a dear man, a good chanter and who was beloved by everyone. He respected everyone and, in return, he was respected by all. Only one son, who immigrated to Eretz Israel, lives amongst us. The second son–in–law was Reb Aaron Kanner about whom we wrote before in this book.

Reb Shmuel Rosen's second son, Reb Yechiel was a fiery opponent of Rabbi Shlomo Shapiro. He died during the prayers wearing his Talit and Tefilin. Reb Yechiel had four sons and three daughters, all of whom resided in Strzyzow with their families. They all perished in the Holocaust. Four grandchildren of Reb Yechiel miraculously survived the Holocaust. They escaped from the train which was carrying them to their death. The Rosens were all Hassidim of the rabbi from Sadigora.

The Schefler Family
by Shlomo Yahalomi

There were three Schefler brothers in Strzyzow: Reb Mordechai Mendel; Reb Shimon and Reb Moshe. Reb Mordechai Mendel was a chanter who assisted Reb Leib Sternberg in shul. He was a devoted community activist. Reb Shimon Schefler was a simple, faultless, pious man and had a good heart. He was one of the Psalmists who recited Psalms every Saturday afternoon, winter and summer. Reb Moshe Schefler was always graciously doing charitable work. In fact, he was murdered by the Nazi together with Reb Shmuel Moshe Groskopft and Reb Yacov Rosen during a meeting in which they were discussing charity matters. May G–d avenge their innocent blood. Remnants of these families survived and live in Israel.

[Page 171]

I also want to mention Basha, the sister of the Scheflers. She was a cook who was hired by the town to cook and bake for every occasion; weddings, engagements and circumcisions. She prepared food that everyone enjoyed.

The Sturm family
by Shlomo Yahalomi

One of the oldest and most respected families in Strzyzow was the Sturm family. The head of the family was Reb Yacov Sturm. His son, Rev Avrohom Itzhok was considered to be among the nobility of the town. He studied Torah at night and wore a silk frock and a colpac (a rabbinical Sabbath fur hat) on weekdays as well as a Talit on Friday nights until after Kiddush. Rabbi Shlomo Shapiro used to say of him that he prayed with such inspiration and devotion that he was often frightened that he might collapse and not be able to finish his prayers. At one time, he served as a community leader and during his term, Rabbi Alter Zev Horowitz was elected as rabbi of Strzyzow. That was after Rabbi Shlomo Shapiro left for Munktach. The second son of Reb Yacov Sturm, Reb Shimon, left town to study with Rabbi Meir Schick, a Torah genius.

Reb Avrohom Itzhok had two sons; one of who married into the big Diamand family. Although his father supported Rabbi Alter Zev, the son was an ardent supporter of the Shapiros. In fact, he married the granddaughter of Rabbi Tzvi Elimelech Shapiro.

Reb Avrohom Itzhok's son–in–law was the assistant rabbi, Reb Alter Ezra Seidman. Reb Avrohom Itzhok's second son had two sons and a daughter. The first son married the sister of the Krosno Rabbi. Reb Avrohom Itzhok's grandson, Reb Yacov Asher, immigrated to Germany and later to the United States. His son lives in Israel and is a professor in the Haifa Technion. A second grandson came from Germany to Eretz Israel and sacrificed his heroic life for the independence of Israel.

The Tenzer family
by Shlomo Yahalomi

The Tenzer family was among the most respected families in town. Reb Hersh Tenzer, the founder of the family, had several sons. He was a Hassid and a faultless person. He possessed a noble spirit and a gentle soul. Reb Hersh was an enlightened man – a perfectionist and very truthful. He was also humble, always had a smile on his face and he loved to study Torah. He married a daughter from the large Diamand family. Reb Moshe, the son of Reb Hersh, was a pious man, an ardent Hassid of the Rabbi from Belz. His wife was the assistant rabbi's sister. Only one son survived and he resides in Israel. The second son of Reb Hersh, Reb Yacov Tenzer, was a clone of his brother Moshe. He was very polite and he was an admirer of the rabbi from Bobow.

There were Reb Itzhok Tenzer and Reb Tuvia Tenzer all with families. They all perished under the Nazi.

Reb Abraham Ever Klagsfed from Krosno was a son–in–law of Reb Abraham Tenzer – may he be remembered favourably. During the war, he almost lost his life when he collected gold in Krosno to pay a ransom demanded by the Nazi from the Jews in Strzyzow. May G–d remember him favourably.

[Page 172]

One of Reb Hersh Tenzer's sons, Reb Zalman, immigrated to Eretz Israel with his wife, sons and grandchildren. Reb Zalman lived a long life in the Holy Land. The majority of the Tenzer family perished in the Holocaust.

[Page 173]

About Daily Life and Trivial Events in Strzyzow

Odd Stories

Gentiles Reciting the Prayer "Shema Israel"
by Itzhok Berglass

It happened one spring, after the snow thawed, and the rains ended. It was twilight on the day of the funeral, when the Priest Yablocinski was buried. The Christians called him "The Old Priest" because he lived to a very old age. (I wrote about him in the story about the excesses in 1898.) Because he was admired by his coreligionists, thousands of people came to his funeral, from near and far. In those days there were no bridges over the Visloka River, which encircled the town. The crossing was done by ferry–boats which were located, one at the end of the town near the village Godowa, and the other a few kilometers down the stream.

On the day of the funeral the river overflowed. The attendant of the ferry–boat was very busy so that Reuven Saphire and his wife who were the concessionaires had to give a helping hand in collecting the passage fee from the passengers. As evening approached, they overloaded the boat and the boat partially sank. The steel cable to which the boat was attached, tore and, instead of crossing to the other side, the boat turned north and was carried away with the tide.

A panic broke out among the passengers on the boat and among those who were waiting for their turn on the shore. The passengers on the boat were helpless and could do nothing to help themselves. The only thing left to do was to pray. In town meanwhile, Reuven's children ran to the Beit Hamidrash to pray for the safety of their parents in front of the open Holy Ark. Their prayers were expressed only by silent crying without words. And the community prayed with them.

On the ferry–boat, the passengers whose lives were in danger whole–heartedly prayed to Jesus and to the Holy Mother. Reuven and his wife sat in a corner of the boat and recited the prayer "Shema Israel." When those who were near them heard them praying in Hebrew, in despair, they too began to pray to the Jewish G–d and repeated the words in Hebrew. Soon the entire crowd began to pray the eternal Jewish prayer, "Hear O Israel." Mispronouncing the words.

The District Commissioner's Party
by Itzhok Berglass

My father had various characteristics that complemented each other. On the one hand, he strictly observed all the divine rules and commandments, both light and weighty ones, like all the Jews. He was a believer in the righteous and a fiery Hassid of the Rabbi from Munkatch. On the other hand, he did some deeds that were considered progressive.

[Page 174]

In his youth, he was a fervent visitor in Rabbi Shlomo Shapiro's house until his departure for Munkatch. He studied Torah day and night and became outstanding and prodigious in his studies. But, at the same time, he also studied the Prophets, realizing that without the knowledge of the Prophets he would not know to write Hebrew. Being aware before his marriage that, eventually, he would take over my grandfather's business, intensively and rapidly he learned Polish and German, two languages which he would have to know in his future business endeavors, from the town's man of knowledge, Reb Hersh Mohrer. He sent his two daughters, my older sisters, Nechama and Chaya Sarah, to the high school in Rzeszow, after they finished the elementary school in Strzyzow. The advantage of this high school was that they did not have to attend in the Sabbath, unlike the local gymnasium. As for me, he did not allow continuing in high school after finishing the elementary schooling but he did urge me to learn the two languages on my own and to study the Prophets. My father did not object to my learning Hebrew using Shevach Volkowisky's letters, which was a popular way of studying among young people desirous of attaining the knowledge of the Hebrew language, and which most parents opposed seeing it as a beginning of going astray, meaning Zionism.

Because of the strictness in observing the Sabbath, my father suffered much in his business relations with important customers in the area. He never agreed to any compromise. In his youth, during his business visits to aristocratic homes, he never agreed to be treated to even a glass of tea. Nevertheless, he never lost a customer because his business had almost a monopolistic position in town. And now, to the main story.

During the Austrian rule, the District Commissioner in Strzyzow was Mr. Zalewski, a noble man both inspirit and behavior. Indeed, he did request from the Jews obedience and help to elect candidates who supported the government, but he never said, "You have to do it because you are Jewish." He showed his gratitude with words and deeds. He soon advanced in his rank and from the small town of Strzyzow, was transferred to serve as the High Commissioner of the big city Przemysl, an important fortress city for the Austrian Empire.

When he was leaving Strzyzow, he was named an honorary citizen. In appreciation, he gave a party for the City Council, Christians and Jews alike. The Commissioner's wife received the guests at the entrance, as protocol dictated, with a handshake. The last to enter were the Jews. (Apparently it was accepted even in liberal Austria that the Jews were always last, as was customary in school to be seated in the last row.) My father was among them. When my father's turn came to shake the hand of the commissioner's wife, he apologized that he did not shake hands with strange women. As a result, after the initial confusion, the others did not have to shake the hand of the hostess. The party ended in good spirits. There was kosher food prepared for the Jews but my father told me afterwards, with bitterness toward the Jewish colleagues, that they did drink the wine.

The morning following the event, the whole town talked about it. Indeed, the "Progressive laughed about it, but the pious praised my father for his principled courage.

[Page 175]

The Thousands That Were Burned
by Itzhok Berglass

It happened in the days of the Austrian rule, when a thousand crowns or five hundred guldens was considered a huge sum and one could exchange them for gold coins within minutes. However, people were careful in doing so because they might lose the small gold coin or mistakenly spend them as hellers (pennies), which shone like the gold ones. Conservative Jews held onto these crowns and guldens and never traded them in until the end of the Austrian Empire.

Reb Moshe Dovid Unger was a plain, rich man, who owned the only soda–water plant in town. He also was a wholesaler, who exported dried mushrooms to the United States, where they were sold by his two sons who earlier emigrated to America. Peddlers who bought mushrooms in the villages sold them to Reb Moshe Dovid. He also traveled often to congressional Poland, and from there exported mushrooms directly to the United States.

Except for the group of cattle dealers who shipped weekly shipments of meat to Vienna, Reb Moshe Dovid was one of the main recipients of large sums of money for his merchandise in Strzyzow. Bank transfers were not customary in those days. Besides, maybe Strzyzow had no important bank through which it would have been possible to transfer huge sums. Neither was the post office able to do it. It is doubtful whether the local post office ever had such large amounts on hand to pay out such transfers. Therefore, money was sent in value registered envelopes sealed with a special wax which was acceptable by the Austrian postal service.

One such shipment which contained several thousands of crowns arrived for Reb Moshe Dovid on a wintery Sabbath afternoon. The mailman delivered the envelope on the Sabbath, being sure that he will get the signature for the delivery on the next day. Since no one in the family could handle money because it is forbidden on the Sabbath, the mailman put the envelope in the kitchen not far from the stove. After a short while, the old water carrier came into the house. He was the Sabbath goy who removed the candlesticks from the table and made the fire in the ovens on the Sabbath in the winter. When he looked for paper with which to start the fire in the stove, he found the envelope which was lying nearby. Happy to find such a finding, he innocently started the fire by putting the envelope under the logs. Soon he began to scream because he got burned from the wax which melted and spilled all over the fire. And the deed was discovered. A panic broke out, but it was too late, the situation could not be remedied.

The Prescription
by Itzhok Berglass

Almost every Jew liked to have a drink of 96 proof spirits on weekdays, during his meal to entice his appetite, and in the Beit Hamidrash on various sanctified occasions, on the Sabbath, after eating fish, and in friends' houses on different celebrations. The Jews were protected by their cleverness in preventing intoxication. They knew that such strong brandy which burns like fire is impossible to over imbibe.

[Page 176]

Reb Tzvi, a simple, faultless Jew, who divided his days between his store and the kloiz of Reb Moshe Leib from Sassov, used to enjoy an extra drink. Understandably, within limits, so as not to get drunk. When he aged, he became ill with pneumonia, a serious illness in those days, which caused many to die. As soon as Reb Tzvi became ill, he asked his family members to give him a drink of spirit to which he was accustomed. His family refused to fulfill his request, despite his pleading throughout his sickness.

Not until his condition deteriorated, did his family tell Dr. Taub, the only Jewish doctor in town (who lived in Strzyzow until the First World War), about Reb Tzvi's strange request. The doctor saw that these are the last hours of the sick man, and he saw no reason to deprive him of this pleasure in his last minutes of life. So he advised the family to give Reb Tzvi the longed-for drink, saying that there is nothing to lose. And behold, Reb Tzvi took one sip from the strong liquid, his eyes lighted u, and it was as if a new living spirit had entered him. After a few hours, he began to perspire and the crisis was over. His condition improved and, after a short time, he fully recovered.

A Conscientious Ignoramus
by Itzhok Berglass

A certain so and so was a wealthy man and a certified ignoramus. Not just an illiterate who envies those who know how to learn a chapter Mishnayoth and a page of Gemara, but a conscientious ignoramus who despises those who spend their time studying Torah. Sometimes he also sided with his fellow simpletons who, in his opinion, were a special class in opposition to the scholars who prided themselves on their knowledge.

Once, a wealthy ignoramus passed away in Strzyzow. The Kehillah and the Burial Society demanded the customary fee from his heirs, according to their financial situation. Then a group of those ignorant organized in defense of the bereaved family to free them from any payment. When they were asked the reason for their strange demand. "Is it not asked from everyone?" they were asked. "Even the heirs of Reb Avrohom Itzhok Sturm, one of the most respected people in town, a scholar and a pious man, had to pay the customary fee." Then the certain so and so replied: "Why do you compare the deceased to Reb Avrohom Itzhok who squandered all his life at the Gemara?"

When the certain individual demolished his small house and built a big two-story house, the work stopped for two days every week, Saturday and Sunday, as it was customary at the construction of a Jewish house. He became angry about the delay for which he blamed the town's scholars and their Torah, saying: "Because of the Sabbaths and the dark bad days (meaning the High Holidays), I could not finish my house on time."

[Page 177]

The "Resolution" by the Rabbis to Observe the Sabbath Twice a Week
by Itzhok Berglass

Reb Moshe was a village man who came to settle in town and made a living as a middleman, in addition to the support from his sons. He was not a great scholar, but he never released the book of Mishnayoth from his hands. Reb Moshe also liked to peek into a newspaper, even though he did not understand everything that was written there.

And behold! Once he read in the newspaper a wonderful thing. At the convention of the Rabbis and activists which took place in the Yeshiva of Lublin, it was decided to have Sabbath twice a week. (That is how Reb Moshe understood the speech of Rabbi Meir Shapiro, the Dean of the Yeshiva. Speaking about the spreading disease of the desecration of the Sabbath by the Jews, Rabbi Meir quoted the sages who said: "If only the Jews would fully observe two Sabbaths, the redemption would be imminent.") Reb Moshe rushed over to Itzhok the confidant of such type of people, and told him the earthshaking news, but Itzhok told him that he was wrong.

Reb Moshe deeply regretted his mistake, and he returned home disappointed, back to his Mishnayoth.

The Relations Between the Jews and Gentiles
by Itzhok Berglass

As I already told in one of my articles about the interrelations of the Poles and the Jews, they were, in general, normal. The relations of the town's wealthy gentiles with their Jewish neighbors were particularly good. Jews were tenants in their houses, conducted business with them, and sometimes they reached the point of real friendship, despite the fact that their spiritual life and traditions were strange to each other. I will further tell about two events related to this interrelationship which I heard from my friend Itzhok Deutch who also told me the aforementioned story about Reb Moshe.

The Jews Extinguished the Fire in a Gentile House
by Itzhok Berglass

On a Sunday afternoon, a fire broke out in the house of the blacksmith, Leopold Gornicki; who lived on one of the town's main streets. It would have been hard to organize help from the gentiles who were resting on their Sabbath and, until the fire brigade who were spread all over town would have gathered, the wooden structure would have burned to the ground with everything in it. Gornicki came out into the street yelling despairingly: "Jews, good neighbors, help!" Immediately, the Jews who lived nearby, including a few lawyers who lived on the next street near the courthouse, organized help and, in a short while, the fire was extinguished with little damage. To express gratitude to the Jews for their deed, Gornicki persuaded the priest to publicize the deed in his weekly sermon, and to celebrate a special Mass on Sunday. The incident and the Priest's sermon made a strong impression on the Christians, and contributed to the improvement of relationship between the two sectors of the population.

[Page 178]

How the Jews Saved Gentile Property during the Flood
by Itzhok Berglass

The cabinetmaker Jan Zamorski, and his wife always intermingled with the Jews, and the Jews were their main customers. Particularly, the wife befriended many Jewesses who were her acquaintances.

Zamorski's house was near the Visloka River whose water was always overflowing. During heavy floods, the houses located nearby had to be evacuated, including Zamorski's house.

Their Jewish friends were always there to assist the family. They carried out valuable belongings and safeguarded them until the water subsided, and the evacuees were allowed to return home.

The cabinetmaker and his wife used to tell everybody that, while the Jews kept their belongings with honesty and returned everything to them on their return home, the gentile friends were disloyal and kept for themselves a big portion of their belongings which they had helped to carry out from their house.

The Zionist Movement and my Road to Zionism
by Leah Loos

I was then a first grade student in the local Polish gymnasium. My studying did not last long because, despite the fact that I did not attend school on the Sabbath and holidays, my parents had to withdraw me from school under the pressure of public opinion. That is to say, the worshipers in kloiz could not suffer that a daughter from a family related to the Rabbi should attend a Polish gymnasium and thus desecrate the purity of the family. My parents were as religious as all the other people in town and, understandably, were concerned that I should not, Heaven forbid violate one divine commandment. I, who was nurtured from my infancy with the spirit of traditional Judaism, knew that it was forbidden to desecrate the Sabbath, not to eat meat and dairy together, and not to eat any non–kosher food. I have observed all the traditions of Passover, Shavuot, Sukkoth, Hanukkah and Purim. Furthermore, I knew about the mourning of Tisha B'Av and all of the other Jewish traditions in general. I was joyful on holidays and sad in days of sadness, without knowing the real meaning of these events.

My parents worried about my traditional upbringing but not about my national consciousness which I received in the Polish school. During the Polish history lessons my heart ached when I leaned about the spiritual decline of my country, Poland, about the tripartite division of the land and the loss of her independence. I was happy about the peoples' trials and tribulations, my people, whose resurrection was expressed in the constitution of May the Third, about the rescue of the Kingdom by Kosciuszko. I was sad about the failure to receive the independence by Dombrowski, and Poniatowski in the rebellion of 1830 and 1863.

[Page 179]

And suddenly a bitter disappointment. It happened on my big holiday, Constitution Day, May the Third. All the students marched in a procession to the church for a special Mass and, afterward, we were supposed to have marched in a parade through the town to a mass meeting in the club house. We, the Jews, did not enter the church, but waited outside, to later join our comrades in the parade. Behold! While standing outside, we were attacked by a group of gentile boys with insults and shouts of: "Jews go to Palestine!" I was very hurt by the attack and the screaming, and it also aroused some feelings in me. I then persuaded myself to get to know more about my own Jewish people, and I approached the Zionist movement which already existed in Strzyzow, and was active among the youths.

In time, I made a turnabout of 180 degrees, and I decided to fulfill the goal of the Zionist movement and to make aliyah to Eretz Israel. But to make aliyah I had to prepare myself and be qualified. Otherwise, what could one do in Eretz Israel? There was only agricultural work available. Well, I thought, I will have to learn the agricultural trade.

There was no organized Chalutz movement in Strzyzow. So I was forced to get farm training privately. I took advantage of the fact that my best friend Sarah Rebhun, the daughter of Reb Yacov, who was a milkman and traveled daily to Count Wolkowitzki's estate to get milk. The trustee of the farm knew me because he was a steady customer in my father's store, and I was accepted by him to work and learn farming.

Of course, I did not tell my parents about it because they would not have agreed to such a childish idea. Under the pretext that I was accompanying my friend, I left the house every day and worked, to the laughter of the female village workers, who were not used to seeing a spoiled city girl, a Jewess, working in the fields. The work was very strenuous for me. I was not used to physical labor, particularly to remain in a bent position for many hours every day. In addition, I could not complain at home about my backache. Everything was done discreetly.

Despite everything, I decided to hold out, no matter what happened. One day the bomb exploded. The trustee, my employer, came into the store as usual to buy yard goods, and during an innocent conversation, he disclosed to my parents about my secret work. His story disturbed my parents and they immediately decided to put an end to my "craziness."

The first casualty was the blue–white collection box from the Jewish National Fund which they threw out. But I was not swayed from my path. In the meantime, I became active in the movement and, a few years later, I decided that it was time to fulfill the goal that eluded me earlier, namely, to make aliyah to Eretz Israel. This time, my parents were forced to agree because I was more mature and I knew that in Eretz Israel I could do something else besides farming.

I trained as a nurse which I enjoyed very much, and I was the first in town to make aliyah and settle in our land.

[Page 180]

Repentance
by Leah Loos

Reb Yeshayahu Mandel was a fiery Hassid of the Rabbi from Munkatch. He was one of the most charitable activists in town. It was already described in a separate article about his charity deeds. Reb Yeshayahu was one of those Jews about whom the sages said: "Ask him for a donation for the temple, he gives, ask him for the golden calf, he also gives." Therefore, when Reb Yeshayahu was approached by three young men and asked to contribute to the Jewish National Fund, he could not turn them away empty–handed. Maybe he was smitten by the young men's enthusiasm for a Jewish National Homeland. The important thing was that Reb Yeshayahu was among the first donors to the fund. But, alas, deep within Reb Yeshayahu, a doubt was gnawing. Should he have contributed or refused? After all it was a Zionist action, and Zionism was completely forbidden, particularly for the Hassidim of Munkatch. Rabbi Chaim Elazar, the Rabbi of Munkatch, was the grandson of Rabbi Shlomo from Strzyzow, blessed be his memory, of whom the Hassidim in Strzyzow had such fond memories, and he was a strong opponent of Zionism.

And behold! Rabbi Chaim Elazer came to Strzyzow in one of his frequent visits. Understandably, Reb Yeshayahu was among those who came to greet the Rabbi, shake his hands, and hand him the traditional Kvittel" (note). And on that occasion, Reb Yeshayahu wanted, once and for all, to get rid of the nagging doubt. He confessed to the rabbi about the sin he had committed.

The Rabbi of Munkatch, in whose eyes event the Agudat Israel was not kosher, can you imagine how he viewed the Zionists" The Rabbi related to Reb Yeshayahu's sin with total seriousness, and he commanded him to atone in order to obtain forgiveness. The nature of the atonement – I do not know. What I do know was that Reb Yeshayahu did not commit such a sin again.

He also had a blue–white collection box which his daughter had brought into the house, and it became the first casualty. Reb Yeshayahu broke the box and threw it out. From then on his daughter suffered very much from her father because of her association with the Zionist movement.

The Deal with the Ukrainians
by Itzhok Berglass

During the elections to the Polish Parliament which were held between the First and second World Wars, the Jewish candidate from our district was a man from the Mizrachi, Rabbi Hirshfeld from Biala–Bielsko. We, the Zionists, worked very hard for the success of his election campaign in our city.

There were two villages near Strzyzow populated with Ukrainians.

Because of the absence of a Ukrainian candidate, they always voted for the Polish Peasant Party.

[Page 181]

One of our comrades who often visited these villages on business told us that he could strike a bargain. For the price of a few hundred zlotys contributed toward building a clubhouse in those villages, allthe people would vote for the Jewish list to assure our candidate's election. We contacted the Central Committee, or maybe the candidate himself, I do not remember exactly, and they advised us to close the deal and promised to pay us back the money we spent.

We, the naïve ones, to whom every request from above was sacred, rushed over and handed the money to our comrade, a few hundred zlotys, to give to the people in the village.

Where did we get the money? Behold! I, the most naïve of them all, was the Chairman of the local Zionist Committee. In addition, I was the only man who could spare the money and nobody at home would even notice. Therefore, I agreed to borrow from my private funds, hoping to be paid back.

The Ukrainians lied to us. They took the money and voted for the Polish Peasant party, and our candidate lost as in the earlier elections. The man who promised to pay back did not keep his promise, and I was the victim. Money from other funds was sacred, and I would not dare to touch it. These funds were always sent entirely to the head office. I had no choice but to consider my money lost.

The Elections to the City Government
by Itzhok Berglass

Our Zionist movement was gradually progressing. In the beginning, we were a tiny group of boys and girls, dreamers, students enjoying every book, Hebrew and secular, as long as it was on a Jewish subject. These books revealed to us new horizons. Eretz Israel was our dream, our oracle, and a trip to Rzeszow to view a Jewish National fund propaganda film about how the Jews labored in Eretz Israel was a thrill for us. (Many parents did not allow their kids to travel.) We were only interested in politics on the national level – not locally. Even during the Austrian rule, we participated in the election campaign only to assist the Central Zionist Committee.

After the First World War, and the decline of the Zionist movement which followed, we were strengthened only with the return home of the young people. Slowly we became a force in the town's public life. The democratization of the city authorities came a few years after Poland became independent. In the elections that followed, Strzyzow as getting ready to elect forty people to the City Council. The forty people consisted of four groups, ten men in each group. The fourth group was elected by all the people who reached their voting age. The third group was elected by the small tax–payers. The second group was elected by the big tax–payers, and the first group was elected by the aristocracy, high government functionaries, academicians with titles, and the religious clerics, the Rabbis, the Priests, etc.

Until then the city had been ruled by the Clerical Party. The mayor was a cabinetmaker, Mr. Konieczkowski who was under the influence of Father Kwieczinski. The ex–mayor, Dr. Joseph Patryn, about whom I wrote before, challenged his opponents. He wanted to reestablish his rule over the city. To achieve his goal, he recruited supporters from every segment of the population. The Jews were present in both opposing parties.

[Page 182]

However, the majority were on Dr. Patryn's side. The personality of the candidates played a bigger role then the partisanship, and the incumbent Mayor Konieczkowski, despite the fact that he belonged to the Clerical Party which was not too friendly to Jews, conducted himself properly toward the Jews during his mayoralty. Therefore, many Jews were counted amongst his friends, acquaintances, and supporters during the election campaign.

We, the Zionists, who by then were able to muster a sizeable force mainly in the fourth group, hesitated in the beginning whether to get involved in the local election campaign as an organization. But in the heat of the election campaign, a meeting organized exclusively for Christians in the church under the Priests' supervision, the speakers for Konieczkowski attacked the Jews. Only then, did we join Dr. Patryn's party and made an agreement with him to add three candidates from the local Zionist Committee, in addition to the Jews he already had on his list. Our candidates were Dr. Chaim Frenkel, the lawyer, Avigdor Diamand, and I.

Every Sunday, elections were held for one group starting with the most populated fourth group. Dr. Frenkel and Avigdor Diamand were elected by the fourth and third groups. I was supposed to have been elected in the exclusive first group. I could not run in the second group because I did not want to compete with my father who ran on Konieczkowski's list. The elections were proportional but majoritarian. Therefore, all who were on Dr. Patryn's list had received the majority votes and were elected. Meanwhile, my father resigned from the second group of candidates in the opposition camp, realizing that the decisive majority of the town was on Dr. Patryn's side. In that case, we the Zionists decided to demand from Dr. Patryn that my name be placed on the second group's candidate list to assure my election, according to our agreement. But Dr. Patryn, who demanded blind allegiance from his supporters, was not anxious to move my name up because of my father's sin, namely supporting his opponent. He already felt strong and he wanted to impose somebody who would be more loyal as a third candidate. Dr. Patryn was urged on by his close Jewish friends. Because I was still single, they found a serious defect in my candidacy. They complained vociferously, "Have you seen such an audacity, a bachelor?"

We fiercely opposed, arguing that only the organization may decide the candidacy and we demanded that Dr. Patryn adhere to our agreement. When we saw that our argument was not convincing, we were afraid that he was liable to do as he wished. We therefore, resorted to the strategy of the election rule which say: If an elected candidate resigns before the nominating assembly which supposed to elect the mayor, the replacement comes not from the alternates but from the opposition list. Thus, at a meeting of the Zionist committee we decided to notify Doctor Patryn that if he would not transfer my name as agreed, as a protest, Dr Frenkel, and Avigdor Diamand, would resign before the end of the elections. When we notified Dr. Patryn our decision, he, who was erudite in all the rules, jumped up as if he had been bitten by a snake. He knew that in such a case, his opponents would be elected.

[Page 183]

The Jew Michael Schitz, and the incumbent Konieczkowski were on the top of the list.

Dr. Patryn's Jewish friends were embittered and voiced an outcry all over town. "The attic will dictate to us who to elect?" (the attic that they referred to meant the Zionist library from where we conducted all our Zionist activities, which was located on an attic.) But, not only did Dr. Patryn, the realist, pout my name on the list, but furthermore, all day Friday before the elections, and early Sunday morning, election day, he visited all his friends and supporters, and asked them not to change anything in the list because he must see to it that I "The audacious rascal" must be elected.

I was elected, and we, the Zionist Committee, felt our strength. From then on no Jewish activity in Strzyzow was done without us, or without our approval.

The Unsuccessful Intervention
by Itzhok Berglass

When Rabbi Alter Zev Horowitz advanced in age, the Rabbinical family began to worry about naming a successor while the Rabbi was still alive in order, that after one hundred and twenty years, the Rabbinical post would not be left empty, even for one minute. They feared that perhaps it would be exploited by the supporters of Rabbi Nechemiah Shapiro, who, by then, had returned to Strzyzow.

Rabbi Alter Zev's family decided to do something out of the ordinary; to strive that the Rabbi's young grandson, Reb Kalonymus, the son of Reb Chaim Yehuda, be named as successor while the old Rabbi was still alive, an action previously unheard of.

According to the bylaws of the Kehillah, a rabbi had to be elected by all the members of the Kehillah Committee, Reb Yacov Greenblatt, the Rabbi's opponent, had the decisive vote.

The District Commissioner, Dr. Malin, who was one of Rabbi Horowitz's staunchest supporters and wanted to help him execute this act, tried to persuade one of the committee members to cross over to the Rabbi's side, to tip the scale in the Rabbi's favor. This member was a representative of the Zionists, my colleague and friend, Reb Avigdor Diamand, who operated his mother's saloon and made a nice living.

Such a business required a license from the District Commissioner's office which Dr. Malin supervised. The District Commissioner could have found a pretext to make trouble on many occasions, and even revoke his mother's license. It was hard for Avigdor to withstand the pressure of the Commissioner. On the other hand, he could not vote against his principles, and particularly against the will of his Zionist voters, the most of whom opposed Reb Kalonymus, because of the local and national politics of his father, Reb Chaim Yehuda. Therefore, Avigdor resigned his seat, and I was next on the list to take his place.

For the Rabbinical family, I was not much better than Avigdor. My family were ardent supporters of Rabbi Nechemiah Shapiro for two reasons. First, in his youth my father was a frequent visitor in Rabbi Shlomo Shapiro's house as he befriended young people, Torah students.

[Page 184]

Therefore, he continued his loyalty to Reb Shlomo's offspring. The second reason was that Rabbi Nechemiah Shapiro was the son–in–law of the Rabbi Yeshayahu Hertz from Dynow, a brother of the Rabbi Tzvi Elimelech, the Rabbi of Blazow, with whom my brother–in–law was a close friend and to whose advice he listened as if it would have been given by Moses on Mount Sinai.

I personally was not involved in the Rabbinical dispute, however, my grievance against Rabbi Alter Zev was the Zionists' grievance against his son, Reb Chaim Yehuda, who was a fiery anti–Zionist.

The Horowitz family, whose struggle for the Rabbinical seat lasted many years, learned how to exploit everything that could be to their advantage. They found something about me which they wanted to try before the District Commissioner would accept Avigdor's resignation.

Reb Feivel Steppel from Sendiszow, my bride's father, (she s my wife now until a hundred and twenty) was a friend and supporter of the Assistant Rabbi in Sendiszow, Reb Yosele Frenkel, who was the son–in–law of Rabbi Alter Zev. Reb Yosele was also the father–in–law of the young man Reb Kalonymus, the candidate for the succession.

Rabbi Alter Zev, even though he served as Rabbi in Strzyzow, did not abandon his rights in Sendiszow from where he came, when his younger brother was nominated as rabbi of Sendiszow. Rabbi Alter Zev saw to it that his son–in–law, Reb Yosele, should be named Assistant Rabbi. Rabbi Alter Zev's family tried to use the friendship of my future father–in–law with Reb Yosele, to persuade me to vote for Reb Kalonymus. They hoped that I would not oppose, especially when the arranged meeting was made in presence of my bride.

I refuted the argument, claiming that according to our Zionist concept, no public office is private or family property, as it was customary years ago. Our representatives have to honor the wishes of their voters. And, as far as I was concerned, they were opposing the Rabbi. I also refused to abide by my future father–in–law's proposal that I too should resign as my friend did. This proposal came from the initiative of the Rabbi's family who was experienced in finding all kinds of options. I argued that my friend was able to resign because he knew that his replacement would not breach the faith of his constituency, but I could not resign because my replacement would be an easy target for persuasion, and this would strengthen the Rabbi's power.

When my future father–in–law saw my steadfastness, he told those who asked to convince me to resign that, in his opinion, I was worse than my friend Avigdor Diamand. Ultimately, the Commissioner refused to accept Avigdor's resignation.

Despite heavy pressure not to resign, Avigdor did not budge. He refused to withdraw his already submitted resignation. Then the Rabbi's family found a way to persuade one of his opponents to vote for the young Reb Kalonymus and tipped the scale in Rabbi Alter Zev's favor. It was seven to five.

[Page 185]

Jewish Contact with the Authorities
by Itzhok Berglass

Generally, we, the Zionists, unlike many Jews, were not happy about contact with the people from the authorities. The authorities were not very interested in what was going on among the Jews except the Rabbinical dispute. The Kehillah Committee, though, had to bring their problems before the Commissioner for his approval. Every time the authorities showed some interest, it was to our disadvantage. They oppressed us because of their hatred for the Jews in general and, particularly, the Zionist, who were less submissive than other Jews. Among other things, they closed our first library, "The Jewish Library," without reason but that caused only a change of name. We reopened the library soon after at the same location with the same books under the name "Hatikva." The library existed until the end. Settling disputes depended on the character of the people with whom we came in contact, and what kind of a problem it was. Further on I will tell about three such incidents.

How the Word "Choshiver" was Changed to "Hashomer"
by Itzhok Berglass

It happened in 1922, when the three of us; my friend Akiba Keh, Avigdor Diamand, and I, conducted the first appeal for the Jewish National fund, and we strove to reach every segment of the Jewish population in town and the Jews from the nearby vicinities, particularly the wealthy ones. We approached the local Jews face to face attempting to influence them with our persuasive power. To prepare the Jews from the nearby vicinities about the forthcoming visit we had written a circular letter in Yiddish. The circular letter began with the words: "Choshiver" (honorable) Comrade! Because we related to every Jew as a comrade who shared with us the goal of realizing the Zionist ideal. In the circular we pointed out the imminent danger that we were threatened with if we did not use the opportunity given to us to rebuild our homeland, without naming the enemy – the Arabs. The circular was signed by the three of us, the activists.

One of these letters which we sent to Mr. Engel, who leased a farm in Blonek near Frysztak, for reasons unknown to us, turned up in the hands of the District Police in Strzyzow, and they, as usual, examined the proclamation. One of the policemen, sergeant Shpitol, knew some Yiddish and claimed to be an expert in all matters concerning the Jews and their lives. When he was requested to look into the text of this circular, he turned t Reb Meir Ber, the only barber in town, who, until his emigration to the United States, extracted teeth and attached leeches to the sick. (That is why he was called doctor.) Since Reb Meir was a clean shaven Jew, they thought him to be an intellectual. Therefore, he was asked to help decipher the letter. Reb Meir who always bragged about his wisdom and denigrated every Jew, did not want to lose is prestige by confessing that he did not understand what was written in the circular which was sent out by the Zionists. Therefore, after much effort by both, Sergeant Shpitol and Reb Meir to translate the circular, they concluded that in Strzyzow existed the organization "Hashomer."

[Page 186]

The word "Choshiver" became "Hashomer." Hashomer was legal in other places but not in Strzyzow, because it was not officially approved by the District Commissioner.

This incident happened not long after the Polish–Russian War. The Jews and, particularly, the Zionists were suspect ted of being disloyal and, that they sympathized with the Communists. In the anti–Semitic press the name Zionist–Bolsheviks was routine despite the absurdity of pairing these two together. Apparently, the police realized that they needed more evidence about our underground activities. Therefore, one Sabbath afternoon (of course, it had to be on the Jewish Sabbath), when the three of us, I and my aforementioned comrades, strolled in the town's marketplace, out came from the police station a large group of policemen, who split into three smaller groups. One group went into my parents' house and two groups into the Diamand house where the Keh family also lived. The policemen made a thorough search in our three houses. At my comrades' houses they did not find anything. All; the material of the local Zionist Federation and the National Fund was in my house because I was then the secretary of the local Zionist Committee and the head of the National Fund. All the documents and my personal correspondence were taken by the policemen who were unable to distinguish what was suspicious material and what not.

The police filed charges with the District Court in Rzeszow accusing the three of us of running an illegal organization. The case was handed over to a judge who came to Strzyzow and summoned us to appear for interrogation which took place in the local courthouse. I was called first, either because the documents were taken from my house, or maybe because of the alphabetical order, since my name starts with a "B". The interrogation was conducted in the presence of the Sergeant Shpitol. The judge asked me to translate everything that was written in Yiddish and Hebrew. On occasion, during the interrogation, the judge made anti–Semitic remarks to which I vigorously protested saying that they were irrelevant to the case. After the interrogation did not produce any material for prosecution, he pulled out the "heavy cannon," the circular which was in his possession, and asked me to translate it into Polish word by word. By then we still had no idea what the charges were.

Therefore, I did not stop at the word "Choshiver" in the title of the letter, but tried to explain to the judge the words pertaining to the danger which was hovering over the Jews. That this did not mean Poland which is our country, but we referred t the Arabs in Palestine. Then the judge demanded to make clear to him the meaning of the word "Choshiver" in the title of the letter. When I told him that the word was not "Hashomer," the judge was dumbfounded and so much more the Police Sergeant Shpitol. They both realized that the accusation which had cost them so much effort had fallen apart.

The judge immediately ended the interrogation, and after I signed the protocol, he also requested the signatures of my two comrades who were waiting for their turn in the hall of the courthouse, without additional interrogation.

[Page 187]

The main victim was the Sergeant Shpitol who proved his ignorance in matters related to Jews. For a long time he was ashamed to look into our faces and distanced himself as much as he could.

The Election to the Polish Parliament
by Itzhok Berglass

As I previously stated, there was a great demand for Jewish votes during the elections to the Austrian Parliament. We were compelled by force, or willingly enticed by agitators to elect the Polish candidates who were close to the authorities. The Polish aristocracy, who then ruled in Galicia, even though they looked down upon the Jews, still needed them and used them to strengthen their influence. Even when they had to forego their candidacy in favor of assimilated Jews in the democratic parties, they still preferred them over the Zionists, because the Socialists and others belonged to the Polish national caucus in the Austro–Hungarian parliament from where the Polish aristocracy was still able to draw their power and influence.

When Poland was resurrected, the strong Polish Parties did not seek the Jewish support anymore, and did not court their votes during the elections. Whenever possible, t he apportionment was shaped in such a way as to decrease artificially the percentage of the Jewish vote and influence. However, in places where it was not possible, representatives of Jewish parties were elected to the Seym (Parliament) and the Senate.

When the Sanacia Party came to power, and the appeasement of the aristocracy followed, they too used the system of the aristocrats and demanded from the Jews to vote for their candidates because they were not popular among the Polish masses, particularly at the beginning.

The Sanacia Party was no less anti–Semitic than the other Polish parties which preceded them in the government and, in the last few years before the war, they officially endorsed anti–Semitism. However, all this did not prevent them from demanding Jewish support during elections. In Strzyzow, as in the rest of the country, there were also such a demand for support and, to soften the opposition of the Jews, particularly the Zionists, they used official pressure, but not too harshly. Despite the anti–Semitic trial in Brest Litowsk and the concentration camp in Kartuz Bereza, Poland was still a light dictatorship, much lighter than other dictatorships which existed during that period in Europe.

Before the elections to the Seym, (I think this was the last election before the Second World War) the District Commissioner, Dr. Malin, a brother–in–law of an important figure close to the "Belveder," the dictator's palace from the days of Pilsudski, sent the police inspector, Mr. Potoczny, to the Zionists in Strzyzow who were influential in town. The inspector was asked to find some infraction of the law and punish them for it in order to prevent Zionist propaganda during the elections.

Inspector Potoczny was a straight forward young man who came from Rzeszow where he was friendly with all the Zionist young men. He came, accompanied by one of the Zionists, and told us that he was forced to obey the order of the District Commissioner. He fined us a small amount which in no way could detract us from campaigning for the Jewish candidate.

[Page 188]

On Sunday, a week after the elections to the Seym and a day before the elections to the senate, we, a group of Zionists, were strolling in the street, and encountered the mayor, Dr. Chmiel, a son of a peasant, who belonged to the Folks Party and switched his affiliation when the Sanacia came to power. The mayor expressed his confidence that tomorrow we will all elect to the Senate the men from the Sanacia. I replied that this wish seemed strange because in all the elections to the Senate since Poland became independent, a Jewish candidate was always elected from our district, and we intend to continue to vote for our candidate. The authorities saw to it that this time n Jew was elected but the District Commissioner did not forget my transgression. In every district the Commissioner was automatically the head of the Public Works department in the district. In the aftermath of the elections, he gave an order to the department to stop patronizing my business, and also persuaded the landowners around Strzyzow to stop buying anything from me. They all went to the Christian store which had just opened to compete with the Jews, in accordance with the official policy that prevailed then to drive the Jews out. But not for long. They did not take under consideration that my brother–in–law Reb Jacov Itzhok Bernstein's, and my business were like my father's in his time, almost monopolistic, and these customers could not adapt themselves to do business anywhere else.

After a short time, the officials from the District Public Works Department who were in charge of the projects decided to return and buy from us again, provided that their superiors would not find out about it. After a while, the landowners also returned without even bothering to hide the fact from the District Commissioner.

The Kindergarten Inspection
by Itzhok Berglass

At the establishment of the Hebrew kindergarten, we did not make any effort to obtain a license from the Board of Education. We were low in funds, and we knew that the Board of Education sometimes made demands that were impossible to meet. We relied on the fact that the gentiles were not interested about what was going on among the Jews, and we took it for granted that no Jew would report us, especially since only a few individuals knew that we did not have a permit. Perhaps we might have succeeded to administer the kindergarten in this manner to the end were it not for the following incident.

Two inspectors, a man and a woman sent by the Board of Education, arrived in Strzyzow to inspect the Catholic kindergartens in town and the nearby villages. These kindergartens were managed by nuns under the supervision of the local priests. There were no automobiles in town. To get from the railroad station to the town and to the nearby villages the inspectors hired the town coachman, Reb Raphael Ber. As it is habitual with coachmen, he started a conversation with them, and finding out the purpose of their visit, he expressed his national pride by telling the inspectors that all the kindergartens they had inspected already and the ones they intended to inspect were nothing in comparison to the Hebrew kindergarten which was supervised by the Zionists. The inspectors who had no Hebrew kindergarten registered in their files were more than happy to oblige, and asked Reb Raphael to them there.

[Page 189]

The Hebrew kindergarten was located in a rented room in the house of Samuel Feit. The inspectors arrived there before noon when all the children were present and the teacher, Elka Shulman, was busy teaching. When the inspectors asked her who was in charge, she mentioned my name in spite of the fact that from an official point of view, I was only a patron. The practical supervision and the daily management were in the hands of a mother's committee under Nechama Gertner's leadership.

The inspectors did not act harshly and did not immediately report the illegal kindergarten to the authorities. They turned directly to me. After a few minutes, they arrived at my store which was crowded with customers. After I took them into my private quarters, they pointed out to me the seriousness of such a violation. I spoke to the inspectors with frankness. I told them that we simply could not entrust our toddlers, especially the girls, in the hands of the Catholic Nuns, and neither could we abandon the children to the peasant maids who hardly know how to read and write. Therefore, we had no choice but to organize a Hebrew kindergarten. Since we lacked the financial means to execute all the governmental requirements for the legalization, we were forced to do it illegally.

The inspectors who seemed understanding and honest, were sympathetic to our motives. But the law is the law and it could not be violated. The inspectors agreed not to report us to the authorities and they also permitted us to continue to operate the kindergarten. They also promised to give us full support in our legalization efforts. I, from my end, promised to begin the process of legalization right away.

I immediately contacted the Central Hebrew School Organization, "Yavneh." Although most of our colleagues were General Zionists, when it concerned traditional upbringing, we always aligned ourselves with the "Mizrachi". We had come very close to achieving our goal, namely, legalization of the kindergarten, which was nonetheless open until the last moments before the outbreak of the Second World War.

This Also Happened in Our Town
(Resurrection of the Dead)
by Moshe Mussler

It is unbelievable when it is told, but it is true that there was a superstitious belief that the deceased gathered nightly in shul to pray. This belief was deep rooted in the consciousness of the townspeople as in all other Jewish towns in Eastern Europe. Not only did the simple folk, women and children believe it, but those mature and knowledgeable in the holy books did not deny the existence of such a belief.

This belief originated from the fact that in most places, the cemeteries were located in close proximity to the shul. The distance between the shul and the cemetery was no more than four meters. The proximity of these two originated during the fifteenth and sixteenth centuries when the majority of the town's inhabitants were Jews, and the authorities did not take the future under consideration.

[Page 190]

The Austrian Kaiser was considered by the simple folk as their protector from the German Jew–haters and the savior from the Polish people, their enemies. Because of our provincial naiveté, it would have been out of place to doubt such a belief. However, the servants of the Kaiser and the loyalists among his officials in the towns away from the Capitol could not tolerate the fact that the melamdim should teach and explain the Jewish Torah to Jewish children to assure the continuity of Judaism. They resented our existence, and all means were "kosher" top hinder our steps.

Every Monday and Tuesday, gendarmes were dispatched to the melamdim alley, to inspect it and verify that they abided by the law and taught the children in spacious, well–lit rooms, as the official schools did. Mainly, they checked whether they possessed a license from the educational authorities. The gendarmes were also supposed to check if the number of students did not exceed the permit. Woe was to the melamed who was caught in an infraction. A fine and arrest was his lot.

Our teacher also could not withstand the rigidity of the District Commissioner's decrees and he was forced to transfer his cheder to the Kehillah room adjacent to the main sanctuary of the shul. This place was off limits to the authorities. Even the Commissioner's rights ended at the entrance. (According to the law they could not enter a church or synagogue.)

If the truth to be told, in the summertime the studying in cheder gave is a little bit of pleasure. The windows were open to the old cemetery and the clean scented air blew in from the hundred–year–old trees which refreshed us, replacing the choking smell from the Rabbi's kitchen which he had also used for a study.

But alas, the opposite was true in the wintertime. The camel–like oven stood in the corner orphaned and ashamed with its coldness. A rich man's fortune could not be enough to heat it up. If Rothschild would have decided to squander his fortune to supply us with firewood, we would have needed to engage an entire division of woodcutters to fill the oven's emptiness.

As soon as the sound of the shofar was heard at the end of Yom Kippur, the cheder in the Kehillah room surrendered itself to the exclusive rule of the Prince of Winter who did not move out from that room until Shavuot. Despite the anger and indignation of the Prince of Winter we persevered. Frozen to the marrow of our bones, we sat there hours upon hours and studied G-d's Torah. Those long winter nights made the task of studying several times harder. The hours were drawn and the cold stiffened our arms until we were not able to move them. Our dismissal always came with rejoicing shouts. While going home we waved our lighted paper lanterns, our own production, spreading light on the winter scenery of the slumbering town.

It was the beginning of the winter when this story happened. Into our cheder arrived a new student who was three or four years older than we were. He came from a nearby village and he barely knew how to put two letters together.

[Page 191]

He replaced his lack of knowledge of our teacher Moses' Torah with a knowledge which had no connection whatsoever to the Pentateuch, and surely not with the Gemara. He was sharp and skilled about cats, dogs and horses, quick in climbing trees. In vain was our teacher's effort to make him participate with us in studying. His peasant brain could grasp nothing of the problems in the Talmudic tractates and Rashi. He found no interest in the "old wives' tales" from the Pentateuch.

The village boy's extra specialty was demonstrated by swiping apples from the peasants' carts that brought them to town for sale. Thanks to his merits we were privileged to say hundreds of blessings a day over those stolen apples, even on plain weekdays.

He, more than any of us, knew how to vanish from the study bench and evade the angry eye of the teacher, He could never restrain himself for more than a half an hour to sit on the bench, when he would suddenly disappear as if the earth had swallowed him...

The Rabbi's lashing and pinching, slid off him like a summer rain. The teacher's hand was powerless in subduing him. That boy's enthusiasm for a card game was as of a Roman gambler. He did not miss any occasion to join a game.

But not always could he find company for a game. It was not enough for him to be free to play cards. A partner was always needed. Otherwise there was no game. Where could he find a partner when we were all subservient to the teacher and burdened with his heavy yoke?

In addition, we were all inexperienced, and did not know how to disappear from the teacher's sharp eye and slip off the study bench. Fear of our parents also existed and could not be ignored.

Besides, the hesitating heart and our conscience did not permit us to violate the clear commandment that studying Torah should not be interrupted – Heaven forbid.

It seemed that this boy was sent to us from heaven to save us from our distress. On the other hand you may have said that Satan's hand was involved. An ingenious idea entered his head, an idea which had been rolling at our feet all along, but we never noticed it until the boy came along. It was only a pity that this geniality was not channeled to the studying of Torah.

As I mentioned before, this was on those nights when we studied in the Kehillah room located near the entrance to the main sanctuary.

Normally, we waited outside until the teacher came, to pass through the gate together and enter the foyer of the shul. The dead who prayed there caused us terror, and none of us dared to peek and see if truly the dead were there. However, the door to the sanctuary was usually closed and only a weak light from the eternal candle could be seen flickering in the darkness through the portal. This weak light spread horrifying shadows on the walls, moving shadows which were spreading and shrinking, forming all kinds of shapes in our childish fantasies. We saw in them what we wanted to see, namely, the deceased wrapped in tallisim, standing crowded together in prayer.

[Page 192]

One such evening, when we were waiting near the gate of the shul for the arrival of the teacher, nobody noticed that the young man from the village was not among us. Finally, the teacher arrived. We went into the foyer, with the teacher walking ahead of us. When we passed before the gate, we were surprised to see it wide open and, on the bimah, is the center of the shul illuminated by a weak light, we noticed a ghost standing wrapped in a talit, rocking heavily with his hands raised above his head.

A terrible shriek escaped from our mouths. The teacher also became terribly frightened of the ghost. We ran as fast as we could not to be called to the Torah. It was believed that whoever is called to the Torah will not outlive the year.

Breathlessly I arrived home and told my father, of blessed memory, about the incident. My father, who was known to be agnostically minded, interrogated me thoroughly and inquired if I had really seen the ghost with my own eyes.

I swore on everything that was holy to me, that it was true, and I was convinced that my oath was absolutely true, that I saw the dead with my own eyes. As additional evidence, I told my father that the teacher had also seen him and ran.

A smile appeared on my father's face, and he remarked as follows: "I am sure my son that this deceased was a live person. What a pity that you did not use a thick stick to convince yourself whether he was alive or dead. I am not surprised that you were frightened. As for the teacher, I have no answer."

Of course, we did not return to the cheder that night. We went into the warm and lighted Beit Hamidrash, and found all my friends gathered in a corner submerged in a card game. It was close to Hanukkah.

On Hanukkah it was permitted to play cards. The winner was the peasant boy.

When the term ended the boy returned to his village as empty of Torah as he was when he came. Only then did he reveal to us his secret, that he was deceased who was praying in shul on that winter night. He and no one else.

It was easy to understand his intentions. He wanted to scare the teacher, and he wanted to evade studying and, have partners for the card game...

Long Live the Kaiser
by Moshe Mussler

It is a rare occasion that a person has a chance to recite the traditional blessing when seeing a King or Emperor. The blessing sounds as follows: "Praised be He who bestowed a part of his Majesty upon a human being." Especially in our days, when the number of Kings and rulers kept decreasing. The people of our town, and yours truly among them, had the honor to meet the Kaiser and make such a blessing...

It happened in 1904, or 1905, during military maneuvers in our vicinity. All the highways and the country roads were swarming with the royal army. There were cavalry, infantry, artillery, and sappers who built bridges. They were escorted by high officialdom that followed them around.

[Page 193]

One morning on a summer day, the town drummer announced an order from the District Commissioner that all residents of the town ought to appear near the railway at the entrance of the town and, when the emperor's train will pass and his Highness will appear in the window, all the bystanders were required to shout: "Long live the Kaiser."

Of course, nobody would have dared to oppose such an order. Besides that order carried its own reward. a) A chance to recite such a rare blessing. b) If his Highness the Kaiser had bothered to come to us, by all means we should give him a venerable reception.

At the determined hour, a stream of elders, youth, women and infants flowed to the railroad. The Rabbi and the head of the Kehillah were among the official invitees to the reception committee at the railroad station. We, the public, were lined up alongside the railway and, with trembling hearts, awaited the arrival of the Kaiser's train.

That day, not only did the Beit Hamidrash dwellers interrupt the studying of Torah, but so did the melamdim. They too came to greet his Highness in whose shadow we sought forbearance.

Before we went to the station, we rehearsed the blessing several times in order that the recital should go smoothly and without a hitch. All eyes were glued to the far distance, longing for that exalted moment of the revelation which was about to occur before us.

Finally, the whistle of the locomotive was heard. Slowly the train appeared from around the bend and passed in front of us in a slow tempo. Franz Joseph I was standing at the window, waving his hand at us. In all the excitement, I forgot to say the blessing, and I was convinced that I did not mention G–d's name in vain.

Who can take the dirt away from your eyes, "Courageous Soldier Schweik," so that you could see that not only you, in your innocence, believed that destiny from above assigned him to be the ruler? We too were naïve and believed in the righteousness of the Kaiser, his ministers, and advisors.

Let us not be ashamed and confess to the truth. We were mistaken about the straightforwardness of our rulers and governors in the past and will be so in the future – until the end of generations.

Books Burned on the Auto–Da–Fe
by Moshe Mussler

It was an undeniable fact that the shtetl Frysztak was near and subservient tour town, had a smaller population, was smitten with poverty and affliction, but was known in the Jewish world no less than our town which was the site of a regional city.

In the past, Frysztak was served by Rabbis who were famous as Torah scholars and sin–fearing people. Righteous women testified that infants soon after they were brought into the covenant of Abraham our Father, refused to be nursed from their mother's breasts unless their heads were covered and the mothers recited the proper blessing over milk.

I myself never saw such wonder. But my mother told me that she heard it from trustworthy women, and it was not a disgrace to believe it.

[Page 194]

No secular books nor a person who joined the new sect called "Zionism" could be found in the periphery of this community. . . This was the official opinion. Unofficially, in the underground, the Zionist bug penetrated their domain and began to shake the town's foundations.

The Young men from this shtetl became contaminated with "atheism." Namely, they shortened their underwear and made their pants longer. They met with the leaders of our Zionist association, and together they concluded that the youth of Frysztak deserves secular education and, for this purpose, it was necessary to establish a branch of our library. Borrowing and reading books would bring them under the Zionists' wings.

It appeared that the satanic power succeeded, despite all the excommunications and Rabbinical fore–swearings, including the special prohibition of the extremist Rabbi who was then famous all over Galicia.

At the helm of the extremists in Frysztak was Reb Chaim Meir who decided to expunge "atheism" from the community.

On a dark gloomy night, Reb Chaim Meir and a few conspirators who volunteer to do the holy deed, broke into the house where the unclean books were kept, loaded them into a wheelbarrow, and carted them off to the community bathhouse where they were sentenced to be burned. Eye–witnesses reported that during the burning, Reb Meir quietly recited the "Kol Chamira" which is usually recited during burning the chometz.

This happened when the Hapsburg Empire was still in existence and people were not free to do as they wished.

As soon as we found out about it, a complaint to the District Court was filed by our lawyer, Dr. Kornhouser from Jaslo against Reb Chaim Meir and his helpers. He was ordered to pay the damage.

Their consolation was that they destroyed atheistic books. But woe is to such a consolation. For their money, new books were purchased and their reign over the youth ceased to exist. The breach in the wall of extremism began to grow bigger and bigger.

Inference
by Moshe Mussler

Reb Shalom Schwartzman was a renowned Hassid, a very pious man, observant of the Hassidic traditions of the Rabbi from Belz. He always raised his voice during the prayers, burning like a fire. Of course, his fight against the young people who joined the Zionists was for the sake of the Lord. Lo and behold, the Rabbi from Belz was one of the fiercest opponents of Zionism.

On one of those days, Reb Shalom turned to my father, of blessed memory, and said to him: "Eliyahu, my apprehension is that your son, (that was I) will go astray, and maybe, Heaven forbid, become a convert…"

My father replied, "I beg your forgiveness, but you are entirely wrong. I will explain it with an inference. If he ignores a few customs which were not established by our ancestors but only recently, well, maybe he is a little bit agnostic and does not believe in nonsense. There are many who do not believe. But, to betray the Torah of Israel – no way. Under no circumstances, he would not go that far."

[Page 195]

From the Distant and Not So Distant Past of Strzyzow

The Man Who Was No Coward
by Shlomo Yahalomi

    Rabbi Alter Zev Horowitz lived in one of the apartments in my grandfather's houses. Reb Shlomo, my grandfather, was one of his staunchest admirers and always stood by him. But personal relationship was one thing and business another. When my grandfather was marrying off one of his daughters and needed the rooms, he asked the rabbi to move. The Rabbi was not anxious to move and took his time. Reb Shlomo kept pressuring him, but the Rabbi kept postponing his move. Behold, the wedding date arrived. The daughter was marrying Reb Joseph, the son of the famous genius, Rabbi Menashe Eichenstein, a son–in–law of the Rabbi from Dzikow, Rabbi Joshua. The wedding took place in Strzyzow, and besides the groom's father, a whole party of holy Rabbis related to both sides came to participate in the happy occasion. My grandfather sat near Rabbi Joshua, the Rabbi from Dzikov and, when he drank l'chaim to the Rabbi, the Rabbi said to him: "I hear that your reverence is evicting my relative from your house." He emphasized the word "eviction." "Eviction?" Replied Reb Shlomo, "If the Rabbi calls this eviction, I cannot help it. I do not want to evict him. I want him to give me back the apartment willingly because I need the rooms." The Rabbi looked at my grandfather's face and into his clever eyes, and told him in a commanding voice, "If your reverence will evict my in–law from the apartment, you may be forced to sell the house."

    My grandfather Reb Shlomo, who greatly revered the righteous Rabbis and frequently visited with them, had a strong character and was not subservient enough to the Rabbis to change his mind when he was convinced that he was right. He thought for a while, figuring out his financial situation in his mind and concluded that normally he was far from needing to sell his house. He girded himself and said in a low voice. "Forgive me, Rabbi, I think I feel secure for this year and maybe for another couple of years that there will be no need to sell my house." When Rabbi Joshua heard his resolute answer, a smile appeared on his face. He turned to Rabbi Alter Zev and said: "I thought that I was dealing with a landlord who is a fool and timorous man, who could easily be intimidated. Since he is not afraid, I suggest you look for another apartment." The result was that my grandfather gave the Rabbi all the wood he needed to build a house, and Rabbi Alter Zev built a three story house in the center of town.

A Proper Answer
by Shlomo Yahalomi

    It was customary in Galician towns to send the Rabbis monetary gifts before every holiday and also for Hanukkah and Purim. My great–great grandfather used to send money to both Rabbis in town. Once he forgot to send Hanukkah–gelt to Rabbi Moshe Leib Shapiro, of blessed memory. After some time, when the Rabbi saw my great–great grandfather, Reb Yacov Kanner, he told him that he owed him a debt. Reb Yacov asked him, "What kind of a debt do I owe you?" The Rabbi replied that he did not get the Hanukkah–gelt gift. Reb Yacov was amused, and said to the Rabbi, "Oh, and I thought that I was sending the Rabbi a present because I wanted to, and now I found out that I owe it to you." After this incident, he ceased sending him any gifts until the rabbi realized the reason, and he apologized to Reb Yacov.

A Clever Jew
by Shlomo Yahalomi

    When Rabbi Tzvi Elimelech Shapiro from Blazow passed Strzyzow on his way to a small town where he was invited for the Sabbath, a large crowd came to greet him at the railroad station. I was also among the crowd. I was nine year–old then. When the Rabbi reached out his hand to greet me, someone mentioned to him that I was the grandson of Reb Shlomo from Zyznow. Said the Rabbi, "Shlomo from Zyznow? He was a clever man." and told the following story.

    Once a woman handed me a donation with a written note to pray for her husband who was in trouble with the law. Knowing that Reb Shlomo from Zyznow has connections with the authorities, I turned to him and said, "Nu, Reb Shlomo give me an advice." (Meaning that he should see what could be done.) Reb Shlomo responded: "The Rabbi took the donation and I should advise?"

The Merchandise is Already Packed
by Shlomo Yahalomi

Once, the Rabbi Joshua from Dzikow came to a shtetl and something unpleasant happened. Namely, nobody came to see the Rabbi with a "Kvittel." The Rabbi joked about it and remarked. "I never saw such a smart town." When the Rabbi was about to leave town and was already at the train station, Reb Hershel Tenzer found out about it, he rushed over to the station to find the Rabbi, and to apologize. When Reb Hershel reached the station and found the Rabbi, he pulled out a "Kvittel" with a donation and handed it to the Rabbi. The Rabbi refused to accept, and said with a smile, "My merchandise is all packed."

[Page 197]

A Powerful Word
by Shlomo Yahalomi

Reb Menashe from Lutcha was known to everyone as an ignoramus. People close to him said that he barely knew how to read the prayers. All his life he worked the land and traded cattle. When he bought a calf, it was for him a child's play to carry it home several kilometers from where he bought it. Indeed, as strong as he was physically, so weak was he in matters connected with the printed words and things related with the "educated Jews." On Yom Kippur, he used to come to town to pray in shul with the "S'chidim" meaning the Hassidim. And, since noble young men knew his qualities, they hid behind his seat in order to hear what he was saying, while looking in his prayer book. And behold, they discovered that Menashe was saying the same word repeatedly.

They stood and wondered why he suddenly favored the simple word "Laasot?" Until Reb Moshe Adest came and explained to the young men the logic. Menashe used to sit near the washstand where the worshippers washed their hands and recited the prescribed blessing ending the word "laasot" loudly, which he had memorialized, and therefore, kept repeating it during the prayers, not knowing anything else to say.

Everything Has To Be Her Way?
by Shlomo Yahalomi

Somebody was sued by Reb Baruch Berglass before the Assistant Rabbi, Yacov Shpalter. After the Assistant Rabbi decided that the defendant had to pay or take an oath that he was telling the truth. The defendant asked for a delay of two days to consult with his wife. When he appeared on the third day before the Assistant Rabbi, he told courteously: "Honorable Rabbi, my wife advised me to pay the money and not to take an oath." Said the Rabbi cheerfully, "If so, than both parties will be satisfied. You will not have to take an oath and Reb Baruch will be paid." The litigant responded softly. "What do you mean that I should give money?" Although my wife advised me to do so, but what about me? Don't I have anything to say about it? Behold! It is written 'He shall rule her.' She wants me to refuse to take the oath, well, I cannot afford not to listen to her entirely. After all she is my wife. But to pay money, this I refuse. I too have something to say about it."

What was Reb Hersh Ber the Sexton Doing?
by Shlomo Yahalomi

When Reb Hersh Ber the sexton was critically ill, Reb Joseph Mordechai, the Assistant Rabbi, came to pay him a visit. "Hersh Ber, vos Machstu?" (How are you doing?) The Rabbi asked Reb Hersh Ber, who all his life was a jester, even then, in time of illness, he did not forget his humor, and responded without even blinking an eye. "Well, ichmach yesoimim." (I am making orphans, meaning that by his dying he will create orphans.)

[Page 198]

The Rabbi's Insinuation
by Shlomo Yahalomi

Again, there was an incident with the Rabbi Baruch Halberstam from Gorlice, the son of Rabbi Chaim from Sandz, who came to Strzyzow to visit his daughter, the righteous Chana, Rabbi Moshe Leib's wife. He too did not receive a venerable reception in Strzyzow. (The Hassidim of Sadigora saw to it.) When he was about to leave town, he was sitting in a carriage harnessed to four horses, and some townspeople were standing around and gawking at the Rabbi. The Rabbi looked once at the people and once at the horses and remarked, "I just now noticed the horses of Strzyzow."

The Righteous Who Never Sinned
by Shlomo Yahalomi

When Reb Shmuel the tailor became ill, the Assistant Rabbi, Reb Joseph Mordechai, went to visit him and, when he saw that Reb Shmuel, an illness was serious, he tried to persuade him to say the confession. Reb Shmuel refused and said: "I have nothing to repent, I have never sinned, I never had time to sin. I always worked and that is all." Reb Joseph Mordechai saw with whom he was dealing, and asked him, "Perhaps you once forgot to recite the evening prayers?" "No!" "Perhaps did you spoke evil?" "And what are those?" "Well," Reb Joseph Mordechai said, "Words that you should not have said." "No!" Reb Joseph Mordechai realized that the sick considered himself completely innocent, righteous, and without a defect. He stood up and opened the door to leave. Outside the door, he said to Reb Shmuel: "If you are that righteous, you have nothing to fear. You may die in peace."

(I heard this story from Reb Moshe Adest.)

Good Morning
by Shlomo Yahalomi

On Hanukkah, the young men use to hide in the women's gallery to play cards all night. Reizl Reicher came in early one morning, kissed the mezuza and announced loudly: Good morning Your Holiness, blessed be thou...

The Story About the Treasurers Who Were Forced to Resign
by Shlomo Yahalomi

Once, a few congregants were dissatisfied with the treasurers of the Beit Hamidrash, and decided to teach them a lesson. One cold winter night, they demolished the oven completely. In the morning, when the worshippers appeared in the Beit Hamidrash and saw what happened, they said: "There is nothing we can do. The treasurers have to go." And that was exactly what happened, they resigned. Remarked the clever Reb Meir Deutch: "Shoiver Oyvim, Umachniya Zeidim." (Quotation from the silent prayer.) They broke the oven and the enemy surrendered.

Reb Baruch Diller Explained That the Willingness is the Essence
by Shlomo Yahalomi

One of the rich men in town used to be called to the Torah for Maftir on Shavuot year after year. Once happened that he was called to the Torah not for Maftir but for another aliyah. Reb Baruch Diller was the treasurer at that time. The rich man hesitated at first to answer the call. "Why he thought to himself, should I forego my traditional part?" Nonetheless he went, but he decided to get even in some other way. When he was asked how much he was donating, he angrily replied, "Nothing!" Reb Baruch tried to explain to the insulted rich man that he part of the reading that he was called to is as important as the Maftir. But the man did not accept any apologies. So Reb Baruch said to him, "Look, you wanted Maftir, in heaven it is considered as if you had it. Because you demonstrated your willingness, you will be rewarded for it. But I did not want you to have it, so you are not to be blamed for it, and you should not blame yourself, because the willingness is the essence.

The "Dreadful Story" about Mother's Earrings
by Shlomo Yahalomi

There was a long–lasting family feud between two sisters over an heirloom inheritance. The dispute was over their mother's earrings that were adorned with diamonds and precious stones. The earrings were in the hands of one sister, Pearl, Benjamin the tailor's wife. She claimed that she was willing to pay her sister Bashi, Mordechai Rosenbaum's wife, half of what the earrings were worth. Bashi refused to relinquish her claim to her "motherâ€˜s earrings" which she considered priceless. They brought this matter before the Rabbi. It went to court and nothing came of it. Subsequently, they agreed to rely on arbitration by mutually acceptable persons. My father was supposed to represent Pearl who had in her possession he earrings, and Reb Hersh Gelanded was the other sister's representative. A Rabbi, the righteous Reb Shmuel Schiff from Niebylec, was to have the decisive vote. My father refused to act in the dark, which meant to judge about earrings without knowing their value. He was also puzzled about where did Reb Itzhok the butcher, the sisters' father, who was known to be poor and destitute all his life, obtain money to buy such expensive earrings for his wife. . . Therefore, my father insisted that Reb Benjamin the tailor travel with him to Rzeszow, the closest big city, to obtain an appraisal from a diamond dealer. Benjamin was also required to keep the trip secret even from his wife. At first, Benjamin suggested that my father go by himself, but he refused. When they arrived in Rzeszow, they went to Mr. Schiff, the famous jewelry dealer, who appraised the earrings at half a gulden. They went to another dealer, Mr. Cuker, and he appraised the earrings at sixty groshen. My father kept his secret for a few weeks and, in meantime, the sisters kept up the dispute. At an opportune time, my father divulged the secret all over town. It appeared that Pearl quickly relinquished the earrings, and Bashi no longer claimed that all she ever wanted was "her mother's earrings." And that put the dispute to rest.

[Page 200]

With or Without a Permit
by Shlomo Yahalomi

There were in town two merchants who dealt with a certain kind of merchandise. We will not name the merchants or the merchandise out of respect. One merchant, when a shipment was supposed to have arrived on the Sabbath, arranged a permit from the Rabbi for unloading the goods. The other did not bother to ask the Rabbi. They both unloaded the shipment. Said Reb Moshe Adest: "There are two who desecrate the Sabbath. One with a special permit from the Rabbi and one without."

What is a Mitzva and How Did Joshua's Spies Cross the River Jordan
by Shlomo Yahalomi

Reb Chaskel Gorgel the melamed, was teaching ten to twelve–year–old students. He used to ask his students all kind of misleading questions in order to sharpen their wits. Once he asked how did Joshua's spies cross the River Jordan? One student volunteered and said, "I know, they were fish." Another time the melamed asked what is a mitzva? The student replied. "A female." He meant to say what we just learned a week before that in married life there were many mitzvot involved.

The boy was nicknamed "female," that name followed him for many years into his adulthood.

He Used Hands WithoutHaving Said the Proper Blessing
by Shlomo Yahalomi

Reb Moshe Reicher, Reb Yacov Kanner's son–in–law, was a pious honest man. He was G–d–fearing, and a strong believer in the righteous, especially in the Rabbi of Belz. Reb Moshe was a taciturn person and never spoke in vain. He owned a grocery store which provided his livelihood. He never spoke ill about anybody and, if he was compelled to say something negative about somebody, he shivered, his face changed, and, at the end, he did not say anything. He used to say, "What is there to say, it does not help." Reb Moshe was quiet, modest, and humble, but once I saw him very distraught, and it amazed me. That was when one of the townspeople called him before t he Assistant Rabbi for litigation. The claimant had angered him so much with his lies and false claims that Reb Moshe could not restrain himself any longer. He rose from his seat, approached his opponent and…hit him with his umbrella. Behold! Wonder of wonders! Not a word came out of his mouth, even though he hit him. Still, he did not utter even a single word. The claimant stood up and yelled, "Have you ever seen such an audacity? He used his hands and did not even recite the proper blessing. Not even one word. He could have at least said "Liar." But hitting without words that is a chutzpa.

[Page 201]

The special "Sabbatical Inspiration"
by Shlomo Yahalomi

Reb M. Z. came from a good family, an offspring of Rabbis and scholars. However, he himself was not a great learner, not in the least. He was a great joker and loved to make fun of everything and everybody. He also liked to get involved in all the problems of the town, to express his opinion everywhere, and oftentimes, he scolded people he did not like. All this took place on weekdays, when he was busy making a living, whereas on the Sabbath, his temper reached its peak. Already on Friday afternoons he became possessed with the Sabbatical inspiration and, if somebody induced him to speak, he said: "Stay away from me. I am already in the murderous Sabbatical inspiration."

The Father and Son's Card Game
by Shlomo Yahalomi

Reb A. Z. was a great scholar and very witty. We will not stop here to give his full description and tell a few things about him because it belongs in another chapter in this book. Here I will only tell a funny and petty story. A.Z. and his sons were involved in a card game in which the players had to beat each other by raising the stakes (in Yiddish "Shlugen"). One of the sons threatened his father and said, "Don't do it! I will beat you." (Ich will dir shlugen.) The father responded by scolding him. "Shigatz! You will dare to beat your own father?"

The Son Sued the Father
by Shlomo Yahalomi

A certain person was very rich. (Out of respect to him and his family, we could not name them.) The man supported his son who often came to visit him to ask for money. Once, the son decided that he would be better off suing his father and claiming part of the property. He claimed that he and his father bought the property in partnership but the father registered the property in his own name only. When the father and son entered the Rabbi's house, the Rabbi, astonished, asked: "What are you doing here with your son?" Replied the father who was distinguished and old, "My son is suing me because I live too long…." As fate would have it, the son passed away before his father.

Reb Hershal'e Schiff's Eye Glasses
by Shlomo Yahalomi

Reb Hershal'e was a veteran Hassid of the Rabbi from Sadigora. He was called Reb Hershal'e B'li Neder.* Because everything he said he added the words "B'li Neder." "Without a Vow." (In this way he avoided ever to say a lie.) For instance: "Tomorrow, B'li Neder, I will get up early. Or, "Tomorrow, B'li Neder I will go to shul. Etc. Etc…. Once Reb Hershal'e lost his glasses. He exerted himself to find them without success. Even after a year had passed, he did not despair, and he continued to search for the glasses. One day a few people were standing in a circle and talking among themselves. Reb Hershal'e approached them innocently and asked, "Are you by any chance talking about my glasses?"

[Page 202]

*B'li Neder was a common expression which the pious used in their conversations in order to avoid promises not able to keep.

Reb Israel Gertner Opposed Buying on Credit
by Shlomo Yahalomi

Reb Israel Gertner was a rich man with a capital "R". He excelled in doing good deeds. When somebody came into his store to borrow money, he would leave his customers and go and bring it to them. However, his son, Reb Menachem Mendel, who lived in Brzozow, was unlucky and always under pressure of his debts. He always owed for merchandise which he purchased on credit, and sometimes he signed his father's name to the notes… His father was angry and complained that he did not care about the money he had to pay. What made him mad was, he said, "Where, and from whom did my son learn to buy merchandise on credit? Why can't he buy for cash like I do?"

Such a "Repentant Sinner"
by Shlomo Yahalomi

There was in town a man who, in his youth, was not very righteous. When he became older, he turned into a "Good Jew" and wanted to be respected. Remarked Reb Moshe Adest, the clever and acute Jew, "This man forgave himself all his sins that he committed in his youth, and he now demands respect for it…"

Yacov or Yacov Chaim
by Shlomo Yahalomi

During the election to the Kehillah Committee, the man in charge of the elections made all kinds of falsifications to prevent the opponents from voting. When Reb Yacov Ziegel (His nickname was "Yacov the Beanstalk" for having an extraordinary long neck), came to vote, it appeared that he was listed Yacov Chaim Ziegel ad could not vote. The Jokers in town joked about him, that by the next elections, his name would not be "Chaim" which means life, but it will be "Yacov Met" which means Yacov the dead...

Every Rabbi Specializes in a Different Sickness
by Shlomo Yahalomi

Elazer the "Guttural" was a simple man, short in intelligence and understanding, but was very honest. He simply believed in G–d. He prayed for the Jews, worried about the sick, and made others write notes to Rabbis with or without the consent of the sick person. He himself did not know how to write. However he knew how to tell about the many miracles performed b y the Rabbi from Tyczyn, the Rabbi from Dukla, and by the Rabbi from Munkatch. And here s a story about one miracle that Reb Elazar used to tell. "Reb A.D. had diarrhea. What did I do? I wrote the Rabbi from M. After a few days, I received a reply that the Rabbi had blessed the sick with speedy recovery, and that was exactly what happened. The sick recovered." Reb Elazer ended the story with an expression of success. "Apropos, why do I tell this story?" He continued, "Because every Rabbi specializes in a different sickness, and the Rabbi from M. is good for diarrhea..."

[Page 203]

Which Fast Was the Best?
by Shlomo Yahalomi

Asked Reb Alter Nechemiah, one of the clever Jews in town. He asked, and answered, "The best fast was the fast of Esther. Why? Because on that day the baking of all kinds of pastries for Purim were done, and during the entire day, out from the ovens came fresh baked cakes and hamantashen, and you could taste each of them to resurrect your lusting heart..."

And What is Called a "Ruined Holiday"
by Shlomo Yahalomi

Reb Alter Nechemiah continued with an ironic wink of his eye. "A ruined holiday is, when it is not raining on Sukkot... "

"We Implore Thee, O Lord, Prosper Us"
by Shlomo Yahalomi

Reb Yacov Eisner was a venerable Jew, pious and kind to fellow men. He was employed as a clerk in the lumber–mill of the partners Johannes–Kracher. After working there for thirty years and reaching his old age, the owners decided to close the mill because it was not profitable anymore, and to keep it going meant losing money. Reb Yacov, seeing his livelihood slipping away, his world darkened around him and his face became thinner day by day. It was true that there was no shortage of good people who tried to encourage him. But no one was able to find an answer to the terrible and simple question. "How will such a dear man live, and from where will his help come?" About two weeks before closing the lumber–mill, on the eighth day of Passover, Reb Yacov was honored with chanting the "Hallel" service. He chanted pleasantly, sincerely, and from the heart. This time he outdid himself. It was obvious that he reached the point of resignation. I still remember the heart–rending melody in which he say the "Pitchu Li." When he got to the words: "We implore Thee, O Lord, prosper us, "he began to cry so bitterly that it tore our hearts. One person who was not such a strong believer said, "If there is a G–d in this world – He has to help Reb Yacov after such a warm prayer.

Well, a miracle did occur. Reb Yacov played the lottery all his life, to his great and happy surprise, he won fifty thousand zlotys. The whole town was in an uproar. Everybody said that when he sang, "We implore Thee O Lord, prosper us," he won the lottery."

[Page 204]

Memories From Strzyzow

In The Days Past
(When Grandfather Married Grandmother)
by Professor Dr. Ch. Lehrman, Strzyzow–Berlin

Half a century represents almost a whole human lifetime. Sometimes it represents even more that the time of man's existence on earth. It represents many years in the history of mankind, in general and less if we look at the same number of years within the boundaries of the twentieth century, taking under consideration the intermittent uproars and world events that have occurred. This is true especially in reference to the history of the Jewish people, whose destiny is eternally connected in a special dramatic form to the occurrence of world events.

A Jewish family that incidentally happened to be drawn into the whirlpool of world history represents a special mirror of the basic changes that occur in the passing times and in the lives of the countries. A Jewish family whose name is not known in the circles of art, science, politics and finance, but is considered a simple family such as we find among the prolific families of Eastern Europe, is considered typical for the whole nation with all recognizable signs of its special destiny, its wanderings and changes. In each such family lives a whole people as in every prominent tree there is included an entire forest.

The term "forest" is abstract when it concerns a great number of trees, which grow and develop in similar conditions. Sometimes a bolt of lightning would strike one of the trees and, half the forest would be destroyed. Yet, the individual tree always represents the reality. The forest is only the concept of individuality of such living reality. The trunk, its roots, and its branches are the product of the earth, the water, and air, wherever they prosper, and they are proof to those who, like them, are fed and were created under the same skies and upon the same earth. Every tree becomes green, deepens its roots, its branches spreading throughout, and its tree–top rises high. The trees represent the whole forest, as every patriarchal Jewish family with its children represents the entire nation. Their multiple destinies, on a smaller scale, reflect the destiny of the Jewish history and symbolize the tragic connection with the great events in the world.

This is the only justification or the attempt made here in the description of the events in the life of such a family who were involved and connected with the stormy days and the climate that brewed in these periods. Alas, the leaves were spread by the wind. Nevertheless, a few branches sunk new roots under new skies and into new ground. They the survivors proved that in spite of everything, they possess a special trait derived from common genes. The offspring speak all the languages of the masters of different lands and, at times, they do not understand each other directly and have to find a common tongue for mutual understanding. Even though they live under different living conditions, their way of life is similar, as a spiritual heritage of the family.

[Page 205]

To execute the writing of these memories was a difficult task for many reasons. For many years the author hesitated to do it, but it always sprang forth in his mind as a moral obligation which should no longer be postponed. The people always came to my mind and I could not forget them, even though they passed on a long time ago. Surely, these people who came to my mind strongly urged me to describe the loveliness of their past. They demanded the perpetuation of their existence and to give a meaning to people that passed, but with humility and obscurity, without any glow or glory.

Therefore, there will not appear in these lines any heroes adorned with victory, nor personality dressed in silk or velvet who passed with great noise and tumult.

I did not come in touch with generals or diplomats. If I accidentally passed one of them, he did not divulge to me his plans or governmental secrets, but spoke to me only about simple, actual problems of the time.

And so, these lines will remain a simple description of simple events of small people, their struggle with their troubles and daily harsh problems, their unsuccessful experiences trying to get involved in the disputes of the strong and the mighty.

These memories will not lead us upon shiny hills, trees and forests do not grow on knolls either, only on green valleys and hillocks. A man's life, his rich feelings and cravings are not discovered in high class saloons but in the lower class of society, in places where simple people still belong.

Whoever was born before the First World War knows about the atmosphere of the days without worry, which was referred to as "The Pleasant Period." At that time Europe was in the height of glory and might. For many decades there was no war, only "there, in the back of Turkey." In the Balkans skirmishes and small wars were taking place. But on the shores of the Seine, Rhine and Danube, life was prosperous. Paris was singing the hovering melodies of Offenbach, and Vienna was dancing to the tunes of Straus and Lehar waltzes which penetrated into the farthest corners of the imperial monarchy. These tunes even reached the other side of the Carpathian Mountains, the last outpost of the monarchy, the land of the Galician crown, with her rich natural resources and her poor Jewish population, whose sole richness was not submerged in the ground, but in the Kingdom above and her messengers of Torah and Talmud on the ground.

There was no bigger contrast in the world than those bearded Jews with fur hats that outwardly resembled Russian peasants but inwardly lived in a religious fantasy world, and had no territorial bounds, but still, in their hearts and with their honesty were faithful to the "Kaiser Franz Joseph," whom they endearingly called "Ephraim Yosl." They loved the Kaiser, their defender, who, in his old age, after the tragedies that had occurred in his household, became a legendary figure.

[Page 206]

His portrait looked down from the walls of public buildings with an expression of satisfaction on his face.

In truth, the mighty empire's ceiling was cracking. Centrifugal forces were waiting for the occasion to be liberated from custodianship of Vienna, and to attain national political autonomy. Except Hungary, the narrow–mindedness and the limitations of the ruling bands prevented them from becoming a modern United States, to solve political tensions, to deepen and draw nearer the existing cultural and human relations. Politically and economically such a federation in the territory near and around the Danube would have been a blessing.

The non–political area, as it was said, all the nationalities represented an illogical but practical unity. The Jewish segment was honored with spreading the spiritual light of Vienna. One of the most shining representatives from the metropolis, Stefan Zweig, remarks in his review, "The world of Yesterday," that the Jewish establishment in Austria in the twentieth century was most decisive. He testified that most names in the field of art and science who made Vienna world famous were Jewish names or of Jewish origin.

Even though it was a strange phenomenon, Jews who lived in other areas outside the Austrian borders also had spiritual bonds with that metropolis because of the Kaiser's facial features, his whiskers, and his formal dress, which was not warrior-like, in contrast to the face of the neighboring Russian Czar, which reflected the rage of the pogroms and anti–Semitic decrees. There was plenty of anti–Semitism among the Polish population also. Even in Vienna itself, there were periodic signs of that dreadful mentality of the fickle Austrians, which produced creatures like Hitler and Eichmann. However, in order to spread this poison, proper climatic conditions were needed, as existed during the crumbling of the proud empire on the Danube, which occurred quietly without fanfare. Until that time, an atmosphere of agreeable tranquility existed because of a fundamental level of political standards. And therefore, the pious black–frocked Jews also enjoyed religious–cultural autonomy, as in the historical days of that nation of thousands of years ago. In many little towns, the Jewish population was a recognizable part of the population. They openly fulfilled their religious life, unhindered in any shape or form. When a wealthy religious citizen donated a Torah scroll to his synagogue, all the worshippers carried the scroll with dance and music throughout the city streets, under the gaze of the local gentile population who did not even turn their heads, unlike the Jews when a Catholic procession passed by. These Jews did not consider assimilation as in Western or Central Europe. There was no higher culture in the area which could attract assimilation and was worthwhile. A few high class respected families sent their children to gymnasiums where they wore fancy uniforms, but the community looked upon them as partial traitors, and avoided any contact with them. Still, when one of those educated appeared later as a doctor or a lawyer, the Jews preferred him to the "Goy" doctor or lawyer, because it was possible to reveal their aches and suffering of their brethren to him in a more effective way, and to more fully confide in him. These professionals also spoke the German–Yiddish dialect, popular even in the Slavic countries, which in the meantime had become a nation.

[Page 207]

Dialects have their own destiny. Sometimes they influence the national bonds more than political borders. The German–Swiss dialect which is still spoken but not written created a stronger border with the northern neighbors than the Rhine River, and it conserved the alliance as all the areas on the German border did. These German speaking people strove to go "Home into their land," during the Nazi regime. This also determined the fate of three hundred thousand Luxembourgians who held onto the Mosel–Franco dialect even though their newspapers were printed in French and German. In this case they were helped by geographical proximity. The Yiddish–German dialect, after being completely detached from the place of origin, served as a special expression of isolation from the area. Jewish refugees from Bavaria and from Frankonia who were tired of the periodic expulsions and pogroms brought with them the dialect to Poland during the reign of King Kazimir, and held on to it as a family treasure. From this dialect alone a literary language developed which became a fine gentle tool for thoughts and feelings. When on the one hand it was used to explain the complicated thoughts and concepts of the Babylonian Talmud, on the other hand, the Jews who settled in Poland and South Russia found it to be a forceful, suggestive, extraordinary way of expressing their sufferings and yearnings. To the narrow–minded and primitive National socialistic forces who mocked the language, to them it sounded like an eastern Jewish Jargon. They did not realize that this language was inherited from poets and men of thought. They turned it into a caricature, into a defiled language for giving orders by judges and hangmen. In Imperial Vienna, they knew very well the meaning of the German language islands which were like pioneers of colonization in the midst of the Slavs under their rule.

The ancient Frankonian dialect became for the Jews a beloved and faithful habit, more so for those who lived among the Slavs. The Polish, Yugoslav, and Hungarian languages were used only in dealings with the non–Jewish world. But on Saturdays these "weekly languages" were banished as were the weekday thoughts and occupations. Then life turned into an imaginary world which was timeless and had grown organically for thousands of years, since Abraham our Patriarch from Ur Kasdim, serving as an inner shield of national independence, protecting those who went into dispersion from their homes and the birthplace of the Holy Scriptures. The process of growth in the Diaspora when the Jews acquired a great deal of culture from the outside, did not change them, Yiddish became a cultural possession of their own. The Slavs influenced Jewish life in the form of their clothing, eating habits, and songs. Also, sometimes the Jews behaved hot tempered like Slavs, or even like Mongolians. But all those characteristics merged and were absorbed in fundamental severity, folksiness, and independent behavior. Still, every man can sense the process of ferment in his heart and arteries, and without knowing it, tensions and contrasts are periodically created in his character. These characters are sometimes a creative force and sometimes simple tensions and contrasting illusions in the inner person and the Jew from Eastern Europe, born in the process of the merger of opposing inherent factors.

[Page 208]

The young couple who entered into a nuptial covenant to last a lifetime at the beginning of this century were entirely different in their outwardly appearance and character. Both were approximately two years old. It was customary to marry very young when they were still uncorrupted, unexploited, and innocent. They marriage was a bond between two families of the same nature and their goal was only to have and rear as many children as possible. Professional matchmakers and people with good intentions used to unite matching families from different places. The heads of the families came to an agreement concerning certain conditions and they surprised their children with the announcement of their engagement. Wealthy families placed their emphasis on mergers with families of scholars, and obtaining a groom well–versed in Talmud. Such a match was considered a great honor which justified the effort. My father's family was considered a family of scholars. My father Chaim came from Przeworsk. Although my mother, Bluma Krantzler from Strzyzow was also a product of a respected dynasty, born to pious people and well–versed in holy books, in my father's family, the knowledge of the Talmud was tied to the art of scribing Torah scrolls, a holy occupation which passed on from generation to generation with the exception of one. The one man who desecrated the dynasty's tradition was my grandfather, Leib, who became the head of a Yeshiva of only a few especially talented pupils. To belong to this group, special strict qualifications were required. Three of my grandfather's sons studied in his Yeshiva. Joseph, who proficiency and acuteness were known wherever he came and who was an authority in all the Rabbinical teachings, won the respect of many Torah scholars. David, the second son, was no less an excellent student. In addition, he had outstanding good looks, a characteristic of which he himself was not aware, and, until his distinguished age, had attracted and influenced young and old. He was the only one among all his brothers and sisters who died a merciful death. As it is said, "One who prayed for his brethren is answered first."

The youngest of all, Chaim, had no desire to overtake his brothers. He was satisfied with the fact that he qualified to study in his father's Yeshiva, even though he was a fast learner and he understood and remembered whatever he studied. But he was more interested in what was happening in the outside world, and used every excuse, legitimate or illegitimate, to sneak off from the Yeshiva, volunteering for all kinds of missions, and performing chores around the house, which in his opinion were preferable to studying in the Yeshiva.

In the street he never stepped aside to avoid the provocations of Polish boys, as his comrades used to do, but he stood up even to the strongest opponent, like David against Goliath and what he lacked in physical strength he accomplished with a surprise maneuver. When a peasant lad once put is two milk cans on the ground to punish the Jew, the Christ killer, Chaim did not go into a wrestling match. He pushed him into a can which overturned, spilling the milk, and the guy fell into his own milk puddle. His wailing for the damage aroused a pity, and the worry for the second can made him forget the Jewish boy.

[Page 209]

As in the above incident, my father during his entire lifetime was in control of every situation. He had the ability to quickly appraise a situation, and react swiftly. In addition, he was excitable and vigorous but he was flexible in regard to mistakes. The sentiment for justice in him did not allow him to act otherwise. He was capable of judging the qualities of a person with just one look, and he took pleasure in imitating the way a person talked. He was naïve and of easy persuasion because he himself could not lie, but still, in important situations he easily recognized the truth, and he was capable in a stunning manner to judge correctly in matters which did not belong in his daily routine. He also possessed good judgment in political matters, and was able properly to assess the situation and to prepare himself accordingly. He foresaw Hitler's intentions and analyzed them when times were still normal, in the years 1935–36, when the world tried to anaesthetize him with the flourishing economy in Germany and when even the Jews who lived in Germany participated without hesitation in the beguiling blossoming of the economy. My father was shocked and angered by the common blindness and when we told him to leave politics alone, that it did not affect him directly, he shouted: "It does affect me! This criminal affects us all!" Regrettably, he was right. At a time that no professional politician believed the general cynicism of the Nazi rule which a few years later exposed its repulsive face, to my father it became his most personal destiny, as he clearly foresaw it in the beginning with helplessness.

But this happened much later, a whole generation later. It was told here only to point out the essential characteristic outlines of my father, the clarity with which he diagnosed people in different matters, his independence in thought and deed, in matters small and large which came to him in his youth and followed him into his old age. Young Chaim's quick and decisive power of thinking and acting often caused him difficulties and friction in the Jewish community in which, after all, there existed certain inherited religious etiquette demanding unconditional obedience to patriarchal customs. This also included matters of arranged marriages which were not a matter of individual choice but rather a matter of the judgment of parents, and their religious–national outlooks. It demanded graceful surrender to the parent's choice having complete confidence that the selected mate would be for life. That is how Abraham our father behaved when he sent his servant Eliezer to select a bride for his son Isaac and it became a patriarchal tradition to those people that these stories were not legends from a distant world wrapped in the spirit of Hassidism but role models that we had to follow. In most cases, these marriages were successful and worked out nicely. Love did not die between them of natural causes as a cynical Frenchman once remarked, but it was a different kind of marriage which was not the norm write about in Western literature. Of course, there were silent tragedies like the one told in the Bible between Jacob and Leah. She was brought to Jacob instead of Rachel whom he really loved. But these tragedies were within the risk of society, and communal way of life, in which the individual was supposed to surrender to the religious national ideal of a careful selection in order to preserve the growth of "a kingdom of priests and a holy people."

[Page 210]

In some way or form, ideas in regards to an individual right to select a mate penetrated into the city of Przeworsk, even though it was only the nineteenth century. The young Chaim who already in his early age became influenced, G–d knows by whom, by new winds that blew all over the world, probably thought of these ideas when his older brothers were married to mates brought to them by others. Maybe he found in the character of our father Jacob, as it is told in the Bible, the determination of a man who was not only "a man who sat in the tents and studied," and he compared himself to him. Anyway, one morning he disappeared from his father's house. He found some transportation which traveled from place to place, and arrived in the regional city of Rzeszow, and from there by train he found himself in Strzyzow.

From the railroad station which actually was only a small barrack it was quite a distance to the town, but suddenly he was standing in the center of town, a huge marketplace, from which narrow streets and alleys branched out in different directions. Everything that happened in this town occurred in the marketplace. There one could hear the news from around the world. One of the side streets led to the house of Moshe Krantzler, a huge estate, surrounded by a garden, bordering on the railroad tracks. On the other side of the tracks an extensive green meadow was spread out on which in the summertime, cows that provided Kantzler family with all their dairy needs, grazed. During the winter the meadow was covered with snow. In March the waters of the Viskoka River overflowed its banks after the ice was broken, and flooded the fields and plains. An unpleasant sea of water extended for several kilometers, spread all around and often interrupted the train movement for several days. Then a small locomotive was sent out on the tracks to survey for any damage. That event marked the beginning of spring. Chaim asked about that particular house. Names of streets or house numbers were not in existence. He went into the house and came into a dark corridor where he saw a big barrel filled with water which Yankl the water carrier brought daily from the well for which he was paid a few red copper coins. Chaim wanted to announce his arrival, so he drew a cup of water from the barrel and recited loudly the blessing over the water. Then he modestly approached the door leading into the apartment. In the first room there was a big round oven, and it seemed that here was spent the ordinary daily life. From the other room a chandelier for the Sabbath candles hung from the ceiling where apparently the Sabbath and holiday meals were eaten. There were beds in both rooms. To be exact, they were sleeping places used as such at night and as benches in the daytime. Around the oven there was a bench which served as a welcome shelter for wayfarers who could not find a place in the barn. There was always a place for those who sought lodging. No one was ever turned away for lack of space. The Krantzlers behaved the same way later when they lived in Germany and France. They gave shelter to outsiders in the hours of the night if they could not find a roof over their heads. They also practiced this tradition later in Eretz Israel. When European refugees arrived, they provided them with places to live. Only now in the modern Israel things have changed, when the offspring of the refugees obtained elegant four–room apartments, there is only room for "Sabbath night parties."

[Page 211]

Chaim went in with extra humility but with determination. When he saw four women he remained standing embarrassed. The woman in the center had blue eyes and wore a wig as it was proper in those times. Apparently the other three were her daughters. One had black hair, the second was blond, and the third one had brown hair. They looked at the young man whose face was covered with a small black beard, with extra curiosity. They thought he might turn around and withdraw, but he did no such thing. He introduced himself with humility, and asked Bluma, his bride–to–be, her name. They all gazed at the blond girl who blushed and did not utter a word. She was average height with bright blond hair and blue eyes like her mother's.

However, her body was more firm, and she had a high round forehead with wide jaws. If someone would have encountered her in the streets of Krakow or Lwow, they would have said, without hesitation, that she was a Polish girl, of pure Slavic race, except for her sharp penetrating look which gave her blue eyes an entirely different expression different from the pale blue pupil of the eyes of real Slavic girls. These pale blue eyes blend into the scenery of their native land where Polish and Russian boys and girls dream, play, and dance carefree. Jewish blue eyes, even though their origin might be Slavic, still their penetration is much deeper. They are deep and unsearchable as the depth of the sea, and they tell about experience of life and sufferings.

While the black haired Sheindl, and Yente the brunette, were smiling looking at Bluma, the blond mother, Molly, solved the general confusion when she said: "Here they come. The men are back from the morning services." The whole street all the way to the marketplace, could be seen through the window, and the women often stared out worryingly observing how the master of the house walked, trying to determine whether he was angry or in a good mood. Today he – and his son Yerachmiel walked with easy, carrying their velvet talit bags under their arms. Both were of middle height, which Chaim immediately noticed because he was tall. One of the men had a short unkempt white beard, and the second man had a fluffy reddish–blond beard which adorned his chin, and of which he was very proud, not allowing them to grow wild. Unlike other pious, devoted illiterates who possessed very little, if any, Torah knowledge at all. Yerachmiel opened the big Talmudical tractate and hummed with his sweet voice the treatise about civil or criminal law, his father's strict facial lines softened, and the eyes of the tiny mother, Molly, sparkled proudly. Even the three sisters conversed in a whisper.

Now father and son entered the house cheerfully, as it was proper and seemly after completion of the morning services. When they saw the strange young man, they reached out their hands with the customary "Shalom Aleichem" greeting.

[Page 212]

They looked around them with surprise, and they immediately understood the whole situation. The face of the master turned gloomy as usual which always aroused the family's anxiety. He furrowed his thick brows and did not know how to approach the unheard of behavior of this future son–in–law, and how to react. Before the master of the house had a chance to become angry, his wife quickly softened his angered mood by reciting a few verses about similar situations in the Bible. She had read these verses in the Yiddish Pentateuch, translated especially for women. Ultimately, he decided that a guest is a guest and, as such, the proper thing to do was to ask him to wash his hands and come to the table. Our Patriarch Abraham did the same, as it is written in the Torah: "And comfort ye your heart, after that ye may pass on." That is the way a Jew, a Hassid, who follows the Torah with its strictures, is supposed to act; otherwise he is not a descendent of Abraham our Father.

Consequently, the three men sat down to the table, and the women served rye bread, butter and strong coffee. Bluma served an extra large cup for the guest. During the meal, the men spoke about various subjects, and Chaim often glanced at Bluma and was in attentive to the conversation at the table. Instead of listening to the conversation, he tried to overhear what the girls were talking about. Finally, because it was not a Sabbath or holiday, and duty required going out to trudge in the villages in search of a livelihood, the host asked Chaim to recite grace after the meal. Still, everyone felt that this breakfast was a festive event and they separated with the blessing "Be well, and go in peace." Later that evening, Chaim returned home to Przeworsk, and announced, "I am satisfied with my bride," and he went to sleep.

Bluma, Chaim's bride, was the oldest and most active among her brothers and sisters. Her iron will and her talents she inherited from her father. Her blond hair and blue eyes came from her mother who was still called "the beautiful Molly," and whose beauty in her older years was expressed by her good–heartedness and love for her fellow man. She quietly influenced her husband upon whom the heavy load of providing for the family rested, and she shared his many worries. He therefore was very strict and ruled his family to the point of instilling fear with his sparkling eyes that seemed to be always angry. He was a land and cattle broker. He had acquired a good deal of property and he lived in his house surrounded by a garden and fields. He possessed very little knowledge outside of what he needed to conduct his business. To read and write in German he did not know. He knew only Hebrew. However, his children were all educated and wrote in a precise calligraphic handwriting, except Bluma. Being the oldest, she had no time to study. She wrote down on paper what was needed, fast, phonetically, and with clarity, without paying attention to neatness or spelling. Arithmetic she did by heart, she had no need for pen and paper. If Bluma possessed her father's commercial instincts and the capability of judging a person's character, she also possessed the fierce strong will and iron consistency, expressed by her absolute, uncompromising religious belief, and she was truthful in any situation without hesitancy. The kind of belief that moves mountains is a most valuable thing in life when it is found in a goodhearted person who has abundant, endless mercy toward the poor and afflicted, as practiced by her mother, discreetly.

[Page 213]

Of course, Bluma's father also fulfilled the religious obligations of good deeds and charity, as it is required of a religious man. He often did more than was normally required of him. His barn was open for lodging for many wayfarers who in the morning were served breakfast and some money for their pockets. These things were done with true piety and this was the result of religious upbringing in which Father Abraham was a role model, since he championed hospitality and feeding the poor. Molly's abundance of love for her fellow man turned the precept of charity into a personal matter, and influenced the character of her children, especially the daughters, Bluma and Yente (Janet). Humane and religious foundations grew in her body and integrated into one block which could not be dislodged by any kind of influence or prompting.

After the wedding of Chaim and Bluma, the young man realized that in the poor social conditions of his native land, his profession as a scribe would hardly provide an existence and everything on the other side of the German border looked better and easier. They heard that the people who immigrated there had succeeded enough to bring over their families. But was this land where Torah observant Jews could live and remain devoted to their beliefs? People often came back for a visit, people who left before, and they returned with smooth, clear–shaven faces, without side–locks, and they looked entirely like authentic Germans. Germans in everything. They wore suits with short jackets in contrast to their relatives, who still wore long coats. Even if there were a few who wore some trace of a beard to show that they were still pious, what would become of the children, who would learn in the German schools and in the streets the German language, and therefore would become estranged from their parents who spoke Yiddish and their Jewish traditions? Would they ask their mother with the same reverence: "Mutter, gib mir coffee," in German as: "Mame gib mir kaveh." In Yiddish? Who knows where this would lead? Would keeping tradition cease together with the change of language? Nonetheless, they tried to solve it by reaching an agreement with Bluma's parents and the Krantzler family that they will try to make an effort and do everything possible that some of the children that would be born would be reared in the grandparents' home. Meanwhile the young couple would establish their Jewish home amidst the dangerous environment. With a distressed soul, Bluma went to Rabbi Moshe Leib Shapiro (although he was not the official Rabbi, he did serve as adviser and spiritual consultant to a select circle of the pious, the "Hassidim"), to ask him if she would be able to use the ritually slaughtered meat there expressing apprehension that the kashrut was not as strict as it was at "home." Not because she was a meat lover. She could as well exist for weeks on fruits and vegetables, but during her pregnancy she was supposed to maintain a proper diet. What should she do? The wise Rabbi responded, endearingly pronouncing her name: "Blumahl'e Blumahl'e! What kind of a response did you expect to hear? Is it not enough that I do not forbid you to go? You want me to preach you morals? Feed yourself according to the existing conditions there, but follow your husband and remain a kosher Jewish daughter!"

[Page 214]

Bluma's heart accepted the faith that the friendly Rabbi with his sly eyes implanted in her. And she never ate bread which was not cut with her own knife, and no butter was used which she did not make herself from milk that she bought directly from the cowshed. In the later years she sent her offspring to fetch her own can of milk from the farmer's house after they observed the milking. These offspring when they grew up were not exemplary children. They often burdened the life of their religious parents but, in principle, they adhered to religious faithfulness, and all things concerning religion.

The small dowry that was promised by the father–in–law was not fully paid. But did Laban the Syrian behaved differently toward Jacob? The anger of a cheated son–in–law was justifiable, but the father–in–law did come up with some mitigating excuses. What was left of the dowry was used for the trip to Germany, and for the food during the first few weeks until they entered Stuttgart, and they were able to find a source for their livelihood.

Stuttgart and many Jewish communities in Swabia, Germany, did not have an outstanding scribe. Therefore, Chaim thought that his livelihood would be easy, as the saying goes: "A profession stands on a golden foundation." And the subject here is a profession for which brains and heart were needed, not only the art of calligraphy like that of a copier in the Middle Ages, who copied all types of ancient texts for which there was no need to be pious and knowledgeable in Torah. An average man, even though he knows his trade, is not allowed to write the holy letter on parchment. A scribe must approach this holy task with sanctity especially before writing G–d's name; he is required to immerse himself in the mikva in order to be clean, body and soul. Therefore, only a few could be found who possessed all the required characteristics, such as artfulness, knowledge and being a Hassid. Stuttgart was lacking such a scribe who could periodically check the Torah scroll for a worn out letter or a blurred word because in such a case, the Torah is unfit to use. The infinite, conscientious attitude toward every serif written in the Torah scroll was being guarded during hundreds, actually, thousands of years, to prevent the tiniest error. And that is how the purity and devotion to each letter was preserved; as it is written in the Torah "Ye shall not add to it and not decrease from it." It was forbidden to correct words that "were not clear," in the Torah, not as the copiers of the Middle Ages did with ancient manuscripts, changing versions of ancient poems, and the present researchers racking their brains to understand them. The revered awe of the Jewish scribes towards Torah scrolls prevented forgery and distortions, even those made with good intentions.

Well, there was no such good professional scribe around and, to Chaim's sorrow, there was also a lack of pious devoted, good Jews in the Wurtemberg area. Not at all as he had imagined. The affluent, liberally–religious communities in the progressive lands of Wurtemberg and Baden, did not pay attention to the condition of their Torah scrolls. Therefore, when a scribe appeared to offer his services, they reluctantly let him check one or two scrolls without being too sympathetic to that profession, and they paid a meager fee.

[Page 215]

Chaim traveled from community to community, stayed away from home a day or two and sometimes even three or four days, ate only what he brought with him. Because he saw the disrespect for the art of a scribe, he doubted if they kept kosher. There was also a deep disregard among the German Jews for the Jews from the east who had just recently immigrated into their midst. This was also a factor in the meager pay for such an important art. They proudly considered themselves to have the upper hand in knowledge in the Holy Scriptures which no one dared to challenge.

Chaim refused to be "inert," to be a scribe without being erudite in world events. He also refused to accept benevolent bread from his German coreligionists. After a few months of unstable life as a scribe, he realized that, even though he could have existed in this profession, it had no "foundation of gold" and he would be forced to live in continuous poverty. Therefore, he searched for a permanent occupation, and he determined that at a time of a flourishing economy in that country which never stopped preparing for the next war, there were possibilities of being prosperous in a field that the locals neglected. These were materials that could be used as raw material for the military industry. Items like: Scrap iron, rags, etc. which in time might bring in huge profits. The junk business had especially prospered in Germany where the people considered the war imminent, unlike other countries, such as France, Austria, and Italy, where it was thought that peace would not be disturbed. At least, it seemed to them that way. There was a short-lived crisis in that sort of business after the First World War, but it soon recovered when the Germans began to prepare for another war. The pockets of little people always depend on world events.

At first Chaim went into this business on a small scale, without any ambitions to subdue the potential economy of the land. This was the only possibility for a young immigrant to attain a relatively moderate existence and to be independent. He refused to depend on his coreligionists who paid so little, and explained their attitude by saying that fixing scrolls was a rewarding deed in itself, and he should expect to be rewarded by G-d. Chaim thought to himself that he does not want to enslave his piety to make a living, but to preserve it as a way of life in his daily adventures.

As time went by, he became a supplier of raw materials for the Germans, and his knowledge in the business broadened. He felt secure enough to bring over his brother and wife, and he took them into the business as partners. The two brothers were inseparable all their lives, until the language of the nations became mixed up as it was during the time of the tower of Babylon, during the period of National Socialism, which drove one brother to emigration, and to a new life, and the second to expulsion to the town of his birth. On the initiative of the two brothers all the Eastern European Jews who lived in Stuttgart joined and became a congregation. Such a congregation of the Eastern European Jews which gathered indiscriminately all the immigrants from all professions existed for some years. But, could they have worshipped with people who did not observe Sabbath and did not keep kosher? In the congregation "Shomrei Shabos" was accepted only those who were truly G-d fearing there was no shortage of people to perform the religious rituals for free. Therefore, no funds were needed. They were self sufficient.

[Page 216]

David, Chaim's younger brother, served as cantor. He was less intelligent than his older brother. He had a slower grasp and less initiative. On the other hand, he had a wonderful voice which brightened the prayer house with godly brightness, so that in the heart of the worshippers there was more light than in all the marble temples in the world. David possessed a shiny appearance, was taller than is brother, faultless, spiritually tranquil, noting artificial, and he did not pay attention to the impression he was bound to make. He won hearts with his childlike sharpness. He did not realize that he personified a figure from the Holy Scripture. He never looked in a mirror, an instrument that causes the sin of self-esteem. While studying the daily portion of the Talmud before the services he was a very passive, even though in religious diligence he was remarkably active. As soon as he approached the pulpit with his head covered with the talit and began to chant, angels began to sing and pray with him.

No wonder then that his fame spread throughout the region, and many communities tried to hire G-d's beloved singer, promising to pay him well. However, David rejected such offers and refused to negotiate, even at times when he needed the money. He adhered to what our sages said in the Book of Ethics: "Do not turn your religious knowledge into a livelihood." Such talents should not chase after fortunes, they should be used only for G-d. The small congregation that the two brothers organized kept growing, thanks to its cantor and his brother, Chaim, the founder whose knowledge of the Five Books of Moses had qualified him to be the Torah reader. In time, their third brother, Joseph, arrived after escaping from the Czarist Cossacks and, since he was a Talmudic scholar, he granted to this little religious community of Eastern European Jews Rabbinic glory and respectful reverence in the eyes of the old established liberal Jewish community.

The three brothers, Joseph, Chaim and David, became the leaders of the Orthodox community without even striving for it. They became the authoritative center for uncompromising Jewish religious life in Stuttgart and its vicinity. These people, even though small in number, adhered to all ritual strictures and Rabbinical laws without fear of appearing absurd. On the contrary, as a result of their inner confidence, they gained unlimited reverence. The three brothers had no intention of ruling others. In their outward appearance they looked alike; they were tall, all taller than their wives. Joseph was blond, his eyes blue like steel.

David had dark brown hair and Chaim was black–haired. All the colors of the Jewish race were represented in the three brothers and their wives.

And meanwhile, children, boys and girls, were born at intervals of a year or two. Every child bore a different complexion and different characteristics. In these characteristics the offsprings' outer appearance reflected the inner contrasts that exited in their parents' contrasts between religious tradition and the strange, suspicious environment, and the daily difficulties that derived from it, and also the strong decisiveness to withstand all challenges, impulses and tasks, broadmindedly, with moderate temper and with loyal simplicity.

[Page 217]

Contrasting Worlds
Vienna–Budapest, August 19, 1966
"Turn My Boat While Sailing Upon the Waves of the Danube"
by Professor Dr. Ch. Lehrman

This small endearing song instilled in me dreadful fright since the fifth year of my life. My little sister brought it from Germany, the distant wonderland, when she came with mother to Strzyzow to take us, the two oldest, "home," after we were left with the grandparents as "collateral." They came to take us to our parents who in our eyes were complete strangers, as were our brothers and sisters who meanwhile had grown and blossomed in Stuttgart. They talked to each other in Swabian, and sang Swabian songs. They also responded in that German Provincial language when our parents spoke to them in ancient upper German, which in the Slavic countries was called "Yiddish."

The little brothers and sisters looked upon us, the brothers from the east, who were dressed in long frocks and adorned with oversized sidelocks, with strangeness and bewilderment, and kept a well–mannered distance from us. They treated us exactly like the Western European Jews treated their coreligionists from the east. It was not because "children" say out loud, what adults whisper, "but rather because it is human nature to consider oneself better that those who just came from far away and such a phenomenon appears at an early age and within the same family."

We the children from cheder looked with amazement at our little brothers and sisters, who were so nicely dressed, spoke so differently from us. They said "Mutter" and "Danke shoen," and had sayings for all occasions like: "Children should not dare to touch forks, knives, scissors or fire."

Everything seemed derived from an orderly world which, until the mass destruction, did not deviate a speck from order and punctuality. We were also attracted to that little song which told us about the Danube and the turning of the little boat. I learned the song easily because of the pleasant tune, but later I always searched for the meaning of the turning boat. And for many years it remained an unsolved puzzle. Finally, I sailed upon the waves of the Danube. After I crossed many lakes and oceans cruised many rivers up and downstream, I realized the farfetched dream which I had longed for all my life. No sailing compared to the sailing upon the waves of the Danube. Here I returned to the scene of my childhood, to that period of brightness which preceded the sobering reality of the present day Eastern Europe. The waters of the Danube are still crossing and flowing through the same countries which had belonged to one mighty but powerless kingdom before. Still, she was a kingdom of glory, the double Austrian–Hungarian monarchy whose emblem was a double–headed eagle, and whose languages were as many as the ethnic nationalities that lived there.

[Page 218]

Galicia, which was almost on the outskirts of the empire and was closer to the banks of the Vistula River, still belonged to the cultural circles of the monarchy on the banks of the Danube. This monarchy disintegrated and turned into anarchy on the banks of the Danube, which lasted until the Red Army arrived in its march of steel, and offered her protection. This protection was accepted with little enthusiasm, and it created the social political unity that exists now.

So was my life, turning on a pivot. I returned to the departure point, to the source, to understand the turning. But it always seemed to me that I was turning on my own pivot. In all stages of my multi–colored, dizzying existence, this was a repetitious return to the source. In all stages of my life, Germany, Switzerland, France, Anglo–Saxon countries, and Luxemburg, where I lived different lives, I always adapted and fit myself into the lifestyle of the area, because I rapidly understood it, often more effectively than the local people who knew their language as they knew their bread and beer. The local people took their life for granted, and their devotion and their trustworthiness was less than that of the newcomer who came from far away and breathed in his temporary surroundings. However, there was always a last opposing force which interfered in the complete integration apparently an external influence, or a spiteful craze, professional or official, which at the decisive moment represented an internal opposition. Out of the consciousness of my soul and the Jewish format which was forged in Eastern

Europe, I defended myself from diving unconditionally into other forms of existence, which I could very well and joyfully accept, observe and absorb without failing to copy them, with one–sided thoughtlessness. I guarded my Jewishness and my religion. Such a thing is very inconvenient in a world which does not tolerate any human society with distinguished merits, in which feelings and thoughts rule equally. An individual who guards his individuality becomes only an onlooker at best. The existence of such limitations is always arousing the suspicion of the masses, and it is more dreadful when a whole society is classified as such, it becomes isolated and self–conscious. It becomes intolerable. This is the source of dislike of strangers of all kind, beginning with anti–Semitism and ending with xenophobia, which are found in the Jewish communities, toward their coreligionists who are different in character.

As a guest and one who has been on both sides of the ocean, I was able to see and prove such phenomenon from experience. The strong rejection that kept increasing and bordered almost on hostility, shown by the German citizens of Jewish faith towards Eastern European Jews, had made an about face, from a historical point of view, when the Eastern European Jews immigrated to the United states and became wealthy. In time they began to treat the recent German–Jewish immigrants the same way. The Carpatho–Ruthenian Jews were treated even in a more severe form by their Hungarian brethren in whom the Magyar national spirit deeply embedded.

The Swiss Jews, even though they are small in number, their economic position is solid and secure. They see themselves as the chosen, because of the fact that over a hundred years they lived in a country which came out unscathed from both World Wars.

[Page 219]

The long–existing superior feeling toward their coreligionists was expressed with that certain Swiss emphasis. Their relations with the few thousand wretched refugees from the Third Reich became tense. They expressed the Swiss way of thought, that the refugees did not fight the Nazi military, and called the Jewish refugees "Swabians" or "Poles." They related to these refugees who had to run for their lives like aristocrats. But to fulfill their religious custom of helping those who came from outside and were in need, they treated them in the same way as the Roman patricians, the semi–barbarians, treated the Greek slaves who were of higher cultural standing, and whose culture and knowledge of the hirelings for very low pay, all "In the name of G–d." A scholar, if he were hired, forfeited not only his copyright, but also the right for personal respect.

I was the only outsider who succeeded in entering the Swiss University during those days of hostility and estrangement; that is to say, to be properly nominated as a lecturer and obtain he right to teach. The reason was that the higher learning institutions were the last liberal outpost of Swiss liberalism and free democracy and I was cognizant and grateful to the teachers of the philosophical faculty in the University of Lucerne. Of course, I would also like to express my thanks to the few Jewish families who did receive the refugees with a refreshing and enlivened breath, in contrast to the frozen faces of the Jewish leaders. After being accepted as a lecturer, I published my letters and, with modest pride, I put after my name the letters P.D. which is the abbreviation of private docent, to at least note my regained sense of self–esteem. The heir to a local Jewish family conceitedly remarked: "P.D. means Poor Devil." In a sense it was true. The description fitted me. Because at that time, I had no account in a Swiss bank. It would have been satisfactory for me to have an account in any bank that did not have the sign "Jews Forbidden." The letters P.D. represented a personal value for me but had no meaning in the eyes of the community leader. To him a refugee was a "poor devil" and should be treated as such. Other values did not exist.

Indeed, they were aristocratic of long ago, those Jewish Helvetian citizens, a selected tribe from among the children of Israel who were at that time pursued and oppressed in the worst manner in Europe. They considered themselves the beloved of the Master of Universe, and a few of them even thought that not only the few thousand Swabs and Poles whom they rescued but rather all of Switzerland, owed them gratitude for their piety and, because of their merits, the land was miraculously saved from war and devastation and that G–d bestows favors to his chosen while they sleep, and when they were awakened from the noise of the tumbling of the "Thousand Year Reich," they realized that their esteem had grown in leaps and bounds without moving a finger, and their wealth had multiplied was it not a sign from G–d who rules from above that he loves them?

There was a slight difference in relations of the Luxemburgian Jewry towards the refugees. They too considered themselves G–d's favored sons. There were about a thousand of them who lived there since the time of Napoleon.

[Page 220]

The war did not stop at their gates, and everybody who felt threatened was forced to flee. More so, the number of Jews increased because Luxemburg had a more humane policy towards strangers and permitted a few thousand Jews from Austria and Germany to enter and wait for United States immigration visas. The number of Jewish refugees was larger than that of the local Jews who had begun as cattle merchants and ultimately established well–based businesses, and saw themselves as outstanding aristocrats in every venue on relations to the recent arrivals who did not speak their language. The sudden influx should have been foreseen by the great rulers of the world, the sober politicians, from Daladier, Stalin, and Chamberlain. Everything happened suddenly, and they did not make it possible for the Jews to leave on time and reach safe shores. The Jews were forced by the occupying authorities to leave immediately and to wander off wherever the wind might carry them, so that the authorities could notify Berlin that Luxemburg had become "the first country in Europe without Jews."

According to the known pitiful policy that ruled in those days, the United States and other democracies had very little interest from a humane point of view to help the pursued Jews, and therefore, they did not reach generous decisions. For the Jews who were born in Luxemburg it was easier to receive immigration visas. In contrast, the refugees for whom Luxemburg was the first stop were compelled to conduct time–consuming negotiations in the American consulate Office until they were unable to emigrate and ended up being deported by the Germans.

After the war, the Luxemburgian Jews, the so–called new Americans, returned to their homes and to their properties and, during the post–war prosperity, they became wealthy. To be saved because they were citizens of Luxemburg seemed to them a special miracle from Heaven. They thought that G–d worried about their well–being, and their reaction to this miracle was not expressed by praising G–d and by pious thankfulness, but by conceit. They considered themselves a beloved, singled–out community of a thousand people. They considered themselves wrongfully, proud Luxemburgians, declaring: "We will remain what we are," a slogan with which the country successfully defended itself for centuries against their imperialistic neighbors. The words of that slogan echoed from the mouths of the returning Jews like a declaration of superiority. The Rabbis and teachers who were in their service but were not natives, had to accustom themselves to that atmosphere and lifestyle, if not they were chastised and chased out.

There were among the strangers some who persistently tried to accustom themselves and to agree with the heroic thousand Jews from that great principality, with their world outlook, living standard, and their relation to the Torah of Moses. These people refused to accept any burden of outside culture. They too remained what they were, and had no need even for Moses or for the true and just Prophets. However, there were a few genuinely pious Jews. One was a great princess whose husband descended from the ruling family of Austria, and she was benevolently inclined towards the ex–citizens of the Kaiser and his empire.

Until I attained this experience and this information, my boat was turning around periodically.

[Page 221]

It turned on the waters of the Rhine, Limat, Moselle, Hudson, and Jordan, often sailed against the current, against the wind, but it did not display its flag accordingly. The boat was in danger of being capsized and broken up. She sighed, she groaned in her conversation with the mighty steamboats which proudly and reposed sailed against the currents, but she always changed her curse anew and stubbornly continued in her special path against the winds and the waves. Now the boat is again turning on the Danube, without deviation from all the revolutions that have taken place on its banks, and she makes her way, telling herself tales.

* * *

Now back to my parents. My father, Chaim, and my mother, Bluma, built themselves in Stuttgart the foundation of a modest existence, but in their hearts they remained "at home" in Galicia, which was filled with the contents of Jewish life that developed unchanged for hundreds of years. There the contents of life were religion, and the purpose of life was fulfillment of the commandments of the Torah. Life's happiness was expressed by celebrating the religious holidays with all their folkloric supplements. The livelihood in the eastern countries remained poor and insecure, and they lived from Sabbath to Sabbath. The paupers could afford a decent meal only with the help of the wealthy. Every house or shed had to have meat and fish for the Sabbath. Otherwise it was considered a desecration of the holy day, a crime for which the haves would be held responsible. Therefore, there prevailed a particular alertness on Friday mornings, and charity was given to all the needy. No humiliation or disrespect was involved by receiving or giving charity. Because without the poor there would not be a chance to fulfill the command "contribution of a tenth to the poor," which ought to be fulfilled in the religious circles. This is a commandment written in the Torah, and which was established by our Father Jacob long before the giving of the Torah. When Jacob was forced to escape the wrath of his brother Esau, after h had fraudulently deprived him of his first born rights, and Isaac's blessing, he made a vow that after his rescue from danger, "And of all that thou will give me I will surely give the tenth unto thee." Therefore, giving to the needy was a duty to fulfill, a commandment from the torah, and was liable to bring shame to the whole community if someone had difficulties enjoying the Sabbath even in the most humble way. In contrast, the government was seen as an abstract monster. Paying taxes t the state was not done as conscientiously as was the giving of charity. The Jews often visualized the government as a dragon with many arms against which you must defend yourself by all means. It was not considered wrongdoing if one act with cunning against the government that kept changing her laws intermittently. However, the precept of charity, the ancient human law, had to be fully implemented, and could not be violated. And in the Jewish world of Eastern Europe, any deviation from that precept was seen as an attack on the law of nature.

Charity was not always given generously, and neither did people always come forward to help willingly. But still, charity was a natural function like walking and breathing.

[Page 222]

The life of the poor segment of the population was very hard, and their livelihood came only from dealing with each other. Only a few were able to dig themselves out from collective poverty. Through commerce and brokerage they won a respectful place in those Easter European countries where these were the only business open to them. Through persistence, these people achieved a certain position of affluence.

My grandfather, Moshe Krantzler, the father of Bluma, my mother, belonged to that stratum. He was a land broker, and he built himself a homestead in which he had a cowshed with several milking cows. The money he saved he made work for him. He lent it to the poor peasants to be repaid after the harvest. His daughters, Sheindl, Bluma and Yente, helped him in the business. What else could they have done until marriage when studying Torah was not required? But the sons, Chaim and Yerachmiel were required to study Talmud and the scriptures to their hearts desire, and to become scholars, and G–d fearing sons, and to be the hoped–for glory of the parents' lives. Not only that, but studying was looked upon as an investment of the family's wealth. Indeed, they would also become desirable grooms for affluent families. Moshe Krantzler was a pious man and an ignoramus. Therefore, he prided himself in his sons the scholars. But, from his successful practical life as a merchant, he also recognized that worldly knowledge was no less important and, therefore, he desired that his sons should also know how to write from left to right and mathematics. The sons used to boast about their calligraphic handwriting which was in style during that period. The youngest daughter, Yente, stealthily learned from her brothers the art of writing and, with the agility; she overtook all of them, even though this knowledge was of no use to a girl. All three of them had a calligraphic handwriting and one could not distinguish between the boys' and the girls' handwriting. Only later did the oldest son adapt a few American letters when through his knowledge of reading and writing, a big wide world came to his attention. He saved money for the passage and went to the new world, and to symbolize his new life he changed his name to "Henry." To his parents, he became some kind of a lost son who shaved like an atheist. To his brothers and sisters, he became a hidden ideal of courage and independence. And for Yerachmiel, his brother, who was pampered and well–guarded in the learning institutions as the only son. Henry became a patron, who ultimately saved his life when he created the possibility to bring him over with his big family to America, at a time when his sisters waited in vain for a helping hand to be rescued from the Nazi flood. And so it happened that while the European Jewry was exterminated a new branch of the Krantzler tribe blossomed across the ocean as in the ancient times through Joseph, the seventy people from the house of Jacob found refuge in the land of Goshen, and there they became a mighty nation.

However, the lost sons did not follow the path which had been paved by Joseph the dreamer, has caused great pain to their parents. Such parents often reach their end in darkness and gloom. The childish stubbornness and the paternal bitterness caused the cutting off of natural bonds. However, it very often happens that these lost sons turned later into saviors and supporters of their parents. How else could any spiritual progress have occurred without these lost sons who deviated from habits that had been sacred, and who had plowed a new furrow for themselves?

[Page 223]

And so, what had happened to Henry Krantzler with his discovery of America was not such a unique occurrence. In 1900, there were many like him who had abandoned the poverty of the Eastern European ghettos, the majority of whom sailed to the land of opportunity, America. Others wandered off to Belgium, France, England or, like Chaim and Bluma, my parents, to Germany.

The millions of Jews who lived between the Danube, Vistula and the Volga, led steady lives for hundreds of years without deviation, within invisible walls in which they locked themselves in. Reading and writing in the Latin alphabet awoke a persistent distrust within Hassidic circles because it was here where the dropout of many began. As soon as the children began to attend secular schools, immediately they missed many hours of religious school, the cheder. After finishing elementary schooling, some were sent to high schools and gymnasiums for another four to six years because, in the Austrian part of Poland, there were no restrictions against Jewish students. In the higher learning institutions, the Jewish children were required to attend on the Sabbath and holidays. They carried their satchels in the street and openly desecrated the Sabbath. They even wrote on Sabbath. In the Orthodox homes, these students were seen as blemished, and as future traitors, and the Orthodox Jews avoided any contact with them. They even avoided obligatory elementary schools whenever they could.

In contrast to the above, every ten–year–old Jewish boy knew how to write the mother language a German–Yiddish in the Hebrew letters, and was well–versed reading the Bible. At the age of three, his hair was shorn, except, of course, the sidelocks which could not be touched, and he began to learn how to read. At five, the boy learned to translate into Yiddish the chapter of the week, and the more capable were taught the Rashi commentary. At six, the boys began to learn the civil law in the Talmud and, a few years later, the marriage relationship according to the Talmud. All that was necessary to learn about life, were learned from the Talmud. Weren't all the problems discussed in the Talmud? Before they were to see things by themselves, they saw everything from the perspective of the Mishna and Gemara. These provided the outlook on all of life's problems for the Eastern European Jews. Since the philosopher, Immanuel Kant, the time and place are the forms of outlooks according to which the spirit of man grasps things, and puts them in certain order. The spirit of the East–European Jew observed the world from the perspective of the time and place when the Mishna and the Gemara were created.

In their world outlook, my parents, Chaim and Bluma, even though they emigrated to Stuttgart, nonetheless, their world outlook remained linked to their parents' home in Strzyzow – to the father's knowledge of Talmud, the mothers firm, unbreakable piety, which constantly demanded sacrifices in every step she took, denying herself pleasure all her life. She became stronger in her belief and did not leave room for any compromise. The question was, would the children who were born in a different environment withstand all the provocations of the secular world around them? Would they also remain solid believing Jews?

[Page 224]

Chaim and Bluma decided to leave their two older sons for a few years at the grandparents' house in Strzyzow. They wanted them to absorb the Jewish atmosphere before they started their secular schooling. Therefore, Bluma went to Strzyzow to give birth to her older son Isaac and this was very satisfactory to Grandpa Moshe and Grandma Molly Krantzler, because at that time, their house began to empty of children, and now the house began to fill up again. A short time later, two more sons appeared – Chanan and Naphtali. Bluma was most appreciated for being so active, awarding three sons in a row. Isaac and Naphtali resembled their mother, blond as flax, and with bluish eyes. The middle one resembled his father. He was black–haired, and his eyes were a mixture of bright brown and green. Elchanan came into this world full–haired, to the great joy of his aunts, mainly aunt Yente, who linked that trait to his Hebrew name "Elchanan" which means a godly gift, and was a good omen for a life of happiness according to her outlook.

Now that the desire to have male heirs was abundantly fulfilled, the birth of a daughter was expected. A short while later a baby girl was born, Roselain, who became the center of attention. She had black hair as h r father desired, and he became instantly attached to her, because the three sons resembled the Krantzler family. Roselain was born in Stuttgart because traveling to Strzyzow for each birth was not easy anymore. And concerning the sons' upbringing, a compromise was reached. The older son Isaac and the second son Chanan would remain in Strzyzow until their Bar Mitzvas, and the other children, starting from Naphtali be raised at mom and dad's house in Stuttgart.

This division which was made with the best educational intentions, and out of thoughtful religious responsibility, more likely caused the estrangement between the two older sons and their parents, and also between the rest of the brothers and sisters, an estrangement which was never remedied. Therefore, when the house in Stuttgart was humming with children, Isaac and Chanan remained outsiders, almost strangers, and their relationship with their parents was strained and tense. In this family as in other families, there existed different layers of assimilation into the German way of life and German habits of thought. The road from the Danube to the Rhine River passes through hundreds of years of Jewish and European history. The road continues from the Middle Ages, with the force of firm belief, but with merciless surrender and the adaptation of the individual to a closed world outlook and until the twentieth century, with its explosive force, which cannot be described, neither favorably or unfavorably.

Isaac and Chanan had filled a vacuum that was created by Bluma, who was merry and full of life when she had left the Krantzler house.

Grandpa Moses looked upon the two tots as the interest on is capital which he lent to my father Chaim. My grandfather, the forceful man who was easily provoked to anger, and was not easy to negotiate with, was stern toward his wife and children, but when he saw his grandchildren, he became radiant and bright. Nevertheless, a certain reservation existed in their relationship toward grandfather whom they called "Zaide."

[Page 225]

They often witnessed his outbursts and became frightened when they saw the man who always related to them with extra love, so forceful towards others. The children also noticed his generosity when giving charity and donations to religious institutions within the community. They did not realize then that the inclination to become angry was already implanted in their hearts and bodies. These senseless, furious outbursts were liable to destroy in one second all the human love which had accumulated during the whole day. From where was such a destructive forcefulness derived? It surely was not derived from being educated in the Holy Scripture which peach love for our fellow man and upon which social life in a small Jewish town was based.

The smallest child in a family is always the most pampered. Chanan the toddler soon realized this and took it to heart. Isaac was two years older than he. Now everyone was busy with little Chanan. In this house he remained the little one for many years. He was the master over the grandparents, uncle Yerachmiel, and aunt Yente. Later, in his parents' house, everything suddenly changed. There were other reasons for the pampering: His delicate looks which resembled the face of a girl and also his being a sickly child. Such a sickly condition would not have been improved with mere old fashioned feeding. If not for beloved grandmother Molly, who did not know tiredness and for whom no sacrifice was too big, Chanan would have died at a young age. I remember since I was two years old, that every time my grandmother became frightened for any reason at all, she wrapped him in a woolen shawl and ran to Doctor Taub, while the child in protest kicked and bounced the body of that weak woman.

This Doctor Taub was not a member of the religious committee in town. He was dressed like a "German," his beard was trimmed and well groomed, not according to the religious etiquette. Also, even though it is not forbidden for a doctor to ride in a carriage to visit the sick on the Sabbath, his calls were not always life–threatening. Therefore, the shadow of a sinner hovered over him, as it hovered over all those elite circles that sent their children to school on the Sabbath instead to shul. And who knew what other forbidden acts they committed from which a pious man shrinks? However, as a doctor, Doctor Taub earned a certain respect in the while community, despite his dubious piety. Eastern European Jewry respected first of all Talmudic scholars. However, they did not deprive reverence to practical people who possessed worldly knowledge.

Little Chanan often visited Doctor Taub, and later he visited other doctors in the area. He even reached Krakow. Apparently, the tendencies of doctors have not changed. They diagnosed him as having an inclination to infirmness, without finding a cure for it. This alone as enough reason for those who were near the child to worry and to take extra care about him. Chanan exploited the situation to his advantage and knew how to benefit from it. He behaved with despotism and without mercy toward the family members who were apprehensive about his sickness and always noticed a change in his face when they treated him gently, and felt happy about it. The child's illness used to disappear overnight.

[Page 226]

The child had a special love affair with his grandmother and, under her protection, he felt infinitely secure and deep down inside, he felt that, because of his childish existence, he could do anything he wanted and would be forgiven. He thought that his impolite cunning was like by his grandmother and other adults. What had seemed strange to Chanan about his grandmother was her wrinkled face which was not as smooth as the faces of the mothers of his playmates. Chanan once asked her meticulously about the difference. The fact that his "mother's" face was also smooth had no meaning for him because she was far away, somewhere in Germany and she only came to visit from time to time. Each time she came, she brought another child with her. Once she brought a blond child with blue eyes whose name was Naphtali. Another time she came with a lovely girl whose eyes expressed amazement at the odd people that she encountered in that small Galician town and at the fact that two brothers who were born here belong to her family. These glorious eyes that belonged to the girl, combed and dressed with much splendor, were willed with confusion and contempt, and always avoided people's eyes.

In time, the children became used to each other and played together, but not without friction. It was harder for the children to relate to the two strange adults who were introduced as mom and dad, although they did look a bit like people from Strzyzow. This father with the black beard looked like somebody from a strange land. We related to him as someone who invaded our domain. Seldom and with hesitation did Isaac and Chanan enter into the back room whose windows faced the fields, and was used by our parents during their visits. Once Isaac left their room and inadvertently slammed the door and provoked father to chase after him into is secret hiding place to demonstrate his fatherly authority. That act proved to the child that indeed that man had invaded the domain which was not his. For many weeks, actually years even, mother could not create the family bond with these two natives of Strzyzow.

Only once before mother's leaving was I struck with a sudden sadness. I snuck off alone into my room and hid my face in the pillow. Mother was forced to leave the carriage, and she came into that room where she awarded me with a long blazing kiss on my forehead, and put a five gulden coin in my hand and disappeared. For a long time afterwards, I felt her blazing kiss, and I was emotional and exited in a most strange way. I wondered about the wonderful feeling which I could not explain to myself. Only after many years, after I grew up and matured the same wonderment returned to me, the same incessant spring of worry and devotion of the parents. By then it was too late. The children became letters, the parent became foster children. If only people would continue to talk to each other, not about others, but about themselves, in order to get closer and to understand each other. Such mutual conversation is not silver but gold, and silence is not even silver but a brooding station for estrangement, for keeping away, for creating mutual animosity and all the ills that occur upon the earth.

Once the whole family arrived from Stuttgart to Strzyzow for a longer stay. Apparently, the log separation from some of the children became unbearable to my parents. And possibly there may have been other problems, like the fight for existence which became harder because of the uncompromising observance of religious traditions.

[Page 227]

My father rented a small store in the marketplace, and the adjacent small apartment might have been sufficient if the two of us would have remained with our grandparents. We still went often to visit them, but only upon their request. When I encountered my father in the street, we looked at each other with great interest, but we did not know what to say to each other. Without uttering a word from our mouths, we passed each other and continued on our way. I have been him sometimes sitting on the steps of his store, waiting for customers, mostly in vain. This showmanship of waiting for customers was not befitting such an energetic and active man. He probably surrendered to his wife's request and tried to return and adjust himself to the Galician household.

Customers seldom came and the ones that came, bought very little. In contrast, a customer appeared one day of whom everyone was afraid. This was Jasiek the "thief in broad daylight." He used to appear every once in a while in this or that store, and he was given whatever he demanded so that he would leave peacefully. Most of the time he was drunk and he waved and played with his knife, so that many closed their shops when they saw him nearby. There was no possible escape from him because the only local policeman always appeared afterwards, making compromises with Jasiek just as everybody else who did not want to bump into him. Alas, he continued the robbing activity with despotism to the distress of the Jewish shopkeepers.

And it happened that he came into the small, modest, new store and demanded money or merchandise from my surprised father. He was accustomed to receive the handouts without explanation from the softhearted Jews who were afraid of his knife. This time Jasiek's time had come to leave with a great surprise, because my father, without hesitation, slapped his face, pushed the astonished man out into the street in not a very gentle way, and locked the door from the inside. The residents of the town assembled in groups and all the neighbors stared and looked in bewilderment at how the terrible Jasiek was thrown out by the quiet, tranquil Jew, who never bothered a fly on the wall, and how the culprit's nose was bleeding. At the sight of the gathered crowd, this bogyman who until now had imposed fear on everyone, decided that it was time to depart. However, he did not depart without an avalanche of dreadful curses in the best choice of words of the Polish language, and threats against my father. The story about this event was told all over town, and there was no mincing words to describe the daring of my father whose life was now in danger. However, none was ready to bet even the smallest sum that, in the future Jasiek would come out ahead. Afterward fear dominated my mother's whole body, fearing for her husband's life. Therefore, she was searching for a way how to avoid a tragedy. Shortly, when Jasiek appeared again, she simply approached him with a question, would he like to have a drink of vodka? She invited him to her apartment near the store, poured several drinks for him and filled his pockets with cakes and cookies. Jasiek could not figure out what was happening to him, and he never showed his face in this area again.

[Page 228]

After this incident my father's stature went up tremendously in the eyes of those who constantly feared that scoundrel. The appearance of my mother, that tiny woman, often saved my father's life from all kinds of characters of Jasiek's type. The business was bad. The only good thing that my father derived from that situation was that he had spare time to devote to studying the Talmud, to which he dedicated a lot of time anyway. The daily income was barely enough for the daily needs. However, the Sabbath was always celebrated festively with fish and meat, plaited challa, deserts and hot cholent. That festive meal lasted a long time, and it included heart rendering songs, in Hebrew and Aramaic, songs in which we thanked G–d for favors he awarded us, body and soul. And, if a poor wanderer appeared in the synagogue as a guest, he was called to the Torah, and then, he was invited home for the Sabbath meal. Sometimes the guest introduced a new tune to an old song. This was so rewarding that it seemed that complete happiness reigned in our house. However, the peak of satisfaction was seen during the Sabbath morning services in the kloiz of the Rabbi from Sassov. The official Rabbi worshipped in Beit Hamidrash. However, the center of study of the aristocratic Jews who stood out with their Hassidic way of life was in kloiz. There they gathered around their Rabbi, an offspring of the Shapiro Dynasty, a delicate man adorned with a white beard and sparkling eyes which expressed love and possessed a warm, enticing voice. The Rabbi often chanted the Sabbath morning prayers. He did not chant with a voice trained according to musical rules. However, his strong voice and the expression of his soul were thrilling, heart rendering and musical by themselves, according to all the principles of traditional form, so that the worshipers, whether they were veterans who knew his chanting, or newcomers, they all were deeply impressed in an extraordinary way by his variations which burst out of his throat and ascended into the heavens. His chanting and his charming personality inspired spiritual life in the Orthodoxy who were around him and increased the number of his followers to the great dissatisfaction of the official elected Rabbi, despite the charm, piety, and scholarly skill that the latter possessed.

The appreciation of the two spiritual leaders in Strzyzow, Rabbi Alter Zev Horowitz and Rabbi Moshe Leib Shapiro, found its expression in the "Mishloach Manot" that were dispatched to them on Purim on silver or glass platters. My brother Isaac and I noticed the difference because we were the messengers of our grandfather. (Aside from this, we also served discreetly as the messengers of the grandmother, who set all kinds of food articles to old women to whom we could not disclose the name of the sender. Their pleasant surprise caused gladness to my soul so that right there I decided to do it again in the future.) On Rabbi Shapiro's plate, a sparkling five gulden coin shone from amidst the sweets, the equivalent of ten crowns, a nice gift considering how little my grandfather's daily expenses were, approximately a penny a day. In contrast, the appreciation of Rabbi Horowitz was expressed with a three gulden coin, just because he was the official Rabbi, and for the sake of peace. In distinction, he had heartfelt bonds with the Hassidic circle of Rabbi Shapiro.

[Page 229]

I too was satisfied with such evaluation of the Rabbis because the black–bearded Rabbi of short stature was the Rabbi to whom we owed official allegiance, but was less admired that the Rabbi with the snow–white beard who was full of life ad youthful feelings, and whose piety was not so gloomy but cheerful and filled with love toward people. He also loved children. Therefore, we, the two Hassidic students, sneaked into his house when our father was invited together with a few other guests after services, and while the Rabbi's wife treated the guests with honey cake and preserves, we suddenly appeared to our father's embarrassment, who felt guilty because of the Talmudic saying, "One guest does not invite another guest." Nevertheless, we felt safe from father's slight anger because of the look and wink of the eyes of this holy and cheerful man who was our stronghold and shelter.

My father often visited the Rabbi's house on Friday nights after the Sabbath meal to mingle with the Hassidim, listen to the Rabbi's torah discourses, and to enjoy the pleasure of the Sabbath by singing songs. My big brother Isaac, who was about seven or eight–year–old, was the firstborn, and, according to the religious rule, he had certain responsibilities, and he was supposed to guide me when I, at grandmother's urging, went to visit my mother and my little brothers and sisters. After I overcame my first apprehension, I developed a good relationship with them, especially with Naphtali, with whom I walked around the room while he sat in a walking chair on wheels. Suddenly, he stood up on his two little feet in the chair and burst out with a joyful laughter for his just–finished journey around the room. I derived great satisfaction from my usefulness in my parents' house, and I wanted to add joy and to entertain my little brother even more. And, as I began my sudden galloping and sudden stopping, I also wanted to surprise little Naphtali with these sudden intermittent movements. The physical law of perseverance was unknown to me then, so I began to gallop with the wheeled chair on which the tot was standing, hoping to hear gladdening laughter. Instead he fell, hurt his forehead on the cement floor, and began spasmodically to cry, which brought my mother running to the scene, terribly frightened. I stood stunned and frightened, thinking that I killed my brother, and I did not know how to escape from that shameful situation, even though it later appeared that it was nothing serious. Then, my mother inadvertently gave me such a furious look, even though she surely did not suspect that I did it intentionally. This fact, together with the lovingness with which she kissed her little one, convince me that in this house, I was a stranger and will remain so in the future.

Embarrassed for such little understanding of the law of physics and life, I was saddened from the loss of affection, and sneaked away from there and ran "home" to grandmother. Without uttering a word, I went to bed. I felt that I had left with my parents a reason for unfavorable judgment of noble mind, just because I was helpless and confused at a time when I was completely innocent. I also felt that there was no chance for me to be accepted by them unconditionally, and that they would not understand my moods the same way my uncle Yerachmiel and aunt Yente understood them in my grandparents' house.

[Page 230]

Therefore, I solemnly decided to remain forever in Strzyzow and to keep a certain distance in relationship with my parents and brothers and sisters.

As a result, I felt no obligation to share anything with Naphtali, who spoke German, the way I shared with Isaac. It was an expression of some inner resistance more or less. One day I had to go on an errand to the suburb of the town. I was accompanied by my little brother Naphtali and, as a reward; I received a great juicy pear. With such a mouthwatering item in my pocket, I began my journey. All kinds of thoughts kept popping up in my mind, how to devour the pear without sharing it with my brother. Although his company leased and entertained me, a pear is a pear. In addition, he was a brother who spoke a different language which meant that he was not such a close relative, contrary to reality. I debated with myself, whether a definite enjoyment of eating the whole pear is better than the doubtful enjoyment of eating only half of it. I kept wondering, "How could I turn my head sideways for every bite of the pear, and how could I take it out and return it to my pocket without being detected?" But before I made my decision, I knew it would not work and I would not be able to escape sharing the pear. "What should I do?" I thought to myself. The saliva filled the cavity of my mouth and demanded to be used in the most proper and useful way. And then, the most rational idea came to my mind. "You know, Naphtali," I said, "Until now we walked side by side for a long time. It was boring. Now, let us walk one behind the other. Something different. We will still be able to converse with each other. And, since I am a little taller than you, I could look forward over your head. Therefore, it is better for you to walk first, and I will follow you. But you should not look back because you are liable to trip and fall. Keep looking forward."

It was not easy to convince Naphtali, but he had no logical reason to refuse my suggestion and he surrendered. We walked, one behind the other and, slowly I ate the fruit. I was careful not to smack my lips. At least, I believed that I was successful not to make any sound. I managed somehow to keep in line walking in a goose step or, maybe, he had his own reasons for doing so, until I made a good–hearted gesture and said to him that from now on we could walk the rest of the way side by side as before.

However, he fiercely refused: "No Chanan, now I want to walk behind you and you should walk ahead of me." A menacing suspicion came to my mind. I became angry at such deceitfulness, and I tried to sway him away from it. But he insisted on changing positions. As far as I was concerned, I had no logical reason to oppose. The fact that I was a head taller than he did not bother him and he just demanded equal rights. This convincing, logical consciousness of just and unjust is our strength and our weakness all our lives. I marched forward and, in my imagination, it seemed to me that I heard the sound of biting into an apple. I had the urge to turn around and to expose his deceit. But he fiercely protested when he saw my slightest movement, insisting on the strict execution of my own cunning maneuver. Resigned, sad and silent, I continued on my way, while Naphtali smacked his lips behind me.

[Page 231]

The pear which was eaten a while ago and was resting in my tummy brought up a bitter aftertaste in light of my fantasizing about the taste of an apple in the present. I felt trapped in my own web, cheated, and, in addition, I did not feel like a straight forward, innocent person. I felt conquered with my own weapon, despite of the higher value of the fruit that I consumed. Somewhere in my heart, I recalled a verse which I apathetically memorized in cheder, that G–d pays the wicked according to his wickedness and traps him in the same trap that he set up for others. My real feelings at that time was, it seemed to me, filled with rage which was directed toward my little, deceitful brother. However, I restrained myself after I thought about the egotism and lack of integrity in my own person. I began to grasp all these traits in my character. What I have memorized and learned in the damp moldy cheder, about the righteous and the wicked which is connected to personal experiences and rises and appears from far distances, even though, much time passes until we comprehend that the practical implementation of principle is in itself an exalted function which a person can hardly manage to execute during his lifetime. To mature means to arrive to that fitting position of correlating the theory with deeds. If we do not reach maturity, barbarism rules, despite of the accumulated knowledge of piles and piles of books.

In light of the above, it is possible to have an explanation for what happened in the land where art was cherished so much, where science developed immensely, in the land which spreads between the Danube and Rhine, where my lifeboat was supposed to have turned around? What is unimaginable is not the fact that the military was trained and specialized to murder women, children, and elderly people. This thing could have been done in any other place after systematic preparation and certain influence. In these conditions murder units could have been established everywhere. What was missing was the brakes against degeneration of the political rulers, the opposition of the men of spirit and all those guardians of science who apparently lacked maturity, and did not make the connection between theory and practice, between knowledge and action.

The value of science exist only when it creates morality. Otherwise it is only a heap of information which could be used for any dangerous purpose. Educational institutions in many countries lack this logical point, possibly because of the disease inherited from the Greeks which the clever idolaters smuggled into the western evangelical countries in a superficial form. A child who grew up in the bosom of Judaism is required, when he intermingles with the western world which is called with a Christian name, to know the gentile contrast, the deep contrast, not only from the aspect of the different superficial science and methods of learning, but also about the basic goal in the face of qualitative life. The sailing on the Danube through Central Europe ought to be, for a conscientious Jewish child, a considerably difficult role which could not be described by the commonly used word, "assimilation." It was a compromise between two worlds which came into existence not by philosophical articles but by groping and searching for the values of life of the Jewish youth who were often helpless.

[Page 232]

The individual activity and the penetrated opposing values and opposed world outlooks concerning basic matters already existed as a result of Jewish children attending secular elementary schools. That is how the silent compromise started in the Austrian area where Polish was spoken, and it continued into Swabian surroundings, where the source of Danube, the majestic river is, which streams undisturbed between blue banks, through various countries uninfluenced by any political changes, singing its eternal song.

[Page 233]

The Holocaust and the Aftermath

The Second World War and the Holocaust
by Itzhok Berglass

Friday, September the first, 1939, was the day that the Second World War broke out. Tension had been felt already in the last days of August, but the tidings that the war had begun came with the German bombings in our vicinity. In the first days, stillness prevailed in the town in the absence of reliable news about the situation. Indeed, the railroad schedule was in disarray as a result of sabotage and bombings by the German enemy. Nevertheless, people, including the Jews, believed in the fighting ability of the Polish army. Everybody was certain in the truthfulness of the government's promises expressed in the appeal for war bonds that we were "Strong, United, and Ready." We also were sure that the military would defend with all their might the defense industry district, located in our area, a triangle bordering the San and Visloka Rivers. On Monday, September the fourth, and the night that followed we still saw a military movement towards the Slovakian border to the south but, at the same time, the first caravans with refugees began to appear in Strzyzow. They came from places near the German border. On Wednesday the stream of refugees increased and grew even bigger on Thursday. On Thursday night, and on Friday, September the eight, Strzyzow joined the main stream of refugees. It was like a river which on its way to the sea, absorbs all the waters of smaller creeks and continues to flow with the main stream. But, in spite of the wave of refugees which included many Poles, government clerks, and policemen, (they all returned after Poland's surrender) the number of Jews was small. During the First World War, the Russians occupied Strzyzow twice. After the Jews suffered during the first occupation because of a casualty in the Mandel family, many families evacuated the town when the Russian came for the second time. The retreat of the Austrian army was slow and orderly, transportation means such as trains and carriages were put at the disposal of the refugees. This time, the Poles retreated in disarray; the trains were out of order because of the bombings by the Germans and sabotage by their agents. To hire a carriage was impossible.

Resides, the majority of the town's Jews, including the Galician Jews, in general, did not think of running. Many of those who ran in the First World War were still alive and did not try now to do it again. Neither did the rich and well-to-do who, for much money, could still have obtained transportation. Only the older people remembered the Germans from the First World War when they were "allies" of the Austrians.

Nobody in Strzyzow read the book "Mein Kampf," and the hearsay about the mistreatment of the Jews in Germany, Austria, Chechoslovakia, did not sufficiently disturb the Jews from Galician cities. Although a few of the German Jewish refugees who settled in Strzyzow had warned against the Germans of today, they themselves remained.

[Page 234]

The Jews were ready to suffer from the Nazis but they were not willing to live the life of wanderers, especially after they had seen the suffering of the women and children refugees who passed Strzyzow. Such Satanic thoughts that the Nazis would annihilate men, women and children were incomprehensible. The rumors were that they were sending young people to forced labor camps. Because of all the above mentioned reasons, only a few families and single men left on foot. Among those who left were the Rabbi, Kehillah leaders, community activists, several young men, and a few wealthy people who feared being taken hostage.

The path of the refugees from Strzyzow led through Dynow, a crossroads city. Thousands of refugees, families who ran out of means to continue their escape, many who were on foot and run out of energy to go any further, and well-known personalities who had not intended to go any further to begin with, were stuck there. (All they wanted was to leave town and be somewhere that nobody knew them.)

Some people who passed Dynow were stuck in Dubiecko. One of the group from Strzyzow, Reb Yechezkiel Ziebner, was killed in that town on his way from the morning services. He was carrying the bag containing his talit and tefilin, a Nazi noticed him, and shot him.

My brother-in-law, Reb Yacov Itzhok Bernstein, remained in Dynow with his three children. He refused to continue because of the Sabbath. After the German victory and the Soviet invasion into the eastern part of Poland, everybody returned to their homes. Again, caravans of refugees, though smaller, were seen moving in the opposite direction. A small number of returnees recoiled, hearing about the atrocities of the Nazis, and decided to wait for the Soviet army which, according to the Soviet-German agreement, were supposed to reach the San River. But the majority came home. Reb David Lieberman who left Strzyzow with his whole family, did not flinch from the maltreatment of the Hitlerists he had experienced, but returned home. On their way home, they prayed with a group of refugees on Yom Kippur. The Germans assaulted them and, wrapped in their taleitim, they were taken into a grove, lined up with their backs to the soldiers, and the soldiers began shooting in the air. Despite such an ordeal, he and his family came home, and he was among the first to be killed, as it will be told further on.

The systematic killing period had not yet begun. But Jewish blood was spilled freely as soon as Hitler's soldiers arrived. In our vicinity, many killings occurred. Six hundred in Przemysl, including Reb Moshe Deutch from Strzyzow. In Dynow – two hundred and thirty people, mostly refugees who were passing through town. The Nazis went from house to house, taking men only. In sendziszow, on Rosh Hashana, the Nazis selected fifty men from among the worshippers in shul and killed them. Five men were brought from Frysztak and killed in Strzyzow. Women and children – they did not touch yet. Those who were returning from the evacuation were in continuous danger. In addition to the Germans, Ukrainian bands attacked the caravans of the refugees, especially those who traveled alone. There were even incidents in which these people found shelter with the Germans while escaping from the Ukrainians. The most dangerous area was near Lesko. There the Ukrainians killed a group of refugees who were returning home.

[Page 235]

Among those killed was a son or Reb Ephraim Kneller. Only a few survived that massacre, finding refuge in a German field-kitchen unit. Tzvi Baumel was killed on his way home. He worked in Krakow before the outbreak of the war. When the Germans were approaching the city, he decided to go home to his father, Reb Benjamin, in Strzyzow. Passing through the town Preclaw, near Mielec, he went into the local Belt Hamidrash with a group of Jews. Soon the Nazis began knocking on the door, when he went to open it, they shot him and he was instantly killed.

The concentration of the refugees in Eastern Galicia was bigger than in other places because the Germans expelled all the Jews from the border towns to the Russian side. However, Strzyzow was forty miles away and had no such luck. The refugees from Strzyzow who were on the Russian side were joined by a few Jewish soldiers who remained in the east when the Polish army fell apart. Most people from Strzyzow were concentrated in Lwow. Help was extended to them by the Schiff family, the Jewelers from Rzezow, and Reb Shalom Wllach, who owned a big liquor store before the Soviets requisitioned it. Their meeting place was in the house of Reb Fishel Goldberg. He was also a refugee from Strzyzow who arrived in Lwow with his entire family, and had a spacious apartment· In his house, the refugees who were lonesome, were warmly received. Especially warm was his wife, Feiga, who was the only mother among the refugees from Strzyzow. In Strzyzow she also used to help poor Jewish wanderers who came to Strzyzow by horse and buggy. She took them into her barn yard and the horses into her stable.

During the nine months that the refugees stayed in Lwow and its vicinity, until their expulsion to Siberia, many of those who were separated from their families returned home illegally. The reports which came from Strzyzow were not bad. Everyone who left his family there was homesick, and it was also difficult to get accustomed to the Soviet way of life. Those who did not return still yearned to do so, but they wanted to do it legally. Most of them were saved by being exiled to where the Nazis could not reach them.

All the returnees to Strzyzow crossed the border safely and arrived home, except one disastrous, shocking incident involving a young woman, the daughter of Reb Elazar Loos. She lived in Dynow and was expelled to the Russian side with the rest of the Jews soon after the massacre. While returning from a visit to her parents in Strzyzow, she was shot by a border guard as a result of a Polish informer. It was not clear whether it was a Russian or a German border guard.

The refugees from Strzyzow attempted to cross the border legally, with a permit from the German-Russian Population Exchange Committee, which was located in Przemysl. Luckily, they did not succeed. Many Jews did cross to the German side with a permit by hiding their Jewishness. Those unfortunate ones were happy to receive a permit and did not know that they were going to a sure death.

The Exchange Committee was transferred later to Lwow, and there they resumed issuing permits to Poles and individual Jews whose families at home provided a confirmation from the German authorities that their return would be useful for the economy.

[Page 236]

Tens of thousands of refugees in Lwow and Eastern Galicia who expressed their wish to return home on the German side, waited patiently, and were sure that the aforementioned Exchange Committee came to Lwow to arrange their repatriation. These refugees wanted their return to take place in an orderly manner. Therefore, they voluntarily organized themselves into groups with a central leadership. They invested much effort in this organization, but luckily, no repatriation took place.

At the beginning of June 1940, all single refugees who registered to return home, were arrested and sent into forced labor camps throughout Russia. At the end of June, all refugee families were put in freight trains and sent off to Siberia, and to the northern provinces of Russia. From among the Strzyzow families, only my family and I were exiled. The Goldbergs and Dr. Frenkel obtained Soviet passports. Also Dr. Chwal, the only Jewish doctor in Strzyzow, who at first escaped alone and later brought his family over during a population exchange, remained in Lwow, and probably perished later with the local Jews. A few single people including the Rabbi of Strzyzow, Reb Kalonymus, escaped and obtained passports. All these people remained in Lwow and its vicinity.

When the Germans attacked Russia in June 1941, and occupied Lwow, all the people from Strzyzow returned home and shared the lot of the rest of the town's Jewry. From the Goldbergs, only two sons survived. The younger son, Elazar, joined the Soviet army. The second son, who studied medicine in Italy when the war broke out, joined the Italian anti-Nazi underground.

Dr. Frenkel, the lawyer, returned home from work one day and found his house empty. His wife and two daughters had been taken away to the place of no return. He survived as Dr. Wierzbicki, with Aryan documents, settled in Krakow and, after the war, served as lawyer for the people from Strzyzow who returned from Russia.

The refugees from Strzyzow who were exiled to Russia experienced all kinds of hardships, imprisonment, hard labor, starvation, sickness, and plagues. Some died and were buried there. These were: Rabbi Naphtali Chaim Halberstam; R. Alter Zev's son-in-law who at one time organized and headed the Agudat Israel in Strzyzow; Rabbi Alter Zev's grandson, Reb Menashe Horowitz, who starved in the labor camp abstaining from eating non kosher food, and on Passover living on the sugar rations only; Reb Gershon Holles, the scholar, died in an epidemic outbreak in the South Asian part of Russia after he had been released as the result of the Stalin-Sikorski agreement. He held onto a gold watch which had been presented to him on the day of his engagement as was customary then in Galicia. Ultimately, the watch survived but not the owner; Reb Aaron Taub died after he was arrested for the second time for refusing to accept Soviet citizenship which the Soviet authorities forced upon the Polish citizens. He was afraid that he would not be able to return to his wife and children. He died from exhaustion serving in a labor brigade; Reb Mordechai Weitman died in Samarkand; One of Reb Alter Yacov Weichselbaum's daughters and her husband died from starvation in Dzambul. People from Strzyzow, who lived there could have saved them, but they found out about them too late; two sons of Reb Feivel Hauben died in a remote collective farm.

[Page 237]

An offspring of the Gertner family who was expelled from Germany and settled in Strzyzow, evacuated from Strzyzow to the east and, after many wanderings, found his death in a Soviet Sovchoz, lonely and abandoned; Itzhok Schliselberg, the translator's second cousin, also died of starvation, after giving away his rations to his young children; Reb Zisha Hirshfeld's daughter from Lutcza near Strzyzow and her husband also died in Russia.

Most refugees from Russia returned from Russia to Poland in the years 1945-46. A part emigrated to different countries, mainly to the United States. The majority settled in Israel.

Only one returnee from Russia did not lived to reach Israel. This was Naphtali Roth who, before the war had been an active member in the Zionist Youth Movement. The climate and life in Russia and the long journey home in the freight trains weakened even more his failing health. He was hospitalized in Poland, where he died after having a day of happiness brought on by the visit of two relatives from Strzyzow.

As soon as the Nazis entered Strzyzow, the maltreatment of the Jews had began. The Nazis beat them, plucked their beards and sidelocks and, with their savage behavior, imposed a deadly fear upon the Jews. They looted the Jewish stores and left them bare. At the beginning the authority was in the hands of the military, headquartered in the palace of Count Wolkowitzki, and also in a few private houses, including the houses of Reb Michael Schitz and Reb Samuel Feit.

By Rosh Hashana, the storm had calmed down a little. Nevertheless, Jews did not worship in the regular prayer houses but in hiding, as the Jews used to do during the Spanish Inquisition, in basements and attics.

On the second day of Rosh Hashana, a shocking incident occurred, which made the Jews of Strzyzow realize that their lives depended on the benevolence of each Hitlerite. The Germans brought five Jews on a truck from Frysztak whom they had taken out from a prayer house, still wearing their taleitim. They were killed in a nearby grove, a place where the town Jews used to stroll on their Sabbaths and holidays. Among the slain was one from the Puderbeitel family whose father was among the two hundred and thirty victims previously murdered in Dynow. There was also one of the Kracher family who owned a stone quarry. They were buried on the same place where they were shot. Later, after the intercession of the Jews from Strzyzow, they reburied the victims in the Jewish cemetery. People said that the main credit for the intercession belonged to Reb Michael Schitz.

Not to let the Jews forget even for one moment the trouble they found themselves in, another ugly incident occurred on Yom Kippur Eve which, fortunately, ended without a tragic result. Wanting to take advantage of the existing relaxation in the last few days, some Jews rushed over to the bathhouse to immerse in the mikva for the holiest day of the year. At the same time, a truck full of German soldiers arrived in town. Apparently, they had the desire to amuse themselves by bullying the Jews. Either they noticed, or somebody had told them that Jews were in the bathhouse, and they surrounded the place. The majority escaped half naked and hid in the area, but a few were caught by the Germans and brought to the marketplace. By then, a group of young Jewish girls came out and implored the soldiers to let the captives go. At the end, the Germans released the captives.

[Page 238]

Days passed filled with fear and worry. The military command was replaced by civilian authorities and the troubles changed to a different format. Instead the savage and wild torments, oppressive decrees started coming, one after another, denigrating the Jews and turning them into dust. The German Commandant Keller was not especially bad, and perhaps he did not add to the decrees that came from above. But there were enough of them to torment the lives of the Jews.

When the administration took over a "Judenrat" was appointed as in all of the cities in occupied Poland, and other countries of Europe. The Judenrat consisted of eight to ten members and served as a liaison between the Jews and the German authorities. Reb Abraham Brav, the Zionist activist, was appointed as head of the Judenrat. The members were: Reb Yacov Rosen, Reb Aaron Deutch, community activists who were members of the latest Kehillah Committee, Reb Elimelech Waldman, the man from Mizrachi, Sheingal from Gorlice, who had moved to Strzyzow and was the brother-in-law of Dr. Samueli, the lawyer. (During the German occupation, many reputable Jews moved to other cities where they were unknown.) A few more were appointed, including two from the exiled Jews from Kalisz who had been brought to Strzyzow. In all the days of existence, the Judenrat in Strzyzow behaved decently. It always stood up for the Jewish people and did all that was possible to ease the Nazi decrees.

Reb Yacov Rosen was killed in Strzyzow and Aaron Deutch was deported from the ghetto of Rzeszow with his family to an annihilation camp. Reb Elimelech Waldman was one of the most active intercessors who negotiated with the Germans. He continued to intercede for his brothers in the ghetto. He believed as the others did, that by intercession, he would be able to annul the oppressive orders. When the Nazis selected his wife and children to be deported to the annihilation camp, they wanted him to remain in the ghetto. But he refused and went with them.

Reb Abraham Brav and Sheingal became active members of the Judenrat in the Rzeszow ghetto. They remained there until the last of the Jews from Strzyzow were gone. They were also the last to be sent to their deaths.

Among the first anti-Jewish decrees was the prohibition to travel by train and, later, the prohibition to leave the periphery of the town. A permit from the local commandant Keller was required to leave town, and during the "good days" of that commandant, it was not difficult to get such a permit. To travel by train, a special permit had to be obtained from the regional commandant in Rzeszow, and could be obtained only through the Judenrat. The Judenrat secured such permanent permit for Itzhok Leib Rosen, who was the only official freight deliverer in town. He could travel unhindered. Later, he was also permitted to get in and out of the ghetto in Rzeszow which had been established earlier, at the time when the Jewry of Strzyzow were still in their homes. In general, Jews traveled only when they were compelled to travel, because traveling was deadly dangerous.

[Page 239]

The next decree was forced labor. The Jews and, to some extent, the Poles were forced to work, each men a few days a week. Sometimes women were forced to work too. The Jews were sent by the Judenrat. Two German companies were active in Strzyzow: "Todt" a military contracting firm, and "Kirchof." Both used to feed the workers and also paid some wages. There were incidents when poor Jews volunteered to work, knowing that they would be fed. The Todt Co. treated the workers better than the Kirchof Company, where workers were beaten and tyrannized. The work was hard labor, paving roads, building tunnels, stone quarrying and unloading freight.

The Jews were also forced to do jobs, which were a part of the Nazi oppressive system. They were forced to remove the gravestones from the cemetery, bury them in the ground and prepare the Land for public parks. The gravestones from the rest of the Jewish cemeteries were removed after the expulsion of the Jews. The better stones were used for paving the marketplace, and the fate of the older stones is unknown.

The worst jobs which were forced upon the Jews were jobs not needed for the German war economy, but were created to humiliate and denigrate the humanness of the Jews. The Nazis made the Jews sweep the streets, do jobs in the quarters of the German soldiers and functionaries to disgrace the Jews. Jewish men and women were nabbed for these works mostly on the Sabbaths and holidays. During these works, the Jews were maltreated, their beards and sidelocks shorn off, and disgraced as much as possible.

Besides the workers from Strzyzow, a thousand young Jewish men from Warsaw, Radom, and Kalisz were also employed in our vicinity. They were organized in labor brigades supervised by Jewish supervisors and escorted by Jewish policemen. They lived in barracks outside of town in temporary labor camps. The Jews from Strzyzow were forbidden to mingle with them.

At the beginning, one of the slave-drivers of the Jews from Strzyzow was the Christian Sabbath Goy, Sibirca, who served the kloiz and the Beit Hamidrash. He was a Petlura man who escaped to Poland after the Bolshevik Revolution, where many of his kind found refuge. He had setted in Strzyzow, and the Jews with their forgiving nature had given him a job and a small house which originally was built for the sexton. Now his time had come to repay the Jews with evil deeds for their good deeds, and to torment them. After some time, he fell into disfavor with the Nazis. He informed that a certain Pole had expressed a dislike for the Nazis, and the Pole, wanting to protect himself, attributed this criticism to Sibirca, and according to Nazi justice, both were sent to a concentration camp. They never returned from there. They were the only two from among the Polish population in Strzyzow who were sent there. The city of Kalisz in northern Poland was annexed to the Third Reich, and its Jews were forced out and some were resettled in Strzyzow. They were housed temporarily in the prayer houses, in Jewish homes or abandoned stores where they lived together with the local Jews. At the beginning, they were supported by the local Jews, and later worked for the Germans and received rations for reduced prices.

Of course, all the orders which the Germans bestowed upon the local Jews were also applied to the Jews from Kalisz. They shared the same fate.

[Page 240]

Until the expulsion to the Rzeszow ghetto, only a few of the young men from Strzyzow were sent to labor camps. These young men were snatched from the streets for this purpose,

During one such action, Itzhok Leib Rosen was caught in Tarnow. Since he had a travel permit, he was released. He also produced a document from a German firm in Sanok, approved by the General Government, stating that he was buying cattle for the German military. Most laborers were sent to Pustkow or Bieszadka, in Western Galicia. The Jews with their vitality pulled themselves together, despite the oppressions and decrees. Although the stores had been looted and abandoned by the owners, still everyone adjusted to the conditions and made an effort to find some livelihood and existence until the storm would pass. Tradesmen kept working and merchants sold merchandise which they had succeeded in concealing from the Germans during the looting, or they brought new merchandise from near and far by endangering their lives. The Jews barely survived. Many bartered household items and valuables for food, which the peasants brought to town, since Jews were forbidden to go to the villages.

The tradition of charity which was always deep-seated in each Jewish heart, expressed itself even more in those very troubled times which the Jews, including the Jewry of Strzyzow, had never before experienced, Everyone who was able to help, helped the needy. However, charitable activity was scaled down to a minimum. It was done in secret because any organized activity except the Judenrat was forbidden, and for violating the Nazi Rule, there was only one punishment – death.

Informers who would benefit from their brother's misfortune did not exist in Strzyzow. There were two Jewish policemen who helped the Nazis execute their ordinances through the Judenrat and, understandably, did not enjoy the sympathy of the Jews in Strzyzow. It was known that one of them used his position to extort money from different people. In spite of that, he was not considered to be like those known disgraceful Jewish "Kapos." Ultimately, they were sent to the Rzeszow ghetto with the rest of the Jews and found their sanctified deaths as the others,

Besides the two policemen, there were a few helpers who worked for the Germans. One of them was a son of the better families in town. They were only simple messengers who obeyed the requests of those who were in charge.

As it was said before, the Jews adjusted to the oppressive life and edicts, hopeful that it would eventually pass. Because of those so-called "quiet days," the Jews did not prevent their family members who were on the Soviet side, from returning home. Some even urged them to come home. Homesickness was a strong factor among the refugees as was the inability to get used to the Soviet way of life. Nevertheless, even in the quiet days, all kinds of incidents occurred which did not let the Jews forget what a mean situation they were in. Worst of all were the killings of people for the smallest violation of the oppressive rules.

Every incident that occurred shocked the population for a while, but they thought that it was only an isolated incident caused by special circumstances, and whoever would succeed to stream through between the wicked waves, would be safe.

[Page 241]

Even during the expulsion to the ghetto, they still thought that, although the situation was difficult and burdensome, their life of suffering had reached its ultimate point. They did not imagine the possibility of total destruction, which had been already decided at the higher Nazi echelon.

The first killing incident had already occurred in 1940. The German Commandant who replaced Keller while he was on his vacation, encountered Reb David Lieberman on the bridge which led to the village Godowa. The Commandant ordered Reb David to report to him at his office. According to hearsay, Reb David wanted to reach Count Filipowicz, with whom he ha done business before, to ask him for food for his family. Reb David vacillated whether to report or not. At the end he concluded that there was no escape. He went and did not return. The Commandant's office was in the house of the Notary Banski. The Hitlerites took Reb David to a nearby field, where he was shot in the neck while he was walking, his body was handed over to his family, and he was given a Jewish burial.

The excesses became stronger after the United States joined the Allies in their war against Germany. On Passover Eve, 1942, eighteen Jewish prisoners were taken out from prison in Rzeszow and executed in the Jewish cemetery, which the Hitlerites turned into a killing field. The victims were all American citizens. Among the killed was Moshe Rosen from Strzyzow, a brother of the Rosen brothers who survived the Holocaust. In that same period, the fur action took place. The Jews were ordered to hand over all the furs in their possession. A short time later, a fur stole was found in Reb Samuel Saphire's house. He was killed on the spot.

The worst incident occurred on May 4, 1942. When a Gestapo unit arrived in town to punish those Jews who escaped East in 1939, before the occupation, but were not exiled by the Soviets, and returned home after the Germans conquered the region of Eastern Poland. Dr· Rosenthal Oas the only one who was found in his home. The Gestapo took him to the churchyard and shot him using their modus operandi, a shot in the neck while the victim walked with his back to them. The rest of the returnees, Yechiel Rosen, Moshe Gertner, and his brother-in-law, Reb Hersh Lichtman, went into hiding as soon as they heard about the arrival of the Gestapo. Then the Gestapo killed six other Jews instead. Some of the victims were found in the house of Reb Samuel Moshe Groskopf, where they had been meeting to discuss charity problems, and the rest were caught in the street. On that day were killed: Dr. Rosenthal, Reb Samuel Moshe Groskopf, Reb Yacov Rosen, Reb Moshe Schefler, Reb Pinches Eisman and one unknown man.

This killing incident depressed the spirit of the Jews, and they never recovered until the expulsion which came soon after. Trains loaded with Jews from Biecz, Jaslo, and Gorlice passed Strzyzow on their way to the extermination camps. They traveled in locked, very crowded cattle cars. The floors were covered with whitewashing lime for disinfection. The women with their babies on their hands all tried to be near the small window gasping for fresh air.

[Page 242]

By then, the Ghetto in Rzeszow was already established. Besides the Jews from Rzeszow, all the jews from the vicinity were brought to the ghetto. The Jews in Strzyzow thought with dread what they could expect. Despite all the troubles, their situation in town was still better than in the ghetto. There, the Jews were hungry for bread and nobody knew what was coming. Like the drowning person who grasps at a straw, so did the Jews. They tried bitterly to escape the expulsion order. The Judenrat did whatever they could, they traveled to the German District Headquarters hoping that their intercession would result in some help.

The Nazis, seeing that the Jews lived in illusion, decided that was an opportunity to be the inheritors of their victims. Although Jews were permitted to take all their possessions to the ghetto where their wealth would anyway fall into the Nazi hands, each individual preferred to be the inheritor, nor somebody else. There was also the possibility that the Jews might conceal valuables in their homes, and the Nazis would not get it. Therefore, with their characteristic cunning, they promised the naive Jews that they could remain in Strayzow for the price of a few kilograms of gold, despite the fact that the Germans themselves were well aware of their intentions.

Despite of the savagery of the Nazis, the Jews believed that perhaps this time the truth came out of their mouths, and a member of the Judenrat, Reb Aaron Deutch, came to the town with an immense and bitter outcry, despairingly appealing to them to extend a helping hand for own rescue. "Jews! Save yourselves, have mercy upon yourselves," he cried. He asked them not to hide the gold articles which were still their possession. When despite all the efforts that were made, the collected gold in Strzyzow did not meet the quota and was not enough to satisfy the Nazi demand, Itzhok Leib Rosen, the only person with a travel permit, was sent to the rich Krosno, a nearby town, with a plea for gold donations to rescue the Jewry of Strzyzow from expulsion.

In Krosno the annihilation process had not began yet. Apparently the Nazis could not possibly create their inferno everywhere at the same time. The Jews there still lived their oppressed lives working, and a few Jewish stores were still open. Only later did the Nazis come around to set up a ghetto in Krosno for the local Jews and for the Jews of its vicinity. The Jews were all murdered in the forests of Udzikan near Rymanow. Upon arriving in Krosno, Rosen turned to Reb Ever Klagswald, the shochet, who was the son-in-law of Reb Chaim Felt from Strzyzow. Despite the fact that the Jews of Krosno were not much better situated, Reb Ever, with the help of other people, succeeded in collecting a considerable number of gold articles and brought it to Itzhok Leib Rosen who was waiting in Reb Ever's house. As soon as Rosen brought the gold to Strzyzow, and when all the gold was delivered to the Hitlerites, they immediately set a date for the expulsion to the Rzeszow ghetto.

In the days of June 26, 27, and 28, 1943, hundreds of peasants with carriages arrived in town. A part were recruited by the Germans to transfer the Jews, and the others came voluntarily, expecting to benefit by plundering the expelled Jews. The Germans set a price of twenty-five zlotys for a one-horse buggy, and fifty zlots for a two horse carriage.

[Page 243]

They allowed the Jews to take with them everything to the ghetto. They knew that everything the Jews took with them would fall in their hands anyway.

In total, one thousand and three hundred men, women and children were expelled from Strzyzow.

Filled with despair, the Jews loaded all their belongings on the carriages believing that they would live in the ghetto a long time. Some took with them the leftover merchandise, which they had succeeded to hide from the Nazis to barter for food, and the tradesmen took their tools.

The exodus to Rzeszow lasted three days. S. S. men escorted the caravans and on the way killed all the incapacitated, especially the invalids. Mordechai Russ was among those killed. He was an invalid from the First World War, and his legs were amputated. Reb Aaron Borgenicht, the sick and semi-paralyzed, was also killed. It was reported that Reb David Wiener who, during the German occupation, had not left his house but studied the holy books continuously, did not respond to those who came to expel him. Whether they were Germans or their helpers the poles, he did not pay attention to them. They shot him right there in his room.

On the third day, the last day of the expulsion, when almost all the Jews were gone, Reb Itzhok Leib Rosen arrived in town from the Rzeszow ghetto under the pretext that he had to hand over a storehouse of empty barrels which he managed. In truth, he came to retrieve his uncle Reb Chaim Rosen who remained alone in his room and refused to come out, claiming that he preferred to die in his room rather than in a strange place. Rosen reported that all the Jewish homes were broken open and looted for whatever there was left and, in the air, the wind carried feathers from Jewish beddings which the pilferers tore searching for valuables. The Polish collaborators kept tab on each Jew in town. As a matter of fact, as soon as Rosen arrived in town, the mayor Wladislaw Gornicki, inquired about his business and also mentioned that his uncle had not left yet. Itzhok Leib Rosen succeeded in convincing his uncle to go with him, and he also witnessed the expulsion of the last Jews, Rabbi Nechemiah Shapiro, who was forced out from his house together with his family, to the sound of the wailing women and grandchildren. Al this did not effect the murderers. Nobody saw the Shapiros in the ghetto. They never arrived there. They were probably killed on the way.

The Nazis were helped by the Polish collaborators, headed by mayor Wladislaw Gornicki. His father, Peter Gornicki, the blacksmith, had always befriended the Jews and, for many years was elected as mayor with the help of the Jews. But the hatred for the Jews had been nourished in his house and passed on to his sons. Gornicki's helpers were all from poor Christian circles who always participated in the pogroms. The wealthy of the town this time had also stood aside, and it was hard to determine their position. The truth is that in the whole town not one Jew was saved. The only one who did hide was sent from place to place until he reached Gornicki's helpers. Ultimately, he was killed when he ran out of means to pay those who were hiding him.

Moniek (Moshe), Reb Aaron Borgenicht's son, was found by a farm worker in Jan Patryn's farm hiding in a stack of straw near the Visloka River.

[Page 244]

From there he went to Patryn's relative, Ignac Patryn, and afterwards to the house of Mrs. Maznicka. Soon somebody informed the police and when they began to look for him, he moved to the house of Wladislaw Uszlicki. He kept paying for the hiding places with valuables which his parents left with their neighbors, Polish intelligentsia. They had handed him only a part of the valuables, retaining the rest for themselves as a safekeeping fee. After he spent all that he had, he was found killed in a water puddle not far from his hiding place.

In 1948, with the new Polish regime, Uszlicki, Maznicka, and a third man by the name Stare, were arrested and brought to trial on murder charges. Mrs. Maznicka died during the trial, and the two others were freed for lack of evidence. After an appeal by the prosecutors, Uszlicki was sentenced to life imprisonment but after his appeal, he was freed again for lack of evidence. A few years later, one murderer was sentenced by Heaven, and his head was severed when he fell under a train.

According to my supposition and my knowledge, the Christian citizenry in Strzyzow could have been divided into three categories. The first category comprised of those who were hurting for the Jews but were powerless to do something about it and lacked the moral force to help them. The second category consisted of those who were happy about the Jewish calamity, thinking to themselves, "They got what they deserved." Many of these people collaborated with the Nazis and helped them to hunt for Jews in hiding. The third category were the apathetic who worried only about themselves and did not care what happened to their neighbors with whom they lived for many generations. Nevertheless, these people also benefited from the misfortunes of the Jews. They took advantage when they bartered with the Jews, exchanging valuables and merchandise for food, and subsequently they inherited their stores, homes, and their belongings, which were abandoned by the Jewish owners after the expulsion.

The hatred for the Jews had not ceased even after the expulsion. In 1943, a group of young Jews, natives of Strzyzow and its vicinity, came to Strzyzow from the Rzeszow ghetto. They were the remnants of the ghetto. They were used for different jobs before their deportation to forced labor and annihilation camps. The Rosen brothers and Elazar Loos were among the group who came to dismantle barracks in the suburbs of the town and, on this occasion, they exchanged clothing and other articles for food to take with them to the starving ghetto. The people from Strzyzow reported them to the Germans and they barely escaped with their lives, never to be sent to perform such jobs again.

The Jews from the ghetto who worked in the vicinity and returned daily to the ghetto were sent from time to time to clean homes, which were vacated by the owners after they were sent to their deaths. During such cleaning, they found articles of clothing, which they later bartered for food. They took this food into the ghetto with the consent of their German foremen who kept a considerable portion for themselves. This time when the local Poles reported the Jews, the German foremen were also arrested. Later it was discovered that the informers and the local police had also not reported what they confiscated from the Jews but kept it for themselves.

[Page 245]

To emphasize the hatred for the Jews, here is a story about the treatment of a young Jewess, Gitel Shlosman, by a few Christian girls in Strzyzow. Shlosman left the town a few years before the war. She lived during the German occupation on Aryan papers. At the end of 1942, after the expulsion of the Jews, she came to Strzyzow to buy hides from the butcher Mr. Gocek on behalf of her Christian employer. Upon arriving in town she was recognized by a few Christian girls her age, who asked for her purpose for coming to a place where there were no Jews. Not withstanding her pretense that she did not know them, the girls did not leave her alone until she reached the butcher's store. They waited for her outside the store, and she was finally forced to escape through a back door to a village where she stayed overnight in a farmer's house. She left town early morning amidst great danger again, because the man who bought her the train ticker at her request had recognized her at last moment. The girls reported the incident to the German police, and the butcher complained to the merchant in Krakow for sending a Jewess who caused him entanglement with the German police.

That is how isolated Jews were pursued and hunted by the Poles, helping the Germans in their destruction.

The Rzeszow ghetto was set up in those streets which had been mostly inhabited by Jews before and the Nazis had concentrated all the Jews from Rzeszow and the nearby towns and villages. The living conditions in the ghetto was as in all other ghettos. The crowding was terrible. They suffered starvation, sickness, and hard labor, plus daily edicts and many other misfortunes. The worst of them was the frequent "Actions" the selections of transports to the annihilation camps.

The young people, upon arrival in the ghetto, were issued labor cards. The laborers were forced to work mostly in the stone quarry in Zarnowo.

The Nazis began the liquidation of the ghetto soon after the arrival of the Jews from Strzyzow. They were helped by Polish policemen and also by Jewish "Kapos" imported from Warsaw, Kalisz, and other cities.

The elderly were not sent to the annihilation camps but killed locally. If the younger family members refused to separate from their loved ones, the Nazis killed them together.

That way the whole family of my sister Nechama was killed together with my mother Yocheved, refusing to separate Killed were: My sister Nechama Bernstein, her husband Reb Yacov Itzhok, their two sons, David Dov and Elimelech Shlomo, and the little girl Bina. May G-d avenge their innocent blood.

The families of the people who worked outside the ghetto were put in the transports which passed Rzeszow on their way to the annihilation camps. They were taken to the railroad station at Staroniwa which was the second station to Rzeszow, on the Rzeszow-Jaslo line, where they joined the transports. Before boarding the train, they had to line five in a row. The first in the row had to pay fifty zlotys, per person for the fare, in total two hundred and fifty zlotys, despite the fact that all their money was extorted from them before in different ways and the possession of money was prohibited. People were killed for possession of money, Chaya, the daughter of Reb Aaron Deutch, was killed in the ghetto for possessing cash.

[Page 246]

Also Chaya Scheinman, Reb Chaim Mandel's daughter, and her daughter Frumet died for such a crime. And now on their last voyage to their extinction, whoever could not pay the fifty zlotys was killed on the spot. The wretched were led to the train in broad daylight in the middle of the street surrounded by S. S. men and Gestapo who kept hitting them with truncheons and riffle butts indiscriminately, women, children, and elders. If somebody stumbled on the way, he or she was shot and killed immediately. If the victims did not march in a straight line, they were beaten savagely. Relatives of the fallen were not permitted to stop for a moment to help their dear ones. They were forced to continue in line to the death train.

While the Jews were marched to the trains, sidewalks on both sides of the street were crowded with Poles who cheered this calamity of the Jews and jeered the afflicted, as it should be recorded for eternal abomination – the Jews were led to die to the sound of: "Your end has come, Jews!" After each such action, the road to the Staroniwa station was strewn with corpses.

After each selection, the lucky ones who remained to continue to work, were transferred to the eastern part of the ghetto until the next selection. It was called the ghetto of life. There were instances when those who remained in the ghetto succeeded in bringing with them family members and hiding them. But in their absence, the Nazis kept finding them and sent them away to their extermination. This happened to Chaya Rosen, the mother of the Rosen brothers.

The Jews knew about their fate. Nevertheless, they hoped, or deluded themselves, and believed, rather wanted to believe, the words of their tormentors, that the deported were only resettled to other places where they would be working. Upon arriving in the annihilation camps and before their annihilation, the Nazis forced their victims to write letters to their relatives who remained in the ghetto saying that they were working and feeling well. These letters were distributed all over the ghetto.

On December 11, 1942, only four thousand people remained in the Rzeszow ghetto which had thirty thousand people before, consisting of Jews born in Rzeszow and nearby towns and villages. On that day, the last transport was shipped out to an unknown annihilation camp. The camp in Belzec, where the majority of the Galician Jewry, including the Jews from the

Rzeszow ghetto, were sent, had been liquidated already. The remnants of the ghetto in Rzeszow were put into a passing transport from the ghettos Tarnow and Bochnia. One hundred fifty people had been squeezed into each car. There were seven cars containing one thousand and fifty people.

From the ceiling of each car a rope was hanging, and the S. S. man announced that anybody who was tired of living can put an end to it with this rope. But the people still clung to their hopes. The last members of the Judenrat with its leader Reb Abraham Brav were also on this train.

Reb Samuel Felt, the young man, Itzhok Leib Rosen, his brother Samuel, and Chaim Adest, who were from Strzyzow, and one man from Bochnia who had jumped from trains several times before were in the same car.

[Page 247]

It was two o'clock in the morning. As soon as the train left Rzeszow, the man from Bochnia climbed over the heads of the people to get to the little window. Because of the density in the car he could not have done it otherwise. Then with pliers, which he had hidden in his clothes, he cut the barbed wire over the window and jumped from the train. After him two more from Tarnow or Bochnia jumped out. Zechariah Yaffe from Czudec, a little town near Strzyzow, followed them. He was the fourth man. Yaffe had survived the ordeal. Samuel Rosen and his older brother Itzhok Leib were the fifth and the sixth, the last ones to jump. They jumped despite the protests and shrieks of a few women who were afraid that on account of their escapes, the S. S. men would take revenge on the remaining victims. Chaim Adest, a healthy young man from Strzyzow had refused to jump despite the coaxing of the Rosen brothers. He was convinced that having a vital profession for the war economy (he had learned the plumbing and mechanical trade while preparing to make aliyah to Eretz Israel), he would get work wherever the Nazis sent him. Reb Samuel Feit refused to jump because he did not want to live anymore his wife Rachel, and their only son, Joseph, had been sent away in a previous transport. His younger daughter stayed behind in the ghetto and his older daughter escaped from the ghetto with Aryan papers, as it will be told further on.

About one hundred fifty people jumped from that death-train, Including the Rosen brothers from Strzyzow, Yaffe from Czudec, and the young man Ritter from Lutcha. Ritter was a grandson of the hero from blood libel in the days of the Kaiser Franz Joseph I, a story written earlier in this hook. This young man fled back to his village Lutcha, where he was later killed.

Far two days after jumping the train, wounded and bleeding, the Rosen brothers and Zachariah Yaffe circled around in the area until they succeeded to sneak back into the Rzeszow ghetto and were happy to be among their brothers again.

All the Jews who escaped from that death train returned to the get despite the fact that their lives in the ghetto were in constant danger. For the moment, this was the safest place. Outside of the ghetto, with a few exceptions, they were surrounded by Polish enemies who were ready to hand over a Jewish body to the Germans for the price of a half kilogram sugar, or even without being rewarded at all. The Poles were happy to help in the annihilation of the few remaining individuals who were hunt like wild animals. When during the dismantling of the barracks in Strzyzow, Elazar Loos, the son of a respectful family, was asked by the mailman, Ludwiz Kolodziej, why he did not run away? He responded: "Where to, and far how long will I succeed to be alive? There is no escape for a Jew."

Most of those who jumped off the train on November 15, 1942, survived and safely returned to the ghetto. Upon arriving there, the three from Strzyzow found the remaining Jews still there.

Characteristically, the behavior of the Nazis was such that the Director of the ghetto accepted favorably the escapees, and even more so they were accepted by the local projects foremen, despite the fact that they knew that these people had escaped from the death trains.

[Page 248]

Although the Hitlerites were united in their goal of the oppression and killing of the Jews, still, everyone looked out for his own interests and the job he was responsible for. Every German was afraid that not having a job, he would be sent to the eastern front. At this time neither woman nor children were deported, but only young people, this caused them to be short-handed. Therefore, they were happy to accept the returnees in order to continue to use their labor and remain on their jobs. Nothing would be lost by killing the Jews later.

There were no incidents of organized resistance in Strzyzow. The town Jewry went as did the majority of European Jewry towards their deaths without active resistance. Jews had fought as soldiers in the Polish army against the Germans. After the Poles' defeat, no resistance was possible or rational. Before the German defeat in Russia, no one rebelled. Even people who lived on their own land did not rebel, and rebellion was impossible for the Polish Jewry who lived among a hostile population. Even though the Poles were enslaved by the Nazis, the majority adapted themselves to the enslavement without their individual lives being in danger. Not only did the Poles failed to help the Jews, in many cases they helped in their annihilation.

In addition to the above, the strong rulers, the Nazis, planned the killing of the Jews with deceit and hypocrisy. Before they directly attacked the powerless and defenseless Jews, they broke down their spirit and power of resistance gradually. They proclaimed their strong hatred for the Jews but the decision would have caused an armed resistance even in the difficult conditions of the Jews as the remnants of the ghettos and the partisans did. This was not a war with the Jewish people but contemptible murder by ambush.

Whenever possible, they took the aged, the women and children for annihilation, at the time when the men and youth were at work. By lying to the victims, they hid their true intentions and induced in them hope until the last moment. Any resistance, the smallest one, was a sure death, and every Jew hoped that by endurance he would survive until the end of the war. They believed that the killings were only partial and not aimed at all the Jews. On the other hand, there were many people who waited for death as a redeemer after loosing their families. Many men from Strzyzow, when the Nazis asked them to remain in the ghetto in order to exploit their labor until their turn would come, did not agree but joined their families on their last journey.

There were two incidents of resistance in Strzyzow which ended in the death of the resistant, in fact, they hastened their end.

The young man, Moshe Thim, was nabbed by a few German soldiers while they were washing their military vehicles at an open well. They tried to force him to do their job. He forcibly resisted and hit them back with their own weapons. At the end, they overpowered him and brought him to the commandant. This happened in the so called "good days" of Commandant Keller. When the boy's father, Reb Kalman the tailor, who worked for Keller and the rest of the officers, found out about it, he went to Keller and pleaded for the life of his son.

[Page 249]

Keller could not forgive the young man for having the audacity to strike the superior German soldiers, or maybe he was afraid to free such a person. On the other hand, Keller could not withstand the pleas of the unfortunate father who had served him faithfully all this time. He did not pronounce his sentence but he sent the boy to the District Commandant in Rzeszow. Moshe Thim never came back to his parents.

The second incident occurred during the actions in the Rzeszow ghetto when the family of Reb Samuel Saltzman from Niebylec was led to the railroad station, Staroniwa, for deportation. Reb Samuel Saltzman was strong and young, and the Nazis wanted him to stay behind and continue to work for them.

However, he refused and joined his family. On the way, an S. S. man who escorted the transport, struck his wife. Reb Samuel the Jew, a native of Niebylec whose Jews were known for their pride and strength, of whom the peasants were always afraid, had already escaped once from the Germans for some small infraction of their decrees. He could not endure the mistreatment of his wife by an S. S. man. He attacked him and struck him with severe and powerful blows. Another soldier from the convoy who marched behind, shot him in his neck like the "heroes" of that period, and killed him instantly.

In the forest near the village Pstrongowa, on the road between Strzyzow and Sendziszow, small groups of Jews with their families were hiding. They oftentimes attacked Nazis. But these were people Rzeszow, Czudec, Niebylec, and not from Strzyzow. In 1943, one of these groups attacked the police in Strzyzow and demolished the Station. In this action, a partisan by the name Vilf was killed. Officially he belonged to the Jewish police in Rzeszow, but secretly he was a member of the anti-Nazi underground and helped his brothers. Part of those in hiding survived and came out together with their families after the Red Army liberated the area.

The heroic deed of a native of Strzyzow who settled in another town should also be mentioned. This was Reb Menachem Groskopf, the son of Reb Samuel Moshe, a known silver ornaments maker for taleitim. Reb Samuel Moshe Groskopf came from Sassov, whose people were well-known as ornament makers. Reb Menachem was raised in Strzyzow and was an alumnus of the Belt Hamidrash. He married a daughter from Brzostek near Tarnow and settled there. He lived the traditional life of the older generation, namely, he studied Torah mornings and evenings, and in the daytime he was engaged in commerce to feed his family. Menach Groskopt was also active in the community. When the Germans occupied the town he was nominated as head of the Judenrat. As usual they demanded that he supply people for the forced labor camps. Reb Menachem, the warm-hearted Jew, could not do it, and he told them that he will not hand over Jews for hard labor and affliction and, if it is necessary, he himself was ready to go. This was at the beginning of the German rule and Reb Menachem could have hoped that by obeying the Germans, he would not be harmed. Nevertheless, he performed his heroic deed and the Nazis killed him right there for resisting their edicts.

Somewhere else in this book, Reb Itzhok Leib Rosen reported a verystrong resistance to a Jewish "Kapo," despite their brutality in helping the Nazis to inflict pain on their own brothers, there existed some possibilities for a favor by influencing them through their relatives and through the inner Jewish rulers. Because of that fact, Itzhok Leib was saved, as he told in his article.

[Page 250]

After the above-mentioned deportation, there were no more families in the ghetto. Only men and youths remained who were sent in groups to work in the area and later to forced labor camps where the conditions were similar to death camps. Being in the ghetto, the few lonely people from Strzyzow stayed together and, if possible, lived together until they were separately sent to other camps. The Rosen brothers, Elazar Loos, Yacov Adest, Nechemiah Felber, two sons of Reb Levi Kalb, Menachem Lieberman, Naphtali Diamand and others lived together.

Naphtali Diamand was once sick and could not go to work, which often happened to many others. But this time, on returning from work, his colleagues did not find him in the room and on his bed there was a bullet and blood stains. During the daily inspection, the Nazis could not forgive him his absence from work because of his illness, and they killed him in the room.

The Rosen brothers were among the few from Strzyzow who remained alive. They were sent from camp to camp. From the labor brigade in the ghetto, they were transferred to the labor camp Huta Komarowska, which was affiliated with the Rzeszow ghetto and administered from there. The Lieberman brothers, Itzhok and Leibush, the sons of Reb David Lieberman, and Nechemiah Felber were also in that camp. A day before their arrival, the young man, Mordechai Beitler, Reb Leibush Beitler's son, was killed during an attempt to escape. The two Lieberman brothers became sick with typhus, and were taken back to the ghetto, but were never seen again. The Rosen brothers together with Menachem Lieberman and Nechemiah Felber were taken to the camp Kochanowka and later to Pustkow. From there the oldest Rosen Yechiel, was sent to a camp unknown to me, and the young men Itzhok Leib and Samuel Rosen, Menachem Lieberman, and Felber were sent to Plaszow, and from there to Mielec. In this camp, which was exclusively Jewish, worked about three thousand men in the airplane industry. When the Russians were approaching, the above-mentioned four from Strzyzow were sent to a salt mine in Wieliczka and later to the famous annihilation camp Auschwitz. Luckily, there was no room for their transport, so they were sent to Limeritz which was in the Sudetenland. Menachem Lieberman was sent from there to Dachau and was not seen again. The two Rosen brothers and Nechemiah Felber were transferred to the Mathausen camp, which the guards themselves called "Murderhousen." This camp had three branches, the main branch, Branch No. 1 and Branch No. 2. Branch No. 2 was the worst of the three, and was burned by the Americans as soon as they came, with the intention of wiping such horror off the face of the earth. However, with their action, they did a service to the Nazis who were interested in forgetting their treacherous actions. In that camp, the people from Strzyzow encountered two more from Strzyzow, the brothers, Wolf and Nechemiah Hauben. Both of these men and Nechemiah Felber succumbed a few days before the liberation, after years of pain, hunger, beatings and hard labor.

[Page 251]

They collapsed under the last horrible edict which was bestowed upon them.

This was the decree of disinfections ("Entlausung"), which was done in the following manner: Lining up thousands of people naked for six hours outside in thirty degrees below zero temperature, and having to walk through rows of cold showers. For each four persons, there was only one blanket, and only a few fortunate people had on a pair of torn shoes.

Three thousand five hundred people succumbed to this blow, and the three people from Strzyzow among them. In the labor camp Shiwna, Yacov Felder succumbed. He was sent there from Rzeszow, after his family was deported to the annihilation camp in one of the transports.

The two Rosen brothers were liberated by the Americans on May 5, 1945, and met in the American Hospital another man from Strzyzow, Eisik Welisz-Guttenberg, who lived in Zmigrod before the war, and is currently in the United States.

Of all the inhabitants of Strzyzow who were under the Nazis, only eight survived: The Rosen brothers, Yechiel, Itzhok Leib, and Samuel Reuven Greenbaum, Elazar Loos, David Schefler, Pearl Rosen, the Rosen's sister, and Hinda Felt.

Stone quarry in Zarnowo, the Rosens and Samuel Feit obtained two Christ birth certificates – the Rosens for their sister Pearl, and Samuel Feit for his daughter Hinda. With these documents they escaped to Krakow. After the arrival of a few young Christians from Strzyzow to Krakow, these girls were in danger of being recognized, so they left Krakow and went to Berlin where they posed as Polish girls until after the war. There they found themselves many times in danger as a result of the allied bombings of the Germans.

Reuven Greenbaum was also moved from one camp to another. From the Rzeszow ghetto he was sent to Bieszadka, from there to Pustkow, to Auschwitz, Glejowice, Grossrosen, Limeritz and, finally, to Mathausen the worst of them all. With his luck, they did not let his transport in for lack of room. Ultimately, he was sent to Theresienstadt, where he met Elazar Loos, and there he was liberated. After the liberation, he was sent to Buchenwald, which by then became an American camp for the liberated. Thanks to his youth, he received an entrance permit to Switzerland, and later immigrated to the United States.

Elazer Loos who went through hell-fire in the German camps was liberated in Theresienstadt. He visited Strzyzow after the war, but as a result of all the sufferings he went through, his health failed and he did not realize his dream of going to Eretz Israel and joining his sister there. He died in the Displaced Persons Camp in Landesberg, Germany. About David Schefler, his sister Shoshana Ginsberg will write about him. Natives of Strzyzow who were stranded in the German occupied eastern part of Poland and survived were the following: Gitel Shlosman whom we mentioned before, Joseph Reich, a grandson of Reb Eliezer Loos, Shimon Mandel, a grandson of Reb Yeshayahu Mandel, Joseph Weinberg, and Dr. Tzvi Hersh Eisner.

Joseph Weinberg, who lived in Lwow until the outbreak of the war, was in the camp of Janow, which was named the "School of Murderers," because that was where the S. S. men and the Gestapo received their education in murder and brutality.

[Page 252]

It was reported that the commandant of the camp used to stand on the balcony of his house armed with a rifle and, surrounded by his family, he showed off his marksmanship by shooting Jewish children who were thrown in the air by his subordinates. His little daughter stood near him and begged her father to continue to play which so amused her. The commandant ordered the Jewish inmates to turn around and killed them with a shot in the neck as it was customary with the Nazis. He imposed such a terror on the inmates that they always obeyed his orders despite the fact that they knew that obeying was sure to bring their death. Joseph Weinberg had prepared himself for a long time for such an order and he decided to disobey. When he did, the commandant slapped his face, but did not kill him. Joseph was later in Auschwitz and there he was active in helping his troubled brothers. According to the testimony of one of the witnesses, an inmate in that camp, the architect M. Kubowitzki, Joseph Weinberg jumped from a train transporting him to an annihilation camp. He ultimately survived by a miracle from the Russians who wanted to kill him together with a group of Jews as German spies. The group was looking for a resting place after being liberated.

Joseph Reich, the son of Adela Loos, who was the daughter of Reb Eliezer Loos from Strzyzow, moved with his parents from Rzeszow, the town where they lived before the war, to Jaslo, his father's birthplace. The pursued Jews falsely believed that by changing towns, their luck would also change and they would be able to survive. Details about his survival will be in the article of his aunt, Miss Leah Loos.

Shimon Mandel, Reb Benjamin's son, found himself at the outbreak of the war in Strzyzow, at his grandfather, Reb Yeshayahu Mandel's house. After a while, disguised as a Christian boy, he successfully reached his parents' house in Dombrowa near Tarnow. Having been moved around in German concentration camps, he was liberated in Theresienstadt, where he met Elazar Loos, and later settled in Israel.

Dr. Tzvi Eisner, Reb Yacov Eisner's son, who grew up in his parents' house in Strzyzow, together with his wife, were hidden in a bunker during the Nazi occupation. At the end, he left the bunker, and with Aryan documents in his hands, he moved into the lion's den in the Ukraine, place of arduous hatred of the Jews, and survived. Presently, he lives in Poland and works as a doctor.

Also in Western Europe, France, and Belgium, many from Strzyzow perished, and only a few were fortunate enough to be saved from the Nazi hands during the occupation of those countries. One of them was Moshe Mussler who lives in Israel with his family and participated in writing this memorial book. He also wrote about his and his family's sufferings and rescue during the Holocaust.

In the life-threatening days and destruction, the strong family ties expressed themselves with exaltation. Sons did not abandon their parents, grandparents, but went with them to the annihilation, even though occasionally they could remain in their places and stay alive, according to the false hope instilled in them by the Nazis. Parents who could not escape the Nazi hell, tried to extract their children to prevent their suffering and pains.

[Page 253]

It was told in this book by Rabbi Chanan Lehrman that his parents who were forced to return to Galicia from Hitler's Germany, succeeded in smuggling out a young girl together with their own children. Shulamit Greenwald nee Hasenkopf tells how her father, Reb Michael Hasenkopf from Strzyzow, (the translator's uncle), who could not leave Germany, implored her: "Do not remain here. Leave as fast as you can." The only request of Reb Samuel Feit, who remained in the death train during the escape of the Rosen brothers, was that they watch over his young daughter Hernia, who was left in the Rzeszow ghetto.

Yenta Gertner, the daughter of Reb Israel, stayed in Germany until she succeeded, after much hardship and great effort, to take out her three sons and sent them to the western countries. Only then did she come to Strzyzow to join her husband Reb Joseph Berger. Strzyzow had seemed to them to be temporarily safe. Their fourth son had been sent before to Eretz Israel where he lives now and, from him, r obtained the details of his mother's effort. The youngest, Zachariah, went with a group of children to Holland on August 31, 1939, one day before the out break of the war, and, from Port Hak-Van, two hundred fifty children sailed in a Dutch ship to the British port of Dover. Upon the arrival of the ship, under the darkness of night, the British refused to permit the children to disembark, until the Christian Dutch captain threatened to sink the ship, with its passengers and staff, to the abomination of the whole world. Under this menacing pressure, the manager of the port contacted his superiors in London. When the leaders of the British Jewry, including Lord Herbert Samuel, found out about it, they successfully interceded with the Interior Ministry and obtained the necessary permit.

Children in Captivity

During the Holocaust, many Jewish children were handed over into Christian hands to rescue them and keep them from the inhuman sufferings that was the fate of their parents. Further on, I will tell about two cases of handing over children from Strzyzow to Christians.

The first was the child Aryeh, the son of Mordechai and Vita Popper, the daughter of Reb Eliezer Loos. When his mother, Vita, found her tragic death, as it was told before, the child was four years old and lived with his father in Przemysl, where most of the expelled Jews from Dynow lived. After the city was occupied by the Nazis and the tormenting of the Jews began, the father was sent to work on the railroad and could not keep the child with him. To give him to another Jewish family became dangerous and, therefore, he gave the child to a Polish family which, for a sizeable financial reward, took care of him. At times when Mordechai was marching to work in a convoy under the escort of the Nazi soldiers, his nanny would bring Aryeh out to the street so that the father could see his dear son. According to Mordechai's sister-in-law, Miss Leah Loos, the father was sent with his nephew, Joseph Reicho to Auschwitz and his son remained with the Christian woman. Until this day, his whereabouts are still unknown. Whether he lives somewhere as a gentile, not knowing about his Jewishness and the great respected family from which he originated, or, whether he was handed over to the Nazis and murdered, nobody ever found out.

[Page 254]

Children in Captivity

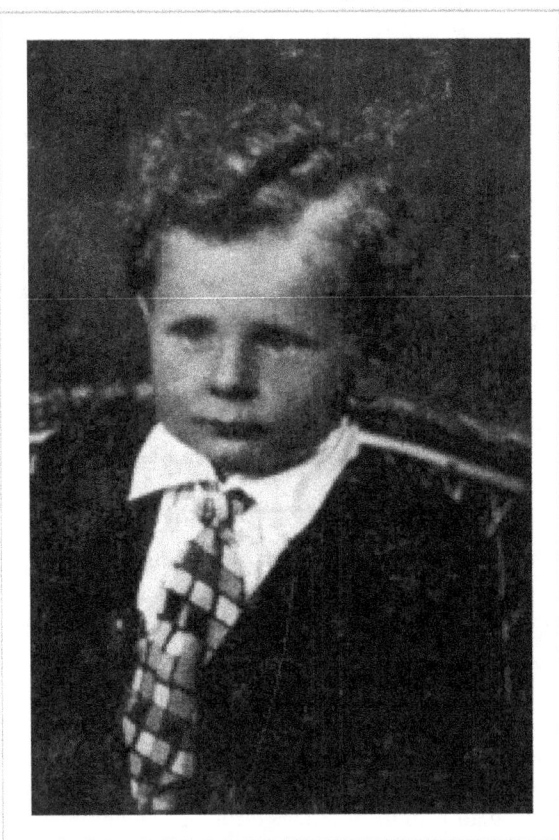

The child Aryeh,
the son of Mordechai and Vita Popper;
the grandson of Reb Eliezer Loos from Strzyzow

*Nechama Gertner with her son Israel,
the grandson of Reb Israel Gertner,
from Strzyzow*

[Page 255]

Nechema and Moshe Gertner's son, Israel, who was just recovering from scarlet fever, prevented his mother from leaving Strzyzow before the Germans approached, as she planned to do. She wanted to protect him from the hardship of travel. The father Moshe, escaped by himself to Lwow. He was not exiled by the Soviets in June 1940, but returned to Strzyzow after the Germans occupied the eastern part of Poland in 1941. Their fate, his wife's and his, were the same as the rest of the town's Jewry.

After our return from Russia in 1946, we heard unconfirmed rumors, that before their deportation to the ghetto, the mother handed over the child Israel, who was then six years old, to her Christian maid who came from a village near Niebylec, and who had taken care of him in his childhood.

In Strzyzow which I visited for a short time, I was not able to find out anything, and, it was unsafe to loiter around in the remote villages. With the savage hatred of Jews which prevailed at that time, only death could have been found. Then and after my arrival in Israel, I did promise a sizeable amount of money to several Poles in Strzyzow as a fee for helping me trace down the child, without results. Neither were the many Jewish institutions which were active in Poland able to obtain any positive results.

In 1966, a cousin of the boy, Moshe Berger, from New York, without the knowledge of the Polish language, visited Galicia and reached the village near Niebylec, in order to search for a trace of his lost cousin, Israel. From conversations with the villagers, he concluded that surely the child was given to the Christian woman, but he could not find her. Therefore, the child's fate remains unknown.

After the War and the Holocaust

Some of the Holocaust survivors and repatriates from Russia visited Strzyzow after the war. There were different motives for the visit, but the main motive was the yearning for home, the spiritual need to bid farewell to the birthplace which, along with everything that was dear to them, they had "temporarily" left years before. Before leaving the native land to begin their new life, they wanted to see for the last time all those places which reminded them of their dear ones, and of the good life when they were young. I was one of those visitors.

I went to Strzyzow not without fear. A big part of the Polish Population related with open hostility to the few Jews who came out from hiding. The Poles were particularly hostile to those Jews who had returned from Russia whose number seemed to the Poles ten times greater than it was actually. Hostile remarks were often heard about the large number of surviving Jews. The popular rumor spread among the Poles was that Poland supplied Russia with coal in exchange for their supply of Jews.

[Page 256]

There were incidents in which Jews, women among them, were taken off the trains by force and killed. Individual Jews, while visiting their hometowns for the same sentimental reasons as mine, were killed. The murderers did not know nor did they care, that those lone ones rescued from fire, the Holocaust, were leaving their homeland en masse and, that to the majority of refugees that returned from Russia, Poland served only as a transit station on their way to the wide world. From Szczecin, where thousands of repatriates were concentrated Jews were escaping nightly in trucks and sometimes by ship through the Oder-Elba Canal to West Berlin. This escape was carried out with the silent agreement of the Polish authorities and by the bribery of the Russian-German border guards. The Jews had to beware only of the Jewish-Communist activists because the escapes had undermined the existence of all kinds of committees, which the Communists had organized. The enemies of the Jews did not take into consideration that through the open Polish-Czechoslovakian border, a continuous stream of Jewish refugees was flowing to Austria and Italy. In their strong hatred of the Jews, the anti-Semites murdered Jews at the borders during their escape, though they knew that in a few hours they would have left Poland forever. Such a killing occurred before the mass exodus through Szczecin and Klacko, while the Jews were still Looking for escape routes. As soon as we crossed the Polish border on our return from Russia, we were shocked to hear the news of the murder of a group of young men who tried to cross to Slovuakia on their way to Eretz Israel.

In Rzeszow, where a small number of survivors had settled after they came out from the bunkers and tried to find some livelihood, a pogrom took place in 1945. These Jews were later transferred to Krakow under the protection of the Red Army, and there they became victims of a pogrom, which occurred shortly after their arrival.

My niece Henia and I came to Rzeszow on Our way to Strzyzow in 1946, a short time after the pogrom in Kielce. The air was saturated with hostility toward the Jews but in Rzeszow itself all was quiet. A few native Jews who returned from Russia had settled in a Jewish house and had organized some kind of a Jewish committee, which drew support from Jewish welfare organizations. The committee had a small cafeteria and provided lodging for the needy. In addition, there were in Rzeszow people from the surrounding towns and villages who waited for the liquidation of their affairs in their hometowns. The new Polish merchants, perhaps some of those who had mocked and jeered the Jews when they were led to their deaths in 1942, and who had organized the pogrom in 1945, now enjoyed this concentration of Jews who had no intentions of staying, but meanwhile were good customers in their stores, restaurants and lodgings.

As soon as entered the Primitive train on the Rzeszow-Jaslo line which passes through Strzyzow, we immediately encountered strong hostility toward the Jews. In the car, three "innocent" Peasant women were talking about the Jews who had disappeared. Of course, they did not realize that those who were sitting nearby were Jews. During the conversation, one said to the other with an expression Of satisfaction, "Their end has come," and the other responded, "I am glad."

We traveled the road well-known to us from before the war, and got out at the dilapidated Strzyzow station.

[Page 257]

As soon as we left the railroad station, we saw the last Jewish cemetery, which was located on a hill not far from the station. There was no sign of the concrete wall, which surrounded the cemetery nor the gravestones. In one place where Rabbi Alter Zev Horowitz was buried, a Pile of rubble was visible. That is all that remained of the Rabbi's tomb.

We walked to the town, feeling as if we were returning to the home which we only left yesterday Nothing changed, everything was so close to our hearts. This can only be expressed with a Yiddish word, "Heimish." Then the pain awakened with more strength, and the wound which was not healed yet opened again. The same house, the same courtyards, and the same stores, only our brothers and sisters were missing. From the Poles only a few were missing, those who passed on in a natural way, but not even one Jew could be found. All the stores had new owners, but many stores still had the same merchandise as before. In our store I found merchandise which had been there when i left in 1939. All the Jewish houses and dwellings were occupied by new residents who also used the furniture of the previous owners.

Here are the changes that did occur. The house of Reb Aaron Kanner, the adjacent Beit Hamidrash, including the small house where the Christian "Sabbath Goy" used to live, were all demolished. This demolition had brought the end of the Beit Hamidrash alley, which had been the spiritual center of the Jewry in Strzyzow. Instead a broad street was opened which continues through the old Jewish cemetery all the way to the northern hills. The brick fence and the concrete wall, which surrounded all three cemeteries, were entirely destroyed. Only the old oak trees in the old cemetery survived. The two adjacent cemeteries were turned into a public park which is used by the neighbors. Nobody knew of the whereabouts of the old gravestones.

The shul remained intact, desolate, as an eternal witness to Jewish life for generations. In addition to the disturbance of the Jewish remains in their graves, the gravestones from the cemetery were used for pavement of the marketplace Maliciously, the gravestones were layed with the inscriptions up.

Witness to Jewish life in town were also the houses that were built by Jews, including the three structures which served the community: The kloiz of Reb Moshe Leib Shapiro and his son Nechemiah, the Talmud Torah and hostel for the poor, and the community bathhouse. The Jewish houses are now occupied by Christians who also inherited the household articles. The community buildings are serving the Christian population.

A few mute remnants also remained, namely, the copper candelabras and the brass chandeliers in the shul, which I mentioned before in the chapter about the prayer houses.

During the First World War, the Austrian authorities wanted to confiscate these candelabras. This took place during the action of collecting all the copper and brass articles for the war effort. The copper roof of the Catholic church in Strzyzow was then replaced with galvanized sheet metal. With great difficulty the Jews did succeed in preventing the confiscation of these candelabras, claiming that they were an inner part of the shul. Before the Germans occupied Strzyzow, a few young men hid those items to prevent their confiscation. The unfortunate did not know that they should first preserve their lives. Apparently, these articles are still hidden somewhere.

[Page 258]

In one of the Christian cemeteries, there are graves of two young Jewish girls who were brought to town by the Germans after the expulsion of the Jews. They were killed and buried without markers on their graves. I was told that there are Christians who bring flowers to the graves on All Saints Day.

During our visit, remodeling was going on at the prayer house of Reb Moshe Leib Shapiro. The building to whose perfection he had devoted so much aptitude, was being prepared for the use of voluntary fire fighters brigade. And that is what it is used for at present.

On the eastern part of the marketplace, three homes were destroyed because the Nazis did not like their aesthetic looks.

In the center of the market is a tomb of Soviet soldiers who fell during the battle with the Germans for the liberation of the town. The tomb was surrounded with a small garden, and at present it is enlarged and engulfs the whole marketplace. For years the City Council and the clergy fought to liquidate the marketplace and turn it into a public park, but the Jews had opposed it. The store owners and tradesmen, with the help of the local inhabitants, succeeded to fail the idea, which would have meant deprivation of their livelihood.

At present, the park does not bother anyone. The town is asleep. No commerce, no traffic, perhaps because of the semi-Soviet regime, or because of the absence of the effervescent Jews. The weekly market is still on Tuesday. However, it lasts only two hours with a meager participation of peasants from the villages, and it does not last as before, from morning to evening.

We were received in town with politeness. The offices, which we had visited to arrange the return of our home, did everything to alleviate the formalities as quickly as possible. The meager funds which we had received from the sale of the house provided us just enough money to buy food and lodging during our stay in Poland, and provisions for the trip to a safer shore. We stayed in town three days, but we slept only one night in the house of Dr. Adam Patryn, the nephew of the deceased Doctor Joseph Patryn, the ex-mayor of the town. Like his uncle, he and his family were friendly towards the Jews. During the anti-Jewish boycott campaign, his mother took in as a business partner Reb Heshel Diamand, and for that reason, the stop of the annual religious procession near her store was cancelled. Dr. Patryn himself attended a wounded Jew who was hiding in the forests during the German occupation, which was a very dangerous act.

We left the town never to return, like all who visited their hometowns after the war. Few individual Jews returned and settled in the towns of Galica and Central Poland, and, from a Jewish perspective they live atropic lives, almost like the Spanish Marranos crying to hide their Jewishness. Some even paid with their lives, for yearning to live in their birthplace. In Strzyzow nobody settled. The heir to the Jewish community was the Town Council, and later the Soviet Style City People Committee. This is the situation on town at the present.

[Page 259]

In the oldest Jewish cemetery a public park was planted. On the second and the third cemetery, which were used by the neighbors as vegetable gardens, a school was erected. Since there was no vacant space around, and foundations in Poland have to be deep, the skeletons were removed from the graves and deposited in one place.

The shul was originally planned to turn into a flourmill, but instead it was turned into a storage room for the local cooperative. In 1959, the Peoples Committee of the town decided to destroy the shul and build a public building. However, the Commissioner in charge of historical landmarks from Rzeszow District opposed, and declared that the building is sound, despite being neglected since 1939, and should be preserved as a landmark. He suggested to improve the structure and to use it for administrative or cultural purpose. After painstaking intervention of the Strzyzow organization in Israel and with their agreement, it was decided, according to information received by us, that the shul became the regional museum.

During the compilation of this book, the shul is still used as a storage room, and it is not known which proposal will prevail – the Central Authority's, which helps to preserve Jewish landmarks in many other bigger cities, or the local authority. Particularly, in such a remote provincial place, which strives to erase the memory of Jews, and has not hesitated to destroy old buildings and the desecrate cemeteries, as mentioned before.

In 1959, the gravestones were removed from the pavement of the market, apparently, by an order from higher authorities and, also as a result of our organization's intervention. After the gravestones had been lying in a pile for two years, they were moved to the hill where the last Jewish cemetery was located, except the ones, which fell apart because of their usage as pavement for close to twenty years. The cemetery is being used for farming by different people, mainly city employees.

To the Talmud Torah building, another floor was added, and it serves as a medical clinic for the townspeople.

Lately, the Jewish bathhouse was also renovated, and it is used by the public under the People Committee's supervision.

1967

Ultimately, the central administration prevailed and the shul in Strzyzow remained intact. It was renovated in 1966. Some interior changes were made and it was turned into a city library. These are the changes that were made:

The two entrances from the south side were partially blocked and made into windows. The stairs which led to the women's balcony were demolished. Two new entrances were created, one from the east side, where the holy ark used to be, and one from the western side. Inside the main sanctuary, a balcony was build around all four walls with stairs leading to them from the inside. Only the center of sanctuary remained untouched.

[Page 260]

The four columns with the vaulted ceiling remained in its original height. The rooms around the main sanctuary were also remodeled. Out of the school room, the Kehillah room, and women's section, one large conference room was made. The interior of the shul was painted a uniform white color which covered up all the murals painted by the Garfulnkel family, and also the excerpts from Psalms which were engraved in the wall since the eighteenth century. Only the leviathan which was painted two hundred years ago and was recently restored with great effort by Polish artists remained in place. In front of the two entrances there are signs in Polish: "The Central Public Library in Strzyzow." The fact that this building served as a prayer house for the Jews for four hundred years is not mentioned because there was no one in Strzyzow to see to it, unlike Krakow or even a smaller town like Lancut.

Shortly, two other houses near the shul will be demolished. The house of Reb Reuven Saphire which is located on the right side of the lawn in front of the shul, and the house of Reb Yacov Kanner on the left side. On these lots the city intends to build a large commercial center. The city originally planned to construct such a building on the vacant lot, after demolishing the shul, but failing to get permission from the authorities, they still found a way to build the building which will include the lot in front of the shul.

During the renovation of the shul, when the brick wall on the south side of the structure separating the stairwell from the women's gallery was demolished, an opening to the stairs leading to the attic was found. There the Poles found the attic full of used and torn books. These books had been there since I was a young man, and they had kept piling up because of the large size of the attic. Nobody ever bothered to bury them as is customary with used and torn Hebrew books. Polish scholars who were conducting research about the Jewish life, which had disappeared, found out about those books and so did we. We heard rumors that four hundred holy books were discovered in the attic of the ancient shul. After we checked it out, the true character of this find became clear to us.

The presence of the Jews in Strzyzow is being forgotten. Once in a while, some Jew living in Poland reaches Strzyzow, trying to buy Hebrew books, candlesticks, and chandeliers, which can be found in gentile houses, the heirs of the Jews. One who recently visited Strzyzow was the brother of Reb Reuven Saphire.

It is understandable that our contact with our birthplace, which we still visualize as the effervescent Jewish town, will eventually cease because we have no interest in the new gentile Strzyzow.

One more person from Strzyzow survived the Holocaust. This is Joseph Baumel, the son of Benjamin. He and his brother Tzvi, lived in Krakow and, at the outbreak of the Second World War, attempted to return home to their parents in Strzyzow. Tzvi was killed in Preclaw near Mielec and Joseph came home.

A week before the expulsion of the Jews from Strzyzow to the ghetto in Rzeszow, he returned to the place where he worked before in Krakow, a big Jewish business, which was now administered by a German. He hoped to be able to work there.

[Page 261]

Unfortunately he was caught by the Nazis and was sent to Plaszow and other camps. During a transport he jumped from a death train, which was going to Auschwitz, winding up in Mauthausen, where he was liberated. After the end of the war, he met a girl co-worker from before the war, who was with him in one of the camps and who he thought was dead. He married her, and they immigrated to the United States of America.

[Page 262]

Words of Contemplation and Thoughts

Judaism and Nationalism
by Rabbi Israel Frenkel, Toronto, Canada

This article is dedicated to the memory of the martyrs, my wife Esther, daughter of Reb Shlomo Diamand; my daughters Rachel and Sarah, my sons Shlomo and Shalom who were killed in Lwow in 1941, for the sanctification of the Divine Name, by the savages, the Nazis and their helpers, whose names should be obliterated forever.

The horrible and fearful Holocaust, the impressions of which are carved with a steel etcher in everyone's heart, had revealed and exposed the cultural consciousness of Esau, and manifestly proved that secular knowledge is not a sufficient means to education the sleeping animal in the human being. There is nothing in the human being that can curb his natural inclination to plunder and murder. It is clear that what was pathetically called progress was only an outward appearance, blinding the eye from seeing the animal in mankind, who as soon as he smells blood, shakes his back, kicks with his legs and rushes to satiate his passion exposing his nude image and his true character.

The same thing is lacking in Jewish Nationalism which was created in the same form. The force that is needed which could restraint he inner dismantling of the spirituality, causing assimilation and loss of the meaning of the word "Nation," of which the Diaspora had become a scaffold and the dispersion throughout all the corners of the globe had often times offered various material convenience in exchange for assimilation. Our history confirms such a fact by the disappearance without a trace of the ten tribes who sailed into the mighty sea of the Assyrian people. They were the Samaritans who adopted the strange cult during the reign of Jerubaam, even before the general dispersion, refusing to surrender to the holy authority of the Temple in Jerusalem.

The nationalism of the Samaritans was insufficient to stand as a barrier against the plague of assimilation, but such was not the case in the Kingdom of Judah. Because Judah held on firmly to the Hebrew traditions and culture, it was not swept away with the torrent and did not fall victim to the craze of disintegration which plagued the Kingdom of Israel. In fact, after seventy years in Babylonian exile, Zerubavel, Ezra and Nechemiah, made the declaration about the return to Zion which provoked the declaration of Koresh, the ruler of Babylon, resulting in the building of the Second Temple and the restoration of the political life of the Jewish people in their land.

[Page 263]

Thanks to the spiritual center in Yavneh and its scholars, the well from which the soul of the people drew its spiritual food, and their glow, which illuminated the darkness of the exile, and the hearts of the afflicted, made them believe in a glorious future after the coming of the Messiah, which turned into the "I believe" of all Jews. This has preserved our energy and enabled us to reach this point at a time when within other nations, religion and nationalism are sovereign ideas. The states are separate from religion because religion engulfs many nationalities. Our religion engulfs our nation alone, as it is said: "This nation alone shall dwell without consideration of others." Israel and the Torah are one. Blood relationships do not make the Jews a people. Extremism and racism are strangers to Judaism. Racism by itself stems from Darwinism which denies the Teachings of the Torah of Moses, which begins with: "And G–d created man." David King of Israel was the grandson of Ruth the Moabite who accepted the ethics of Judaism recognizing the Torah's world outlook without external material enticement. When she said, "Your G–d is my G–d," she became part of Israel's body.

[Page 264]

Territorial boundaries do not define Jewish nationhood either. Besides the mysterious holiness of our land "Upon which G–d's eyes had been cast from the beginning until the end," the borders serve only as an insulator to prevent infiltration of alien influence. Within their borders the Jewish people can fulfill their aspirations and their characteristic life undisturbed, without being socio–economically dependent upon gentile rules, a first step toward spiritual surrender, which ends up in complete assimilation. The criterion of natural Judaism is based specifically on deeds and obedience, on ways of thoughts and actions, whose roots were derived from the great and rich past of the people, and the mental inclination of the gentle Jewish soul, nurtured by the historical idealism hidden in the Book of Moses.

Even before the conquest of our land, when the Israelites wandered in the desert and stood at the foothills of Mount Sinai, when they had repudiated the Egyptian rituals, the voice of Moses, the leader of our people, was heard: "Today you became a nation." By receiving the Torah the nation had been crystallized and became a whole unit. It would be considered a betrayal of the people and their national values to turn away from the Torah, Heaven forbid. Nationalism without a Jewish outlook and idea, and without religion is like a body without a soul, not able to exalt the Jewish soul to its desired level.

Rabbi Israel Frenkel, Toronto, Canada

Until now my words were addressed to the Jewish youth, "to the boy and girl only." Now I would like to turn the coin to the other side: "To the mature man and woman." Already at the end of the nineteenth century, there were anti–Semitic politicians in Austria and Germany who developed a concept, defining the Jews a sect of believers observing Jewish religion. With such a concept they wanted to solve the Jewish problem with the kiss of death, by burning the soul out of the existing body. It attracted the assimilated and they became faithful partners of this concept in order to fight Zionism. To our sorrow, the premise of depriving the nationality had also found many sympathizers among the Orthodox segment of our people, who were apprehensive that Zionism might penetrate the wall of the Beit Hamidrash and would negatively influence the religious youths. For the same reason, the Orthodox also opposed emigration to the United States which, as it appears now, was destined by Providence. The increase of the Jewish community in the United States through mass immigration had saved the American Jewry fom assimilation.

[Page 265]

We witnessed the same phenomenon following the development of the Jewish community in Eretz Israel and the forming of its religious image. The Jewish people's strong will to live and the Divine promise: "And even when they (the Jews) will be in the land of their enemies, I will not despise them, and will not abhor them, to be destroyed," was stronger than the artificial wall that some Jews erected between their heart and brain, between the body and soul, between nationality and religion, The self negation in different countries of the Diaspora did not reduce even one iota the hatred of the Eternal People by the world. It also did not stop the national feeling of the youths. Also, the seekers of social justice among the nations, the dreamers of a new world, and their leader Karl Marx, in his stigmatizing chapters about the character of Judaism, are trying to describe Judaism in an unfavorable light. They are depriving the Jewish people of their national character. According to his teacher

Marx, Stalin the student, in his pamphlet, "The problems of Nationalism" negates the nationhood of the Jewish people, relying on Marx' quotations.

However, the sub–sequential force of the Zionist movement, its growth, the flourishing progress of the settlements in Eretz Israel, the people's fight for freedom, and the ocean waves of the exoduses, has eradicated the above false idea forever. As a result of these historical events, Stalin changed his mind, according to Gromyko's declaration in the United Nations, and the recognition of the Jewish State. And if the gentiles could change their minds, more so those Jews who kept their distance and had a negative opinion toward Zionism, causing division – they surely ought to change their minds and negative stand toward the resurrection movement of the people and its spirit. Nationalism and Jewish religion are identical and both are derived from the same source – the Torah of Moses, the foundation of which the claim to our land is based. And, without the land, we cannot carry on the wholeness of the Torah.

Judaism has taught us to love mankind. Our people were crowned with titles such as merciful, shy, and benefactors. Judaism is a synthesis of the people's heart and its brains. Its symbol is the head phylactery opposite the brain, and the hand phylactery opposite the heart, which shall not be separated. Judaism requires turning severity into a form, to sacrifice the body on the altar of the nation for the eternal soul of the people, for the existence of the nation, and sanctification of the Divine Name.

The brain of the nationalistic Jews should be influenced from the spirit of the Torah, the soul of Judaism. The religious Jew should comprehend with his intellect the importance of the national factor which is Judaism's body. The Jew who believes shall rest and repose on the seventh day because on this day G–d rested. The nationalistic Jew should do the same because his forefather had protected him for generations. The religious Jew should put on his prayer shawl and tefillin as a devotion to the Divine, and the nationalistic Jew as a devotion to: "Thou shall respect thy father and mother," and, "Thou shall not abandon the teaching of thy mother."

[Page 266]

The platonic division between religion and nationalism is a disturbing factor in national unity, and its demolition is in order.

A Partial Answer, Regret and Guilt
by Rabbi Israel Frenkel, Toronto, Canada

This article is dedicated to the tragic death of my mother, Chana Turner, in the ghetto Kozow, and to my brother, Tzvi, his wife Hassah, and their son Baruch. Blessed be their memory.

The heart of every Jew is replete with Job's sufferings, and some time filled with Job's complaints against G–d. Let the believing reader find in these lines a partial answer to his complaints against Providence.

Years have gone by since the awful tragedy occurred. This was a national tragedy and a tragedy for thousands of individuals. The nation was somewhat compensated for her losses through the establishment of the sovereign State of Israel in the holy land and the return of its sons to their home. A celebrated beginning of total redemption and also a small consolation to the individuals, the surviving remnants, each of whom can declare: "I was there and saw the suffering." However, for the nation or the individual, it is still a long way from a complete recovery. We are even further from understanding the horror of the tragedy which we witnessed, and of which we were a part. Once in a while a "severe complaint arises in our hearts against Heaven, "and everyone is like Job from Biblical times who objected and wondered about G–d's justice. Therefore, an attempt will be made here to enlighten the impasse, according to this writer's outlook, an outlook to which he arrived immediately after the Shoah, and which has been growing stronger inside of him from then until the present.

As it is known, the nature of a person is a synthesis of material and form, of human wisdom and instinct. He always stands at the crossroads between good and evil. He can freely choose between t hem, as our sages said, "The path a person follows – he is led to." If his godly part, his wisdom, overtakes instinct, he overpowers his bestiality and becomes a free man, not a slave to his passions. Then he is an ethical thinker, a whole person. However, if his instinct dominates his wisdom, he becomes a slave to his bestial passions. His spirit becomes warped, he loses G–d's image, and his wildness surpasses even that of the beast.

This freedom of choice to select a path in life is one of the cornerstones of the holy Torah, which is based on "There is law, and there is a judge." The leadership from above, Divine providence, is in command of everything around us. However, it is different with man's actions. Good or bad deeds are not controlled by a higher dictate. "He does not dictate bad or good." A person is unhindered and is free to perform good or bad deeds, from which he himself is responsible. And it is up to heavenly justice to punish man for his bad deeds, and reward him for his good ones. This is the primary religious principle referred to as: Reward and punishment.

On the basis of the above theory that a person has the freedom of choice, free to perform humanitarian deeds or, in the alternative, he can rob and murder, therefore, we come to the conclusion that, if a person finds himself in a dangerous situation, he must make a choice and do everything possible to escape from that danger that is hovering over him and not rely on miracles. This was formulated by sour sages: "Every ting depends on Heaven except deeds. When you see a crooked path, beware, and G–d will assist you." Here we reached the partial solution to our problems.

[Page 267]

Is there a more dangerous situation than a small minority living among a grim, hostile population that is always ready to destroy them? In such a dangerous situation, it was an elementary religious commandment to do something to alleviate that problem and escape from that place, as Jacob did when Laban's face changed and gave him that hostile look. G–d told him, "Return to your fatherland," and leave this dangerous place. From that, one should draw the conclusion that whoever closes his eyes to danger can only blame himself. The individual or community finds himself in a situation of abandonment by G–d.

Just as in regard to the flood, G–d had told Noah one hundred and twenty years earlier to build the ark. And Providence had sent Jeremiah, the messenger, with a warning, half a century before the destruction of the Holy Temple. The return to Zion Movement was also created by Providence to awaken the European Jewry from their sweet dreams, and take them away from the flesh pots. They refused to see that around the golden calf there were animals with human likeness that were waiting for the proper moment to destroy them. When some of those nationalistic messengers came to us from a "distant place" because they came from assimilated circles, but we should have understood that they were sent by G–d. The Zionist Movement engulfed assimilated families also, whose children became fighting pioneers. "The sound of the masses is like the sound of the Almighty." It was G–d's message to save them from the crematoriums in their future. In fact, the Jewish settlement in Eretz Israel remained unscathed by the blood–flood, just like Noah's ark during the flood.

Was it not a sign from G–d when, after the First World War in which we lost more blood than others, Balfour appeared with his declaration for a Jewish Homeland in Eretz Israel? The gates of Palestine were open for years but, unfortunately, we refused to leave the golden calf and the flesh pots of Europe. Our leaders also committed a sin because they chose the comfortable but risky way of, "Stay put/do–nothing attitude." Forgetting the teachings of the Torah: "And you will be blessed in all your endeavors," the leaders refused to recognize the sign of G–d.

In conclusion, we must say that the tragedy that befell our nation is not as some would like to interpret it as G–d's punishment. However, it should remind us of our guilt for being passive to the oncoming danger. We continued to live in a sea of hatred at a time when it was hinted from Heaven to escape and make aliyah to Eretz Israel, the land on which, "G–d set his eyes on from the beginning to the end."

Even now we try to return to our stupidity and cling to the defiling nations. We are returning to the danger and we sit among the gentiles whose bestiality may burst out tomorrow or the next day. There are some people among us who try to wrap this thing in piety. They are looking for the beard on the faces of the Israeli leadership, and if they do not find it, they kick the State.

[Page 268]

Let us not search in the faces of the Israeli leadership for the features of the high priests who served in the Holy Temple. The leaders' greatness expresses itself in that they know how to stand up to the enemies who are at our gates. Great is the suffering even now that the Jewry of Poland, Lithuania, Galicia, and the majority of the Hungarian Jewry are not with us in

Israel. How can we correct this sin? By returning to the homeland in Eretz Israel. This will be the consolation for the destruction. This will be the answer to our disturbing thoughts which keep pestering us. A great danger hovers over us. Statehood or slaughter. Let us select Statehood.

Our Strength Against a Hostile World
by Rabbi Israel Frenkel, Toronto, Canada

The world's nations have utilized all kinds of methods in order to force us to disintegrate and cease to exist. They use paradoxical controversial distortions on our account to motivate the nations to exhibit their hatred for the Jews. Simultaneously, with the wild shut, "Take revenge!" for the supposed ritual killing of a Christian child during the pogrom in Kielce, was also heard the beastly roar about the Judeo–Communism. From the left we were crowned with the title of international capitalists and from the right with the title international Communists. It makes no difference whether the distortions are believers or atheists, conservatives or progressives, we always remain the weak, gentle people, always the scapegoat, the lightning rod which ought to divert the anger of the masses from their rulers who direct their rage upon the helpless, defenseless, Jewish citizens.

However, the strong will to live possessed by the Jewish people, that stiff–necked nation, refused to resign from their historic existence, and would not give up their hopefulness for a bright future. The trials and tribulations that the Jewish folk organism had to endure, that their tormentors imposed upon them, did not break or weaken their drive for continuity. The desire for moral and spiritual resistance has risen even more, in spite of the painful suffering, as the Torah says in Numbers I, v. 12, "But in the measure that they afflicted the same, so it multiplied and so it spread itself out."

After the Second Destruction, Rome celebrated the destruction of Judea at the gates of Titus. They thought that the end had come for the nation. However, soon the sun began to shine from Sura, Nahardea, and Pumpedayta, the Talmudical universities where the bloodied organism of the Jewish people was healed, the nation's soul was forged, and the will to live was refreshed to await a future full of hope, and refused to give up even one iota of belief in the eternity of Israel. At a time when not even a trace of the Roman Empire remained, we awoke to a spiritual life by creating the Babylonian and Jerusalem version of Talmud, which glued together the loose parts of the persecuted Jewish people from Babylon and Eretz Israel into one unit.

When the Crusaders tried through pogroms and murder to break the stubbornness of the Jewish will to live, a bright star began to shine from the Jewish scholars of Spain. The well–known Golden Era which introduced new horizons of wisdom and thoughts for the Jewish soul, crystallized itself in the thirteen "I believes" of Maimonides. These thirteen statements refreshed with hope the Jewish lamb which spread throughout the world and strengthened the belief in a promising future.

[Page 269]

When the Ukrainian Hitler, Chmielnicki, committed his brutal blood–shed from the Jewish body, the nations of the world thought that we had despaired and our stubbornness was broken forever. But soon a great light speared in the darkness: The Hassidism of the Baal Shem Tov, of blessed memory, which shined into the downtrodden Jew, brought an uplifting of the Jewish soul. The Jew drew power, belief, and assurance in a brighter morning, and looked with abhorrence upon his tormentors.

After the blood–flood, the last gruesome catastrophe of the European Jews, our enemies thought: "Their hope is gone." They were sure that after such a bloodletting from the body of the Jewish nation it will remain powerless, and Jewish struggle for self–determination was shattered forever. However, despite our enemies, with help from above, the grandchildren of the Hasmonian, with incomparable heroism and might, the modern–day Macabees jumped into a holy war with enthusiasm, and fought for the existence and continuance of the body and soul of the Jewish nation and they did not fear for t heir lives. Because the dying of Jewish heroes possesses a high moral idealistic sense, our present–time Macabees, with their readiness to die, have removed the diaspora shame of being led like sheep to the slaughter.

The quiet noise of lamentation and the roaring rivers of blood from our holy martyrs in Europe disturbed the conscience of some of the righteous gentiles who sinned by being passive to the Jewish tragedy. The millions of souls of our martyrs were seeking an amendation and a reason for the Holocaust. Therefore, the Israeli heroes who spilled their blood on the battlefields during the war for Independence have given an amendation and content to the holocaust in Europe. Their blood had touched the victim's blood.

Martyrdom and the Sanctity of Life
by Rabbi Isaac Glikman, author of Holocaust and the Revival

Dedicated to the memory of my older brother, Joel, and his family
May G–d avenge their innocent blood

It was told: When Rabbi Yossi, the son of Kisma, became ill, Rabi Hanina, the son of Tradion, came to visit him. And Rabbi Hanina said, "Brother, don't you know that the nation which rules us was predestined by Heaven? And I heard that you are openly engaged in studying the Torah, with people gathered around you. You are also holding a Torah scroll on your lap." The sick responded, "Heaven will have mercy." Said Rabbi Hanina, "I am talking reality and you are telling me that Heaven will help. I will be surprised if they will not burn you together with the Torah scroll." It was told that a few days later Rabbi Yossi passed away and the biggest personalities of Rome came to his funeral.

[Page 270]

On their return, they found Rabbi Hanina engaged in studying Torah, a large crowd around him, and he was holding a Torah scroll on his lap. He was brought before the Romans who tied him up together with the Torah scroll, put branches soaked in water, and put them on his chest to delay his expiration. His pupils told him: "Open your mouth and let the fire enter you." Their intention was to hasten his death and lessen his pain. Then Rabbi Hanina responded: "The one who gave me life should take it away. I cannot do it." A Roman by the name of Kalztoniri said to the Rabbi: "Rabbi, if I would make the fire bigger and take off the wet woolen sponges, would you recommend me to obtain a reward in the hereafter?" Said the Rabbi. "Yes! I swear." Soon the fire grew bigger, the wet sponges were removed, and Rabbi Hanina expired. Another Rabbi lamented: "Some gain a reward in the hereafter in a second, and some have to serve G–d all their lives." (Excerpt from the Talmudical tractate, Avoda Zarah, pg. 18.)

Two basic things stand out from the above tale which described the spiritual image of Rabbi Hanina, who had reached the highest level of sanctification. The first part of the story shows us the greatness of the virtue to love G–d and his torah which burned inside him like a flaming fire. It prodded him publicly to defy the ruler's order forbidding the study of Torah, without considering the danger to his life. When Rabbi Hanina was asked why, he responded that G–d's commandment is to study Torah. He did not even try to defend himself in order to save his life, as if he were just waiting for the chance to sacrifice his life on the altar for the holiness of G–d and his Torah. Yet, the second part of the story is no less amazing. It extends the principle of the sanctity of life that prevented the Rabbi from hastening his death, even though he was in great pain and on the verge of dying. At his student's suggestion to open his mouth, he said: "Life is not the domain of man. It belongs to the one who had given it." The reason the other Rabbi cried was not that Rabbi Hanina had refused to hasten his death, but rather, that Rabbi Hanina, in his horrible suffering, was forced to help the Roman, his brutal executor, received a reward in the hereafter for relieving him from his suffering and hastening his expiration.

Two commandments, one parallel with the other, have come down from heaven to the people of Israel and imprinted their mark on them. "And I shall be sanctified among the children of Israel." (Leviticus XXII, 32,) "And ye shall keep my statues and live with them." (Leviticus, XIII, v. 5.) According to Halacha: "Not ye shall die with them, did G–d say, but live with them." The first commandment re quests sanctification of his Name, and the second commands us to preserve and guard our life regardless of the circumstances or situation, as long as it is not connected with the sanctification of his Name. These two commandments conquered the Jewish heart. They penetrated t he depths of the soul and became personal characteristics of the people, which protected them from spiritual and physical annihilation. On one hand, the spilled blood for the sanctification of the Divine Name during all generations was a kind of bloodletting from the nation's organism which strengthened her spirit and healed her soul.

[Page 271]

And, on the other hand, the strong guidance for the continuity of life, despite all physical and mental suffering involved, guarded the people from physical annihilation. The ability to adapt to the conditions of diasporal life, filled with humiliation and bitterness, and the strong will to continue to live, even though we had to bow down to let them trample on our backs, those commandments guarded us from annihilation and suicide.

Our sages drew the same moral from Rabbi Akiba when his ship broke up at sea. He was asked the question: "Who saved you?" He answered, "A board from the ship happened to come along, and to every wave which came at me, I nodded with my head." And from that response, the sages concluded the following: "If the wicked attacks you, you shall nod your head at them." This became the policy of the Jewish people in their diasporal life. This policy had brought the wrecked ship of the Jews through the stormy waves of the tyrants and the wicked who threatened to sink her during all the years of the dispersion, until the ship reached safe harbor.

Every once in a while we hear criticism from the younger generation in our land about the passivity of the holocaust martyrs in relation to their annihilators, who led them like sheep to the slaughter; words as sharp as stabbing swords which desecrate the honor of the martyrs whose destruction resulted in the establishment of the State of Israel. Their ostentatious words are accompanied by, "If we would have been there…" And they do not tremble nor feel the extent to which their remarks are deprived of basic reality, missing understanding and historical sense. The example Rambam used in his Guide For the Perplexed (Part II, sec. 17) is known to contradict those who believe in antiquity and take as evidence natures existence after the creation, believing that nature existed in the same way during the formation or prior thereto. It is the same as though someone compares the living condition and natural development of a child after his birth to the natural growth and development of a child after his birth to the natural growth and development in his mother's womb. The Holocaust martyrs had suddenly found themselves in the mouth of a savage animal who had trampled great nations and mighty governments. The martyrs had no arms or shields. They had been dispersed and dwelled among a gentile and hostile population. They knew well that rebellion had no chance to succeed and would have been suicidal. To satisfy feelings of vengeance by killing a few cursed Nazis would have caused immediate death and horrible torture for thousands of Jews.

Undoubtedly, if the victims would have been given a chance to survive for the price of betraying their faith, they would have followed in the footsteps of the martyrs from past generations and would have given their lives away. But the German Amalekites declared war on Israel and his G–d, and did not give his victims the opportunity to sanctify the Divine Name. They, the victims, preserved the purity of their faith and carried on their duty to live until the last minute. They returned their souls to their Creator, believing that they had merited to be the ones who drank the poisonous cup of the tribulations of the dispersion to the end, and the spilled blood fulfilled the faithful function which repeats itself in Jewish history.

[Page 272]

The expression of the Prophets came through in one short sentence: "In thine blood thou shall live."

It is true that they did not survive the flood of blood and fire but, with their deaths, they bequeathed their lives to the People of Israel. Therefore, arise and honor the martyrs of the Holocaust. Because of their blood we are alive.

I Shall See the Holocaust Before My Eyes Forever
by Shlomo Yahalomi

The question, "Why does the righteous suffer and the wicked prosper?" Is as old as the universe. Already the master of the Prophets, Moses our Teacher, asked G–d: Let me understand yours ways. (Exodus XXXIII, v. 11). According to our sages, the intention of this questioning by Moses was, "Why is it that some righteous men prosper and some suffer….and why is it that some wicked men prosper and some suffer? (Talmud tractate Brachot, pg. 7). Also Jeremiah asked: "Why are the wicked successful?" And there is no harder question than this one. Despite all the answers that have been given, this question remains and has never been fully solved. There is a vacuum among the thinkers of the world. And, if this is asked by every generation and they have never diverted their mind from it, more so, this question is asked by our generation, the generation of the Holocaust. And this question will probably be asked in the future until the Revered Name will reveal he reasons for it, and all mankind, not only the believers, will see that, "G–d's ways are just and all his deeds are benevolent." However, it is true and correct that G–d's thinking is not as ours and we are not competent to understand his ways or to reach the depths of his thoughts. As Rabbi Nachman from Braclaw had already expressed in his sharp remark, "What kind of a G–d would he be if Nachman would understand Him?" Nevertheless, plenty of pleasant thoughts were expressed and much was said about the puzzling question, even though it was not explained completely. However, these thoughts and explanations made it easier for us to digest one of the greatest curiosities. We will briefly mention a few principal answers which have been given by our sages, adding explanatory comments from commentators and writers, and a little bit from this writer too.

1. The Creator of mankind has created a world with everything in it. He created mankind with wisdom and has given him true learning, the Torah of Life, which guides and shows mankind which way to follow and the required deeds, fulfill G–d's commandments, and despise wickedness. Although G–d can force mankind to fulfill his commandments, he has given him a free choice to distinguish between good and evil. If man chooses the good, he merits his reward in the hereafter. And, if he chooses wickedness, he is punished. Yet, if G–d would reward the righteous and punish the wicked in this world, this would invalidate the whole principle of free choice because man would be afraid to sin and, perforce, would choose to be good. Therefore, G–d conducts the world in an ambivalent way. One righteous man prospers, and the other not. The same is true with the wicked.

[Page 273]
From this ambivalence the free choice between denial and belief is derived, between the fulfillment of G–d's commandments and their disregard. If the human being is free to choose as he wishes, he is responsible for his deeds and there is a punishment and reward, mainly in the hereafter.

2. Let us quote the sages in their own words: "Just as the wicked is punished for the smallest infraction in the hereafter, so is the righteous man punished for the smallest infraction in this world. Just as the righteous are paid a reward in the hereafter, even for the tiniest good deeds, so are the wicked rewarded for any tiny good deeds in this world." (Talmud, tractate Tamid, pg.11.) Again, the sages have said: "The Almighty brings suffering upon the righteous in this world so they would be rewarded in the hereafter. He bestows favors upon the wicked in this world in order to torment and denigrate them to the lowest level in the hereafter." (Talmud, tractate Kidushin, pg. 40). And the ages continued: "G–d is exacting with the righteous and holds them accountable for each little wrong that they committed in order to secure their tranquility, and the best reward in the hereafter. The wicked, he rewards for the little good they do in this world and holds them accountable for their wickedness in hereafter." There are many more sayings on this subject throughout the Talmud and the Zohar. To sum up what the sages have said in our own wordsis: G–d pays the wicked in this world so that they would have no reward in the hereafter because over there, therewards are so great that they do not compare to the rewards of this world. In contrast, the righteous man's punishmentfor a sinis much greater in hereafter than in this world. And that is how Rashi comments on the sentence:
And He pays his enemies in order to deny him."
3. So far we have considered the traditional teachings. However, in the mystical teachings, in the Kabbala books, the "righteous suffering" is explained as follows: There are no new souls in our generation. They have all been in this world once or many times before. And if it so happens that a person had sinned in this previous life and, after his departure, G–d had mercy upon him, he is lowered again to this world in order to pay for his sin and cleanse his soul. Therefore, it is possible that height become righteous and honest. Fulfilling equally the small and large commandments, yet he could still suffer because of t he sins of his previous life.
4. By what has been previously said we are establishing without doubt that the righteous man suffers and the wicked prospered. However, many of our ancestors cast doubts, whether what we see as good and evil is in fact so. The source of this opinion comes from our sages, and we will explain it in detail. Let us begin from the verse in Genesis I, v. 31. "And G–d saw everything He made, and behold it was very good." The Commentator comments on it as follows: At first glance, everything we see in this world is seen with our eyes. At first glance, every thing we see in this world is seen with our eyes. We do not know if the bad we see or the good is absolute, because we see only what happens now but we cannot see the consequences of these events. Therefore, we cannot judge whether it is good or bad. What we consider bad may result in good.

[Page 274]

And G–d saw what he made means G–d who sees and can look until the end of the generations. He can see everything he made, not part of it. "Behold it was very good." G–d knows that everything is very good. "Day unto day pours forth speech, and night unto night reveals knowledge." It happens that you are full of wonderment and question about the Divine's ways and you cannot understand the phenomenon of daily life which seems to you as an obscure puzzle, but you have to realize that the "day of the future will eventually come in place of the "day" which has passed. "Pours forth speech" means that the day of the future will explain, interpret, and reveal knowledge about the "night" of today and tomorrow. It will expose the obscure and remove the doubts. Many occurrences are so obscure that they do not make sense and are not logical. You see only obscure lines but, "At the end of the world is the solution." End of the world means in the far future. "This world is not as in the hereafter." In this world you say blessings on good tidings and on bad, but in the hereafter there is only the best. Why? Because in this world our lives are short and we cannot see the end results of bad things, but in the hereafter, where the end results became known, that is where everything is good and beneficial.

"And Joseph shall put his hands upon thine eyes." (Gen. XLII, v. 4) When Jacob's sons sold their brother Joseph to the Ishmaelites, it was a big event in that period, a horrible tragedy to our Father Jacob from which he refused to be consoled. However, the future showed that this tragedy became a great source of happiness because "G–d considered it a favor." "And Joseph shall put his hand upon his eyes" means that the misfortune of Joseph showed that humans are short–sighted and cannot see the end of G–d's intentions. As it is said: "Man's days are short and filled with wrath." (Job XII, v. 1.) Since man is short–lived, he cannot see the shaping of history to the end. Therefore, he is full of rage and bitterness. (According to the book <u>Wisdom and Morals</u>.)

How precious are the words of Reb Moshe the Scribe, the author of <u>Chatam Soifer</u> who explains that: "And thou shalt see my back but my face shall not be seen," means that G–d's ways are visible but are only understood later, a long time after the fact. But, when these events occur, they are not understood and often times seem strange and unjust, Heaven forbid. On the phenomenon of the treatment by G–d of the righteous and the wicked which sometimes undermines the belief in G–d, Rabbi Aaron Levin of blessed memory, may G–d avenge his blood, commented on "Let me see I beseech you, Thy glory?" What was G–d's response? "I will cause all my goodness to pass before they face," which meant that G–d will show Moses all the facts as they occur in their entirety, and it will prove to you that, "I will be gracious to whom I will be gracious, and I will show mercy to whom I will show mercy." Because I have mercy for those who need mercy, and I am gracious to those who need graciousness.

Rabbi Yanai said it in one and succinct sentence. "We cannot pass judgment about the welfare of the wicked and the suffering of the righteous." Wise men do not ponder a problem which they cannot solve completely.

However, all that we have heretofore discussed has concerned individual righteous men.

[Page 275]

The matter is entirely different when we approach the dreadful chapter of the Holocaust. The words "Six Million" hang in the air before our eyes, engraved with letters of blood, fire, and clouds of smoke from the furnaces and gas chambers, in which they were tortured and died. The parents, wives, sons, daughters, brothers and sisters, millions of people from the House of Israel!!!!! The horror of the Holocaust to which there is no similarity in all the chains of terrible persecutions which have followed our hunted people during close to two thousand years of dispersion–there is no explanation for it. And, although we are forbidden to question the virtues of G–d, blessed be He, surely every believing Jew ought to think that G–d is right. We should not proclaim, as, to our sorrow and shame, extreme Orthodox Jews proclaim, that this was a punishment from Heaven for our sins! Even though G–d is righteous, we should not denounce our purified martyrs. As it is said in Deuteronomy XII, v. 7. "Ye shall not do so unto the Lord your G–d." On which the commentator Rim comments, "Do not say yes to your Lord your G–d, and do not justify every tribulation."

Here is what Rabbi Yehuda said about the quotation in Jeremiah IX, v. 9. "Who is the wise man who understood why we lost our homeland" This question was asked the sages, the Prophets, and the angels, and nobody seemed to be able to explain why, until G–d himself gave the explanation, as it is written: "And G–d said because they abandoned my Torah." At the outset those words seem puzzling: What is the difficulty in answering the question why was the land lost? That the sages, the Prophets, and the angels could not answer. Essentially, every child who studies in school, if asked why we lost our land would answer, because Israel sinned. So, why didn't the sages and the rest of them explain it? A deep thought is hidden in Rabbi Yehuda's words. He wanted to point out that the sorrow and humiliation of the sages was so great and the embitterment so strong that, despite the fact that they believed and knew that G–d is righteous and His judgment is just, they did not want to openly justify the destruction. They could not restrain heir distress and say that the Jewish people deserved such a harsh punishment. They did not dare to accuse Israel and, therefore, they did not answer that question.

Only the Holy, blessed be He, He himself could have said, "Because they abandoned my Torah." Nobody else could have said it. No sage, no Prophet, and not even an angel. And if somebody would challenge this and say: If, on one hand, we are obligated to admit that G–d is just, and, on the other hand, not to justify the Holocaust, then, does this mean we should not think about the holocaust altogether, and it should be forgotten? To this we will respond and say: Heaven forbid! Such a thing will not take place among the Jews. On the contrary, the horror of the Holocaust cannot disappear from before our eyes – not even for one second. If we forget, we will add another Holocaust to the original Holocaust. It would be a sin to ourselves and our nation. Let us explain this subject.

When trouble befall an individual or upon a whole nation, there is, in addition to the negative, also a positive side. As it is written:

[Page 276]

"Tribulations cleans all the sins from man." (Talmud, tractate Brachot, page, 5) Tribulations awaken man from his sleep and urge him to recount his deeds, and to ask himself: "Why?" Why did it happen? What were the reasons for it? And, if he keeps pondering his question continuously and if it brings him to draw the true moral and the rightful conclusion, corrects what needs to be corrected, and he does not continue in the previous mistakes, this is considered the positive side of the tribulations. But, if afflictions do not wake man up, do not cause him to recount his deeds, and are not a factor and a strong lever to pick him up from his slump, from the life that he lived until now, then they were only empty pains that did not produce any positive results.

The conclusion that we derive from the above is as follows: Not to preach publicly about sins connected with the Holocaust, but every individual should think of himself and ask himself why and do some soul searching. Then he will find many answers to his questions.

Everyone should beat his own chest and not the chest of others. And that is the right conclusion and the proper moral. Everyone who does not want to holocaust which befell our people to have occurred in vain, should remember: "And I shall see the Holocaust before mine eyes forever."

Remembrance and Forgetfulness
By Samuel Nachum Frenkel, Toronto
son of Esther, the daughter of Reb Shlomo Diamand from Zyznow

According to medical science the process of forgetfulness is a natural process which accompanies the mortal from the day of his birth until he leaves this world.

Just as the parts of the body degenerate and lose their vitality with the approach of old age, so do the brain cells and many nerves become rigid and weaken the memory.

However, when parts of the body degenerate, they express themselves in all types of diseases which interrupts the normal function of mankind and causes pain. There are symptoms which serve as a warning that healing action is needed. But with forgiveness, this is not so.

Forgetfulness is free of any symptoms, and the body does not feel any pain or discomfort. There are certain forms of mental illness for which forgetfulness is a remedy. It is well known that physicians of the psychoanalysis school of thought inject the mentally ill with special drugs to hasten their forgetfulness and to rehabilitate to a normal life.

Yet, if forgetfulness is a blessing to an individual, it is a curse and a tragedy for society. "REMEMBER, DO NOT FORGET" is a warning with which our Torah is replete, is addressed to the whole nation in general because forgetfulness means the kiss of death. Therefore, the people needed harsh warnings against it. Contrast this to the quotation "A promise is made to the deceased that he will be forgotten from the heart." Without this promise the Jewish individual who painfully remembers the past could not find the energy to begin building a new life. Then came the eternal commandment, "Remember" which warns the people not to expel from their heart the memory of the holy martyrs of our nation and to eradicate the memory of the Amalekite.

May the memory of the holy martyrs be blessed and their souls be forever bonded in the bond of life with the martyrs of all generations.

[Page 277-8]

Samuel Nachum Frenkel, Toronto, Canada

[Page 279]

Written by Survivors

Woe is to Me for Those Who Perished
In Memory of My Family – Obliterated in the Holocaust
by Itzhok Berglass

Millions of our brothers were annihilated. However, the sorrow for the millions does not soothe the pain of the individuals for their close family members who were among the victims. The pain hurts even more because almost my whole family could have survived if not for the mistake of my sister and brother–in–law. Also for reasons beyond their control, my wife's family could have survived.

My sister and her husband acted humanly, but their mistake was ascribing to the enemy any human feeling and that the brutality of the Nazis would be beyond comprehension.

My brother–in–law, Reb Yacov Itzhok Bernstein, who was Nechama my older sister's husband, left Strzyzow on Thursday, September 7, 1939, with his three children, David Dov, age seventeen Elimelech, age fourteen, and their daughter, Bina, age six. He reached Dynow his birthplace, and stopped at his parents' house where his mother and his brother–in–law the assistant Rabbi of the city, Abraham Shorr, lived. During the whole day, Friday, he could not find transportation in order to continue his escape. Only at the end of the day, as soon as the Sabbath closed in on them, did they find an opportunity to continue. Most refugees, learned, pious people, Rabbis and scholars among them, traveled on the Sabbath, recognizing the life threatening situation. But my brother–in–law, the fearful and the pious one, refused.

He remained in Dynow until the Germans entered the town. He survived the bag massacre when the "Knights" killed two hundred and thirty men. At that time they did not touch women and children. Thereafter, he returned to Strzyzow to my mother and sister by horse and carriage which was sent for them by my sister. They lived in Strzyzow relatively quietly for a short time. This was during Commandant Keller's rule. Later they suffered together with all the townspeople until the bitter end.

The family was killed in the vicinity of Rzeszow because it was not worthwhile for the Nazis to deport my old mother Yocheved to an annihilation camp. She was killed locally, like all the old people, together with the rest of my family. Who refused to be separated from her.

The younger sister Chaya Sarah Feivusz, lived in Sanok, with her husband Abraham Itzhok, and two children, Yacov and Ruth. In order to get rid of the Jews who lived near the newly established German–Soviet border, the Germans expelled all the Jews to the other side of the San River, before the Russians arrived. Only a few Jews went into hiding to wait until the storm of the expulsion would be over. My sister's family was among them, despite the fact that at the beginning, they did plan to leave.

[Page 280]

They were packed and just waited for a horse and carriage to take them to the other side of the San River.

At the beginning of the occupation, they too lived a relatively quiet life until the annihilation began. When they felt that the peril was nearing, they built themselves a bunker together with the baker owner, Diller, who was the son–in–law of Reb David Dembitzer from Strzyzow. They built the bunker in a big oven in the baker and lived there a few years under excruciating conditions, constantly afraid of being discovered. They lasted almost until the liberation of the city by the Red Army, but a few months earlier the Nazis discovered the bunker and killed all of them.

The circumstances of the survival for the eight people of my wife's family could have been different. They were going to be exiled by the Soviets like us but, for some reason were not sent away and were killed during the Holocaust.

My father–in–law's family, refugees from Sendziszow, had expressed their desire to return home as we did and, therefore, would have been exiled on the same Friday, at the end of June 1940, when we were arrested to be sent away. But my father–in–law became ill and was operated on in Zolkiew. Therefore, he, his wife, Frieda, and son Eliezer, were spared from exile.

A short time later after the operation, my father–in–law passed away, and my mother–in–law along with her son remained in Zolkiew until the occupation by the Germans after the outbreak of the Soviet–German war. They were among the first to be killed before the others were sent into the ghetto.

My brother–in–law, Reb Abraham Taube, the husband of my wife's sister Chana, in whose house we lived before our exile to Siberia, was a very rich man. Almost all the rich people in town were sent into exile by the Soviets to places where the

Germans had not reached. My brother–in–law was sure that he too would be exiled with his family and, for a long time was packed and waited. Unfortunately, the Soviets did not touch them.

He was a goodhearted man, benevolent to the needy, even to those who later collaborated with the communists. The soviet authorities did not know the local population and, in order to distinguish between the average people and the rich, they received advice from those whom my brother–in–law helped. These people remembered their benefactors among which my brother–in–law belonged, and they saw to it that my brother–in–law was left alone.

That is why my brother–in–law remained in his house, worked in his specialty, managing the big forests which were nationalized by the Soviets, until the German occupation.

My sister–in–law Chana, with her brother and their mother, were soon killed. My brother–in–law jumped off a train which was transporting Jews to the annihilation camp. He was shot at and died in horrible pain. Their two sons, Joseph, age seventeen, and Moshe, age thirteen, were tortured to death in the Janow camp known for its disgrace.

My wife's older sister, Leah Millstein, was an active public servant in women's charitable organizations and in the Free Loan Society, in Lwow.

[Page 281]

She was the wife of a rich manufacturer, a partner in the famous beer brewery in Kalisz. She did whatever was possible to escape the Soviet exile. During the Nazi occupation she reached Warsaw on Aryan documents, and there she disappeared without a trace.

The only member of my wife's family who had no chance to survive was her brother and his family. He was a timber merchant and, during the annihilation, he escaped with his wife Bilha, into a village where they were hidden by a forester, a Christian acquaintance. He exploited them as much as he could, and then handed them over to the Nazis.

Of all my family and my wife's family, only those who were exiled by the Russians, survived, since they were out of reach by the Nazis.

My Family
by Shoshana Ginsberg nee Scheffler

My father Shimon Scheffler, and my mother Sheindl, were religious people, as were the majority of the people in town, and, in that spirit we children were raised.

Even though our parents were very religious, they did not put obstacles in our paths when we joined the pioneers of the Zionist Youth Movement, and aspired with all the others to immigrate to Eretz Israel. Our parents understood our feelings that we, the youth, could not continue to live in the Diaspora, in an atmosphere of hostility, deprivation, and frequent pogroms. They themselves hoped some day to join us.

To our regret their aspirations of joining us did not materialize. They sanctified with their deaths the divine Name, together with my brother Moshe and my relative Shoshana Gelbwachs, who was adopted by my parents just before my sister and I immigrated to Eretz Israel.

My brother David survived the German concentration camps but his health was ruined going through so much suffering. When he arrived in France after the liberation, he died after a prolonged illness. G–d shall avenge their blood.

My Mother
by Pinchos Klotz–Aloni

The well–known folk song "Mein Yiddishe Mame," always reminds me of my mother. Everyone knows his mother. Mine was just like yours, like everyone's mother. And when I happen to think about another cordial song, "A brivele De Mamen," I feel that I have sinned, I have written very few letters to my mother.

When I left my mother, more than thirty years ago, I left with the enthusiasm of a twenty year–old man with the thought of discovering a new world, and, if not, to help build a new world. I thought very little about the fact that I left at home such a dear mother who longed for me and waited for a letter.

[Page 282]

Now I would gladly write to her, but where is she? Where is my mother?

In the past, mothers were brought to a decent burial, and everyone knew their burial place. They had a gravestone which carried their holy names. But my mother do I know where her blood was spilled? Maybe her blood was not spilled at all? Maybe she was gassed to death in a gas chamber? Or, maybe she went to the ovens alive? Therefore, the pain is much heavier when you do not know what happened to her, where her bone disappeared.

And from my memories I draw pictures about my childhood when my mother showed so much love to me, when she protected me from my strict father's punishments. She was always covering up for me, taking the blame herself, because she knew that the things my father considered mischievous were not mischievous at all. All I wanted to do was to go to the river for a swim or run to the woods to play and, when I became older, I wanted to read a book. My father refused to recognize all these things. According to him, a Jewish boy ought to sit in cheder or Beit Hamidrash, study Torah, and not spend time foolishly.

However, my mother understood well these "foolishness" but I did not know to appreciate her greatness, her good–heartedness. Now, when I do understand it so well, she is not here anymore. Regretting does not help, and neither does beating my chest. All that is left in my memories is the vision of her, her bright portrait, which I will never stop revering and respecting as long as I live.

You see, my dear mother, these few lines that I wrote as a tribute to you are a tribute and a Kaddish for all the Yiddishe Mames, because they all were alike, they all possessed the same merits, the same attributes. May the radiant vision of the "Yiddishe Mame" appear before us from the tragic past like a light tower in a stormy sea to shine upon our paths in our present life.

Father Said: Do Not Remain Here
by Shulamit Grinwald–Hasenkopg

I arrived in Eretz–Israel from Frankfurt, Germany, at the end of October 1938. How much I longed for that day, but how bitter were the circumstances through which I finally merited to immigrate. For years I belonged to the Zionist Pioneer Youth Movement, and I was getting ready for a life of realization in Eretz Israel. My emigration documents arrived on Rosh Hashana 1938. The formalities were all arranged. The crates with my baggage were already sent and my suitcases were packed and ready. My mother was crying about the fact that our family was being torn apart, but I was joyful. I was looking forward to my departure. It was customary that on a day when a group of Zionist youth departed, relatives and friends came to the railroad station, singing Hebrew songs, dancing the Horah, not paying attention to the hostile looks of the Nazi onlookers. Thus my day of departure was approaching, it was set for Monday, November 3, 1938.

[Page 283]

And behold, on Thursday, my uncle came home with bad news. He had heard that Jews of Polish origin were expelled from nearby Wiesbaden. We were filled with anxiety. My mother, as usual, had already prepared everything for the Sabbath. We anxiously went to sleep. At five in the morning I was awakened. I heard a voice from my parents' room. "Get dress immediately! The whole family! You are being expelled to Poland," I got up and went into the next room. Two German policemen and one secret policeman in civilian clothes were standing there. "Oh! Here is one more Jewess." A policeman said. My father pleaded with the not to chase out such small children in the street in such a cold and rainy morning. There were three little brothers in our family. But to no avail. On the insistence of my father, they postponed my expulsion for three days because of my emigration papers. The whole family was ordered out. We were stunned. We woke the brothers. I helped mother to pack a few things. I went up to the attic where the wet laundry hung. It was frozen stiff because of the cold night. I still remember to this day the packing of the wet and frozen laundry. My little brothers were told that they were going for a train ride, and this, understandably, made them happy. In one half hour we were ready because the policemen kept rushing us. They were pressed for time. They had a lot of work to do expelling all the Jews from Frankfurt.

I embraced my family, and the policemen locked the apartment. I was allowed to take my suitcases with me. The policemen escorted my family to a transit station. It was five in the morning. I a sixteen–year–old girl, was left alone in the street in a pouring rain, a suitcase in each hand. I was perplexed. I did not know where to turn. I was sure that all my relatives were expelled. Suddenly, two Christian women passed by. They did not even see my face, but one said to the old in a happy voice, "It is really a nice day. They are throwing the Jews out in the street." Only then did I begin to cry in that gloomy morning. Bitterly crying, I took the two suitcases, and went to the "Pioneer House," to my instructors. They were still asleep, and I woke them up. I told them what happened. The immediately woke up the youngsters who they thought were designated to be expelled. They packed their belongings and provisions, including warm blankets. When the police came, the youngsters were taken away, leaving the food and the warm clothes behind.

The Sabbath passed in depression. I was supposed to leave Germany Monday. On Sunday I met my father. The Poles did not let him cross the border and he was returned to Frankfurt, Germany. The police gave him back the keys to the apartment. I met him in the street and silently embraced him. We were speechless. We walked home together. He opened the door and, in the kitchen, the food for the Sabbath was still on the shelves. All the beds looked as if the people had just slept in them. Suddenly my father began to tremble, a cold sweat covering his face. He began to vomit and he fainted. I pulled him, my strong, husky, and tall father, into bed. He then broke into a spasm and said: "Do not remain here! Go away from here quickly. We are all doomed. Only you have a chance to survive." Those words were a prophesy.

On that Monday, three youngsters, all by themselves, went to the railroad station. The station was empty. We sat in a corner and cried.

[Page 284]

In Munchen the train filled up with emigrants, but the depression did not fade away. Only when the train passed Rusbach, the border station, and left the German land, did a sudden change of mood overcome us. Everybody began to sing: "Masel Tov Jews, we are going home." This was a song which came from the heart, never to be forgotten.

The Bitter Account
by Shlomo Yahalomi

This is not a day for singing
Rather take a sheet of paper and write an elegy
(Reb Yehuda Halevi)

It happened the second day of Shavuoth 1947, in a Displaced Persons Camp, in Ferenwald, Germany. The synagogue was filled to the fullest capacity, actually overflowing. Outside the synagogue, hundreds of worshippers who had survived fire and frost, men, women, and orphans, waited to say Yizkor. They were getting ready to pour out their sadness and bitterness before the Master of the Universe. I was standing on the pulpit immersed in my thoughts, wondering how I would be able to fulfill my obligation and memorialize so many untainted martyrs, and also those who passed away of natural causes. I was duty bound to memorialize my parents, grandparents, my wife of my youth and our children, my sister and family, uncles, aunts, and so many colleagues who disappeared without a trace. And I did want to remember them all. Who would if not I? My heart was shrinking from pain and sorrow, my head weighted heavily upon my shoulders as if a huge mountain was pressing it. How can I roll these rocks off my chest? And suddenly, I remembered a heart–warming story about one of the ancient Rabbis of Strzyzow, Rabbi Elimelech Shapiro. And this is how the story is told:

Once during the High Holidays, the Rabbi took his prayer book in his hands and approached the pulpit to chant. The Rabbi chanted all day, but the prayer book remained open on the same page where he had opened it at the beginning of the day. When the Hassidim saw it, they were puzzled and asked him for an explanation. The Rabbi responded with a story. That in the days of the Baal Shem Tov, there was a Jewish man who was a tax collector for the master of the village. The man had a wife and one son. When the parents of the boy passed away, the master took him into his home and raised him as a Christian. Years later, when the boy found out that his parents were Jewish, he decided to run away and return to Judaism. When it became known to him that Yom Kippur is a day of pardon and forgiveness, the boy escaped to the nearest town and went to the synagogue. This was just before "Kol Nidrei." He saw that most people wore white, and prayed with tears in their eyes. He was very moved. He took a prayer book in his hand and, with tears in his eyes, he said: "Lord of the Universe, I do not know how to pray, I do not know what to ask for. Take this prayer book and read what it is appropriate to read because you know it all.

[Page 285]

Rabbi Tzvi Elimelech paused for a second and continued: "So did I. I took the prayer book in which the prayers are according to the holy Ari's version. It is full of mysterious and wonderful secrets which I absolutely do not understand.

Therefore, I opened it and put it before G–d, without turning the Pages, and said: "Master of the Universe, you have before you a prayer book according the holy Ari's version, and you know everything."

This is the story that came to my mind which relieved me from my confusion. Like that boy who returned to Judaism, I meditated, "You, G–d, knows everything at a glance." Suddenly a shriek escaped my mouth: "Yizkor Elohim," (Remember O G–d).

From that time on, every time I say Yizkor, I recall the above story. And that is how I memorialize all the souls. Also now, I intend to list with blood and tears all the victims that were sacrificed on the altar of the Nazi inferno, I know that I cannot remember everyone. But I rely on the Almighty who knows and remembers everything.

I will not write about my parents who died in the prime of their lives because they died of natural causes and I wrote about them in another place in this book. Here I will tell about those who were killed for the sanctification of the divine Name. First let us remember my companion, the wife of my youth, the enlightened, talented, and clever, Leah, the daughter of Reb Eliezer Licht from Brzostek, near Jaslo, in Western Galicia. The Licht Family was a well–respected family, and my father–in–law was an enlightened, and pious man. He established and led an exemplary Jewish home. All his sons and daughters were known for their education and exemplary behavior. My wife was the youngest of them all, and she was called "The brains of the family." After our marriage in 1936, we settled in Brzostek, and lived there for three and a half years, a life of happiness and tranquility, until the outbreak of the Second World War. The war brought an end to all our hopes and destroyed our home.

On the first day of the war, the enemy bombers appeared in the skies over our town. The fright was enormous. Many of the residents told me that, "Jews like you" meaning men known for their wealth, should escape because they will be the first victims. People were also convinced that the Nazis would not hurt women. Therefore, in order to spare the wife and the children, it was advisable for the men of the house to leave. Even my clever wife had begged me to go, first to my birthplace, Strzyzow, where my brother Heschel the head of the Kehillah was living and, later to escape together wherever we would decide. After much hesitation I left Brzostek, and a week after the outbreak of the war, I reached Strzyzow. This was September 8, 1939. I did not find my brother in Strzyzow because he had left a few hours before my arrival. While I was standing and regretting that I did not find him, the door opened and he walked in. It appeared that on his way, somebody told him that I was on my way, so he immediately returned. He wanted us to plan together what steps we should take. My brother was lucky to secure one seat in the car of Count Bilitcki, a Christian estate owner. He owed money to my brother and, therefore, he offered him a place in his car to travel to Lwow.

[Page 286]

My brother insisted that I should take the seat and he would somehow manage to find transportation. I refused. I was sure that he was endangering his life and finding a seat, even in a horse drawn cart, would be next to impossible. Finally, he surrendered. We separated with hugs and kisses, hoping to meet soon after Hitler's defeat.

Saturday night rumors spread that there would be heavy fighting between the Polish and German armies in the vicinity of Brzoztek because of the hilly topography. I decided without hesitation that I should not be here in Strzyzow while my wife, who was pregnant, was on the front line. Early next morning I returned to Brzostek. And, simultaneously, the Nazis occupied the city. I spent two months under the Nazi occupation. I will not go into details of my experience during these two months. Ultimately, my wife and I, and my relatives, concluded that the Nazis did not hurt women and children and I must go away. And so, on October 31, 1939, I was on my way. And here again I am skipping over many details about my wanderings and prisons in Lwow, Odessa and Charkov, hard labor in Siberia, and on and on. I received a letter and then a package from the wife of my youth. Despite the horrible situation in which they found themselves, she successfully ended her pregnancy and bore us a son.

"Life" in the Nazi inferno turned into hell. The sufferings have increased day after day. The savage German animals began to hurt women also. Everyone felt that the end was imminent, but still a spark of hope flickered in the hearts of the hunted and the tortured. My wife who possessed a lot of energy and was known as a clever woman refused to sit idle and wait for the bitter end. When the "actions" began at the end of 1942, she escaped from Brzostek with our daughter Sarah to the Krakow ghetto. (The infant son Joseph Chaim had died before because of the horrible living conditions.) She bleached the little girl's hair blond and, whoever did not know her and saw her golden curls, thought she was Aryan. After a short time in the Krakow ghetto, she escaped to the Bochnia ghetto where her sister was living. In time, she found out that there was a way of obtaining emigration papers for a large sum of money by taking the place of another woman. She was able to pay more than the other woman was willing to pay. (This woman survived although at that time, she was unwilling or unable to pay such a large amount. Still she did manage to survive notwithstanding the suffering she went through.) My wife obtained the much sought–after travel papers and, with a few more "lucky" people, she was put on a train which was supposed to take them abroad. Instead, the train arrived in the infamous Plaszow camp. Soon after their arrival, the cursed Nazis murdered all of them. May G–d favor their memory with all the rest of the untainted martyrs and avenge their spilled blood.

My sister Eta, was one of the attractive, educated, clever, and polite daughters of Strzyzow. When she learned she remembered. Whether this was our Prophets or the "Pan Tadeusz" (A famous Polish poem by Adam Mickiewicz), she knew it all by heart. Even though she was a little more educated than other girls, they never envied her. They loved her with their souls. It was all because of her gentleness and good–heartedness.

[Page 287]

She was easy–going and loved everybody. She strictly adhered to the Fourth Commandment, "Honor thy father and thy mother." After my father passed away, she watched over my mother as if she were the apples of her eyes. She married a good man with a heart of god, as the saying goes. He was an enlightened man with many virtues. His name was Reb Aryeh Leib, the son of Reb Benjamin Beinish Halevi Federbush, from Dzikow. The Federbush house was a house of Jewish glory. Both my sister and her husband were very charitable. A woman survivor from Dzikow has told me that my sister had sent back to Strzyzow her entire hope chest to a poor girl friend who was going to be married, and bought herself an entire new wardrobe. If there was in town a poor Bar Mitzva boy, she used to provide all the food for the festive meal. And the way she behaved, so did her husband. Despite being busy in his business, he always found time to spare to do something for the poor. He chaired the Food for Poor Committee and distributed the vouchers for lunch or dinner to the poor, as it was customary in many Galician towns. And G–d had blessed them with prosperity and with a lovely dear son whose name was Joseph Chaim, after my father. The boy astonished everybody with his looks and charms. What can I say in conclusion? That my sister and her husband's house was a rich and happy home. They gave charity, practiced kindness as befits a true Jewish home, where G–d's Torah and good deeds was their pedestal. And then the horrible war began.

The Nazis occupied Dzikow a few days after the war began. Dzikow and its vicinity was considered by the Nazis an important area and they ordered the Jews to leave town. On Sukkoth 1939, all the Jews were expelled, my sister among them. They went to Radomysl and then to Lwow. In Lwow they suffered greatly both materially and because of my sister's illness. Still they worried about me and as soon as they found out that I was sentenced to hard labor and was sent to a remote labor camp in Siberia, they managed to send me a few packages. Later I found out that, not only did they send packages to me, but also to other relatives. What a food package meant in those days knows only he who suffered as we did. I also received a few encouraging letters which strengthened my spirit. Despite my sister's sad and bitter situation, her letters were a work of thought and style. I was astonished at her ability to do such writing in days of such hardships. Her last letter was imbued with sorrow and sadness on one hand, and cheerfulness on the other hand. Ending her letter she signed off with, "Eta the daughter of Dvoira who needs a complete recovery."

Soon after the outbreak of the Soviet–German war, when the Nazis marched into Lwow, they committed excesses and massacres on the Jews. My brother–in–law, my sister and child escaped, and returned to Dzikow. There they stayed until August 1942. On the fifth day of the month of Av, they were expelled to Baranow. They were forced to march on foot, men, women, children, old people and infants. In Baranow my sister's in–laws were murdered. From there they were taken by train to Dembice. In Dembice they took away my sister's son, Joseph Chaim, and killed him right there before his parents eyes. They refused to do my sister the "favor" of killing her first. In the camp of Dembice, the Nazis concentrated 58,000 people.

[Page 288]

On the seventh day of the month Av, they selected 600 men. One hundred were sent to Rzeszow, one hundred and fifty to Tarnow, two hundred to Pustkow, and one hundred and fifty back to Dzikow. My brother–in–law was in the last group. My sister was late killed with the rest of the fifty eight thousand. Only about fifty people survived the Holocaust.

After all that my brother–in–law went through and what he saw, he became dejected. He constantly held his little boy's clothing under his arms. He worked slave labor in Dzikow. In addition to all the tortures, he was forced to sing Polish and Yiddish songs for the cursed and the wicked because he was an excellent singer. Ultimately, he was also murdered. Before his death, he handed to somebody his son's clothing and told them to watch over his son.

See G–d and look. See my pain, sorrow, and broken heart while I write these stories, avenge their spilled blood.

My heart shrinks from pain when I begin to continue the bitter account memorializing the victims that my brother Heschel sacrificed on the altar of the Nazi inferno. He too lived a respectful and happy life. He lived as the majority of Jews lived throughout Poland and Galicia. The Holocaust destroyed his house and ruined everything he owned. But it is my duty to name the victims.

My sister–in–law, my brother's wife of his youth, Hinda, was the daughter of Reb Joseph Saul Halevi Weidenfeld, from Limanow, a well–known noble family. After my brother was forced to escape to the Russian side, his wife with their two sons, the beloved Joseph Chaim and Isaiah Itzhok, remained in Strzyzow. My brother's wife, Hinda, was a fine, good–hearted woman. Her relationship with our mother Dvoira was spotless. She revered her like her own mother. After my mother passed away, my sister and I lived together with my brother. She treated us motherly and cordially. That fact was known in the whole town. For a certain period, the situation in Strzyzow was bearable. It even reached the point that all the wives whose husbands were on the Russian side, secretly asked them to return home. Hinda too had written my brother and asked him to return. However, my brother refused to abandon me as long as I was an inmate in the Russian jail. He hoped that he would be able to do something about it. He remained in Lwow and, due to that fact, he remained alive. If he would have returned, he would have perished in the Holocaust. It did not take long and the situation in Strzyzow became bad. The persecutions became worse day after day, and in the bitter end, they perished together with the whole town in Belzec. May G–d remember them favorably and avenge their blood.

The list is not complete yet. I am duty bound to memorialize the martyrs related to my present wife, may she live until a hundred and twenty. Her name is Dvora, the daughter of Reb Menachem Mendel Eisen from Wielopole.

My father–in–law, Reb Menachem Mendel, was born in Ropczyce. He was a grandson of Reb Shmaryahu, a pupil of the famous Rabbi Shlomo Zalman Frenkel from Wielopole, who once said to his Hassidim, "During my absence you can ask Reb Shmaryahu for a blessing." My father–in–law inherited from his grandfather the purity of belief and his piety.

[Page 289]

He gathered in wanderers and the book of Psalms never left his hands. He was active in the Visit the Sick Society. Survivors have testified that he was no less G–d fearing and possessed as many good virtues as his brother Reb Shlomo, the Assistant Rabbi in Wielopole, to whom even gentiles came to litigate. My father–in–law and his brother perished in the Holocaust. G–d shall avenge their blood.

Also my mother–in–law Chana, their children: Yacov Shmaryahu with his wife Miriam and their children, Abraham, Bina and Shragai Feivel; Rachel with her husband Mordechai Pinchowski from Strzyzow, their children: Eliezer, Chaya Pearl, Frieda with her husband Itzhok Weiser; their daughters Miriam and Breindl. The son Isachar, and also the son Aaron David, who escaped to Russia, but disappeared without a trace and was never heard from. Beside my wife, another son and daughter survived and are now in the United States. They all were scholars and observant Jews.

In addition to all the dear ones from my immediate family, many more martyrs perished from the big families of Diamond, Kanner and Eisen. Aunts and uncles, among them my uncle Reb Nathan Kornreich from Bukowsk, who was my mother's brother and his wife Gnendl, who was killed by the Poles as soon as the Nazis came. The list would probably reach in the hundreds. Many whom I remembered are listed in the list of the martyrs at the end of this book.

I want to express my gratitude to the one who is above us in heaven, for my survival. My wife Dvoira and I have two daughters who are dear to us. So did my brother Heschel merit to make a new home and he has a lovely wife and two sons who are following in G–d's ways.

Father Reb Chaim Itzhok Kalb
The Son of Reb Tanchum Yacov of Blessed Memory
by Ben Zion Kalb

Who has the perception and the pen to record the history of our generation, a generation born, raised and educated in a shtetl, at the end of the past century, and was swept with the torrent of the First World War into the West, became integrated with that new world, and with the ascent of Hitler, his name shall be obliterated forever, has made aliyah and settled in Eretz Israel? Who could have been able to withstand such powerful storms which this period bore but an outstanding scholar? Only he who absorbed the inner dynamic of the living Judaic Torah, was able to withstand all those changes of life. And such a person was my father, Reb Chaim Itzhok Kalb.

He was the son of Reb Tanchum and Sarah. Reb Tanchum was the shochet in Strzyzow, an enlightened man who was revered by all the people. He spent his childhood in abject poverty. To avoid being recruited into the army, he went to Hamburg, Germany, to stay with a relative. In Hamburg, he gave Talmud lessons to the rich Orthodoxy. The way of life there which was so different from his small town, had deeply impressed him and bore in him a yearning for values with which Judaism was blessed.

[Page 290]

On his return home, he married his wife Rachel, had two children, and soon the global storm placed him in Bohemia. There he established himself in the business world and became the founder of the Orthodox Kehillah in Teplice. His spouse and he were not spared sadness and sorrow, when three of their children were taken away from them as a result of different diseases.

Soon his cleverness was publicly known and, when any dispute occurred, whether legal, personal or material, the townspeople turned to Reb Chaim Itzhok for advice. How else can you signify an outstanding scholar if not by his ability to translate his knowledge in practical daily use? He mixed well with people and he was especially beloved for his chanting. He preserved his clear voice until the last days of his life.

When Hitler came to power, my father was well–established economically, he branched out into many businesses and was a wealthy man. He managed to salvage only a fraction of his wealth, before it was too late, in order to start a new life in Eretz Israel.

He was seriously injured as a result of a car accident. He lived four more years, thanks to his considerable energy and love for life, defying all medical prognoses. He died on is eightieth birthday.

The People of Israel Shall Live!
by Leah Loos

How many Jews survived the Holocaust in which six million perished? Not many tens of thousands, one from a town, maybe two from a family. Without using the word "miracle" to describe the manner of the survival of each Jew, hundreds of volumes would not be enough. This was an enormous event unknown in world literature because mankind had never experienced such a Holocaust until the appearance of Asmodeous–Hitler.

I would like to describe here, within the limited frame of this memorial book for the martyrs of Strzyzow, the history of one survivor, a remnant of a family close to one hundred people.

My mother Sarah's family of the Holles Dynasty, had lived for many generations of Strzyzow and its vicinity. My father Eliezer, of blessed memory, came from a little place near Lancut. His large family lived in Strzyzow and Rzeszow. During the Holocaust my parents and my brother Elazar remained in Strzyzow. Also my cousins, my mother's brother and his family, my father's nephew, Reb Ephraim Kneller with his family, remained in Strzyzow.

From this entire family only one person survived, my older sister's son, Joseph Reich. How they all perished is already told in this book. I just want to tell how this single remnant survived. During the selection, when the Nazis separated the young people into two groups, those to be sent to forced labor and those to be sent to their annihilation, both my older sister's son and daughter were selected to be sent to a labor camp, my sister's son, Joseph, left his parents, but my niece, Henia, refused to separate from her parents and went with them to the annihilation.

[Page 291]

My brother Elazar, was sent to a labor camp. He went through all the hardships in the ghetto and camps. Although he broke an arm, he managed to stay alive. In Theresienstadt, after the liberation, he contracted typhus. His body overcame this disease too. However, his mind was damaged and he became depressed. He managed to contact me. I was then in the service of the Allied Forces in Italy. He received my encouraging words and the news about our nephew's survival. He expressed his wishes to come and settle in Israel. But the British ruled our land and the fate of the Jewish survivors was in their hands. In order to make aliyah, they had to obtain permission from the British. This disappointment depressed him even more and until I was able to take some steps to speed up his illegal aliyah, he put an end to his life. I erected a gravestone for him in Landesberg, Germany, and this is the only gravestone in our family.

My cousin, the son of my mother's sister, Meir Holles, lives in the United States. During wartime, I was in constant contact with him. In every letter he expressed fear about the fate of our family. He deluded himself with false hope that perhaps somebody from his family will survive. His spirit broke after he found out the bitter truth that no one from his family escaped the inferno. He too put an end to his life. He was lonely. From his family, the Fradels and the family of Elazar Wurtzel, six children with their own families, no one survived.

My sister Vita, left her residence in Dynow after the first massacre. She with her husband, Mordechai Popper, and son Aryeh, who was four years old, moved to Przemysl. There, while crossing the San River, my sister met her death from a Russian or German bullet. She wanted to bring provisions for her family. My brother–in–law stayed in the Przemysl ghetto with his little boy and my nephew, Joseph, the son of my other sister. They worked and managed to hide the child for some time. When the last action began against children, my brother–in–law gave away his little boy to a Christian family for a sizeable sum. The boy was five years old, and he himself chose a non Jewish name "Tadek." I was told about the amazing instinct he had to preserve his life. Like all of the actions, he felt what was happening around him, so he ran away and hid in a huge soup barrel in one of the food–serving places. He remained there until the danger passed, and then he returned on his own to his father.

I have no information about the fate of this child. The only survivor, Joseph, my nephew, does not know the name of the Christian family or their address. All of my efforts and searches brought no results. Did the Christians hand him over to the Gestapo? This question is constantly on my mind.

During the final liquidation of the ghetto in Przemysl, my brother–in–law and my nephew were loaded into a train which supposedly was destined to go to Auschwitz. They have hidden in their boots some break–in tools with which they broke open the car and jumped off the train. About one hundred Jews were killed by German bullets. Joseph and another man survived and reached the forests near Tarnow. The other young man was injured in his knee.

[Page 292]

For a week they roamed around in the woods, alone, hungry and depressed, until they reached the point of apathy and unwillingness to live. One day they noticed a pair of horses in the woods. Joseph's companion who was a village boy knew that at noontime the owner of the horses was bound to appear to water the horses. They waited for him. When the owner came, Joseph appealed to him to give them food and shelter, especially to help his wounded comrade.

They did not expect a positive answer. They were sure that the gentile would report them to the Gestapo for the reward of a kilogram sugar or salt. To their great surprise, not only did he not report them, but he returned from his house with a basket loaded with precious food and cigarettes which his wife had prepared for them. These people should be remembered for generations to come. The name of the peasant family, these gentle souls, was, Michael and Maria Wlodek, from the village Lenkowice, near Tarnow. These farmers hid the boys in a bunker under the threshing floor. They fed and clothed them for a year and a half until the liberation. Even though they were very discreet about having Jews under the house, their lives were in constant danger, because their house was swarming with S.S. men, and the neighbors could have reported them at any moment or even their own children or servants. If only there would have been more Poles like these farmers, many more Jews would have survived. After the liberation, my nephew, Joseph Reich, went to our house in Strzyzow, to his parents' house in Jaslo, with the illusion of finding someone alive. He found no one. Nothing interested him anymore in Poland. He contacted the Jewish underground organization to help him reach Eretz Israel illegally, knowing that I, his aunt, lived there. I was in Italy at that time as a volunteer in the British Army. There I heard about his survival and found him in a Displaced Persons camp in Padua, Italy. He immigrated to Eretz Israel via Aliyah Bet, settled there, established a family, and his two children will be the continuation of our family. The people of Israel will live!!!

In Memory of My Parents
Who Perished Somewhere in Poland
by Dr. Chanan Lehrman, Rabbi of West Berlin

My parents were simple, humble and unpretentious. Their only aspiration was to live a decent, straight life in the spirit of the Ten Commandments, and to implant the same principles in their offspring.

My father, as evidenced by his last name, came from a scholarly, rabbinical family, going back many generations. He refused to use his Torah knowledge as a tool to earn a living. Therefore, he became a small–caliber merchant. My father was always happy with what he had and lived from day to day being grateful to G–d for each day. Several hours a day he devoted to study the words of the Torah which he also taught to his children, fulfilling the commandment, "And thou shalt teach them diligently unto thy children." He did not leave the task of teaching to the professional teachers.

[Page 293]

Such were his ideals and his virtues. His heartiest honesty was accompanied by his alert cleverness and intuition which had kept him away from frivolity. My father was blessed with an endless resource of good–heartedness and with a sense of humor which did not leave him in his most difficult moments.

He found a helper in the person of his spouse, my mother, who was energetic, strong–minded, and sharp–witted in her practical life. Her devotion to others which had no limitations was known to everyone. Her appearance, her stature, and her alertness, in spite of her shaky health, stood out in endless vitality and left a deep impression on whoever had a chance to meet her. To raise nine children, each of whom had a different character, was for her a simple matter. Even to feed them from her own labor during the years of the First World War, when my father was mobilized, was not too difficult for her. She still had time left to help her neighbors, help the sick, and console the poor. Not only with words, but with deeds. When someone brought into the house one, two or even three poor people to be fed, she welcomed them with a smile. "Nothing to it. One more mouth, one more spoon of water to add to the soup." Because of her belief, she could move mountains. Such belief is what we intellectuals arrogantly call extremism. Was it not extremism when, at the height of 1914–1918 War, she did not even once conceded the lighting of the Sabbath candles, one for each member of her family?

She was always able to obtain these candles which had become increasingly scarce. And every time, after she finished the candle lighting ceremony which was for her a symbol of renewal of the covenant with G–d, her heart was filled with joy because she considered t his covenant the destiny of her family. And, if a child's life was in danger, she felt certain that her love for G–d would not disappoint her and it will be the source of her rescue. Her perseverance was so strong that even a Commandant of a concentration camp could not withstand it. When one of her children was in t hat camp, she managed to free him without money and without "contacts," only by the power of her tears. When my parents, two elderly people, were expelled from Germany to Poland together with their youngest child, she managed to get the child out from that miserable country which later turned into a gigantic valley of death. G–d kept his covenant which my mother had made with him during the Sabbath candle lighting. My parents fulfilled their obligation toward G–d. They blessed their children and taught them ethical virtues and they knew that their children were on safe shores, although scattered throughout the four corners of the globe. This was their last comfort when they approached their tragic end. Behold, here they were again lonesome, hiding in a cellar beneath a factory, with potatoes their only provision. Only one food package out of five had reached them from abroad. They continued to live only by the strength of hope that the day would come that their family would be together again.

The suffering continued. The winter of 1941–42, the last before the terrible slaughter, had brought them to the brink of despair, without heating, clothing, or food, in a stage of complete weakness, a critical shriek escaped from their mouths, with greater bitterness than the shriek of Job.

[Page 294]

But this was only a momentary weakness which flashed upon us with a blinding light, revealing the situation they were in, which they kept covering up with calming words not wanting to disturb us.

The last postcard was dated July 1942, which doubtlessly was smuggled out, simply notifying us in a few words written in haste and with a trembling hand, that they were transferred to a place without a persona address, but not to worry about their fate. From then on, we did not receive any communication. Their pain, like the pain of thousands of others, ended. Only now are we beginning to familiarize ourselves with their sufferings. Their destiny was the destiny of many millions and I would like to ask your forgiveness for telling this personal story which nowadays is nothing but a banal problem. Our imagination is not capable of grasping the awe and the dreadfulness which giant numbers symbolize. The image does not react until the event is personal. I would like to ask your permission to revere my parents' memory by which you will become participants in memorializing all the victims from all the nations. The custom of Jewish tradition demands that on the remembrance day of death of one's parents, "Kaddish" should be recited, a prayer that praises and exalts the will of G–d, candles should be lit to symbolize the power passed on from father to son and spread the spiritual light which might bring peace to the world. I doubt if I will ever find out the exact day of my parents' departure, but my lectures beginning today and hereafter, will be about the relation between logic and belief and it will be given in a traditional spirit. This will be my humble contribution to the collective light and all this is because of the spark that my parents lit in me. (The last section of this article is an excerpt from my lecture on November 9, 1944, at the Lucerne University in Switzerland, on the subject of "Jewish thoughts in the History of Philosophy.")

The author of this article is a grandson of Reb Moshe Krantzler from Strzyzow who, at that time, was a lecturer in the above–mentioned university.

Memories from My Father's House
by Seryl Fishler–Mandel

Oft times when I walk in the street and come across a man wearing a beard with sidelocks, on a gentle face from which the radiance of the divinity shines, a shiver goes through my body. The vision of my father, of blessed memory, appears before my eyes.

My father was a G–d fearing man. All his faculties were immersed in studying and teaching to others the Holy Torah.

The small business which my family owned after the First World War, suffered very much because my father treated it very lightly, feeling that the store was not worthy of devoting too much time. Therefore, the burden fell on my mother's and children's shoulders, and we derived very little livelihood from the store.

The daily program of my father began at three in the morning. At this early hour he got up and went to the Beit Hamidrash. He always stopped on his way at the mikva, and soon after, he sat down to his studies.

[Page 295]

The sound of his humming was heard all around him, and everyone knew that Reb Chaim Mandel is studying already. He taught the Talmud to young men, Mishnayoth to the adults, merchants and tradesmen. His sweet voice and the Sassov traditional songs filled the vacuum of the Beit Hamidrash when he chanted on the Sabbath and holidays.

My father of blessed memory, used to make pilgrimage to the Rabbi from Munkatch where he taught Torah to the Rabbi's son–in–law who is now the Rabbi of Holon, Israel. He sat in as an arbitrator in much litigation, being known for his acuteness.

After the passage of Rabbi Moshe Leib Shapiro from Sassov, who live in Strzyzow, my father of blessed memory, together with Reb Yeshayahu Mandel, Reb Samuel Moshe Groskopf, and Reb Chaim Yacov Nuremberg, all of blessed memory, continued the Rabbi's traditions and his court was preserved under the leadership of Rebbetzim Chana, until their son Rabbi Nechemiah returned from Vienna and inherited the Rabbi's place.

My mother, may she rest in peace, had suffered with great humility because of her worries for a livelihood. There was a houseful of small children. Only with the help of my grandparents was the family able to exist until the children grew up and helped in the store.

My younger brother Naphtali, of blessed memory, had intertwined Torah with ethics, and also obtained a broad, general enlightenment.

I, as a young girl, joined the General Zionist Association and my goal was to make aliyah to Eretz Israel. It is hard for me to describe how great my suffering was because of the negative attitude to Zionism in our home and, even my studying Hebrew was met with objection.

I was convinced that there would not be any possibility for me to make aliyah directly from my home to Eretz Israel. Therefore, I left my parents' house in 1931, and, just before the ascension of the savage, I reached Berlin.

The moment I entered Germany, I energetically concentrated my efforts to obtain a permission certificate. My efforts were fruitful and thanks to it, I am now able to write these memories here in Israel. I showed the way to my family which remained in the Diaspora. But only one sister followed me and is at present with me. My sister Mina, may she rest in peace, who also was an active Zionist, was supposed to have come from Warsaw with the last illegal group. However, she did not board the ship. She was apprehensive that the ship would not reach her destination. She was fated to remain with my family until the bitter end.

[Page 296]

My Holy Father the Martyr, Reb Abraham Kalb the Shochet, of Blessed Memory
by Ben Zion Kalb, New York

My master, my father the teacher, t he martyr, Reb Abraham, the son of Reb Tanchum Yacov, told me that he was the grandson of Reb Kopel from Lykowa, a descendant of Rashi. On the gravestone of my great–grandfather, Reb Avremah'le Nobitnitzer, was inscribed as follows: "A holy and godly man who blew the shofar for Rabbi Hersh from Rymanow." My father was holy and untainted while alive, before he was murdered by the Nazis. Torah and prayer, benevolence and devotion to G–d, had filled his life since he was first able to understand. He did everything with amazing exhilaration. Whoever heard my father express his inner soul during his chanting of the High Holiday prayers, "Malchuyot, Zichronot, Shofrot," or "Kol Nidrei," remembered it all his life. He did everything with holy fieriness and excitement, fulfilling the precepts of eating matzo, sitting in the Sukkah, lighting the Hanukkah candles, etc. He was like the "eternal fire which burned on the altar and never went out." I never saw him go to bed or get up in the morning, even when he was tired. His mysterious melody at the midnight prayers was filled with yearning for the living G–d and it always woke me up in the middle of the night. His powerful belief in G–d was most convincing, more than all the logical and philosophical proof. He cleaved to the righteous and to Hassidism. He frequently visited the Rabbis: Rabbi Yechezkiel from Sieniawa, Rabbi David Moshe from Tchortkow, and his son, Rabbi Israel, also the Rabbi from Ostrowce, and other world famous Rabbis. He was attached to them with all the threads of his soul.

During the Holocaust, when, with the help of G–d, I successfully rescued over three thousand Jews, men, women, and children, I needed to sign all kinds of messages in order to organize such a holy task, I always signed "Ben Avraham." I was sure that thanks to my father's merits who taught me to put my life on the line for our people, I was able to complete such a holy task successfully. The last time I saw him at the end of 1939, he told me to take with me the small Talmud that we possessed. When I told him that the Talmud is not very popular with the Gestapo, he responded with excitement, "Torah shields and saves." I took it with me, and this is the only object left from my father. The Nazis murdered him near an open grave in the cemetery in Newmark.

My mother, Sheindl, was murdered together with my father. She was the daughter of Reb Bezalel who had been a shochet and Assistant Rabbi in Sczucin for fifty years. The simplicity with which she believed in G–d and her good deeds were well–known. When she gave charity, she did not want anybody to know. My sister Malka, her husband Moshe Halperin, a pious scholar, and their five–year–old son Bezalel, were all murdered.

[Page 297]

May G–d avenge their spilled blood. My older brother, the martyr, Menachem Mendel, was very charitable. He revered our father and mother very much. When the Gestapo came to take him away, my mother told him to jump out of the window and escape but he said, "And what about you?" He was afraid that if he would escape, they would kill our parents instead. He did not realize that our parents would be killed later anyway. That is how they were all killed. May G–d avenge their blood, and may their merit shield us and all of Israel.

In Memory of My Father and My Town
by Menachem the son of Moshe Kandel–Nuremberg

"I remember thee and I growl" about you my native town, which I left forty years ago. You were wiped off the face of the earth, and you are no more.

My town, my dear town, how can I forget you? You are fresh in my memories as you were on the day when I left you. I still remember the marketplace all the streets and alleys, filled with charm and beauty.

I recall in my memory all the revered citizens, the scholars, the simple and faultless folks, they all were people of faith, straightforward, innocent people.

It comes to my mind the remembrance of the old shul, the kloiz, and the Beit Hamidrash, which were filled with scholars, delighted young men and boys who diligently studied torah, and out of those walls the sound of Torah was heard. This effervescent life which so strongly pulsated was cut off by the cursed Nazis, savages in the form of humans. They all perished during the Holocaust in the fire which engulfed the entire House of Israel. And from my eyes tears are dripping for the destruction of our nation.

Let me commemorate my father, Reb Moshe, the son of Reb Itzhok Eisik Nuremberg, who was one of the outstanding people in town. He stood tall both ways, physically and morally. An outstanding scholar who knew Talmud, was an authority in the ritual rules and strictures. My father was well acquainted in the Responsa, and he was a teacher and instructor to Israel. Many people came to his house for advice and enjoyed his resourcefulness. He was a fiery Hassid of Rabbi Yechezkiel Halberstam from Sieniawa, and he also dabbed in writing and left manuscripts which have not seen the light yet. He ended his days as Assistant Rabbi in Keln, Germany. May his memory be blessed.

This article was written on the day of his yahrzeit.

[Page 298]

In Memory of My Family
by Ruth Kremerman–Russ

My father, Reb Aryeh Leibush Russ, and my mother, Rachel Yidis, were typical of the previous generation. They opposed my aliyah to Eretz Israel and I did it without their blessing. My dream to make aliyah materialized but my happiness was mixed with sadness because I had to leave my parents when they had not yet recovered from the loss of their only son, Abraham. My brother Abraham died when he was only twenty–three years old. My sister Sarah with her husband, Moshe Blau, was planning to follow me. My brother–in–law was supposed to immigrate as a Rabbi but the British Mandatorial Government had cancelled the Rabbinical privileges for aliyah and they, with their three children, remained in the foreign land. They were all annihilated by the Nazis, and I never merited seeing them again. May G–d avenge their blood.

In Memory of My Father, Sister with Her Family,
Why, O Why, Did It Have to Happen?
by Harry Langsam

My mother, Fruma Ryvka, of blessed memory, died at the prime of her life, leaving five orphans the youngest of which I was only six months old. Until 1939, when the horrors of the Holocaust befell upon Israel, I always envied other children for having a mother, and inwardly carried a grudge against G–d for taking her away at such a young age. But having survived the Holocaust made me realize that maybe G–d did it because she was a righteous woman and he wanted to spare her so much suffering.

My father, Reb Yacov, the son f Reb Tzvi Elimelech, was a tall, handsome man. His face was adorned with a dark, chocolate–colored beard, and the last time I saw him, in October, 1939, his beard was sprinkled with a few gray strands.

My father was a pious, deeply religious man, but not a fanatic. He understood that the world is moving forward, and one cannot stop progress. He himself was an avid reader of the "Yiddishe Toghlatt," an Orthodox newspaper published by Agudat Israel. He never objected to seeing a child reading a Yiddish book or newspaper. But he never permitted any of us children to deviate, Heaven forbid, one iota from the basic religious principles or rituals.

My father was a Hassid and admirer of the Rabbi from Munkatch, and all the Rabbis from the Dynow Dynasty, with whom we were related through Reb Pesach Langsam from Jawornik, from whom the Dynow Dynasty originated.

When the Second World War began on September 1, 1939, I was working in Tarnow. My brother Simcha lived in a nearby town, Zabno, and my oldest sister Beila with her family, lived in Dombrowa, also not far from Tarnow.

[Page 299]

Friday, September 1st at eight o'clock in the morning, was a moment that I will never forget. The owner of the paper–bag factory where I worked, Reb Wolf Getzler, had just walked in and headed straight for the electrical box. He pulled the switch to stop the machines and said, "children, the war has begun."

On Saturday, when I walked in the street with some friends from the Religious Zionist Organization, we were nabbed by Polish soldiers and taken to dig bomb–shelters. This was the first time in my life that I was forced to desecrate the Sabbath. A short while later, by the intervention of the Jewish community leaders, we were released, promising to appear voluntarily the following day to continue the building of bomb–shelters for the civilian population.

Sunday night, September 3rd, Tarnow was bombarded all through the night with destructive and incendiary bombs. The whole town was on fire. The next day, early in the morning, the entire population began to evacuate the town. People with worried faces, red–eyed from a sleepless night, and loaded with packs of their belongings, were going somewhere without a definite direction. There was total chaos.

I hurriedly joined the stream of refugees leaving behind my meager belongings, thinking that I would soon return. I went to Zabno, where my brother Simcha was working in a bakery. My intent was to bring him to Tarnow and from there to evacuate with all the others eastward, stopping in Strzyzow to see our father.

The road was swarming with evacuees, and every few minutes we had to ditch in to the fields because the German planes were machine–gunning the civilian population. When I arrived in Zabno, my brother was gone and I was told that he went to Dombrowa to join my sister's family. So, having no choice, I set out in the direction of Dombrowa. I walked a day and a night until I reached Dombrowa. I was happy to find my brother and to see my sister with her family. For three days we debated amongst ourselves what to do. We simply did not know how to handle the situation, whether to evacuate or not. There were all kinds of contradictory opinions. Older people who lived through the First World War were against leaving, pointing out, a) we could not run faster by foot than the motorized German army, and b) being a refugee is very difficult. Therefore, we decided to remain in Dombrowa. On Friday, September 8th, the Germany army marched in, and took the town. A dark night began for the Jewish people.

The High Holidays were upon us. The prayer houses were all locked up by decree. The Rosh Hashana and Yom Kippur services were conducted secretly out of the Germans eyes. My brother Simcha and I had not heard anything from our father. Therefore, we decided that I should try to reach Strzyzow. Soon after the first two days of Sukkoth were over, dressed as a peasant boy, I started out on my journey to see my father. It was a distance of eighty kilometers, and a very dangerous journey. I had very little money and a few packages of cigarettes on me. Cigarettes had become a scarce commodity at that time. I arrived in Strzyzow on a Friday afternoon, it was Hoshana Raba. The first unpleasant welcome into town that I received was to see a group of Jewish young men working at forced labor under the supervision of the Sabbath Goy, Sibirca, who was among the first of the gentiles to take advantage of the situation and show his hostility towards the Jews.

[Page 300]

Of course, my father was happy to see me and to hear about the well–being of my brother, my sister and her family. Only from my sister Golda had we not heard anything, nor did we know her whereabouts. A few days later, a mail smuggler brought a note from her which said that she was fine and was in Lwow. She hinted that we should join her. My father and I decided that I should return to Dombrowa and plan together with my brother and sister what to do next. Traveling for a Jew was very dangerous because Jews were forbidden to use transportation. Only angels watched over me and were my guardians. Soon after I reached my brother and sister in Dombrowa, I began to insist that the only thing to do is to escape to the Soviet side. My brother hesitated. He tried to find all kinds of excuses to hold me back. His main reason was fear of becoming a refugee. In the meantime, the Germans went ahead with their oppressive orders. They issued an order that all males ages 18 to 60 have to register. This convinced us both that the time to escape had come. We decided to go to Strzyzow first to see our father and, from there, to reach the San River on the German–Soviet border. Again, by sheer luck we had no trouble reaching Strzyzow. We told father about our decision and he gave us his blessing. Nobody suspected that it was as dangerous for the older people to remain under the Nazis as it was for the younger people, and nobody could even imagine that the Jewish people faced a total annihilation. Before we left home, our father told us: "As a father, how can I urge you to wander off into the unknown but, on the other hand, there is too much risk for you to remain here. Therefore, go with the grace of G–d and do not forget Him. But please try to be back home for Passover. I hope by then Hitler will be dead and we will celebrate the seders together." We have never forgiven ourselves for not taking our father with us.

It was raining heavily. The hills surrounding Strzyzow were covered with low clouds and it seemed as though the hills were hiding their embarrassment for being forced to leave them. We said good–bye to our father, to our town, to our birthplace, with a trembling heart and tears in our eyes. We never saw our father again. Oh G–d! Please avenge his innocent, untainted blood

During the imprisonment in Soviet Russia, I received one postcard from my father in response to my letter. He wrote that he was not hungry, that Reb Mordechai the baker helps him with bread, and he was wondering why we were in a labor camp. He perished with all his brothers and sisters from Strzyzow, apparently in the annihilation camp of Belzec.

My sister Beila, her husband, Naphtali Einhorn, with their three little darling boys: Tzvi Elimelech, Itzhok and Yehuda Zev, who resided in Dombrowa perished somewhere in Poland. She was married into a big branched–out family, the Einhorns, and the Apples, who also lived in Dombrowa, but none of them survived.

Finally, I want to mention my aunt, Tova Feldmaus, who was my mother's sister, her three children: Hersh, Elazar and Gitel. Their young spilled blood should never be forgiven.

[Page 301]

As I wrote before, a good angel watched over me, my brother, and my two sisters, four offspring of my father did survive. We all established families, bore children and grandchildren. As the Prophet said: "The perpetuity of Israel is infinite."

Days and Years in Strzyzow
by Chana Schiff–Shmulewicz

First I would like to reminisce about my childhood, about the days of my attendance in the elementary school. From the scholastic point of view, I like the school very much, but being Jewish with Christians all around me had caused me much suffering. One particular incident which left a great impression upon me happened in school in history class. My teacher had asked me a question and I gave her the right answer. Soon thereafter, she asked a Christian student from an intellectual Polish family a question, but the student failed to respond. The teacher was shocked and remarked loudly that her heart ached seeing that Polish history flows from the mouth of a Jewish girl, but the Polish girl was ignorant and did not know anything about her own national history. This remark which contained so much anti–Semitism deeply impressed me. When I told my parents about the incident, they did not think that it was out of the ordinary. They advised me to get used to these facts and, in the future, not to get upset over such incidents.

That is how I spend my years in school, years of open discrimination by the teachers against the Jewish students. The Polish students did not stand passively by. As a result of their upbringing at home and school, they always looked at us disdainfully and most of them teased us and called us insulting names. But in most cases we kept quiet. Thus, in our hearts we had accumulated a bitter pain which influenced us in our future and guided us in finding something that contained a challenge and satisfaction. This was the Zionist Movement in our town.

After we graduated from school (seventh grade), we found ourselves in a vacuum. We were without a goal and with nothing to do. The only avocation in town was around the Visloka River. There we spent hours in Jewish company, we conversed and red books. I remember well the day when a few of the young sons in town, Elazar Goldberg and Joseph Schiff, (I did not know then that he was to be my husband.) asked us to join the Hebrew Youth. In that period, the membership of this movement was small and consisted mostly of boys. The home of that group was in the club of the Zionists, named "Hatikva," which was located in the big house of Reb Shlomo Diamand, blessed be his memory. His grandson, Reb Shlomo Yahalomi (Diamand), is very active in the compilation of this book. The Chairman of the Zionist Movement was Itzhok Berglass who invested much time and effort in this book, and even now continues as the Chairman of the Natives of Strzyzow and Vicinity Society. Thanks to these two, this book which is so dear to us came into existence.

We soon became adapted to the movement. We found in it what we were looking for, namely, ideals.

[Page 302]

We began to work for these ideals and derived great satisfaction. Our main goal became now to make aliyah to Eretz Israel. Our first instructors were Joseph Weinberg and Pinchos Klotz and, from them, we absorbed the love for our land. We had many groups and one of them studied Hebrew under the guidance of Mr. Hersh Shapiro. After he made aliyah, we were taught by Libka Greenblatt, Mr. Elimelech Waldman, and others, whose names I do not remember. They all perished in the holocaust. May their memory be blessed. Later on, we ourselves began to instruct the younger members of the movement.

We worked several years in the movement and, ultimately, we went to a training kibbutz which was required in order to be qualified for aliyah. The day of our departure was approaching. On one hand, our hearts rejoiced immensely at the prospect of making aliyah to Eretz Israel and, on the other hand, we were moved with the thought that soon we would have to separate from our families and colleagues.

On Thursday, January the 4th, 1935, in the early morning, a day wrapped in cold and snow, we began our journey. To the railroad station we were escorted by our parents, brothers, and sisters, and our comrades from the organization. My grandmother, Esther Hinda Berger, who was known for her wisdom, also came to the station in spite of her advance age She was the wife of Joshua Berger.

One year after my emigration, my husband's parents, Reb Levi Itzhok Schiff, and his wife Ryvka, also emigrated with their youngest son, David. Reb Levi Itzhok was one of the active leaders of the Kehillah in Strzyzow and a fiery Hassid of the Rabbi from Sadigora. My husband's older brother, Meir, who was very devoted to his parents, his wife Dvoira, and their little daughter, Chaya Leah, remained in Strzyzow and they all perished in the holocaust. They planned to follow us but they and many others like them did not make it.

My husband's house was known in town for its hospitality. Almost every Saturday night and holidays, the Hassidim used to gather in Reb Levi Itzhok's house to celebrate the yahrzeits of their Rabbis. The house used to fill up to the fullest capacity. The Hassidim used to tell Hassidic tales and enjoyed the festive meals prepared by my mother–in–law, Ryvka, who was a righteous woman. She was helped by her mother–in–law, Chaya Leah, and by Dena Brauner, the wife of Zalman Brauner. My in–laws have continued their traditional hospitality here in our land My father–in–law became active and was one of the founders of the Natives of Strzyzow Society in Israel.

Now I would like to commemorate my parents. My father Reuben Shmulewicz, may G–d avenge his death, was a G–d fearing man and easy–going with others. He did not seek reverence or money, only love for the Torah and love for his fellow Jews. He studied Torah day and night, and participated daily in studying Mishnayoth with Reb Shalom Schwartzman.

Yom Kippur in our house has left a deep impression in my memory; I remember that on Yom Kippur I did not see my father from the beginning of "Kol Nidrei" until the closing prayers "Neilah" the next day. All that time he spent in Beit Hamidrash, contemplating the holy books. My mother was a good–hearted woman, devoted to her children, and known for her charitable activities. Blessed be her memory.

[Page 303]

I would like also to mention a few people from Strzyzow that were our neighbors, people of charity and good deeds, as my mother used to tell me. Like Reb Moshe Scheffler, known for his help to the poor and the sick. Reb Mordechai Schwartz, the baker known for his benevolence and whose bakery was open to all the hungry. Reb Mordechai's son, Eliezer, followed in his father's footsteps and possessed the same virtues. He lived in our land for many years and passed away a prolonged illness.

Of all the comrades of the Zionist Movement, only a few survived and they are here, living with us in Israel, thanks to the fact that they were fortunate to immigrate before the outbreak of the war.

We left behind in Strzyzow many comrades with hope to meet here in our land. These were boys and girls who contributed so much to the Zionist Movement in Strzyzow and they could have contributed much more of their energy and strength in the development of our homeland,. But, they were waiting for the entrance visas into our land, the cursed war broke out which prevented the materialization of their dreams. From among my girl friends, I would like to remember my best friend Leah Rosen. She was waiting to immigrate to Eretz Israel, and meantime her life was cut short by an untimely death. She was my best friend. This happened only a few months after my aliyah. I was deeply shocked and her memory never left me.

I would like to memorialize here a few more sons and daughters of Strzyzow. They all were cut down in the prime of their lives, by the savage Nazis: Miriam Zanger, Ryvka Kresh, Rachel Diamand, and many more boys and girls who were known for their talents. Their memory is always with me, and I will never forget them. May their memory be blessed.

Eta Hacker
(From the Landesman–Diamand Family)
by Shlomo Yahalomi

Eta was born to her parents, Reb Asher Leml and Miriam Landesman, in or about the year 1885. Miriam was the daughter of Reb Shlomo from Zyzow. Eta was orphaned at a young age. She was a very sensible and clever woman, with a gentle spirit and a delicate soul. Her life was not strewn with pleasantness. Before the Nazis came to power, she lived a modest and honest life in Vienna, Austria. Then, with the ascension of the Nazis, she was forced to leave Vienna and, after much wanderings, she arrived in the United States. Eta always remembered her parents, her origin, and the Jewish spark remained with her all her life.

After a prolonged illness, she passed away on the thirteenth of the month Teves, 1964, in New York. According to her will, she was flown to Israel and buried near the Rabbi Ashlag, of blessed memory. She left all her possessions to orphanages. May her memory be blessed forever.

[Page 304]

How I Found Out About the Town of My Origin, Strzyzow
by Shlomo Neumann
From the Adest Family

One day when I was in the office of our kibbutz, I overheard a chavera by the name of Tenzer, mention that her family came from Strzyzow.

Strzyzow! – I jumped up surprised, that is the place where my father's family came from. Through her I got in contact with the Society of the Natives from Strzyzow in Israel and obtained the memorial book about the martyrs of Strzyzow. I was surprised to find that the name Neumann was not mentioned in that book.

This brought me to write what little I know about my family.

Our father, Reb Moshe Aaron Neumann, of blessed memory, was born in Strzyzow in the year 1882, the son of Shlomo Neumann from Strzyzow. To the best of my knowledge, our grandfather was a contractor who built houses. He also dealt with timber. According to my oldest sister Chana, who remembered my grandfather as a very old man, he lived to the age of one hundred and fifteen years. He passed away in 1920, after the pogrom in Strzyzow. Until the pogrom he is said to have been a healthy upright man with a long white beard. He is said to have been born at the time of Napoleon, and passed away after the First World War. He was heavily beaten during the pogrom, when the hooligans claimed that a Polish child had been murdered and he was suspected to being a party to the murder. Our grandmother was called Odess before she married, and was a teacher of young girls. Our father Reb Moshe Aaron Neumann, fought in the Austrian Army during the First World War, and was a prisoner of war. He married my mother Chaya, who was born in Rzeszow, and my three sisters, Chana, Toni and Gina, were born in Strzyzow. After the war, my family moved to Magdeburg, Germany, where I was born. Our father taught Jewish children and prepared them for their Bar Mitzva. He also was the founder and leader of a shul.

Our mother, Chaya, of blessed memory, passed away in 1933.

We stayed in Magdeburg until my father was transported by the Gestapo to Poland and interned in Zbonszin, on the Polish–German border.

My sister Toni, of blessed memory, who was in Poland at the outbreak of the Second World War lived in Krakow. During the war, my father lived together with her in Krakow and in 1942, they both moved to Strzyzow. This was the last time we heard of them…My oldest sister, Chana, of blessed memory, managed to get to England just before the war broke out. She and her husband, Fred, of blessed memory, are buried in England.

My sister, Gina, came to Palestine and settled in kibbutz Rodges. She later left the kibbutz to study nursing. In 1949, she was sent to France to work in refugee camps for displaced persons who were waiting to immigrate to Eretz Israel. Toni fell ill and remained in France where she married Abraham, who recently passed away. Today she lives in France.

[Page 305]

I succeeded to escape to England at the age of thirteen. During the war and until 1947, I was in a Youth Aliyah Hachshara Center, and from there I went to Israel on that famous boat "Exodus." When I finally managed to get to Israel, I joined our chaverim from England and together we established Kibbutz Lavi. I was married in Lavi to my wife Rosi, and we have three children, two girls and a boy.

Bat Sheva, my oldest daughter, is married to Ronni, and they have two children. They live in Ranana where my other daughter Irit, also lives. She and her husband Motti have four children.

Our son Moshe Aaron, lives in Lavi, is married to Sarit, and has two sons.

The reason for my parents' immigration to Germany from Poland was the fact that my father hated Poland, as he told me the evening before he was expelled to Poland by the Gestapo.

My parents were Zionists. My mother's family who lived in the United States sent us tickets to go to America before Hitler came to power in Germany, but my mother, of blessed memory, would not hear of it. After this incident the family in the United States broke off all contact with us, even during the Holocaust.

[Page 306]

From The Legacy Of The Martyrs

Naphtali the Son of Reb Chaim Mandel...
May G–d Avenge His Blood

Excerpts from Naphtali's letters to his colleague and student, Chaim Mohrer in Eretz Israel.

(First Letter)

Time grabs a person with a strong grip and does with him as it wishes…and only occasionally does a person isolate himself from the tumultuous life into a corner, remaining with his soul, until he feels how much he distanced himself from real life and feels emptiness in his soul. Sometimes his soul cries from the depths of his heart, and laments for its devastation. The latent yearnings attack he person for the times that have passed him by.

And now, my beloved, I came to alert you that being in the Holy Land, the metropolis of G–d's Kingdom, the land that G–d claims to be eternally His…remember, my loveable Chaim, that you left your native land and came into a new environment, between those who call themselves leftists and rightists, where the licentiousness is tremendous. Therefore, Chaim, watch your actions and watch over your soul…Remember how the Talmud comments on the verse, "You created darkness and it became night, : which means, that this world resembles night…Make an effort to set aside time for studying a page Gemara or to read the Books of Ethics. Avoid the crowds who are immersed in emptiness because you are in a place where nobody knows you and the temptations are immense. Therefore, not associate with them, with the people who have o sense to distinguish between day and night.

With me personally, there is nothing new. I study Talmud daily, the tractate of Yoma, and the commentaries, the Bible, and philosophical books, the Rambam, The <u>Obligation of the Hearts</u>. There I find consolation and the healing of body and soul.

Sunday, Chapter of the week, "Bechukatay." 1936.

(Second Letter)

Here is our shtetl, dear Chaim, everything is the same. G–d continues to lead his world monotonously. The annual guest, the winter, has arrived and, when the people or the animals breathe, a white steam emanates from their mouths. The sidewalks in front of Bunim's candy story is already littered with the shells of pumpkin seeds and inside the store, they are busy studying the game of billiard. Suddenly, tables with six holes, six balls, and long sticks appeared in all the candy stores. The whole game consists of trying to knock the balls into the holes. You cannot imagine what is going on with that billiard. The cursing and foul language of these loathsome creatures, these "scholars." Their acuteness and proficiency is unimaginable. is

[Page 307]

The noise that coming out from Bunim's candy store can be heard in heaven. G–d shall have mercy and help Nechemiah "Crook" (Felber) learn the game. If not, he may destroy the whole world. The jokes and senseless conversations during the game are worthy of being published in a special edition to show that the existence of this world is justified…

At the other "Rabbi's" store, in the story of Reb Shmuel Rosenbluth, may he be blessed with a long life, the clientele is more revered, and more G–d fearing." Samuel himself puts together combinations, adds mysterious mathematical ciphers, and the book of "Zohar" is always open on the table in the store. He is deeply immersed in reading a spicy romance.

Saturday night, the chapter of the week, "Miketz," 1937

Why Did G–d Punish Me So Severely?
by Eta Federbush–Diamand

Oh yes, my dear Liba, it is true. My dear mother, the love of my soul, is no longer alive! The brutal death has snatched away from me my most precious treasure which was concealed deeply in the inner chambers of my heart and soul. The earth has covered my dearest possession in this world. My mother's heart, the heart of an angel, has stopped beating. Is it not awful? Is it possible to describe such a great loss? Can I possibly put on paper what is going on in my heart? In my crushed and broken heart? There was always before my eyes a sacred purpose: "Mother," to live for her, to look after her, and to watch over her like the apple of my eye. It seems to me that where it concerns reverence for my mother, I did everything possible. I devoted my youth to her. In the last few weeks, I did not leave her for a moment, day and night. I invested all my power and energy to help her, but to no avail. Why had G–d punished me so severely? Apparently, I deserve such a punishment. Well let us not question G–d's ways.

Do you know what my life consist of now? It is a life with the image of my dear mother which is engraved deep in my heart. The only thing that gives me repose are the tears that I shed for her…After my father passed away, she was the father and the mother, the foundation of our house. When this foundation collapsed, what is there left to do? To cry and cry.

Be well and shed tears for the fate of your dear friend who became orphaned.

This an excerpt from a letter written by Eta Federbush to her girlfriend, Liba Tucker in 1934.

[Page 308]

Excerpt From a Letter
Written to Leah Loos in Eretz Israel
by Liba Greenblatt and Sarah Alta Mandel

My good friend!

Many thanks for the warm Mazal Tov that you sent me. You are wishing me that you hope soon to be able to convey these congratulations to me in person over there in "Ha–Aretz." May G–d fulfill your wishes. Meanwhile I see no hope for the materialization of this goal because my husband's position enables us to make a living and we are afraid that over there, we would not be able to find a livelihood with our meager funds. The needs of a family are bigger than those of a single girl. But still, we are not resigned. Maybe the conditions will improve in the future and we will be able to settle in Eretz Israel.

A few weeks ago your mother told me that you intend to write letters to us. So we are waiting impatiently because we are curious to know how your true spirits are, how your life is individually,, and what the spiritual and material situation of the children of Israel is in general. But your letters have not arrived yet and, in the meantime, I am moving to Rymanow. Therefore, when your letter will finally arrive, I will not be able to read it. I will have to rely on Sarah Alta, to learn the contents of your letter and this will not be satisfactory to me. Therefore, please hurry up and send letters. Maybe I will still be here in Strzyzow and, if not, please write me another letter which would make me very happy.

I will be leaving Strzyzow soon after the holidays and I wish to find in my new life what we all dreamed about–happiness.

Be well, healthy, and write soon.

From your friend who sends regards from myself and my husband whom you never met. He is a good Jew, and he is interested in everything that is happening over there.

Yours, Liba

I too thank you for the greeting card and send my best wishes. I am too busy now to write more because I am preparing the seders for Passover. I am waiting impatiently for your letter. Write soon.

Sarah Alta

[Page 309]

Letter From the Nazi–Occupied Territory
by Eta Falk–Dembitzer

Strzyzow, March 16, 1941
To Sarah and Itzhok Berglass.

My dear friends!

I apologize for not writing sooner, even though I know how important it is to hear from home but I am devastated after the tragedy that happened in my immediate family. Therefore, I could not concentrate my thoughts and sit down to write a letter. This postcard was written two months ago, and I just found it today in a drawer. I decided to mail it anyway.

I am not writing too much news because I do not go outside and nobody comes to visit me. Everyone has his own troubles and does not want to listen to somebody else's troubles.

I have recently seen your entire family. Thank G–d they are all well. Also Chaya from Sanok paid a visit and she is also well. I also heard that Mrs. Gertner had received a postcard from you, and was happy to hear that you are in good health. Please write some more. Kisses from the bottom of my heart.

Eta

A Letter to Itzhok Berglass in Pimia, Siberia
From Chaya Feirush–Berglass

Sanok, February 24, 1941.
My dear brother!

A week ago I was in Strzyzow to observe our father's yahrzeit. Nechama and I with David and Elimelech went to the cemetery. Thank G–d, we are all healthy but mother misses you. She carries around in her pocket the few postcards she has received from me.

Did you hear anything from your relatives in the United States? We wrote to them. Maybe they would like to help me emigrate. By all manes. We advise you to go. We advise you to go. But we know that it takes time. We do not hear from you too often. We are well and have had enough food

Kisses for everyone.
Chaya

[Page 310]

A Letter to Itzhok Berglass in Pimia, Siberia
From Nechama Bernstein–Berglass

Strzyzow, February 25, 1941.
Dearest brother and family!

For some time we did not hear from you nor from Henia. The postcards which you sent through Paltiel Kneller's father–in–law have not reached us. Please write directly to us. Write us a card every week but do not add Yiddish words because it takes long to receive them. Chaya was here to observe the yahrzeit of our father, blessed by his memory. We all went to the cemetery and prayed that we should be together again. Thank G–d we have our health. Sometimes we all regret that we are not together over there with you because togetherness is much better. What is Ryvka studying? She is probably a big girl now. Does Rachel remember us? Bina is always kissing her picture.

Where do you live? In a city or in a village? What is your occupation? Henia lives in a village and her husband Eliezer is a lumberman. Heschel Diamond is also there, somewhere. But he has not written anything. Let Sarah and the children add a few words.

We kiss you all and wish to see you soon.
Nechama

A Plea for Support to the Secretary of the Strzyzow Society in the United States
From the Assistant Rabbi in Strzyzow, Rabbi Yacov Shpalter.

To the revered, charming, and generous Reb Samuel Mussler.

Since I had very friendly relations with your father, of blessed memory, I dare to take the opportunity to bother you with my request.

I am and had been the Assistant Rabbi of Strzyzow for the last fifteen years. I was accepted by all parties in town. Even though it is a small town, I still made a meager living because the town was not as poor as it is now. Recently, the town became so impoverished that my income fell to the lowest level, and I do not have any other resources for a livelihood. My salary was reduced. In one word, I am simply broke. I have daughters whose time to get married is long overdue. However, I have no dowry for them, not even a small dowry. Therefore, I decided to present before you, the Strzyzow Committee, my plea. My beloved friends, champions of generosity, look into this matter, look into my bitter situation. It is not in my character to ask for charity. If the problem would be food only, I would be satisfied with bread and water and would not stretch out my hands to ask for charity. But the problem is dowry for brides who are long overdue and, therefore, I am forced to do whatever possible.

[Page 311-3]

I have lived in Strzyzow for the last fifteen years and worked as an Assistant Rabbi. Therefore, I dared to call on the natives of Strzyzow who are known for their character and merciful feelings. The people from Strzyzow always helped the needy, myself among them. However, the situation in town became so bad that help is not forthcoming. Therefore, I am turning to you, revered committee. Have mercy and contribute to my daughter's dowry, at least a hundred dollars. As a reward for such a great mitzva G–d will bless you with prosperity and success in all your endeavors. G–d will favorably fulfill your hearts' wishes. I am concluding my words with great hope for your help.

I am addressing my plea especially to you Mr. Mussler. I remember your father, of blessed memory, very well, and his gentle personality, and merciful feelings. Surely, the fruit of such a fine tree inherited the same merits. Therefore, consider my bitter situation. I am drowning. I am hopeful that you will help the Committee decide in my favor, and the Almighty will give a helping hand.

The Assistant Rabbi in Strzyzow
Yacov Shpalter

A pleading letter for support to Samuel Mussler, secretary of the Strzyzow society in the U.S.A. from the assistant Rabbi Yacov Shpalter

[Page 312]

Letter of recommendation from Itzhok Berglass to the secretary of the Strzyzow society in U.S.A. about help to assistant Rabbi Yacov Shpalter

---

Letter of Recommendation
from Itzhok Berglass

Dear Comrade, Mr. Mussler!

Our Assistant Rabbi, Yacov Shpalter, asked me to verify that what he stated in his letter is true, since only few of the emigrants from Strzyzow know him. I hereby confirm that everything he wrote is true. Rabbi Yacov Shpalter is an old man. He has served us as Assistant Rabbi for the last fifteen years. At present, he finds himself in a critical situation. The reason for it is that the funds of the Jewish Community have decreased for several reasons. Therefore, his salary is very small and it is hard to live on it even by our low living standards. The Jewish population is very poor. The Assistant Rabbi has no other income, and is inconceivable that he will be able to marry off his daughters. He deserves to be given the help he asked for.

Please give my regards to all my friends and to my cousin, Mr. I. Berglass. I conclude my letter with reverence.

Itzhok Berglass

[Page 314]

Letter of recommendation from Abraham Tenzer to the Secretary of the Strzyzow Society in U.S.A. about help to assistant Rabbi Yacov Shpalter.

[Page 315]

Letter of Recommendation
from Abraham Tenzer

To my old and very beloved friend!

Our sages wrote: "The world is based on three principles: Torah, worship, and kindliness." As you probably still remember, our shtetl is known for its piety. People studying Torah, praying with devotion, but the fulfillment of acts of kindliness comes a little harder because of poverty in our town. Providence wasted the completion of the three above–mentioned merits. Therefore, he made you immigrate to the United States and find there a good, free life. You ought to be thankful and fulfill the great mitzva, doing acts of kindliness. You should express your gratitude for going to the United States, as Joseph did to his brothers for going to Egypt. This should enable you to extend a helping hand to your impoverished brethren of Strzyzow. Dear beloved brothers! You cannot imagine the present situation. It cannot be described on paper. In this case it is a man, a great scholar, who is satisfied with as little as possible. He served us for the last fifteen years, his salary keeps decreasing, and nobody here is able to help him. It is a great merit to help a Jew, especially a great scholar. And in addition, he is also in need of dowries for his daughters which are, as described by our sages, a mitzva without limitations. We should not and cannot permit girls to remain unmarried. I plead with you, do not ignore it. Dear brothers! Make an effort and support this man, Rabbi Yacov Shpalter, and as a reward for your charitable deed, the Creator will help, fulfill, and answer all your prayers. You will become prosperous and live happily and in richness. G–d willing we should be able to convey to you only good news. This is the wish of your acquaintance and best friend. Please give my regards to all our landsleit, especially to Mr. Mussler, and Zalman Berglass who, I heard is very generous.

Abraham Tenzer

Letter from the Free Loan Society in Strzyzow
To the Strzyzow Relief Committee in New York

Strzyzow, March 23, 1939.
Dear Secretary!

We received your letter dated March 14, addressed to Dr. Frenkel and me. I have not responded before today because I waited until my anger subsided. I decided not to mention the other problem again. The fund assigned by you has not yet arrived but we hope to receive them any day. As soon as the funds will reach us, we will immediately call a meeting of the Committee to distribute the funds and send them to Zbonszin. Since your listing was not accurate and addresses were missing, we turned to Shalom Flaumenhaft who sent us an exact list of all the addresses of the people from Strzyzow.

[Page 316]

Whereby we found one more person from Strzyzow, namely, Reb Samuel Feit, the son–in–law of Yechiel Rosen. Of course, we will send him some funds also. According to Shalom Flaumenhaft, it appears that only six families live in the refugee camp and the rest live privately.

We will send the money to Zbonszin individually by mail because to send a special messenger would cost us over one hundred zlotys. From Strzyzow to Zbonszin is very far. It takes fifteen hours by express train. An exact list of the recipients will be sent to you around Passover time and also a report about the activities of the Free Loan treasury.

We would like to confirm with great satisfaction that our treasury has received credit of 500.00 zlotys from the Joint Distribution Committee in Warsaw with a long–term repayment plan, which means that the first payment will be due in the years 1947–1948. As you can see, our business with the "Joint" are not too bad. They would even be better if they would give us more money. From the previous credits that we received from "Joint", we have already paid back one hundred fifty zlotys. The activities of our Free Loan Society are regular, namely, as soon as money comes in, we loan it out. We will send you the monthly balance sheets, and also the minutes of our meetings.

Next month the annual membership meeting will take place, where a new leadership will be elected. It is quite possible that a new committee will be elected and the old one will retire.

Dear friend. Secretary! Since you have helped the poor in Strzyzow and those expelled from Hitler–land, for which you deserve sincere thanks, you should now begin to do something for the Free Loan Society. We need a continuous infusion of funds. The number of applications is increasing steadily.

About Strzyzow, there is nothing important to report, and about what is going on in Poland, you probably read in the newspapers. Regards from the people in Strzyzow who are wishing you and all our friends a joyful Passover.

Abraham Brav

[Page 317]

The Vicinity

The Little Towns
by Itzhok Berglass

In the district of Strzyzow, there were three little towns which were connected to Strzyzow as the regional city. The largest of these towns was Frysztak, which was called by her Jewish residents "Frystik." It was located on the highways Strzyzow–Jaslo, and Strzyzow–Krosno. There were more Jews in Frysztak than in Strzyzow and were the majority there. There were very few Christians in that town and until the rise of official anti–Semitism during the rule of the "Sanacia Party," there was always a Jewish mayor in Frysztak. The last mayor who served many years was Reb Tzvi Yare.

The main source of livelihood in this town was the weekly market which took place on Thursday and was primarily a cattle market. Merchants and farmers, sellers and buyers, came to this Market Day from far and near.

In its spiritual life, Frysztak was different from Strzyzow. The difference was that Frysztak was such an extreme city that it did not allow the penetration of the Zionist Movement but at a very low level, it was headed by Shlomo Schmidt. We wrote already about the burning of the secular books.

The second small town was Czudec called, in Yiddish, "Tchitch." It was located on the way to Rzeszow. This town had the same characteristics as Strzyzow, only on a small scale. It had commerce, wealth, scholars, Hassidim, and also the Zionist Movement.

Czudec's livelihood was derived from dealings with the rich farmers in town and vicinity, who owned huge estates and, also, with the biggest landowners in that area, Polish aristocrats.

The Youths in Czudec were more liberal–minded than the youths in Strzyzow and, in the Zionist Movement, they put more emphasis on their social life. They had a dramatic group which Strzyzow lacked, they had also developed a stronger pioneering spirit and, thanks to that spirit, many people from Czudec now live in Israel.

The third nearby town was Niebylec, in Yiddish it was called "Nebalitz." They had a Kehillah, a Rabbi, and other clergy. In the last generation, they had among them merchants, scholars, and Hassidim, as in any other Galician shtetl. Of late, they even had a Jewish doctor. But, of all the four towns in the district of Strzyzow, Niebylec looked more like a village than a town. Once, the majority of its Jews were simple people, believers, and strong adherents of mitzvot, but behaved like peasants. They were mostly cattle and horse traders, highly conceited with an inclination for skirmishes, imitating the behavior of small Polish aristocrats. Until the war broke out, many of Nibylec's cattle and horse traders played an important and respected part in the market in Frysztak.

[Page 318]

The distinctive feature of this town was the Jewish estate of Reb Joseph Asher Wallach, with its huge cross standing in the center of the garden which was left by the previous owners. Reb Joseph Asher Wallach, the pious Jew, could not remove the cross from the garden and lived in its shadow all of his life.

The Villages
by Itzhok Berglass

There were many Jews in the surrounding villages who continued to live there until the final years, in spite of the great exodus in the years before the Second World War. Most Jewish families were deeply rooted in these places for generations. They had all kinds of occupations, small store–keepers, trades–people, peddlers, middlemen, tavern keepers, and also buyers of farm produce and forestry. They had contact and dealt with the estate owners in the area. These estate owners conducted most of their business through the Jews who lived nearby. Some Jewish dealers reached a high rank in the world of commerce which engulfed the whole region, like Reb Hersh Resler from Tolkowice and Reb Shlomo Diamond from Zyznow. Every village Jew had a small farm of his own, like his neighbor the Polish peasant. There were also a few larger Jewish estates, like the estate in Rozanka which, for generations, belonged to the Diamond family, and the Glinik estate which belonged to Reb Abraham Mendel Berglass, the patriarch of the Gertner and Deutch families in Strzyzow. Berglass was charitable and well–respected in town because after every harvest he provided food for the poor in Strzyzow. Ultimately, both estates passed into Christian ownership.

In shtetl, everybody knew each other and felt a part of one entity but, in the village, every Jew stood out as an individual. To him, Christian farmers used to turn for advice and help and, in many cases, they trusted the Jew more than their own

Christian brother. The Jewish townspeople knew all the Jews from the villages only by their first names and the names of their villages, never by their last names. The village Jews were also distinguished from their brothers in town in their spiritual life. There were among them people who hardly knew how to pray or recite Psalms, and some were ignorant altogether. Only a few knew how to study the chapter of the week, a chapter of Mishnayoth, or Talmud. Hassidim and scholars among these Jews were a rarity. In some villages, the Jews organized a quorum on Saturdays and Holidays to pray together. Only a few came to town for the High Holidays. When they had a quorum, they always hired somebody from Strzyzow to chant for them and lead the prayers. In general, they were as observant as the townspeople. They observed the small and the large rituals, in spite of being isolated. Often times they were only one or two Jewish families in a whole village. They did not mingle with the gentiles and their houses were Jewish in all details. They kept strictly kosher, observed the Sabbath and holidays, and their children were sent to Strzyzow to study and, on rare occasions, also to obtain higher education.

[Page 319]

The incident of the conversion of two sisters in Rozanka was an exception. In the final years there were a few young men who belonged to Zionist groups and associated with the youth of Strzyzow.

In any case, all the village people dreamed about settling in town, and some realized their dreams. Many of the Jewish population in Strzyzow lived once in a village or were descendants of village people.

The Village Lutcza
by Itzhok Berglass

Lutcza was different from other villages because of the many Jews that lived there. They had several quorums which used to congregate on the Sabbaths and holidays in the estate of Reb Yechezkiel Wallach and, after he passed away in the house of his sons until the Holocaust. Lutcza was a huge estate which occupied an area the size of a large village with a population of thousands of people. For many years this estate was very neglected by the previous aristocratic owners until Reb Yechezkiel Wallach bought it. Previously this estate was leased and managed by Reb Eliyahu Bilut. Reb Eliyahu was a fiery Hassid of the Rabbi from Dynow. He behaved like the Polish aristocrats. He related to his workers and to the farmers with conceit. The workers and the farmers from the village were used to such treatment since feudal times. Reb Eliyahu used to leave the estate for long periods of time. However, unlike the Polish aristocrats who traveled to the big city or abroad to live the life of pleasure, Reb Eliyahu visited with Rabbis, especially during the months of High Holidays which fell during the harvest season of the Polish farms. Reb Feivel Adest, the clever man from Strzyzow, used to call Reb Eliyahu "The Hassidic Vagabound."

There were rumors in Strzyzow that the Rabbi from Dynow promised Reb Eliyahu that someday he would be able to buy the estate from the Christian owners. But my father, when told about those rumors, vigorously denied them, stating that, "If the Rabbi had promised it to him, it would have surely come true." (Hassidim believe that the righteous request and G-d fulfills)

At the end, Reb Eliyahu left the estate broke, and it was purchased by Reb Yechezkiel Wallach. Reb Eliyahu and his descendants bore a grudge towards the Wallach family forever, and for years they tried to harm the Wallachs.

Reb Yechezkiel, in contrast to his predecessor, related to his subordinates with humility and simplicity, took good care of his possession, and lived a conservative life. The only luxury he allowed himself was proper matches for his sons and daughters. His sons–in–law came from good scholarly families and for daughters–in–law; he searched only for daughters from good families. All his sons and sons–in–law worked with him on the estate. With Reb Yechezkiel's help, his son, Joseph Asher, was able to purchase the estate in nearby Niebylec, and is son–in–law, Reb Yehuda Schiff, obtained the large farm, Lunek. His grandchildren were all educated like city children. He engaged melamdim to study with them Torah, and tutors for secular education. One grandson, Reb Zisha Hirshfeld, was a Zionist representative in Lutcza and vicinity.

[Page 320]

Reb Yechezkiel Wallach passed away of old age and was buried in Niebylec, the Kehillah to which Lutcza belonged.

Details about what happened to the Jews from these little towns and villages during the Holocaust, and who survived, are unknown to me. The only thing that I do know is that they disappeared like all the other Jewish communities. Only a few have survived.

In the village Godowa, near Strzyzow, a young man, Yacov, the son of Aryeh Leibush Diamand, was hiding until he was caught by a local farmer who brought him to the Nazi police, and he was killed by them.

The grandson f Ritter who was the victim of the blood libel, a story which was previously told in this book, was killed in Lutcza. He was one of those who jumped from the train which left Rzeszow ghetto on November 15, 1942. The Rosen brothers jumped from the same train, this young man went back to his village and hid until he was recognized by some Poles, and he was killed by them. Reb Abraham Wallach, heir to the estate was also killed in Lutcza. He lived in Krakow and came back to his village to hide. From all the Wallach family very few survived. One grandson, Reb Shlomo Wilner, survived by hiding in Lutcza and a few others escaped and were exiled in Russia. In Rozanka, Reb Chaim Resler and part of his family survived hiding in a farmer's house, except his wife and son who left their hiding place. They were lured to come out of hiding by a peasant woman who knew of their hiding place but could not report them to the Gestapo, not wanting to endanger her relatives in whose house the Resler family was hiding. She took revenge, and she succeeded at least to kill part of the family.

The Jewish Villagers were the Pillars of Benefaction
by Shlomo Yahalomi

The settling of the Jews in villages was an important factor, not only by establishing roots in all parts of life in Poland, but also by helping find occupations and livelihood in the cities and in the villages also. This settling was needed and desirable for the benefit of the Jews who lived in the big cities and small towns. Whoever is well–versed in Hassidic history in Galicia knows that some Rabbis wanted to forbid the Jews to live in villages. The reasons being their apprehension for the safety of single Jewish families among ninety–nine percent gentiles, and the fear for the gentile influence upon the Jewish family members. The major worry was the problem of educating the children. In contrast, there was famous s Tzadikim who looked favorably upon and even enticed many Hassidim to settle in villages. Their reasoning was that at that period and until the last years it was easier to make a living in the villages. Many of our brothers have found their livelihood in the villages by farming, peddling and in the logging industry. The village people were used also for a way station for the wandering Jews. The desire of the Rabbis was that there should be at least one Jewish family in each village, where a traveler could stop to pray, have a meal, and find lodging.

[Page 321]

Therefore, Rabbi Shlomo Zalman Frenkel from Wielopole told Reb Aryeh Leibush Diamand from Dobrzechow that his four sons should each settle in a different village. And they did exactly what the Rabbi had told them to do. Reb Yacov settled in Wyscka, Reb Moshe in Ruzanka, and Reb Akiba in Kozlowa. The fourth son later settled in Pstrongowa. Such cases were many in Galicia, where people obeyed the request of the rabbis and therefore were blessed with a decent living, many even becoming rich men. On the other hand, there were many who struggled to make a living. But they all served as a way station for the wayfarers, fulfilling the commandment of hospitality. Some of these village Jews were also scholars, pious men, at peace with G–d and their fellow men. Of course there were many among the villagers who were ignoramuses, but they were humble and knew their place. By then, the so called "Democracy," which disturbed the great society and put "Progress" ahead of Torah, had not ruled yet.

In the section "Ancient Families in Town," I listed many village people but in this chapter, I would like to include the ones I missed before.

Reb Eliyahu Bilut from Lutcza
by Shlomo Yahalomi

Reb Eliyahu was the lessee of the estate and the village Lutcza. He ran the estate as though he had been a squire from birth. He liked to play the role of a ruler, and so did his son. His son Yair trained the farmers to address him "Sir" or "Master." But, with all of the above, Reb Eliyahu was a Hassid and admirer of many Galician Rabbis, like rabbi Chaim from Sandz, rabbi Itzhok Eisik from Ziditchow, and many more. He was a lavish contributor to charity and all worthwhile causes, wherever he came, he presented himself with an open hand and great reverence. When my grandfather was a young man, Reb Eliyahu helped him become accustomed to visit the righteous and he took him to visit the Rabbis from Sandz and Ziditchow. In the early part f this book an interesting episode that happened to my grandfather and Reb Eliyahu on one of their visits to Sandz was told. With all due respect to Reb Eliyahu's charitable deeds, and his Hassidism, he lagged behind the other Jewish estate owners in knowledge, and ability to manage his domain properly, and everything that went with it. The result f his shabby management was that he was forced off of the estate and his offspring became dependent on others. I knew one of his sons who, despite reaching low esteem, had not resigned himself and demanded to be treated with superiority. Whoever stood before him was expected to stand at attention, the thoughts and deeds of a person are sometimes puzzling…

[Page 322]

Reb Yechezkiel Wallach from Lutcza
(He was a Diamand on his maternal side)
by Shlomo Yahalomi

Sometimes after Reb Eliyahu Bilut was forced off of the estate, it was purchased by Reb Yechezkiel Wallach. Wallach became the master of the village and also the richest man in the vicinity. Reb Yechezkiel was a simple, purposeful man, but clever, and a man of action. A straightforward man, unpretentious, he always believed in the Almighty in his own way. When he prayed, he locked himself in his room and nobody was allowed to enter and disturb him in his prayers. This fact was known by the other gentile estate owners, and they avoided visiting him at that time of day. And if somebody did come, he had to wait until Reb Yechezkiel finished his prayers. Once unexpectedly a rabbi from the Ropczyce Dynasty came to Lutcza to see Reb Yechezkiel and he, too, had to wait. Later Reb Yechezkiel apologized, and the Rabbi responded, "On the contrary! I like it. It is a very nice custom."

Interesting stories were told about Reb Yechezkiel's cleverness, and here is one of them told to me by Itzhok Deutch. There was one Jewish girl among the servants, who was not attractive and not too young. She managed the household and her main job was to watch the kashrut. In those times, it was very hard for such a girl to get married. If she would have at least had some money to cover her deficiencies, well, perhaps – but she was very poor. And she kept aging and aging to the sorrow of her friends. Behold, an incident occurred. Reb Yechezkiel lost a thousand American dollars, a huge sum even for a rich man like Reb Yechezkiel. He regretted the loss. After a few days, the girl found the money and immediately returned it to Reb Yechezkiel. He was stunned by such an act and he appreciated the great temptation which this poor girl had gone through. However, he decided to punish her for her "stupidity." Giving back to him the money he never hoped to find. What did he do? He called in a gentile boy and told him to take a stick and hit her, but very lightly. And then he gave her the thousand dollars. The girl later established a family with the money.

Reb Yechezkiel Wallach had sons, daughters, and many grandchildren. He married them off into the most respected families. One of his sons–in–law was Reb Zisha Hirshfeld, the son of Reb Moshe from Rozwadow. He was a distinguished scholar and he was sharp. He knew by heart every complicated segments from Ketzot Hachoshen, a book about religious strictures and Jewish customs. Most offspring of Reb Yechezkiel perished in the Holocaust. Only a few survived.

[Page 323]

The Large Diamand Family
by Shlomo Yahalomi

About the large Diamand family we already wrote in the section about the ancient families in Strzyzow. I only want to add a few details. Almost every member of this family owned a Torah scroll which had been specially written for them. My grandfather, Reb Shlomo from Zyznow, had two Torah scrolls and in his house, they prayed with a quorum. Reb Abraham Diamand from Pstrongewo had four Torah scrolls and gave charity lavishly. Most of the Diamonds' were like him. When the Russians occupied Galicia during the First World War, they accused Reb Zalman Diamand from Wysoka of spying for the Austrians. He was saved only by a miracle. Reb Zalman was one of the first victims during the blood libel pogrom. One of Reb Zalman's sons, Reb Yacov, was surrounded in a house by Poles who planned to kill him. He succeeded in sneaking out and hiding in an abandoned flour mill, immersed in water all night. He survived because the gentiles did not think of looking for him there. Next morning he jumped into a train which was on his way to Jaslo, and from there, he escaped to Germany. At present, Reb Yacov Diamand lives in Israel with his family. Reb Zalman passed away in 1937, but his wife and the rest of his offspring, all perished in the Holocaust. G–d shall avenge their blood.

[Page 324]

Memories from the days of the Holocaust

The cup of sorrow from which I drank during the Holocaust years
by Moshe Mussler

Tranquil and quiet were the years that my family and I spent in the rich and cultural metropolis of Belgium. I was a member of the teaching staff for the Hebrew curriculum in the elementary and Hebrew High School "Tachkemoni" which was supervised by the Kehillah in Antwerp. This school was certified by the government and it was under the control of two authorities: the government's and the Kehilla's. But one authority did not interfere with the other. We, the teachers of Judaic studies such as Hebrew, Bible, Talmud and Jewish history, taught our subjects and the secular teachers who were not Jewish, taught secular subjects.

Our livelihood was comfortable. Besides our monthly salary, we had some additional income from private tutoring and Bar Mitzvah preparations for boys who did not attend this school.

The Jewish parents related to the teachers with reverence, unlike the relationship between the Polish Jews and the melamdim. It was a well–known fact that whoever was accepted to teach in that school was well qualified.

On May 10th, 1940, German military columns invaded Belgium. Even before that day, a feeling of helplessness weighed heavily upon the Jewish community in this country. We knew that under the German rule, our situation would become desperate. The rich who possessed Belgian passports or some other privileged documents had already left the country. However, the majority of the Jews stayed.

Two days later, a door to rescue opened. I was among the first to be pushed into a train which was going to take us across the French border. The adventures that we experienced during the voyage, I have already described in an article published in one of the newspapers in Israel, which also contained some autobiographical details.

We travelled across French territory for eight days until we reached a village near the Spanish border. The French government provided us with lodging in abandoned houses and allocated for our monthly support.

At the beginning, the French related to us as unfortunate refugees who were forced out of their homes, leaving everything behind and escaping. But after the conquest of France when the rule passed on to the German collaborators, our situation changed drastically. Thanks to German propaganda, the relations between the population and ourselves also changed for the worse, as if we, the Jews, were to blame for their defeat.

Interestingly enough, on one of those days, I happened to overhear an innocent conversation between two women. One told the other: "The end of all these Jews who arrived en–masse into France will be that they will all be deported to Poland, their native land, and there, they will find their deaths". This was a prophesy that fully materialized.

[Page 325]

In the meantime, we sat tranquil in that border village, inclined to believe that we would remain there until peace came. The summer was coming to an end and we began to prepare ourselves for the winter. We were about one hundred and eighty kilometres from the Spanish border. But it was unthinkable for us to endanger ourselves by crossing the Pyrenean Mountains and seeking shelter in Spain. The situation was uncertain. All kinds of rumours circulated among the refugees. Some said that the Spaniards were handing over the refugees into German hands and, indeed, there were such incidents. Some told us that there were robbers in the Pyrenean Mountains who took the clothes off our backs and left them to the ravages of the wild animals or to die from exposure in the mountain wilderness.

A few days before Rosh Hashanah 1940, we were put for the first time into a refugee camp. We spent seven months in this camp. This is not the place to describe camp life, how hard it was to live with masses of people who, although they were all Jews, were gathered from every corner of Europe. It was a life of idleness and degeneration. However, in a certain way, we were still free to come and go and were not forced to work. Many returned illegally to Belgium because of rumours that had reached us in that the German authorities did not harm the Jews and even allowed them to work. Not only that, but some were even becoming rich….Ultimately, their ashes were scattered over the fields of Treblinka and Auschwitz.

We began to feel hunger in this camp. Luckily, I still had some money in my pocket and could obtain something outside of the camp to satisfy our hunger.

In April 1941, we were transferred to the Rivesalt Camp, closer to the Spanish border. In that camp, we immediately felt a change in relations to the Jewish refugees by orders of the German conquerors. In that camp, hunger ruled forcefully. Famine left its marks on our souls. We walked around like shadows. They forced us to work but not at hard labour. Everyone according to his ability. I would like to point out that most functionaries, including the guards, did not maltreat us. Except for a few single incidents, they related to us decently in comparison to the conditions that existed in other occupied territories, especially in Eastern Europe.

Thanks to my knowledge of several languages, I worked in the post office and was required to censor the mail and cross out everything critical about the Vichy government. Understandably, I left two words intact for everyone I erased, just to do my duty as a censor. Whoever received such a letter knew exactly what our situation was. In one of the letters that passed through my hands, I found the address of a family who lived freely in a small town and whose son was a student of mine in Antwerp.

I wrote to the mother of the student. I knew that she was a woman of valour and able to intercede on my behalf. I asked her to find me a job as a farm hand which might result in my release from the camp.

The woman saved my life and the lives of my family. She did not rest until she obtained a work contract for me. In August of that year, I was released from camp and moved to the village of Lelan in the Terva District where I became a farm hand.

[Page 326]

I can assure you on my own behalf that I was not an outstanding farm worker. From where could I possibly have obtained any knowledge of tilling and sowing? Did my father own land? I did not study agriculture in cheder and, besides, life in the camp had devastated my health. Nevertheless, I invigorated myself and kept working.

Three months passed until I succeeded in obtaining the release of my spouse and my children. We settled in the village and, considering the place and time, it was excellent. Well, not entirely.

Due to our long wanderings and especially the camp life, my wife became ill and her life was hanging on a thread. How she managed to recover in a time when medicine and nutritious food were in short supply, in addition to the mental stress and constant fear in which we had found ourselves, is a puzzle to me to this day.

We were the only refugee family and the only Jews in that remote village. I have to admit that, in spite of the anti–Jewish propaganda by the Vichy government and the villager's knowledge that we were Jews, they all related to us as the unfortunate who were driven out of their home for no reason at all. By the way, let me point out that my sons and daughter spoke fluent French. The villagers found no blemish in us and supported us by selling us all the food we needed.

There were a few Jewish families in a nearby town that, like us, arrived from Belgium and some were from the French territory which was occupied by the Germans. Periodically, we visited this town and they reciprocated our visits. We spent almost a whole year in this village in relative tranquillity. Only weak echoes reached our ears as to what the Germans and the Vichy rulers were plotting against us. We did not know anything about the fate of the Jews in German–occupied countries. Who could have imagined that somewhere in Europe, total extinction was declared on every Jew?

In the early morning of the 15th August, 1942, the farmer, my employer, woke me up and told me that policemen were waiting for me in the yard.

There was nowhere to run and it did not enter my mind that I was in any danger. I did not have a skeleton hidden in my closet, I did not engage in black marketing and I also had not spoken against the Vichy government. I felt innocent. Why would I run?

We were novices, innocently believing like children that there was justice in this world. And for that, six million of our brothers paid with their lives.

The gendarmes did not handcuff me. They helped me pack my belongings and when I asked why and for what reason they were taking me away, they meekly responded: "an order from higher up to take you someplace".

I was brought to my quarters where my family lived. There I found my wife and children waiting for me, surrounded by policemen as I was. The policemen took us to the nearby town where we found all the Jews assembled at the police station. The French people were standing in groups and were looking at us.

[Page 327]

A few among them openly expressed their disgust at the arrest. Almost everyone shared our sorrow and blamed the German rulers who had conquered their country and had oppressed them as well.

On that day, throughout France, all the Jews who were citizens of Poland, Germany, Czechoslovakia and the rest of the countries occupied by the Germans, were arrested except those Jews who were French or Belgian citizens. In other cities, those functionaries who belonged to the French underground notified the Jews about what to expect. However, only few believed them and hid. The majority did not believe that the decree would be put into action, and even if they would have believed it, where could they have possibly hidden?

We were transferred to the district town where we found about two hundred Jews who had already been arrested in the little towns and villages of the surrounding area. The majority had never tasted life in a camp and they did not realize that this might be the last station in their lives. Apathy, inactivity and mostly, not knowing what lay ahead of us, overcame us. With little courage, we could have saved ourselves but our senses became blunted and the will to live was taken away from us. The master of the people had abandoned us to be killed and Satan had gained the upper hand.

We were brought to camp De Gurs also known for its obloquy. Few survived there. In that camp the best of the best from Manheim's Jewish community in Germany, perished. They were exiled to this camp by order of the Germans in 1940 after the conquest of France.

This camp was located at the foothills of the Pyrenees and during the winter months, it became one big swamp.

The members of the Manheim Jewish community who were brought into the camp during the cold winter could not withstand the bad weather and, when the first frost came, they fell like flies. These were mainly children and the elderly. Silent witnesses to that tragedy are the heaps of earth around the camp. These wretched have not even been rewarded with a monument, unlike the millions of their brothers who died in the valley of death in the camps of Poland. Under these heaps are the graves of the unknown who took their last breath in that cursed region.

Into that camp we were brought. There are no words that can describe our feeling after the gates closed behind us. The guards treated us as if we were dust on the roads and the clerks of the Vichy government treated us as if we were a bunch of criminals who were liable to destroy the country and kill their leaders.

Even though we had some camp experience, we sensed in our subconscious that we would all die unless we succeeded in being released as soon as possible. Depression and despair, helplessness and hopelessness of escaping from the claws of the human savages, took control over us.

I have not eaten for two days. I walk around like a sleepwalker from barrack to barrack and stare into the faces of my brothers and sisters, remnants of all the Diaspora from Eastern and Western Europe. Sheep for the slaughter – our children – like lambs, trail their mothers. They soon would fertilize the thirsty land with their bodies. The well of tears had dried up and the skies above us were like copper.

[Page 328]

Hope came to an end.

Among the crowd of refugees, I encountered a man who was married to the granddaughter of Pearl Gertner from Strzyzow and also the son of the rabbi from Brzozow near Strzyzow. I think that his name was Reb Yacov Itzhok Weber. He lived in Antwerp and wound up in France where he was caught with other refugees. We barely exchanged greetings and went our way, each in the opposite direction. He strongly believed in our survival and that we would leave this camp eventually and that the wicked hand would not be allowed to do with us as he wished. His wife and children, one son even wore long side–locks, put their faith in him. They believed that the merits of their father the rabbi and the merits of their righteous ancestors would protect them. I wished that their belief would not disappoint them.

Meanwhile, I be–friended Rabbi Ansbacher whom I knew from the Rivesalt camp. He was also brought here and for the time being, he served as rabbi for the camp. Rabbi Ansbacher was also convinced that we would be expelled to some camp in Poland but that there was no danger to our life.

Since the rabbi knew that I was a Hebrew teacher, he came up with the idea of organizing a study group. Because of it, perhaps a door to safety might open for me too as a clergyman. There was a group in that camp to whom the expulsion order did not apply such as South American citizens, Jewish veterans who found in the French army, etc. He promised me that he would do everything he could to save me from expulsion.

We walked alongside the fence and during our walk, he asked me to clarify some grammatical terms in Hebrew. I doubt if I was able then to explain properly those grammatical terms, but at least I found an interest to take my mind off the situation.

One morning, we were asked to appear before the French officials whose numbers had suddenly doubled on that occasion. We had to appear before them one–by–one and they would decide our fate. My eyes visualized the official's face as the Angel of Death who, by lifting his sword, decrees a person's life or death.

One Jew, a native of Germany who was called in to appear and while standing in front of the official who had not yet lifted his hand in deciding whether he would live or die, collapsed and died. A doctor was rushed to his side but his efforts were in vain. Another heap of dirt was added to the French soil where the body of a nameless Jew was buried. At least his ashes were not scattered. But the heap will remain there forever.

I too with my family passed the same official and the verdict was that we would remain in camp for the time being because of the doubts on my citizenship. These doubts were the reason why we were among the living of today.

Meanwhile, many transports left the camp to an unknown destination; among them was the son of the rabbi from Brzozow with his family and some acquaintances from Belgium. The truth is that the French did not know the destination of these transports. These actions were wrapped in a veil of secrecy and obscurity. The truth will remain a secret that only a few later came to investigate.

[Page 329]

These few are either dead or they are ashamed to admit that indeed, the French officials did know the purpose of these transports. Therefore, they remained silent. This is a blemish which cannot be removed. It clings to the body of the nation and, preferably, should never be known.

We remained two more weeks in camp De Gurs. One blue morning, they told us, a group of fifty or maybe sixty people, that we would be sent back to the Rivesalt camp and there a decision would be made as to our fate.

This group consisted of a rabbi, one of the great personalities of Germany, converted women who wore their crosses so that they would be visible to everyone and the remainder were people with doubtful citizenship. My family and I belonged to the last group.

That evening before our journey, we were treated to a lavish meal. Such meals are usually reserved for people sentenced to die. We could not believe our eyes. Even cigarettes were distributed to us – an article that was difficult to obtain at any price. On the other hand, we were thoroughly searched by the police and everything that could be used to commit suicide was taken away from us.

Armed guards with loaded weapons guarded us and prevented any contact with the rest of the refugees. Only Rabbi Ansbacher and a Catholic priest were allowed to get near us. We sat through the night, the Rabbi and I, and spoke about everything related to Judaism except about my fate and what was in store for us. At day–break we were ordered on board trucks which took us to the railroad station.

After travelling for about an hour we became convinced that, indeed, the train was going in the direction of Rivesalt and we breathed a sigh of relief. This camp, where we had spent almost a year, was well–known to me and I was hoping that since we did get out from the De Gurs camp, we would find some opening, even one as small as the eye of a needle, to escape from this camp too. I had a hopeful feeling. Who can predict the turn of fate?

On my arrival in the camp I encountered an acquaintance from Antwerp, one of those who deeply believed in Providence and that there was a "Leader of the world". When he saw me he embraced me with such enthusiasm that, to a certain extent, I began to share his belief. He had just arrived from Belgium and had not settled in yet. This man, who knew no foreign language but Yiddish, when he heard about what I had gone through in the camp De Gurs, advised me what to say when I would appear before the officials that would decide my case.

This man did not survive but he saved me and my family with his advice and, as long as I live, I will never forget his name.

And now I would like to clarify my citizenship problem. I had in my possession a marriage certificate which I had received on the day of our civilian marriage in Ode–Mora, Transylvania. In this document, there is no mention about the country of my origin, which was Poland, thanks to the bribe which my father–in–law gave to the Romanian clerk in order not to delay the wedding. In addition, my wife had an expired Romanian passport but I made it "kosher" after a minor correction at the last minute. I also had my children's birth certificate that they were born in Belgium.

[Page 330]

When my turn came to appear before the official who was empowered to decided everyone's fate, whether to deport or not, I claimed that I was a Romanian citizen, that my children were Belgian citizens and, according to instructions of the Vichy government, we should not be deported.

The clerk claimed, relaying on information he found in the camp files from the previous time when I was in Rivesalt, that I was a Polish citizen and decided to deport me. But my wife and children were free to go. I insisted that I was never in Poland and it was probably a mistake.

I fought for my life. It was not enough that I had suffered in the country where I was born but and after I had left and disowned her, she still kept pursuing me.

Ultimately, the clerk decided, without my knowledge, to hand over my case to an inquiry committee for a decision. When I left the office, I met Abraham Kanner from Strzyzow. He had decided to escape from the camp and not wait until he would be called to appear before the official. "I have enough money to bribe the guards", he said "and most importantly, I am alone without my family". Indeed, he disappeared on that same day from the camp.

Meanwhile, Rosh Hashana 1943 arrived. In the evening, we congregated in one of the barracks. Words could not describe the prayers and the tears that were shed during the chanting of the prayer. "Now Lord, our G–d, put thy awe upon all whom thou hast made". We prayed for our lives that hung on a thread. Our souls twitched and implored. Angels and the distressed participated in our supplication which split open the gates of heaven. I mused: Who among us will merit acceptance of his prayers?

At daybreak on the second day of Rosh Hashanah 1943, a voice came through the loudspeaker: "Pick up your belongings and report to the square near the office of the camp commandant. Hurry".

About six hundred men, women, elderly people, youngsters and children; people who suffered poverty and hunger; a wretched community, trampled by the imbecilic, heartless, merciless police and camp guards, reported to the front office and waited for their verdict.

The southern sun spread her rays upon this oppressed mass and the cliffs of the Pyrenean Mountains were illuminated with a glowing light. For the second time in history, these mountains looked upon Jewish masses at their feet.

About four hundred years ago, these Pyrenean Mountains witnessed Jewish masses leaving Spain on the other side when they were dispersed into the Diaspora to France. Now France was also going to exile them. Thousands expired then and now, so many casualties on the same track.

We sat on our bundles and waited. Everyone was immersed in his own thoughts and tried to figure out this world. Finally, they arrived – those in whose hands our lives were pending. We lined up in alphabetical order. The official, with a list in his hand, called out names and the ones that were called went over to the other side which was fenced–off and guarded by armed guards. I did not even notice when the official approached the group in which I was standing with my family. My senses were confused. I became numb and my eyes gazed into a vacuum.

[Page 331]

I suddenly woke up and noticed that the official had passed us by and had gone to the group behind us. Neither I nor my family were called out to go over to the other side. Were we saved? I dropped to the ground and my lips muttered a prayer which could not be found in a prayer book. A thanksgiving consisting of a few words that breaks out from the heart only at a time when you feel that your life is in danger.

From the six hundred people who were standing in the square, only twenty–six were spared the expulsion on that day. Why? And by whose merits? Would we merit leaving this camp and be freed from the horrible nightmares which weighed heavily and cut deeply into our soles and wounds that would never heal? Who knows the mysteries of destiny?

At sunset, we bid farewell with our eyes to our brothers and sisters who were taken by trucks to the railroad station and from there to a place from which only a few merited to return.

Two days later, my family and I were released from the camp and returned to our village, but our sufferings had not ended yet.

In November of the same year, all of France was occupied by the Germans and the hand of the occupant rested heavily upon us. Fear of deportation became more realistic. All escape roads were blocked. We were apprehensive and could not rest day or night. Our lives hung on a thread and we were aware of it. Luckily, our neighbours stood by us and many times we found shelter in their houses. Periodically, I stealthily went to a farmer's house and listened to the broadcasts from London. I listened to the description of the annihilation of the Jewish community Bialystok by an eye witness. This broadcast was so shocking that I was barely able to return home.

We spent a year and a half in constant fear. Until this day, I am still puzzled. How did we survive the malicious hand? I intentionally avoided telling in detail what we went through after our second release from Riversalt camp. Even though we were forced to move from one farmhouse to another, to hide in barns and were almost caught once by the French police, all the above is like a drop in the ocean in comparison to what the deportees to the east had suffered before find their death in the gas chambers.

Fortunately, the relations with the French people toward us changed for the better, especially in the provincial towns and villages and they helped us hide from the eyes of the German occupiers.

In August 1944, the wicked rulers were defeated and the hour of our liberation arrived. We walked upright again like the other citizens. In May 1945, we returned to Antwerp where we had lived before but to my sorrow, my two sisters Sarah and Leah with their families and also my brother Joel were not alive anymore. They found their deaths somewhere in the valley of death – Poland – with the rest of the martyrs of our people. Also, my brother Abraham and his family perished.

In the month of Adar 1946, I made Aliyah to Eretz Israel to join my son and daughter who had preceded us. Blessed be He that we lived to fulfil the mitzvah of Aliyah and to live in our land. For a few years, I taught high school and the Ulpan on Mount Cansan. Because of my illness, I was forced to retire. Blessed be G–d that we were worthy to see the flourishing of our land.

[Page 332]

My son is a member in a religious kibbutz in the valley of Beit Shean and my daughter works for the government and is married to a bank clerk. All my grandchildren, except one, were born in Israel and they are the consolation in our lives.

At the edge of the Sheol
by Shlomo Yahalomi

I stood at the edge of the Sheol.
And faced the abyss, extinction and obliteration;
Perplexed, filled with anguish.
I will perish here in these wastelands.

About apace was the distance between me and death …
For my last request I already was asked…
In silence, I confessed all my transgressions.
My soul was immersed in drops of tears.

How dreadful is this weeping valley!
If to die you decreed, oh G–d!
Please, not here! Not in this forsaken corner.
Keep me alive until my return home, and then…

Behold, G–d listened to my prayer.
And the Angel of Death did not touch me;
Therefore, I express praise and glory
And will be forever thankful to G–d.

These verses were written in the spring of 1942 in the Soviet Russia on a collective farm; "Trudovik" somewhere in Kazakhstan. It was after my recovery from typhus in spite of the doctor's prediction to the contrary.

On the third anniversary of my exile
by Shlomo Yahalomi

Three years I have not seen my house.
Three years I wander and browse.
Three years spread with bitterness is my bread.
Three years sleepless are my nights in bed.

Three years since my life is dark, not bright.
Three years my days are dark as night.
Three years my eyes from tears are wet.
Three years G–d's punishment I have met!

[Page 333]

For three years my misfortunes have doubled
With prison, slavery, sickness and trouble.
Why, G–d was this brought upon me?
And how many years of pain are still in store for me?

Three years my blood like water was spread – –
G–d in heaven, have my redemption sped – –

Seven Rosh Hashanahs
(Memories from the Veil of Tears)
by Shlomo Yahalomi

With Awe and fear
Rosh Hashanah 1939, in Brzostek, Western Galicia

These were real and fearful days. Only four days had passed since Hitler's soldiers came to town and they had already established their new order with "German precision". For instance, they demonstrated their defiled strength by organizing an "efficient" police force and imposed fear and anguish upon the whole vicinity. Most Jewish people already learned from their personal experience what this new order consisted of. One of the first steps of the Nazi was to turn the shul into a storage room and a part of it into a stable. In addition to the personal worries of the Jewish families, another worry was added – the High Holidays were approaching. "Good" Christians whispered into their Jewish friend's ears that the Nazi were getting ready to maltreat the Jews and run wild, just because it was the High Holidays. In spite of great danger, nobody was planning to acquiesce, not to pray and blow the shofar in a quorum. "Not on the life of the Nazi will such a thing happen!" Reb Moshe Walter said. This faultless man, a Hassid of Rabbi Itzhok from Szczucin and a descendant of the Ropczyce Dynasty, did not believe that the war had really begun …. When I saw him on the first day of the war after we had already seen the German bombers in the skies, I said to him: "Nu, Reb Moshe?" He opened the palm of his hand and pointed to the centre and said: "There will be no war!" Reb Moshe and many like him was sure that we would soon see the defeat of the Nazi and, therefore, we should not flinch by not praying in a quorum because we would feel ashamed all of our lives and would never forgive ourselves. Therefore, it was decided to organize a few minyanim.

Not to arouse the anger of the oppressor, we arranged prayer houses in the alleys and remote corners of the town, of which we had plenty in Brzostek. We took as many precautions as possible. We put guards to watch all four corners of each house where prayers were conducted. On each side, a girl stood and looked out for approaching Nazi. Every thirty metres, a girl stood guard within a radius of one hundred metres.

[Page 334]

The girls would notify each other if they saw a dog coming and warn the worshippers. In such a moment, we would interrupt the prayers and were ready for "whatever would happen". When a sign was received that the coast was clear, we continued to pray, filled with extraordinary fear until we finished the prayers.

It was hard to conduct such prayers and even harder was the mental exertion – the gnawing doubts which depressed body and soul together. How far we were from reality when we recited: "He subdueth the people under us and all the nations under our feet". How great was the distance between the reality and our reciting the verse: "And therefore extend they fear O Lord, our G–d over all thy works". With guards having to stand watch outside…? Still, when we finished our prayers without a serious disturbance, we thanked G–d and sang with the melody of the rabbi from Ropczyce the song: "Strengthen Us Today", as though nothing had happened. Only one among us did not sing – Reb Fishel Goldman – an intellectual of the older generation who was a natural pessimist. He said: "If I would be sure that at least half of us that are congregated here will remain alive, I would sing like you. But I doubt it very much. That is why my heart aches". This time, this pessimist was right. And how right was he? From approximately forty people, men and women who participated in the prayers that day, only I who conducted the services survived to write these memoirs.

Purim in jail
by Shlomo Yahalomi

On the first day of the Hebrew month of "Vei" Adar 1940 (the second month of Adar which falls in a leap year is called Vei Adar), I said to my comrades in misfortune that Purim was approaching and regardless of our situation, we ought to celebrate as it is written: "And those days should be remembered and observed in every generation". The reaction to my announcement was scepticism and astonishment and even a light smile appeared on some of the faces. Not only did the partially religious oppose my suggestion but even Nathan Ginsberg, the pious and G–d fearing (may G–d avenge his blood) also gave me a cold shoulder and said: "What kind of a Purim can this be? How can we celebrate Haman's defeat which happened thousands of years ago, when his decree about our annihilation is materializing right before our eyes?" But, little by little, I convinced everyone that we, the ones "who are sitting in the darkness and in the shadow of death, bound in the chains of pain" were supposed to celebrate Purim which reminds us that every Haman ends up on the gallows.

Another colleague and I were delegated to work out some special programme for Purim in jail. On that evening, we sat forlorn and debated with what and how we could celebrate Purim. We realized the "tangible" of the question. Therefore, we could only fulfil the commandment "spiritually". How and with what would we create a Purim atmosphere in our cell which was as big as a chicken cup?

[Page 335]

There were all kinds of propositions especially one proposed by Mr. Gendelman from Katowice who stood out for his wonderful fantasies and odd visions. We finally agreed to a programme which we did not fully realize because we had forgotten that we were inmates in Soviet Russia and that they suspected us of being spies.

In a depressed mood, entirely "in–Purim–like", we, a minyan of Jews, sat on Purim eve in our cell. Some sat on beds, or at least something resembling beds, some on the floor or under the so–called "beds". There was no room for us to sit in a circle. We were solemn as though it were Yom Kippur Eve before Kol Nidrei. I began to read the Megillah with a low voice, like the recital of the "Amidah". I was afraid that the warden, our comrade Sergei, might hear us. I read: "once upon a time in Shushan" and at that point, I was interrupted by the blacksmith from Gorlice who asked: "When did this wonderful Mordechai live?" Of course we did not have a Megillah. I read from my memory. And I responded to the man that Mordechai lived a few thousand years ago. Hamans we have in each generation but a Mordechai? ... And just when I wanted to continue, the door opened and comrade Sergei angrily yelled: "What is going on here? What kind of propaganda is this?" I tried in vain to explain and to calm him down and said that no "propaganda" was going on, but he insisted: "it is very bad!" Two hours later, a higher official came, opened the door and called out: "Whose name begins with the letter D?" (The majority of the prison officials could not pronounce our last names). When I said that my name was Diamand, he said: "Let's go" and we left the cell.

I was not sure whether this call had anything to do with the reading of the Megillah or, by coincidence but I was being called for interrogation. My heart was pounding and I was worried as to what was going to happen. Most of all, I feared that our planned Purim programme would be disturbed. While I was immersed in my thoughts, two guards took me into a windowless taxi and we travelled about half an hour until we stopped in front of a huge and splendid building which was occupied by the N.K.V.D. The guard led me into a small room where an "interrogator" with a face and eyes of a Jew sat. After a moment of silence, the interrogator began. First I was asked to state my name, my parents' names and then the main questions such as: why did I cross the border without permission? Did I know that I was breaking the law? I told him that I ran from a sure death. I ran from the Nazi and in such a moment I could not ponder the legality of my deed. I also expressed my amazement about the possibility of punishing people who were forced to leave everything behind and escape over the border. Of course, he ignored my amazement and passed on to the more serious questions. "Why did you come to spy in favour of the Nazi?" When I expressed my great surprise that they could suspect a Jew of espionage for the Nazi, he responded: "On the contrary, because of the fact that the Nazi sent Jews to spy as they would not be suspected". Understandably, I could not deny such logic. Therefore, the only thing left for me was to deny that I was a spy. He again asked me if I desired to remain in the Soviet Union after the war. I did not respond for two reasons: a) He would not believe me; it would have only aroused more suspicion.

[Page 336]

b) I had made up my mind to tell the truth and only the truth. Therefore, I said: "As the situation is at present, I could not answer that question because I have not been free even one day in Russia and I do not know if life is good or bad." He understood the sting in my response and reacted with a "Yes" as though his conclusion that I was a spy was correct. He asked me what my occupation in Poland was. I knew that everyone who was asked such a question claimed to be from the working class. I decided not to lie for the following reasons: 1) He would not believe me (all the guards I encountered had said that I did not look like a proletarian and that my soft hands testified to it). 2) By telling the truth I might win his confidence and he would believe my words. He asked many more questions but I want to concentrate only on the last dialogue between him and me.

"Are you religious?" – "Yes, Comrade Interrogator!" He continued: "My mother was also religious she always attended prayers in the synagogue. Tell me is it true what a Jewish man from Lesko told me that it is forbidden to put out a fire on the Sabbath?" "No" I replied: "When it is dangerous you are supposed to put it out". He asked: "Do you believe that there is a G–d?" I answered: "Yes!" and he followed with: "Can you see him?" I replied: " What kind of G–d would He be if I could show Him to you?" He asked: "Can you prove that there is a G–d?". I thought about this question and replied: "Can you prove that there is not?" He furrowed his brow, thought for a while and said: "Yes. The pros and cons are even".

After this dialogue he told me to go. I left him escorted by two guards and thanked G–d that everything went smoothly.

Next morning somebody suggested that we get revenge on the only Haman among us. A filthy Ukrainian who hated us stood out for his wickedness and could not suffer the "Jews". He mainly always quarrelled with Rothman from Brzozow who was his neighbour. Rothman angered him with his recital of Psalms. The revenge was that Rothman yelled in the ears of the Ukrainian the quotation from the Psalms: "G–d shall avenge the gentiles". The Ukrainian became angry and began cursing all the Jews. Rothman reacted loudly too until the warden opened the door and took the Ukrainian into solitary confinement. (A dark cellar with all kinds of "conveniences"). We, the Jews, rejoiced even though the joy was not complete. The guard warned us that if we did not quiet down he would take us all into solitary confinement. Having no choice, we sat all day without saying a word until evening came and the guards changed.

I will never forget that evening. We sat and talked about all the miracles and wonders that G–d had bestowed upon us in every generation. We also held a Torah discourse on the theme of the day which was "Purim". The Galician blacksmith suggested that we forget about the situation in which we found ourselves and to tell Purim jokes and anecdotes to cheer each other up. We unanimously agreed to his proposition and began to be merry, telling jokes until we forgot that we were in prison.

[Page 337]

After the merry–making was over, the sighs came back again.

To finish off the celebration, I told a story which I had heard in my childhood. Reb Israel from Ryzin, of blessed memory, (the founder of the Sadigora Dynasty), spent one Purim in jail and longed very much to fulfil the mitzvah of giving presents to friends, as is customary on Purim. Since he was the only Jew in the cell, he hoped all day long for a visitor to realize the fulfilment of the mitzvah. When the day passed and he still had not fulfilled the custom, he became very sad and tears came to his eyes. The Rabbi lifted his eyes to heaven and said: "Master of the Universe! I am sending you my untainted tears as a gift as it is customary". With this story we ended this unforgettable evening and ten Jewish prisoners in an Odessa jail sent tears as a gift to our Father in heaven.

These tears were the ones which strengthened and encouraged us and gave us hope that we would overcome all our tribulations and sorrows. We began to prepare ourselves for the upcoming Passover.

Passover
The festival of freedom in prison
by Shlomo Yahalomi

Actually, I began to think about the upcoming Passover holiday two months before. There was nothing much to prepare because I did not have the slightest hope of obtaining matzos. My only worry was how to subsist without eating chometz. The only thing that I could do was to refrain from consuming the daily fifteen grams of my sugar ration, which by law, was supposed to have been twenty grams and save it for Passover. I saved about nine hundred grams of sugar. With this sugar and with hot water which was also part of our "food", I was preparing to live through Passover. The night before Passover Eve, I fulfilled the mitzvah of searching for chometz. However, I did not use a candle because there were no candles in the cell. I recited the customary "Kol Chamira", clearing the bread which we did not have. My thoughts were directed towards clearing the misery from the face of the earth and turning it to dust. On Passover night we prayed the Maariv prayer and recited the "Hallel" with the festive melody of the rabbi from Ropczyce, but in a subdued voice. When I reached the verse: "Open Thy gates of justice", I thought to myself, "M–d! Please! Open the gates of the prison.." After prayers, I made "Kiddush" over a few grams of sugar and recited: "You have chosen us from among other people and given us the season of freedom". Later, I began to conduct the Seder and ten imprisoned Jews celebrated the holiday of freedom under locked doors, iron grills on the windows and guards that guarded these wretched escapees from the darkness and shadow of death. Tear drops fell from my eyes and the big oppressive and painful question hovered in the air: "Mah Nish Tanah, what has changed?"

How was this Seder different from the others? The Ukrainian who had had a very good day because he had eaten all of our rations also wondered and asked: "Mah Nish Tanah?" Why are the Jews, in spite of their tears, in a festive mood and I, who have the whole world on my side, am sad?

[Page 338]

And the guard who watched our door and peeked in every few minutes through the little peephole, also wondered why in the cells that were occupied by gentiles there reined gloom whereas from the cells of the Jews a subdued song could be heard. He stood astonished and grumbled: "What kind of people are they? I do not understand". Nathan Ginsberg, the pious and fiery Hassid of the famous rabbi from Tchortkow and Itche Rothman from Brzozow, addressing their questions toward Heaven, also asked over and over: "Mah Nishtana?" The writer of these lines has authored a prison version of the Haggadah and began: "We were slaves in Poland, Lithuania, and Romania and refused to leave. The matzo that we are not eating on this Passover symbolizes our missed opportunity to make Aliyah, despite all the warning signals. Why do we eat "Maror" and plenty of it? Because we refused to leave our "sweet" life in the Diaspora, afraid that we might be forced to taste a little bitterness while settling in Eretz Israel". And so I kept reading the Haggadah, adjusting it to our situation until I reached the end of the song "Chad Gad–Yaw" where G–d executed the Angel of Death who pretended to be our "redeemer".

Luckily we were not disturbed in our extraordinary adventure, celebrating our freedom while actually being enslaved, neither by the guard nor by the Ukrainian who was with us in the cell. For a while we managed to forget ourselves and despite everything, we felt a little spiritual freedom. However, I was not worthy of observing the entire Passover. On the third day after living on sugar and water, I became sick and was taken to the infirmary where I finished my disrupted; kosher Passover in Soviet Russia.

Rosh Hashana 1940 in the Odessa prison
by Shlomo Yahalomi

Between Rosh Hashana 1939 and Rosh Hashana 1940, I came a long way and changed my "residence" several times. A certain period I spent under the "courteous" protection of the Nazi. Two weeks I "rested" in one of the courtrooms of Lesko Lukawice, Galicia when the N.K.V.D. (Soviet Secret Police) guards watched over me so that I would not be harmed... I spent three months in Lwow in the infamous prison: "Brigidki". From there I was transferred to a "new apartment" in the Odessa prison in Russia. In this place I celebrated the High Holidays and the Sukkoth holiday of 1940. Two weeks before Rosh Hashanah, the Ukrainian chief warden, Vasily Ivanovitch, was fired and replaced by a Jew, Gregory Isaacovitch. Soon after the new warden took over, we felt that some activity was going on within the prison walls. Not a cell was left untouched. People were taken out and replaced by others. Our Jewish brothers who tend to see the shadow of a mountain as a real mountain, like to see the shadow of salvation as real. And since the changes that were made in most of the cells consisted of Jews being left in each of them, at least ten or more, the Jews thought that this was not just incidental but a clear intention of the new warden, who was one of us. People said that his intention was that the gentiles should not disturb us and thus enable us to concentrate on our Rosh Hashanah prayers to our heart's desire.

[Page 339]

I did not know what was going on in the other cells but I was certain that there were faithful Jews in every cell who prayed. In our cell, I was the benefactor of the prisoners, the inmates who sat in that darkness and shadow of death. There were no prayer books. I was assisted by my memory with which G–d had graced me. I knew several versions. The versions of Ropczyce, Dynow, Sandz, Munkatch and Sadigora. But I used none of them. I conducted the prayers in an entirely new version; a special prison production. Each word was drained with blood, tears and pain. This time we did not sing at the end of the prayers: "Strengthen Us Today". Instead of a song, a heavy sigh emanated from everyone's mouth.

Shavuoth night, 1941
by Shlomo Yahalomi

I was in a labour camp, Mostovice Yaravtze, in the northern district of Archangelsk. Even though I was forced to work on the Sabbath many times, I could not resign myself to the idea that on Shavuot, the Festival of Receiving the Torah, I would have to work. Therefore, I tried to negotiate with the head of the work brigade to release me from work the following day, after I succeeded to convince him that I could keep a secret and he could rely on me. I "arranged" with him that I would not go to work and would remain in the barracks "sick". This was my "Emendation of Shavuot night".

That night I could not sleep. No matter how hard I tried to forget the present, I did not succeed. Sad thoughts sprang forth in my mind and, from time to time, a heavy sigh escaped from the depth of me. This angered my ignorant Georgian neighbour who could not understand what I was missing in this camp which, according to him and his experience, was one of the best camps. I told him, with a pretended seriousness, that I was worrying that perhaps I might be transferred and be forced to leave this camp. And who knows where they might take me?

"You are right" the Georgian said. "Indeed, it is something to worry about.

Broken and crushed, I got up in the morning from my 'bed'. After I washed my face with cold water and dipped my soul in my tears, I returned to my place. I covered my head with a blanket and prayed, oppressed and broken–hearted. In general, daily life and the hard labour in particular had not been inspiring and cheerful. More so on the Sabbaths and holidays, my sadness increased many–fold. I reminisce about the exalted joy and the festivity of a holiday in my little town and the sadness of this holiday made me numb. Therefore, I poured out my emotions in humming my prayers. When I had finished my prayers, I took off the blanket from my head. I searched with probing eyes in every corner of the barrack as if I wanted to see where I was.

I washed my hands and began reciting the Kiddush over a slice of bread as follows: "These are G–d's holidays". At this moment a bitter thought came to my mind. Are these G–d's holidays? I approached a corner where two Poles were playing chess. Like every neutral onlooker, I became involved in the game which relaxed my mind a little. But this relaxation was very costly to me.

[Page 340]

When I returned to my place, I discovered that my only winter coat had been stolen. And again, I came to think: "Are these G–d's holidays?" I began to investigate and I found the thief: a young Russian – but not the coat which was already in the quarters of the head of the brigade who had delegated the thief to do such a fine job. This fact did not surprise me at all. It was not the first time such things happened in camp. Actually, I would have gladly agreed to part with the coat in exchange for being released from working on Sabbath and holidays. Interestingly enough, the young thief was brutally beaten by the head of the brigade for have confessed to the crime.

"There is always a silver lining" as the saying goes. After the theft, I felt completely free and decided not to work on the second day of the holiday either. I was sure that the head of the brigade would not dare say a word. After all, I had hinted to him that the deed that his messenger had done was the same as if he himself would have done it. The thought that I would also rest on the following day aroused in me a feeling of alleviation and particular satisfaction. I slowly regained my composure.

In the evening, we, a group of Jews, sat around an over–turned empty barrel of herring which served as a table and we spoke about the events of the day. There was also a Torah discourse and a song which was composed by the famous Avish Meir from Sandz was sung with the words from a liturgical poem. A wonderful melody, passion pouring out of the soul to the Creator and expressing our confidence in the Protector of Israel and his Redeemer. I also recited the Archangelsk version of the poem "Akdamuth" – a poem which is customarily recited on the Shavuot holiday. I recited the original words interwoven with Russian words in rhyme, making fun of our miserable camp life. I sang it with its traditional melody and there was happiness in our corner. And, when I was asked by a friend who now lives in Israel, how does such happiness come to such a place? I responded: "These are G–d's holidays".

In my diary from those days which is in my possession now, I wrote this episode under the title "Shavuot, 1941, these are G–d's holidays".

Rosh Hashanah, 1941
In the collective farm "Mocry Maidan" near Saratov
by Shlomo Yahalomi

One year passed that was filled with events. During the year, I managed to receive a sentence of which my comrades were envious. Only three years of hard labour in a Siberian labour camp. The Russians called such a sentence "child's play"; only children were punished so lightly. After the Sukkoth holiday of the previous year, my voyages began. I spent a short time in the prison in Charkow. Next was a tour of the entire Archangelsk District (a total of nine months hard labour). The amnesty was proclaimed pursuant to the agreement between the Soviets and General Sikorski, the head of the Polish government in exile. I wandered from one place to another, from one station to another. Vologda, Gorky and Yaroslawl until a few comrades and I reached the collective farm "Mocry Maidan". Despite the fact that we were free and liberated, it was harder to find a minyan to pray than it was in prison.

[Page 341]

The leader of our brigade, Shachanov, had threatened us with all kinds of persecutions for being absent from work on the High Holidays. Therefore, all of us were afraid to disobey him. Both nights of Rosh Hashanah we prayed with a minyan. However, the daytime prayers I prayed alone in a house of a Russian religious woman who put her room at my disposal for two hours. During the ten days of penitence, we were suddenly summoned to report to the town of Sergach for mobilization into General Ander's Polish army. At least, that is what we were told. I became apprehensive that with our, luck we would be forced to travel on Yom Kippur. For a train to travel half a day and then stand still for two days, was a common occurrence in those days. There was also a chance that we might become stranded in the middle of nowhere or, with our luck, the train might just keep on traveling without stopping. But, thank G–d, nothing extraordinary happened. We arrived in the city of Arzames on Yom Kippur Eve and the train stood idle all during Yom Kippur. We continued our journey after Yom Kippur was over. Meanwhile, I had a "happy" Yom Kippur, pardon the expression. The railroad station in Arzames was swarming with people; men, women, children and soldiers. In a corner, a group of tortured, broken and depressed Jews stood and prayed. They thanked G–d for His graciousness, for making it possible for them to pray and to recite their confession with great humility, beating their chests while saying "Al Cheth".

Go ahead. Pray!
Rosh Hashanah 1942. District Takmak. Kazakhstan
by Shlomo Yahalomi

After spending a few months in General Ander's Army and wandering all over Kazakhstan, Uzbekistan and Tadzhikistan, I finally arrived, together with many other exiles, in Kish–Mish near Takmak. There, an epidemic of typhus broke out among Jews and non–Jews of which fifty people died. Soon after Passover, I began working in the collective farm of "Trudovik" and later in one of its branches. When the High Holidays approached, there was not a shadow of doubt about letting us pray. We intended to organize public services in Kish–Mish anyway. In this city, there were many Russian Jews who had escaped from places which the Nazi had conquered and had found shelter here in Kish–Mish. And they too were hungry for a little "Yiddishkeit". One week before the High Holidays, I was surprised by a sudden visit from the brigade leader, Bogomolov, with the unhappy news that I was being transferred together with other people to another branch of the farm – Tchik–Par. This news was very depressing. I was apprehensive that after I left no one would organize public services in Kish–Mish. Having no choice, I packed my belongings and reported to Kish–Mish – the centre of the collective farm, thinking that there I would decide what to do next. After my arrival in town I went to the home of one of the local Jews and there I found a treasure – the book of Kings. I was very happy because since my arrest, I had not held a holy book in my hands. I remembered reading somewhere that some saintly personalities, when they were in doubt about something and could not decide what to do, they opened a book and what was written on that page they did accordingly.

[Page 342]

So I decided to do the same thing. I opened the book and found a prayer of King Solomon. I thought to myself: my name is also Solomon. This must be an omen that I should remain in Kish–Mish to conduct the prayers on Rosh Hashanah so that the people could hear the prayers of Solomon. I dodged being sent to Tchik–Par where the rest of my group had been sent and remained in town.

The first night of Rosh Hashanah we conducted the services without a hitch. However, the next morning, a man from the N.K.V.D. suddenly appeared and angrily came over to me – the leader – removed my tallit from my head and yelled in anger: "What is going on here?"

I responded with pretended audacity: "What is the matter with you? Are you a Trotskyist? As far as I am concerned, Communists have nothing against religion. Stalin has said so. Only Trotsky said that Communists ought to fight religion until it is wiped out". When the man from the N.K.V.D. heard such a respond he thought for a while and went outside to seek advice from his comrade with a higher rank. After a few minutes, he returned and softly said: "Alright. Keep praying".

"In the land of the free"
Rosh Hashanah 1943. "Peat Enterprises" in the district of Dzambul
by Shlomo Yahalomi

Another year passed by and it was not strewn with roses. During that year I actually stayed in one place but in reality, I travelled a great deal on business connected with my job. I was the traveling representative of the "Peat Enterprise" which took me throughout Great Russia and reached the famous Tien Shau Mountains. The management even tried to send me to a remote and forsaken corner, surrounded by mountains and cliffs, to build a new highway for my Russian fatherland. But at the last moment, I managed to get out of it. (In Russian, one must know how to take care of "things". Without knowing how, you cannot survive even one hour). During this year, I was almost sentenced to prison or to forced labour again for refusing to accept a Russian passport but, with G–d's help, I was saved. A great many Jews from several European countries worked in this enterprise and planned to pray publicly on the High Holidays. We were sure that this time everything would be in order, because almost all of the leadership were in our pockets. From Director Zeeman to Chief Engineer Seltzer who is now working as an engineer in the city of Tel–Aviv. Although he was a refugee he had a lot of influence. Also, engineer Karp, a brigade leader and a few foremen. But, apparently, Providence wanted to put me to the test again – a very serious test. On the eve of Rosh Hashanah, I was summoned to Director Zeeman's office where a man from the N.K.V.D. was present. They told me: "You want to pray? Please! Take a week or two week vacation – go wherever you want and pray there. But do not organize public services here! Your Jews will neglect their work on the High Holidays. They will pray with you and we will have to try you for sabotage". Clear and direct – no more and no less! I kept quiet for a moment and said: "I prayed under the Nazi and was not harmed.

[Page 343]

Here in the land of freedom and justice, I would be punished?" The man from the N.K.V.D. looked at me with an angry face. It seemed that I hit the target. It was obvious that he was restraining himself from showing any emotional signs. After a deep silence which lasted half a second, he said as though speaking to himself: "Cunning". "You can go now". The director said: "remember what you were told here. You have your orders. That is all".

Despite the fact that a few friends of mine did try to dissuade me from my decision to organize public services on the High Holidays and to conduct them, I did not give in and again for the sole reason that I knew if I would not do it, there would have been no prayers. I, therefore, announced that services would take place. Most local Jews came to the evening and morning services which took place in our barracks and the services passed without any hindrance or obstruction. We were not disturbed.

However, the director, sticking to Soviet principle: No work, no bread – did punish us. We did not receive our bread rations for those two days of Rosh Hashanah. After Rosh Hashanah, when the director saw me, he asked me what I had prayed for. I told him: "we prayed for a good year for us and also for you, Comrade Director, in spite of the fact that you deprived us of our bread rations…"

"Well alright, you will get it". The same day we received three bread rations.

The director and the management resigned themselves to the situation and did not even try to influence us not to conduct public services on Yom Kippur. On Yom Kippur eve, a few brigade leaders asked me to begin the "Kol Nidrei" services a little later because they too wanted to attend. This was a real sanctification of the Divine Name. Not only Jewish leaders came but non–Jewish as well and communist youth leaders were among them. The closing prayer: "Neilah" was most exalting. All the emotions of our aching hearts were poured out in our prayers. Until this day, I still hear the resounding shriek that came out from the depths of the exiled and the forsaken Jews who declared in the land of atheism, in spite of everything: "The Lord is G–d".

Whenever I meet with people who worshipped with me at that time, I am asked: "Do you remember our declaration that 'The Lord is G–d'?

United with my brother once again
Rosh Hashanah, 1944. Dzambul
by Shlomo Yahalomi

The year which had just passed brought with it a happy and exciting occasion for me. I met my brother Heschel. I had already heard that my brother was alive as of July 1943. I found that out from Yechezkiel Diamand from Rudnik. While I was in Bystrowka on "official business", he came over and greeted me happily and called out my brother's name. When I responded with astonishment that I didn't know him, he said: "Why are you pretending? Were we not together in the labour camp?" I immediately understood that he mistook me for my brother Heschel because we resembled each other very much.

[Page 344]

But I did not know the whereabouts of my brother, nor his address. In March 1944, I received a letter from Itzhok Berglass in which he informed me of my brother's address. During that year, I was mobilized again into a labour army from which I managed to escape. I wanted to reach my brother in Dzambul. I therefore tried to get into the Red Army and, while traveling to the assigned place, to disappear in Dzhambul. After a few unsuccessful tries I finally reached Dzhambul – actually a collective farm near Dzhambul, where my brother was living. I have much more to tell about our meeting after having been apart for so long, but I would like to concentrate only on the theme: "Rosh Hashanah".

This time I was not the only one who was getting ready for the High Holidays. Thousands of Jews who lived in that area, refugees from Poland, Lithuania and other countries as well as Jews from every corner of Russia joined us. There I found people who knew me from the camps and also from before the outbreak of the war. In Dzhambul I also merited to become the "Public messenger" (cantor) and chanted all the prayers on Rosh Hashanah and Yom Kippur before a big crowd of people from various Diasporas. It is impossible to describe and to imagine how we prayed.

Although we did not know everything that had happened to our brothers who had remained under the Nazi, we already knew that something terrible had happened beyond human imagination. The crying had ascended to the heart of Heaven because of the sound of the cries and sighs. The rooms that had been put at our disposal by Reb Ever Englender from Kosno, one of the richest men there before the outbreak of the war could not absorb such a big crowd of worshippers. Many remained standing outside. There were many curious onlookers who were deeply shocked and had tears in their eyes.

In spite of the great sadness and the sorrowful mood, the services were conducted as in the earlier years. We sang when we were supposed to sing all the traditional melodies and added a few new ones which had been composed during our wanderings. And, at the end, we sang even louder the finale: "Today you have strengthened us".

Rosh Hashanah 1945
The last Rosh Hashanah in Soviet Russia
by Shlomo Yahalomi

Our hopes that we would be able to live in Dzhambul until the end of our exile were only an illusion. We thought that we would not have to continue to wander until we, the Polish citizens, would be permitted to return to our land, Poland. It was not to be. The authorities again began to pester the pursued and tortured Jews. They forcibly mobilized them into all kinds of labour camps which were called: "Labour Army". After I was mobilized several times and managed to get out, and after my brother was forced to flee from Dzhambul and move to Alma Ata, I too escaped and joined him in Alma Ata. There we found a new world. It was evident that we did not find a free world but we found dear brethren from all corners of Russia – a larger number than anywhere else. There were Hassidim of Lubavitch, Bratzlav, Chernobyl, Trisk and many others. There were only a few scholars among them but they were virtuous and had warm hearts – Jewish hearts. They went out of their way to help the Jewish refugees from Poland and other countries. Their emotions were mixed both with love and envy toward us because we were less afraid of the Soviet regime and organized public services wherever we could, from which they also benefitted.

[Page 345]

Despite the fact that we were told at our arrival in Russia that "nobody ever leaves", we kept our faith and believed that we would get out. Of course, the Polish refugees had organized a big quorum for the High Holidays as they did in the previous years. About a thousand people participated in the services. The location was small so the majority of the worshippers were forced to remain outside. There was something new in this years' services. Part of the chanting was done by a Russian Jew from the Ukraine – a fiery Hassid of the rabbi from Lubavich. Even though he was not blessed with a good voice, his chanting was warm, clear and untainted. Many Soviet citizens participated in the worship. I chanted the Mussaf prayers which deeply impressed the Russian Jews. "We have not heard such chanting for many years", they said. The fire which was latent inside of the Russian Jew had awakened and began to burn again. The founder of the communist party in Eretz Israel who had returned to Russia and there repented, was also present among us. His name was Yacov Meirson. Many of those who participated in these services and merited to make Aliyah recall these services with tremble and holy anxiety. These services turned into a great demonstration in the land of atheism. It was declared at this grand forum that the G-d of Israel lives and exists even in Russia.

Memories from the land of Exile
by Itzhok Berglass

It was summer of 1940. The excitement among the refugees from Western Poland, the majority of who were Jews who found themselves in the Eastern part of Poland under the rule of the Soviets, was very great. Although during the registration which had taken place a few months earlier, the refugees had declared their willingness to return to their home towns from which they fled or were expelled, this declaration had not been given wholeheartedly. They would have preferred to have been left alone and not asked again. However, they had to answer this question on the registration form. Most of the refugees were persons who had left their families, parents, brothers, sisters and especially wives and children, on the German side. These refugees knew that Soviet Russia was hermetically sealed. Therefore, they were apprehensive that, by expressing the desire to obtain a Soviet passport, they would be cut off from their families forever. Even those refugees who had been expelled by the Nazi before the arrival of the Russians were attached to their birthplaces where they still had relatives. They overcame the fears and having no alternative, they expressed their agreement to return to Nazi occupied territory.

The German Resettlement Commission had arrived in Lwow and the refugees had organized themselves in town and district committees but the Germans did not give any sign of activity. All they did was to issue passage permits to Poles who had applied for them. A few permits were issued to Jews whose relatives, on the German side, provided recommendations from the German authorities that they were needed for the German war economy.

[Page 346]

In the last few weeks before the Soviet exile, the Soviet authorities ordered those refugees who had declared their willingness to accept a Soviet passport, to settle in certain towns, at least one hundred kilometres from the German border. From this order, we concluded that something was going to happen.

One day, all refugees without families who had refused to accept Soviet passports, were arrested and a few days later, on a Friday night at the end of June, all of the families in the same category were also arrested. The individuals were sent to forced labour camps and we, the families, were loaded onto cattle trains under heavy N.K.V.D. convoy and shipped out to far distances throughout Russia. The wagons were filled to capacity. Each wagon had a few benches which were supposed to serve as beds. The toilet was located in the centre of the wagon. As soon as we got into the wagons we caught lice. Apparently these wagons had already been used for human shipments without having been disinfected.

From Zolkiew were we lived, the train travelled through Lwow eastward. As soon as the journey began we were exposed to the "integrity" of the Ukrainian farmers when they brought food products to the stations and demanded from us, people behind bars, exorbitant prices, several times their market value. We also felt the warmth of our Jewish brethren who were not allowed near us because we were the ostracized. In spite of this, they overcame their fear and handed us food and cookies for the children through the barred train windows.

We travelled northeast to Chelyabinsk. During our voyage we also learned a lesson on the Soviet way of life. When our train passed close to a passenger train, a Jewish passenger told me: "I want you to know that in this country there is no return from exile". And he rushed off. From Chelyabinsk, they took us with the Trans–Siberian train eastward and despite the hard conditions, we were happy to keep on travelling endlessly for fear of the future when we arrived at our destination. After eighteen days of travel, our wagons were detached from the Trans–Siberian train and the next morning of the nineteenth day, we reached our destination and were unloaded at the Kamaratzga station.

The location of our exile
by Itzhok Berglass

The station and the final place of exile at which we arrived two days later was in the district of Krasnoyarsk which stretches from the North Sea to the Mongolian border. In Kamaratzga we were divided into several groups; received food and remain overnight sleeping in a public building. The following morning we were sent to our final destination some sixty kilometres south of the railroad. Women and children were sent by trucks and the men by wagons which were pulled by tractors used to transporting steel rails for the railroad. At midnight, we reached the village of Narva and were put into the culture hall. Most of the inhabitants of the village were Estonians who had assimilated and become Russians. They were exiles from the time of the Russian Czar and had named the village after the Estonian port from where they came.

[Page 347]

In the village we were joined by an official nurse whose main function was to watch over the children and the frail. She "encouraged" us by saying that all those under her charge would not last long because the winter temperatures reached –50Â° and the summer heat reached to +40Â°. Mosquitoes and all types of insects sucked human blood and poisonous snakes teemed everywhere even in the houses. We later found out that everything she said was true. However, miraculously, we held out until our liberation, with a few exceptions.

From the village of Narva we were sent deeper into the forest, some twenty kilometres, in groups which were hurriedly assembled from the people with whom we had lodged in Kamaratzga. Our group consisted of eighty people – men, women and children. These barracks were built years earlier by Ukrainians who had lived near the Polish border and had been exiled to prevent fraternization with their brothers on the Polish side. After they settled permanently in collective farms, the barracks were then occupied by Austrian Socialists who had fought against Dolphus and, after their defeat, had escaped to Russia – the land of socialism – where they were then exiled to Siberia. Then came the members of the International Brigade from Spain where they had fought and were defeated by Generalissimo Franco. They too were exiled to Siberia. Just before our arrival, Polish aristocrats – rich land owners from Eastern Poland and Polish government functionaries that had been exiled before us, divided the big barracks into small rooms for each family. We inherited these rooms.

The quarters into which my family and I moved into consisted of one large room and two small chambers. In one of these small rooms, a Pole was still living with his family. He was the only one who remained after all the Poles had left. It was terribly crowded. Along the walls there were two-tiered plank beds which served as our bedroom and between these plank beds was a narrow passage. Our boarders were huge rats that ran around fearlessly among us, nibbled from our meagre food and all kinds of insects that nourished themselves with our blood. On rainy days, water leaked through the room and the main "beneficiaries" were those who slept on the upper banks. My eight-year old daughter and I were among them.

After three days of rest, we were recruited for work.

The place was called Pimia. In the near future it was supposed to have been turned into a city, a central place for the whole area and especially for logging. Our first job was to build a narrow railroad track to enable the government to transport the timber out of the woods and onto the Mona River which flows into the Yenisei. From there, the timber could be shipped throughout Russia and the world.

Until then, the transportation of timber was only possible in the spring when the snow had thawed and water levels rose in all the tributaries flowing into the Mona River. All the labour done by the exiles and under the supervision of local people was aimed at this central purpose.

We worked hard digging, stone quarrying, timber cutting and cutting up the timber. Women who did not volunteer for work were pursued by a militiaman and forced to work. He used to hunt for them, always appearing on a horse with a whip in his hand and the women, seeing him approaching, would sometimes escape into the thickness of the forest.

[Page 348]

These were the conditions we lived in. In the wintertime, when the swamps were frozen and with considerable risk, a part of our group was sent further into the woods. They came out in the fall, after the liberation, which was the result of an agreement between Stalin and Sikorski after the Nazi attacked the Soviet Union.

The protest
by Itzhok Berglass

The exiles did not accept their suffering lying down. We lived under the Soviet rule for a short time and we spiritually could not agree to the injustice that was being done to us. We were naÃ¯ve and thought that if we were exiled in Siberia we had nothing to fear. We did not consider: "that there was another Siberia from where you can never get out". With these words, we were threatened once by the local lumber-mill manager who complained that we were slovenly in our work. We also did not realize that this exile had saved our lives. Like Joseph in the Biblical times, we would have to be thankful because "G-d did us a favour. He saved many people".

We wrote three identical memos and sent them to the three famous people in Lwow whom we knew had been activists and had cooperated with the Soviet rulers. We sent letters to the Polish writer, Vanda Vasilevska, professor Panczeszin who had defended Jews that had been pursued during the Polish regime especially Jewish students that had been attacked by their Polish colleagues – the Jew haters, and to Professor Studnicki who we also knew before our exile.

The memos were written in a sharp tone against the authorities. We complained that instead of treating us like refugees that had escaped the sword and as it is customary all over the civilized world, they took us out in the middle of the night like criminals and sent us into exile. Therefore, we asked their intercession to bring us back from exile.

I was the initiator and author of the memos. I signed it first and after me, all the heads of families in our barracks also signed the memo.

Fortunately, these letters were not released by the people to whom they were addressed. But we did receive a heart-warming letter from Vanda Vasilevska. She told us that what had happened to us was well-known and that there were efforts being made to correct the injustice. The response from Professor Panczeszin was more formal but with a promise to help. The third one did not respond at all.

As time went by, we became accustomed to our situation. As the saying goes in Yiddish: "When you get used to troubles you live with them happily". But, we never gave up hope that someday we would get out of Siberia. That was what kept us going and we held out until our release.

"Give thanks to the Lord for He is good"
by Itzhok Berglass

When in other places it was still summer, in Siberia it was already fall. It rained frequently with cold winds blowing and the living conditions became worse – worse than in the hot summer months. Our upper bank, my daughter's and mine, was located near the door which was frequently opened and closed, day and night. Eighty–eight people kept coming in and out. The leak through the roof worsened and it became almost unavoidable for my daughter not to catch a cold. She became ill with severe angina.

[Page 349]

I was notified of my daughter's illness while I was at work in the field. Soon after work, I went straight to Narva to the clinic which was attended by a young doctor and a medical assistant. I told the doctor that I was afraid that the angina might develop into diphtheria. I was asked to pay for the use of a horse and the medical assistant rode out to my barracks. He diagnosed it as only a severe form of angina. He wrote out a prescription and told me to get it filled the following morning at the pharmacy.

I took the prescription early in the morning and went to see the militiaman who was in charge over us to tell him that my wife had to remain with the child and that I needed permission to travel to the village to pick up the medicine. The exiles were not permitted to leave the place without a permit. The militiaman was still asleep so I went to the foreman and asked him to release me from work. Such a release could also be used as a pretext to travel without a permit. He refused. In desperation, I jumped on to the small train which was going to Narva to pick up some workers. One of the foreman's helpers demanded that the train engineer stop the train and forcibly remove me but he refused.

When I returned home and handed the medicine to my sister–in–law, I was immediately put on trial for my crime. The Judges were: my foreman, the militiaman and the head of the district militia who often visited our village. The district officer accused me of arbitrarily leaving work and travelling with a permit. I responded by asking him if he any children and when he responded affirmatively, I told him the whole story. I showed him the doctor's diagnosis and asked him how he would have handled the situation. He immediately released me and told me to return to work.

Two days passed and on the Friday, my sister–in–law again appeared at my workplace and told me that I must bring the doctor again because my daughter's illness had worsened and that she was very sick. The doctor refused to come claiming that he had diagnosed her correctly the first time and that there was no other medicine available, only that which he had already prescribed. With sadness and great worry about the fate of my daughter, I went back to the train to return home. I fed her myself with a slice of turnip which a Russian travelling with me had offered after I had not eaten all day. I walked the four kilometres from the train to the barracks in the dark, on a lime path that had many holes in it. I fell several times in the mud praying in my heart that for the pain I suffered, I should merit to find my daughter alive.

When I opened the door of the barracks I became frightened by the quietness that prevailed. My wife told me to relax and that the crisis had passed. When the situation had become worse, my daughter had haemorrhaged and, because of this, the clotted breathing passages had opened up and her temperature had gone down. As to the quietness that prevailed in the barracks, she explained that it was because our brothers–in–trouble kept as quiet as possible so as not to disturb the sick child.

I was late for the Friday night prayers but I still began to pray and to recite the welcome Sabbath song: "Give thanks to the Lord for He is good". It was not an ordinary prayer welcoming the Sabbath which is recited every Sabbath eve, but it was a thanksgiving from the bottom of my heart for His benevolence. Tears were dripping from my eyes and they were tears of gratitude and joy.

[Page 350]

The holidays in Siberia
by Itzhok Berglass

Our lives were difficult and primitive. Our thoughts concentrated only on work and on how to obtain food. We wore rags because the clothes we had brought with us were bartered away to the local people in exchange for food. Our spiritual food consisted only of a prayer book which contained the Psalms. We subscribed to the Yiddish Communist paper: "Truth" from Moscow but instead, they sent us the "Truth" that was printed in Kovno. I also had in my possession the Five Books of Moses from which I taught my little daughters the Hebrew alphabet and a few words in Hebrew to prevent them from forgetting what they had learned in the Hebrew school in Strzyzow. From our traditional Galician Jewish life, we became forcibly estranged but it was unthinkable for us not to observe the Jewish holidays, especially the High Holidays. We were still negotiating our release from work on Rosh Hashanah with our foreman, the man who had refused to let me go to pick up the prescription. (He had changed and had become another person after I befriended him). Our neighbours, who lived in the barracks a few kilometres away, preceded us by turning to the head management of the company which was under the leadership of a Jew from Krasnoyarsk. These men were all devoted Communist Party members and they opposed any religious activity. Therefore, they categorically refused our plea and watched us closely so that we should not succeed in our effort to be released from work on those days that were holy to us. Normally, they fell behind in supplying empty wagon trains on which we loaded the excavated rocks and gravel and caused us a loss in wages. This time, they sent more wagons than usual and gave order to return the empty wagons immediately after they were unloaded at their place of destination. But it happened otherwise. When we returned to the stone quarry with the empty train, the train de–railed and the tracks came apart. Similar accidents often happened but on a smaller scale and people never got hurt. This time, the de–railing was more serious and even though no one was hurt, a few days were needed to repair the railroad. My immediate foreman, who would have been ready to release us from work, if not for the fear of his superiors, was happy and said: "Your G–d did it".

The following three days we did not work: Thursday the first day of Rosh Hashanah; Friday, the second day and also Saturday. We sat at our working place on a hill and enjoyed the warmth of the autumn sun. When we came home in the late afternoon, we prayed the Mussaf prayer at our ease.

After Rosh Hashanah, we began to worry about Yom Kippur which was coming soon. Ultimately, we agreed with the foreman to trade Yom Kippur for another working day. Yom Kippur was on a Saturday and we agreed to work on the Sunday, our usual day off. The foreman knew that according to the ruling ideology, this was not permissible. Therefore, he left that day under some pretext and went to the regional village of Narva.

[Page 351]

We did not leave our barracks but we began to pray. When the militiaman who often came to our working place saw that our group was missing, he came galloping on his horse to our barracks and there he saw a show that he had never seen in his life. All the men were wrapped in their taleitis and the women were with them. In response to his question, we told him about our agreement with the foreman. He did not agree and demanded forcefully that we leave immediately for our work. When we did not respond to his command, he took out a list with our names and asked everyone individually if he would obey or not. The first man he asked agreed to obey. I was the second to be asked. Before I replied, I consulted quietly with the others and we decided to go out to the job but not to work.

As soon as we agreed to leave, he rushed off to see the foreman. When he could not find him, he turned to his assistant, a young Pole who knew about our secret agreement with the foreman. The assistant told the militiaman that the foreman had agreed and that there was no work for us to do. Next, the militiaman turned to a construction foreman. He refused to accept us for one day and also did not want to act against his comrade, the other foreman. He was a Russian intellectual who had asked me once to teach him Hebrew. He was exiled because when the German–Soviet war broke out and while in a drunken state, he said that he was going to fight the Germans for his fatherland but not for Stalin. He was sentenced to die but was later granted a reprieve and was sent to the front on the first firing line. After having been wounded, he was sent into exile.

The militiaman (who we called "commanding officer") did not want to jeopardize his good relationship with the foreman, so he relented. We returned home cheerfully and continued the fasting and praying until the end of the day.

On Sukkoth holiday, we were meritorious to have a Sukkah, which was the envy of many of our brothers in Russia. Near our barracks there was a little unfinished house without a roof. Covering it was no problem in the thickness of the forest. Therefore, we made the blessing over a slice of bread "to sit in the Sukkah" under the cover of snow.

We did not eat Chometz on Passover. The Jews from Zolkiev, the city from where we were exiled in Siberia, had not forgotten us. They sent a small package of matzos to each family. They were paid for it by our relatives who had remained there and the people, who did not have any relatives, received the matzos for free. We, the lucky ones, that is three families in all, received an extra package of matzos from our cousin, Elimelech Eisenstadt, may G–d avenge his blood. He lived in Brody not far from the little town of Radziwlow where the major Polish matzo industry was located. We also prepared some potatoes and what was missing, we filled with a ration of hunger.

Just before Passover, we moved from the shared barracks to individual quarters – two families to a room. Every room conducted its own seder, expressing hope for better days and being able to join our families who remained in Easter Galicia under the Soviet rule and those in Western Galicia who were under Nazi rule.

[Page 352]

The majority of the exiled merited returning to Poland but of our families who were left there, we did not find anyone alive.

Memories of the first days of Poland's occupation by the Nazi
by Simcha Langsam

As soon as World War II broke out, on September 1, 1939, utter chaos prevailed all over Poland. The population distanced itself from the borders of the Third Reich. The declaration by the commander of the Polish Army, Ridz Smigly, that the enemy army would not be allowed to touch even a button which belonged to the Polish people, had nurtured hope in the hearts that, in a few days after the German defeat, the Poles would return to their place as conquerors.

The first bombs that fell over the cities and villages caused great confusion and panic among the population. The wandering of the masses began. The highways and roads were replete with refugees, mostly whole families with their belongings. Some were in motorcars, some on horse–drawn carriages and some on food amidst the Polish army who retreated like sheep without a shepherd, not knowing where to go and where they were. The German airplanes flew low and shot at the refugees. Thousands of casualties fell among them women and children.

In that confusion, Jewish refugees who were Polish citizens stood out in particular. They panicked. They were confused and stupefied from the German "blitzkrieg" on the one hand and the hostility of the Poles toward them on the other hand.

All the wandering ended when the German overran the refugees. Some even gave bread and candies to them and told them to go home.

The Polish refugees returned immediately to their homes. However, the Jewish refugees who already knew that all their belongings at home had been stolen by their Polish neighbours and that in some places, the Germans had already begun their bloody actions, were not in any hurry to return but were searching for means to unite their families who were separated during the wandering. Among all those Jewish refugees, there were very few people from Strzyzow and its vicinity, because the town was not located on a strategic or main crossroad. Among the stream of refugees was my brother, Yechezkiel, who now lives in the United States and I, the writer of these lines. We became stranded in Dombrowa and stayed with our sister Beila, may G–d avenge her blood. (She perished with her husband and three children).

Like all refugees, we looked for a way to return and unite with our father who had remained alone in Strzyzow.

Traveling by train in those days was very dangerous for a Jew. The danger stemmed more from the Polish passengers than from the Germans. Therefore, we kept postponing our trip from day–to–day.

Dombrowa, the neighbour of the big city of Tarnow, followed the events in that city. It was relatively quiet in Dombrowa itself, except for the nabbing of Jews for all kinds of work.

[Page 353]

At the end of October 1939, news reached us from Tarnow that in the streets of the city, proclamations were announced as part of the Nuremberg anti–Jewish laws. The Nazi restricted the Jews from moving about in town, they shore the beards off of Orthodox Jews and made a thorough registration of all Jews in town. They nominated commissars into Jewish businesses and ordered the Jews to wear a Star of David, and also display the Star of David in the windows of Jewish stores. Horrible tidings came of killings of Jews without any reason.

Upon receiving such news, gloom began to reign among the Jews in Dombrowa. Panic increased when, on the first day Sukkoth, a group of Jews were kidnapped. Only a part of this group returned to their families and the rest were killed. After this incident, people avoided walking in the streets and gathered to pray at the rabbi's house and in a few other private homes. The tension reached its peak after the incident that occurred on Hoshana Raba. After the services in the rabbi's house, we received news that the Germans were nabbing Jews to work and that eight people who had been nabbed the day before, had been shot. The worshippers rapidly dispersed into their homes. My brother–in–law, the husband of my sister Beila, and I lay down in bed and put various medicines nearby. (The Germans were very afraid of contagious diseases). Within minutes, we heard knocking of boots on our door and yelling in the street. A shudder went through our bodies and we anxiously awaited that was to come. With the butt of a rifle, the door broke open and a German with the face of a rapacious animal yelled: "Juden Heraus! Get out to the market place!" We dressed in confusion not knowing what was going on around us. Having no choice, we left the house in the direction of the market which was already filled with people. Seeing what was happening, a thought came to my mind to run faster but in the opposite direction. While running, a few more joined us and among them was Benjamin Mandel, the son of Reb Yeshayahu from Strzyzow who lived in Dombrowa. And that is how we reached a grove outside of town. In the grove we found a few more people mostly young men like us. The fear and panic that prevailed in that small group was indescribable. This was the first time that we were separated from the Jewish community, and did not know what our fate would be. At sunset, the wife of one of the escapees arrived with the good news that the danger was over and that the majority of those that had been nabbed had already returned home. That night, we conducted the Hakafot in the rabbi's house. The feeling was more like Tisha B'Av than Simchat Torah. After this horrible experience, a suggestion came up among the worshippers that it was time to escape from the German occupied territory to the Soviet side. The rumours were that the Russians would probably move on to the Vistula River and, with the Germans retreating, danger hovered over us, especially for the young people. The next day, a group of young people left Dombrowa in the direction of the Soviet border. I went to Tarnow and from there, I intended to reach Strzyzow to say farewell to my father and march off to the Soviet side with my brother Yechezkiel. In order not to be recognized as a Jew, I cut off my side–locks, put on a cap worn by gentiles and, by train from Tarnow through Rzeszow, I reached Strzyzow.

[Page 354]

My fright during the trip on the train was indescribable. Here and there I recognized a disguised Jew like myself sitting in a corner, looking out the window and pretending to enjoy the beauty of nature. My ears alertly absorbed the conversations that were carried on among the gentile passengers. The topic of the conversations was the "Jews" and the loss of the Polish fatherland. Thanks only to these conversations, they could not hear the beatings of our hearts and they did not notice the paleness of my face and the changing of colours according to the subjects of their conversations.

I reached Strzyzow in the evening hours and was welcomed by my father, may G–d avenge his blood, and by my brother Yechezkiel, may he live a long life, who had reached Strzyzow by foot during the Sukkoth holiday. My father told me about the relative quietness that prevailed in Strzyzow, except for two incidents. Jews were brought from Frysztak and shot by the Gestapo in the Christian cemetery and the bodies were later handed over to the Burial Society. The second incident was that the Germans had turned the shul into a dormitory for the cavalry, including their horses. After a few days, they handed it back to the leader of the Kehillah, clean and tidy.

The situation in Strzyzow
by Simcha Langsam

In daytime, the Jews moved around freely, or almost. At sunset they locked themselves in their houses with closed shutters over the windows and closed gates. The next day was market day. I went out to the market with the purpose of meeting my colleagues and thinking that maybe they would like to join us in our escape to the Russian territory. I was astounded to see the prosperous commerce that was going on. All the Jewish stores were open and filled with customers as in peace time. I saw a different world here, different to what I saw in Tarnow and other cities. Maybe this imaginary quietness held back the Jews of Strzyzow, especially the young people, from leaving their homes and fleeing while there was still time. I did not encounter the same fright and fear of annihilation the way I had in other places. During the day I met a few of my comrades and told them what was happening in other cities. I explained to them the danger they should expect but, to my amazement, I did not find the desired attentiveness to my proposition. Israel, the son of Yechiel Friedman, replied: "Do you think that the Germans will slaughter all the Jews? You can see for yourself that, thank G–d, the situation here is bearable. We are alive for the time being and G–d will help us in the future". I spoke with Naphtali, the son of Reb Chaim Mandel. He simply jeered at me: "What? Go to the Russians? Are they better than Hitler?" When I told him what was happening in other place and explained the dangerous situation for the young Jews and that we could come back after the Russian Army would conquer all of Poland, he replied: "You have slightly convinced me that the situation is serious but I will tell you the truth. I have never lived outside of my parent's home and I am not used to taking care of myself. More so, in such dangerous times, I cannot separate from my family, even If for one day, and who can fore–tell what the morrow will bring?"

[Page 355]

I was shocked to hear such words. Were their eyes blinded so much that they could not see what was coming? There was nothing to do for me but to say good–bye and I went about our own preparations for the journey to the Soviet side, which seemed to be the only rescue at that time. When father found out that none of the young people accepted our proposition, he tried to convince us to remain with the rest of the town because there was a common destiny for all. But when he saw that our decision was unchangeable, he inclined to agree but under one condition – to see rabbi Nechemiah's approval, may G–d avenge his blood. Our father was an intimate friend and he knew where the rabbi was hiding. We arrived in Reb Shlomo Auerhun's house where the Rabbi hid after the Germans began to inquire of his whereabouts. After a few seconds, the rabbi entered in all his splendour but the expression of love and the smile on his face that was always there whenever he spoke with small or big people, had disappeared. Instead, a gloom covered his face. The gloom of suffering, not so much personal as the sadness of the whole community and maybe the suffering of the entire Jewish nation. After a deep sigh, he stretched out his hands and greeted us with the traditional "Shalom Aleichem". Breathless, he listened to our report about the situation of the Jews in other cities and of the maltreatment of the Jews by the Nazi. We talked about the purpose of our coming and asked him for his approval and blessing. With a heavy heart but clear–sightedness, the rabbi replied: "Dear children! Who is wise enough to know? We have nobody to lean on but our Father in Heaven. To spill our hearts in prayer and supplications, the Almighty will help us. I too wish I could leave this place. May G–d endow you with success wherever you turn and may G–d guide all your endeavours and watch over all of Israel". He pressed our hands with the blessing: "Go in peace". He escorted us with his eyes lifted toward heaven, praying and supplicating for our fate and the fate of his flock. On the way home, we stopped to say good–bye to the rabbi's son, Reb Shlomo. He expressed the same opinion as his father and said: "It is hard to advise which way to go. I join in my father's blessing. May it be G–d's will that we merit a complete redemption and the end to our troubles should come soon".

Our father waited anxiously for the return from our visit to the rabbi. When he heard about the rabbi's approval, tears began to flow from his eyes. After a few minutes of silence he said: "Kinderlech. This separation is very hard for me, who knows…" The next few words stuck in his throat. He later continued: "I know how hard it is to be a Jew in Russia. For Heaven's sake. Remain Jews and be good Jews". He could no longer speak. After a while he added: "For your betterment, I give you my blessing for your journey to Russia". We tried to assure our father that G–d willing we would come home for Passover and that as soon as the Russians would move forward, we would be the first to return. The next day, we began to supply the house with all kinds of provisions such as soap, salt, matches, etc. that should have sufficed our father for a few months. Tuesday, October 25th, 1939 – a day on which G–d used the word "Good" twice during the creation, we left behind us everything that was dear to us, hoping that on our return we would find everything in order and our father well.

[Page 356]

We travelled by train to Jaslo. There we lodged in a Jewish hotel near the train station. (I think the owner's name was Canin). The owner welcomed us warmly and offered cordial hospitality. Despite the fact that all his rooms were requisitioned by the German officers, he found a place for us. Early the next morning, we put on the tefilin and prayed an abbreviated prayer because we were in a rush to reach Sanok on the border. The owner of the hotel was polishing the officers' boots while he gave us directions and sent us off with the traditional: "Go in peace and come in peace". At noon–time, we arrived in Sanok and were welcomed by a Gestapo agent in civilian clothes who spoke Polish. He stopped us in the street with the question: "Jews, where to?" I began to stammer and replied that we were going to the Jewish Kehillah. He asked for identification so I showed him a membership card of a religious organization. He then asked us if we were carrying arms and, after a light search in our back–packs, he gave us the order: "Turn right on that street and then left on the other street and there is the Jewish Community building. Stay inside. Do not wander in the streets otherwise you will meet your bitter end".

In the Kehillah we found about three hundred Jews sitting with their belongings. They had already been waiting for two days to cross the San River. Because of heavy rain falls, the river had swelled and had made it impossible to cross over to the Russian side. In another room, I saw a German officer playing cards with the Jewish community leaders. I found out from people that the gestapo in Sanok were being bribed to look the other way while the Jews were crossing the river and while playing cards the bribe took place. At sunset, we found out that that night we would cross the San and that it was the Gestapo's order. They could not risk such a large concentration of Jews in one place. We lined up in a column and everyone with his pack on his back began to march. There were women and old people among us. From somewhere, a score of Poles suddenly appeared and escorted us with jeering and laughter. One played a harmonica expressing joy that: "the Jews were leaving for Palestine…" At midnight, we crossed the river and were arrested by the Russian border patrol.

[Page 357]

Memories
by Simcha the son of Yacov Langsam

And the Lord said onto Moses: "Write this for a memorial in the book and Rehearse it in the ears of Joshua…"

G–d had awarded two precious gifts to those he created when he blew into them the breath of life. What you do not like to remember you forget by force or forgetfulness and what you don't like to forget you remember by force of memory.

I have a special affection for the second gift because whenever I remember an event that occurred in my life, my desire to thank and to proclaim the greatness and the wonders of the Almighty increases. Therefore, it is my duty and my holy command to write the memories of the period when the world brought down the Holocaust upon our people from which I and a very few fortunate Polish Jews survived.

My brother Yechezkiel and I, together with hundreds of Jews, went on a journey to seek refuge from the claws of the Hitlerist bands in 1939. After many travails about which I told in a previous chapter, we arrived in the city of Lesko. This city is located on the other side of the San River which, at that time, was the natural border–line between the Polish territory occupied by the Soviets and the Polish territory occupied by the Germans.

By the lights of German search lights, we crossed the San River which was overflowing. It was a shocking sight. Under the cloak of the darkness of night, a group of Jewish people – the elderly, women and infants among them, were stranded in water which reached up to their chins. Their clothes and belongings were wet and the danger of drowning was imminent. It was the rainy season. "I am drowning. Please help me. I am a father of small children" pleaded an older man with his last breath. Indeed, with great effort, I successfully brought him ashore.

Excited, shocked and wet to the marrow of our bones, we found ourselves on the shore of the noisy river in Soviet territory. Some of the refugees who had already tasted the taste of death under the Germans were kissing the ground of the free land. Some recited the morning prayers. There was a strange feeling, a feeling of joy mixed with sadness. On one hand, although we could still see the Germans on the other side, we were out of their reach. On the other hand, our hearts were filled with a new worry: what was going to happen to our dear ones who remained in the hands of the murderers?

The border guards that carried light arms welcome us with a repeated request: "Quiet!" (We did not know then that silence in that land is the means of survival).

Heavily guarded, we were brought into a large movie hall in the city of Lesko.

[Page 358]

We were told that we were arrested for investigation into the purpose of our coming, whether it was espionage for the Germans. We encountered rabbi Kalonymus, the young rabbi of our town among the arrested. He was very depressed but he told us that something was being done on his behalf. To our joy, he was freed after a few days as the result of the intervention of a few Jewish communists who had recommended his release.

From Lesko, we were transferred by the N.K.V.D. authorities to the city of Lwow and imprisoned in the famous "Brigidki" prison. After a thorough search of all parts of our bodies, all "forbidden" articles were confiscated. We were dispersed throughout the prison in different cells – about seventy or eighty in a cell, cells which in normal times would hold twenty–five prisoners. The fact which depressed us the most and caused much pain to the imprisoned was the confiscation of the tefilin. The Jewish communists threw all the tefilin into a big pile in the prison yard. A shudder went through our bodies when we saw what was happening to something so sacred to us for generations. We felt that this horrible war was also a war against the Jewish soul. We realized that this denigration act was a special "treatment" against the Jews. We protested to those in charge but their reply was: "Our land is a free land. You can pray undisturbed but the prison is not a church!"

One of the prisoners did smuggle in a pair of tefilin and that news encouraged us. Most of the prisoners had forgotten what they had gone through lately and found consolation in these phylacteries.

It is hard to describe the first night in prison on a bank–bed made of boards. Despite the exhaustion of the last few days, nobody slept a wink. At daybreak and after fulfilling a few prison regulations, we all lined up for the donning of the tefilin. People who had never in their lives donned a tefilin lined up. Everybody recited the blessing and handed the tefilin to the next in line. We did it in a corner, out of sight of the jail guard. There were in our cell people from Frysztak, Jaslo, Krakow, Tarnow and Rzeszow, but none from Strzyzow. We later found out that the son of the assistant rabbi from Sendziszow was in one of the cells. I was told that he had refused to eat any food except for bread and water. He was very depressed and suffered from all kinds of aches and pains.

Once in a while, I succeeded in sending him a carrot or a piece of sugar which was given to me by a Jewish prisoner from Bukhara who worked in the kitchen. It was only by accident that I found out that he was Jewish. I saw him once moving his lips before his meal and so I asked him: "What are you mumbling?": "I pray", he replied. When I asked him to say the prayer louder, to my astonishment, I heard him recite the blessing "Netilat Yadayim". That is all that is left in my memory from my father's house, blessed be his memory. "I am Jewish" he said in Russian because he did not speak Yiddish.

There were about two quorums of Jews in my cell. We tried to encourage each other and we sought consolation in all kinds of discourses in Torah and in the words of our sages.

During that period, I befriended a man from Rzeszow – Reb Samuel Nachum Emer – a peculiar type, about whom I will tell further on.

[Page 359]

After I spent three months in Lwow, I was transferred to the Ukrainian prison if Kiev, Charkov and others. With each transfer, I was separated from the people with whom I had found a common language. Especially painful was my separation from my brother Yechezkiel. He was sent to another prison and I did not know his whereabouts until the liberation.

In order to understand how much our looks had changed, I would like to tell here an interesting episode. In the cells, besides the Jews, there were also non–Jewish inmates – Polish anti–Semites and other extreme nationalists who hated the communists in Poland and preferred the Nazi. They waited for them for years before the outbreak of the war.

Suddenly the door opened and the guard ordered us to move over and make room for more inmates. A few people came in, frightened, with torn and shabby clothes, some Jewish and some not. All of them were searching with their eyes to spot an acquaintance, a relative or just an ordinary Jew. I too looked at the newcomers and noticed a Jewish face and soon began a conversation: "From where is a Jew? How long ago did you leave Poland? How is Jewish life in Poland?" and many other questions. After I finished questioning my neighbour, he heaved a deep sigh and began to reply to my questions. He suddenly burst out with a cry: "Simcha! Simcha! Don't you know me? I am Samuel"! I mobilized all my brain cells but could not recognize this bearded young man who looked my age and who, only a few months earlier, had prayed with me in the synagogue and had strolled down the streets together on a Sabbath afternoon. I could not believe the changes that had occurred in such a short time. When he saw that I could not recognize him he told me that his name was Samuel, son of Reb David Lieberman from Strzyzow. At present Samuel resides in Petach Tiqua, Israel. After being together for twenty–four hours, the separated us again.

Zitomir
by Simcha Langsam

On the outskirts of the town there was an isolated three–story building surrounded by a wall and watchtowers on each corner. This was a prison and in it the authorities assigned me together with thousands of other Jewish residents.

In the cell with me were a few young men who belonged to the Zionist Religious Youth Movement; the rest of the inmates were elderly observant Jews. In the first few days, we felt only depression and despair. We were cut off from the whole world without a newspaper, without any contact with our families and we did not know what was happening on the front lines. We worried about our families that had remained in the hands of the murderers. Hunger, filth and sleepless nights imprinted on us a horrible impression. Continuous nightly interrogations and the threats of the interrogators that tried to force confessions of spying from us, for which we could be sentenced to fifteen or twenty year's imprisonment, brought mental suffering upon us. All the above sufferings united us; the religious young men and the observant Jews into one large family in our daily prison life. All these shared factors were the source of our unity.

[Page 360]

The most uniting force in our group was Reb Samuel Nachum Emer, of blessed memory. This man encouraged us and instilled in us a belief and confidence in the eternity of Israel. He strengthened in us the belief in redemption because of the merits of the Tzadikim and the founders of Hassidism. He led collective conversations and also conversed with each of us individually. Reb Samuel took it upon himself to be the spiritual leader during our denigrated life and despairing moments. Reb Samuel had an extraordinary personality and a wonderful disposition. He lived in Rzeszow where he had left his family.

He was about forty or forty–five years old, a great scholar, pious and a strict observant of all the commandments even when it caused him pain. What he allowed others, he did not allow himself. His memory was astonishing. He never forgot anything he learned. He remembered entire Talmudical tractates, the Psalms, etc. During the eleven months that we were together, he had not eaten anything besides bread and water. The rest of the observant inmates ate everything except for cooked meat. Although our menu did not contain meat, if the soup had any meaty taste, we refused to eat it. Reb Samuel succeeded in uniting around him a group of twelve young people who did not eat chometz on Passover. Reb Samuel believed that the troubles that befell the Jews were pains before the final redemption. He was an admirer of the rabbi from Koloszyce. He strongly opposed Zionism. He taught us daily from his memory a chapter of Mishnayoth or a chapter of Gemara. We prayed daily with a minyan and our cell served as a spiritual centre for the entire prison. He made sure that we would remember at least one section of prayers in case we were the last Jews to survive. "Who knows", he said: "If we are not the last Jews alive, upon who was imposed the task of carrying on the Jewish spark?" he urged us not to be frightened of any sacrifice and that "keeping the fire burning on G–d's altar was not easy". "I am convinced" he continued, "that the prayers that we pray daily from our hearts to the creator and the acceptance of the yoke of His Kingdom will be our shield and our sword". His ornate thoughts were divulged in secret to his closest friends only. "No matter what! I have to write prayer books by hand and prepare a calendar for several years ahead so that, Heaven forbid, you shall not desecrate the High Holidays or the regular holidays until G–d will have mercy upon us and enable us to live as true Jews, in body and soul". "Who knows if I will be still around? I doubt if I will be worthy of surviving". We sat for hours figuring out all the details of how to fulfil Reb Samuel's wish, how to supply him with paper, pen and ink. It was not an easy task in prison. Samuel Nachum took upon himself to supply the paper. The jail nurse related to him with a special respect. She called him: "the Jewish rabbi". Reb Samuel exploited this relation and always asked her for a powder against headaches. He successfully hid the wrapping paper. (An inmate was not allowed to possess any paper). I stole a pen from the interrogator's desk during the long hours of my interrogations.

[Page 361]

We also found a way to obtain ink. In the hall of our jail, there was a desk at which the jailers used to sit and on that desk, there was an inkwell. Before going out for our daily walks, we prepared small pieces of cotton. The custom was that we were escorted by two jailers ahead of us and two in the back. When we passed the desk, we dipped the cotton in the inkwell and, upon returning to our cell, we added a few drops of water to it in a cup and so we had ink. Of course, all the activities were carefully executed because being caught committing such a crime could have brought upon us heavy punishment. To ensure complete secrecy, we hid the writing materials inside a broom which was made from willow twigs. Nobody would have thought to look in such a place. With revered piety and fear for the authorities, but anxious for the mitzvah, Reb Samuel sat down in a corner and began to print with small print on pages the size of 5x7cm. Reb Samuel Nachum sat days and nights and did the holy work. His pupil watched the door with alert and would notify him when the guard was approaching. Two months of vigorous work ended when prayer books containing the entire weekly and holiday prayers, the "Amidah" for Rosh Hashanah and Yom Kippur and even Akdamuth for Shavuot were before us. Lon Lag B–omer, we prepared ourselves for a modest celebration – the receiving of the "Sidurim". Reb Samuel's face glowed with happiness. We all became emotional. We gathered in a corner and Reb Samuel turned to us with a trembling voice: "Dear children", he said and tears began to flow from his eyes. Filled with emotion, we joined him in cries that tore at our hearts. Cries that were choked before they could be heard for fear of being heard by the guards. We were grasped with the holy atmosphere of the Judgment Day as though we were preparing to establish the foundation of our People's continuity and deciding who shall live and who shall die. Reb Samuel Nachum continued with a choking voice. "In these days, when Jewish blood became worthless, who knows if anybody still remained there that could join us in our crying? We were separated from everyone who was dear to us, from parents, mothers, brothers and sisters, women and infants". At this point, he strengthened his voice: "My heart is tearing apart when I realize that a big part of our nation could have saved their lives if they would have listened to the beat of salvation… I have to confess that a big part of our nation is guilty in our tragedy. We have not understood and have refused to respond to the call of the few on the rebuilding of our homeland. We postponed our redemption with our own hands. And now!" Here he turned to the younger segment: "I don't know if I will merit entering again into G–d's congregation but you probably will, I believe. Please! When the times come, abandon the Diaspora. Do not remain in strange lands even at physical cost. For Heaven's sake, remove all the bounds with the bitter Diaspora and establish a new life in the Holy Land and with it, you will speed up the complete redemption for you and for future generations".

With trembling hands, Reb Samuel Nachum handed the Sidurim to everyone in the group and said: "That is our most precious treasure – the prayers in which we spill our hearts out before the Creator of the World. These Sidurim that I am handing over to you should accompany you wherever you go until the Redeemer will come and redeem the remainder of Israel".

[Page 362]

This is the title page of Reb Samuel Nachum's prayer book with the dedication to Sicha Langzam:

"This prayer book I wrote as a gift for my dynamic friend, the revered and accomplished young man, Simcha Langsam, when we were imprisoned in Zitomir, Russia in 1940.

G–d shall bring us out from here and bestow upon us a complete redemption.

Samuel Nachum Emer From Rzeszow

[Page 363]

Reb Samuel Nachum opened the last Siddur and requested us to repeat after him. He began to recite the prayer "Avinu Malkeinu". When he reached the verse: "G–d our King, have pity over us and over our babies and small children. Dot it for the sake of those who perished by fire and water for the sanctification of Thy Name", he loudly began to wail. However, he was compelled to stop for fear of the authorities. "How hard it is", he said. "The fact that we cannot even cry aloud. There is nothing harder and more painful than that which we cannot do whilst others are allowed to do. Nevertheless, boys, this is the greatness of the Jewish people. In every generation they rise up to annihilate us and the Holy blessed be He, saves us from their hands. All shades of Hamans impose upon us physical and spiritual decrees, mock us and scorn us among the nations, gloom our skies, darken our days and it seems as if the end has come. But at these times, our people exalt themselves heroically with the highest exaltation and exemplary self–sacrifice. They escape the different furnaces even though wounded and injured, but strong in their belief that they must produce from amongst themselves, redeemers and deliverers, to prove to the wicked world, that in spite of everything, the People of Israel must live and exist. Go forward powerfully and you will be helped".

After the ceremony, I stood silent for a few seconds with my prayer book that I had just received. In my mind, my father's image appeared – Reb Yacov, the son of Tzvi Elimelech, a descendant of the rabbi Tzvi Elimelech Shapiro Dynasty from Dynow. I remembered the last few hours in our house before our separation as he stood before me. His tender white forehead, his long golden and slightly curled beard that adorned his sad face, and the tears that were flowing from his eyes. With trembling hands, he handed us the tefilin and the prayer books to pack among or belongings. The echoes of the words that came out of his mouth when he handed the tefilin to my brother Yechezkiel and me were still in my ears. "My sons, most beloved and dear to me! Every time when trouble befalls us, our nation becomes weaker. It is the duty of every Jew to block it and fence it off. I fear, my sons that Heaven forbid… (he had trouble finishing his sentence). "A need will arise that you will have to sacrifice your lives for 'Yiddishkeit'. Remember, do no separate from the tefilin. If you will guard them, they will guard you". We kissed and embraced with extra love, and his tears kept flowing down his cheeks as though he wanted to implant upon us his thoughts and engrave them in our memory.

These memories came to my mind in that moment when I pressed the new prayer book to my heart with its small pages and miniature letters which was written by Reb Samuel Nachum Emer. May their memory be blessed.

G–d has privileged me to build my house in the State of Israel where I came to rest and put down my roots. I was privileged to bring with me the prayer book which accompanied me throughout the waste plains of Siberia and to exhibit it in the Generation–to–Generation Museum which is located in Heichal Shlomo in Jerusalem.

In this memorial book which perpetuates all the holy and untainted souls from our city, I would also like to commemorate the beloved exalted, and untainted soul of Reb Samuel Nachum Emer, of blessed memory. May he always be remembered. Amen.

[Page 364]

Ben Zion Kalb saved many Jewish lives during the Holocaust
by Shlomo Yahalomi

In this short article I would like to write a wonderful chapter which deserves to be glorified because the main hero is a native of Strzyzow. Ben Zion Kalb, the son of Reb Abraham Kalb, of blessed memory. This story is about the rescue of thousands of Jewish people from brutal killing by the Nazi – may their names be obliterated. This story deserved to be written in a more revered space in our book and in a more detailed way because of its importance, not only for the people of Strzyzow but also for the history of the Holocaust and the rescuers of Jews in general. However, for reasons that I cannot bring forth there, I received this material at the last moment when this book was almost finished. It was the will of the Divine Providence that Ben Zion, the friend of my youthful years when we sat and studied together in the Beit HaMidrash and fought the battle of Torah, came for a short visit to Israel. Only then did I convince him that these rescue stories should be told. Henceforth, I received this material from him with some pictures. For lack of time and space, I could not publish everything, only the most important facts. I feel obliged to point out that besides the letters and documents that I saw, and of which a few copies were included in this book, like the confirmation of the Jewish Agency, the letter from the Rabbi of Bobow and also the letters from Rabbi Micha Dov Weismandel, of blessed memory, Izhok Zukerman and others. I myself interviewed a few people who livewith us in Israel who witnessed the rescue activity and they confirmed the truthfulness of this story.

The war caught up with Ben Zion Kalb, his brother Mendel and his parents in Nowy Targ. They moved there from Strzyzow over forty years ago. (Approximately in the late 20's). Two months after the outbreak of the war, he concluded that there was no future in Poland and decided to escape before it was too late. He obtained travel documents to Altendorf, Slovakia and from there he went to Kazmark. In Slovakia, Jews were relatively free and they thought that the wickedness would not reach them. To make a living, people smuggled wares and foreign currency across the border. Ben Zion was forced to do the same thing and therefore had constant contact with occupied Poland. Thanks to this contact, he knew what was happening to his brothers, the children of Israel and the fate that awaited them in the future. He knew that not only the German Nazi but the Poles too were eternal haters of the Jews and were waiting for the occasion to get rid of them. Ben Zion tried to take his parents and brother, Mendel out, but his parents refused to leave and Mendel refused to leave his parents. Consequently, Mendel was murdered in Rabka on July 21, 1942 and the parents in August, 1942.

When the situation in Slovakia worsened as well and the Nazi began to send Jews to work, Ben Zion claimed that this was not work, it was
death.

[Page 365]

Letter from the Jewish Agency

> The Jewish Agency for Palestine
> Palestinsky Urad   Bratislava, December 18, 1945
> Bratislava   ....
> Telefon ....
> N/196./45.
> To whom it may concern:
>
> We are hereby certifying the activity of Mr. Benzion Kalb, Bratislava, carried out in the years 1943 and 1944, cooperating with our illegal working groups in Slovakia for the liberation of Jews confined to Polish Ghettoes and concentration camps, whereby we also state that you have introduced such measures as to enable the first people to come across the borders.
>
> Hereby we wish also to emphasize that it was due to your cooperation that a number of children could be saved. As a matter of fact, 103 children under the age of 30 were liberated in the course of three weeks.
>
> We were fully aware of the fact that in connection with your activity you were exposed to persecution by the Gestapo and have been imprisoned in Bratislava.
>
> For this stannah and self– sacrificing collaboration, you have deserved the fullest appreciation of the Klall.
>
> Ustridry Svaz Cionistky   Palestine Office of the Jewish Agency
> Bratislavk   Palestinski Urad
>   Bratislvka

[Page 366]

However, few believed him. The majority helped to send their children to "work" to Auschwitz. Ben Zion did not let the community leaders rest and he finally convinced them to start an urgent rescue operation. Thanks to his business contacts with non–Jews in Poland, he was able to dream about a widespread rescue operation with the help of his non–Jewish messengers. With the help of one righteous gentile, Jan Malec from Zefisco (then Poland and now belonging to Slovakia), and some other means, Ben Zion succeeded in bringing over to Slovakia three thousand people, including two hundred children aged two months to six years. This was a dangerous action. Once Ben Zion travelled with his gentile helpers and was arrested and held in prison for two weeks. Miraculously he escaped. He was in hiding for six months in a cellar and had gone through hell. (G–d willing, we will tell about these events in a separate book which I hope to publish). More than once, he was forced to leave the children alone in the woods for the night and the next day he had to search for them and found them almost frozen to death. Several times, they were almost caught by the Nazi but the gentile Jan Malec, who knew all the pathways in the woods, succeeded in bringing them out undetected.

Of course, just by bringing the children over from Poland to Slovakia, the rescue action was not complete. We knew that the wickedness would reach Slovakia as well. But when? Maybe soon? Again, much devotion and work was needed to complete the job. Almost every transport of children had to be hidden among the gentiles until safe houses were found for them. And here, I would like to mention favourably Mrs. Bartoshek, a gentile woman in whose house Ben Zion Kalb hid and through whose husband he sent letters to the rabbi, the famous rescuer Reb Micha Dov Weismandel, the author of *Min Hameizar* and Reb Shlomo Stern. Rabbi Weismandel put him in contact with the underground organizations that participated in the rescue operation. Members of that organization were, among others, Mrs. Fleishman, the famous heroine; Dr. Newman; Dr. Duks; Ben Zion Gotlieb from the Mizrachi; Egan Roth and Mr. Korminski. When Ben Zion returned from Poland and described the hopeless situation there, at first they did not believe him. Even those who did believe did not know how serious the situation was. It is interesting to quote an excerpt from a letter written by Rabbi Weismandel to Ben Zion: "Please, do whatever is possible to put the children who have just reached you into kosher homes, truly pious so that Heaven forbid we should not lose them to strangers. They are the few who are left and we shall watch over them that they remain pious with G–d's help". However, Ben Zion did not heed his advice. On the contrary, he did the opposite. He understood that in non–Jewish homes the children would be safer. But he also hid some children in Jewish homes. Ben Zion Kalb was in contact with Jewish leaders in Pressburg and he pressured them to help bring over more Jews. The people from Pressburg contacted Switzerland, the United States and Eretz Israel. Great sums of money were needed. Dr. Wallstein, who now lives in Israel, took care of the finances. In his continuing efforts in the rescue operation from Poland, Ben Zion Kalb organized the smuggling of many Jews from Slovakia to Budapest, Hungary, through Preshov and Kashau. There the Jews joined a Polish organization pretending to be gentiles, until ten years after the war.

[Page 367]

The second from left is Jan Malec, the most important messenger in the rescue operation. He himself rescued 635 people including 200 orphans. At his right is his son, and at his left are his relatives.

[Page 368]

What a pity that there is no list of the survivors who went through this smuggling route. I would like only to mention a few of them. The first survivor was Ben Zion's bride, Clara Lieber. After super–human efforts, Ben Zion finally located her and kept contact with her. In one letter, she wrote to him that if he would not sent Jan Malec (the gentile chief smuggler), she would travel to his brother Mendel. (Which meant she would be killed). She was in Bochnia. Her rescue was very expensive. She was the first who dared to go and she showed a dangerous way on how to leave Bochnia. After her successful escape, many followed her. Subsequently, it was enough to pay the smugglers between ten and eighty dollars per head. Persons who had money paid and if not, others paid for them. Many times Ben Zion paid out of his own pocket. Other survivors were: Rabbi Shlomo Halberstam from Bobow; his brother Reb Yechezkiel; the son of Reb Moshe Stempel who was Reb Feivel Stempel's and the old Rabbi from Bobow's grandson. He now lives in London and is the head of a Yeshiva. The police tried to stop their car and shot at them. With them were six more children – the children of the Rabbi from Sucha who was the grandson of the Rabbi from Sandz. Reb Moshe Shenfeld, the son–in–law of Reb Itzhok Meir Levin; Eliezer Unger; two sons of Mordechai Weinberg from Krakow (who was the son of Reb Berish, a famous Hassid and a wealthy man in Krakow. The sons of Reb Mordechai Weinberg now live in Israel and they served in the Israeli Army and Navy. Their uncle, Reb Joel Kremer told me about them. Also rescued were the Smith sisters, relatives of Reb Moshe Bleicher; the assistant rabbi in Krakow and Eva Eckstein from Rzeszow. Reb Jonah Eckstein and Mrs. Stern took care of the children until they were safe.

Had there been enough money, it would have been possible to save many more children. On the next pages, there is a letter from "Antek" – Itzhok Zukerman and Tzivia Lubetkin who confirm this fact. The above were ghetto leaders in Poland. Ben Zion Kalb also suggested helping them to escape but they refused. They refused to abandon their brothers. Dr. Bornstein, who is at present head of the Neurological Department of the Beilinson Hospital, told my wife that Ben Zion had proposed to help him escape but he refused to leave his wife behind. Many other famous people have given testimony that Ben Zion Kalb had rescued many lives. The last but not least of witnesses is the present Rabbi of Bobow, Rabbi Shlomo Halberstam who called him: "the war hero in the field of saving Jewish lives". As indicated at the beginning of this article, this is only a synopsis but a highly qualitative chapter for which I would like to be credited as publicizing the deed of Ben Zion Kalb in this book. This article came about as a result of applying a little pressure after which he agreed to tell me a few details about his activity, accompanied with documents verifying what he had told me.

I would like to add that it is an honour for our shtetl that, not only did no one collaborate, Heaven forbid, with the Nazi but they were willing to sacrifice their lives for the rescue of our brethren – the pursued and afflicted. I want to point out that Ben Zion was not the only one with such deeds. There were other natives from Strzyzow who were active after the Holocaust in the rescue of Jewish children from gentile hands. About that rescue, Itzhok Berglass wrote in another place.

[Page 369]

And the holy martyr, dear Reb Mendel Groskopf, our landsman who the Nazi nominated as head of the "Judenrat" in Brzostek where he lived, handed over a list with one name only: His own. He overcame temptation and refused to deliver Jews into the damned, wicked hands… He was murdered on the spot. He was the first martyred victim and he surely bequeathed much honour on our shtetl.

Letter from Rabbi Weismandel to Ben Zion Kalb

Blessed be He   Friday, Chapter of the week: "Ki Tetzeh" 1942.

Peace and blessing to my charming friend who pursues justice and kindness, Mr. Ben Zion Kalb. May his candle continue to burn!

I received your letter. And what can I say? What can I tell? We are facing destruction. We should all say: "We are to be blamed" because there was a time when we could rescue many more if we would have had the funds. My heart and body are broken in fragments. And now I plead with you, do whatever is possible to rescue what is left. Maybe you still have some means left? In the time of fury we think that all is lost. But later it appears that there is still a few who were in hiding and can be rescued. Therefore, we need immediate transport. We need messengers to appraise the situation, to see what can be done. You should contact Mr. Grayer, may his candle continue to burn. He might advise how it may be done and the Almighty will assist, protect and help.

One more favour I would like to ask. Please, do whatever is possible to put the children in kosher homes because they come from truly pious people, in order to keep them from strange hands. The children are the few that are left to us and we are obligated to see that they remain pious until the complete redemption will arrive.

I will be waiting for a response. Give regards to Yechezkiel; Mr Grayer; Mr. Berger; Reb Joseph and all the rest who are involved in this big, holy mitzvah.

Your friend
Micha Dov

[Page 370]

Copy of Rabbi Weismandel's letter

[Page 371]

Ben Zion Kalb with Reb Mordechai Weinberg's two sons that he rescued

Clara Lieber, Ben Zion Kalb's bride

A postcard from the Valley of Death

[Page 372]

A group of children rescued by Ben Zion Kalb
The adults: standing from left to right are: Eva Ekstein, Jonah Ekstein and Mrs. Stern who took care of the children

Two children who were rescued by Ben Zion Kalb and Mrs. Stern

[Page 373]

Original letter from Itzhok Zukerman and Tzivia Lubetkin

[Page 374]

A postcard from the valley of death

February 23, 1943.

My dearest!

Last night I received your postcard which wandered a week or more to find me. I was not able to describe my happiness. I am still perplexed. Apparently, as you did not expect to hear from me, so did I not expect to hear from you. But let us get serious. As you see, I am, thank G–d, well but the physical conditions are very hard. My girlfriend received Hungarian citizenship from her relatives and, therefore, her condition has improved a lot. If you could do the same, it would help me too. I have nothing more to write about except that I very much miss you. Now that I know that you are well, I would very much like to see you. When you will write to your friend Jasiek, who brought me once the silk stockings, ask him in my name to come to see me. I have a lot to tell him. I am concluding my writing with the plea – try and respond immediately. Do not let me wait. Write to the same address and I hope it will reach me in the same situation that I am now.

Kisses, Clara

Letters to Ben Zion Kalb from Taivia Lubetkin and "Antek" Itzhok Zukerman, leaders in the Warsaw ghetto

Dear Comrades!

We received your letters. Many thanks. We were moved about your worry for our existence. Regrettably, notwithstanding our willingness, all of us cannot come to you. We are busy here with rescue activities and defence. The lives of thousands of Jews and our self–respect depend on our work. We thank you and all the rest of our friends wherever they are, from the bottom of our hearts. Maybe the day will come and we will see each other. Who knows? We will try that…(name unreadable) should come to you accompanied by Mordechai, her husband. Geller left two months ago to Hanover to a concentration camp for foreign citizens. So far, we have no information of his whereabouts. What we heard is that they all went to Auschwitz and were killed there. Do you have contact with Schwalbe in Switzerland or Joseph Katyanski in Hungary? Have you any contact with a group of comrades of ours from Zaglebie who should have arrived in Hungary? Lease, contact us whenever it is possible. You must help us to organize a staff, to search for border smugglers to enable us to transport children who are still alive. The man who was sent by you to take me and Tzivia wanted to take us for free but as to the others, he demanded one hundred dollars in gold for each person. This is a huge sum. It comes to sixty five thousand zlotys in our currency per head. This is awful and terrible. For such a price, not many can escape.

But everyone who survived until now wants to escape. Remember! The lives of the remnants of Israel in Poland depend on your activity. Do whatever is possible to help us. If you can, inform Eretz Israel about us. We live and act however we can.

In the name of the remaining survivors.

Itzhok Zukerman (Antek) and Tzivia Lubetkin.

[Page 375]

Letter from Izhok Zukerman "Antek" to Ben Zion Kalb

[Page 376]

Letter from the Rabbi of Bobov to Ben Zion Kalb

[Page 377]

From the ghetto house in memory of Itzhok Katznelson

To the revered Mr. Ben Zion Kalb in New York.

Sir!

A tourist from Brazil, who came to Israel via New York where he met you, paid us a visit this week. From his statement it became clear to me that you were one of the Slovakian–Hungarian committee members who sent to us a special messenger in 1944. That man told me that you possess the response letter. We would be grateful if you could send us a photocopy of that letter. We would also be grateful if you would be willing to put into writing the details of that part of the action within the frame of the general activity of the rescue committee of which you were a member.

With thanks and blessing.

Itzhok Zukerman (Antek)
Rosh Chodesh Kislev, 1969.
Blessed be His Name

From Rabbi Shlomo Halberstam of Bobov
1501–48th street, Brooklyn, New York.

Great peace for my dear friend, the marvellous war hero in the field of the rescue of Jewish lives, Mr. Ben Zion Kalb, whose pseudonym then was "Ben Abraham". May his candle keep burning.

It is my desire with all my heart and soul to repay my debt to you for your work in the years of fury and destruction, to testify and inform mankind of your heroism. To inform the children and grandchildren that you were merited by the blessed Name with such great merits to be the saviour of many hundreds of Jewish lives. According to information I have received, thousands of men, women and children from Poland escaped via Slovakia to Hungary from the Nazi claws, may their names be obliterated.

You found a path and contacts in the border area. You sent gentile messengers across the border. And many times you travelled by yourself to the border to rescue children from villains, and they pursued you.

[Page 378]

as with the orphans of my holy grandfather from Sandz, the boys of the Rabbi from Sucha, may G–d avenge his blood. Also with the sons of my brother–in–law, Reb Moshele Stempel, of blessed memory. You successfully escaped, miraculously and by the grace of G–d.

I will never forget your devotion to the cause, putting yourself in a dangerous and life–threatening situation where, in your every stride or step, there was only a thin thread between life and death. You walked daily among the hegemonic Germans, may their names be obliterated. You used different tricks in order to save the lives of our wretched brothers, putting your own life on the line in a way which is hard to believe when told.

And I am a witness to your rescue mission because I myself with my brother Yechezkiel David, shall he live, and many members of my family, escaped through the route that you opened and with the help of your messengers.

Behold I am signing off with a blessing. May G–d pay you for your deeds, blessed be your share for meriting it. And this came from the energy and instilment of your father, the Rabbinical Hassid distinguished in Torah and piousness, Reb Avrom the Shohet of Strzyzow, may G–d avenge his blood. Your father was a pupil of the holy and righteous one, the Rabbi of Bobow, of blessed memory. From him you learned the attributes of love for Israel and the devotion to Jewish souls. I wrote this letter as a testimony and remembrance for your sons and future generations. Each generation shall praise your deeds. G-d shall send you his holy help that you should live and bring forth an honest and blessed generation. May you succeed wherever you turn and we shall soon all merit to see the consolation of Zion and Jerusalem, the salvation of Israel. Amen.

[Page 379]

My last Simchat Torah in Strzyzow
by Harry (Yechezkiel) Langsam

The last High Holidays which are called in Hebrew "Yamim Noraim", the Days of Awe, were truly awful days. They were filled with fear for the rapacious Nazi animal that had just recently completed the occupation of Poland.

When World War II began, I resided in Tarnow where I was working in a paper bag factory. My brother Simcha and I were expecting to hear from our father, of blessed memory, who remained in Strzyzow. But, having no news about his well–being troubled us immensely and we therefore decided that I should try to reach Strzyzow by foot, ignoring the danger that hovered over a Jewish boy wandering through villages void of Jews.

I knew the road from before the war when I had travelled by horse and buggy with Reb Leibush Diamand. I dressed up in peasant clothes so as not to arouse suspicion. I left on my journey heading for Strzyzow. From Tarnow I went to Pilzno, then to Brzostek, Frysztak and into Strzyzow, a distance of fifty miles. The road was peaceful without any unpleasantness. Between Pilzno and Brzostek, I lodged in a Jewish house. At first the owner refused to let me stay because of the orders of the Gestapo which forbad lodging to strangers. But I had no choice. I could not continue because of the seven o'clock curfew. The man risked his life and let me stay. It was Friday morning, Hashanah Raba, when I reached Brzostek and went into the house of Reb Mendel Groskopf who was a native of Strzyzow. (In another part of this book, his heroic death for the sanctification of G-d's name was described in detail). We prayed the morning prayers and I witnessed a heart–breaking scene when Reb Mendel put on the table a dried–up lulav from last year in commemoration of better times. Everyone cried bitterly remembering those previous holidays. I reached Strzyzow at three o'clock that afternoon.

In the evening, it was Shemini Atzeret Eve and we gathered in the house of Michael Schitz to conduct the services and make the Hakafot which resembled more closely to prayers in a mourner's house than to the festivities of earlier years. My heart ached when I recalled the joyous Hakafot, the colourful flags with the red apples and the burning candles on their tops, the exaltation with which Rabbi Nechemiah Shapiro had conducted the Hakafot and the children pushing each other in order to be able to kiss the little Torah scroll with which the Rabbi made the Hakafot. With love and devotion did the Rabbi bend down to each child, trying not to miss anyone. The Rabbi had a special affection for his little Torah scroll and never separated from it. He ordered a special suitcase and wherever he travelled, the Torah was always with him.

We felt that under the brutal rule of the Nazi who flooded us with a sea of hatred, it would be impossible to live. The Jews were not liked before, but now we were abandoned altogether. For that reason, we decided to leave Strzyzow after the holidays, to leave this damned land and wander off to the eastern part of Poland which was occupied by the Soviets and where, at that time, Jews were not oppressed. On Tuesday, October 25th, 1939 my brother and I left our home, our birthplace, with the hope that we would return shortly and find everybody safe.

[Page 380]

When we left rain was pouring as it usually did in that part of Europe. It seemed that nature was crying with us. I looked around, stared at the house where I was born, at the muddy alley and bid farewell in my thoughts to my shtetl and its wonderful scenery, the hills, the groves, the river and also to her Jews and to the very few good gentiles. I also summed up and recalled the pain I had gone through in this place. There were also some good and happy times, but not too many.

We were frightened of the unknown road which we still had to pass under the German rule. The life–threatening danger was immense. On the other hand, we were scared of the life under the strict Soviet regime. We cursed all those who had brought such misfortune upon us. Our father, of blessed memory, escorted us a short distance and expressed his wishes to see us back home soon for the Passover Seder. To our sorrow, that was the last time we saw our father and we never saw the rest of our family who remained under the German occupation.

Memories from the days of horror
Jumping off the death–train
by Itzhok Leib Rosen

Midnight, November 15–16, 1942. We were transported by train to the annihilation camp. The train consisted of twenty–one cattle cars. Fourteen cars came from Bochnia and Tarnow and seven cars with Jews from the ghetto in Rzeszow were attached at the railroad station in Rzeszow. Each car contained approximately one hundred and fifty people. With us were the last members of the Judenrat from Strzyzow – Abraham Brav and Sheingal and also Samuel (Mulik) Feit and Chaim Adest, both from Strzyzow.

When we passed the village of Krasna, about thirteen kilometres from Rzeszow, an older man from Bochnia rose, a man who had already experienced several escapes from death–trains, and uttered these words: "Fools! Why are you standing here? Where do you think they are taking you?" And he forced his way to the small opening, pulled out a pair of pliers hidden in his boots and cut the barbed wire that covered the opening. The man jumped out and, thanks to him, we also jumped.

It tears my heart apart when I think about these two people from Strzyzow – Mulik Feit and Chaim Adest, a boy as tall and as strong as a tree. I begged them: "Jump!" but they refused. What a pity. The poor souls did not believe that they were being led to their deaths. I myself was afraid to jump but I heard my brother Samuel shouting from the outside. He had already jumped so I instinctively followed him. Mulik Feit yelled after me. I heard him very clearly: "Take care of my child!" His younger daughter Hena was still in the ghetto.

[Page 381]

Among the escapees was a young boy from Lutcza and Mr. Yaffe from Czudec, in the vicinity of Strzyzow. The boy disappeared immediately and I later found out that he did not survive. In the early morning we went into a barn, gave the peasant five hundred zlotys and were given a bowl of soup each and a bottle of home brew. In the afternoon, the peasant scolded us and demanded that we leave his premises immediately because German policemen had arrived in the village. This was not true but we had no choice. We had to leave. We decided to return to the ghetto in Rzeszow. The peasant directed us to the highway leading to Rzeszow. We walked toward the ghetto and nobody noticed us.

Before entering the ghetto, Mr. Yaffe wanted to stop at a gentile friend's house. However, we did not find him home. His wife was very frightened and told us to hide in the pig–pen where we spent a few hours. Meanwhile, the woman went to look for her husband whom she found in a salon and he came home dead drunk. He took us out from the pig–en and asked us to lie down on his bed, but we refused. We spent the night in deadly fear and in the early morning, the man sent his wife and six children into the street to see if it was safe. We followed them and jumped over the fence of a house which belonged to the famous jeweller, Zuker, into the ghetto. In the ghetto we encountered one hundred and fifty people who had jumped from the train that night but the man from Bochnia who had cut the wire was not among them.

We lived in the ghetto until May 1943. Much has been written already about our lives in the ghetto and the bitter experience we went through. I would like only to mention one episode:

A Polish officer by the name of Pasek helped us contact our sister Pearl who lived in Berlin on Aryan documents. During the time that we spent in the ghetto, we had received about ten letters. We received each letter in mortal terror and we thanked the Almighty that they had not fallen into the hands of the Gestapo. We were lucky that there were no Jewish informers in the ghetto.

Although it is very depressing to reminisce about these troubled times, on the other hand, it relieves a burden from my heart.

The struggle with the Jewish "Kapos"
by Itzhok Leib Rosen

After the great expulsion from the ghetto in Rzeszow, which took place on November 15, 1942 only four thousand people remained in the ghetto. One day upon returning from work outside the ghetto, we noticed an excited crow that was milling around one area of the ghetto. This part of the ghetto was called "Drukerruvka". The Kapos were extorting contributions from everyone. When I came closer I was hit in the face by a Kapo's whip. The Kapo was a local Jew from Rzeszow – Mr. Kleinmintz. There were not many local Jewish Kapos anymore. Most Kapos were from Lodz and Kalisz. Not realizing what I was doing, I hit him back and he fell. I quickly ran home but mistakenly entered another house where I encountered a few more Jewish policemen, including the sadly infamous "Itchele" from Kolbuszowa. I hit him too and he fell down the stairs.

I was finally overpowered by a few policemen and taken to the German command post which was located in the same building as the Judenrat.

[Page 382]

The entire ghetto was in uproar. It seemed like a revolt. Luckily there were no Germans in the ghetto when I was brought there. While I was led by the policemen, we encountered Mr. Lubasz, a well-known and beloved Jew in the Rzeszow ghetto. The man knew me from before the war. He calmed down the placement and he followed us until we reached the Judenrat. Meanwhile, as I found out later, other policemen caught my younger brother Samuel who was only fifteen years old and they took revenge on him by beating him savagely. When we came into the Judenrat, Abraham Brav and Sheingal, the two remaining members of the Judenrat in Strzyzow and also members of the Rzeszow Judenrat, happened to be there. They saved my life by taking me out of the hands of the placement because by then, German policemen had arrived in the ghetto. Brav and Sheingal locked me up in the office of Dr. Kleinman, the chairman of the Judenrat, and kept me there for an hour until the arrival of Dr. Kleinman. Faking anger, Dr. Kleinman scolded me. I denied and showed a receipt proving that my contribution had been paid. And that is how the matter ended. My brother and I realized that our lives had been saved by a miracle.

My second encounter with a Kapo occurred in Huta Komarowska camp. This camp was under the command of the German commander – Shubke – who was not a bad man. When a group of people were sent to Strzyzow to work there, demolishing unused barracks, they bartered some clothes for food and he was forced to arrest us at the insistence of the local gentiles. He was afraid that the local gentiles might report him to higher authorities. But after he was convinced that all the gentiles were interested in was taking the food away from us and that they had no intention of pursuing the matter further, he immediately released us. However, there was one commandant in the Huta Komarowska camp – the infamous Schmidt (whose trial is taking place right now in a German court). He was helped in his cruelty by the Jewish Kapos – the brothers Rybner, Mr. Straucher, Elimelech Kirschenbaum and others. We worked very hard cutting timber and during the work we were brutally tortured by this commandant and his helpers, the Kapos. Once we complained to commandant Shubke and he called in the Kapos and reprimanded them for their bad treatment. The next day the Kapos were mad at us and took revenge. They ordered that every second day would be penalty day, which meant working without food and without our shirts at a time when the mosquitoes were sucking our last drop of blood. If someone attempted to straighten his back or stopped working for one second, he was beaten with a truncheon over his back. The worst of them all was Elimelech Kirschenbaum. He was later shot by the Russians. Once, when he came near my brother Samuel and raised his truncheon, I jumped close to him with the axe in my hand and said to him: "Elimelech – if you touch my brother your end will be right here". My anger affected him. He let go of my brother but he threatened that he would settle with me when we returned to the camp.

[Page 383]

While walking back to the camp we searched our souls for advice. "Should we try to escape or not? What should we do?" We also shared our thoughts and wanted to hear the opinion of my older brother, Yechiel, and Mendel Lieberman, the son of David Lieberman from Strzyzow. The brother of the Kapo, a fine young man (he now lives in Israel), advised us not to run. There was nowhere to run. The Poles were pursuing every Jew. This man kept scolding and reprimanding his brother the Kapo all the way back to camp until the Kapo finally agreed to swallow his pride and not report the incident to the commandant. And that is how the problem was solved and we were saved again.

"Yiddishkeit" in the German concentration camps
by Itzhok Leib Rosen

Excerpt from a letter written in Sao Paulo, Brazil. 10th day of Kislev, November 15th, 1964.

Today is Sunday and we have the day off. It is also November 15th when Brazil celebrates Independence Day. I remember that twenty–two years ago, on November 15th, 1050 Jews were sent away. My brother Samuel and I were among them. Abraham Brav, Samuel Feit and a few more from Strzyzow were also in that transport.

Yes, my friends, one cannot forget, especially we who suffered will remember for ever what we went through and what we witnessed. These memories will be with us until the last day of our lives.

Now, if you wonder whether we had tefilin in the camps? Yes. I remember very well. I had my tefilin which I received on my Bar Mitzva day. I took them with me to the ghetto in Rzeszow. In May, 1943, I brought them into the concentration camp. From Huta Komarowska we were transported to Kochanowka and were required to go naked through the disinfection chamber. We were ordered to hold our shoes over our heads. I hid my tefilin in the shoes and that is how I managed to bring them into the camp. We were assigned to block number 2. There were only two blocks each housing about two hundred and fifty Jews – a total of five hundred men.

Everyone in our block wanted to don the tefilin and pray in them but no one was anxious to risk his life by keeping them. For a whole month we spent nights donning the phylacteries, each person taking his turn. To avoid suspicion, we had to do it at night because at six in the morning, we had to appear for a head count. Until someone from the outside noticed that something suspicious was going on in our barracks. The Nazi chased everyone out, searched the barracks and found the crime. However, nobody said that the tefilin belonged to me. From that day (this was beginning of 1944) until liberation, we completely lost count of the Jewish calendar and almost forgot about Yiddishkeit. From Pustkow we were shipped to Plaszow, from there to Bochnia, onto Mielec and finally to Wieliczka. The Russians were closing in on the Germans but they did not let up on the victims. In Wieliczka we were slaving in the airplane factory which was located underground in a salt mine. However, the factory had very little success for the Germans.

From Wieliczka the German ran with us to Flosenburg and on to Limeritz in Czechoslovakia not far from Theresienstadt.

[Page 384]

There we met Mendel Lieberman and Nechemiah Felber from Strzyzow. Lieberman was sent to Dachau and I never saw him again. I met Felber again together with Wolf Mandel and Nechemiah Hauben from Strzyzow in one of the last and worst camp – Guzin 2 near Matthausen. All of them succumbed during the last horrible murder action, the so–called "Entlaussung" (disinfection).

Somehow we felt that the High Holidays were approaching but were not aware of the exact date. I dared and asked an S.S man if he happened to know when the Jewish New Year would be. He told me that not far away there were some Jews working from the Theresienstadt ghetto about whom we did not know.

One day I risked my life and secretly crawled over to that group from the Theresienstadt ghetto and asked them about the High Holidays. However they did not respond. I did not give up. On my third try the ghetto Jews threw me a little note that tomorrow would be Yom Kippur. That is how we found out the Jewish date. Since then, we kept track of the Jewish dates together with the troubles that had just begun anew because we were shipped to Matthausen (Murderhausen).

The horrible years. 1942–1945
By Hilda Mandel
daughter of Samuel (Mulik) Feit

As one of the few survivors of the Holocaust from Strzyzow, I was asked to contribute a few lines to describe my survival.

It is difficult for me to write about it and I never did until now. I always felt guilty for being the only one alive from my wonderful immediate family that consisted of my father Samuel (Mulik) Feit, my mother Rachel, sister Henia and brother Joseph. I am the older daughter Hinda, (Hilda) Mandel.

Let me begin from the time when my family was expelled to the Rzeszow ghetto in the summer of 1942. On arrival at Rzeszow we were put in a tiny and dark room with many other people. Shortly after, rumours started to spread about sending us to labour camps from which no one had returned. Daily, there were lists of people who were ordered to report and they were taken away to an unknown destination.

My father and I were taken each morning to a work brigade that was assigned to work on roads or railroads but we never worked together, always in separate places. We left the ghetto heavily guarded and returned in the evening. That lasted a couple of weeks. We also went through a selection (left meant immediate death and right a few more days to live).

One evening they announced that all women with children not yet thirteen years of age had to report in the morning. That meant my mother and my little brother Joseph. There was also a list with names to report and my name was on the list.

That evening my father, of blessed memory, gathered us together to say goodbye. However, he handed me a document of life which consisted of a birth certificate of a deceased Polish girl. He handed it over to me and said: "I hope with this document you will be able to survive. Take a chance". He was able to secure this document while on work detail.

[Page 385]

The next morning while we were being marched out of the ghetto to go to work and while crossing the fields, I simply left the ranks, rolled and rolled on the ground, hid in bushes and walked away. I still think to this day that G–d made the soldiers blind for the moment of my escape. I should say our escape because I had a companion. This was Pearl Rosen from Strzyzow.

While we were hiding, we saw a column of people – our brothers and sisters – being led to the railroad station and for the last time, I had a glimpse of my mother and brother being led to the trains.

We purchased tickets to Krakow and we were on our way. I had a friend from the gymnasium in Krakow who helped us finding a temporary job in a military hospital. At this time I assumed the name of Barbara Czapczynska which was on the birth certificate. After weeks of living in deadly fear of being discovered, we decided to volunteer for work in Germany. We were accepted and they shipped us to Berlin.

I stayed there for three years in the lion's den, working in an office until the end of the war. I know my description sounds cut and dry. However, this is only an outline of my survival from 1942 to 1945. A lot of suffering and pain, physical and emotional went into these years and after and it just never stops. I miss my parents, my sister and brother and I will to the end of my days.

I know we all have scars that never heal. I know I have.

May G–d avenge their untainted blood. They shall never be forgotten.

Surviving in the Lion's den
By Pearl Strengerwoski–Rosen

At the outbreak of World War II, my brothers and I with our mother, of blessed memory, were all living in Strzyzow except for our older brother, Yechiel who was mobilized in the Polish army to defend the "fatherland". Soon thereafter, we lost trace of him and did not know whether he was alive or not.

When the situation became clear to us, that is, we began to hear what was happening to the Jews – being tormented and later annihilated, many of the younger people ran away wherever they could; many crossing the border to Soviet–occupied territory. Few Jews went into hiding but the majority remained in Strzyzow and resignedly waited their fate under the Nazi regime. Jews were exploited and used for hard, physical and denigrating work. The Germans needed cheap slave labour for their war machine. Our family remained in Strzyzow. My brother Itzhok Leib and I, with the youngest brother Samuel (Shmulik), took care of our sick mother. The burden of providing food for the family fell on the shoulders of my brother Itzhok Leib and me.

Meanwhile, we were informed by a messenger that my oldest brother was alive and hiding in a small town, Nowosielce, not far from the border town Sanok. I went there with my older brother's documents and brought him home. This was illegal and had to done secretly because the Germans grabbed all returnees from the Russian side and killed them as being communists. Luckily they did not find out about him and he survived. A short time later we were expelled to the Rzeszow ghetto together with the rest of the Jews from Strzyzow.

[Page 386]

The situation in the ghetto became very difficult. The Germans concentrated Jews from the whole area into the ghetto. The Germans tormented the ghetto Jews and inflicted pain and suffering upon them. The poor suffered the most not having the means to obtain any food to sustain life. The daily life–threatening situation continued.

The Germans began to deport people to the annihilation camps. In one of the selections, I was among those to be shipped out. With great danger and difficulty, my friend Hinda Feit and I succeeded to escape from the ghetto and went to Krakow on Aryan documents. In Krakow we had a Christian friend, a classmate from school, who helped us find jobs as nurses in German hospitals. I worked in one hospital and Hinda in another. When it became dangerous to be recognized by someone from Strzyzow, we both "volunteered" to be sent to Germany for work.

With great hardship we finally reached Berlin, the lion's den. In Berlin my friend and I were separated and began working as clerks in an office because of our knowledge of the German language. This all happened in 1942.

Although we worked in separate places, we did manage to keep in contact. I saw before my eyes the Angel of Death many times. We were required to wear the letter "P" on our clothes as Polish slave labourers. Once I forgot to attach the letter to my clothes and it just so happened when an Allied air raid took place. Somebody reported me and I was summoned to a higher authority. Not knowing the reason why I was being summoned, I was very frightened. I was sure that I was discovered as a Jewess. I took farewell of my friend Hinda Feit and reluctantly went to report. I was sure that I would be killed. But when they asked me why I was not wearing the letter "P", I breathed a sigh of relief, because I realized that for such an offence, the punishment was not so severe. There were many such instances when my life was hanging on a thread.

My friend and I were in Berlin until the end of the war. We lived through heavy bombardments and our lives were in great danger – ironically from friendly bombs. At the end of the war, we were perplexed. We did not know where to go or which way to turn. I decided to return home and search for my family. I jumped on the first freight train which was going in the direction of Poland. After eight days, I reached Rzeszow and was reunited with my oldest brother Yechiel and my dear friend, Hinda Feit.

[Page 387]

"Kol Nidrei" in Auschwitz
By Joseph Weinberg

The sad days of the horrible autumn brought one plague after another. As soon as people arrived they immediately met their destiny. From the older numbers, there were few left. A wild craze dominated the Germans. The worse the news which came from the front, the wilder and more blood–thirsty they became. It seemed that they were taking revenge on us for their unfortunate defeats on the battlefield. Every few days they ordered us to run naked and the weak ones were picked for the ovens. They resigned victims apathetically went into the barracks from where they were taken to the ovens. The rest of us were resignedly trudging daily to–and–from slave labour. We knew that tomorrow or the next day we would share the same fate. Every day there were new arrivals. From all over Europe, wretched people were brought here for annihilation. We became used to the stench of burning bodies. It became part of the natural scenery of the wonderful surroundings. The beautiful mountains were like a crown for the camp. Every morning, dew covered the grass and from the nearby river, a whisper was heard in the still of the night as if it was bringing secrets from a distant world and from the starts in the skies. Trembling leaves on trees, crops in nearby fields were moving in harmony with the breeze and bright clouds which were created by the smoke that came out from the crematorium ovens all became one entity.

The beautiful scenery from the other side of the fence pained me. We were here where everything was dead. With deep resentment, I observed the fantastic sunset. Nature mocked our destiny. And so passed one frightful day after another. However, a sliver of hope was hidden deep in the heart. Maybe! I clung with the last threads to life. The day did not pass entirely without hope.

For several days, whispers reached us from the women's camp. They were not taken out to work anymore. They were locked up behind the barbed wires. Stories were circulating that many women were covered with scabies and a big selection took place. At night, wild wailing was heard as if thousands of people were being slaughtered. The German Kapos who knew what was going on told us that four thousand women were selected to be burned and were packed into one barrack naked. The women lay there one on top of another without food or water. They raised the roof with their bodies and the S.S. men kept shooting at them like rabbits.

That night we could not fall asleep. Next day was Yom Kippur Eve. Tragic were these days of awe!

In the morning we found out that Berlin had ordered not to burn the women but to heal their wounds. A small ray of hope stole into my heart. Maybe after all! After the evening count, we were supposed to gather for the Kol Nidrei prayer. We had promised ourselves for a long time that this year we would conduct Kol Nidrei services.

[Page 388]

A thick fog covered the skies on that morning. The fog disappeared at noon and it began to rain. The sun was hidden in the clouds. Heaven cried all afternoon. Now, just before Kol Nidrei, the heavens calmed down a little bit. The rain stopped and sadness was all around. The sun felt guilty and did not dare to appear.

From all the blocks, people came to the block of the Jewish elder. People were lying in the bunk beds, stood in the aisles, pressed to each other and hung onto each other. Everyone who felt his Jewish heartbeat came. Even the block elders and the Kapos. They belonged to the elite. But now they stood among the ordinary prisoners. Fear befell them. Even the German block elders and Kapos, the horrible murderers became silent. They avoided passing the barracks. For some reason, today they became frightened of the Jews.

The Rabbi was chanting. He was a new arrival. Acquaintances had helped and supported him. So many Rabbis had perished. At least let one Rabbi survive.

Wrapped in the tallit, the Rabbi prayed the preliminary prayer before Kol Nidrei. Clear was his voice. We, the prisoners around him, froze. We felt that we were the sacrificial lambs who had put our bodies on the altar to be burned for the sanctification of G–d's name. Through the broken walls of the barracks, I looked out and saw the chimneys of the crematoriums from where smoke was mounting into the sad skies. I heard the sound of the Rabbi – not a sound that came from the heart but as if the heart itself had opened and cried: "And with the little blood and milk that is left in us we pray". We stopped and repeated the same verse again. We emphasized the word: "little" and gathered repeating after him the two words: "our blood and milk". And suddenly, someone yelled: "The blood and milk of our parents, our children and relatives". Tears were dripping from everyone's face. The sobbing poured out like a river, even the stone–hearted could not resist crying anymore. I did not cry. I could not take my eyes off the smoke coming from the chimneys. I felt tiredness in my bones. In the barracks was an unbearable heat.

When the Rabbi began: "with the permission from above", I was carried off into another world. It seemed to me that I was sitting in a catacomb in Spain and seeing the auto–da–fe, the horrible Torquemada, the wretched Jews who were burning for the sanctification of the holy Name and the smoke of the burned ascending into heavens. I heard the "Shema Israel" that the black wrapped souls took with them. I saw people clothed in black, masked and coming into the catacombs. "To pray with the sinners", the Rabbi continued. The black–clothed people from my vision. I heard the Rabbi say: "From this Yom Kippur on", and suddenly there was silence. A dead stillness reigned in the barracks. Nobody was praying. Nobody was crying anymore. As if all the people became speechless.

However, from the outside, frightening wailing was heard. On the road that runs alongside the barbed wires, women were being led to the ovens. The sounds of the truck engines overpowered the sound of the lamenting and naked women. Among the gathered here, there were many who had their dear ones among those women.

[Page 389]

Everyone was lying still as if they were trying to recognize a familiar voice. Through the open gate we saw how the victims stretched out their arms toward Heaven and pleaded for mercy. The screaming became louder. We were all in a state of shock. The Rabbi was the first to awake from the numbness that overtook everybody. He interrupted Kol Nidrey and began the prayer: "Unetanei Tokef Kedushat Hayom". His voice was heard in the stillness of the barracks as if an echo was responding to the wailing of the women. His voice sounded clearly and when he reached the verse: "who shall perish by fire" – a lamentation came out of everyone's throat, repeating the Rabbi's words as if from the world beyond. "Who shall perish by fire" the Rabbi kept saying but his voice was drowned out as if the worshippers were trying to rescind the verdict of the tragic fire. But the engines did not stop humming as more and more victims were brought to the ovens.

"And who by fire?" The people did not stop screaming. The voices of the wretched integrated with the men's prayer. As if hypnotized, they repeatedly yelled: "who will perish by fire?" As if they wished that the fire should absorb them too. And suddenly, in the middle of the prayers, the sound of the shofar was heard. Someone was blowing the shofar. The shofar woke up the people as if from a dream. First silence overtook the barracks. I heard my heartbeat and soon everyone was crying. While the worshippers were crying, the shrieks of the naked women reached the heavens. The sound of the bells was heard signifying that we had to return to our barracks. We were hurrying not to be late. In the block where we prayed, near the stove which we turned into a pulpit, the Rabbi, the shepherd of the flock, lay dead, wrapped in his tallit. There he breathed his last breath.

The crematoriums, which were surrounded by a grove, were burning all night. The ovens were not big enough.

[Page 390]

My road of suffering
By Reuven Greenbaum

Being under the German rule in Strzyzow, I shared the suffering with my family and we were sent off to Rzeszow together with the rest of the Jews. In one of the many transports which were sent to Belzec were my parents. They were sent there to be annihilated. The moments of our separation will remain with me all my life, when my dear mother handed me her jewellery which she had inherited from my grandmother Golda. Among them was a long, golden chain with the watch which she had received on her wedding day and the Sabbath diadem studded with pearls and diamonds. Possibly, she had saved my life with this jewellery. It enabled me to buy bread in the different concentration camps. A message from my sister in Belzec was delivered to me by an S.S. man. I was grateful and rewarded him for it. How naïve I was. I did not know that this was part of the Nazi scheme to calm down the relatives of the victims and cover up their evil doing. Reuven Greenbaum I was sent away from the Rzeszow ghetto before the Nazi finished their destruction there. First, I was sent to Bieszadka, from there to Pustkow. From Pustkow to Auschwitz near Gliwice, Grossrosen and finally to Matthausen, the worst of them all. Luckily, the camp was overfilled and they did not let us in. So I was sent to Limeritz. I finished my trail of suffering in Theresiendstadt where I met Elazar Loos. And there I was liberated. Reuven Greenbaum After liberation, I was sent to Buchenwald which became an American camp for the liberated. I was very young – a teenager and, therefore, I was allowed to settle in Switzerland because they had agreed to take in children. From there I immigrated to the United States where I live until this day.

[Page 391]

For The Homeland

The Fighters
by Itzhok Berglass

Natives of Strzyzow and their offspring were among the builders of the homeland and among those who fought for her liberation from foreigners. People from Strzyzow participated in every battle of the Israeli Army. I will not write about this subject in a broad form because here, in Israel, fighting for our land is self–understood. I will write only about one incident which occurred in the days of the renewal of the Jewish spirit during World War I which, at that time, was not such a routine occurrence.

Yacov Feingold,
of blessed memory
by Itzhok Berglass

Yacov was among the first who volunteered for the

Brigade. He lived in the United States with his parents, Reb Simcha and Tova. The love of Zion he absorbed at home from his parents and from his brother who organized the Zionists in Strzyzow. Yacov did not only preach Zionism to others but also practiced it himself. Before he left to join the Jewish Army, he spread the idea of volunteering for the Jewish Brigade among all his friends. After World War I, he remained in Eretz Israel, married a daughter from Strzyzow, Ms Tzilah Beller, an off–spring of the Holles family, and lived there all his life.

Translation of the postcard from Yacov Feingold.

To the Laterbaum Sisters
by Itzhok Berglass

Revered comrades! You will surely forgive me for not coming to Newark to take farewell from you. It was simply impossible for me because I was busy propaganding the cause of the Jewish Legion. I am conveying to all of you a hearty goodbye and will return to our land where they may continue to live a free Jewish life. We are leaving New York for a long, long, voyage. Be well. Give my regards to the Silver family and all other friends.

Your comrade.
Yacov.

[Page 392]

Yacov Feingold, of blessed memory, in the uniform of the Jewish Brigade

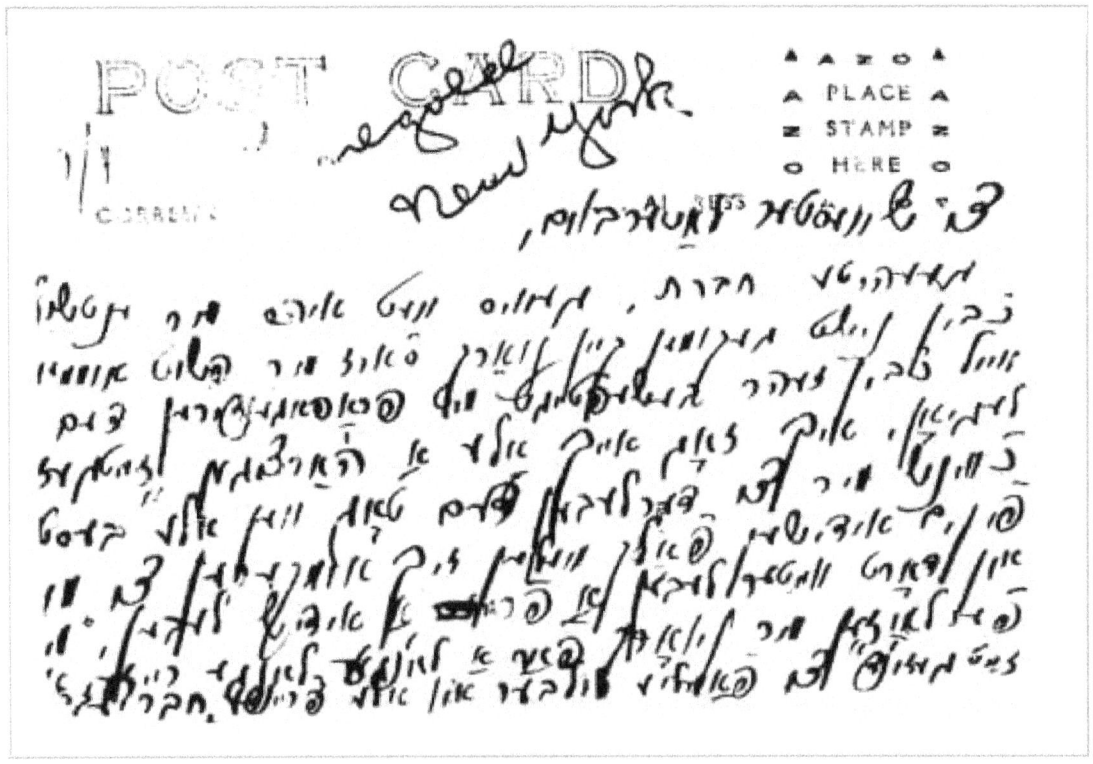

A postcard from Yacov Feingold to the Laterbaum sisters

[Page 393]

The Casualties
by Itzhok Berglass

The wars and the enemy extracted a bloody ransom from the natives of Strzyzow. A few of them were among those who fell in action. Here are the ones we knew:

Meir Mordechai Gutwirth, of blessed memory. He was nineteen years old. He was one of the first persons from Strzyzow to die in Eretz Israel. Shlomo Yahalomi wrote about him in his article, "Reb Shalom Schwartzman". According to his spiritual upbringing, he was not an active fighter but he fought for the homeland just by his presence and he fell for the land.

Joseph Asher, of blessed memory
The son who did not forget and will not be forgotten
by Leah Laos

Leah Loos, his cousin, writes about his life and his heroism. Joseph Asher was the grandson of Reb Yeremiah and Liba Asher, and the great–grandson of Reb Chaim Israel and Necha Gitel Sturm from Strzyzow. He was born on September 28th, 1924 to his parents Adela and Shlomo Asher in Breslau, Germany where his parents had immigrated to from Strzyzow. He fell while fighting for the independence of Israel in the battle of Kula on July 16th, 1948.

Joseph the child received both a traditional and secular upbringing. The harmonious family gave him much warmth and love and equipped him with moral values which left their impression on his personality. His happy childhood was disturbed at a very early stage with the ascent of the Nazi in Germany. This proud Jewish child witnessed the brutal persecution of the Jews. He saw with his own eyes the burning of the shul which he regularly attended and his ears heard the songs of the S.S. troops who audaciously marched in the streets of his native town and sand: "when Jewish blood drips from our knives the German heart rejoices". The injurious humiliation of man and Jew had penetrated deeply and fermented in his gentle soul. The ever–merry and joyful child became taciturn and pensive. He kept quiet, gnashed his teeth and wore his dreams.

Zion was not a strange idea to a child who was raised in a traditional and observant home. The resurging echoes of Zion which was being built anew, reached him through his sisters who belonged to the Zionist Youth Movement. From his father who was a soldier in the Austrian Army during World War I, he heard the tales about military actions, and he dreamt.

He dreamt of reaching Eretz Israel. There, we would have our own army and by that time, he would be a grown man and, as a Jew, he would naturally serve in the Jewish army. His dream materialized. On Passover 1939, he and his family arrived in Eretz Israel. They left Germany with the last train. He easily adapted himself to the new conditions in the land; to the new language and new comradeship. Soon, the gentle and good–looking boy earned admiration and love from all those around him.

Understandably in school, he joined the boy scout organization and stood out with his diligence, ability and courage. From the working youth movement he graduated into the Hagenah and there they imposed upon him important duties despite his youth.

[Page 394]

Joseph Asher

[Page 395]

Most of his time he devoted energy and willpower to those activities. From the Hagana he was sent into the civil guards. There, a brand new chapter began in his life, in the life of the young Joseph. Training with arms, manoeuvres, night watch and galloping on horse throughout the land. He got to know and love every village and isolated settlement with its inhabitants and his body clung with more exaltation to the land, to love and guard her. He was devoted to his duty with all the threads of his soul. When the bloody excesses broke out and after the United Nations decided to divide Palestine, Joseph was the first in Ramat Gan to volunteer his full service to Hagana. His past command position with them prodded him to take this step. When his parents and sisters, worrying for his safety, asked him why he had to be the first, he replied: "without a first, there is no second. And why should I not be the first?"

In the training camp, he was in charge of turning the new illegal immigrants who had just disembarked from ships, into trained Israeli soldiers. There was not another one like him in that job. In the very short time he had at his disposal and out of scared, persecuted, stoop–backed and suspicious people, he produced brave and proud Jewish soldiers. They regained their self–respect and self–awareness and the purpose for which they were being prepared to fight became clear to them.

However, Joseph's effervescent personality did not find satisfaction in what he was doing. He wanted personally to participate in the battles and not just prepared others to fight. He joined a battle unit as a platoon commander and took part in the heaviest battles. Although they were much older than he, all his subordinates admired and revered him. The discipline in his unit was exemplary. His personality enthused his men because he was always the first in every dangerous place.

He was a devoted son and brother, giving all his heart and soul to the family. He often appeared at home on short furloughs to calm his worried family but soon returned to his duty. Ne never talked about his actions and the dangerous situation in which he always found himself.

After the first cease–fire, he took part in a bloody battle with the goal of opening the road to Jerusalem. This was Joseph's last and desperate battle. A small number of men, poorly equipped and without food and water, were defending these hills of Kula. For twenty–four hours, they were surrounded on all sides by the Arab Legionnaires who were equipped with the best

English armour and artillery. A hail of bullets and artillery shells came down on that handful of young men and killed them one–by–one.

Joseph fell just a few hours before the second cease fire. He managed to hand over the command to assistant and to say: "Shalom".

Twenty–eight dear young men were slain on those hills of Kula. A village of Yemenite Jews was established on the hills of Kula and named "Hill of the Twenty–Eight". The Yemenite rabbi, eulogizing on memorial days, says: "The people of this village, even though they are weak physically, cling to this land with love and stubbornness. Despite the difficult conditions of this place, thanks to the inspiration of the ambitious young men who sacrificed their lives to redeem this land from enemy hands for us and our children".

Joseph's favourite saying used to be: "A homeland is not a piece of land on which one sets a price and bargains over". And Joseph surely did not bargain over the price.

[Page 396]

Michael Kalb

[Page 397]

My brother Michael Kalb,
of blessed memory
by his brother Aryeh

My brother Michael, may G–d avenge his blood, the son of Chaim and Reisl, was born on 18th January, 1931 in Teplice, Czechoslovakia. He made Aliyah with his parents in March 1939. He studied in the Talmud Torah and in the Tachkemoni School in Bat Yam and later studied optometry in Tel Aviv. At the same time, he continued his education in evening courses in the Beni Akiba Gymnasium. He was talented and humble. The diary that he kept since he was six, attests to the fact that he was always examining and judging himself and trying to forge his character to stimulate his duties and respect with devotion to the homeland and the aspiration of the nation. At the age of sixteen, he sought acceptance into the Hagana and, when he became impatient with the delay of a response, he followed his comrades into the underground of the Jewish fighters. He was caught by the British Police posting anti–British proclamations but was released on bail. He spent several weeks philosophically resigned to the punishment he was about to receive. Nonetheless, in his diary, he expressed his confidence that the British rule would not last as long as his sentence. To pacify his family who was fearful for his fate, he arranged a release from the underground and promised to settle in a village after his release from prison. He was sentenced in 1947 to leave town for a year and left to Shfaiyah to join his brother. When five of his comrades were slain by the British near Raanana, he could hardly contain himself, wanting to return to the underground to seek revenge.

After the United Nations' decision to divide Palestine, and then the ensuing Arab riots, he joined the Palmach. He was trained in the Negev. When he was under siege by the Arab Legionnaires, he bore the suffering with love and he later returned to the lowland and took part in the battles. He resisted the suggestion of his superior who wanted to withdraw him from the battles because of his young age and to send him to train as a nurse. He participated in the battles and bore the distress of hunger and thirst and the loss of his best friends, heroically. The boy of seventeen had become a veteran soldier. During the bombardment of Rishon, L'Zion and Hulda, he removed the wounded and the dead from under the rubble without waiting until the bombardment had ceased. On July 7th, 1948, just before the second cease–fire and while standing guard near a bunker in Zirah at the approach to Jerusalem, he was fatally wounded by a bullet from an Egyptian sniper and fell. He was buried in Hulda and his remains were later transferred to Mount Herzl in Jerusalem. May his soul be kept among the immortal souls of Abraham, Isaac and Jacob.

[Page 398]

Moshe Lehrman

[Page 399]

Moshe Lehrman,
of blessed memory
by Aryeh Kalb

Moshe was the son of Reb Itzhok Lehrman and the grandson of Reb Moshe Krantzler, of blessed memory, from Strzyzow and a descendant of a family of Torah scholars. We will reprint the articles which were written in a pamphlet on his personality and his active life. The pamphlet was published in memory of the fallen in the battle of Dvima on the Jordanian border. This was a surprise attack by the Jordanian murderers from an ambush on seven of our soldiers who were on a routine border patrol.

Moshe was born in 1937 in Tel–Aviv. In his childhood he was an excellent student in the religious school – Moriyah. He was outstanding in studying Gemara and secular studies. From elementary school, he went on to attend the City Religious Gymnasium where he was also among the best students, again mainly in Talmud study where he had shown an immense capability in memory and acuteness. When he reached the seventh grade, he selected a more realistic approach to his studies but did not neglect the holy teachings. He was active in social life and joined the Beni Akiba. After his Master's Degree, he began to study law at the Hebrew University in Jerusalem. Here too he received high grades and earned scholarships. He was beloved by everyone especially by his comrades in military training for which he volunteered in spite of the fact that his physical condition was limited. May his memory be blessed.

Parting
Eulogy by Rabbi M. Shapiro
by Aryeh Kalb

Do you remember Moshe! Our last conversation? I asked you to do your daily chores starting from the light ones and gradually shifting over to the hard ones, step–by–step and not tackle the hard ones at once. It is not in a man's character to skip and jump. But you said: "Behold, there is inside me a treasure of strength and energy that are capable of embracing the world. Therefore, I do not want to split them into splinters. I wish to perform one mighty deed in which I could activate all my strength and energy".

And I claimed that laziness speaks from your throat, that you knew well that there was not any might deed before you. Your only desire was to evade the daily chores. But now, Moshe, with an agitated and broken heart, I come to let you know that you defeated me. You really searched for something high and mighty. You did not dole out your love for the people but you gave all of yourself the way you wanted to do it.

The brutal situation in which a defiled hand cut down the plant that G–d planted, should we divert our furious gaze to the defiled hand?

Come and see the heavenly language about such incidents. Our sages have told us that a Rabbi Akiba's execution, they combed his flesh with iron combs. Is there a more brutal situation than that? A defiled hand combs the flesh of Rabbi Akiba. G–d's martyr? What was the reaction in heaven?

[Page 400]

An echo was heard which said: "Be happy, Rabbi Akiba". Heaven did not pay attention to the defiled hand but to the cut–down plant. To him it was said: "Be happy". This was the reaction of Heaven to such a brutal and critical situation. Do you think that only Heaven is capable of reacting that way? People too are capable of reacting the same was as it was further told by the sages that Papus also said: "Be happy Rabbi Akiba that you were caught studying Torah". Therefore, one can see that humans can also reach such a feeling.

Moshe! In your youth, you opposed everything you did not like, so why are you silent now? Permit me, Moshe to presume that your silence is a sign of your agreement with what I have just said. Therefore, I would not turn to the defiled hand, but to you I will speak with the heavenly language. "Be happy Moshe that you were killed for the sanctification of G–d, the people and the land". And let us part with the verse: "Go and rest and you will stand by our destiny until the end of the days".

My comrade Moshe
by Shlomo Levi

Wednesday evening after the murder of the seven in Dvima, I was one of the visitors in the house of the bereaved. An atmosphere of death was all around us. Choked lamentations of disaster pierced the prayers of the people who came to pay respect to the deceased in the parents' house. The picture of the slain son was on the table in the centre of the room as was a letter from the University authorities awarding him a scholarship and a booklet of lectures edited by the slain, along with other mementos. The heart was broken by the rigidity of destiny which cut down the lad in the upswing of his youth. "Moshe is not here anymore", his father lamented with a broken heart, choking permeated with horror and deep pain, as if unconsciously confirming the fact of which we were all painfully aware.

Moshe, we all remember him. Average height, wide shouldered, his pale face indicating tranquillity, his yarmulke sitting sideways on his sparse hair, his faded glasses and a stubble of a beard. His looks were a little mature for his age. Wearing simple but immaculate clothes, he always walked slightly bent, swaying to both sides. I remember how he walked slowly in the halls of the university, with a slightly dilapidated black leather attachÃ© case, filled with outdated notes.

His inner character matched his outward appearance. Good–hearted, friendly, straight–forward and honest with those with whom he came into daily contact, sensitive in his relations to his fellow men, humble and conservative in his behaviour. These were his traits. He was clear–minded, without deviation or obscurity.

Moshe was Orthodox. However, he was one of the religious young men whose orthodoxy did not interfere with other youthful activities. On the contrary, he was active in sports and took special interest in professional sports literature. His belief was pure and sincere.

[Page 401]

His piousness did not express itself only in a yarmulke or other outward symbols, even though he strictly observed them. His inner belief told him when to alleviate and when to be strict in fulfilment of mitzvoth. However spent time with Moshe in the army, even for a short time, knew that he never used his religiousness as an excuse to lighten his duties.

In his studies he was very fundamental. Being proficient in the Hebrew sources enabled him to obtain acuteness and profoundness in his secular studies. He was not one who studied the same thing a hundred times but one who studied once and fundamentally. The saying of Socrates that: "Informed means to know that you are uninformed" was his motto. He never boasted about his knowledge. He was humble and learned from everyone. No wonder that success followed his life. In the finals in his first year in the university, he won a high scholarship and the same thing happened in his second year. Who knows how far he would have gone? Moshe was one of the students who had to worry about his economic status. The financial situation at home and his high moral standards did not permit him to be supported by his parents. Moshe knew he had to earn a living. His scholarship was not sufficient so he had to spend much of his precious time working. He did not flinch from any physical work and was not selective in his search for a job. This fact was known to all. However, the domain of work did not interfere with the domain of Torah. His work never suffered because of his studying and vice–versa. It was a perfect intertwining between work and learning and he still found time to edit lectures – an activity that existed for years at the duplication centre under the auspices of the Student Union. Moshe invested much labour, energy, perseverance and reliability in editing these lectures. Only he who worked with Moshe side–by–side knew to appreciate his thoroughness in his work, the depth of his understanding and devotion to grammar. The outer appearance was as important to him as the inner text. How angry he became when he discovered a mistake in the text. His good comradeship, his ever–readiness and the spirit of goodwill were his characteristics in every cooperative work. Every step of Moshe was fundamentally planned. Every stage in his progress was subject to his critical evaluation and purposefulness. It is painful and sad that this inclination brought him closer to his death. Moshe was appreciated by the command of his unit. They knew that according to his physical condition, he was not required to participate in certain training exercises, but the voluntary spirit that was throbbing inside him and his ambition made him a good military man.

And so, far from daily pettiness, Moshe met his death. Moshe left this world. The news about his departure hit all his friends and acquaintances like a thunderbolt. On the day of the funeral, friends gathered in the modest quarters of his parents. I was among those who came to express condolences. I felt obligated to say a "few words" but I suddenly realized that I was speechless.

[Page 402]

Tzvi Navon,
of blessed memory
by Shlomo Levi

Tzvi was the son of Eta of the Mohrer family; the grandson of Tzvi Mohrer, one of the intellectuals in Strzyzow of the previous generation. Tzvi was a fighter pilot and was killed in a crash. The greatness of the loss to the Israeli Army was expressed in the condolences of his commanding officer to his family. He said: "Our military is also among the mourners and are in need of consolation". We are quoting below the eulogy of his friend and the poem by his sister, Chaya who was twelve years–old at the time of his death. It w

as published in his memory in the youth journal – "Maanit" dated July 1956.

Tzvi Navon, of blessed memory
On the shloshim of his death
by Zalman

A son of the cooperative village of Ein Vered who fell in action.

How cruel destiny is that we, the comrades of Tzvika who accompanied him throughout the years, are required to write the chapter of his short life, the story of Tzvika's life, who only a few days ago was among us. He excelled us with his freshness, energy, smile and good nature.

Tzvika was blessed with many talents with which not every boy is blessed. As a kindergartner, little Tzvika was flexible, alert, his hair shorn like a girl and he became the King of the forest. He climbed and jumped from one tree to another like Tarzan, without mishap. His contours intertwined with the trees. He actually hovered over them. It is possible that then already he possessed the inner push to choose his way in the future. Later in school, he stood out with his talent as a good student. When the class was examined in mathematics or science, Tzvika was happily cruising around outside because the teacher had asked him to, being apprehensive that other students might copy his answers. His high grades were given to him without the need to be examined. He stood out not only in the academic subjects but also in calisthenics and all kinds of sports. Who can forget his walking on his hands to the delight of the whole group, performing somersaults, jumping on boxes with great leaps with the perfection of an acrobat? There was no sport team in which Tzvika would not participate.

Ten years of studying ended and everyone went his own way. Tzvika enrolled in the technical school of the Air Force in Haifa because his inclination was toward a technical profession and science. He was accepted into the school on a scholarship which he received after a difficult examination. In the technical school, Tzvika also became an outstanding student and he decided to join the Air Force after finishing the technical school.

Despite the fact that Tzvika studied in Haifa, he never missed a Sabbath at home. He loved his little brothers, his parents and his comrades on the farm. He enjoyed studying and always told in detail and with great talent about his adventures during the week. We loved to sit around and listen to him. We enjoyed the way he spoke.

[Page 403]

Tzvi Navon

[Page 404]

After graduation, Tzvika did not stay long at home. After a hard struggle with his parents, he volunteered for the Israeli Army. He joined the Air Force and began to put into practice what he had learned. After a short period and with a strong will and effort, he succeeded in achieving his goal. In the Air Force, Tzvika's thoroughness and strong will were discovered and it enabled him to overcome all hardships. How we all rejoiced when the happy moment arrived and he came home adorned with his pilot's wings. A mature young man appeared before us upon whom we all could rely.

And from then on, Tzvika never missed even one Sabbath at home, at the club and with his comrades. Every Friday night, he was the first among the dancers and it was a pleasure to look at him. His dancing was filled with energy and youth, his light movements, his flexibility and his charm. He was the centre of every gathering, and on a Thursday evening, the horrible news was received: "Lieutenant Tzvi Navon fell in action. He was twenty and a half years old". Woe to us! Tzvika is gone!

To my brother
by Chaya Levin

Fly bird of steel
Fly to the distant clouds.
On your wings are resting
The souls of youths,
Among them one is dancing.
One who jumps about –
This is the soul of my brother!

Stars illuminate the night,
The sun illuminates the day,
All, all, all, everything.
All became sad and black.
A star shined, a star fell.
The world became dark.
The world was crushed.
Keep flying bird of steel.

Fly bird of steel,
Fly magic bird,
You enchanted young manhood,
Pure youth,
Whiteness of youth.
Keep flying bird of steel.

[Page 405]

Aaron, the son of Yacov Kanner

[Page 406]

Aaron, the son of Yacov Kanner,
of blessed memory
by Chaya Levin

The son of a respected and ancient family in Strzyzow – Reb Aaron – his grandfather was the brother of the well–known Reb Yacov Kanner from Strzyzow who settled in Germany where he established a large branch of the Kanner family. All their sons and daughters with their families perished during the Holocaust. We are quoting here the few words which were dedicated to the memory of Aaron, of blessed memory, in the memorial book which was published in honour of the fallen members of Kvutzat Masada in the Jordan Valley of which he was a member.

Aaron Kanner
by Chaya Levin

Aaron was born on July 20th, 1920 in Leipzig, Germany. He was a high school graduate. In his youth he was a member of the Gordonia–Maccabee Hatzair. He was one of the leaders in the movement. His personality served as a role model and an example to others. Just before the war began he moved to Belgium and immediately joined the pioneer movement. When times became critical, he moved to Switzerland. There he became a counsellor to young Zionist groups who had concentrated in that country before making Aliyah. In 1945, as soon as the Swiss borders opened, he immigrated as a member of the "Swiss Group". He was immediately mobilized to guard duty and defence. He made himself available for the armoured unit and participated in Hagana actions in his district. Aaron was also a supernumerary policeman. He studied in military theory and, during the bloody Arab excesses, participated in the battles for the Galilee and the Jordan Valley. He fell in Zemach on May 18th, 1948 during the decisive battle over the Jordan Valley. He was laid to rest in the cemetery in Dganiyah Alef.

Chanan Abraham Kalb,
of blessed memory
by Chaya Levin

With sorrow we had to add one more victim who fell for the Homeland. He was a member of a family who had already lost one son about whom it was written in a previous chapter. Chanan Abraham, of blessed memory, was the son of Aryeh Yehuda and Rachel Kalb, a grandson of Reb Chaim Itzhok and Shoshana Kalb. A native of Jerusalem. He died at twenty–three while escorting an excursion group of students from Herzlia Gymnasium on the eleventh of Adar, 1948. Their auto bus drove over a landmine in Minchol Rechem. He was a second lieutenant in active duty, an engineer, sportsman, dancer, lover of nature and scenery. A wonderful son to his parents, brother and comrade to his two sisters. A delightful person full of energy, straightforward and beloved by everyone. He left for another world. May his memory be blessed.

[Page 408]

The Destruction of Frysztak

How the Nazis annihilated a Hassidic Shtetl
by Menashe Unger

Reb Shlomo Schmidt from Frysztak, Western Galicia, recorded in his diary which I have in my possession and described in detail how the defiled Germans bit by bit destroyed the Jewish population of the Shtetl until the judgment day arrived, the 3rd of July, 1942, when the "Master Race," may their name be obliterated, finally decided to solve the "Jewish Problem" as they called it, to kill all the Jews in Frysztak.

The final action by the German murderers was also done with the accuracy for which they are famous for. Every group was ordered to stand separately at the annihilation place, the cattle market. And that is how Reb Shlomo described this black day in his diary.

"All night long I could not sleep. I thought about the Judgment day, which was coming upon us. Last night I bathed my children, changed their underwear, trimmed their fingernails, in case they were killed, Heaven forbid, I wanted them to be purified beforehand. Freida Gitel Kuperberg, passed by our house and showed me that she was wearing shrouds. Itzhok and Necha Tepper did the same. Everyone walked with his family. I went to the cattle market accompanied by my eighty-year-old mother, my wife, and children. According to the order of the Gestapo, each group stood separately. Those who worked for the Albert firm separate, the Todt firm separate, the workers in the Judenrat and the Social Self-help workers were also separated. The women and children of husbands who worked for the above firms were also separated. My son Tzvi was with the Judenrat personnel. The policemen checked that no one was missing. The chief of the police, Tepper, came to Samuel Baldinger and told him that Chaim Broner was missing, and gave an order to bring him out, because unless all the Jews were accounted for, all the Jews would be shot. It seems that until the last moments, Reb Shlomo Schmidt and probably all the rest of the people did not believe that this was the end. After five minutes, Itzhok Tepper with Henoch Meisler returned and stated: 'When we came to Chaim Meir's house, he was not there. We went up to the attic and found him sitting and reciting Psalms. His beard and side-locks were still intact. We told him to come with us and he said: "I am not going!" We told him that if the Germans will find him, he will be shot. He responded: "I am not going! It is my wish to be shot while reciting the Psalms. All my life I could not visualize a more beautiful death. Is there a more beautiful death than dying for the sanctification of the Holy Name while reciting Psalms?

"Polish policemen surrounded the square. I knew immediately that we were in a bitter situation, that we were not only taken to work, but that our lives will also be taken away.

"They arrived at six o'clock in the morning sharp.

[Page 409]

The District Commissioner, Dr. Gens, the Gestapo Chief Rachnitz, and the assistant Augustin, with twelve German policemen, equipped with truncheons and guns in their hands.

"The Gestapo Chief and the District Commissioner approached the Judenrat and asked Samuel Baldinger and his assistant, Israel Aaron Berglass, if all the Jews are present. The District Commissioner ordered that everyone over sixty should leave the place. My mother also left. I was relieved and thought that they were being released to go home. Suddenly I saw a German policeman grab with his truncheon the neck of Yacov Ressler and drag him on the ground. A second policeman did the same to Reb Bezalel Lev, and so did a third policeman. He dragged the sick son of Feivel Gross. Gitel Gotlieb became paralyzed right there. She was lying on the ground and the policemen stooed there and kept hitting her head until she lost consciousness. Then he took her away, dragging her on the ground with a truncheon. A policeman was standing near Reb David Epstein's mother-in-law, tearing down her headscarf. When the headscarf fell on the ground and she bent down to pick it up, the policeman hit her over her head. She kept putting it on and he kept hitting her until she fainted. The sanctification of the Holy Name by this pious woman brought to mind the story about the Shapiro brothers from Slavuta in Peretz's book, "Three Presents."

Reb Shlomo Schmidt continues his story in his diary: Dr. Gens approached the Kehillah leaders, and with his truncheon he grabbed one of them, Mr. Goldfisher, by his neck and dragged him like they drag a dog. He was the cashier in the Judenrat. Dr. Gens ordered Goldfisher's sister with her five children to step out, tore off her wig with his truncheon and sent them to the over sixty group. While the woman with the children passed by the policeman, they were beaten murderously. Wolf Riger's wife and Joseph Sperber's wife with her three children were also beaten savagely.

"The Gestapo Chief Rachnitz, took Mr. Brav, Mr Mussler, and Mr. Puderbeitel and put them in a separate group. Then Dr. Gens asked, "where is Schmidt with his family?

I pretended that I did not hear him and slowly moved away. In the meantime, I was put among the workers. They added another twenty-five people to our group. They kept taking people off the marketplace. Some people's documents were stamped as workers, and some were sent with the transport. It was eleven o'clock a.m. Trucks began to move in and they were loaded with Jews. The Jewish policemen were throwing children into the trucks like potatoes. They counted how many there were on each truck before leaving, one truck, two, three, four. No crying or screaming was heard. People were stunned. It was as quiet as a cemetery. From time to time a sound was heard of people falling into the trucks, and the sound of beating the people who refused to climb on the trucks. I saw how they threw children on the trucks aiming in such way that they would fall back on the ground. Dead or alive, they were thrown on the truck again.

"The District Commissioner appeared on the marketplace. It was already twelve o'clock noon. The heat was intimidating, and we were still standing on the same spot. The four trucks had returned, escorted by a few policemen, and they began loading again. The Commissioner ordered all orphans to step out. The orphans obeyed the order, among them my sister's children, Beila Broner's children. Hersh, Israel, Chana and Sarah. Their father Yacov was standing in our group. Hersh, the thirteen year old, called his father quietly: 'Daddy, I did not pray today. I am also hungry! Daddy, Daddy!' As long as I will live I will keep hearing the lamenting sound in my ears.

"Empty tucks returned again. The District Commissioner called out names:

"Samuel Baldinger with his wife and chidlren, Yacov Brav, Kalman Wagshal, Wolf Riger, Israel Aaron Berglass.

"The District Commissioner asked who is a barber. Feivel Seiden stepped forward. He ordered to cut out a swastika on those heads that had ample and bushy hair. Then he ordered them to hand over silk, rings, knives and pocket mirrors. Everyone put on a pile all the things they owned. Trucks arrived to take us away. We were about one hundred and fifty people. When we arrived in Piskow, the Assistant Chief of the Gestapo, Mateus, said that we arrived too late. We continued to travel. We thought that they were taking us to Warzyce to be shot. We recited the confession and asked forgiveness from each other. However, our trucks returned to Frysztak.

"On that day, Friday, July the 3rd, 1942, the German murderers killed three-fourths of the Jewish population in Frysztak.

The Rabbi from Koloszice in Frysztak during the Holocaust
Menashe Unger

The Rabbi from Koloszive was killed by the German murderers on the second day of Chol Hamoed Sukkoth, 1942.

Nowhere is it mentioned in what city he was killed and where he was when the Nazis occupied Poland.

However, I have in my possession a manuscript, a rare handwritten diary, written by Reb Shlomo Schmidt from Frysztak, covering the first day of the Nazi occupation until the day when almost all of the Jews of the four hundred families were annihilated by the Germans. Only a few individuals, among them Reb Shlomo Schmidt, his wife and daughter, Chaya Rappaport, miraculously survived.

Reb Shlomo Schmidt was the Mizrachi leader in Frysztak and was a member of the Kehillah committee. (He passed away a few years ago in New York). His daughter, Mrs Rappaport, brought to me this diary which is an important historical document, and there we found the information about the Rabbi from Koloszice, Rabbi Chune Halberstam, who at the beginning of the war escaped to Frysztak where his father and brother served as Rabbis.

Reb Shlomo Schmidt wrote as follows:

"September 5, 1940, Rabbi Chune Halberstam, the Rabbi of Koloszice, has arrived from Rzeszow. I went to see him, to hear some news, and to inquire why he came here.

"The Rabbi told me that he was forced to leave Rzeszow because he could not stand by and see the afflictions that the Germans kept piling upon the Jews.

[Page 410]

They were thrown out of their apartments, their furniture confiscated, and thousands of Jews were dragged to hard labor, hungry, barefoot, and in torn clothes. And not only were they not paid for their labor, they were being tortured and humiliated. 'So I decided that, sine I could not help them why should I stay there? I would rather be in Frysztak, a small town, and I also heard that the situation here was not too bad. Although there is plenty of trouble here too. But you cannot compare this trouble to what the Jews of Rzeszow were going through. Since the days of Awe are approaching and in Rzeszow it would have been impossible to pray with a quorum, at least here I will have a quorum and also be able to use the mikva, and be able to study the Torah....' "However, in Frysztak, too, the Germans have began to torment the Jews horribly.

"A month later, October the fifth, 1940, Schmidt wrote in his diary, that the Beit Hamidrash and the shul were closed. The Germans had shot many Jews there, so the Jews were afraid to go there to pray. They pray in private houses or in prayer houses tucked away in alleys.

"When Yom Kippur Eve had arrived, the Jewish Committee leaders persuaded the Nazi Truppen Fuehrer Hantzeldorf, and the chief of the labor office, Radel, that the Jews would deliver one hundred people instead of fifty so the work could be completed by midday and thus enable the Jews to attend the Kol Nidrei services. However, at ten o'clock, ten more railroad cars arrived loaded with steel bars, and the Germans did not allow the Jews to leave until the cars were unloaded. Then Reb Shlomo Schmidt went to the Rabbi of Koloszice to look for Jews to help in unloading the train, and, Reb Shlomo Schmidt wrote: "I came to the Rabbi and saw him sitting at the table surrounded by people, eating the final meal before the Yom Kippur fast. I began to complain and said to him: Is this fair? Jews might be forced to desecrate Yom Kippur, Heaven forbid, and you are entertaining people here? Send everyone immediately to help the others unload the steel from the train. Then the Rabbi said: 'He is right,' and ordered his children to go to work. And when the Hassidim saw the Rabbi's children went to work, everyone went.

"But the Germans did not free the Jews, Schmidt wrote in his diary.

And, if the jews would have left, the Germans in charge had orders to shoot and kill anyone who dared to try to leave.

"The Jews were forced to work all day Yom Kippur. And when Mr. Schmidt came to the prayers, they were praying Mussaf. Reb Shlomo continues his diary, "When the Rabbi asked us what was happening, we told him about the dangerous situation in which we had found ourselves. He commented: "You can be assured that by not being able to pray, you achieved more than those who prayed all day!"

On March the fourth, Mr. Schmidt wrote in his diary: "The Sturmführer Erwin Klassen came to him and asked him how much a Torah scroll did cost before the war. I told him five hundred zlotys. Then the Sturm Fuehrer said, that if I will give him five thousand zlotys, he will return the two Torah scrolls, which he had taken away from Joseph Engelhard. I told the German: The community is poor. Nobody has that kind of money. I went to the Rabbi from Koloszice and told him the story that the Sturmführer demanded five thousand zlotys for the return of two Torah scrolls.

[Page 411]

The Rabbi said: 'According to the rule, we ought to redeem the holy scrolls. But, in this case, we should not do it because the German would continue to extort money from Jews. It is better not to give in.

In the same diary, the suffering that the Rabbi went through, how he lived in hiding, and also how his son perished, are described.

The Holy Headscarf
by Chaim Lieberman

In the chronicle about Jewish martyrdom, there is a story about a yarmulke over which a Jew died for the sanctification of the Holy Name.

Our great poet and writer, L. Peretz, wove the story about the yarmulke into a beautiful poem and, through this poem, did this exhilarating story penetrate and remain with love in many Jewish hearts.

Many Jewish women quietly in their hearts envied the men and their destiny to have been blessed with such a story about martyrdom over a yarmulke because, after all, a yarmulke is an exclusive male affair.

However, now women can be consoled that they have become equal with the men. What happened with a man and his yarmulke, has now in the present Holocaust, happened with a woman and headscarf.

The story with the yarmulke was as follows. In Slavuta, Czarist Russia, there were two brothers. The Shapiro brothers were printers of holy books. They also printed the famous "Slavuta Talmud" edition among other books. There used to be certain quotations in the Talmud, which were disliked by the Christians. They claimed that there are insulting references to Christ, which showed disrespect for their god. Christian rulers forced the Jews to delete these quotations from the Talmud. These deletions were marked in the Talmud with the word "deleted". It so happened that the Czarist authorities accused the Shapiro brothers of inserting the previous deletions in some editions of the Talmud. Therefore, they were punished with a horrible punishment. To march between two rows of soldiers. The punishment was implemented in the following manner: Two long rows of soldiers lined up facing each other, and each soldier held twigs freshly soaked in water. The Jews had to march half naked between the soldiers while the soldiers whipped them with the twigs. One brother marched through and came out with bleeding wounds. Then the other brother began marching and, when he was almost through and only a few steps remained to the end of the agony, he discovered that the yarmulke was missing from his head. Of course, a pious Jew would not walk bareheaded. He returned more than half way to retrieve his yarmulke to cover his head. Meanwhile the soldiers kept whipping his naked body while he marched back and forth in the same track. However, this time the Jew did not make it to the end of the line. He fell dead.

J. L. Peretz tells in his poem, "Three Gifts" of how a sinner was sent down from heaven to be a wanderer in order to atone for his sins. He found the above-mentioned yarmulke and carried it with him to heaven. And for that he merited being let into paradise.

[Page 412]

Times have changed but Jewish suffering does not change. A similar story happened in our days. However, this time the martyr was a woman not man. It happened not with a yarmulke, but with a headscarf.

It happened in Frysztak, in a small, pious shtetl, located between Sandz and Krakow. This town consisted of many Hassidim and scholars.

When the bloody Nazi wave had spread all over Poland, it also flooded this kosher little shtetl, Frysztak, of approximately two thousand souls. The gruesome Nazis inflicted horrible vengeance everywhere, but in every place in a different manner, according to the individual fantasy of the murderers. In Frysztak, the judgment day was on July the 3rd, 1942. An order was issued by the Gestapo that all Jews with their families must appear on that morning, at six o'clock sharp in the cattle market, and whoever did not appear, would be shot.

And the selection began. It was a selection of who should live and who should die. The ones who were selected to live should work and die later.

The ones who were selected to die were ordered off the place. They were dragged by their necks with hooked canes. Before that no one was allowed to move. For every turn or move they were murderously beaten. This scene was described in detail by an eyewitness, Reb Shlomo Schmidt, in a previous chapter. Reb Shlomo Schmidt, a community leader survived the Holocaust and told this story in a letter to his landsman in New York, Mr. Samuel Mussler from Strzyzow.

Among the victims, there was an eighty-year-old woman whom the Germans had beaten murderously until she lost her consciousness, while she was trying to put her headscarf back on her head. The Germans dragged her away from the marketplace, threw her body on a truck, and she was taken to the woods with others to be killed. The headscarf remained on the ground. The Germans have won.

And, if such a Jewish soul was hovering at that time over the marketplace like in the story of J. L. Peretz, he would probably have picked up the holy headscarf and delivered it to Heaven, and would have earned entrance to paradise.

However, this old woman was not the only saintly woman on that day in Frysztak. The whole community was holy. As much as each German was brutal and defiled in his own way, so were the Jews of Frysztak holy, each in his own way.

There was a Reb Chaim Broner who insisted on dying while reciting Psalms in the attic. His last words were: "In all my life I could not have imagined to die a more beautiful death. That is exactly what happened. The police came and found Reb Chaim Meir reciting Psalms. They cut his beard and sidelocks, dragged him out to the marketplace and, like Rabbi Akiba was killed by the Romans, so was he killed by the Germans. They killed him and his five sons.

The martyrs, Samuel Last, his wife, Chava Leah, with their six children. Chava Leah came to the marketplace and said: During the night I bathed all the children, trimmed their fingernails, gave them clean underwear to wear, in case, Heaven forbid, they were killed, they will be purified beforehand.

[Page 412]

Chava Leah gave her six children, like Chana gave her seven sons two thousand years ago for the sanctification of his Holy Name. She had no more to give. And another woman who overheard Hava Leah's statement, said: "Me too. I also purified myself and put on shrouds. In case they will kill us, let us die in shrouds." The German District Commissioner noticed that Mendel Schmidt was talking with Reb Fishel Beigayer. He called over a Gestapo man and ordered him to give each of them twenty-five lashes on their naked body. They were whipped until they were bleeding but not a groan came out of them.

This story and thousands of other details, to the shame of the Germans and dignity of the Jews, was told in that long letter which was sent by the surviving community leader, Mr. Schmidt, from Frysztak.

That is how this pious, righteous shtetl, Frysztak, perished for the sanctification of the Holy Name.

Some day when a Jewish writer will write about the martyrdom of the shtetl Frysztak, like Peretz wrote about the Slavuta brothers, he should write that righteous souls from heaven came hovering over the marketplace in Frysztak on that day and picked up not only the headscarf and the hair of Reb Chaim Meir's beard, but also the souls of the entire shtetl, and flew with them to heaven, and put them before the chair of the Almighty.

Names:

BALDINGER	Samuel	& family
BERGLASS	Israel Aaron	
BRAV	Yacov	
BRONER	Chaim	
BRONER	Yacov	& Beile and children Hersh, Israel, Chana and Sarah
EPSTEIN	David	
BEIGAYER	Fishel	
GOLDFISHER	Mr.	
GOTLIEB	Gitel	
GROSS	Feivel	
HALBERSTAM	Rabbi Chune	(Rabbi from Koloszice)
KUPERBERG	Freida Gitel	
LAST	Samuel	& Chava Leah, and 6 children
LEV	Bezalel	
LIEBERMAN	Chaim	
MEIR	Chaim	
MEISLER	Henoch	
MUSSLER	Mr.	
MUSSLER	Samuel	
PUDERBEITEL	Mr.	
RAPPAPORT	Chaya	daughter of Reb Schmidt
RESSLER	Yacov	
RIGER	Wolf	
SCHMIDT	Mendel	
SCHMIDT	Reb Shlomo	
SEIDEN	Feivel	barbe
SPERBER	Joseph	

TEPPER	Itzhok	and Necha
TEPPER		The chief of the police
WAGSHAL	Kalman	

[Page 415]

List of the martyrs of Strzyzow and vicinity

This list was prepared by the survivors of Strzyzow, Itzhok Deutch, Simcha Langsam (Israel) and with the help of Yechezkiel (Harry) Langsam, Los Angeles, U.S.A. It was checked and corrected by Itzhok Berglass.

We invested great efforts to vitalize our memories in order to register the names of the martyrs.

We tried very hard to the best of our ability not to leave anyone out of those who perished in the Holocaust, especially those who did not leave a relative or friend.

The Committee sent out registration forms to all people from Strzyzow in Israel and abroad, to register their relatives, neighbours and acquaintances. And so, relatives registered relatives and neighbours registered neighbours. Still, there was a possibility that we did not receive the exact details, mainly the relationship where it concerns little children, parents and grandparents.

The untainted souls which were listed together with those who were not, may their souls be bound in the bond of life, and the memory of their sacrifice will never be forgotten by us.

Of Thee I cry, My eye is shedding a tear

By Simcha, the son of Yacov Langsam

Our sages said that one of the sounds that are heard throughout the world is the sound of the soul which leaves the body during the departure of a person. And if this is true with one person and during a natural death, it is truer when the untainted souls of a whole community, elders, women, toddlers and youths have separated from their bodies by unnatural, brutal deaths.

The echo of the sounds of the martyrs of Strzyzow and vicinity during the Holocaust, especially during the last minutes of their lives, has not vanished from our ears for over twenty years.

Their image and the sounds of our parents, sisters and brothers keep calling to us: "Earth, do not cover our blood".

Their last request were the sounds which called to us: "See vengeance upon our murderers". Their last plea was: "We are dying as Jews. Please say Kaddish for us".

We cannot point out from which of the victims was heard such a plea, but surely it was the wish of all who were trussed upon the altar of the nation. Such wishes were expressed by our dear ones in their last requests to the Jewish people in general and to the survivors of Strzyzow in particular.

[Page 416]

If a tragedy befalls and a member of the family dies, no one can console the relatives of their great tragedy. Everyone stands around broken and crushed but, in time, life returns to normal. It is all natural. "The earth covers it and man forgets". But it is not so with the martyrs of the Holocaust who met their brutal destiny and did not merit to be buried by the Burial Society, according to Jewish tradition. And, we the survivors are unable to gather their remains, wrap them in a tallit, put them in a casket and give them a Jewish burial because their ashes were spread by the Nazi all over the fields of Europe. Therefore, we are duty-bound to gather the letters of the names of the holy and untainted souls and to perpetuate them in this memorial book, published in Zion, the land of their dreams and thus fulfil our obligation also to those who left no heir to recite Kaddish.

By putting together this holy list, we were given a part in creating a bond with our dear ones. Not only by lighting a candle and saying Kaddish one day a year during our generation, but also, all those from Strzyzow and vicinity who now live in Zion and in the Diaspora will be able to open this book someday and recognize the names of their parents and their grandparents in the holy community in which a bustling Jewish life existed for hundreds of years. There were spiritual people, simple people, rabbis and Tzadikim, scholars, righteous women and school children. All these were trussed to be sacrificed for the nation. They were killed and annihilated, suffering suffocation deaths in the gas chambers, burned or buried alive in camps built by the Nazi in Chelmno, Belzec, Sobibor, Treblinka, Auschwitz and others.

It is a holy obligation to the individual and the public not to forget those whose memory is imprinted deep, deep in our hearts.

With a quiver of holiness do we stand the survivors of Strzyzow and vicinity, in solidarity with all untainted souls who sanctified the Name of Heaven with their lives and deaths.

Itgadal V'yitkadash Sh'mey Rabba

[Pages 417-432]

The Martyrs
Transcribed by Linda Richman

Surname	First name(s)	Other Surnames	Remarks	Page
ACHT	Fredich (Ephraim), and his mother			417
ADER	His wife and daughter			417
ADEST	Eisik, the son of Feivel, his wife Sara Ryvka, and son Chaim			417
ADEST	Pinchos, son of Feivel, and his family		Germany	417
ADEST	Yakov, son-in-law of Levi Joseph WIND, and his wife Bracha	WIND		417
ADLER	Abraham, son-in-law of Feivel ADEST, his wife and son	ADEST		417
ADLER	Joel, son-in-law of the Assistant Rabbi Alter Ezra SEIDMAN, his wife Esther and daughter Malka	SEIDMAN	Pilzno	417
ADLER	Israel, son of Joel and his wife		Tarnow	417
ADLER	Pinchos Yakov, son of Joel, wife Necha Leah, sons Zev, Eliyahu, Alter Ezra, and daughter Chana		Tarnow	417
ALSTER	Leah, widow of Joseph, daughter Necha, sons, Joshua and Zev Wolf, his wife Hinda nee KRAUS	KRAUS		417
AMEIS	Abraham, son-in-law of Yakov SCHITZ	SCHITZ		417
AMKRAUT	Yechezkiel, son-in-law of Elazar WURTZEL, his wife Yenta, sons Dov and Baruch	WURTZEL		417
ANDERS	Toza, daughter of Tzvi Hersh PFEFFER, her sons Leon and Manfred	PFEFFER	Expelled from Germany/killed in Riga	417
APPERMAN	Dr. APPERMAN M. and son			417
ASHER	Liba, widow of Jeremiah, daughter of Necha Gitel STURM	STURM		417
ASHER	Zelig, son of Liba, his wife Miriam (Mirl) nee ZIMMER, daughters Malka and Eta	ZIMMER	Sandz	417

AUERHOUN	Shlomo, son-in-law of Moshe David UNGER, his wife Feiga and daughter Chana	UNGER		417
BAUMEL	Benjamin, son-in-law of Hersh RESSLER, his wife Hinda, daughters Liba and Feiga, sons Israel, Moshe and Tzvi Hersh	RESSLER	Death of Tzvi Hersh, See p. 235	417
BAUMEL	Joshua, father of Benjamin, and another son		98 years old, lived in Czudec	417
BEITLER	Leibush, his wife, and sons, Shlomo Aaron Shmuel, Nechemiah, and Mordechai			417
BER	Raphael, his wife Yehudit, daughters Gitel and Leah, and son Moshe Yehuda Leib			417
BER	Yakov, Raphael's brother, his wife and daughter.		Lwow	417
BERGER	Esther Hinda, widow of Joshua			417
BERGER	Eta, daughter of Michael MINTZ, her husband and son	MINTZ	France	417
BERGER	Joseph, son-in-law of Israel GERTNER, his wife Yenta	GERTNER	Expelled from Germany/killed in Strzyzow	417
BERGLASS	Abraham Menachem, son of Hersh Ber, his wife, daughter, and son, and a daughter of Hersh Ber			417
BERGLASS	Yocheved nee GUTTMAN, the widow of Baruch	GUTTMAN		418
BERNSTEIN	Pinchos, son-in-law of Israel GERTNER, his wife Rachel, son Shlomo, one more son and a daughter	GERTNER	Krakow	418
BERNSTEIN	Yakov Itzhok, son-in-law of Baruch BERGLASS, his wife Nechama, sons David Dov and Elimelech, and a daughter Bina	BERGLASS		418
BLECH	Abraham, son-in-law of the Assistant Rabbi Alter Ezra SEIDMAN, his wife Liba, daughters Sarah and Leah with her husband	SEIDMAN	Limanow	418
BLECH	Izhok, son of Abraham, and his wife Sarah			418

BLAU	Moshe, son-in-law of Aryeh Leibush RUSS, his wife Sarah Freda, sons Meir, Chaim Eliezar, and one more son	RUSS		418
BLOCH	Elazar, son-in-law of Moshe Shmuel FRIEDMAN, with his family	FRIEDMAN		418
BIRNBACH	Baruch, grandson of Zelig ADEST, his wife Berta and two children,	ADEST	Germany	418
BORGENICHT	Aaron, son of Itzhok, his wife Hena, son Moshe, daughter Zisl (Zenia)		Death of Moshe BORGENICHT, See p. 243	418
BORGENICHT	Itzhok, son-in-law of Pinchos KANNER	KANNER		418
BARTH	Mordechai, his wife, son Moshe, daughter Beila			418
BEVAS	Joshua, son-in-law of Mordechai RUSS, his wife Rachel	RUSS		418
BOMBACH	Samuel, son-in-law of Elazar WURTZEL, his wife Adela	WURTZEL	Rzeszow	418
BRAUNER	Zalman, his wife Dina, daughter Ryvka, her husband and child			418
BRAUNER	Moshe, son of Zalman, and his family		Vienna	418
BRAV	Abraham, son-in-law of Alter NECHEMIAH, his wife Henia, daughter Eta	NECHEMIAH		418
BRUDER	Meir Hersh, son-in-law of Yakov SCHITZ, and his wife Pearl	SCHITZ		418
BRAV	Brother of Abraham, with family		Sandz	418
BRAV	Abraham, cousin of Mordechai BRAV, with his family			418
CHWAL	DR. CHWAL, his wife and daughter			418
DAN	Elimelech, son-in-law of Joseph Bendit ZILBERMAN, his wife, sons, Moshe and Leibush, and a daughter	ZILBERMAN		418
DEMBITZER	David, son-in-law of Hersh RESSLER, and his wife Zelda	RESSLER		418

DEMBITZER	Eisik, son of David, his wife Tova nee WEINBERG, and a son	WEINBERG		418
DEUTCH	Chana, widow of Wolf, daughter of the Assistant Rabbi Alter Ezra SEIDMAN	SEIDMAN		418
DEUTCH	Aaron, son of Chana, his wife Hinda Leah nee STERNBERG, daughters Chaya, Rachel, and Yehudit (Yiddis)	STERNBERG		418
DEUTCH	Chaya Kreindl nee BAUMEL, wife of Itzhok, their daughters Ryvka and Rachel, son Hersh Fishel.	BAUMEL	Itshok DEUTCH survived	418
DEUTCH	Joseph, son of Chana, his wife Tzila nee GUZIK and son Zev.	GUZIK		418
DIAMAND	Aryeh Leibush, son of Shlomo, his wife Edel, and daughter Rachel, also a son Yakov, with his family		Shlomo was from Zyzonw	418
DIAMAND	Baruch, his wife, sons Israel and Naphtali, and four daughters			418
DIAMAND	Chana Rachel, widow of Shlomo Zalman, her sons Aryeh Leibush, with his wife Eta, Joseph Mordechai and Abraham. Daughters Nina (Nechtche), and Reizel, also Elazar the son of Reizel		Shlomo was from Wysoka/Reizel was killed while smggling food to camp inmates	418
DIAMAND	Hersh, son of Feivel, his wife, their son Moshe, his wife and son			419
DIAMAND	Hinda nee WEIDENFELD, wife of Heschel, their sons Joseph Chaim and Yeshayahu Itzhok	WEIDENFELD	Heschel DIAMAND survived	419
DIAMAND	Joseph, son of Aryeh Leibush, with his family		Swilcza	419
DIAMAND	Keila, the widow of Akiba Shmuel, son Tzvi Hersh with his family. Son Zev Wolf with his family. Daughters, Eta and Sheindl with their families		Berlin, Blazo	419
DIAMAND	Leah nee LICHT, the wife of Shlomo Yahalomi. Their daughter Dvora and son Joseph Chaim	LICHT	Shlomo Yahalomi-DIAMAND survived	419

DIAMAND	Malka, first wife of Mendel the son of Chana Rachel, also his daughter Shulamit (Zelda)		Mendel DIAMAND survived	419
DIAMAND	Pearl, daughter-in-law of Joseph DIAMAND and son Yakov		Krakow	419
DIAMAND	Reisl (Reizhe), widow of Moshe, her son Aryeh Leib, his wife, and their daughters. Her son Avigdor and his wife Chaya nee HOLLANDER	HOLLANDER		419
DIAMAND	Reisl, daughter of Aryeh Leibush, her husband, sons Joseph, Mordechai and Abraham		Dubiecko	419
DIENSTAG	Gerson, his wife, son Shimon, another son, and two daughters			419
DILLER	Baruch, son of Itzhok, his wife Sarah			419
DILLER	Baruch, son-in-law of David DEMBITZER, his wife Sheindl	DEMBITZER	Sanok	419
DORNBERG	Abraham, son-in-law of Levi Joseph WIND, and his wife Ronia	WIND		419
DRESEL	Daughter of Shimon GROSS, her son Joshua, and a daughter	GROSS		419
DYM	Chana, widow of Yakov, sons, Moshe, Chaim, Joseph. Daughter Fruma, and another daughter			419
EHRLICH	Elchanan and his wife Chana			419
EINHORN	Naphtali, son-in-law of Yakov LANGSAM, his wife Beila, and their three sons, Tzvi Elimelech, Itzhok, and Yehuda Zev	LANGSAM	Dobrova	419
EISMAN	Moshe Pinchos, son of Yehuda Nathan		Szczawnica	419
EISNER	Chana, widow of Yakov, her son Ptachyah		Rzeszow	419
EISNER	Meir Raphael, son of Chana, his wife Ryvka, and a son			419
BODNER	Daughter of Chana EISNER, her husband and daughter	EISNER		419
ETTINGER	Malka (Mala), her son Eliezar, and two daughters			419

ETTINGER	Shlomo, his wife Sarah, his son Leib, Leib's wife, and their son Moshe.			419
FALK	Baruch, son-in-law of David DEMBITZER, his wife Eta	DEMBITZER		419
FASS	Hersh Leib, his wife, their daughters Mindl and Ryvka, with her husband			419
FEDERBUSH	Aryeh Leib, his wife Eta, nee DIAMAND, the sister of Hershel and Shlomo, and their son Joseph Chaim	DIAMAND		419
FEIBER	Miriam Gitel, granddaughter of Moshe David UNGER, and her son Tzvi Hersh	UNGER		419
FEIGENBAUM	Israel, son-in-law of Moshe MANTEL, his wife Pessil, and their children	MANTEL		419
FEIT	Chaim, son-in-law of Hershel TENZER, his wife Miriam, son, Yeshayahu, and their daughters, Malka, Freidl, and Gitel	TENZER		419
FEIT	Joshua, son of Chaim, and his wife			419
FEIT	Necha, daughter of Shlomo DIAMAND, the widow of Chaim Hersh FEIT	DIAMAND		420
FEIT	Samuel, (Mulik), his wife Rachel nee PROPER, son Joseph, and a daughter Henia	PROPER		420
FEIT	Samuel, son-in-law of Yechiel ROSEN, his wife Sarah, and daughter Chana Reisl	ROSEN	Germany	420
FEIVUSH	Abraham Itzhok, son-in-law of Baruch BERGLASS, his wife Chaya Sarah, their son Yakov, and a daughter, Ruth	BERGLASS	Sanok	420
FELBER	Yakov (Yekel), his wife Pearl (Pesha), sons Elchanon and Nechemiah, two daughters and Pearl's brother			420
FELBER	Nathan, son of Yakov, with his entire family			420

FELDER	Zisl, widow of Fishel, the daughter of Yechiel ROSEN	ROSEN		420
FELDER	David, son of Zisl, with his family		From Berlin/David poisoned by business partner	420
FELDER	Yakov, son of Zisl, his wife Henia nee GARFUNKEL, and their sons	GARFUNKEL		420
FELDMAUS	Tova, daughter of Chaim HASENKOPF, her sons, Hersh and Elazar, and a daughter Gitel	HASENKOPF		420
FISHMAN	Adolph, son-in-law of the Assistant Rabbi Alter Ezra SEIDMAN, his wife Hena, and two sons	SEIDMAN	Rzeszow	420
FLAUMENHAFT	Shalom, and his wife		Germany	420
FLEISHER	Leib, his wife Dresel, son Hersh Elimelech, another son, and a daughter			420
FLEISHER-TETELBAUM	Meita, widow of Moshe, Leib FLEISHER's brother, Malka Tzivia her daughter, her husband, surname TETELBAUM and son Yakov	FLEISHER, TETELBAUM	Frysztak	420
FRENKEL	Dr. Chaim Frenkel's wife, their daughters Lusia and Yadwiga (Yadzia)		Dr. Frenkel survived	420
FRENKEL	Esther, wife of Rabbi Israel FRENKEL and daughter of Shlomo DIAMAND. Her sons Shlomo, Shalom, and daughters Rachel and Sarah	DIAMAND	Rabbi FRENKEL survived	420
FRENKEL	Joseph (Reb Yosele), son-in-law of Rabbi Alter Zev HOROWITZ, and his wife Chana	HOROWITZ	Asst. Rabbi in Sedziszow	420
FRIEDMAN	Chaya nee KRAUT, widow of Yechiel, their son Israel, and daughters Chava, Seryl, and Pearl	KRAUT		420
FRIEDMAN	Leib, son-in-law of the Assistant Rabbi Joseph Mordechai WIENER, his wife Nechama, sons Abraham, David, Chaim, and Pinchos with all their families	WIENER	Leib and Chaim were both Shochets	420
FRIEDMAN	Menachem, son of Moshe Samuel, and his wife		Expelled from Germany, killed somewhere in Poland	420

FRIEDMAN	Tova, daughter of Moshe Samuel, with her family			420
FRIHMAN	Chaim, son of Menashe, his wife Gitel, a son and daughter		Krakow	420
FRIHMAN	Michael, son of Menashe, his wife Chaya, a son Menachem, and a daughter			420
GARFUNKEL	Aaron, his wife Rachel nee STERNBERG, and son Ben Zion	STERNBERG		421
GELANDER	Hersh, son-in-law of Baruch DILLER, his wife Ryvka, daughter Seryl and another daughter, sons Shamai and Menachem	DILLER		421
GELBWACHS	Shoshana, niece of Sheindl SCHEFLER	SCHEFLER	Raised by SCHEFLER family	421
GERTNER	Leah nee BERGER, widow of Israel GERTNER, their daughter Alta, her husband and children	BERGER	Tarnow	421
GERTNER	Chaim, son of Leah, his wife Beila nee BERGER, and son Joseph	BERGER	Krakow	421
GERTNER	Menahem, son of Israel, his son Joseph, and the rest of his family		Brzozow	421
GERTNER	Menachem, brother of Israel, his wife, their sons Samuel and Leibush, and a daughter			421
GERTNER	Moshe, son of Israel, his wife Nechama nee WEISBERG, and their son Israel	WEISBERG	p. 255 "treatment of children", re son Israel	421
GLICKMAN	Joel, son-in-law of Baruch DILLER, his wife Leah, son Yechiel, and a daughter	DILLER		421
GLITZER	Shalom, son-in-law of Menachem RIMER, his wife Leah, and a son	RIMER	Rzeszow	421
GOLDBERG	Fishel, his wife Feiga, their daughter Rachel, sons, Eliyahu and Mordechai, with his wife Leah nee DIAMAND	DIAMAND		421
GOLDBERG	Nechama, sister of Miriam PINCHOVSKI nee GOLDBERG	PINCHOVSKY		421

GOLDMAN	Abraham, son-in-law of Zelig ADEST, his wife Dvora Sarah, their daughters Malka, Miriam, Eta, their sons, Itzhok and his family, Mendel and his family, Elimelech and his family, and Yakov, their youngest	ADEST	Holland, Dembice, Wysova	421
GOLDBERG	David, son of Abraham, from a previous marriage, with his family		Somewhere in an unknown country	421
GOLDMAN	Leib, son-in-law of Feitel LAST, his wife and sons	LAST		421
GOLDSAND	Yechezkiel, son-in-law of Leib STERNBERG, his wife Eta, son Yakov, another son and daughter	STERNBERG		421
GREENBAUM	Chaim, son-in-law of Yakov HEGEL, his wife Hinda, daughter Esther, and son Leibush	HEGEL		421
GREENBAUM	Mordechai, son-in-law of Yehuda Nathan EISMANN, his daughter Fruma and her husband	EISMANN		421
GREENBLATT	Yakov, his wife, sons Yechezkiel and Samuel Zanvel, his wife and daughter			421
GROSKOPF	Samuel Moshe, his wife Seryl, their son Menachem and his wife		Brzostek/ Death of Menachem, See p. 249	421
GRUBER	Yehuda, his wife Ryvka and daughter Chava			421
GRUBER	Beila nee AUERHOUN, wife of Eliezar GRUBER, and their son Moshe David	AUERHOUN	Eliezar GRUBER survived	421
GUZIK	Menachem, his son Moshe, Moshe's wife Frieda nee GRUBER, and daughter Feiga	GRUBER		421
GUZIK	Michael, son-in-law of Menachem, his wife Hena, and son Tushik		Yaslo	421
GUZIK	Zisl, daughter of Menachem GUZIK, witth her husband			422
HABER	Shimon, his wife, daughters and son Elisha			422
HAGEL	Baruch, son of Yakov (Yantche), his wife, and daughter Lusia			422
HAGEL	Michael, son of Yakov, his wife Adela and daughter Gala			422

HALBERSTAM	Yakov, son-in-law of Rabbi Alter Zev HOROWITZ, his wife, son Ben Zion, and two daughters	HOROWITZ		422
HALPERIN	Moshe, son-in-law of Abraham KALB, wife Elka, and son Bezalel	KALB		422
HASENKOPF	Michael, son of Chaim, his wife Sarah, their sons, Abraham Yakov and Mordechai Poppel		Frankfort, Germany	422
HASENKOPF	Rosa, wife of Yakov HASENKOPF, son of Chaim, daughter Frieda, and son Zelig	HASENKOPF	Yakov escaped to Israel/family killed in Germany	422
HAUBEN	Abba, and his daughters			422
HAUBEN	Lipa, his wife, their sons Meshulam, Israel, and Akiba, and a daughter Dena			422
HAUBEN	The widow of Feivel, her sons Yakov (Yekel), Nechemiah and Yechiel			422
HAUBEN	Elazar, son of Feivel, his wife, and a son			422
HAUBEN	Zev Wolf, son of Feivel, his wife, and a son.		Germany	422
HECKER	Gabriel, son-in-law of Nathaniel SCHLISSELBERG, his wife Ryvka, and four children	SCHLISSELBERG		422
HENIG	Moshe,, son-in-law of Levi Joseph WIND, his wife and a son	WIND	Rzeszow	422
HOLLES	Simcha, grandson of Itzhok BERGLASS, his wife Mindl	BERGLASS	Expelled from Krakow/killed in Strzyzow	422
HOROWITZ	Rabbi Kalonymus-Kalman, his wife Tzivia nee FRENKEL	FRENKEL	The last Rabbi of Strzyzow	422
ICHEL	David, son-in-law of Yakov REBHUN, his wife Leah, and their sons, Abraham and Meir	REBHUN		422
ICHEL	Aaron, brother of David, his wife, and two children			422
ISERLES	name unknown, wife, and two sons			422
ITZINGER	Yakov, son-in-law of Menashe FRIHMAN, and his wife Chaya	FRIHMAN		422
KALB	Abraham, son of Tanchum Yakov, and sons			422

KALB	Levi, son of Tanchum Yakov, his sons: Tanchum, Tzvi, Hersh, and Menachem Mendel, and daughters: Chaya, Sluva and Mindl		Nowy Targ	422
KALB	Menachem Mendel, son of Abraham, his wife, and son Bezalel			422
KALB	Shabtai, brother of Tanchum Yakov, and his wife Malka (Mala)			422
KANNER	Avish			422
KANNER	Asher Pinchos, his wife Miriam nee KLAUSNER, and their family	KLAUSNER		422
KANNER	Naphtali, and his wife Hizel			422
KANNER	Pinchos, son of Naphtali, and daughter Ryvka			422
KANNER	Samuel Joseph, his wife Sarah nee ROZENCVEIG with their family	ROZENCVEIG	Germany	422
KANNER	Joseph Bendit, son of Israel, and his sister Beila			422
KANNER	Yakov, his wife Rachel nee STIEGLITZ, and daughter Tova	STIEGLITZ	Tova died of a heart attack during attempted escape to Switzerland. Part of German KANNER families exiled to Zbonszin, Poland & killed there, others killed in France	422
KANNER	Ryvka, daughter of Tzvi Hersh KRACHER, and her husband	KRACHER		423
KARP	Hersh, his wife, his son Feitel, and a daughter with her husband and children			423
KARP	Meshel, son of Hersh, his wife and daughter			423
KARP	Shlomo, a relative of Zalman BRAUNER, his wife, and children	BRAUNER		423
KAUFMAN	Esther, widow of Yechezekiel, andd son Samuel			423
KEH	Ryvka, widow of Abraham, and daughter Czarna GOLDMAN	GOLDMAN	Bialistok	423
KEH	Akiba Yakov, son of Ryvka, his wife and son Abraham		Rzeszow	423
KEH	Ptachyah, son of Ryvka, his wife Golda nee FEIT, and a daughter	FEIT		423

KESSHTECHER	Yakov and his entire family.		Rzeszow	423
KESSHTECHER	Leibush, son of Yakov witth his entire family			423
KETT	Widow of Shimshon, her sons, Gershon and Abraham Leib, and daughter Ryvka			423
KINZLER	Abraham, grandson of Yakov KANNER	KANNER		423
KAGSWALD	Abraham Ever, son-in-law of Chaim FEIT, his wife Malka (Mala), their daughters: Doba, Rachel, and Gita, and a son Yakov	FEIT	Kroano	423
KLEIN	Joseph, his wife Leah, and daughter Yehudit, son Chaim Hersh with his wife and family			423
KLEINMINTZ	Tobias, son-in-law of Menashe SCHWALB, with his wife Sarah, and children	SCHWALB		423
KLOTZ	Joseph, his wife Elka nee FRIEDMAN, daughter Shprintza RIBSHEID, her son Samuel and daughter Sarah	FRIEDMAN, RIBSHEID		423
KLOTZ	Leibush, his wife Golda, their children Moshe, Samuel, Yakov and Beila			423
KNELLER	Ephraim, son-in-law in the HOLLES family, with his wife and children: sons Paltiel, Eisik, Tzvi Hersh, and daughter Adela with her husband. Also, the widow of Joseph KNELLER	HOLLES	Joseph KNELLER died in Russia	423
KORNREICH	Nathan, son-in-law of Shlomo DIAMAND, his wife Gnendl, their sons Nathan and Aryeh Leibush, and daughters: Bluma, Rachel, Reisl and Leah.	DIAMAND		423
KRACHER	Tzvi Hersh, his wife, their daughter Leah, and sons : Moshe and Mordechai			423
KRACHER	Pinchos, son of Tzvi Hersh, and his wife Batyah (Basha).		Barnanowicz	423
KRAUS	Eliyahu, his wife, their sons: Abraham, Moshe Leib, and a daughter Zisl			423

KRAUS	Joseph (Osik), his wife Leah, their daughter Hinda, and sons Moshe and Tuvia			423
KRAUS	Michael, his wife Leah nee REIN, sons Mordechai, Raphael, Moshe, and a daughter	REIN	Mordechai/eldest son, Moshe/youngest.	423
KRAUS	Shlomo, and his wife Bluma			423
KRAUS	Chana			423
KRAUT	Benjamin, his wife Chana, daughter Ryvka, son Samuel, his wife and son			423
KRAUT	Gitel, widow of Yehuda KRAUT, her daughters Reisl, and Esther. Another daughter, surname WILD, and her little girl.	WILD		423
KRESH	Samuel, and his wife			423
KRZESZOWER	Son-in-law of Leib EISENBEG, and his wife	EISENBERG	Rzeszow	424
KRIEGER	Elimelech, son-in-law of Israel Yakov MILLINGER, his wife Feiga, and son, Yehuda Leibush	MILLINGER	Rzeszow	424
KRYM	Moshe, and his wife Esther		Germany	424
KRYM	Benjamin, son of Moshe, his wife Frieda, and children		Germany	424
KUFLIK	Itzhok Moshe, son-in-law of Feitel LAST, his wife Yehudit, their sons, Simcha and Samuel, daughters, Sarah and Shpriza	LAST		424
KUFLIK	Samuel, son-in-law of Israel KANNER, his wife Chana, and son, Israel	KANNER		424
KULIK	Mishkit, widow of Eliezer			424
KULIK	Meshhulam, son of Mishkit, his wife Esther nee MILLER, daughters, Breindl, Chava, and one more daughter	MILLER		424
KULIK	Moshe, son of Mishkit, his wife Ryvka nee ROSENBLITH, sons Ber Meir and Elazar	ROSENBLITH	Rzeszow	424
KULIK-MARCH	Sarah, daughter of Mishkit, wife of Mordechai March.	MARCH	Mordechai MARSH survived	424

KUPFER	Mendel, his wife, their son Moshe, and a daughter			424
LANDAU	Chana, daughter of Necha Gitel STURM, and daughters Dreisel and Eta	STURM	Sandz	424
LANDESMAN-TZIMET	Chana and her husband Hersh	TZIMET/LANDESMAN		424
LANDESMAN-COHEN	Feiga, daughter of Chana, her husband, and daughters	COHEN/LANDESMAN	Sendziszow	424
LANDESMAN	Yakov, son of Chana			424
LANGSAM	Yakov, son-in-law of Chaim HASENKOPF	HASENKOPF		424
LAST	Feitel, his wife, his son Shlomo, his wife nee GETZ, and a son	GETZ		424
LAST	Michael Leib, brother of Feitel, his wife Chaya Rachel, daughter Freidl with her family			424
LAST	Eliezer, son of Michael Leib, and daughter Leah		Rzeszow	424
LAST	Chana, daughter of Michael Leib, with her family		Sandz	424
LEHERMAN	Chaim, son-in-law of Moshe KRANTZLER, with his wife Bluma	KRANTZLER	Escaped from Germany/killed in Strzyzow	424
LEHRER	Chaim, son-in-law of Joseph DIAMAND, his wife Pearl, sons, Meshulam, Zalman, and Yehuda-Yidl	DIAMAND	Antwerp	424
LEIBEL	Moshe son of Zimel. Zimel was the son-in-law of Israel KANNER.	KANNER		424
LEIBEL	Jonah, brother of Zimel, his wife and sons			424
LEIF	Zisha, son-in-law of Batyah SCHEFLER, his wife Chava, sons Shimon and Itzhok	SCHEFLER		424
LEITNER	Shimon, son-in-law of Baruch DILLER, his wife Yehudit, and daughter.	DILLER		424
LEVINSON	Tzadok, son-in-law of Joshua SELIGMAN, his wife Tova, son Joshua, daughter Chana, and two more daughters.	SELIGMAN		424

LICHTMAN	Hersh, son-in-law of Israel GERTNER, his wife Ethel, daughters Reisl and Pearl	GERTNER		424
LIEBERMAN	David, brother-in-law of Israel GERTNER, his wife Malka, sons : Menachem, Itzhok, Leibush, and Aaron, daughters : Ethel, Mindl, and one more daughter	GERTNER		424
LOOS	Eliezar, his wife Sarah, nee HOLLES, and son Eliezar	HOLLES		424
LUSTGARTEN	Menachem Mendel, son-in-law of Yakov REBHUN, his wife Sarah, and a son	REBHUN		424
MANDEL	Chaim, son-in-law of Joshua BERGER, his wife Kreindl Bracha, son Naphtali, daughters Mishkit and Sheindl. Also, daughter Sarah Alta with her family.	BERGER	Dukla	425
MANDEL	Zev Wolf, son of Chaim, his wife Rosa, sons Herzl, Joshua, Saul Joseph, daughter Golda Hena.		Dukla	425
MANDEL	Yeshayahu, brother of Chaim, children Pinchos, Chaim, and Sarah		Czudec	425
MANDEL	Ryvka, brother of Chaim, wih his family.		Sandz	425
MANDEL	Yeshayahu, his wife Pesia, their daughter Alta, with her husband. Also, daughter Leah, husband Moshe Yakov, and daughters			425
MANDEL	Benjamin, son of Yeshayahu, his wife and son		Dombrowa	425
MANDEL	Wife of Reuven Zelig MANDEL, daughter-in-law of Yeshayahu		Reuven Zelig MANDEL survived	425
MANDEL	Shimon, son-in-law of Reuven SAPHIRE, with his family.	SAPHIRE		425
MANTEL	Alter, his wife, and daughter Sheindl			425
MANTEL	Sarah, widow of Moshe MANTEL, and her son Joel			425

MEISELS	Shimshon, son-in-law of Aaron KANNER, his wife Chaya, son David, and a daughter	KANNER		425
MILBAUER	Tzvi, his wife Bracha (Berta), and a son Nachum			425
MILLER	Shimon, son-in-law of Fishel DIAMAND, his wife Mania, their sons Fishel, Mendel, and Joshua. Their daughter Dena with her husband and son	DIAMAND		425
MILLINGER	Israel Yakov, son-in-law of Joseph DIAMAND, wife Gitel, son Fishel, daughter Malka (Molly)	DIAMAND	Przeworsk	425
MINTZ	Abraham, son of Michael			425
MINTZ	Joshua, son of Michael, his wife nee STURM, and a daughter	STURM		425
MINTZ	Rochma, daughter of Michael MINTZ, with her entire family		Lancut	425
MOHRER	Leibush			425
MOHRER	Mendel and his brother Shlomo			425
MUSSLER	Miriam, widow of Hersh Hisel, her son Yechezkiel, daughter Leah with her husband, and two sons			425
MUSSLER	Zelda, widow of Eliyahu, and her son Elieazer, daughter Sarah with her family, and daughter Leah PUSTELNIK with her husband	PUSTELNIK	Sarah, Joel and Leah were in Belgium	425
MUSSLER	Abraham, son of Eliyahu, with his family			425
MUSSLER	Joel, son of Eliyahu, and his two sons		Belguim	425
MUSSLER	Joseph, son of Miriam, his wife, and two sons		Frysztak	425
NECHEMIAH	Alter, his wife Leah (Lantche), nee DIAMAND	DIAMAND		425
NECHEMIAH	Tzvi Hersh, son of Alter NECHEMIAH, his wife Yenta nee KRAUT, and a son	KRAUT		425
NECHEMIAH	Zev Wolfe, son of Alter NECHEMIAH, his wife, a son and daughter		Expelled from Germany/killed in Strzyzow	425

NEUMANN	David, son of Shimon, and his family		From Wysoka, Jaslo	425
NEUMANN	Moshe Aaron, from the ADEST family, and his daughter Toni	ADEST		425
NETZER	Leah nee MOHRER, her son Hersh, his wife and a daughter	MOHRER		425
NUREMBERG	Chaim Yakov, his wife Reisl, son Elimeleh with his family. Daughter Yachet Cohen with her family	COHEN		426
ORBACH	Pinchos, son-in-law of Feitel LAST, and his wife	LAST		426
PELTZ	Nathaniel, his wife Yehudit, daughter of Hentche REIN, and son Yakov	REIN		426
PESSEL	Baruch, son-in-law of Eprhaim KNELLER, wife Vita, and children	KNELLER	Gorlice	426
PINCHOVSKI	Moshe, his wife Miriam nee GOLDBERG, daughter Esther	GOLDBERG		426
PINCHOVSKI	Mordechai, son of Moshe, his wife Rachel nee EISEN, son Elieazer, daughters Chaya and Pnina	EISENBERG		426
PINZEL	Peretz, son-in-law of Yakov STURM, his wife Ryvka and son Zelig	STURM		426
POPPER	Mordechai, son-in-law of Eliezer LOOS, his wife Vita Feiga, and son Aryeh.	LOOS	Dynow/Also, see page 253.	426
REBHUN	Yakov and his wife			426
REDLER	Itzhok, his wife Dayche, daughters, Rosa and Gitel			426
REDLER	Shlomo, son of Itzhok, his wife, their son Tzvi, and a daughter			426
REDLER	Zalman, son of Itzhok, and his wife.			426
REICH	Shlomo, son-in-law of Eliezer LOOS, his wife Adela, and daughter Chana	LOOS	Rzeszow	426
REICH	Chaim, father of Shlomo, his wife Beila nee WURTZEL, son Baruch, and one more son	WURTZL	Jaslo	426

REICH	Chana, her sons, Moshe, Yakov, and Meir			426
REICH	Hersh Leib, his wife Mindl, and three daughters			426
REICH	Tuvia, his wife Mindl, and daughter Rosa			426
REICHER	Moshe, son-in-law of Yakov KANNER, his wife Leah, their sons Kalman, Shlomo, Joseh, and one more son	KANNER		426
REICHER	Menachem Mendel, son of Moshe, with his entire family		Germany	426
REIN	Hentche, widow of Hersh Ber		Hersh Ber was the Sexton.	426
REIN	Shlomo, son of Hentche, his wife Dobra, two sons and a daughter			426
RESSLER	The wife of Chaim RESSLER, and daughter-in-law of Hersh RESSLER and her son Hersh		Lured from hiding, reported and killed.	426
RIMER	Menachem Mendel, son-in-law of the Assistant Rabbi Alter Ezra SEIDMAN, his wife Malka, daughters Sheindl and Chaya	SEIDMAN		426
ROSEN	Joseph Hersh, son of David, and his wife Bath Sheva			426
ROSEN	Menachem Mendel, son of Joseph Hersh, his wife, his son David, daughter Pearl, and one more daughter			426
ROSEN	Joel, son of Joseph Hersh, with his family.		Belgium	426
ROSEN	Yakov, son of Joseph Hersh, his wife nee KANDEL, son Alter Zev, daughters Neche and Mindl	KANDEL		426
ROSEN	Beila, widow of Ben Zion, son of Yechiel ROSEN, her son Moshe			426
ROSEN	Chaim, son of Yechiel, his son Gertzel, daughter Rosa with her husband			426
ROSEN	Israel, son of Yechiel, his wife, a son and a daughter		Sanok	426

ROSENBAUM	Mordechai, his second wife, widow of Ber WEINER, son of the Assistant Rabbi, Joseph Mordechai WEINER	WEINER		426
ROSENBAUM	Samuel, son of Mordechai, his wife Chana nee SHEFLER, daughter Batyah (Basha), and son Dov Yakov			427
ROSENBLITH	Rizha, widow of Elazar ROSENBLITH			427
ROSENBLITH	Itzhok Meir, son of Rizha, and his entire family		Rzeszow	427
ROSENBLITH	Samuel, son of Rizha, his wife Rachel nee SCHWARTZ, son Elazar, and a daughter Ryvka Meitel	SCHWARTZ		427
ROSENTHAL	Dr. Francziszek, son-in-law of Gabriel WASSERMAN, his wife Chava, and a daughter.			427
ROSNER	Abraham, son-in-law of Joseph KLOTZ, his wife Chana, daughters Rachel and Gisela, and son Naphtali	KLOTZ	Belgium	427
ROTH	Benjamin, son-in-law of Michael Leib UNGER, his wife Feiga, and daughter Sheindl	UNGER	Sheindl escaped from Rzeszow ghetto. Discovered and killed.	427
ROTHSTEIN	Chaya Dobra, daughter of Moshe David UNGER	UNGER		427
RUBENFELD	Moshe, his wife, and a son			427
RUBENFELD	Michael, his wife Hentche nee KULIK, sons Dov Ber and Joshua	KULIK		427
RUBISH	His wife and a son			427
RUSS	Aryeh Leib, his wife Rachel Yehudit (Yiddis)			427
RUSS	Mordechai, brother of Aryeh Leib, his wife Miriam, their sons Eisik and Akiba			427
RUSS	Israel, son of Mordechai, and his wife			427
RUSS	Bath Sheva, daughter of Mordechai, and her husband			427

RUSS	Chaim Meir Yechiel, son-in-law of Rabbi Nechemiah SHAPIRO, his wife Fruma Ryvka, andd their children	SHAPIRO	Stary Sol	427
SALOMON	Brother-in-law of Mordechai and Abraham BRAV	BRAV		427
SAMUEL	Samuel, son-in-law of Elazar WURTZEL, his wife Reizl, their daughter Freidl, and one more daughter	WURTZEL		427
SAMUELI	Dr., his wife, son Daniel, and two daughters			427
SAPHIRE	Shlomo, son of Reuven, and his family		Jaslo	427
SAPHIRE	Samuel, son of Reuven, and his wife			427
SAPHIRE-HOCHDORF	Daughter of Reuven, widow of Leibush HOCHDORF, her son Shimon, and two daughters	HOCHDORF		427
SCHACHER	Eta, daughter of Feiga STERNBERG from her first husband, Feivel SCHACHER.	STERNBERG		427
SCHEFLER	Batyah (Basha), sister of Mordechai, Moshe and Shimon.			427
SCHEFLER	Joshua, son of Batya, his wife Eta, their daughters Betti and Leah			427
SCHEFLER	Beryl, his son Samuel, and a daughter			427
SCHEFLER	Moshe, his wife Pearl Leah, and a daughter Gitel			427
SCHEFLER	Mordechai Mendel, brother of Moshe, and his wife Pearl			427
SCHEFLER	Simon, brother of Mordechai Mendel and Moshe, his wife Sheindl nee GELBWACHS, their sons : David and Moshe	GELBWACHS		427
SCHEFLER-CUKIER	Chaya, daughter of Mordechai Mendel, daughters Dvora, Doba and Freidl	CUKIER		427
SHEINMAN	Israel, son-in-law of Chaim MANDEL, his wife Chaya, their daughter Fruma, and sons Itzhok and Joshua	MANDEL		427

SCHIFF	Kalman Yakov, the son of Tzvi Hersh, his wife Esther nee MANTEL, their sons Mordechai and Shlomo, and daughters Hinda, Ryvka and Reisl.	MANTEL	France	428
SCHIFF	Meir, son of Levi Itzhok, his wife Dvora, and daughter Chaya Leah			428
SCHIFF	Bracha, widow of Yakov, daughter of the Assistant Rabbi, Joseph Mordechai WIENER. Her sons Joseph Mordechai, David Hersh, and daughters Ryvka and Mindl	WIENER		428
SCHIMMEL	The son of Moshe Itzhok		Killed somewhere in Germany or France	428
SCHITZ	Michael, son of Yakov, his wife Malka, sons Moshe, Dov Ber, Shlomo and Israel. Daughters, Dvora and Gitel			428
SCHITZ	Noah, son of Yakov, with his family		Rzeszow	428
SCHLISSELBERG	Nathaniel, and his wife Alta Risha			428
SCHLISSELBERG	Yechezkiel, wife Chana nee RUBIN, and their daughter	RUBIN	Germany/Yechezkiel survived	428
SCHLISSELBERG	Elchanan, son of Nathaniel, hiis wife Tova, and son Aryeh			428
SCHWEBER	Simcha, his wife nee WILNER, son Joseph from her previous marriage,	WILNER		428
SHMULEWICZ	Reuven, son-in-law of Joshua BERGER, his wife Ryvka, son Shlomo, daughters : Breindl, Pearl, Rachel and Malka	BERGER		428
SCHREIBER	Noah, son-in-law of Moshe MANTEL, his wife Pearl, sons Itzhok and Hersh, daughters , Chaya Chava, Malka and Hena	MANTEL	Gorlice	428
SCHREIBER	Bracha, wife of Samuel		Samuel SCHREIBER died in Russia.	428
SCHWALB	Menashe, his wife Yenta, sister of Baruch BERGLASS, their sons Nachman and Aryeh Leibush with their families	BERGLASS	Niebylec and vicinity	428

SCHWALB	Esther, daughter of Menashe, her husband and children			428
SCHWALB	Family from Lutcza		They lived in Nadvorno	428
SCHWARTZ	Mordechai, his wife Golda Leah, daughters Shprintza and Hena, sons Hersh and Joseph			428
SHWARTZMAN	Widow of Leib SCHWARTZMAN, her sons, Joshua and Moshe Yakov and daughter Sarah			428
SEIDMAN	Moshe Meir, son of the Assistant Rabbi Alter Ezra, his wife Chava nee DIENSTAG, sons Benjmin Zev and Fishel, also Abraham from his marriage to Hena, and Abraham's wife	DIENSTAG	They lived in the vicinity of Lwow.	428
SEMELIS	Joshua, his father, his wife, daughters Tova and Beila,, one more daughter, and two sons		The father lived with them.	428
SHAPIRO	Rabbi Nechemiah SHAPIRO, and his wife Tila		The Rabbi from Sassov.	428
SHAPIRO	Yeshayahu Naphtali Hertz, son of Rabbi Nechemiah, his wife Reisl, and their children		Dukla	428
SHAPIRO	Shlomo, son of Rabbi Nechemiah, his wife Ryvka, and children			428
SHAPIRO	Tzvi, and wife Sarah, daughter of Ryvka ZILBER, and their daughter Feiga	ZILBER	Tzvi SHAPIRO survived.	428
SHEINUK	Ephriam, son-in-law of Joseph DIAMAND, his wife Sarah, son Moshe, and daughter Reisl	DIAMAND	Rzeszow	428
SHEINGAL	Brother-in-law of Dr. SAMUELI, with his family	SAMUELI	Gorlice/in Strzyzow Judenrat	428
SHEPS	Daughter of Yakov GREENBLATT, her son, and daughter	GREENBLATT		429
SHPALTER	Yakov, his wife, two daughters, and a son		The last Assistant Rabbi of Strzyzow	429
SPRINGER	Israel Mendel, son-in-law of Yechiel ROSEN, his wife Ratza, daughters Pessil, Feiga, and the rest of the family	ROSEN		429

STEINMAUER	Aaron Joseph, son of Moshe Itzhok, daughters: Esther, Hena, and Sarah Feig. Also two granddaughters			429
STEINMETZ	Yakov, son-in-law of Moshe RUBENFELD, his wife, and two sons	RUBENFELD	France	429
STEINMETZ	Shimon, his son Samuel, his wife, and sons, Moshe and Joseph			429
STEINMETZ	Leah, daughter of Shimon, her husband and son			429
STEINMETZ	Tzvi, son of Samuel, with his family			429
STERNBERG	Hentche, widow of Leib, the daughter of David ROSEN	ROSEN		429
STERNBERG	David son of Hentche, his wife nee HAGEL	HAGEL		429
STERNBERG	Chaim, son of Hentche, with his family			429
STERNBERG	Samuel, son of Hentche, his wife and daughter			429
STURM	Necha Gitel, widow of Israel STURM			429
STURM	Elazar, son of Necha Gitel, his wife Chaya nee STORCH, and daughter Reisl	STORCH		429
STURM	Yakov, son of Necha Gitel, his wife Sheindl nee FIHRER, and a son with his family in France.	FIHRER		429
STURM	Joshua, son of Yakov his wife nee KRIEGER, and a son	KRIEGER		429
STURM	Yakov, his son Menachem with his family, daughter Feiga Chana with her husband Baruch Eliyahu			429
STURM	Yakov, brother-in-law of the Assistant Rabbi Alter Ezra SEIDMAN, sons, Chaim Asher and Moshe, and a daughter Eta	SEIDMAN	Dubiecko	429
SZPRUNG	Zisl (Zosia), daughter of Ryvka KEH, her husband, and a son Abraham	KEH	Bialistok	429

TAUB	Ryvka, wife of Aaron, daughter of Israel and Leah GERTNER, , her daughter Yenta, and son Israel	TAUB	Aaron died in Russia.	429
TEITELBAUM	Malka Rosa, widow of Shimon TEITELBAUM, her son Shlomo and his wife			429
TENZER	Abraham, son of Hershel, his wife nee DIAMAND	DIAMAND		429
TENZER	Joshua, son of Abraham, with his family		Jaslo	429
TENZER	Moshe, son of Hershel, his wife Yocheved nee WIENER, sons, Chaim, Naphtali Tzvi, Joseph Mordechai, and Shalom Jonah. Daughters Golda and Malka	WIENER		429
TENZER	Hena, wife of Itzhok, their sons Menachem Mendel and Israel Tzvi, daughters Freidel and Beila		Itzhok TENZER survived.	429
TENZER	Itzhok, son of Yakov, and his family		Lodz	429
THIM	Kalman, his wife Tila, sons : Mordehai, Joseoh, Moshe, and daughter		Death of Mordechai, see p. 248.	429
THIM	Eliyahu, son of Kalman, his wife, and son Moshe,			429
TUCHMAN	Joshua, son-in-law of Feivel DIAMAND, his wife Reisl, and a son,	DIAMAND		429
TURTELTAUB	Moshe, brother-in-law of Fishel GOLDBERG, his wife Feiga , and her son, Eliyahu, from a previous marriaage,	GOLDBERG		429
UNGER	Michael Leib, and his wife Hena Rachel			429
VEGG	Abraham, and his son Joshua		Szedlisko	430
WACHNER	Moshe, son-in-law of Liba ASHER, his wife Eta Reisl, sons Chaim Israel and Akiba, daughters Risha and Esther.	ASHER		430
WALDMAN	Elimelech, son-in-law of David WIENER, his wife Sarah, and two daughters	WIENER		430

WALKER	Yerachmiel, son-in-law of Shimon TEITELBAUM, his wife Tova, and two daughters	TEITELBAUM		430
WASSERMAN	Emil, his wife and a daughter			430
WASSERMAN	The widow of Gabriel WASSERMAN, brother of Emil			430
WEBER	Yakov Itzhok, his wife nee GERTNER and sons	GERTNER	Belgium	430
WEICHSELBAUM	Elimelech, his wife Tzipora nee MEISELS, daughters, Rachel, Shprintza, and Feiga, sons Shlomo, and Shimon	MEISELS		430
WEICHSELBAUM	Rachel, widow of Alter Yakov, son Aaron, daughters, Frieda Reisl, (Belgium). Dora Gitel with her husband and son.			430
WEIDEN	Kalman, son-in-law of Naphtali KANNER, his wife Shprintza, son Aaron Hersh, daughters, Rachel and Miriam	KANNER		430
WELISH	Hersh, his wife Miriam nee GUTTENBERG, and a son Chaim Samuel	GUTTENBERG		430
WEINBERG	Zev Wolf, his wife Chana Dvora nee RUBIN, son Alter Chaim, his wife and daughter, daughters Breindl and Feiga, with husband and daughter	RUBIN		430
WEINBERG	Moshe, son-in-law of Joshua BERGER, his sons Joshua, Yakov, and Elieazer, and a daughter Feiga	BERGER	Sandz	430
WEINER	Joseph, wife Chana, daughter of Shlomo ETTINGER, and a son	ETTINGER	Lwow	430
WEISS	Elazar, son-in-law of the Assistant Rabbi Alter Ezra SEIDMAN and his wife Sarah	SEIDMAN		430
WEITMAN	Joseph, son-in-law of Tzvi Hersh SCHIFF, his wife Sarah Ryfka, their sons, Hertzel and Moshe, daughters Hinda and Malka	SCHIFF		430
WEITMAN	Dvora, wife of Mordechai, the son of Joseph		Mordechai died somewhere in Russia.	430

WIENER	David, son of the Assistant Rabbi, Joseph Mordechai			430
WILNER	Shlomo, son-in-law of Zalman BRAUNER, his wife Bath Sheva, son Israel, another son and daughter	BRAUNER		430
WIND	Levi Joseoh			430
WIND	Moshe, son of Levi Joseph, his wife nee DIAMAND, and sons	DIAMAND	Rzeszow	430
WOLF	Joseph, son-in-law of Menachem GUZIK, his wife, and two sons	GUZIK	Vienna	430
WURTZEL	Moshe, son of Elazar, his wife Liba, son Baruch, daughter Freidl		Rzeszow	430
YAROSH	Hersh, his wife, and two sons,			430
ZAGNER	Michael, son of Zalman, son-in-law of the Aassistant Rabbi Alter Era SEIDMAN, and his sister Esther ZAGNER	SEIDMAN		430
ZALESZITZ	Sarah, daughter of Leah			430
ZALTZMAN	His wife, a son, and a daughter.		Re their deaths, see p. 249	430
ZANGER	Meir, son-in-law of Shlomo DAMAND, his daughters, Miriam (Mania), and Ryvka. Ryvka, Meir ZANGER'S seCond wife is the daughter of Reuven SAPHIRE	DIAMAND/SAPHIRE		431
ZEIDLER	Yakov, his son Tuvia, his wife and four daughters			431
ZEIDLER	Joshua, son of Yakov, and his wife		Rzeszow	431
ZEIDLER	Freidl, daughter of Yakov, and her husband		Rzeszow	431
ZIEBNER	Yakov, son-in-law of Levi Joseph WIND, and his wife Hena	WIND		431
ZIEGEL	Yakov, son-in-law of Berish HOLLES, his daughters, Freidl, Gitel, Seryl, and a son	HOLLES		431
ZIEGEL	Naphtali, son-in-law of Chaim HASSENKOPF, his wife Dvora, and son Israel	HASSENKOPF	Tarnow	431
ZIEGEL	David, son of Naphtali, his wife Beila, and four children		Dombrowa	431

ZIEGEL	Menachem, son of Naphtali, his wife Berta, and children		Tarnow	431
ZIEGEL	Moshe, son of Naphtali, his wife Chaya, son Aaron, and daughter Ryvka		Tarnow	431
ZIEGEL	Chana Mindl, daughter of Naphtali, and her husband		Tarnow	431
ZILBER	Ryvka, widow of Moshe Aaron, daughter of Hersh RESSLER	RESSLER		431
ZILBER	Joshua, son of Ryvka, his wife Seryl, nee ETTINGER	ETTINGER		431
ZILBER	Menachem, son of Ryvka, his wife Necha nee DIAMAND, and son	DIAMAND		431
ZILBER	Pinchos, son of Ryvka, his wife Nesia nee HAME.L	HAMEL	Rymanow	431
ZILBERBERG	Menachem, son-in-law of Elazar WEISS, wife Gitel, son Alter Ezra	WEISS		431
ZILBERBERG	Widow of Naphtali Chaim NUTMAN, her son Naphtali, and two daughters	NUTMAN		431
ZILBERMAN	Joseph Bendit, his wife, sons Wolf and Yakov, and two daughters			431
ZILBERMAN	Shlomo, son of Joseph Bendit, his wife Bina nee WEICHSELBAUM-LICHT, their sons Samuel Moshe, and Yakov Hersh (Heschel)	WEICHSELBAUM-LICHT		431

Jews from the Villages in the Vicinity of Strzyzow

The Families: DIAMAND, FELBER, HIRSHFELD, LANDESMAN, REICH, SCHWALB, STEINMETZ, WALLACH, WILNER, ZILBERMAN and others.

The Jews from Kalisz were expelled and killed in Strzyzow

Frysztak

These names were registered by their relatives from Strzyzow

Surname	First name(s)	Page
DEUTCHER	Joseph, his wife Malka, their sons Alexander, Shlomo and Mordechai, daughter Reisel	431
FESSEL	Aaron, son-in-law of Joshua BAUMEL, his wife Chaya, son Shlomo, and daughter Beila	431
SCHENKEL	Israel, his wife and sons: Joseph, Aaron, Naphtali, Gershon, and daughter Hadassah	431
SEIDENFELD	Itzhok, his wife and daughter	432
FRIEDMAN	Sarah	432
TEPER	Sarah	432

Czudec

These names were registered by their relatives from Strzyzow

Surname	First name(s)	Page
BAUMEL	Berish, son of Joshua, and his wife Chava	432
HAUSNER	Hersh, and daughters : Rachel, Chava, and Kreindl Bracha	432
HAUSNER	Samuel Yakov, the son of Hersh, his wife Pearl, son Menachem, and daughters Ryvka and Chana	432

HAUSNER	Israel David and his wife Ryvka	432
RUBENFELD	Menachem Mendel, his wife, son and daughter	432
WEISS	Chaim, his son Elimelech, his wife, son, and daughter	432

[Page 433]

The departed in the Holy Land

On this page I would like to fulfil my duty and pay respect to the people of Strzyzow who passed away and are buried in the Holy Land.

> Michael BIRNBACH, Shlomo, the son of Tzvi Hersh DIAMAND, Menachem Mendel HASENKOPF, his wife Sarah née ADEST. Yacov HASENKOPF, the brother of Menachem, Shlomo Zalman TENZER, his daughter Golda TISHLER, Chaim KALB, his wife Shoshana REISL, Ethel LEV née KANNER (LUTCHA). Reuven Zelig MANDEL, the brothers Baruch and Elazar NUREMBERG, Simcha FEINGOLD, his wife Chana, their son Israel with his wife, Eliezer Yacov KLAPPER, Abraham Itzhok KANNER, his sister Tova BILDER, Chaya Fruma Ryvka RABINOWITZ, Rabbi Baruch I, RABINOWITZ's wife, Shalom SCHWARTZMAN, his wife Sarah née SCHIFF, Pessil SHIMMEL and her sons Abraham and Mordechai, Levi Itzhok SCHIFF, his wife Ryvka née HOROWITZ, Moshe SCHLISSELBERG, Itta HACKER née DIAMAND, granddaughter of Shlomo DIAMAND who died in the United States and according to her will, was buried in Jerusalem and Menachem Felber. Itzhok, the son of Baruch BERGLASS. (His name was added by the translator)
>
> **May their memory be blessed**

[Page 434]

In Memory of our Brothers, the Jews of Strzyzow

The monument

To the Jews of Strzyzow and vicinity who were killed in the ghetto of Rzeszow, in its surrounding area, in the annihilation camp of Belzec and in unknown camps and places, and who did not receive a Jewish burial and surely no gravestone was erected in their memory.

Also, to the Jews who died of natural causes during generations until the Holocaust and were buried in our cemeteries and whose gravestones are no longer in place.

The only monument that was erected in their memory is the plaque which was installed in the cellar of the Holocaust on Mount Zion, Jerusalem by the Organization of the Natives of Strzyzow in Israel.

The Torah Scroll

There is in possession of the Organization of the Natives of Strzyzow, a Torah scroll with a silver crown and a breast–plate which is housed in the Beit Hamidrash of the Rabbi of Holon, Rabbi Baruch Rabinowitz, the grandson of Rabbi Moshe Leib Shapiro, of blessed memory. On the crown and on the breast–plate names of martyrs of Strzyzow are engraved and on the cover of the Torah scroll, a dedication to the memory of the martyrs is also inscribed. The plaque on Mount Zion, the Torah scroll, its crown, the breast–plate and this memorial book are the only monuments that memorialize the people of Strzyzow.

Translator's footnote: The Torah scroll mentioned before was later transferred to the sanctuary of the Hillel Zeitlin religious school in Tel–Aviv. The school promised to observe the annual yahrzeit of the martyrs of Strzyzow by lighting candles, saying Kaddish and studying the Mishnayoth for the martyrs' souls.

May the memory of the Martyrs be blessed forever.

[Page 435]

*The Torah scroll was placed in the shul of the H. Zeitlin Religious School.
In appreciation, the students will observe the Yahrzeit and say Kaddish for the martyrs of Strzyzow.
The memorial plaque was installed in the Holocaust cellar on Mt. Zion in Jerusalem.*

[Page 436]

Memorial prayers conducted by Shlomo Yahalomi at the plaque for the martyrs of Strzyzow

Itzhok Berglass lights the candles during the memorial service for the martyrs

[Page 437]

The memorial service which took place on July 13th, 1966 on Mt. Zion, Jerusalem for the martyrs of Strzyzow.

Shlomo Yahalomi eulogizing the martyrs in the synagogue on Mt. Zion

[Page 438]

The memorial service of Mt. Zion for the martyrs of Stryzow

[Page 439]

Remnants of the Jewry of Stryzow at the memorial plaque on Mt. Zion

[Page 440]

The text of the inscription on the plaque

This monument is a testimony to the martyrs of Strzyzow, Galicia (on the Visloka River) and vicinity who perished and were murdered for the sanctification of the Holy Name in the days of the Holocaust in the years 1939–1945. May G–d avenge their innocent blood.

Their holy memory is preserved in the heart of the survivors of the community and the Jewish people, forever. May their souls be bound in the bond of the living.

The Yahrzeit and Memorial Day is on the 25th day of the month of Tamuz.

The Organization of the Natives of Strzyzow and vicinity

[Page 441]

Remnants of the Community

Natives of Strzyzow throughout the world
by Itzhok Berglass

This article will be very superficial and possibly may contain some inaccuracies because we lacked clear information about our natives who are spread throughout the world. Even in countries where there are large concentrations of our brethren, we did not find anyone to write about people from Strzyzow who settled there. However, this fact does not free us from the obligation of writing an article at the conclusion of this book after having described the town, its inhabitants and the Holocaust in which our Kehillah was wiped out and after which the few remaining survivors have spread into many countries.

Only a few survived from those Jews who lived in Strzyzow until the outbreak of World War II. The majority remained in town when the Germans took control and from those, a few young men who were sent to German labour camps and two young girls on Aryan papers, survived. From the few of our townspeople who escaped East to the territory occupied by the Russians and were not exiled, three people survived: One, on Aryan documents after his family was taken away during his absence and were annihilated somewhere. A second man returned to Strzyzow after the Germans occupied Lwow and survived in a German camp and the third one succeeded to join the Soviet Army. From the army he was transferred to a prison and later into labour camps. He finally reached Eretz Israel. Of the people who illegally returned to Strzyzow during the short Soviet–German peace period, no one survived. The majority of the refugees from Strzyzow in Soviet Russia were exiled to distant places and forced into labour camps. A part of those could not withstand the hard living conditions but the majority of these refugees remained alive. Among them, there is only one family who remained intact: husband, wife and two daughters – the only pre–war family from Strzyzow who is living in Israel.

Natives of Strzyzow live all over the world thanks to the immigration during the fifty years that began in the second half of the previous century until the beginning of the war in 1939.

[Page 442]

The memorial plaque for the martyrs of Strzyzow in Brazil

Memorial plaque for the Holocaust martyrs and heroes who fought for Israel

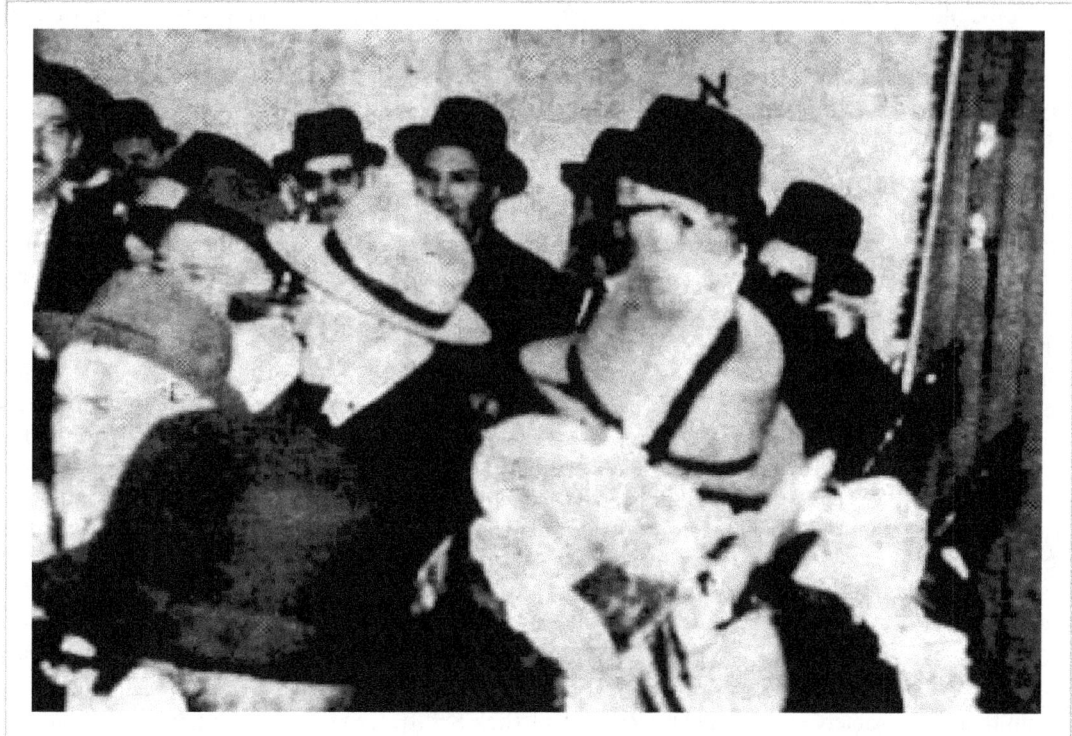

The consecration of the synagogue Machzikei Dat in Sao Paulo, Brazil built by Leib Rosen from Strzyzow

[Page 443]

Most of the immigrants who went to the United States and Germany were mainly single, young men from poverty-stricken families and from the middle class who could not find a place in their parents' home or entrepreneurs who looked for enchantment in the big world. Family people emigrated only after their effort to establish a livelihood failed. For longer periods, they immigrated to the United States and for shorter periods to Germany. They went and returned several times. They left the families in town and sent home money for support.

Entire families or daughters rarely emigrated. In general and until World War I, emigration was not popular. Long-standing families, respected families, were embarrassed to emigrate and even to be supported from such sources. Despite the fact that money does not smell, it did not seem to have the same value as money earned with sweat at home. Also, a dowry of a girl which came from an emigrant did not earn the same respect as the one given by parents who saved it up during many years of hard work and thrift. This situation changed after World War I when many Torah-educated young men began to immigrate to Germany. Young men, scholars, enlightened people and also families who struggled to make a living especially the people who had evacuated from Strzyzow during the Russian occupation, did not return. Reb Leib Eisenberg, a Torah scholar, settled in Vienna. Joseph Wolf, the son-in-law of Menachem Guzik, became rich in his new place. Reb Moshe Itzhok Schimmel, the Hassid who immigrated to Germany, became very wealthy. Reb Hersh Pfeffer, an educated man, owned a printing shop in Strzyzow and, after his departure, there was never another printing shop in town. Reb Chaim Laufer, the scholar and intellectual known for his sweet voice, and others.

After the war, there was a turnabout. Emigration increased. It became natural and people were not ashamed of it anymore. Besides the two emigration places, the United States and Germany, a few also went to Belgium, France, Switzerland, England and South America. Some also went to Upper Silesia which belonged to Poland. Then emigration began to Eretz Israel – every possible way, legally or illegally. Aliyah and emigration continued until the outbreak of World War II.

Israel

At present, there are about one hundred and forty people from Strzyzow in Israel. There are a few families in which both parents came from Strzyzow. However, the majority were single people who got married and established families outside of Strzyzow. There were no cases of Aliyah made by elders or Hassidim to live out their last years in the Holy Land. There are only a few Jews of the older generation: Reb Levi Itzhok Schiff who brought his whole family with him. Reb Shimon Leitner who came by himself bought some property but went back to Strzyzow. Reb Shalom Schwartzman came with his wife Sarah, née Schiff, the daughter of the Rabbi from Niebylec and his grandson Mordechai. They settled in Meah Shearim, Jerusalem. They made Aliyah influenced by the spirit of Zionism without even realizing it. Zionists, pioneers, members of Zionist youth organizations that made Aliyah were mostly single and settled in towns.

[Page 444]

They did not organize into groups or join a Kibbutz. The number of people from Strzyzow in Eretz Israel increased after Hitler's ascendance to power. Then, several families who had immigrated to Germany came to Eretz Israel. Finally, the majority of the Holocaust survivors, particularly those who returned from Russia and also families who survived in the Western countries, came to Eretz Israel after several years of wandering.

During World War II, when the number of people from Strzyzow in Eretz Israel increased, Reb Levi Itzhok, who saved his family by making Aliyah and had been previously an activist in the community of Strzyzow, tried to organize all the Strzyzow natives, as other cities had done. He did not succeed because those who came from Germany claimed that they were German refugees since they had left Strzyzow a long time ago. After the war when the first refugees arrived, mainly those who came from Russia, Reb Levi Itzhok Schiff tried again and this time he succeeded in organizing the Society of Natives of Strzyzow in Israel. The timing was perfect. The new immigrants arrived one by one, found an address where to turn to and get help and guidance. After the establishment of a free loan committee, they were also helped financially. The house of Reb Levi Itzhok, with the help of his wife Ryvka, was open to receive guests from Strzyzow who were in need and he himself exploited his circle of friends to help the immigrants to find living quarters and a job. The nature of Reb Levi Itzhok Schiff was always to befriend people and he therefore organized around him some kind of a committee, mainly of the people who came from Germany who, despite distancing themselves from their native town, were close to him spiritually and he succeeded in influencing them to join the society.

The first committee of the society was headed by Reb Levi Itzhok Schiff. He served as president for about ten years – from 1950 to 1959. His assistant and right-hand man was the secretary Elazar Nuremberg. The committee members during the years were: Shlomo Asher; Pinchos Aloni (Klotz); Michael Birnbach; Itzhok Berglass; the brothers Joseph and Eliezer Gruber;

Menachem Hasenkopf; Shlomo Yahalomi-Diamand; Chaim Kalb; Simcha Langsam; Chana Langerman; Seryl Fishler; Israel Pfeffer; Itzhok Lanner; Tzvi Sternberg and others.

The committee's main action was to establish the organization which exists until this day and its activities consisted of organizing annual memorial services to honour the martyrs of our town, to support needy members and to establish a free loan fund which loaned funds for several years to new immigrants who arrived after the war.

Levi Itzhok led the organization even when the rest of the committee members withdrew one-by-one and even after secretary Elazar Nuremberg passed away. At that time the only activity of the society was the maintenance of the annual memorial services which was helped by Pinchos Aloni and Eliezer Gruber.

In 1958, Reb Levi Itzhok Schiff could not continue to be active anymore. At the annual gathering on 25th Tamuz, 1958, a temporary committee was elected and on 3rd of Tevet, 1959 a general assembly was called during which new leadership was elected.

[Page 445]

The new committee consisted of: Pinchos Aloni; Itzhok Berglass; Eliezer Gruber; Shabtai Hausner; Golda Tishler; Shabtai Hausner; Golda Tishler;Shlomo Yahalomi-Diamand; Chaim Kalb; Simcha Langsam and Seryl Fishler. At the meeting which took place on 11th of Tevet, 1959, I was elected Chairman and Treasurer; Pinchos Aloni secretary and Shlomo Yahalomi were put in charge of caring for the perpetuation of Strzyzow.

At the next assembly, two additional members to the committee were elected: Leah Loos and Joseph Schiff.

This committee is still in existence and is active in the regular activity of the society. We settled the financial problem and arranged a thorough registration of all natives of Strzyzow. The Free Loan Committee ceased to exist by itself but in time of need we supported the needy. We successfully intervened and prevented the demolition of the shul in Strzyzow and also initiated the removal of the gravestones from the movement in the market place of Strzyzow. We were helped by the Polish-Israeli Friendship Society during the friendly period. At that time, public opinion was still a factor and our appeal to the Polish Consul, Mr. Antony Bido and to other public figures was a big help. The main activity of the committee was devoted to the perpetuation of our martyrs, our community in general, so that it should not sink into oblivion after a generation.

Shlomo Yahalomi, who was responsible for the perpetuation, arranged with the help of Tuvia Weiden, the brother of Kalman Weiden from Strzyzow, the installation of a memorial plaque in memory of our martyrs and community in the Holocaust Cellar on Mount Zion in Jerusalem. On the plaque, the established annual Memorial Day, 25th of Tamuz, is inscribed. The annual memorial services takes place on this day. Several times the services took place near the plaque. In spite of the fact that we are small in numbers, we are still able to arrange memorial services, give expression of sorrow and demonstrate our spiritual bond with the martyrs on our own. Reb Chaim Kalb, of blessed memory, excelled in this endeavour until his last day. And Reb Shlomo Yahalomi with his capabilities plays an important role in fulfilling his duty.

The pivotal event in the perpetuation activities was the publication of this memorial book in memory of Strzyzow and its vicinity. There were many obstacles. First, we were forced to overcome the apathy and doubt of our own power even among those capable colleagues to participate in writing the book and to gather materials. We also needed to obtain a great sum of money in order to publish such a big book, rich in content for such a small Society. (Strzyzow had only three hundred and fifty Jewish families). Help from abroad was very small. There is no organized Strzyzow Society worthy of consideration anywhere, not even in the United States. The technical preparations, the difficult work of proof-reading and editing, was all done during several meetings of the editorial committee and then the burden fell on two persons – the writer of this article and Shlomo Yahalomi to successfully bring the publishing to the end.

The Strzyzow Society in Israel is the most organized group, better than in any other country. The natives of Strzyzow, including the second generation, are involved and even excel in the life of our Homeland.

[Page 446]

Shlomo Yahalomi authored two books on Torah subjects: Pninei Torah and Pninei Avot which were published in two editions and were very well accepted in religious circles. Teachers in religious schools are often quoting these books in their lectures about Judaism. He also writes articles in newspapers and magazines. Reb Shlomo Yahalomi is active in the National Religious Party and charitable institutions. He also gives speeches and lectures. Moshe Mussler, who was a Hebrew teacher in Belgium, translated books in Israel from French and Flemish into Hebrew. Rabbi Baruch Rabinowitz not only serves as Rabbi of the City of Holon but also takes part in the spiritual life of Israel by speaking and lecturing. The writer Ryvka Gurfein, née Steinmetz, and the journalist Zev Schiff, the son of Mordechai, grandson of Reb Levi Itzhok, are famous and have received several awards. One can find people from our town in kibbutzim, colonies, working in institutions, in commerce and trade, also in academics, from elementary to high school and higher learning institutions. You will also find people from Strzyzow in the staff of officers in the military and police force.

Footnote of the translator: All the activities listed in the above article took place in the sixties. At present, the Strzyzow Society no longer exists due to the passage of the majority of its members to their eternal rest. In fact, in 1988, less than a minyan showed up for the memorial service.

The United States of America

As I remarked in the beginning of this chapter, it would have been desirable that someone who lived in the United States and knows more about the lives of the people from Strzyzow in the U.S. would have written about them. Since no one came forward, I am forced to write about them myself. Even though it might not be completely free of errors.

The immigration to the United States began at the end of the nineteenth century, mainly unmarried men with very few young women and even fewer families. The first immigrants soon adapted themselves to the American lifestyle but did not break off contact with their town of origin, especially not with their relatives who remained in Strzyzow. In time, a Society of Natives of Strzyzow was established which was headed by wealthy people who succeeded to climb up to the higher ranks both socially and materially. However, the inspirer of the society was the Secretary. The first Secretary, who was well-known to us, particularly for his vigorous activity for the people of our town, was Samuel Mussler. On behalf of the organization, he extended help to individuals and charitable institutions in our town in the period between the two World Wars. Tremendous was his help to the remnants who had survived the Holocaust in Europe and those that had returned from Russia. In the small archive left in his legacy, there were many letters and pleas for help from the people of Strzyzow, many thank-you letters for help extended by him and receipts for packages he had sent. I also heard that he had helped new immigrants, people from Strzyzow who had arrived in the United States, after the Holocaust.

[Page 447]

The Secretary of the Strzyzow Society in the United States. Mr. Samuel Mussler

Itzhok (Irving) Lev meeting David Ben Gurion

[Page 448]

He also helped the people from Frysztak, the birth place of his wife. After he passed away, Tzvi Unger, who until then was his assistant, took over and became Chairman and Secretary. He was the representative of Strzyzow in the United States at a time when the community in Strzyzow did not exist anymore. The American Society helped the society of Israel very much during the leadership of Reb Levi Itzhok Schiff.

While he was alive, Mr. Mussler had broached the idea of publishing a memorial book for the martyrs of Strzyzow. He collected some funds for this purpose and Tzvi Unger continued to carry on with the idea. However, their approach, financial and organizational, was not practical, and there were no competent people able to put the idea into action. Subsequently, the funds collected for publishing the book came into our treasury.

After Tzvi Unger passed away the organization in the U.S.A. became even weaker despite the activity of Jacob Diller who had also been a committee member before. At that time, after the war, a few survivors from Strzyzow arrived and among them were: Heschel Diamand, the last presiding officer of the Kehillah in Strzyzow; Ben Zion Kalb, the hero who had saved Jews especially children from the Nazi claws; Rabbi Shlomo Chaim Horowitz, a grandson of Rabbi Moshe Leib Shapiro from Strzyzow (he passed away not too long ago), and others. People to whom we solicited and who had cooperated with financial help, with material and the distribution of this book were: Jacob Diller (he recently passed away); Heschel Diamand and Reb Shlomo Nuremberg. These are the last members of the Natives of Strzyzow Society in the United States. They made an effort to help us in our work but did not succeed in reviving the Society of the Natives of Strzyzow, like other city organizations, despite the fact that the people from our shtetl would have gladly accepted the renewal of such an organization. Not having such an organization, they joined the societies of their spouses who came from other cities in our vicinity. There are individual reasons. Also, conditions in the United States are not the same as they are in Israel. There are very few left of the first generation of immigrants. The American lifestyle and the great distances between the cities and even in New York, relatives do not meet too often. All these are factors in not being able to organize. We found direct contact with many of the people from Strzyzow and sent them the memorial book.

Of their past and present situation, we have very little information. We do not know their economic situation, who succeeded and who did not. I am writing here of the activity of two people from Strzyzow who are known to me; one because he is my cousin.

The first person is Menachem Tzvi Baim, of blessed memory from Frysztak, the husband of Sarah Dembitzer, the daughter of Reb David from Strzyzow. He was a rich and generous man, open-handed to charity but his main deed was his rescue work. When the Nazi took the rule of Germany in their hands, he rescued from there many families who had immigrated to Germany from Strzyzow, by arranging entry visas. He turned his house into a transition place, provided jobs and helped them adapt to the new land.

[Page 449]

The second man was my cousin, Itzhok (Irving) Lev who carried my grandfather's name, Itzhok Berglass. He became very successful but he had not forgotten what he had learned in his youth, his Zionism, and he energetically distributed many Israel bonds. He brought huge amounts to Israel to develop the land and he therefore met with all the members of the Israeli government.

Canada

There are a few people from Strzyzow who live in Canada. I think that the first immigrant to that country was Sheindl Ameis with her sons Yacov and Eliezer and daughters Esther and Ryvka. She immigrated in the years between World War I and World War II. At present, residing in Canada are the above-mentioned family Ameis, the Holocaust survivors Rabbi Israel Frenkel, a son-in-law of Reb Shlomo Diamand from Zyznow, his son Samuel Nachum and their relatives Hena and Gita Propper, grandchildren of Reb Shlomo Diamand; the grandchildren of Reb Nathaniel Schlisselberg. Also, Israel, the son of Reb Moshe Pinchovski lives there too. The brothers Abraham and Israel Kraut; the sons of Reb Yehuda and probably Abraham Reicher. Sheindl Ameis passed away recently. We also heard that Dr. Leon Deutch, the grandson of Wolf Deutch lived there but now only his widow with her family live somewhere in Canada. No more information about our brethren in Canada was made available to me.

Latin America

I have no information about natives from Strzyzow in Latin American countries except for Brazil. However, there is hearsay that in Argentina a granddaughter of Reb Fishel Felder and her daughter Hena with her family as well as Sheps, the son-in-law of Reb Yacov Greenblatt who emigrated alone as his family had perished in Strzyzow, now reside here. In Uruguay Rose Gans lives, the daughter of Reb Michael Leib Last, with her family and her sister-in-law, Shprintza, the daughter of Reb Mordechai Rosenbaum, the offspring of Reb Hersh Feit from his daughter Sarah and Meir Kornreich, a grandson of Reb Shlomo Diamand from Zyznow. In Venezuela, Yacov Adest resides with his sister Bina, the children of Reb Ephraim Samuel Adest. Menachem Mendel Kanner, a son of Israel who escaped from the Nazi died in one of these countries.

Brazil

There is a group of people from Strzyzow who reside in Brazil. The first who arrived there was Joshua, the son of Reb Moshe Schefler with his wife Batyah, the daughter of Reb Mordechai Mendel Schefler.

[Page 450]

The interior of the synagogue

The Synagogue "Machzikei Dat" in Sao Paulo, Brazil

[Page 452]

    He brought over his relatives, his brother Abraham with his wife Ryvka and later, Abraham Moshe Felder, the son of Reb Fishel Felder, with his wife Sarah who was the sister of the Schefler brothers and, after the Nazi came to power, Moshe Felder's sister, Tzipora Mohrer with her family emigrated there from Germany. After World War II, the survivors of the Holocaust, the brothers Itzhok Leib and Samuel Rosen and their sister Pearl Strongerovski also immigrated to Brazil. They are all cousins of Moshe Felder. Moshe's father was disappointed with his son because he had refused to study Torah. So he taught him a trade as a "punishment". However, being in a strange land, he returned the respect to his father by behaving like a son of a Hassid. He lived in a forsaken little town three hundred miles from Sao Paulo and he turned his house into a central Jewish home, bought a Torah scroll and turned on room into a prayer house. He and his wife fulfilled the mitzvah of hospitality to strangers and the lonely Jews from that area come to their home for the High Holidays. About fifty people used to gather in his house. He died young and his wife Sarah with her sons left Brazil and settled in Kfar Sold, Israel. They did not evacuate the place even in the dangerous days of the Six-Day War.

    After the war, Rabbi Baruch J. Rabinowitz settled in Brazil. He is the grandson of Rabbi Moshe Leib Shapiro from Strzyzow. He came to Brazil via Eretz Israel and served as Rabbi in Sao Paulo. While there, the strong opposition by Yechiel Rosen toward Rabbi Moshe Leib's son, Shlomo, during the rift between Sandz and Sadigor was forgotten and the grandchildren of Reb Yechiel Rosen befriended the grandson of Rabbi Moshe Leib as natives of the same city. Later, Rabbi Baruch J. Rabinowitz left Brazil and immigrated to Israel at the same time that young Samuel Rosen also immigrated to Israel. Itzhok Leib Rosen, Samuel's older brother, lives in Brazil where he has become very successful and is active in the Jewish community, especially in its religious life. This activity, to which he devotes much time, energy and financial support, gives spiritual satisfaction to his soul which years to make Aliyah. Lately, thanks to Itzhok Leib Rosen's effort and large donations, the Synagogue Machzikei Dat was built in "Bam Netira" a section in Sao Paulo. It was previously housed in a rented building. In the synagogue, a plaque in memory of the martyrs of Strzyzow was installed. And so, another monument was added in memory of the holy martyrs of our town in the distant land, Brazil.

Itzhok Borenstein, the editor of the Yiddish newspaper "Der Nayer Moment", after touring the synagogue Machzikei Dat, wrote in an article that Sao Paulo became richer with a new shul. The shul is not big but very beautiful. Her name is Machzikei Dat. On Rosh Hashanah, the prayers are led with good chanting and the shofar was blown by Reb Itzhok Leib Rosen, the founder of the shul. Itzhok Leib was also the biggest contributor to this memorial book.

In the thirties, Simon, the son of Wolf Deutch, escaped from Germany via France to Brazil and there he passed away. Yacov Tzvi Millbauer on whose estate near Strzyzow a big group of Mizrachi chalutzim received their training, also lives in Brazil. There is rumour that Joel, the son of Hersh Leib Fass resides in Brazil with his family.

[Page 453]

Remnants of the Community in Europe

Poland

Poland is our native land. At present, only three people born in Strzyzow live there despite the fact that almost all Holocaust survivors returned to Poland immediately after their liberation. Also, those who returned from Russia, except one who arrived in Palestine from Russia via Teheran, passed Poland on their journey to the wide world. In general, they did not stay too long in Poland. The majority liquidated whatever there remained to be liquidated and hurriedly left illegally. Some tried to establish themselves and left a little later or waited for a more comfortable way to escape into the Displaced Persons Camps in Germany. Only Joseph Weinberg became a communal activist.

As I wrote in the article "The Holocaust and the Aftermath", he was active in helping his brothers in Auschwitz, according to the testimony of eye witnesses. Joseph Weinberg began his activity before the end of the war soon after he had jumped from a death train which transported the Auschwitz inmates west to places that were not yet liberated.

In February 1945, Weinberg became the head of the Jewish Committee in Upper Silesia which was re–occupied by the Polish and Soviet Armies. His main task was to protect German Jews and half Jews from mixed marriages who had suffered from the Nazi and, who now, when they came out from hiding, were pursued by the Soviets who considered them to be Germans. He established an old age home and children's home and, in 1945, he illegally transported all the children via Romania to Eretz Israel.

For this activity, which was in opposition to the official policy of the Polish government, he was fired. But it did not stop him from being active. Together with Rabbi Kahane, the Chief Rabbi in the Polish Army, he founded the Union of Religious Communities in Poland and served as its leader until 1946, when he left Poland.

During that period, Joseph Weinberg was also active in discovering and redeeming Jewish children from gentile hands and, beginning at the end of 1945, he shipped them to England and to Sweden.

In the action of rescuing children, he was helped by our landsman, Menachem Mendel, the son of Zalman Diamand from Wysoka near Strzyzow. Menachem Diamand who had arrived earlier and settled in Katowice where he worked and lived before the war knew the system of the temporary Polish rulers. He also helped individuals who arrived from Russia penniless and were without a roof over their heads. The three people who remained in Poland were: Dr. Chaim Frenkel, a lawyer; Dr. Eisner, the son of Yacov Eisner and Dr. Abraham, the son of Israel Adler, a grandson of the assistant Rabbi, Alter Ezra Seidman.

Dr. Frenkel, whose wife and daughters were taken away while he was at work, left Poland after the war and reached Constantia in Romania to make Aliyah to Eretz Israel. There he changed his mind even though in his youth, while he had studied in the university, he was an active Zionist.

[Page 454]

He realized that he was getting on in years, did not speak Hebrew, etc. At the end, he returned to Poland and his adopted Polish name of the Nazi period. At the beginning, he was successful in his law practice, helping the returnees liquidate their properties and now, if he is still alive, he probably lives a denigrated life like the rest of the remaining Jews in Poland.

Germany

Once, Germany was the second destination of emigrants after the United States. After the rise of Hitler, almost everyone left. A part was expelled to Poland and concentrated in the Zbonszin camp on the Polish border. In that camp, Menachem Manes Friedman's wife died.

Later, all the refugees in that camp dispersed throughout Poland and a few families came back to Strzyzow, their birthplace. A few families came directly from Germany to Strzyzow. They all perished in the Holocaust. The rest of the people who immigrated to Germany came to Eretz Israel, or immigrated to the United States, South America, France and a few children to England. A few families remained in Germany. There was also a case in which the husband escaped to Palestine leaving behind his wife and children having no idea that the Nazi would annihilate innocent people and surely not women and children. Their names are on the list of martyrs in this book. From those who remained in Germany, only one person survived, Yechezkiel, the son of Nathaniel Schlisselberg. He went through Auschwitz, Buchenwald, Scheinbeck, Oranienburg and others. His son was sent before the war to England with a group of Jewish children. His wife Chana, née Rubin and daughter Freda perished in the camps.

After the war, people from Strzyzow appeared again in Germany. These were survivors from camps, those who came out from hiding and those who came back from Russia. The way to the free world was through the German Displaced Persons Camps. The camps were administered by our own people. Many Jewish parties became active again. Especially outstanding was Shlomo Diamand who became a member of the Central Committee of the Mizrachi and Hapoel Hamizrachi. Munich became the central place for all displaced persons and for all active Zionist parties. Munich was also the capital of the American Occupational Forces. Shlomo Diamand was also a member of the editorial staff of the party gazette: "The Yiddishe Shtimme". Unlike in Poland, none of the people from Strzyzow remained in Germany.

I am informed that at present, two or maybe three families whose origin were from Strzyzow, now reside in Germany. One is Dr. Elchanan Lehrman, the Chief Rabbi of West Berlin and professor of Roman philology and its Jewish influence in Wurzburg. He is a grandson of Reb Moshe Krantzler and, in his childhood, he was raised in his grandfather's house. He succeeded in developing his talents after immigrating with his parents to Germany. After completing his many studies, mainly Jewish knowledge, he lectured in the universities of Lucerne and Bar Ilan. He also served as Chief Rabbi of Luxemburg and was made an honorary citizen by the Duchess. Thanks to his many books and articles about Judaism which were well received by the critics, he reached his present position.

[Page 455]

His wife is a writer and polyglot who manages the Language Department in the European Parliament which is located in Strasburg–Luxemburg. A second man from Strzyzow is Yekutiel Zalman (Sali) Feit, the son of Samuel Feit, a scholar who was the son–in–law of Yechiel Rosen. About the third man, I have no clear information. I only heard that he lives in Dortmund alone and discreet about his Jewishness. His name is Mendel–Max Laufer, the son of Reb Chaim Laufer from Strzyzow.

England

Few people from Strzyzow live in England. Moshe Yacov, the son of Michael Leib Last and his brother Abraham live there with their families. Hada, the daughter of Leib Eisenberg and Bat Sheva Weichselbaum, the daughter of Alter Yacov, also live there. They settled there before the war. Some say that Joel, the son of Yacov Greenblatt, escaped from Germany to the United States and afterwards immigrated to England where he now lives with his family.

Belgium

A few families from Strzyzow lived in this country until World War II. Moshe Mussler worked as a Hebrew teacher in the Tachkemoni School. He later brought over his brother Joel and his sisters, Sarah and Leah. They got married and lived there until the Holocaust. In addition to the Mussler family, David Goldberg with his family and a relative, Shlomo Turteltaub, also lived in Belgium. Furthermore, the son of Joseph Hersh, Joel Rosen and Yacov Itzhok Weber, a son of one of the rabbis from Brzozow who married the granddaughter of Pearl Gertner from Strzyzow. One of the anomalies in Galicia from the days of the rift between the Hassidim of Sandz and the Hassidim of Ryzhin–Sadigora was that such a little town like Brzozow had two rabbis; one general rabbi and the second especially for the Sadigora Hassidim. Joel Mussler and his sisters, Joel Rosen with his wife and Yacov Weber with his family all perished in the Holocaust. However, David Goldberg and his son Joseph died of natural causes.

At present in Belgium the rest of the Goldberg family reside, as well as Chaim Last and Leib, the son of Pinchos Adler, a great–grandson of the assistant rabbi Alter Ezra Seidman. Some say that Shlomo Turteltaub who escaped to the United States returned to Belgium. How they are doing there I don't know. Also, it is unknown to me if other people from Strzyzow live there.

France

To France, only a few single people immigrated. In 1930, Kalman Yacov Schiff arrived there when he returned from his unsuccessful voyage to Brazil and brought over his entire family. Later, his brothers Berish and Mordechai followed him. Then, a few immigrated directly from Strzyzow and also some people from Strzyzow who had lived in Germany came to France after Hitler's ascendance to power.

[Page 456]

Finally, a few survivors of the Holocaust and refugees who came back from Russia settled here. Just before World War II and even during the war, many of our brothers came to Eretz Israel. Of those who remained, a few perished in the Holocaust and some survived in France and Switzerland. During the Vichy rule in France, my teacher Moshe Nuremberg passed away and lately Eisik Mintz. Nathan Hasenkopf, the son of Reb Chaim Hasenkopf, the grandfather of the translator of this book, survived the Holocaust with his family by being hidden by a farmer in a rural village. Nathan Hasenkopf passed away recently but his wife and his daughter Nicole live in Dijon, France. His son Maurice with his wife lives in Israel. At present those residing in France are: Madeline Bren, née Mintz; Joseph Groskopf and his wife Leah, née Brauner (she recently came to Israel); Joseph Weinberg; Shlomo Wilner from Lutcza near Strzyzow; his brother–in–law Hirschfeld; Yechezkiel Winer; Reisl née Landesman; Yechezkiel Nuremberg with this sister; Menachem Mendel Kandel–Nuremberg with his sister; Esther Schneider; Eliyahu Yehuda Kanner; Pinchos Schimmel; Berish Schiff; and the children of Kalman Yacov Schiff. The people from Strzyzow in France are not organized but they keep close, close than those in the United States because the country is smaller and the majority live in Paris. Menachem Kandel–Nuremberg helped us to distribute this memorial book. I have no information on their social or material status. They seem to be average people. Outstanding among them is Joseph Weinberg who succeeded in business and is participating in Jewish communal life and Zionist activity. At the beginning when he arrived in Paris after the war, he was General Secretary of the Zionists and editor of its newspaper. Since 1965, he has also served as General Secretary of the German concentration camp inmates. He has published books in Yiddish and French on subjects of the Holocaust.

Switzerland

There are only three families from Strzyzow origin who reside in Switzerland. Mrs. Hena Riger–Lichtig from the Weichselbaum family and her daughter Rosa and family. Despite her old age, Hena Riger is very active in charitable institutions and also supports Yeshivot and charitable institutions in Israel. During World War II, Helen Hindler, the daughter of Yacov Langsam from Strzyzow, the translator's sister, found refuge in Switzerland with her husband after having escaped from Vienna. After the war, they immigrated to the United States and settled in Los Angeles. Also residing in Switzerland is Moshe Yacov the son of Reb Yeshayahu Mandel who at one time divided his residence between Italy and Switzerland. He visits his relatives in Israel annually and he enjoys the Israeli atmosphere which he lacks in his strange land.

[Page 457]

Italy

There were some people from Strzyzow, survivors and returnees from Russia who stopped temporarily in Italy on their way to the Holy Land, but none of them settled here. Most of the people made Aliyah and the rest immigrated to the United States. At present, only one man from Strzyzow lives here: Dr. Menachem Goldberg, the son of Fishel. He studied medicine in Italy when the war broke out. He became a member of the Italian Anti–Nazi underground and survived the Holocaust. Goldberg came to Israel but went back to the country where he had lived for so many years.

Austria

Almost nowhere in the old Austro–Hungarian Empire did people from Strzyzow reside except in Galicia and Vienna. One of my cousins lived in Hungary in the town of Munkatch. Chaim Kalb remained after World War I in the city of Teplice, Czechoslovakia where he was very prosperous. However, after the ascendance of Hitler, he came to the Holy Land and two years ago, he passed away. Leml, the son of Getzel Landesman, settled in Vienna before World War I. Eta Hacker, the granddaughter of Shlomo Diamand from Zyznow and Gitel Tuchman, the daughter of Mendel Guzik, also lived in Vienna. All the evacuees from Strzyzow who came to Vienna returned home after the war. Rabbi Nechemiah Shapiro remained for some years in Vienna but return to Strzyzow in the early thirties. Reb Leib Eisenberg, Joseph Wolf and later, Yacov Diller came to Vienna after World War I. Also, Moshe Brauner went to Vienna and worked for Yacov Diller.

Yacov Diller escaped to the United States. Moshe Brauner's family perished. He was the only survivor. He came to Israel and later left for the United States where he worked again for Yacov Diller. However, he passed away a short time later. Eta Hacker also escaped to the United States where she died and her body was buried in Israel. The whereabouts of Leib Eisenberg is unknown. At this time, the following people live in Vienna with their families: Naphtali Eisenberg; Fishel Adler and his wife who are the grandchildren of the Assistant Rabbi from Strzyzow, and the above–mentioned Gitel Tuchman.

This brings us to the end of the memorial book of the Strzyzow Kehillah.

One of the goals that we strived to achieve was the perpetuation of the memory of the martyrs of our Kehillah. We are confident that this book will also be a family heirloom in every family that originated in Strzyzow, and future generations will read it and will be impressed to read about their ancestors, about the honest, faultless and gentle–spirited Jews that lived among gentiles and lost their lives in martyrdom. The reader will feel close to them and will also hand down this book to the next generation. And, when a book about the Polish Jewry will be written, we will have made a sizeable contribution and, thanks to our book, our Jewish shtetl whose memory is so dear to us will not be forgotten.

[Page 458]

To the conclusion of this book
by Shlomo Yahalomi

Upon the completion of this memorial book of Strzyzow, what can I say? Had we merited having Strzyzow and all other holy European communities remain intact, and we would have written a book about life in those communities, we would have been required to say the blessing: "Shechiyanu" at the completion of the book. However, to our great sorrow, when the reason for writing this book is the destruction and disappearance of our shtetl and the other holy communities, we were forbidden to say the blessing. But just as we are required to praise the Lord for the good, so are we required to praise Him for the bad, regardless of the great pain and sorrow in our hearts. Let us be thankful to G–d that we did survive to write the history of our town and its children.

It would be a violation of the truth if we would have claimed that we wrote everything that should have been written about our shtetl. However, G–d is our witness that we did everything possible not to abuse anyone, not the community and no individual. I hope that we fulfilled our obligation. If we failed, it was not our fault. It could be because we were not capable or because we did not have enough books and documents from the previous generations. We took it upon ourselves to do it because there was no one else to do it.

Although the purpose of writing this book was to describe the past on our shtetl and the perpetuation of her untainted martyrs, we also found it necessary to write about the present, about the survivors who live in Israel and other countries. For this benevolence, we are surely obligated to thank the Creator that he left a remnant of our shtetl. Those who survived the Holocaust are duty–bound and obligated to remember those who perished. The images of our ancestors should remain before our eyes and we should follow their brightness all of our lives and act and perform good deeds as they did so that our ancestors would not be ashamed of their grandchildren.

It is true that it is hard to reach their stature. Our sages said that if our forbearers were angels, we should be human. But, in any case, we are not allowed to distance ourselves too far from the ways of our parents. A person should always ask himself: "When will my deeds be equal to my parents' deeds?" Commented Rabbi Yacov from Sadigora that it means: "When will my deed reach the quality of my parents' deeds and not distance ourselves from them". It is clear that we survived not so that we should, Heaven forbid, distance ourselves from our parents, but to continue the chain of previous generations; to secure the continuity of a nation which lives by the principles of justice and progress – true justice and progress – not spoken idly but the justice of our Prophets, teachers of all generations.

And if the subject is the future, we should realize that as a result of the Holocaust and the great destruction that befell our People, the centre of our existence moved to our Holy Land, the State of Israel, the source of our pride and hope.

[Page 459]

If truth be told, thanks to our yearnings of thousands of years that are expressed in our prayers three times daily, "May our eyes behold they return in mercy to Zion", we preserved in our hearts and beings the love, longings and attachment to Zion. We created the Zionist Movement, the political and the practical return to Zion, the rebuilding of a big part of our historical Eretz Israel. It is also true that the biggest reason for the declaration and the recognition by all nations of the State of Israel was the great destruction and annihilation of our people by the murderous Nazi hands. Even the wicket amongst the world leaders were not able to ignore the mass destruction that befell the Jewish people in Europe, the savagery of it and therefore, were forced to agree to compensate the victims by voting for the establishment of the state of Israel.

True, the hand of Providence was involved. But it was done with miracles wrapped in natural appearance. The "Great Hand" of the Master of the Universe made it happen for the merits of the martyrs and the sacrifices of the fathers and children. By rebuilding the land and fighting for its independence, we lived to see the establishment of Israel which is the beginning of the complete Messianic Redemption.

Since the destruction of the Holy Temple, two tremendous events in Jewish history occurred in our times: the Holocaust and the Salvation. As much as the destruction was in colossal proportions and beyond anyone's imagination, so was the miraculous salvation beyond our expectations. The fact that the resolution of the United Nations to divide Palestine was passed by two–thirds of its members, and was accepted by the majority of the Zionist leaders, seemed entirely impossible to achieve.

If the Arabs would have also agreed to this plan, we would not have been able to live and exist in our land. (The area being so small). They would have sabotaged us on every step. Our conquest of the Arabs in the wars and the many wonders and miracles has all exceeded our expectations and hopes. The Blessed Name has performed miracles and kindnesses for us at every step. The refusal by the Arabs to divide the country, their subsequent defeat, the hundreds of thousands fleeing in panic from the land, is surely a cause of praise to emanate from our mouths: "Were our mouths filled with song as the sea, and our tongue with ringing praise as the roaring waves... we would still be unable to thank the Lord our G–d".

All that was written above could actually have been the finale of our book if... If this book would have been written before the Six–Day War. But something else happened. Great, wonderful, fearful occurrences took place. Great in their proportions, both qualitative and quantitative, greater even than the ones that we have already told here. It is fitting here to tell what Rashi told his grandson, the Rashbam. He confessed that if he would have had time, he would have written a brand new commentary on the Bible considering the things that happen daily. The kindness of G–d that surrounds us and the signs of Messianic Salvation which continue to appear before our eyes, demand from us to change from time–to–time the content of our writings because they become outdated. (For instance: the end of the article written by Ami Feingold in this book – "They were buried on Mount Olives and no one visits their graves because it is located on the other side of the border".

[Page 460]

Now Mount Olives is liberated. More so, whatever happened in the Six–Day War overshadows everything that happened in the War of Independence. The early miracles are pale when compared to the later miracles. The windows in Heaven opened widely and we saw the revelation of Godliness in the holy war. Our generation will tell the next generation not only about the wonders and the miracles but also about the heroism and sacrifice for which there is no comparison in the entire world. The greatest wonder is, according to the testimony of the Chief of the victory, Itzhok Rabin, that the crown of victory belongs mainly to simple soldiers many of whom in their daily lives seem to be modest young men. In the Six–Day War they became lions and even stronger. And those who in peace–time were men of questionable character suddenly turned into idealists and gave their souls for the people and the homeland.

Should we not repeat the words of the Baal Shem Tov? "Happy are the people who know the joyful sound". How good it is for a people that the ordinary soldier knows how to lead a war – not only the general!... That is what happened in the war for our independence. "Who bore these to us?" How did this happen? That children of persecuted and tormented Jews, pursued for thousands of years and who were a synonym of cowardice – how did these children become heroes and destroy so many better armed armies? Of course, everyone has an "explanation". It was natural. But, a very important reason has to be added, and maybe this was the core? G–d the Almighty helped us. It was true that our children and brothers fought heroically. Everyone at his post with such incomparable devotion. However, the most powerful drive was the Holocaust. The Tragedy. And, because of the Holocaust, our children fought the way they did and because of the Holocaust, the Almighty helped us.

Let us have a clear understanding about what we said before: The great misfortune that happened in our generation – the vision of the annihilation of six million Jews in such a gruesome way – stood before the eyes of our soldiers – the heroes. Everyone saw before him the six million martyrs. They also saw what other nations, the bad and the "good" ones did for us. Steadfast was their determination. It will never happen again! No more Auschwitz! Not in our generation or in the future generations. No! We will not be led like sheep to the slaughter ever again. Jewish blood will not be cheap anymore! A high price will have to be paid for it. The free–killing of Jews has ended. We will fight the enemy and even if, Heaven forbid, a Jew will die, it will be expensive. That was the decision. No more abandonment. This has brought forth the heroic deeds of our soldiers – to achieve the astounding and absolute victory.

This was one aspect of the victory. The second aspect was that the Almighty too has decided that no more will his children be abandoned to savage beasts!... Even though we strive to understand and explain, the painful question which torments our brains is – why? Why did G–d do it? Why did G–d allow the slaughter of his people? And there is no answer that could make it clear to us. One thing is clear though and which nobody can deny – G–d gave us the victory in the war against the Arabs as partial compensation for the destruction of the house of Israel during Hitler's rule.

[Page 461]

It is also true that for the merits of the Holocaust and for the holy devotion of our children, we did merit such a tremendous victory. Miracle and nature walked hand–in–hand and brought us the salvation. And, I also want to point out that the biggest miracle was that we did not rely on miracles.

At the conclusion of this book, we would like to declare that G–d's kindness has not yet ended. It is not the end of the salvation and consolation that G–d has in store for us. Only the blind and the deaf are not able to see or hear that the voice of G–d is power, the voice of G–d is splendour. His strong hand will lead us to the complete redemption. It is worthwhile to recollect the story which is told about Rabbi Levi Itzhok from Berditchev, of blessed memory. Every year, after reciting the Lamentations on Tisha B'Av, he threw away the lamentation book to be buried in the cemetery among the unusable letters. He said: "Heaven forbid that we should need them next year. It would mean that we do not believe in the coming of the Messiah soon". The writer of these lines would like to say the same thing. Until we will have this book bound and distributed to the people of Strzyzow, the Holy Messiah will arrive and we will merit the complete redemption in our days. Amen.

Tel–Aviv, the month of Nisan, the month of Redemption. 1968.

[Page 462]

Update on Strzyzow

This letter was sent to me, the translator of this book, by my childhood colleague, Mr. Ephraim Shpalter, the grandson of the Assistant Rabbi of Strzyzow.

Mr. Shpalter lives in Israel. He received the letter in April, 1987 from Mr. Adam Kluska in Strzyzow, in response to a letter that was written by Mr. Shpalter to the city authorities in Strzyzow.

From/ Adam Kluska
Strzyzow 38–100
29 Tolnove Street.

Revered Mr. Ephraim Shpalter, Israel.

Your letter addressed to the City Hall in Strzyzow was brought to my attention since I am Mayor of the City and also Secretary of the Fraternity of the City of Strzyzow.

I was glad to be able to fulfil, if only partially, the request from a past resident of Strzyzow. Enclosed you will find copies of photographs from 1930. A picture of the second grade elementary school; the school that you attended and a group picture from 1928 of the Jewish Community Leaders in Strzyzow with the Rabbi as well as a landmark view with the shul in it. I will also give some information concerning the Jewry of our city. I hope these pictures will serve as a modest souvenir to you since, as I understand it, you have none.

The information about the Jewry in Strzyzow is as follows: The shuls in Strzyzow, Czudec and Niebylec (Czudec and Niebylec were nearby communities) have remained intact as a perpetuation of Jewish culture, despite the storms of the war. We remodelled them and made some interior changes and they now serve as libraries. In the shul of Niebylec, the whole interior was remodelled and it looks very nice. The shul in Strzyzow was also remodelled and the painting of the "Leviathan" on the ceiling above the bimah was completely restored. It is now serving as a rich library with which we pride ourselves. However, the shul in Frysztak was destroyed by the Germans at the beginning of the occupation. At that time, the Germans tormented the Jews in different ways. They beat them, killed them for the smallest infraction, shot at them, robbed everything they owned and restricted their movements. The Germans forced the Jews to do hard, physical labour and the Jews were required to wear the start of David on their clothes. If not, they were threatened with death.

In the winter of 1942, the occupation authorities in Rezszow demanded that the Jews hand over all furs and warm clothing which they needed for their soldiers on the Eastern front. That is how the Jews became abandoned and unprotected by any law. Their destiny was in German hands.

[Page 463]

In the days of June 24, 25 and 26, 1942 the Germans expelled 1355 Jews to the Rzeszow ghetto and from there, they were transferred to the annihilation camp in Belzec. At the same time, the Jews from nearby towns of Czudec and Niebylec were also expelled.

In the summer of 1942, the Jews from Frysztak and Wisznowa were brought to the forest near Jaslo and killed by the Nazi. A monument in their memory was erected at that place.

Poles hiding a Jew were threatened with a death sentence. In spite of that fact and thanks to the help of a few Polish families, a few Jewish individuals were rescued and left Strzyzow after the war.

The Investigation Commission of War Crimes and collaboration with the Germans took testimony from witnesses on the dreadful deeds of these criminals but the results of the investigation and the destiny of the criminals are unknown.

The dreadful and brutal actions of those individuals linger in our memories to this day and we cannot reconcile with the thoughts that such people will not be apprehended and punished.

In 1967, a Fraternity Society and a museum were established in Strzyzow. The memorabilia which we gathered is still in storage until the building to house the museum will be completed. It will take a few more years. The location of the museum will be in the centre of town. In this museum there is also a small Jewish section which contains several pictures and holy books. In reality, there is not much left. A few Jewish gravestones remained in the last Jewish cemetery on Mount Zarnowo where there now exists a settlement. There is a park with a monument and nearby is a pile of remnants of gravestones that were used by the Germans to pave the market–place and were removed after the war. But the cemetery is not enclosed. Lately, some Rabbi from New York and the Editor of the "Folks Shtimme" in Warsaw, who is also the presiding officer of the Jews in Poland, has shown an interest in the cemetery. And so, I am concluding my short information. I would like to point out that I am very happy to be able to help out by sharing the details which are known to me about the Jews of Strzyzow. Please confirm receipt of this letter and the pictures. I wish you health and the best.

With reverence,
Adam Kluska

[Page 464]

A memorial to Chudnov,
in the district of Zitomir, U.S.S.R.
by Harry Langsam

At the conclusion of translating this memorial book of the martyrs of Strzyzow, I had an inner feeling that something was not complete.

In my wanderings during the Holocaust years throughout the wastelands of Russia, I was fortunate enough to have met my life–long companion and together we succeeded in raising a traditional Jewish family, despite the Nazi savages who had planned to solve the "Jewish Problem" forever.

My wife, Anna Langsam, née Muravina, is of Russian Jewish parentage. Her parents were mercilessly murdered by the Nazi with the help of Ukrainian collaborators and I was never fortunate enough to have met them. The claws of the Nazi hordes reached the Jews who lived in all the shtetls of the Ukraine. Therefore, it is incumbent upon me to commemorate the martyrs of the towns in general and, in particular, the shtetl of Chudnov – the birthplace of my wife.

Soon after the Nazi occupied Chudnov, at the end of July, 1942 they ordered all the older Jewish people to report to the Firemen's Club and to bring all their belongings and valuables with them. They were kept there for three days without food and water. On the third day, they took the victims to a grove outside of town where freshly dug graves awaited them. On this day, the Nazi killed all the older population of the town including the parents of my wife. The young people who had remained in town were used for hard labour until September 22 which was Yom Kippur and on that day, the Nazi killed the rest of the Chudnov Jewish population. Small children and babies were thrown in a well alive! Among the victims who were killed on that day was my wife's sister with her family. G–d! Avenge their innocent blood.

In the following lines, I will commemorate the few victims whose names are known to me: My father–in–law, Zelig Muravin, the son of Leib who is remembered by his daughter as a devoted Jew who donned his tallit and tefilin daily as late as the early thirties, when religious practice was already forbidden.

My mother–in–law, Fruma, a hard–working woman and a devoted mother to her children.

Their oldest daughter, Esther, her husband Joseph and their children Itzhok, Sonia and Chaim.

Their second daughter Sheindl, a teacher with her husband and child.

My wife's aunt Eidl, her daughter Sheindl, her son–in law Aaron Roitman and grandson Wolf who was an officer in the Soviet Navy and fell in battle against the enemy.

Last but not least, my brother–in–law Joel Muravin who heroically gave his life fighting the fascist enemy. At the outbreak of the Soviet–German War in 1941, he was badly wounded. After being released from hospital, he joined his two sisters, my wife and her older sister Rachel, who by that time were forced to evacuate from their home in Kiev to the Caucasian Mountains. Being a semi–invalid, Joel could easily have remained with his sisters and continued with them on their journey to Siberia, their final destination.

[Page 465]

However, he insisted on re–enlisting in the Red Army: "to take revenge for the murder of his parents. As a Jew that is where he belongs". This in spite of the painful anti–Semitic encounter that occurred on the front line when he was injured in battle. While he was lying on the field, losing his blood, a group of Red Army soldiers were resting nearby. One soldier told his comrades that he sees a wounded soldier nearby. Another soldier responded: "Leave him alone, he is a Jew". This was within earshot of the wounded Joel Muravin, my brother–in–law.

Luckily he was picked up by someone else and not left to die.

In conclusion, I would like to remember my second brother–in–law, Moshe Portnoi who died in the prime of his life, after going through the travails of the horrible war. His heart finally gave up. He came home with several awards and medals for heroism on the battle field.

"May G–d remember the souls of the saintly martyrs who gave their lives for the loyalty to their nation". (From the Yizkor prayer).

The above–mentioned information about how the Jews from Chudnov were killed was obtained from a witness, a Jewish woman who survived the massacre. Mrs. Bludaya, the only woman survivor was not hit by a bullet; she just fell into the ditch and remained there until dark. She was later hidden by a gentile woman until liberation.

[Page 466]

Pictures from Stryzow

The title page of the book Sova Smachot authored by Rabbi Menachem Mendel who served as Rabbi in Stryzow before he left for Tarnov

[Page 467]

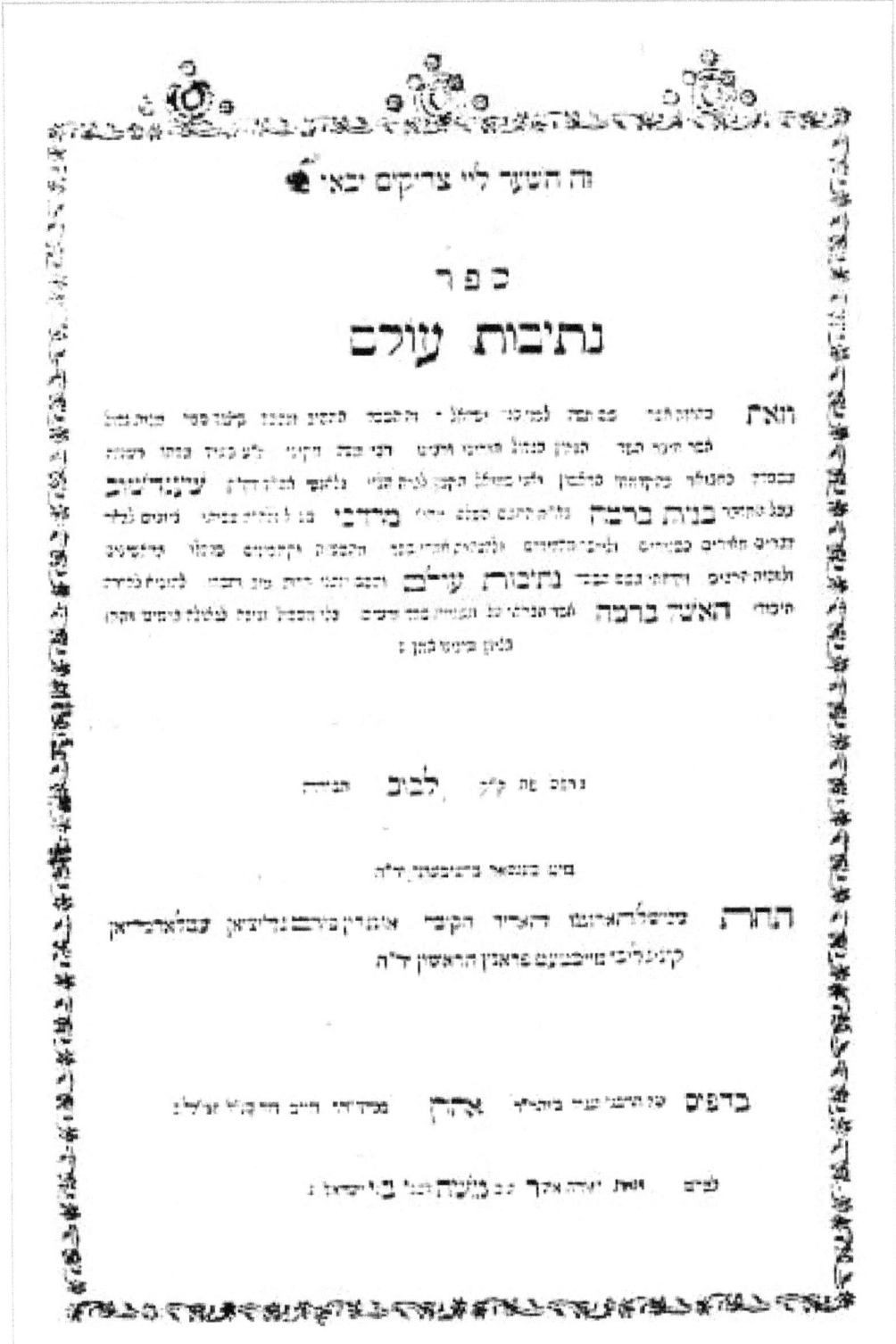

Title page of the book Netivot Olam authored by Shmuel Halevi who was the Rabbi of Stryzow and Szedziszov

[Page 468]

Title page of the book Buyot Berama, authored by Rabbi Samuel Halevi Galanti. It was published in the year 1901

[Page 469]

The title page of the book Toldot Noah which was mentioned by Reb Shlomo Yahalomi, in the article about the assistant rabbis in Strzyzow

[Page 470]

The title page of the book Olam Echad authored by Rzbbi Eliezer Fishel

The Shul before the Second World War

[Page 471]

The Shul after the Holocaust

The North side and the West side of the Shul

A corner in the women's gallery

[Page 472]

Entrance to the foyer

Stairs leading to the women's gallery

Entrance into the main sanctuary facing the Ark

Paintings on the vaulted ceiling

Composition of pictures on the vaulted ceiling, based on excerpts from the ethics of our Fathers

[Page 473]

The interior

The interior

The interior

The Leviathan painting on the vaulted ceiling above the Bimah

378 The Book of Strzyzow and Vicinity

The Leviathan painting on the vaulted ceiling above the Bimah

Various art work on the walls of the interior in the sanctuary including popular chapters of the Psalms engraved on the walls

[Page 474]

[Page 475]

David's Tower   The burning bush

Daniel in the Lion's Den   Jonah inside the fish

Rachel's tomb   The caves of the patriarchs

[Page 476]

The Shul remodelled after the Holocaust serving as a Library

The new entrance

Entrance to the foyer

The north-west entrance where the Ark used to be. Notice the reconstructed attic.

[Page 477]

The remodelled interior of the Shul in Strzyzow after the war

[Page 478]

The foyer

The conference room

The inside stairwell

[Page 479]

The marketplace before the War

The widened street where the Beit Hamidrash alley used to be

The Kloiz in Strzyzow serving now as a fire station

[Page 480]

General view of the town

General view of the town

The south-west corner of the marketplace

The houses of Rabbi Horowitz and Unger family

[Page 481]

The marketplace after the war with the steeple of the church

The house of Fishel Goldberg

The Talmud Torah

The house of Reuven Saphire on the north side of the marketplace

[Page 482]

The house of Shlomo Diamand (from Zyznow)

Part of the house of Yacov Kanner

The north-west corner of the marketplace

[Page 483]

The Clubhouse "Sokol"

Building from left is the elementary school. Next to it is the house of the District Commissioner, and the small house in the centre is the house of Baruch Diller.

The "Crooked Inn" which was leased by a Jew from Count Wolkowicki

[Page 484]

A village near Strzyzow

The emblem of Strzyzow

The grove "Lentownia". A place where people strolled on Sabbath afternoons.

[Page 485]

At the railroad station. The Unger family and friends saying goodbye to their relative, a visitor from the United States of America.

The narrow crossing over the Visloka

The new bridge over the Visloka River

[Page 486]

The Zionist Youth organization, Hanoar Hazioni

The Beitar Convention in Strzyzow, Passover 1930

The group of Zionist Revisionists

[Page 487]

The command of the Beitar in 1934

*Sitting from left to right: Ch. Gruber, T. Shefler, CH. Mohrer and Shoshana Shefler
Standing: at left: Chana Auerhhun; at right, Shprintza Schwarts*

A group of comrades from Hanoar Ha-Ivri

*Standing: from left to right: Naphtali Zilberberg, Shlomo Zaleshitz and Israel Diamand
Sitting, from left to right: Naphtali Diamand and Chaim Dym*

Kvutzat Shoshana in the Hanoar Ha-Ivri. 1930

Sitting from left to right: Ryvka Ameis, Leah Rosen, Chana Shmulewicz
Standing, from left to right: Hinda Bloch, Kresh, Ryvka Roth, Miriam Feit, Rachel Diamand

[Page 488]

"Hanoar Ha-Ivri" in 1932

"Hanoar Hazioni" in 1932

Hanoar Hazioni in 1933

[Page 489]

Hanoar Hazioni in 1934

Sitting from left to right: R. Shmulewicz, J. Schiff, CH. Shmulewicz, Ch. Dym and S. Kupferman
Standing in the middle row, from left to right: Seidler, Schefler, Felber, Kraus, Seidler, M. Shmulewicz and unknown
Upper row from left to right: unknown, Sh. Shmulewicz, G. Keith and A. Diamand

The girl group "Akiba"

The Hazamir group in 1927

Sitting from left to right: E. Gruber, M. Schiff, F. Schacher
Standing from left to right: B. Nuremberg, I. Russ, P. Kanner and H. Nechemiah

[Page 490]

A farewell party for two comrades

In the centre of the picture sitting in the second row are the Zionist leader Tzvi Shapiro. At his left is Sh. Zaleshitz. At his right, Eliezer Schwartz, who were leaving for Palestine

A farewell party for Beila Auerhun before her departure to Eretz Israel

Student of Business course at an outing

[Page 491]

A family celebration in the house of Moshe David Unger
Sitting in the centre is the bride and groom

Stamps of various institutions in Strzyzow

Stamp of the Jewish Free Loan Society 　　　　　*Stamp of the City Hall and the signature of the mayor*

Stamp of the Zionist Group, Hanoar Hazioni

Stamp and signature of the Jewish Registrar

[Page 492]

A certificate issued by the Jewish National Fund to Leah Loos in 1925, certifying the planting of trees in Eretz Israel

Contact between Strzyzow and Eretz Israel through the Red Cross. This letter was a response to an inquiry made by Leah Loos about her family. Of course the response was positive...

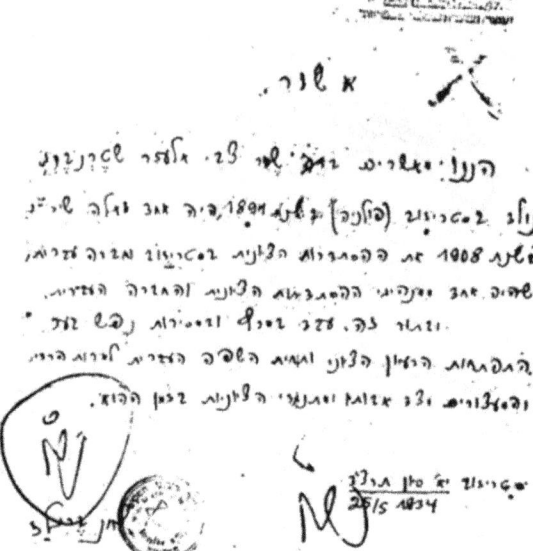

Confirmation of Zionist membership issued by the Zionist Committee in Strzyzow to colleagues who were seeking permits to immigrate to Eretz Israel

[Page 493]

Mendel the water carrier

The brothers Mendel and Shlomo Mohrer, freight carriers

The city policeman.

The mail carrier

[Page 494]

Pictures from Stryzow (cont.)
Gravestones which were removed from the market place

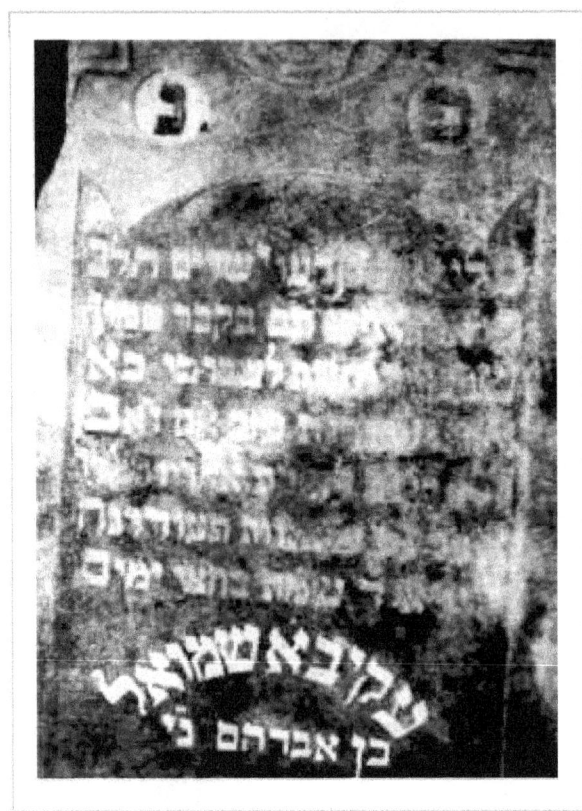

Gravestone of Akiba Shmuel Tenzer

Gravestone of Reb Hersh Schiff

Unidentified broken gravestone

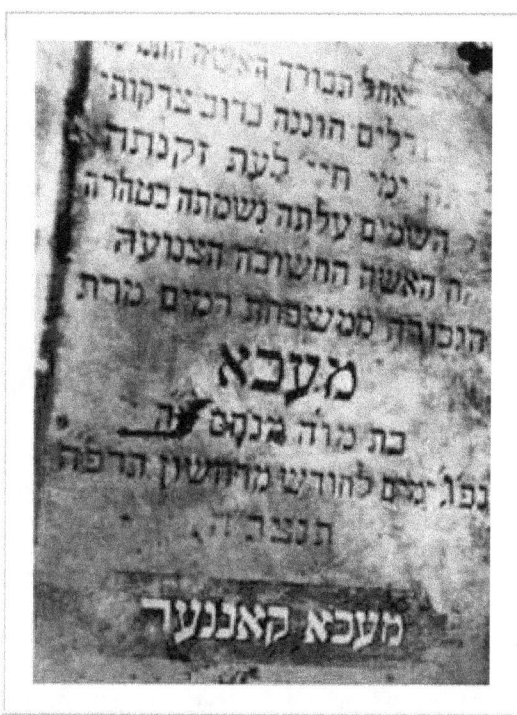

Gravestone of Mecha Kanner

[Page 495]

Pile of gravestones in the market place after their removal from the sidewalks

The desecrated gravestones were placed in the location of the last cemetery

The gravestone of Yechiel Rosen

The neglected cemetery

[Page 496]

Broken gravestones

The old Jewish cemetery was turned into a public park after the Holocaust

[Page 497]

Memorial Pages

In memoriam of the missing victims, with respect to those who are alive

Photographs of families and single people*

*Rachel Bernstein,
Israel Gertner's daughter*

*Aaron Borgenicht, his wife Hena,
their son Moshe and daughter Zisl (Zhenia)*

[Page 498]

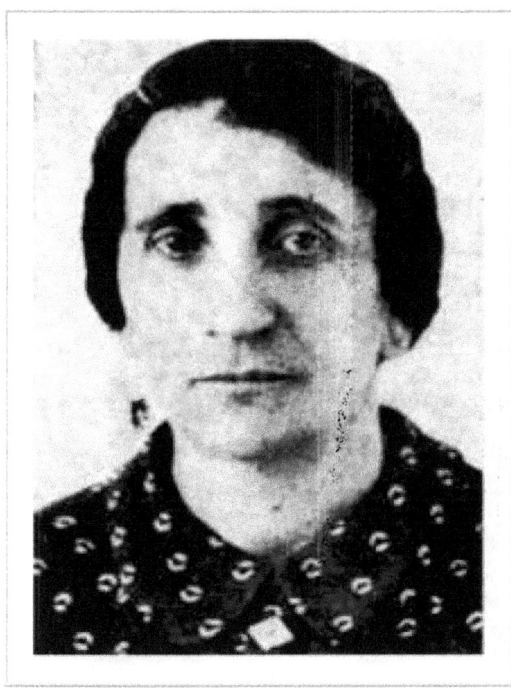

Nechama Bernstein-Berglas, daughter of Baruch Berglas

Tzipa Lev, née Berglass and Chaya Feivush, daughter of Baruch Berglass

David Dov, the son of Yacov Itzhok and Nechama Bernstein

[Page 499]

The Gruber Family

Yehuda (Yidl) Gruber as a young man

First row: Hena April, sister of Ryvka Gruber, Yehuda, his wife Ryvka Gruber
Second row: Freda Gruber, her husband Moshe Guzik, Chaya and Fliezer Gruber

Moshe and Freda Guzik with their child.

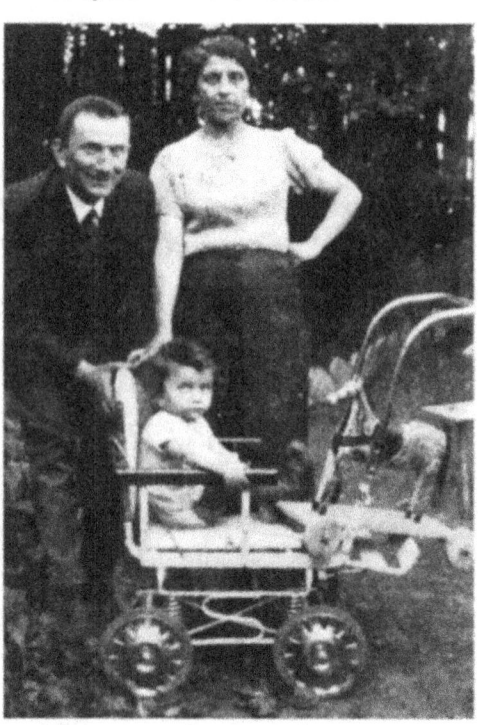

Eliezer and Bella Gruber and their son M. David

[Page 500]

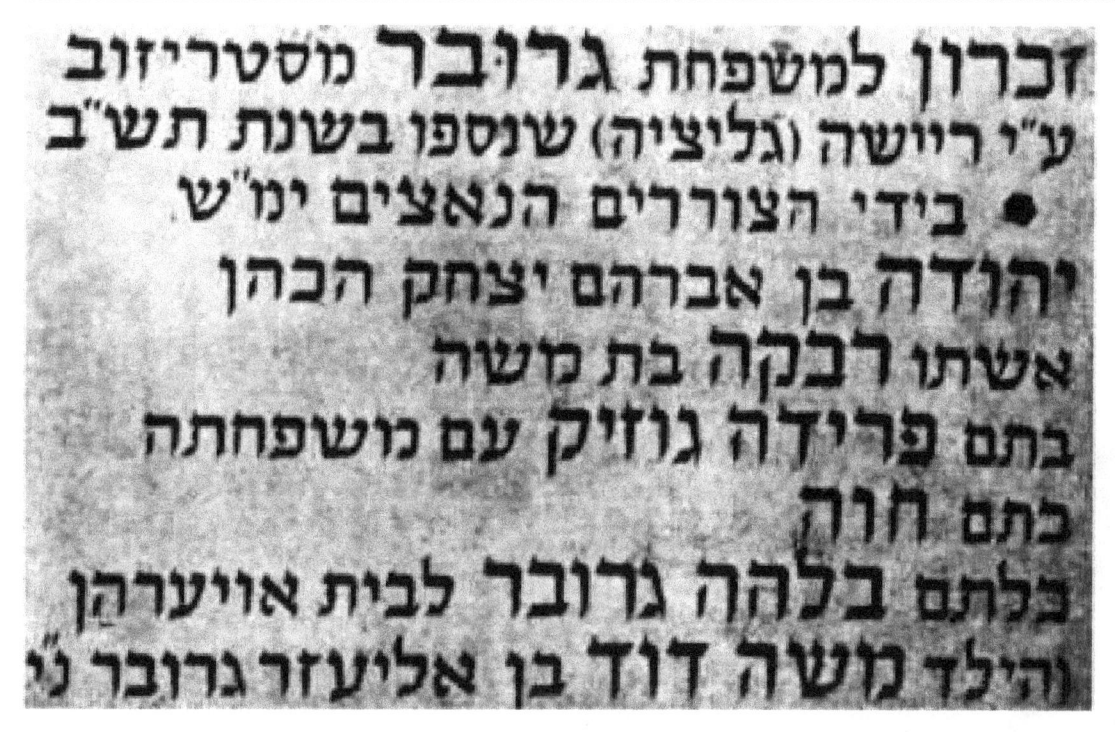

This memorial plaque was installed by Eliezer Gruber in the new synagogue of Ramat Hadar, near Ramat Gan. It says: In memory of the Family Gruber from Strzyzow near Rzeszow (Galicia), who were wiped out in 1942 by the Nazi foes, obliterated shall be their names.

Chaim Samuel Guttenberg

Moshe, the son of Yacov Dym

[Page 501]

Eliyahu, the son of Fishel Goldberg

Feiga and Fishel Goldberg

Mordechai, Elazar and Leah Goldberg

Rachel, the daughter of Fishel Goldberg

* All the names on the pictures are listed from left to right

[Page 502]

Necha Diamand, daughter of Zalman

*Reisl Diamand,
daughter of Shlomo Zalman*

*Chana and Shlomo Zalman Diamand
from the village Wysoka*

Aryeh Leibush Diamand with his bride on their wedding day. He was the son of Shlomo Zalman.

Shmaryahu Diamand from Lutcza

[Page 503]

Joseph Chaim Federbush, the son of Eta and Aryeh Leibush

Joseph Chaim Diamand, his wife Dvoray with her mother, Chana Katz and children Shlomo and Heschel

Eta and Aryeh Leib Federbush

Hinda, the wife of Heschel Diamand and boys

[Page 504]

Nathan Kornreich, his wife Gnendl, née Diamand, and their children

Eta Hacker née Landesman, granddaughter Shlomo Diamand

Rabbi Israel Frenkel, his son Samuel, Nachaum, daughter Rachel, son Shlomo and his wife Esther née Diamand

[Page 505]

Yacov, the son of Aryeh and Pearl Diamand, his mother, his sister and brother

Dr. Akiva Samuel Milgraum-Diamand, the son of Joseph

Yacov (Yantche) Hagel and his wife Golda

[Page 506]

> My father Wolf died in 1939, my mother Chana Dvora née Rubin, my sister Feidzi, her husband, her little daughter. My brother Alter Chaim, his wife and his little daughter – they all perished in the Holocaust. Also my sister Breindl who died in Strzyzow in 1941

Joseph Weinberg, the only survivor of his family, inscribed this monument in this memorial book for his martyred family

Alter Chaim Weinberg

[Page 507]

Aaron Hersh, the son of Kalman Weiden and his uncle Tuvia, his father's brother

Kalman and Shprintza Weiden

*Tzvi Hersh Yare,
the last Jewish mayor of Frysztak*

[Page 508]

*Abraham, the son of
Reb Tanchum Yacov Kalb*

*Chaim Itzhok, the son of
Tanchum Yacov Kalb*

Malka Halperin, the daughter of Abraham Kalb on her wedding day

Menachem Mendel Kalb, the son of Abraham

[Page 509]

Menachem Mendel and Ben Zion Kalb, with their sister's child

Malka Halperin, née Kalb, with her son Bezalel

Menashe Frehman

The assistant Rabbi Moshe Nuremberg

[Page 510]

Sarah, the wife of Eliezer, from the Holles family

Eliezer (Leizer) Loos

The children of Eliezer and Sarah: Vita Feiga, Adela, Elazar and Leah

[Page 511]

Bluma Lehrman, the wife of Moshe Nachum Krantzler

Chaim Lehrman, the son of Aryeh Shalom

The children of Yacov and Fruma Ryvka Langsam, née Hasenkopf, at their mother's grave. Simcha and Yechzkiel Langsam and Beila Einhorn, née Langsam, and Golda Miller, née Langsam

[Page 512]

Naphtali, the son of Chaim Mandel

Chaim Mandel

Kreindl Bracha, Chaim Mandel's wife

Zev Wolf, the son of Chaim Mandel, his wife Rosa and their sons, Saul Joseph and Tzvi

[Page 513]

The children of Israel and Chaya Sheinman, the grandchildren of Chaim Mandel

Mishkit and Seryl, Chaim Mandel's daughters

Reuven Zelig, the son of Yeshayahu Mandel

[Page 514]

Zelda Mussler's daughters: Sarah and Leah. In the centre is the daughter of Shimon Mussler from Lezajsk and Abraham Mussler

Zelda Mussler, the widow of Eliyahu

Tzvi Hersh Pfeffer

Simcha Feingold and his wife Tova

[Page 515]

Samuel (Mulik) Feit and his wife Rachel, née Propper

Joseph Feit and Samuel Rosen in their boyhood

Rachel and Mulik's children: Hinda, Joseph and Hena

[Page 516]

Sitting: Elka Klotz, the daughter of Moshe Shmuel Friedman, Sprintza Klotz with her children Sarah and Moshe Shmuel, and Joseph Klotz
Standing: Joseph's daughters Sarah and Chana and a son, Pinchos

*Hersh Nechemiah,
his wife Yenta, née Kraut*

*Ruzia, the daughter of Yehud
and Gitel Kraut, with her child*

[Page 517]

*Aryeh Leibush Russ, his wife Rachel Yehudit and daughters Sarah, Freda and Ronia
(Ruth)*

Sarah Blau, daughter of Aryeh Leibush Russ, her sons: Meir and Chaim Elazar

Aryeh Leibush and Mordechai Russ at their father's grave

[Page 518]

Children: Ryvka Berglass and Feiga Shapiro
Upper row: Eta Falk, née Dembitzer, Sarah Berglass and Sarah Shapiro

Tzvi, the son of Menachem Mendel, Baim, son-in-law of David Dembitzer was inscribed in this memorial book by his wife Sarah and their son, Jessy

The grandchildren of Hershel Resler: Sheindl Dembitzer, Tova Dembitzer, Eta Falk, Feiga Falk, Sarah Shapiro, Chaya Kreindl Dembitzer, Ryvka Deutch

[Page 519]

First row: Chana Deutch and granddaughter Chaya
Second row: Hinda Leah and Aaron Deutch with Rachel

Itzhok and Chaya Kreindl Deutch

Hinda Leah, the wife of Aaron Deutch and their three daughters, Chaya, Yehudit and Rachel

[Page 520]

The family of Aryeh Leib Sternberg
Leib Sternberg's grandchildren: Yacov, Samuel's daughter, Chaya and Ben Zion
Middle row: Hentche and Leib Sternberg with daughter Rachel Garfunkel
Upper row: Hinda Leah Deutch with Rachel and Rachel Goldzand with Eta

The Sternberg family at the gravesite of their father

[Page 521]

Necha Gitle, the wife of Chaim Israel Sturm

Chaim Israel Sturm

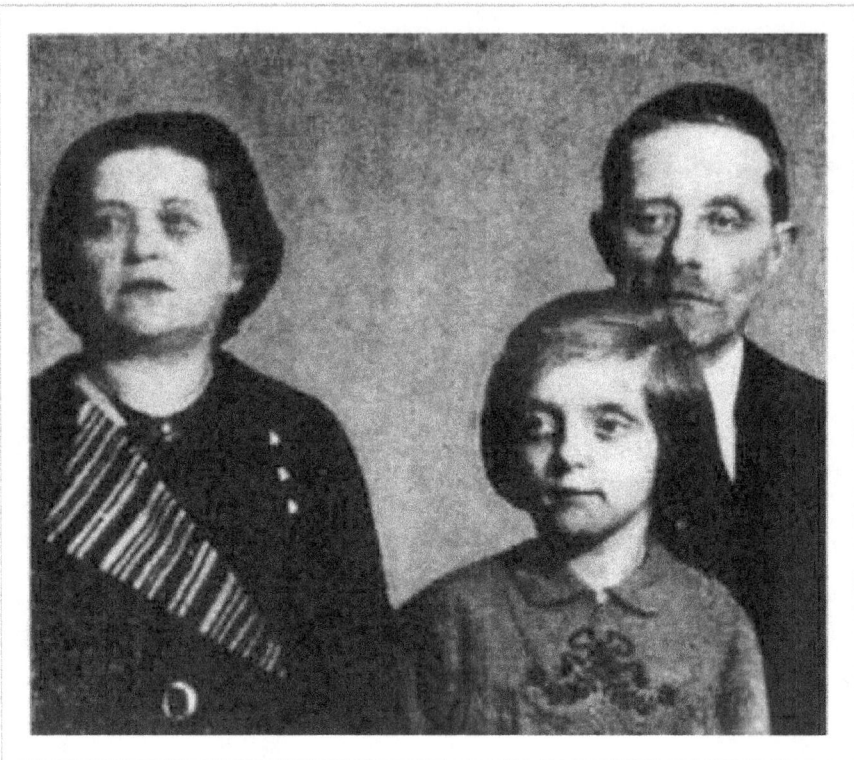

Elazar, the son of Chaim Elazar Sturm, his wife Chaya Sarah and daughter Reisl

[Page 522]

The Sturm and the Asher families

*Sitting: Alta Risha and Nathaniel Schlisselberg, with their two grandchildren
Standing: Ryvka, Nathaniel's daughter and their son Elchanan*

[Page 523]

Kalonymus Saul and Tzirl Blum, the parents of Ryvka Schiff

Tzvi (Hershale) Schiff and his wife Chaya Leah

The family of Levi Itzhok Schiff
Sitting: Necha Horowitz, mother-in-law of Meir Schiff, Ryvka, the wife of Levi Itzhok
Standing: David Levi Itzhok, Meir and Dvora Schiff

[Page 524]

Yacov Sturm   *Deiche, the wife of Itzok*   *Itzhok Redler, the sexton*

Chaya Schitz and her daughter Sheindl Ameis were inscribed in this memorial book by the children and grandchildren, Ryvka-Roth-Ameis and Yacov Ameis

The Shmulewicz family
Sitting: Ryvka and Reuven Shmulewicz, Esther Hinda Berger
Standing: Breindl, Rachel Chana, Pearl and Malka

[Page 525]

Moshe David Unger, his wife Hena Rachel, Pearl and Mordechai Mendel Schefler

Benjamin Roth, his wife Feiga, née Unger

*The Schefler family
Sitting: Shimon and Reisl Schefler
Standing: Joshua, Sarah, David, Shoshana, Tzvi and Moshe*

[Page 526]

The family of Batya Schefler
Front row: Leah, the daughter of Joshua and her sister Batya, Betty the daughter of Joshua
Second row: Shimon and Itzhok Leif, Chava and Zisha Leif, Eta and Joshua Schefler

Pearl Leah Schefler

[Page 527]

Reisl Diamand, the wife of Moshe, Leah, née Diamand, the wife of Alter Nechemia and their granddaughter Tosha

*Eta (Tosha) Brav, Eta Diamand, Chaya Diamand, Hinda Diamand,
Hena Brav-Nechemiah Golda Keh-Feit*

[Page 533]

*Sitting: Vita Loos, Reisl Wirtzel, Rochma Mintz
Standing: Sarah Rebhun, Sarah Alta Mandel, Liba Greenblatt, Leah Loos and Gelander*

Granddaughters of Baruch Diller, daughters of Mendel Rosen and also the granddaughters of Aaron Joseph Steinmauer

[Page 534]

Front row: Chava Gruber, Hena Henig, unknown, Yacov Tenzer's daughter and Leah Reicher
Second row: Henia Bernstein, Leah Kracher and Dena Miller

Leah Reicher, Dena Miller, Chava Gruber, Leah Kracher and Henia Bernstein

[Page 535]

Sitting: Feivel Schacher, Aryeh Diamand, Mendel Zilber
Standing: Mordechai Schiff, Israel Russ, Benjamin (Benia) Dembitzer

Sitting in front row: Eta Diamand, Shoshana Schefler and Ryvka Kraut
Second row: Rubenfeld, Friedman, Malka Mintz and Chaya Springer
Standing: Feiga Kaufman, Mindl Reicher, Eta Hagel

[Page 536]

Front row: Mishkit Mandel, Esther Gruber, Sheindl Dembitzer
Second row: Ethel Liberman, Sarah Klotz, Feiga Gruber
Third row: Leah Mussler

Standing: Mishkit Mandel, Ethel Lieberman,
Tzipora Gruber and Adela Kneller
Sitting: Leah Mussler and Sheindl Dembitzer

[Page 537]

Tova Weinberg, Tzipora Gruber, Sheindl Dembitzer and Esther Gruber

Sitting: Zukier, Shoshana Schefler, Ryvka Kraut.
Standing: Gitel Rothstein, Feiga Kaufman, Shprintza Schwarts, Rubenfeld, Mindl Reicher and Eta Mohrer

[Page 538]

Sitting: Samuel Kaufman and Chaim Dym
Standing: Abraham Mussler and Joseph Schiff

Sitting: Israel Schiff
Standing: Joseph Schiff,
Abraham Mussler, Eisik Russ

*Sitting: Miriam Zanger, unknown, Miriam Feit,
Chana Shmulewicz and Rachel Diamand
Standing: Shlomo Zaleshitz, Israel Diamand and Elazar Goldberg*

[Page 539]

Glossary

"A BRIVELE DER MAMEN"	A letter to my mother. Yiddish folk song
AGUDAT ISRAEL	Hebrew for Union of Israel. Orthodox Jewish Movement
AL CHET	Hebrew for the sin, confession prayer recited on Yom Kippur
AL HANISIM	A prayer which is recited on Hanukkah and Purim
ALIYAH	Hebrew for immigration to the Holy Land
ALIYAH BETH	Clandestine immigration to the Holy Land
ALIYAH L'TORAH	Ascent to the platform where the Scripture reading takes place
AMALEKITES	The descendants of Amalek the grandson of Esau. Exodus ch.17
AMIDAH	Silent prayer which is recited thrice daily
ASMODEUS	An evil spirit in Jewish legends
AVINY MALKEINU	Hebrew for our Father, our King. A prayer which is recited on the High Holidays.
BAIS YACOV	A religious school for girls
BAAL SHEM TOV	Israel, the son of Eliezer. 1700–1760. Founder of a pious movement
BAR MITZVA	A Jewish boy who has reached thirteen. The age of religious duty and responsibility
BARTENURA	Meaning Rabbi Ovadia from Bartenura. A commentator of the codification of Jewish oral law
BARUCH ATA	Hebrew for praise Thy Name. The beginning of every blessing
BEIT HAMIDRASH	House of prayer and place of study of sacred books
BELVEDERE	The residence of the Polish Head of Government
BIMAH	Platform in a synagogue on which stands the desk from which the Scriptures are read
BLUE WHITE BOX	Collection box distributed by the Jewish National Fund
BNOS AGUDAT ISRAEL	Young women's section of the Orthodox Jewish Party
BRIT	Short for BRIT MILAH. The religious rite of circumcision.
CAPO or KAP	A concentration camp inmate in charge of other inmates
CHAD–GAD–YAW	Aramaic song which is sang during the Passover Seder
CHALLA	A traditional loaf of rich white bread for the Sabbath

CHEDER	Hebrew for room. A one–room religious school
CHEVRA KADISHA	Hebrew for Holy Society who takes care of the deceased
CHMIELNICKI	A Ukrainian massacre organizer, especially of Jews in the seventeen century
CHOL HAMOED	Light holiday on Passover and Sukkoth between the first and the last days of the holiday
CHOMETZ	Leavened foodstuff that may not be eaten on Passover
"CHOSHIVER"	Yiddish for Your Reverence
CHULENT or TCHULENT	Yiddish for food stored in the oven for the Sabbath noon meal
CHUMASH	The first five books of the Bible
CHUPPA	Wedding canopy

[Page 540]

ELUL	The last month of the year in the Jewish calendar
ERETZ ISRAEL	Hebrew for the Holy Land
EREV PESACH	On the eve of Passover
EREV YOM KIPPUR	On the eve of the Day of Atonement
ETROG	A yellow citrus fruit resembling lime used during procession in the synagogue on the Harvest Festival in the autumn
GELT	Yiddish for money
GEMARA	The second and supplementary part of the Talmud
GOY	Gentile. Plural Goyim
GYMNASIUM	Secondary school in Poland
HACHSHARA	Hebrew for preparation. Training before immigrating to Israel
HAFTORAH	Hebrew for conclusion. It is the lesson from the Prophets recited immediately after reading from the Pentateuch on the Sabbath
HAGGADAH	Narrative of the Exodus read at the Passover seders
HAGANA	Jewish self–defence during the British mandate in Palestine
HAKAFOT	Procession inside the synagogue during the celebration of rejoicing the ending and beginning of reading the Scriptures
HALACHA	Laws or ordinances not written down in the Scriptures but based on oral interpretation
HALLEL	A part of the Jewish religious services consisting of Psalms 113–118 inclusive recited or sung on certain festivals

HALUTZ, plural HALUTZIM	A Jewish pioneer in agricultural settlements of modern Israel
HAMAN	A Persian official who sought destruction of the Jews and was hanged when his plot was exposed
HAMAVDIL	A Saturday night song which is sung after the departure of the Sabbath
HANUKKAH	Jewish festival commemorating the redemption of the Temple on 165B.C
HASSIDIM	Members of pious Jewish sect originated in the 18th Century in Poland
"HASHOMER"	The watchman
HASKALA	Hebrew for enlightenment. A movement among the Jews in the other half of the 19th Century
HASMONAIM	A High Priest with his sons who revolted against the Greeks
HEIMISH	Yiddish for friendliness
HORA	Lively Israel folk dance
HOSHANA RABA	The 7th day of the Harvest Festival
HOSHANOT, plural HOSANNA	Hebrew for praise to G–d
IN SHUL ARAAN	Yiddish. A early morning call from the sexton to come to the synagogue
JUDENRAT	German for Jewish Council appointed by the German authorities to administer the ghetto
KABBALA	An occult philosophy of certain Jewish Rabbis in the Middle Ages

[Page 541]

KADDISH	A mourner's prayer praising G–d
KAPAROT, plural KAPARAH	A symbolic ceremony taking place before the day of Atonement in which the sins of a person are transferred to a fowl – a white hen or rooster
KAPO	See Capo
KASHRUTH	The dietary regulations of Judaism
KEHILLAH	The leadership of a Jewish Community
KIDDUSH	Benediction recited over wine
KINDERLECH	Yiddish for children in an endearing manner
KLEZMORIM	Yiddish for orchestra

KLOIZ	Yiddish for house of prayers
KOL CHAMIRA	A prayer which is recited on Passover Eve while clearing away the leavened food
KOL NIDREI	The prayer of atonement recited at the opening of the Yom Kippur services
KOSHER	Fit to eat according to the dietary laws
KREPLACH	Yiddish for small casings of dough filled with ground meat, boiled and served usually in soup
KRIAT SHEMA	Declaration of the basic principle of Jewish belief recited thrice daily
KUGEL	Sabbath delicacy. A crusty baked pudding made of potatoes or noodles
KVITTEL	Yiddish for note. Folded note addressed to a Rabbi containing a special request or wish that the Rabbi should pray for
LAG B'OMER	A Jewish holiday observed on the 18th day of the month of Iyar
LANDSMAN, plural LANDSLEIT	Fellow countryman/men
L'CHAIM	To live, cheers
LECHA DODI	Hebrew song welcoming the Queen of Sabbath
LEVIATHAN	Bible, sea monster or a whale
LULAV	Hebrew for palm branch used in the procession in the synagogue during the Harvest Festival
MINYAN	Hebrew for quorum. A properly constituted group for a public Jewish prayer of at least ten Jewish males
MISHLOACH MANOT	Hebrew for sending gifts, a tradition observed on Purim holidays
MISHNAYOTH	The first part of the Talmud containing traditional oral interpretation of scriptural ordinances
MITZVA	Fulfilling a commandment
MIZMOR SHIR	Hymn from the Psalms (Ps.ch.30) sung on Hanukkah
MIZRACHI	A religious Zionist Organization
MUSSAF	The last part of the Sabbath and holiday services
MAARIV	Evening prayer
MAFTIR	The last part of the Scripture reading on Sabbath and holidays
MAIMONIDES	Rabbi Moshe Ben Maimon. 1135–1204. Physician and philosopher in Egypt
MAH NISHTANA	Hebrew for what is different? The beginning of the four questions asked by a child at the ceremony celebrated on Passover night

[Page 542]

MAOZ TZUR	A Hanukkah song
MAROR	Hebrew for bitter herbs eaten during the ceremony on Passover night
MARANOS, plural of MARANO	In the Spanish Inquisition, a Jew forced to profess Christianity in order to escape death
MATZA, plural MATZOT	Flat unleavened bread eaten during the Passover
MEGILLAH	Hebrew for scroll. The story of Esther which is read on Purim is called Megillah
MELAMED, plural MELAMDIM	Hebrew for teachers
MELAVEH MALKA	Literary: escorting the Queen. A Saturday night meal in honour of the outgoing of the Sabbath Queen. (Sabbath is endearingly called the Sabbath Queen)
MENORAH	Seven branch candelabrum. A traditional symbol of Judaism
MENTCHEN, plural for MENTCH	Yiddish for a human being
MIDRASH	Rabbinical commentaries and explanatory notes on the Scriptures
MIKVA	Ritual bath in which Orthodox Jews immerse themselves for ritual purification
MINCHA	Afternoon services
NEILAH	Concluding services on the Day of Atonement
NKVD	Soviet Secret Police
NETILAT YADAIM	Blessing which is recited during hand washing before a meal
NETUREI KARTA	An extreme religious sect in Jerusalem
NU!	Yiddish expression. Well! Come on!
OR HAGANUZ	Ancient Hebrew Hanukkah song
PILSUDSKI JOZEF	Polish General and statesman. 1867–1935
PINKAS plural PINKASIM	Daily Journal of a Jewish Community
POGROM	Russian for an organized persecution and massacre
PURIM	A Jewish holiday. The feast of lots celebrated on the 14th of Adar
PUSHKE	Yiddish for collection box
RAMBAM	Abbreviation of Reb Moshe Ben Maimon. See Maimonides

REB	Hebrew title for Sir or Mister
REBETZIN	A Rabbi's wife
RESPONSA	A compilation of questions and answers on Jewish laws
"REVEE"	Hebrew for forth – the fourth person called to the reading of the Scriptures on Sabbaths and holidays
ROSH HASHANA	Jewish New Year
SABBATH GOY	A gentile who helps to do things that Jews are forbidden to do on Sabbath and holidays such as starting a fire or turning lights on
SEDER	Ceremony celebrated at table in the home on Passover night
SHA GOYIM	Be quiet! A scolding expression when people converse during religious services
SHALOM ALEICHEM	Peace to you. Traditional Jewish greeting
SHAVUOTH	The Feast of Weeks. A Jewish holiday
SHEIGATZ	Yiddish for impudent boy
SHEKEL	An ancient monetary unit
SHEMA ISRAEL	The opening of the declaration of the basic principle of Jewish belief proclaiming the absolute unity of G–d
SHEMINI ATZERET	The eight–day of solemn Assembly celebrated after the seventh day of Harvest Festival
SHEOL	(Bible). A place in the depths of earth conceived of as the dwelling of the dead
SHMALTZ	Yiddish for fats
SHOCHET	Ritual slaughterer
SHOFAR	A ram's horn blown in synagogues on Rosh Hashana and at the end of Atonement Day
SHOMREI SHABOS	Jews who strictly observe the Sabbath
SHUL	Same as synagogue
SHTETL	Yiddish for a little town
SHTREIMEL	Fur hat worn by some Orthodox Jews on Sabbaths and holidays
SIMCHAT TORAH	Rejoicing the Torah. A Jewish festival that marks the end and the beginning of Scripture reading
SLICHOT	Midnight or early morning services beginning a week before Rosh Hashana
SPIEL	Yiddish for play
SUKKAH, plural SUKKOTH	A Temporary structure with a roof of leaf boughs or straw built by Jews for the Harvest Festival commemorating the tabernacles of the exodus

TALIT, plural TALEITIM	Jewish prayer shawl
TALMUD	The collection of writings constituting Jewish laws
TALMUD TORAH	Institution where Jewish children are taught the Scriptures
TANAI	Learned person who participated in the collection of writings and establishing the Jewish law after the destruction of the Second Temple
TASHLICH	A prayer which is recited on the second day of Rosha Hashana near a water or sea
TEFILIN	Phylacteries. Small leather cases containing passages from Scripture and affixed to the forehead and to the left arm by male Jews during morning services on weekdays
TISHA B'Av	The ninth day of the month of Av. A fast day commemorating the destruction of the First and Second Temples
TORAH	The whole body of Jewish religious literature
TOWN DRUMMER or ANNOUNCER	Ordinances were made known by using drums in the market place in order to gather all the inhabitants
TUV B'SHVAT	Jewish Arboretum Day observed in the Holy Land
TZADIK, plural TZDIKIM	Righteous people
TZITIT or TZITZIOT	Woollen fringes attached in the four corners of a prayer shawl or small ritual garment
UNETANEI or UNESANEI TOKEF KEDUSHAT HYOM	An important prayer during the High Holiday services
UR KASDIM	An ancient Babylonian place where the Patriarch Abraham was born
YARMULKE	Scull cap worn by Jewish males
YEHUDA HALEVI	A Hebrew poet
YESHIVA	A college for Talmudic studies
YID	Yiddish for Jew
YIDDISHE MAME	Jewish mother
YIDDISHKEIT	Jewishness, spiritual feeling of being Jewish
YITGADAL VEYITKADASH SHMEI RABA	A prayer, praising G–d, recited in synagogue by mourners and also during the burial of a family member
YIZKOR	Memorial Services for the departed
YOM KIPPUR	Day of Atonement
ZAIDE	Yiddish for grandfather

ZION	The hill in Jerusalem on which the Temple was built
ZIONISM	Movement for re–establishing and at present supporting the Jewish national State of Israel
ZLOTY, plural ZLOTYS	Monetary unit of Poland
ZOHAR	Mystical commentary on the Pentateuch

[Pages 545-557]

Name Index From Original Book

Surname	First name(s)	Page(s)
ABRAHAM	Yacov, Rabbi of Sadigora	98, 99, 117, 134, 169, 170, 201, 302, 458
ACHT	Dr.	56
ADEST	Bina	449
ADEST	Chaim	246, 247, 380
ADEST	Ephraim Samuel	449
ADEST	Feivel	166, 169, 319
ADEST	Moshe	166, 197, 200, 202, 319
ADEST	Yacov	55, 166, 250, 449
ADEST	Zelig	116, 166
ADLER	Abraham Dr.	453
ADLER	Fishel	457
ADLER	Israel	453
ADLER	Leib	455
ADLER	Pinches	455
AGNON	Shalom Yacov	79
ALTEROWICZ-SEIDMAN	Moshe Meir	449
AMEIS	Eliezer	449
AMEIS	Esther	449
AMEIS	Ryvka	449
AMEIS	Sheindl	449
AMEIS	Yacov	449
ANDERS	General	341
ANSBACHER	Rabbi	328, 329
ASHER	Adela	393
ASHER	Jeremiah	393
ASHER	Joseph	393, 395, 397
ASHER	Liba	393

ASHER	Asher Shlomo	393, 444
ASHER	Yacov	171
ASHLAG	Rabbi	303
AVISH	Meir from Sandz	340
AVROM	from Nobitnitz	296
AUGUSTIN		409
AUERHOUN/ORHUN	Beila	88
AUERHOUN/ORHUN	Chana	89
AUERHOUN/ORHUN	Shlomo	355
BAAL	Shem Tov	9, 11, 124, 266, 460
BALDINGER	Samuel	408-410
BALFOUR		267
BARTOSHEK		366
BAUMEL	Benjamin	169, 235, 260
BAUMEL	Joseph	260
BAUMEL	Tzvi	235, 260
BEIGAYER	Fishel	414
BEITLER	Aaron Samuel	70
BEITLER	Leibush	250
BEITLER	Mordechai	250
BELLER	Tzilla	391
BELZ	Rabbi	25, 100, 135, 171, 200
BER	Meir	152, 153, 185
BER	Raphael	188, 189
BERGER		369
BERGER	Esther Hinda	302
BERGER	Israel Aaron	65, 67
BERGER	Joseph	253
BERGER	Joshua	302
BERGER	Moshe	255
BERGER	Zachariah	253

BERGLASS	Avrom Mendel	166, 318, 321
BERGLASS	Baruch	29, 40; 71, 114, 115, 132, 166, 197
BERGLASS-FEIVUSH	Chaya	42, 65, 66, 173
BERGLASS	Hersh Ber	166
BERGLASS	Israel Aaron	409, 410
BERGLASS	Itzhok	42, 79, 88, 115, 157, 164, 172, 179, 233, 301, 309, 312, 313, 317, 344, 345, 369, 415, 442, 444, 449
BERGLASS	Rachel	309
BERGLASS	Ryvka	310
BERGLASS	Sarah	56, 309, 310
BERGLASS	Yocheved	245
BERGLASS	Zalman	315
BERNSTEIN	Bina	245, 279, 310
BERNSTEIN	Elimelech Shlomo	245, 279, 309
BERNSTEIN	David	245, 279, 309
BERNSTEIN	Henia	256, 310
BERNSTEIN-BERGLASS	Nechama	42, 173, 245, 309, 310
BERNSTEIN	Yacov Itzhok	50, 73, 75, 87, 188, 234, 245, 279
BEZALEL	from Szczucin	296
BIALIK	Chaim Nachman	52, 70, 79, 130, 148, 274
BIDO	Antony	445
BIER	Shlomo	151, 152
BILDER	Tova	330
BILITCKI	Count	285
BILUT	Eliyahu	99, 100, 319, 322
BILUT	Yair	321
BIRNBACH	Michael	444
BLAU	Moshe	298
BLAU	Sarah	298
BARUCH	Rabbi from Mezibush	128
BLEICHER	Moshe	368

BLUDAYA		465
BOGOMOLOV		341
BORGENICHT	Aaron	243
BORGENICHT	Moshe (Moniek)	243
BORNSTEIN	Dr.	368
BORENSTEIN	Itzhok	452
BRACH	Rabbi Saul	126
BRAUER	Dr.	163
BRAUNER	Zalman	38, 88, 109, 302
BRAUNER	Dena	302
BRAUNER	Moshe	475
BRAV	Abraham	29, 53, 88, 238, 246, 316, 380, 382, 383
BRAV	Mordechai	51
BRAV	Tzvi Hersh	29, 37, 39
BRAV	Yacov	409, 410
BRAN	Madelaine	456
BROIDE	Leib Rabbi	59
BRONER	Beila	410
BRONER	Chana	410
BRONER	Chaim Meir	194, 408
BRONER	Hersh	410
BRONER	Israel	410
BRONER	Sarah	410
BRONER	Yacov	410
BULOK	Priest	63
CASIMIR	King of Poland	51, 207
CHAMBERLAIN		220
CHATAM	Soifer	274
CHMIEL	Dr.	188
CHMIELNICKI		269
COOK	Chief Rabbi	134

CUKIER	Jewelier	199
CZAPCZYNSKA	Barbara	385
DALADIER		220
DEMBITZER	David	29, 169, 280, 248
DEMBITZER	Eta	53, 88
DEMBITZER	Sarah	448
DEUTCH	Aaron	29, 238, 242, 245
DEUTCH	Chaya	245
DEUTCH	Itzhok	107, 176, 322, 415
DEUTCH	Joseph	55, 88
DEUTCH	Leon	449
DEUTCH	Meir	198
DEUTCH	Moshe	234
DEUTCH	Rachel Leah	88, 303
DEUTCH	Shimon	452
DEUTCH	Wolf	17, 29, 444, 452
DEUTCHER	Moshe	53
DIAMAND	Abraham	167, 323
DIAMAND	Akiba	55, 167, 321
DIAMAND	Akiba Samuel	166, 167, 321
DIAMAND	Aryeh	51, 53, 65, 167, 16
DIAMAND	Aryeh Leibush	166, 167, 320, 321,
DIAMAND	Avigdor	41, 53, 88, 158, 167, 168, 181-184, 185
DIAMAND	Baruch	55
DIAMAND	Chana Rachel	89
DIAMAND	Dvoira	97, 167, 288
DIAMAND	Feivel	38, 89
DIAMAND	Hersh	167, 321
DIAMAND	Hinda	288
DIAMAND	Heschel	18, 29, 113, 121, 167, 310, 343, 448
DIAMAND	Isaiah Itzhok	288

DIAMAND	Joseph	51, 55, 89, 97, 118, 119-121, 131, 167, 321
DIAMAND	Joseph Chaim	286, 288
DIAMAND	Leah	285
DIAMAND	Menachem Mendel	453
DIAMAND	Moshe	29, 167, 321, 322
DIAMAND	Moshe Yacov	167, 321
DIAMAND	Naphtali	55, 250, 303
DIAMAND	Rachel	89
DIAMAND	Reizi	167
DIAMAND	Sarah	166
DIAMAND	Shlomo from Zyznow	94, 167, 195, 262, 276, 301, 318, 321,-323, 457
DIAMAND	Shlomo Zalaman	321
DIAMAND	Shmaryahu	321,
DIAMAND	Yacov	166, 320, 321, 323
DIAMAND	Yechezkiel	343
DIAMAND	Zalman	321, 453
DILLER	Teacher	67
DILLER	Baruch	30, 88, 134, 199
DILLER	from Sanok	280
DILLER	Itzik'l	98, 99
DILLER	Jacob-Yacov	448, 457
DOLPHUS		347
DOMBROWSKI		179
DOV	Ber	138
DUKLA	Rabbi	202
DUKS	Dr.	366
DYM	Chaim	303
DYM	Moshe	55
DYM	Yacov	43
DYNOW	Rabbi	319,
EICHENSTEIN	Joseph	195

EICHENSTEIN	Menashe	195
EICHENSTEIN	Rabbi Yehuda	168
EICHMAN		206
EINHORN	Beila	298, 300, 352, 353
EINHORN	Itzhok	300
EINHORN	Naphtali	300
EINHORN	Tzvi Elimelech	300
EINHERN	Yehuda Zev	300
EISEN	Abraham	289
EISEN	Aaron David	289
EISEN	Bina	289
EISEN	Chana	289
EISEN	Isachar	289
EISEN	Menachem Mendel	288
EISEN	Miriam	289
EISEN	Shmaryahu	288
EISEN	Yacov Shmaryahu	289
EISENBERG	Hada	455
EISENBERG	Leib	443, 455, 457
EISENBERG		457
EISIK	the sexton	31, 76, 144, 145
EISENSTADT	Elimelech	351
EISMAN	Pinches	241
EISNER	Tzvi Hersh Dr.	251, 252, 453
EISNER	Yacov	56, 203, 252, 453
EKSTEIN	Eva	368, 371
EKSTEIN	Jonah	368, 371
ELI	Dovid the Melamed	43, 78, 92, 146, 14
ELIEZER	Rabbi Fishel	11
ELAZAR	the "Guttural"	202
ELIMELECH	Rabbi from Lezajsk	11, 12

EISMAN	Yehuda Nosen	78, 149
ENGEL	Samuel	168
ENGEL	from Frysztak	185
ENGELHARD	Joseph	411
ENGLENDER	Ever	344
EPSTEIN	David	409
EMER	Samuel Nachum	358
FALK-DEMBITZER	Eta	309
FASS	Hersh Leib	452
FASS	Joel	452
FEDERBUSH	Aryeh Leib	287,
FEDERBUSH	Benjamin Beinish	287
FEDERBUSH	Eta	286, 307
FEDERBUSH	Joseph Chaim	287
FEINGOLD	Ben Ami	51, 459
FEINGOLD	Chana	330
FEINGOLD	Israel	330
FEINGOLD	Moshe	51
FEINGOLD	Simcha	51, 164, 165
FEINGOLD	Tova	391
FEINGOLD	Yacov	165, 391, 392
FEIT	Chaim	62, 242
FEIT	Henia	253, 380, 384
FEIT	Hinda	251, 386
FEIT	Joseph	247, 384, 385
FEIT	Rachel	56, 247, 384
FEIT	Samuel	189, 237, 246, 247, 251, 253, 316, 380, 383, 384, 455
FEIT	Hersh	449
FEIT	Sarah	449
FELT	Yekutiel Zalman	455
FEIVUSH	Abraham Itzhok	279

FEIVUSH	Chaya Sarah	279, 309
FEIVUSH	Feivush Ruth	279
FEIVUSH	Yacov	279
FELBER	Nechemiah	250, 384, 407
FELDER	Abraham Moshe	452
FELDER	Fishel	449, 452
FELDER	Henia	449
FELDER	Sarah	452
FELDER	Yacov	251
FELDMAUS	Gitel	300
FELDMAUS	Elazar	300
FELDMAUS	Hersh	300
FELDMAUS	Tova	300
FISHIER	Seryl	294, 444, 445
FLEISHER	Chana	89
FLEISHER	Sarah	89
FLEISHER	Shimon	110, 11
FLAUMENHAFT	Shalom	315, 316
FRANCE	Generalisimo	347
FRIEDBERG	Michael	2
FRIEDMAN	Chaim	28, 69
FRIEDMAN	Rabbi Israel	296
FRIEDMAN	Israel	365
FRIEDMAN	Leib	20, 41, 70, 87
FRIEDMAN	Mendel Mannis	68, 69, 454
FRIEDMAN	Rabbi David Moshe	296
FRIEDMAN	Pinches	69, 70
FRIEDMAN	Seryl	86
FRIEDMAN	Yechiel	354
FRIEDMAN	Moshe Shmuel	46, 82
FREIWIRTH	Jonah	88

FRENKEL	Dr.	79
FRENKEL	Chaim Dr.	4i, 181, 236, 315, 453
FRENKEL	Rabbi Israel	262, 263, 44
FRENKEL	Baruch	266
FRENKEL	Esther	262, 276
FRENKEL	Hassa	266
FRENKEL	Shalom	262
FRENKEL	Sarah	262
FRENKEL	Shalom Chaim	320
FRENKEL	Rachel	262
FRENKEL	Joseph	166, 288
FRENKEL	Rabbi Shlomo Zalman	166, 288
FRENKEL	Samuel Nachum	276, 277, 449
FRENKEL	Tzvi	266
GANS	Rosa	449
GARFUNKEL	Aaron	37,
GARFUNKEL	Samuel	37,
GELANDER	Hersh	30, 38, 88, 116-18,
GELBER	Dr.	11
GELBWACHS	Shoshana	281
GELERNTER	Rabbi Israel	13
GELLER		374
GENDELLMAN		335
GENS	Dr.	409
GERTNER	Chaim	148, 162-64,
GERTNER	Israel	40, 162, 166, 202,
GERTNER	Israel (child)	252, 254
GERTNER	Menachem	202
GERTNER	Moshe	241, 255
GERTNER	Nechama	56, 189, 254, 255
GERTNER	Pearl	328, 455

GERTNER	Yenta	253
GETZLER	Wolf	299
GINSBERG	Nathan 334	338
GINSBERG	Shoshana 251	281
GLATT	Eliezer	64
GLIKMAN	Rabbi Isaac	269
GLICKMAN	Joel	50, 269
GOLDBEIG	Elazar	236, 301
GOLDBERG	Feiga	89, 235
GOLDBERG	Fishel	89, 91, 235, 457
GOLDBERG	David	91, 455
GOLDBERG	Leah	90
GOLDBERG	Menachem Dr.	457
GOLDBERG	Sarah	90
GOLDFISHER	Dr	409
GOLDMAN	Abraham	70, 116, 148, 166
GOLDMAN	Dvoire Sarah	116, 166
GOLDMAN	Fishel	334
GOLDMAN	Itzhok	70, 116, 148
GOLDMAN	Mendel	70
GOLDMAN	Tzvi Elimelech	70
GOLDMAN	Yacov	70
GORGIL	Yechezkiel	72, 87, 200
GORNICKI	Leopold	176
GORNICKI	Peter	243
GORNICKI	Wladislaw	243
GOCEK	Butcher	245
GOTLIEB	Ben Zion	366
GOTLIEB	Gitel	409
GRAYER		369
GREENWALD	Shulamit	253, 282

GREENBERG	Uri Tzvi	4
GREENBLATT	Feiga	88
GREENBLATT	Joel	51, 162, 163, 455
GREENBLATT	Liba	302, 308
GREENBLATT	Samuel Zanvel	88, 162, 163
GREENBLATT	Yacov	29, 162, 449, 455
GREGORY	Isaacovich	338
GREENBAUM	Reuven	251, 390
GREENBAUM	Yehuda Nusen	78, 149
GROSS	Feivel	409
GROSKOPF	Joseph	456
GROSKOPF	Leah	456
GROSKOPF	Menachem	69, 249, 369, 379
GROSKOPF	Samuel Moshe	89, 112, 170, 241, 249, 295
GRUBER	Chava	55, 89
GRUBER	Eliezer	55, 88, 444
GRUBER	Joseph	444
GRUBER	Yehuda	38
GURFEIN	Ryvka	446
GUTTENBERG-WELISH	Eisik	251
GUTWIRTH	Meir Mordechai	134, 135, 158, 159,
GUZIK	Menachem Mendel	443, 457
HACKER	Eta	89, 303, 457
HAGEL	Eta	89
HAGEL	Golda	390
HAGEL	Yacov	61
HALBERSTAM	Rabbi Baruch	198
HALBERSTAM	Rabbi Chaim	11, 14, 19,
HALBERSTAM	Rabbi Chune Koloszyce	137, 360, 410, 411
HALBERSTAM	Rabbi Moshe	168
HALBERSTAM	Naphtali	59, 73, 236

HALBERSTAM	Shlomo, Rabbi of Bobow	171, 364, 368, 376-78
HALBERSTAM	Ychezkiel, Rabbi of Sieniawa	100, 122, 137, 296
HALBERSTAM	Yechezkiel David	368, 378
HALLER	General	63
HALPERIN	Bezalel	296
HALPERIN	Malka	296
HALPERIN	Moshe	322
HAMAN	(Bible)	334
HANTZELDORF		411
HASENKOPF	Chaim	456
HASENKOPF	Maurice	456
HASENKOPF	Michael	253
HASENKOPF	Nathan	456
HASENKOPF	Menachem Mendel	433, 444
HASENKOPF	Sarah	433
HAUBEN	Feivel	236
HAUBEN	Israel	70
HAUBEN	Nechemiah	250, 384
HAUBEN	Wolf	250
HAUSNER	Shabtai	445
HENIG	Moshe	38
HERBERT	Lord Samuel	253
HERSH	Rabbi of Rymanow	98, 296
HERSH	Ber the Sexton	197
HERTZKES	Meir	150, 163
HERZL	Theodor Dr	122
HINDLER	Helen	456
HIRSHFELD	Rabbi	180
HIRSHFELD	Moshe	322
HIRSHFELD	Zisha	237, 319, 322, 456
HITLER		8, 19, 41, 138, 206, 269, 290, 354, 444, 454, 456, 460

HOCHDORF	Leibush	110, 111
HOCHDORF	Shimon	70
HOLLES	Eisik	28, 143, 144
HOLLES	Gershon	236
HOLLES	Joseph	168
HOLLES	Rabbi Joshua	13
HOLLES	Meir	291
HOLLES	Rabbi Shlomo	168
HOLOSHITZ	Heschel	154-56
HOROWITZ	Rabbi Alter Zev	10, 16, 19, 20, 25, 26, 29, 36, 38, 39, 50, 66, 73, 100-02, 120, 170, 171 183, 184, 195, 228, 233, 236 257
HOROWITZ	Chaim Yehuda	26, 66, 183 184
HOROWITZ	Golda	64, 65, 67
HOROWITZ	Rabbi Itzhok	120
HOROWITZ	Rabbi Joshua	195
HOROWITZ	Rabbi Kalonymus	19, 26, 183, 184, 236, 358
HOROWITZ	Menachem Mendel	13
HOROWITZ	Menashe	236
HOROWITZ	Naphtali, Ropczyce Rabbi	11, 13, 19, 98, 102, 103, 107, 108, 120, 168
HOROWITZ	Naphtali Chaim	236
HOROWITZ	Rabbi Shlomo Chaim	448
ISRAEL	Rabbi of Ryzhin	14, 87, 117, 337
ITZHOK	Rabbi of Krakow	11
ITZHOK	the butcher	199
ITZHOK	Eisik from Ziditchow	321
JABLOCINSKI	Priest	50, 59, 63, 172,
JAWORSKI	Leopold Dr.	53
JOHANNES	Moshe	56, 203
JOSHUA	Rabbi of Dzikow	195, 196
KAHANE	Chief Rabbi	453
KALB	Abraham, Schochet	296, 364,
KALB	Aryeh	397, 406

KALB	Ben Zion	296, 364, 366, 369, 371, 372, 374, 377, 448
KALB	Chaim Itzhok	289, 397; 406, 433, 444, 445, 457
KALB	Chanan Abraham	406, 407
KALB	Levi	250
KALB	Menachem Mendel	297, 364, 368
KALB	Michael	396, 397
KALB	Rachel	290, 406
KALB	Reisl	397, 406
KALB	Sarah	289
KALB	Tanchum Yacov	289, 296
KALB	Sheindl	296
KAMINER	Abraham	257
KANDEL	Menachem	297, 456
KANDEL	Moshe	297, 456
KANNER	Aaron	37, 96, 97, 168, 170
KANNER	Abraham Itzhok	330, 433
KANNER	Avishal	96, 97, 168
KANNER	Beila	160
KANNER	Chana	160
KANNER	Chaya	160
KANNER	Dvoira	168
KANNER	Eliyahu Yehuda	456
KANNER	Freidel	159
KANNER	Israel	63, 159, 160, 168
KANNER	Itzhok	159, 168
KANNER	Joseph Bendet	159
KANNER	Menachem Mendel	449
KANNER	Moshe	168
KANNER	Pinches	90, 168, 169
KANNER	Yacov	29, 157, 159, 168, 169, 200, 405, 406
KANNER	Yacov Nathan	110, 111

KANNER	Yehuda Leibush	168
KANNER	Yehudit	159
KANT	Immanuel	223
KAISER	Franz Joseph I	59, 146, 151, 155,
KARP	Engineer	342
KARP	Israel Leib	73
KATZNELSON	Itzhok	377
KEH	Abraham	29
KEH	Akiba	185
KEH	Yacov	54
KELLER	Commandant	232, 248
KIMMEL	Alexander	67, 68
KIRSCHENBAUM	Elimelech	382
KLAGSFELD	Abraham Ever	171
KLAGSWALD	Ever	171
KLAPPER	Eliezer Yacov	433
KLASSEN	Erwin	411
KLEIMAN	Dr.	382
KLEINMINTZ		381
KLOTZ	Joseph the Sexton	41, 114
KLOTZ	Pinches	81, 281, 302, 445
KLUSKA	Adam	462, 463
KNELLER	Eisik	70
KNELLER	Ephraim	70, 235
KNELLER	Itzhok	70,
KNELLER	Paltiel	70, 310
KOLODZIEJ	Ludwig	247
KOPEL	from Lykow	296
KOPITCIUK	Jasiek	92, 227
KONIECZKOWSKI		51, 181, 182
KOMARNO	Rabbi	160, 161

KORMINSKI		366
KORN	Elimelech	37
KORNHAUSER	Dr	194
KORNREICH	Gnendl	289
KORNREICH	Nathan 289	449
KORNREICH	Meir	449
KOSCIUSZKO	Tadeusz	179
KOCIELA	Joseph	93,
KRACHER	from Frysztak	237
KRACHER	Leah	55, 89
KRACHER	Pinches	70,
KRACHER	Tzvi	56
KRANTZLER	Bluma	208
KRANTZLER	Henry	222
KRANTZLER	Molly	211
KRANTZLER	Moshe	222, 294
KRANTZLER	Sheindl	211, 222
KRANTZLER	Yente	211, 213, 230
KRANTZLER	Yerachmiel	211, 225, 229
KRAUT	Abraham	4449
KRAUT	Benjamin	199
KRAUT	Israel	449
KRAUT	Pearl	199
KRAUT	Samuel	198
KRAUT	Yehuda	198, 449
KREMER	Joel	368
KREMERMAN-RUSS	Ruth	298
KRESH	Ryvka	303
KUBOWITZKI	M	252
KUPERBERG	Freida Gitel	408
KUTYANSKI	Joseph	374

KWIECINSKI	Priest	181
KRYM	Moshe	68
LANGERMAN	Chana	444
LANDAU	Leib Dr.	67
LANDESMAN	Asher Leml	303,
LANDESMAN	Getzel	457
LANDESMAN	Miriam	303
LANDESMAN	Reisl	456
LANDESMAN	Yacov	70
LANGSAM	Anna	464
LANGSAM-MILLER	Golda	85, 300
LANGSAM	Fruma Ryvka	298
LANGSAM	Harry-Yechezkiel	1, 84, 111, 354, 357, 359, 363, 379, 415, 444, 464
LANGSAM	Pesach	12, 298
LANGSAM	Simcha	298, 299, 352, 357, 362, 379, 415, 444, 445
LANGSAM	Tzvi Elimelech	298,
LANGSAMYACOV		298, 363, 415, 456
LANNER	Itzhok	444
LANCUT	Rebetzin	109
LAST	Abraham	455
LAST	Chaim	455
LAST	Chava	413, 414
LAST	Feitel	123-25
LAST	Michael Leib	449, 455
LAST	Moshe	455
LAST	Samuel	413
LAST	Shlomo	123-27
LATTERBAUM	Sisters	391, 392
LAUFER	Chaim	443, 455
LAUFER	Mendel	455
LEHAR		205

LEHRMAN	Chaim	208, 211-6, 221-4
LEHRMAN	Elchanan Dr.	204, 224, 225, 226,
LEHRMAN	David	216
LEHRMAN	Isaac	224, 226, 228, 229
LEHRMAN	Itzhok	399
LEHRMAN	Joseph	208, 216
LEHRMAN	Leib	208
LEHRMAN	Moshe	398, 401
LEHRMAN	Naphtali	224, 226, 229, 230
LEHRMAN	Roselain	226
LEVI	Itzhok from Berditchev	10, 461
LEV	Bezalel	409
LEV	Itzhok (Irving)	447, 449
LEV	Ethel	433
LEVI	Shlomo	400
LEVIN	Aaron	Rabbi, 274
LEVIN	Itzhok Meir	368
LEVIN	Nathan	Rabbi, 65
LEVIN-MOHRER	Eta	402
LEVIN	Chaya	402, 404
LICHT	Eliezer	285
LICHTMAN	Hersh	241
LIEBER	Clara	368, 371
L~EBERMAN	Chaim	412
LIEBERMAN	David	234, 241, 250, 359,
LIEBERMAN	Itzhok	250
LIEBERMAN	Leibush	250
LIEBERMAN	Menachem	250, 383, 384
LIEBERMAN	Samuel	359
LOOS	Adela	252
LOOS	Elazar	70, 92, 235, 247, 2

LOOS	Eliezer	251, 252-54, 290,30
LOOS	Leah	91, 179, 252, 253,
LOOS	Sarah	308
LOOS	Vita	53, 88
LUBAVITCHER	Rabbi	345
LUBETKIN	Tzivia	368, 371, 377
LUBASH		382
MALEC	Jan	366, 368
MAIMONIDES	Moshe, Rambam	131, 139, 148, 260, 306
MALIK	Rabbi Hersh Leib	128
MALIN	Dr.	183
MANDEL	Benjamin	252, 353
MANDEL	Chaim	70, 71, 104, 114, 126, 127, 169, 246, 295, 306, 354
MANDEL-FEIT	Hilda	384
MANDEL	Kreindel Bracha	127
MANDEL	Mina	295
MANDEL	Mishket	88
MANDEL	Moshe Yacov	112, 169, 456
MANDEL	Naphtali	127, 295, 306, 354
MANDEL	Reuven Zelig	55, 433
MANDEL	Sarah	308
MANDEL	Seryl	126
MANDEL	Shimon	21, 169, 251, 252
MANDEL	Wolf	69, 127, 384
MANDEL	Yeshayahu	41, 87, 127, 128, 169, 180, 251, 252, 295, 353, 456
MARGALIT	Joel	98
MARGOLIS		62
MARIA	Theresa	78
MARX	Karl	265
MATEUS		410
MAZNICKA		244

MEIRSON	Yacov	345
MEIR	Rabbi from Premishlan	124
MEISLER	Henoch	408
MENACHEM	Mendel from Tarnow	11
MENDELTHE	Rabbi from Kook	10
MENDELE	Rabbi from Rymanow	10, 107
MENASHE	from Lutcza	197
MESHULAM	Rabbi of Tishmenitz	11
MICKIEWICZ	Adam	286
MILBAUER	Tzvi Yacov	452
MILGRAUM	Akiba Samuel	167
MILLSTEIN	Leah	280
MIKOPNIK	Major	152
MINTZ	Abraham	89, 169,
MINTZ	Eisik	456
MINTZ	Michael	169
MINTZ	Shlomo	169,
MOHRER	Chaim	55, 89, 306
MOHRER	Eta	55, 89, 402
MOHRER	Mendel	156, 157
MOHRER	Shlomo	156, 157
MOHRER	Tzipora	452
MOHRER	Tzvi	47, 55, 173, 402
MOHRER	Zalman	29
MOSHE	Rabbi Yechiel	11
MURAVIN		464
MURAVINA	Esther	464
MURAVIN	Itzhok	464
MURAVIN	Joseph	464
MURAVINA	Sonia	464
MURAVINA	Fruma	464

MURAVIN	Joel	464, 465
MURAVIN	Leib	464
MURAVINA	Rachel (Raya)	464,
MURAVINA	Sheindl	464
MURAVIN	Zelig	464
MENDELSOHN	Moshe	12
MUSSLER		409
MUSSLER	Abraham	146
MUSSLER	Eliezer	104
MUSSLER	Eliyahu	194
MUSSLER	Joel	331, 455
MUSSLER	Leah	473
MUSSLER	Moshe	86, 143, 324, 446,
MUSSLER	Samuel	41, 310, 311, 3 315, 413, 446, 448
MUSSLER	Sarah	331, 455
NACHMAN	Rabbi from Bratzlav	2
NAPHTALI	Rabbi from Mielec	96
NAPOLEON		220, 304
NAVON	Tzvi	402, 404
NECHAMA	wife of Eli Dovid	92
NECHEMIAH	Alter	29, 47, 71, 80 203, 321
NECHEMIAH	Hena	53, 88
NEWMAN	Dr.	368
NEUMANN	Bat Sheva	305
NEUMANN	Chana	305
NEUMANN	Chaya	305
NEUMANN	Gina	305
NEUMANN	Moshe Aaron	305
NEUMANN	Odess	305
NEUMANN	Rosi	305
NEUMANN	Irit	305

NEUMANN	Shlomo	305
NEUMANN	Toni	305
NUREMBERG	Baruch	55, 88, 433
NUREMBERG	Chaim Yacov	46, 70, 90, 104, 12
NUREMBERG	Elazar	433, 444
NUREMBERG	Itzhok Eisik	297
NUREMBERG	Moshe	69, 297, 456
NUREMBERG	Shlomo	456
NUREMBERG	Yechezkiel	456
NUTMAN	Israel	20
NUTMAN	Rabbi Naphtali	20, 68
OFFENBACH		205
ORENSTEIN	Joseph	14
OLVA	Jan	22
OLVA	Mikolay	22
OSTROWCE	Rabbi	296
PANCZESZIN		348
PASEK		381
PATRYN	Adam	258
PATRYN	Jan	108, 244
PATRYN	Ignac	244
PATRYN	Joseph Dr.	51, 110, 119, 162, 181-183
PERETZ	Itzhok L 52	92, 409, 412-414
PETLURA		239
PFEFFER	Hersh	52, 443
PFEFFER	Israel	444
PHILIPOWICZ	Count	250
PILSUDSKI	Jozef	187
PINCHOWSKI	Chaya	250
PINCHOWSKI	Eliezer	289
PINCHOWSKI	Rachel	289

PINCHOWSKI	Mordechai	289
PINCHOWSKI	Israel	449
PINCHOWSKI	Moshe	449
PINSEL	Peretz	54
PONIATOWSKI	Jozef	179
POPPER	Aryeh	253, 254, 291
POPPER	Mordechai	253, 254, 291
POPPER	Vita	253, 254, 191
PORETZKY	Dr.	56
PORTNOI	Moshe	465
POTOCHNY		187
PRESSER	Yacov	89
PROPPER	Gita	449
PROPPER	Hena	449
PUDERBEITEL		237, 409
RABIN	Itzhok	460
RABINOWITZ	Baruch Rabbi	127, 446, 452
RABINOWITZ	Fruma ryvka	433
RACHNITZ	Chief	409
RAPPAPORT	Chaya	410
REBHUN	Sarah	54, 179
REBHUN	Yacov	179
REDLER	Itzhok	112
REICH	Jospeh	251-53, 290-92
REICH	Henia	290
REICHER	Abraham	449
REICHER	Leah	89
REICHER	Moshe	156, 200
REICHER	Reisl	198
RESSLER	Chaim	320
RESSLER	Hersh	169, 318

RESSLER	Yacov	409
RIDZ	Smigly	352
RIGER-LICHTIG	Henia	456
RIGER	Rosa	456
RIGER	Wolf	409, 410
RITTER	58	320, 247
ROITMAN	Aaron	464
ROITMAN	Eidl	464
ROITMAN	Wolf	464
ROSEN	Itzhok Leib	21, 138, 240, 242,
ROSEN	Chaim	243
ROSEN	Chaya	90, 243
ROSEN	David	170
ROSEN	Joel	62, 170, 455
ROSEN	Joseph Hersh	62, 170, 455
ROSEN	Leah	303
ROSEN	Mendel 28	69, 71, 113, 170, 2
ROSEN	Moshe	250
ROSEN	Samuel	90, 170, 246, 247, 250, 251, 380, 382, 383, 385, 452
ROSEN	Pearl	251, 381, 385
ROSEN	Yacov	29, 69, 71, 113, 170, 235, 241
ROSEN	Yechiel	90, 170, 250, 251, 316, 382, 386, 455
ROSENBAUM	Basha	72, 199
ROSENBAUM	Mordechai	43, 72, 199, 449
ROSENBAUM	Shprintza	449
ROSENBLUTH	Elazar	161
ROSENBLUTH	Rizhi	41, 89, 161
ROSENBLUTH	Samuel	307
ROSENTHAL	Dr.	250
ROTH	Bunim	306
ROTH	Egan	366

ROTH	Naphtali	54, 55, 237
ROTH	Pessil	55, 89
ROTHCHILD	Baron	13, 190
ROTHMAN	Itzhok	336, 338
RUBIN	Joseph	168
RUDEL		411
RUSS	Abraham	298
RUSS	Aryeh	298
RUSS	Rachel	298
RUSS	Roni	89
RUSS	Bat Sheva	89
RUSS	Mordechai	243
RYBNER	Brothers	382
SADIGORA	Rabbi	98, 99, 117, 134, 169, 170, 201, 302, 458
SAFRIN	Fruma Ryvka	28
SALTZMAN	Samuel	249
SAMUEL	Canter from Ustrzyki	116
SAMUELI	Dr.	238
SAPHIRE	Reuven	110, 172, 260
SAPHIRE	Samuel	241
SHACHER	Feivel	55, 88
SHACHER	Joseph	41, 89
SCHEFLER	Abraham	449
SCHEFLER	Batyah	171, 449
SCHEFLER	David	251, 281
SCHEFLER	Joshua	449
SCHEFLER	Mordechai Mendel	76, 170, 449
SCHEFLER	Moshe	170, 241, 281, 303, 449
SCHEFLER	Ryvka	449
SCHEFLER	Shimon	170, 281
SCHEFLER	Sheindl	281,

SCHEFLER	Tzvi	55, 281
SCHIFF	Berish	455, 456
SCHIFF	Bracha	20
SCHIFF	Chana	301
SCHIFF	Chaya	302
SCHIFF	David	302
SCHIFF	David Hersh	87, 201
SCHIFF	Joseph	55, 301, 445
SCHIFF	Joseph Mordechai	70
SCHIFF	Kalman Yacov	455, 456
SCHIFF	Levi Itzhok	20, 30, 63-6, 87, 302, 433, 443, 444, 446, 448
SCHIFF	Meir	70, 302
SCHIFF	Mordechai	87, 88, 170, 446, 455
SCHIFF	Ryvka	87, 302, 433
SCHIFF	Yehuda	319
SCHIFF	Yacov	20, 129, 135
SCHIFF	Samuel	199
SCHIFF	Jeweliler	199
SCHIFF	Zev	446
SEIDMAN	Alter Ezra	20, 28, 80, 106 160
SEIDMAN	Benjamin	160, 161
SEIDMAN	Moshe	20, 51, 160, 161
SHICK	Meir Rabbi	171
SCHITZ	Michael	29, 183, 237, 379
SCHLISSELBERG	Chana	454
SCHLISSELBERG	Freda	454
SCHLISSELBERG	Itzhok	237
SCHLISSELBERG	Moshe	433
SCHLISSELBERG	Nathaniel	449, 454
SCHLISSELBERG	Yechezkiel	454
SCHLOSMAN	Gitel	245

SCHMIDT	Mendel	414
SCHMIDT	Moshe	408
SCHMIDT	Shlomo	317, 408, 409, 411
SCHMIDT	Tzvi	408
SCHMIDT	Commandant	382
SCHNEIDER	Esther	456
SCHREIBER	Noah	46
SCHREIBER	Samuel	70
SCHWARTZ	Eliezer	303
SCHWARTZ	Mordechai	300, 303
SCHWARTZBART	Itzhok Dr.	53, 66
SCHWARTZMAN	Meir Mordechai	70
SCHWARTZMAN	Moshe	59, 69, 73, 86, 158
SCHWARTZMAN	Moshe J.	130
SCHWARTZMAN	Risha	130
SCHWARTZMAN	Sarah	433, 443
SCHWARTZMAN	Shalom	54, 70, 71, 87, 100
SCHWARTZMAN	Yetta	130
SCHWEIK	Soldier	193
SELIGMAN	Joshua	65
SELTZER		342
SHALOM	Rabbi from Kaminka	12
SHALOM	from Prohobeshnitz	128
SHALOM	Aleichem	52
SHAPIRO	Brothers	400, 412
SHAPIRO	Rabbi Chaim Elazar	14, 25, 82, 104, 126, 127, 139, 168,172 180, 202, 295, 298
SHAPIRO	Chana	127, 198, 295
SHAPIRO	Chaya Fruma	14
SHAPIRO	Rabbi David	12
SHAPIRO	Rabbi Elazer	12-14, 24, 168
SHAPIRO	Rabbi Meir	176

SHAPIRO	Rabbi Moshe	399
SHAPIRO	Rabbi Moshe Leib	14, 19, 26, 27, 36, 39, 96, 106, 124, 155, 195, 198, 213, 228, 257, 258, 295, 452
SHAPIRO	Rabbi Nechemiah	19, 20, 27, 28, 36, 75, 103-08, 127, 128, 140, 141, 143, 183, 184, 243, 251, 295, 379, 457
SHAPIRO	Sarah	56
SHAPIRO	Tzvi	54, 68, 170, 302
SHAPIRO	Rabbi Tzvi Elimelech	11-13, 24, 73, 98, 103, 104, 123, 125, 127, 196, 284, 285, 363
SHAPIRO	Tzvi Hersh	14, 25, 68
SHAPIRO	Rabbi Shlomo	12-14, 19, 21, 24-6, 28, 37, 69, 87, 90, 91, 98, 99, 124, 170, 171, 173, 183, 184, 355, 452
SHAPIRO	Elazar Rabbi	171, 184
SHAPIRO	Tila	28
SHAPIRO	Tova Chava	13
SHAPIRO	Rabbi Yeshayahu	28, 184
SHEINGAL	238	380
SHEINMAN	Chaya	246
SHEINMAN	Fruma	246
SHENFELD	Moshe	368
SHEPS		449
SHIMMEL	Abraham	433
SCHIMMEL	Itzhok	443
SCHIMMEL	Mordechai	433,
SCHIMMEL	Pessil	433
SCHIMMEL	Pinchos	456
SHIPPER	Leibush	164
SHIPPER	Nechama	164
SHMELKIS	Rabbi Gedalyahu	59
SHMELKIS	Rabbi Itzhok	122
SHMUEL	the tailor	198,
SZMULEWICZ	Reuven	302
SHORR	Abraham	279

SHORR	J., Canter	117
SHPALTER	Ephraim	20, 106, 462
SHPALTER	Yacov	20, 28, 71, 106, 10
SHPITOL	Sergeant	185-87
SHUBKE	Commander	382
SHULMAN	Elka	47, 188, 189
SCHWALBE		374
SIBIRCA		239
SIKORSKI	General	236, 340, 348
SIENKEWICZ	Henoch	135
SMIDT	Sisters	368
SPERBER	Joseph	409
SPRINGER	Feiga	89
STALIN	220	236, 265, 342, 348, 351
STEMPEL	Feivel	368
STEMPEL	Moshe	368, 378
STEPPEL	Eliezer	280
STEPPEL	Feivel	184
STEPPEL	Frieda	280
STERN	Shlomo	366
STERN	Mrs	368, 371
STERNBERG	Leib	37, 38, 76, 170
STERNBERG	Tzvi Elazar	51, 53, 61, 90, 444
STOILOWSKI	Priest	59, 61, 91
STRAUCHER		382
STRAUS		205
STRAZOWSKI		22
STRENGEROWSKI-ROSEN	Pearl	385, 452
STUDNICKI	Professor	348
STURM	Avrohom	171, 177
STURM	Chaim Israel	393

STURM	Joshua	88
STURM	Mendel	69
STURM	Necha Gitel	393
STURM	Shimon	171
STURM	Yacov	23, 69, 171
SUCHA	Rabbi	368
SZARO		244
SYRUP	Tzvi	53
TAUB	Dr.	225
TAUB	Aaron	237
TAUBE	Abraham	280
TAUBE	Chana	280
TAUBE	Joseph	280
TAUBE	Moshe	280
TZCHWAL	Dr.	236
TCHORTKOW	Rabbi	338
TEITELBAUM	Rabbi Moshe	11, 68
TEITELBAUM	Malka Rose	91
TEITELBAUM	Nachman	90, 91
TETELBAUM	Shimon	90, 91
TENZER	Abraham	29, 71, 171, 314, 315, 321
TENZER	Hersh	171, 172, 196
TENZER	Itzhok	51, 52, 171
TENZER	Mordechai	70
TENZER	Moshe	171
TENZER	Shlomo Zalman	172, 433
TENZER	Tuvia	171
TENZER	Yacov	171
TEPPER	Itzhok	408
TEPPER	Necha	408
TISHLER	Golda	433, 445

TORQUEMADA		388
TROTZKY		342
TUCHMAN	Gitel	457
THIM	Kalman	248
THIM	Moshe	248
TUCKER-ROTH	Liba	3d7
TURNER	Chana	266
TURTELTAUB	Shlomo	455
TTVI	Hersh from Ziditchow	12
TYCZYN	Rabbi	202
UNGER	Eliezer	368
UNGER	Hena Rachel	41
UNGER	Hersh	448
UNGER	Moshe David	175
USZLICKI	Wladislaw	244
VASILEWSKA	Vanda	341
VASILY	Ivanowich	338
VILF		249
VITAL	Chaim	11
VOLKOVISKY	Shevach	173
WAGSHAL	Ralman	410
WAGNER	Nicole	456
WALDMAN	Elimelech	55, 238, 302
WALLACH	Abraham	320
WALLACH	Joseph Asher	318, 319
WALLACH	Shalom	235
WALLACH	Yechezkiel	54, 319, 320-22
WASSERMAN	Breindl	47, 88
WEBER	Naphtali Hertz	162, 163, 291
WEBER	Yacov Itzhok	328, 455
WEICHSELBAUM	Alter Yacov	236, 455

WEICHSELBAUM	Bat Sheva	455
WEIDEN	Kalman	445
WEIDEN	Tuvia	445
WEIDENFELD	Joseph Saul	288
WEINBERG	Berish	90, 91, 368
WEINBERG	Chaim	88
WEINBERG	Feiga	53
WEINBERG	Joseph	88, 251, 302, 387
WEINBERG	Mordechai	368, 371
WEISER		289
WEISS	Elazar	20
WEISS	Sarah	20
WEISMAN	Abraham Pinchos	20
WEISMANDEL	Micha Dov	Rabbi, 364, 366, 369
WEITMAN	Mordechai	70, 236
WIENER	David	20, 70, 122, 243
WIENER	Isachar	20
WIENER	Joseph	19, 28, 69, 123, 13
WIENER	Yechetkiel	456
WIELKOPOLSKI	Stanislaw	22
WIERZBICKI	Dr.	236
WILNER	Israel	54
WILNER	Mordechai	59
WILNER	Shlomo	320, 456
WIND	Levi Joseph	137, 138
WLODEK	Maria	292
WLODEK	Michael	292
WOLKOWICKI	Count	22, 23, 67, 179, 23
WOLF	Joseph	443, 457
WURTTEL	Elater	96, 104, 112, 121,
WYZIKOWSKI		61, 62

YAFFE	Zachariah	247, 381
YAHALOMI	Dvora	289
YAHALOMI-DIAMAND	Shlomo	5, 9, 10, 21, 41, 42, 51, 68, 96, 114, 121, 165, 167, 195, 272, 284, 320, 332, 334, 364, 393, 444-46, 454, 458
YEHUDA	Halevi	164, 284
YOSL	from Brzozow	73
ZAGNER	Zalman	47
ZALEWSKI		174
ZAMORSKI	Jan	179
ZANGER	Miriam	302
ZEEMAN		342
ZIEBNER	Yechezkiel	232
ZIEGEL	Chaim Yacov	202
ZUKIER		381
ZILBER	Joshua	169, 170
ZILBER	Moshe	88, 170
ZILBER	Pinches	88, 170
ZILBER	Sarah	53, 88, 170
ZILBERMAN	Wolf	69
ZUKERMAN	Itzhok	368, 371, 374, 375,
ZVEIG	Stephen	206

[Pages 558-560]

Photographs from Strzyzow (Original Book Pages)

The shul in Strzyzow	1
Reb Chaim Elazar Shapiro, the Rabbi of Strzyzow-Munkatch	15
Reb Alter Zev Horowitz, the Rabbi of Strzyzow.	16
Reb Wolf Deutch, the most active Kehillah leader.	17
Reb Heschel Diamand, last presiding Kehillah leader.	18
Copy of a report card and certificate of award.	44
Rules and regulations for students attending the Talmud Torah.	45

The Hebrew kindergarten and nursery.	48
A class in the Polish elementary School.	49
Places where the alleged blood libel took place.	64
The Bais Yacov School for girls.	74
Children in captivity.	250
Rabbi Israel Frenkel from Toronto.	263
Reb Samuel Nachum Frenkel, Toronto.	277
Title page of a prayer book written in a Russian prison.	362
Jan Malec, his son and relatives.	367
Clara Lieber, Mordechai Weinberg's sons, and postcard from the valley of death.	371
Children who were rescued by Ben Zion Kalb.	371
Yacov Feingold, and his postcard.	392
Joseph Asher.	394
Michael Kalb.	396
Moshe Lehrman.	398
Tzvi Navon.	403
Aaron, the son of Yacov Kanner.	405
Chanan Abraham Kalb.	407
Memorial Plaque which was installed in the Holocaust Cellar.	435
The Torah Scroll.	435
The lighting of the memorial candles by Itzhok Berglass.	436
Memorial services for the martyrs of Strzyzow.	436
Shlomo Yahalomi, eulogizing the martyrs.	437
Memorial services in the Holocaust Cellar.	438
Remnants of the Jewry of Strzyzow.	439
The Secretary, Samuel Mussler, and Irving Lev, meeting Ben Gurion.	447
The synagogue in Sao Paulo, the interior of the Synagogue and the consecration of the synagogue.	450
The memorial plaque for the martyrs of Strzyzow, and for the six million Jewish martyrs.	451
Title page of the book Sova Smachot	466
Title page of the book Netivot Olam.	461
Title page of the book Bnuyot Berama	468

Title page of the book Toldot Noah	469
Title page of the book Olam Echad, and the shul before the war	470
The remodeled shul	471
Interior paintings in the shul	472-475
The entrances after the remodeling	476
The new look of the interior	477-478
The marketplace before the war, the Beit Hamidrash alley and kloiz	479
General view of the town, house of the Rabbi and the Unger family	480
The Talmud Torah and Lehavdil the steeple of the church, also the houses of Fishel Goldberg and Reuven Saphire	481
Houses in Strzyzow	482
The club house and the school	483
A village near Strzyzow, the grove "Lentovnia" and the emblem of Strzyzow	484
The river crossings and the railroad station.	485
Youth organizations in Strzyzow.	486-490
A family celebration and stamps of various institutions	491
Various documents	492
Various types in Strzyzow	493
Gravestones of Akiba Shmuel Tenzer, Tzvi Schiff, and Mecha Kanner	494
Desecrated gravestones	495-496
Rachel Bernstein and the Borgenicht family	497
Baruch Berglass' daughters and his grandson David Dov Bernstein	498
The Gruber Family	499
Chaim Shmuel Guttenberg and Moshe Dym	500
The Goldberg family	501
The Diamond family and Yantche Hagel 502-5	
Alter Chaim Weinberg	506
The Weidens and the last mayor of Frysztak	507
The Kalb Family	508
Ben Zion and Mendel Kalb, Malka Halperin with her son Bezalel, Moshe Nuremberg and Menashe Frehman	
The Loos Family	510

Chaim and Bluma Lehrman, and the children of Yacov Langsam	511
The Mandel family	512-3
The Musslers, the Feingolds, and Hersh Pfeffer	514
Samuel Feit and his family	515
Joseph Klotz, and his family, also Hersh and Yenta Kraut	516
The Russ family	517
Hershel Reslers grandchildren	517
The Deutch family	518
The Sternberg family	520
The Sturm family	521
The Asher family and the Schlisellbergs	522
The Schiff family	523
Itzhok and Deiche Redler, Yacov Sturm, and the Shmulewicz family	524
Feiga and Benjamin Roth, and the Schefler family	525-6
Alter Nechemiah, Reizhi Diamand, and group of girls from the Diamand, Brav, and Feit families	527

NAME INDEX
Of this Englsih translation

A

Acht, 312, 463
Ader, 312
Adest, 48, 131, 134, 155, 156, 157, 159, 188, 190, 226, 239, 282, 354
Adest, 312, 314, 320, 328, 341, 463
Adler, 358, 359, 360
Adler, 312, 463
Agnon, 67
Aloni, 6, 68, 212, 350, 351
Alster, 312
Ameis, 354, 399, 444
Ameis, 312, 463
Amkraut, 312
Ander, 253, 254
Anders, 312, 463
Ansbacher, 245, 246
Apperman, 312
Asher, 136, 226, 238, 239, 293, 294, 322, 334, 350, 440, 464, 480, 494, 497, 499
Asher, 312, 335, 463, 464
Ashlag, 226
Auerhhun, 397
Auerhoun, 313, 320, 464
Auerhun, 74, 75, 262, 403
Augustin, 304

B

Baal Shem Tov, 9, 12, 14, 15, 96, 99, 203, 214, 362
Baim, 354, 436
Baldinger, 304, 305
Baldinger, 308, 464
Banski, 184
Barth, 314
Bartoshek, 270
Bartoshek, 464
Baumel, 134, 181, 197
Baumel, 313, 315, 339, 464
Beigayer, 307
Beigayer, 308, 464
Beitler, 59, 190
Beitler, 313, 464
Beller, 291
Beller, 464
Ben Gurion, 353, 497
Ber, 120
Ber, 313, 464
Berger, 55, 57, 191, 193, 225, 272, 444

Berger, 313, 319, 326, 332, 336, 464
Berglass, 1, 6, 11, 22, 29, 37, 39, 43, 48, 56, 60, 67, 74, 81, 93, 105, 124, 126, 127, 128, 131, 138, 139, 140, 141, 143, 145, 146, 147, 148, 155, 180, 211, 225, 230, 231, 234, 236, 238, 239, 255, 256, 257, 258, 259, 272, 291, 293, 304, 305, 310, 344, 348, 350, 351, 354, 415, 435, 497, 498
Berglass, 308, 313, 317, 321, 332, 341, 465
Berish, 75, 76, 272, 337, 339, 359, 360, 489, 495
Bernstein, 44, 59, 62, 63, 148, 180, 187, 211, 231, 414, 415, 448, 449, 498
Bernstein, 313, 465
Berstein, 73
Bert, 120
Bevas, 314
Bialik, 46, 59, 67, 103, 117
Bialik, 465
Bido, 351
Bido, 465
Bier, 119
Bier, 465
Bilder, 341, 465
Bilitcki, 465
Bilut, 83, 239, 240, 241
Bilut, 465
Birnbach, 350
Birnbach, 314, 341, 465
Blau, 222, 435
Blau, 314, 465
Blech, 313
Bleicher, 272
Bleicher, 465
Bloch, 399
Bloch, 314
Bludaya, 365
Bludaya, 466
Blum, 442
Bodner, 316
Bogomolov, 466
Bombach, 314
Borenstein, 356
Borenstein, 466
Borgenicht, 185, 186, 414, 498
Borgenicht, 314, 466
Bornstein, 272
Bornstein, 466
Brach, 466
Bran, 466
Brauer, 128
Brauer, 466

Brauner, 36, 74, 89, 225, 360
Brauner, 314, 322, 337, 466
Brav, 29, 35, 36, 45, 46, 74, 183, 188, 236, 282, 283, 284, 304, 305, 447, 499
Brav, 308, 314, 331, 466
Bren, 360
Broide, 50
Broner, 304, 305, 307
Broner, 308, 466
Bruder, 314
Bulok, 53
Bulok, 466

C

Canin, 263
Casimir, 466
Chamberlain, 171
Chamberlain, 466
Chatam, 466
Chmiel, 148
Chmiel, 466
Chmielnicki, 203
Chmielnicki, 456, 466
Chwal, 181
Chwal, 314
Cohen, 325, 328
Cook, 106
Cook, 466
Cuker, 157
Czapczynska, 285
Czapczynska, 467

D

Daladier, 171
Daladier, 467
Dan, 314
Dayches, 91
Dembitzar, 46
Dembitzer, 29, 74, 134, 211, 230, 354, 435, 436, 449, 450, 451, 452
Dembitzer, 314, 315, 316, 317, 467, 470
Deutch, 19, 29, 43, 48, 74, 88, 90, 141, 157, 180, 183, 185, 187, 238, 241, 310, 354, 356, 436, 437, 438, 496, 499
Deutch, 315, 467
Deutchar, 46
Deutcher, 339, 467
Diamand, 6, 12, 19, 29, 35, 38, 44, 45, 46, 47, 48, 56, 74, 75, 81, 91, 92, 95, 96, 104, 125, 131, 132, 135, 136, 144, 145, 146, 190, 195, 199, 208, 225, 226, 229, 231, 238, 239, 240, 241, 250, 255, 281, 351, 353, 354, 358, 359, 360, 390, 398, 399, 401, 419, 420, 421, 422, 446, 447, 449, 450, 454, 496, 498, 499
Diamand, 315, 316, 317, 318, 319, 323, 325, 327, 333, 335, 337, 338, 339, 341, 467, 468, 496

Diamant, 2
Diamond, 217
Dienstag, 316, 333
Diller, 29, 42, 74, 82, 106, 157, 211, 353, 360, 392, 448
Diller, 316, 319, 325, 468
Dolphus, 258
Dombrowski, 468
Dornberg, 316
Dov, 16, 17, 20, 109, 187, 211, 269, 271, 272, 312, 313, 330, 332, 415, 495, 498
Dresel, 316
Duks, 271
Duks, 468
Dym, 39, 48, 398, 401, 417, 453, 498
Dym, 316, 468
Dynow, 468

E

Eckstein, 272
Ehrlich, 316
Eichenstein, 133, 154
Eichenstein, 468, 469
Eichman, 469
Einhern, 469
Einhorn, 224, 429
Einhorn, 316, 469
Eisen, 217
Eisen, 328, 469
Eisenberg, 350, 359, 360
Eisenberg, 324, 328, 469
Eisenstadt, 260
Eisenstadt, 469
Eisik, 469
Eisman, 185
Eisman, 316, 469, 470
Eismann, 320
Eisner, 48, 160, 190, 191, 358
Eisner, 316, 469
Ekstein, 275
Ekstein, 469
Elazar, 469
Elazer, 143, 160, 190, 490
Emer, 265, 267, 268
Engel, 133, 146
Engel, 470
Engelhard, 306
Engelhard, 470
Englender, 256
Englender, 470
Epstein, 304
Epstein, 308, 470
Ettinger, 316, 317, 336, 338

F

Falk, 230, 435, 436

Falk, 317, 470
Fass, 356
Fass, 317, 470
Federbush, 216, 229, 230, 420, 421
Federbush, 317, 470
Feiber, 317
Feigenbaum, 317
Feingold, 45, 130, 291, 292, 362, 432, 497
Feingold, 341, 470
Feingolds, 45, 499
Feirush, 231
Feit, 43, 48, 53, 73, 148, 182, 188, 190, 191, 236, 282, 284, 285, 286, 354, 359, 399, 432, 433, 447, 454, 499
Feit, 317, 322, 323, 470, 482
Feivush, 415, 471
Feivush, 317, 465, 470, 471
Feivusz, 211
Felber, 190, 229, 284, 341, 401
Felber, 317, 339, 471
Felder, 190, 354, 355
Felder, 318, 471
Feldmaus, 63, 224
Feldmaus, 318, 471
Felt, 185, 188, 190
Felt, 470
Fessel, 339
Fihrer, 334
Filipowicz, 184
Fishel, 9, 15, 75, 181, 249, 307, 308, 315, 318, 319, 327, 333, 335, 354, 355, 360, 371, 389, 418, 463, 464, 469, 471, 473, 498
Fishier, 471
Fishler, 220, 351
Fishman, 318
Flaumenhaft, 45, 236
Flaumenhaft, 318, 471
Fleisher, 74, 90
Fleisher, 318, 471
Fleishman, 271
Franco, 164, 258
Frehman, 427, 498
Freiwirth, 74
Freiwirth, 471
Frenkel, 38, 67, 131, 144, 145, 181, 182, 199, 200, 201, 203, 208, 209, 217, 236, 240, 318, 354, 358, 422, 497
Frenkel, 318, 321, 472
Friedberg, 471
Friedman, 20, 28, 37, 41, 58, 59, 69, 72, 73, 262, 358, 433, 450
Friedman, 314, 318, 319, 323, 339, 471
Frihman, 319, 321

G

Galanti, 369
Gans, 472
Garfunkel, 34, 438
Garfunkel, 318, 319, 472
Gelander, 29, 36, 74, 94, 103, 447
Gelander, 319, 472
Gelber, 15
Gelber, 472
Gelbwachs, 212
Gelbwachs, 319, 331, 472
Gelernter, 16, 17
Gelernter, 472
Geller, 277
Geller, 472
Gendellman, 472
Gendelman, 250
Gens, 304
Gens, 472
Gertner, 37, 43, 48, 117, 128, 129, 131, 148, 159, 182, 185, 191, 193, 231, 238, 245, 359, 414
Gertner, 313, 319, 326, 335, 336, 472, 473
Getz, 325
Getzler, 223
Getzler, 473
Ginsberg, 190, 212, 249, 251
Ginsberg, 473
Glatt, 55
Glatt, 473
Glickman, 44, 63
Glickman, 319, 473
Glikman, 204
Glikman, 473
Glitzer, 319
Gocek, 187
Gocek, 473
Goldbeig, 473
Goldberg, 75, 76, 181, 225, 359, 360, 389, 418, 454, 498
Goldberg, 319, 320, 328, 335, 473
Goldfisher, 304
Goldfisher, 308, 473
Goldman, 43, 59, 94, 117, 131, 249
Goldman, 320, 322, 473
Goldman-Last, 43
Goldsand, 320
Goldzand, 438
Gorgel, 74, 158
Gorgil, 61
Gorgil, 473
Gornicki, 141, 186
Gornicki, 473
Gotlieb, 271, 304
Gotlieb, 308, 473
Grayer, 272
Grayer, 473
Greenbaum, 190, 288, 289
Greenbaum, 320, 474
Greenberg, 8
Greenberg, 474

Greenblatt, 29, 42, 45, 46, 74, 128, 129, 145, 225, 230, 354, 359, 447
Greenblatt, 320, 333, 474
Greenwald, 191
Greenwald, 473
Gregory, 474
Grinwald–Hasenkopg, 213
Groskopf, 58, 73, 185, 189, 221, 272, 281, 360
Groskopf, 320, 474
Gross, 304
Gross, 308, 316, 474
Grosskopf, 91
Gruber, 35, 48, 74, 75, 350, 351, 397, 402, 416, 417, 448, 449, 450, 451, 452, 498
Gruber, 320, 474
Gurfein, 351
Gurfein, 474
Guttenberg, 417, 498
Guttenberg, 336, 474
Guttman, 313
Gutwirth, 106, 293
Gutwirth, 474
Guzik, 350, 360, 416
Guzik, 315, 320, 337, 474

H

Haber, 320
Hacker, 226, 360, 422
Hacker, 341, 474
Hacohen, 101, 106
Hagel, 43, 50, 52, 75, 423, 450, 498
Hagel, 320, 334, 474
Halberstam, 17, 20, 62, 81, 97, 133, 156, 182, 222, 271, 272, 280, 305
Halberstam, 308, 321, 474, 475
Halbersten, 44
Halevi, 368
Haller, 475
Halperin, 222, 426, 498
Halperin, 321, 475
Hamel, 338
Hantzeldorf, 306
Hantzeldorf, 475
Hasenkopf, 191, 351, 360, 429
Hasenkopf, 318, 321, 325, 341, 475
Hassenkopf, 337
Hauben, 59, 182, 190, 284
Hauben, 321, 475
Hausner, 351
Hausner, 339, 340, 475
Hecker, 321
Hegel, 320
Henig, 35, 448
Henig, 321, 475
Herbert, 475
Hersh, 475
Hertz, 28, 85, 129, 145, 333, 494
Hertzkes, 118, 119
Hertzkes, 475
Herzl, 45, 97, 296, 326
Herzl, 475
Hindler, 360
Hindler, 475
Hirschfeld, 360
Hirshfeld, 143, 182, 239, 241
Hirshfeld, 339, 475
Hitler, 11, 20, 38, 57, 86, 109, 128, 164, 165, 180, 191, 203, 215, 217, 218, 224, 227, 236, 249, 262, 350, 358, 359, 360, 362
Hitler, 475
Hochdorf, 59, 90
Hochdorf, 331, 476
Hollander, 1
Hollander, 316
Holles, 16, 28, 113, 133, 182, 218, 291, 427
Holles, 321, 323, 326, 337, 476
Holoshitz, 121, 122, 123
Horowitz, 14, 15, 18, 20, 26, 27, 34, 35, 44, 55, 56, 57, 63, 73, 83, 96, 133, 135, 145, 154, 176, 182, 194, 353, 388, 443, 496
Horowitz, 318, 321, 341, 476

I

Ichel, 321
Isaacovitch, 252
Iserles, 321
Itzinger, 321
Ivanovitch, 252

J

Jablocinski, 50, 51, 52, 53
Jablocinski, 476
Jaworski, 46
Jaworski, 476
Johannes, 48, 160
Johannes, 476

K

Kagswald, 323
Kahane, 358
Kahane, 476
Kaiser, 478
Kaiser Franz Joseph, 50, 115, 119, 123, 164, 188
Kalb, 190, 217, 221, 268, 269, 270, 272, 274, 275, 277, 278, 279, 280, 295, 296, 297, 302, 351, 353, 360, 425, 426, 497, 498
Kalb, 321, 322, 341, 476, 477
Kalztoniri, 204
Kaminer, 477

Kandel, 222, 360
Kandel, 3, 329, 477
Kanner, 29, 34, 53, 75, 81, 90, 124, 125, 126, 133, 135, 154, 158, 195, 196, 217, 246, 301, 354, 360, 390, 402, 409, 497, 498
Kanner, 314, 322, 323, 324, 325, 327, 329, 336, 341, 477, 478
Kant, 173
Kant, 478
Kantzler, 166
Karp, 43, 62, 255
Karp, 322, 478
Katyanski, 277
Katz, 420
Katznelson, 280
Katznelson, 478
Kaufman, 450, 452, 453
Kaufman, 322
Keh, 29, 146, 447
Keh, 322, 334, 478
Keith, 401
Keller, 182, 183, 184, 189, 211
Keller, 478
Kett, 323
Kimmel, 56, 57
Kimmel, 478
King, 199
King Casimir, 44
King Kazimir, 164
Kinzler, 323
Kirchof, 183
Kirschenbaum, 283
Kirschenbaum, 478
Klagsfed, 136
Klagsfeld, 478
Klagswald, 185
Klagswald, 478
Klapper, 341, 478
Klassen, 306
Klassen, 478
Klausner, 322
Kleiman, 478
Klein, 323
Kleinman, 283
Kleinmintz, 283
Kleinmintz, 323, 478
Klotz, 37, 68, 75, 212, 225, 350, 433, 450, 499
Klotz, 323, 330, 478
Kluska, 363, 364
Kluska, 478
Kneller, 59, 60, 181, 218, 231, 451
Kneller, 323, 328, 478
Kociela, 75
Kociela, 479
Kolodziej, 188
Kolodziej, 478

Komarno, 478
Konieczkowski, 44, 144
Konieczkowski, 478
Konieczkowskis, 44
Kopel, 221
Kopel, 478
Kopitchuk, 77
Kopitciuk, 478
Korminski, 271
Korminski, 479
Korn, 34
Korn, 479
Kornhauser, 479
Kornhouser, 152
Kornreich, 217, 354, 421
Kornreich, 323, 479
Kosciuszko, 142
Kosciuszko, 479
Kracher, 48, 59, 75, 160, 182, 448, 449
Kracher, 322, 323, 479
Kramer, 1, 6
Krantzler, 165, 166, 168, 173, 174, 220, 296, 359, 428
Krantzler, 325, 479
Kraus, 401
Kraus, 312, 323, 324
Kraut, 354, 434, 450, 452, 499
Kraut, 318, 324, 327, 479
Kremer, 272
Kremer, 479
Kremerman, 222
Kresh, 226, 399
Kresh, 324, 479
Krieger, 324, 334
Krym, 58
Krym, 324, 480
Krzeszower, 324
Kubowitzki, 191
Kubowitzki, 479
Kuflik, 324
Kulik, 324, 330
Kuperberg, 304
Kuperberg, 308, 479
Kupfer, 325
Kupferman, 401
Kutyanski, 479
Kwiecinski, 480
Kwieczinski, 144

L

Lancut, 480
Landau, 57, 125
Landau, 325, 480
Landesman, 59, 226, 360, 422
Landesman, 325, 339, 480
Langerman, 351

Langerman, 480
Langsam, 1, 6, 7, 15, 71, 72, 90, 223, 261, 262, 263, 265, 267, 281, 310, 311, 351, 360, 364, 429, 499
Langsam, 316, 325, 480
Langsamyacov, 480
Langzam, 267
Lanner, 351
Lanner, 480
Last, 98, 277, 304, 307, 354, 359, 364
Last, 308, 320, 324, 325, 328, 480
Laterbaum, 291, 292
Latterbaum, 480
Laufer, 350, 359
Laufer, 480
Lehar, 480
Leherman, 325
Lehrer, 325
Lehrman, 163, 170, 191, 219, 296, 359, 428, 497, 499
Lehrman, 481
Leibel, 325
Leif, 446
Leif, 325
Leitner, 350
Leitner, 325
Lev, 304, 353, 354, 415, 497
Lev, 308, 341, 481
Levi, 14, 23, 29, 53, 55, 56, 73, 108, 109, 190, 225, 297, 298, 312, 316, 321, 322, 332, 337, 341, 350, 351, 353, 362, 443, 477, 489, 495
Levin, 56, 207, 272, 300, 301, 302
Levin, 481
Levinson, 325
Liberman, 131, 450
Licht, 315, 338, 481
Lichtig, 360
Lichtman, 43, 185
Lichtman, 326, 481
Lieber, 271, 274, 497
Lieber, 481
Lieberman, 180, 184, 190, 265, 283, 284, 306, 451
Lieberman, 308, 326, 481
Loos, 6, 46, 47, 59, 74, 76, 141, 142, 181, 186, 188, 190, 191, 192, 218, 230, 289, 293, 351, 405, 427, 447, 498
Loos, 326, 328, 481, 482
Lubash, 482
Lubasz, 283
Lubetkin, 272, 276, 277
Lubetkin, 482
Lustgarten, 43
Lustgarten, 326

M

Maimonides, 117, 203, 459
Maimonides, 458, 482
Malec, 270, 271, 497

Malec, 482
Malik, 102
Malik, 482
Malin, 145, 147
Malin, 482
Mandel, 23, 37, 48, 59, 60, 73, 74, 86, 88, 91, 92, 100, 101, 102, 134, 142, 180, 187, 190, 191, 220, 221, 229, 230, 261, 262, 284, 285, 360, 429, 430, 431, 447, 450, 451, 499
Mandel, 326, 331, 341, 482
Mantel, 317, 326, 332
March, 324
Margalit, 82
Margalit, 482
Margolis, 482
Marsh, 324
Marx, 200
Marx, 482
Mateus, 305
Mateus, 482
Maznicka, 186
Maznicka, 482
Meir, 308, 483
Meirson, 256
Meirson, 483
Meisels, 43
Meisels, 327, 336
Meisler, 304
Meisler, 308, 483
Mendel, 367
Mendelsohn, 15, 115, 116
Mendelsohn, 484
Mickiewicz, 216
Mickiewicz, 483
Mikopnik, 120
Mikopnik, 483
Milbauer, 327, 483
Milgraum, 132, 422
Milgraum, 483
Millbauer, 356
Miller, 72, 429, 448, 449
Miller, 324, 327, 480
Millinger, 324, 327
Millstein, 212
Millstein, 483
Mintz, 75, 134, 360, 447, 450
Mintz, 313, 327, 483
Mohreer, 42
Mohrer, 29, 42, 47, 48, 75, 138, 229, 298, 355, 397, 406, 452
Mohrer, 327, 328, 481, 483
Montag, 132
Muravin, 364, 365
Muravin, 483, 484
Muravina, 483, 484

Mussler, 6, 38, 64, 65, 66, 67, 86, 113, 114, 115, 116, 117, 118, 119, 120, 121, 123, 127, 149, 151, 152, 191, 231, 232, 233, 234, 236, 243, 304, 307, 351, 352, 353, 359, 431, 450, 451, 453, 497
Mussler, 308, 327, 484
Musslers, 499

N

Nachman, 484
Naphtali, 484
Napoleon, 484
Navon, 298, 299, 497
Navon, 484
Nechemiah, 20, 21, 27, 28, 29, 34, 42, 46, 60, 64, 67, 74, 85, 86, 87, 88, 91, 101, 110, 111, 112, 145, 160, 186, 190, 195, 199, 221, 229, 262, 281, 284, 313, 317, 321, 331, 333, 360, 402, 434, 447, 471, 475, 491, 499
Nechemiah, 314, 327, 484
Netzer, 328
Neumann, 226
Neumann, 328, 484, 485
Newman, 271
Newman, 484
Nobitnitzer, 221
Nosen, 65, 118, 470
Nuremberg, 41, 48, 58, 59, 73, 74, 75, 86, 102, 221, 222, 261, 350, 351, 353, 359, 402, 427, 498
Nuremberg, 328, 341, 485
Nutman, 21, 58
Nutman, 338, 485

O

Offenbach, 485
Olva, 485
Orbach, 328
Orenstein, 485
Ostrowce, 485

P

Panczeszin, 258
Panczeszin, 485
Pasek, 282
Pasek, 485
Patryn, 44, 45, 56, 88, 89, 96, 128, 144, 186, 195
Patryn, 485
Patryns, 44, 88
Peltz, 328
Peretz, 46, 47, 77, 304, 306, 307, 308, 328, 486
Peretz, 485
Pessel, 328
Petlura, 485
Pfeffer, 45, 67, 350, 351, 432, 499
Pfeffer, 312, 485
Philipowicz, 485

Pilsudski, 459, 485
Pinchovski, 354
Pinchovski, 319, 328
Pinchovsky, 319
Pinchowski, 217
Pinchowski, 485, 486
Pinsel, 47
Pinsel, 486
Pinzel, 328
Poniatowski, 486
Popper, 192, 218
Popper, 328, 486
Poretzky, 48
Poretzky, 486
Portnoi, 365
Portnoi, 486
Potochny, 486
Potoczny, 147
Presser, 486
Proper, 317
Propper, 354, 432
Propper, 486
Puderbeitel, 182, 304
Puderbeitel, 308, 486
Pustelnik, 327

R

Rabhun, 47
Rabin, 486
Rabinowitz, 101, 343, 351, 355
Rabinowitz, 341, 486
Rachnitz, 304
Rachnitz, 486
Radel, 306
Rappaport, 305
Rappaport, 308, 486
Rebhun, 142, 447
Rebhun, 321, 326, 328, 486
Redler, 444, 499
Redler, 328, 486
Reich, 171, 183, 190, 191, 218, 219, 261
Reich, 328, 329, 339, 486
Reicher, 123, 156, 158, 354, 448, 449, 450, 452
Reicher, 329, 486
Rein, 324, 328, 329
Resler, 134, 238, 240, 436
Reslers, 499
Ressler, 304
Ressler, 308, 313, 314, 329, 338, 486, 487
Richman, 312
Ridz, 487
Riger, 304, 305, 360
Riger, 308, 487
Rim, 207
Rimer, 319, 329

Ritter, 23, 50, 188, 239
Ritter, 487
Roitman, 364
Roitman, 487
Rosen, 23, 28, 29, 58, 60, 75, 92, 134, 135, 183, 184, 185, 186, 187, 188, 189, 190, 191, 226, 236, 239, 282, 283, 284, 285, 286, 349, 355, 356, 359, 399, 411, 433, 448
Rosen, 317, 318, 329, 333, 334, 487, 492
Rosenbaum, 39, 61, 157, 354
Rosenbaum, 330, 487
Rosenblith, 37, 43, 127
Rosenblith, 324, 330
Rosenbluth, 75, 229
Rosenbluth, 487
Rosenstein, 1
Rosenthal, 43, 184
Rosenthal, 330, 487
Rosner, 330
Roth, 47, 48, 75, 182, 271, 399, 444, 445, 499
Roth, 330, 487, 488, 494
Rothchild, 488
Rothman, 250, 251
Rothman, 488
Rothstein, 452
Rothstein, 330
Rozencveig, 322
Rubenfeld, 450, 452
Rubenfeld, 330, 334, 340
Rubin, 133, 358, 423
Rubin, 332, 336, 488
Rubish, 330
Rudel, 488
Russ, 74, 185, 222, 402, 434, 435, 449, 453, 499
Russ, 314, 330, 331, 479, 488
Rybner, 283
Rybner, 488
Ryzin, 17, 21, 29, 73, 74, 95, 251

S

Sadigora, 488
Safrin, 488
Salomon, 331
Saltzman, 189
Saltzman, 488
Salzman, 43
Samuel, 34, 38, 41, 43, 58, 59, 64, 69, 73, 76, 91, 94, 128, 131, 132, 148, 182, 184, 185, 188, 189, 190, 191, 208, 209, 221, 229, 231, 233, 236, 265, 266, 267, 268, 282, 283, 284, 285, 286, 304, 305, 307, 308, 314, 317, 318, 319, 320, 322, 323, 324, 330, 331, 332, 334, 336, 338, 339, 352, 353, 354, 355, 359, 369, 417, 422, 432, 433, 438, 453, 463, 464, 467, 470, 472, 474, 475, 479, 480, 481, 483, 484, 487, 488, 489, 490, 497, 499
Samuel, 331, 488
Samueli, 183
Samueli, 331, 333, 488
Saphire, 138, 184, 196, 197, 389, 498
Saphire, 326, 331, 337, 488
Schacher, 37, 43, 48, 74, 75, 402, 449
Schacher, 331
Scheffler, 212, 225
Schefler, 48, 75, 135, 185, 190, 354, 355, 401, 445, 446, 450, 452, 499
Schefler, 319, 325, 331, 488, 489
Scheiner, 3
Scheinman, 187
Schenkel, 339
Schick, 135
Schiff, 20, 23, 29, 43, 48, 53, 55, 56, 59, 73, 74, 103, 107, 157, 159, 181, 224, 225, 239, 350, 351, 353, 359, 360, 401, 402, 408, 442, 443, 449, 453, 498, 499
Schiff, 332, 336, 341, 489
Schimmel, 350, 360
Schimmel, 332, 491
Schitz, 29, 144, 182, 281, 444
Schitz, 312, 314, 332, 489
Schliselberg, 182
Schlisselberg, 43, 354, 358, 441
Schlisselberg, 321, 332, 341, 489
Schlosman, 489
Schmidt, 238, 283, 304, 305, 306, 307, 308
Schmidt, 308, 490
Schneider, 360
Schneider, 490
Schreiber, 41, 59
Schreiber, 332, 490
Schwalb, 323, 332, 333, 339
Schwalbe, 277
Schwalbe, 492
Schwarts, 397, 452
Schwartz, 225, 402
Schwartz, 330, 333, 490
Schwartzbart, 490
Schwartzman, 44, 47, 59, 60, 63, 72, 73, 83, 88, 93, 103, 105, 106, 124, 152, 225, 293, 350
Schwartzman, 333, 341, 490
Schwarzbarc, 46
Schwarzbart, 56
Schweber, 332
Schweik, 151
Schweik, 490
Seiden, 305
Seiden, 308
Seidenfeld, 339
Seidler, 401
Seidman, 20, 28, 45, 67, 87, 126, 127, 136, 358, 359
Seidman, 312, 313, 315, 318, 329, 333, 334, 336, 337, 463, 489
Seligman, 325, 490
Selligman, 55
Seltzer, 255

Seltzer, 490
Semelis, 333
Shachanov, 253
Shacher, 488
Shapiro, 14, 15, 16, 17, 18, 20, 21, 23, 25, 27, 28, 29, 34, 35, 47, 48, 58, 64, 69, 73, 75, 81, 82, 85, 86, 87, 88, 90, 98, 99, 100, 101, 110, 112, 122, 133, 134, 135, 138, 140, 145, 154, 168, 176, 186, 195, 214, 221, 225, 268, 281, 297, 304, 306, 343, 353, 355,360, 402, 435, 436, 496
Shapiro, 331, 333, 490, 491
Shefler, 397
Sheingal, 183, 282, 283
Sheingal, 333, 491
Sheinman, 430
Sheinman, 331, 491
Sheinuk, 333
Shenfeld, 272
Shenfeld, 491
Sheps, 333, 491
Shick, 489
Shimmel, 341, 491
Shipper, 129
Shipper, 491
Shlosman, 187, 190
Shmelkis, 50, 97
Shmelkis, 491
Shmulewicz, 224, 225, 399, 401, 444, 454, 499
Shmulewicz, 332
Shorr, 94, 211
Shorr, 491, 492
Shpalter, 21, 28, 60, 87, 155, 231, 232, 233, 234, 235, 236, 363
Shpalter, 333, 492
Shpitol, 146, 147
Shpitol, 492
Shubke, 492
Shulman, 43, 148
Shulman, 492
Shwartzman, 333
Sibirca, 492
Sienkewicz, 106
Sienkewicz, 492
Sikorski, 182, 253, 258
Sikorski, 492
Silver, 291
Smidt, 492
Smigly, 261, 487
Sperber, 304
Sperber, 308, 492
Springer, 75, 450
Springer, 333, 492
Stalin, 171, 182, 201, 254, 258, 260
Stalin, 492
Stare, 186
Steinmauer, 448

Steinmauer, 334
Steinmetz, 351
Steinmetz, 334, 339
Stempel, 271, 280
Stempel, 492
Steppel, 145
Steppel, 492
Stern, 271, 272, 275
Stern, 492
Sternberg, 34, 35, 45, 46, 51, 64, 75, 135, 351, 438, 439, 499
Sternberg, 315, 319, 320, 331, 334, 492
Stieglitz, 322
Stoilowski, 50, 51
Stoilowski, 492
Storch, 334
Stoylowski, 76
Straucher, 283
Straucher, 492
Straus, 492
Strazowski, 492
Strengerwoski, 286
Strongerovski, 355
Studnicki, 258
Studnicki, 492
Sturm, 24, 58, 74, 135, 140, 293, 306, 439, 440, 444, 499
Sturm, 312, 325, 327, 328, 334, 492, 493
Syrup, 46
Syrup, 493
Szaro, 493
Szmulewicz, 491
Szprung, 334

T

Tarphon, 88
Taub, 43, 140, 175, 182
Taub, 335, 493
Taube, 211
Taube, 493
Taub-Gertner, 43
Tchortkow, 493
Teitelbaum, 14, 58, 76
Teitelbaum, 335, 336, 493
Tenzer, 29, 39, 45, 53, 56, 59, 60, 73, 136, 155, 226, 235, 236, 408, 448, 498
Tenzer, 317, 335, 341, 493
Teper, 339
Tepper, 304
Tepper, 309, 493
Tetelbaum, 318, 493
Thim, 43, 189
Thim, 335, 494
Tishler, 351
Tishler, 341, 493
Todt, 183, 304

Torquemada, 288
Torquemada, 494
Trotsky, 254
Trotzky, 494
Tuchman, 360
Tuchman, 335, 494
Tucker, 230
Turner, 201
Turner, 494
Turteltaub, 359
Turteltaub, 335, 494
Tzchwal, 493
Tzimet, 325

U

Unger, 37, 38, 139, 272, 304, 305, 353, 388, 394, 404, 445, 498
Unger, 313, 317, 330, 335, 494
Uszlicki, 186
Uszlicki, 494

V

Vasilevska, 258
Vasilewska, 494
Vasily, 494
Vegg, 335
Vilf, 189
Vital, 494
Volkovisky, 494

W

Wachner, 335
Wagner, 494
Wagshal, 305
Wagshal, 309, 494
Waldman, 48, 183, 225
Waldman, 335, 494
Walker, 336
Wallach, 47, 238, 239, 240, 241
Wallach, 339, 494
Wallstein, 271
Wasserman, 42, 72
Wasserman, 330, 336, 494
Weber, 128, 129, 245, 359
Weber, 336, 494
Weichselbaum, 182, 359, 360
Weichselbaum, 336, 338, 494, 495
Weiden, 351, 424
Weiden, 336, 495
Weidenfeld, 216
Weidenfeld, 315, 495
Weidens, 498
Weinberg, 46, 74, 75, 190, 191, 225, 272, 274, 287, 358, 360, 423, 424, 452, 497, 498

Weinberg, 315, 336, 495
Weiner, 330, 336
Weisberg, 319
Weiser, 217
Weiser, 495
Weisman, 21
Weisman, 495
Weismandel, 269, 271, 272, 273
Weismandel, 495
Weiss, 20
Weiss, 336, 338, 340, 495
Weitman, 59, 182
Weitman, 336, 495
Welish, 336, 474
Welisz-Guttenberg, 190
Wielkopolski, 495
Wiener, 20, 60, 91, 98, 107, 185
Wiener, 318, 332, 335, 337, 495
Wierzbicki, 182
Wierzbicki, 495
Wild, 324
Wilner, 47, 50, 240, 360
Wilner, 332, 337, 339, 495
Wind, 108, 109
Wind, 312, 316, 321, 337, 495
Winer, 360
Wirtzel, 447
Wllach, 181
Wlodek, 219
Wlodek, 495
Wolf, 1, 19, 29, 59, 101, 190, 223, 284, 304, 305, 308, 312, 315, 321, 326, 336, 338, 350, 354, 356, 360, 364, 423, 430, 467, 473, 475, 482, 487, 496
Wolf, 337, 495
Wolkowicki, 392
Wolkowicki, 495
Wolkowitzki, 24, 57, 142, 182
Wurttel, 495
Wurtzel, 81, 86, 91, 97, 218
Wurtzel, 312, 314, 328, 331, 337
Wurtzl, 328
Wyzikowski, 52
Wyzikowski, 495

Y

Yablocinski, 138
Yaffe, 188, 282
Yaffe, 496
Yahalomi, 1, 2, 6, 8, 12, 14, 23, 38, 44, 58, 59, 60, 61, 62, 63, 80, 82, 83, 85, 87, 93, 94, 95, 97, 98, 100, 101, 102, 103, 107, 108, 110, 130, 131, 133, 134, 135, 136, 154, 155, 156, 157, 158, 159, 160, 205, 214, 225, 226, 240, 241, 248, 249, 251, 252, 253, 254, 255, 256, 268, 293, 315, 344, 345, 351, 361, 370, 497
Yahalomi, 496

Yahalomi-Diamond, 1
Yare, 238, 425
Yarosh, 337
Yidis, 222

Z

Zagner, 42
Zagner, 337, 496
Zaleshitz, 398, 402, 454
Zaleszitz, 337
Zalewski, 138
Zalewski, 496
Zaltzman, 337
Zamorski, 141
Zamorski, 496
Zanger, 226, 454
Zanger, 337, 496
Zeeman, 255
Zeeman, 496
Zeidler, 337
Zev, 14, 18, 20, 26, 27, 28, 29, 34, 35, 36, 44, 56, 63, 64, 83, 84, 85, 95, 96, 126, 127, 134, 135, 145, 146, 154, 176, 182, 194, 224, 312, 315, 316, 318, 321, 326, 327, 329, 333, 336, 351, 430, 469, 476, 489, 496
Ziebner, 180
Ziebner, 337, 496
Ziegel, 160
Ziegel, 337, 338, 496
Zilber, 46, 74, 134, 449
Zilber, 333, 338, 496
Zilberberg, 398
Zilberberg, 338
Zilberman, 314, 338, 339, 496
Zimmer, 312
Zukerman, 269, 272, 276, 277, 278, 280
Zukerman, 496
Zukier, 452
Zveig, 496
Zweig, 164

www.ingramcontent.com/pod-product-compliance
Lightning Source LLC
Chambersburg PA
CBHW082007150426
42814CB00005BA/252